The IBOC Handbook

The IBOC Handbook

Understanding HD Radio™ Technology

By
David P. Maxson

ELSEVIER

AMSTERDAM • BOSTON • HEIDELBERG • LONDON
NEW YORK • OXFORD • PARIS • SAN DIEGO
SAN FRANCISCO • SINGAPORE • SYDNEY • TOKYO
Focal Press Is an Imprint of Elsevier

Focal Press

National Association of
NAB
BROADCASTERS

Acquisitions Editor: Angelina Ward
Project Manager: Mónica González de Mendoza
Assistant Editor: Doug Shults
Technical Editor: David H. Layer
Marketing Manager: Christine Degon
Interior Design: Alisa Andreola
Book Composition: Borrego Publishing (www.borregopublishing.com)

Focal Press is an imprint of Elsevier
30 Corporate Drive, Suite 400, Burlington, MA 01803, U.S.A.
Linacre House, Jordan Hill, Oxford OX2 8DP, UK

 Recognizing the importance of preserving what has been written, Elsevier prints its books on acid-free paper whenever possible.

Library of Congress Cataloging-in-Publication Data

(Application submitted.)

British Library Cataloguing-in-Publication Data
A catalogue record for this book is available from the British Library.

ISBN 13: 978-0-2408084-4-4

For information on all Focal Press publications
visit our website at www.books.elsevier.com

07 08 09 10   10 9 8 7 6 5 4 3 2 1

Printed in the United States of America.

Working together to grow
libraries in developing countries

www.elsevier.com | www.bookaid.org | www.sabre.org

ELSEVIER   BOOK AID
International   Sabre Foundation

To Diane—my best friend, wife, and #1 cheerleader—
without whom this book and so much else would not have been possible.

Table of Contents

Contents

Acknowledgments

With an undertaking as large and detail-driven as the IBOC Handbook, it will be hard to know when to stop offering my gratitude for all the support I have received. First, and foremost, this book began as a collaboration between myself and Don Lockett, author of "The Road to Digital Radio In the United States" (NAB, 2004). I am grateful for Don's input, support and graciousness. Unfortunately, his professional obligations prevented him from participating as much as we both would have liked. Chapter 1 contains material Don contributed to the effort.

Chapter 12 is about that black art, AM antennas. I am eternally grateful to Grady Moates of Loud and Clean Broadcast Science, for providing most of the words and meaning to the chapter. His facility with the hardware of radio broadcasting is legendary, as should also be his generosity of spirit. Speaking of legendary, I first met Brian Kroeger, D.Sc., now Chief Scientist of iBiquity Digital Corporation in 1996, then with Westinghouse Wireless. He was presenting a sober, scientific assessment of what the numbers said IBOC could and could not do, and I was hooked. Since then, he has overseen the technical team that made this amazing IBOC technology possible. For me, he has always been helpful and informative. Brian, thanks for carving out a little time here and there to patiently answer my questions. I hope this book does justice to the technology that you and your team developed. As well, I want to single out Jeff Detweiler and Ashruf El-Dinary of iBiquity, and of course, "Mr. IBOC," Glynn Walden, of CBS, iBiquity, and CBS. They have plenty of work to do and still found time to respond to my occasional inquiries.

There are so many who have been riding the IBOC wave since it was just a ripple, some of whom I have had the good fortune to meet or work with. Since I bought my first Shively antenna in the 1980s, I have counted on Bob Surette to fill in the gaps in my knowledge of antennas and filters. He has been generous in sharing his experience with IBOC combiners and filters. Jerry

Westberg of Broadcast Electronics gave Grady and myself very helpful feedback on Chapter 12. Richard Hinkle of Broadcast Electronics, Tim Holt of Bird Technologies, Geoff Mendenhall of Harris, and Eric Wandel, formerly of ERI, whether they know it or not, have been resources for me on topics in IBOC transmission, even before I embarked on writing this book. In particular, thanks to Tim Hardy of Nautel, who on several occasions spent valuable time jotting down his explanations on napkins as we'd talk over signal processing and transmission topics. To my friends at Impulse Radio, particularly Paul Signorelli and David Corts, thanks for the opportunity to learn about digital networks while I was showing you the ropes in the broadcast industry. Mike Bergman of Kenwood U.S.A. Corporation has been an invaluable resource on the receiver side of the IBOC equation. I also sought advice, generously given, from Michael LeClair, Chief Engineer of Boston's WBUR Group, and Editor of *Radio World Engineering Extra*. Ron Rackley, a titan in the AM array field, was also responsive to my inquiries. Thanks to each of you, and all that I have not mentioned.

Also, I salute a good-humored, talented, and professional group—my colleagues who represent their companies on the NRSC subcommittees—who are too many to name here. They have helped make my experience with the IBOC process rewarding. I appreciate, as well, the moral support and technical acumen of the people of the National Association of Broadcasters (NAB) and the Consumer Electronics Association (CEA). In particular, special thanks go to David Layer of NAB and David Wilson of CEA for their direct input to my effort.

David Layer also filled the role of Technical Editor. He volunteered to go through the manuscript with a fine-toothed comb, weeding out awkward wording, factual errors, unnecessary information, and (yes, I admit it) the occasional a-little-too-strident remark. What remains is so much the better for his input. However, any mistakes and misdirection that the reader may find lurking in this work are mine. I encourage you, the reader, to let me know what you think about this book.

On the home front, I am indebted to my family for their perseverance through all the time I stole for writing, and to my colleagues at Broadcast Signal Lab for their dedication to providing good service to our customers and supporting my effort on this book. To my fantastic wife, Diane and my fabulous children, Hilary and Scott, thanks for letting me go for it. To my mom the school-marm and my dad the philatelist, Jane and Irv, you have been good teachers and parents and I am grateful for the tools you have given me.

On the business side, in particular, to my business partner since 1982, Rick Levy, thanks for your constancy, technical and moral advice, and wit over the years. This one's for you:

> *There once was an astronomer from Brooklyn,*
> *Who came to the halls of Harvard to book-learn;*
> *He studied galaxies and suns,*
> *And littered the cosmos with puns,*
> *But it was the radio waves that really got him cookin'!*

My colleague Lew Collins has been a wellspring of knowledge and sage advice; our paths first crossed a few years ago, and I only wish it had happened sooner. Another colleague, David

Peabody, has been a good friend and stalwart for nearly our entire careers. Thanks for your loyalty and independent thinking.

On the production side, let me start with my colleague Aaron Read. We met through a dialog of dueling IBOC commentaries in Radio World and hit it off right away. When I needed a creative, technically oriented, visually astute illustrator, you stepped up and made your magic. Aaron created, and inspired, much of the art in this book. Supporting me in art and manuscript preparation were Ann Connors and Maureen Whelan. Thanks not only for this work, but also for helping me keep my hectic day-job schedule while I was also getting the writing done. At the publisher, Focal Press, I am indebted to Acquisitions Editor Angelina Ward and Assistant Editor Doug Shults for their patience and persistence as deadlines loomed and were rescheduled.

Bob Struble, Chairman and CEO of iBiquity Digital Corporation, which made the HD Radio brand of IBOC technology a reality, responded to my lamentation in 2001 regarding the tremendous possibilities of IBOC and its seemingly slow progress at the time. He asked for my patience and counseled that HD Radio technology would "let a thousand flowers bloom." Ironically, this common paraphrase comes from Mao-Zedong's hundred flowers movement at the beginning of the cultural revolution, "let a hundred flowers bloom, and a hundred schools of thought contend." This book is one of those flowers. Thanks, Bob.

And finally, to you, the reader, nothing is more gratifying than to hear, "I learned something; thanks." I hope I have succeeded in putting the pieces of a huge puzzle together in an interesting way. Check out *www.ibocbook.com* for what may develop.

David Maxson
June 2007

Introduction

Until this book was written, there has not been a thorough explanation of the inner workings of the In-Band On-Channel (IBOC) technology in one place. Dozens of articles in the trade press and technical papers at industry symposiums constitute the IBOC story. It may be hubris on my part to think that this technology could be wrapped up in a book, but I have done my best to do so.

Using the National Radio Systems Committee (NRSC) IBOC standard (NRSC-5-A) as a framework, this book introduces the complex layers in what makes it work. The reader does not have to be a digital signal processing engineer. On the contrary, the book is aimed toward individuals with a technical bent, and a curiosity about digital radio, American style. The first two chapters set the context and the history of IBOC. In the following chapters, things get more technical. The book focuses on IBOC, the generic technology that is the subject of the NRSC standard, and it integrates the specific implementation that is IBOC, the HD Radio™ technology of iBiquity Digital Corporation.

Several knowledge threads are woven through the book. First, the role of a standard-setting process is often misunderstood among those who have not participated in one. This book paints a picture of the rigorous NRSC process that led to the IBOC standard. Second, to create a standard requires protocols and specifications. As the book steps through the layers of the NRSC-5 *protocol stack*, the relationship between what a standard says, and what a manufacturer's implementation does, may become apparent. People often ask questions about why a technology works a certain way, or why a feature hasn't developed as expected. The answer often lies in the complex relationship between the standard, the equipment manufacturers, the broadcasters, and the consumers who are both buyers of radios and listeners of them. Broadcast engineers configuring their equipment and programming their transmission gear may have "Aha!" moments when the reasons for the way things are become apparent. Individuals listening to their IBOC receivers and looking at their displays may grasp the subtleties that determine what the technology does in today's receiver and what the possibilities are for tomorrow.

Third in the book is the subject of digital systems. A protocol stack invokes multidisciplinary knowledge. In plainer language, as one progresses from the *information* input at the top of the stack to the *radio signal* that comes out the bottom of the stack, the processing tasks require different types of engineering. Although this book contains a detailed treatment of the IBOC process, it is also a case study in digital systems. The principles that apply to IBOC apply as well to other digital communications media. Protocols that define services must have certain characteristics, while protocols that define transport mechanisms have other characteristics. Often, the features of tried-and-true technologies are borrowed and molded to the IBOC application—such as characteristics of the Open Systems Interconnection reference model, the functionality of streaming modem protocols, the use of virtual ports to establish communications, and the like. The design of an open system also relies on myriad techniques to balance the reliability of the service with the information rate it can provide. IBOC technology exploits signal processing techniques common to digital communications in general. This book presents and explores such concepts such as scrambling, Forward Error Correction (FEC), convolutional coding, Reed-Solomon coding, frequency diversity, time diversity, pulse shaping, matched filtering, Fourier Transformation, quadrature modulation, and the like.

In presenting detailed technical information, I attempt to work the concepts in a manner that will not tax one's math skills. There are places where math is what it is all about, and the equations are there to be dissected. However, even where there are equations, it is my hope that the concepts will still come across if the reader only gives the math a cursory look.

Finally, there should be plenty of "news you can use" for technical people involved in IBOC technology. The book is populated with useful tables, figures, and lists, as well as explanations of how to do things on the transmission side of IBOC.

I crave reader feedback. Check out *www.ibocbook.com* to see how readers can participate.

—David Maxson

SECTION I

BACKGROUND

1 IBOC Digital Radio and the State of the Digital Radio Industry

Conversion to Digital Radio Broadcasting is well underway in the United States. The arrival has been accompanied by a series of technological and regulatory events. This book was written to provide a look at In-Band On-Channel (IBOC) technology from the inside, out. IBOC technology is also discussed in the context of its implementation by the company that brought it to market, iBiquity Digital Corporation (iBiquity). Receiver and transmission equipment manufacturers make and market numerous products licensed by iBiquity under the "HD Radio™" brand name. At points in the book we thresh out the nature of the IBOC transmission protocol and its relation to products that bear the HD Radio trademark. The first two chapters provide a top-level view of the context of IBOC. Chapters 3 through 11 go into the nuts and bolts of the National Radio Systems Committee's NRSC-5 IBOC standard and how the technology works. The final portion of the book touches on other aspects of the technology.

In the first section of this first chapter, "What Is IBOC Radio?" we go over the "services" that are the foundation of IBOC capabilities. In the next section, "The Digital Radio Environment," we take a snapshot of the digital radio broadcasting industry to provide a global picture of DAB and IBOC technology. In "Digital Radio Transmission Technologies" we look at the other technologies in the arena. Finally, in "A Context for IBOC," we discuss IBOC in the context of the regulatory arena and the marketplace, paving the way to Chapter 2.

Following Chapter 2, we dig deeply into the NRSC-5 Standard and the way IBOC works, beginning with an overview of the standard in Chapter 3. Chapters 4 through 11 break out various components of the standard and explore them in depth.

What is IBOC Radio?

IBOC is a form of terrestrial radio broadcasting that employs sophisticated digital radio waveforms that can deliver compact disc-like quality sound, free of interference and noise to radio listeners. The term *IBOC* is an acronym for In-Band On-Channel digital radio, a term that describes the use of the existing AM and FM analog broadcasting bands and channel schemes for the digital transmissions. "HD Radio" is a trade name for AM and FM IBOC digital radio systems, a trademark of iBiquity Digital Corporation, the sole proponent for a comprehensive AM/FM digital radio broadcasting (DRB) technology in the U.S.A. iBiquity licenses the mark to companies that want to use iBiquity technology and that earn, through rigorous testing, the HD Radio brand identity.

The term *Digital Audio Broadcasting (DAB)* is a trademark of the Eureka-147 digital radio system, which originated in Europe and is more commonly used in Europe, Canada and Asia. Eureka-147 was the first commercially available digital radio broadcasting system. It requires broadcast spectrum outside the traditional AM and FM bands and as such is characterized as a "new band" (as opposed to in-band) system. Non-IBOC digital radio solutions, including Eureka-147, often require more bandwidth or channel space per station than is currently allotted in the U.S. AM and FM bands, resulting in a requirement for new spectrum. No new radio bands were available for free over-the-air terrestrial radio broadcasting in the U.S., driving the evolution of an IBOC technology that operates within existing AM and FM bands.

The IBOC digital radio transmitter system encodes incoming analog sound into a binary form for transmission. With IBOC radio, a digitally modulated signal shares the radio station's channel with the existing analog signal (the analog signal is called the *host*). See Figure 1.1. In this fashion, each radio station, AM and FM, is able to broadcast is digital signal.

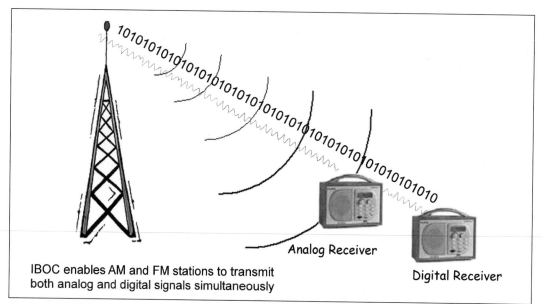

Analog Receiver

Digital Receiver

IBOC enables AM and FM stations to transmit both analog and digital signals simultaneously

Figure 1.1 IBOC Digital Radio Transmission

Services Overview

While digital radio offers distinct advantages over analog, including mitigation of transmission artifacts, digital audio quality alone is not enough to guarantee radio industry investment and support for conversion to digital radio technology, or to ensure consumer adoption in the marketplace. Hence, a number of digital features and enhancements are supported by digital radio that enable broadcasters to provide added value for public service and commercial revenues. These features are transmitted on the IBOC digital signal as "services." The word "service" has a particular meaning in the digital communications and networking world. The Federal Telecom Glossary defines the term in a cumbersome way:

- In the *Open Systems Interconnection – Reference Model*, a capability of a given layer, and the layers below it, that a) is provided to the entities of the next higher layer and b) for a given layer, is provided at the interface between the given layer and the next higher layer.

Chapters 3 through 11 decompose the various IBOC services in substantial detail. For now, suffice it to say that services are the rules that permit types of information to be passed through the IBOC radio channel. The types of information whose services we are most concerned with are the program audio streams, their respective program associated data, and other kinds of data. The specific names of the services offered on IBOC transmissions are:

- Main Program Service   MPS
- Supplemental Program Service   SPS
- Station Information Service   SIS
- Advanced Data Services   ADS

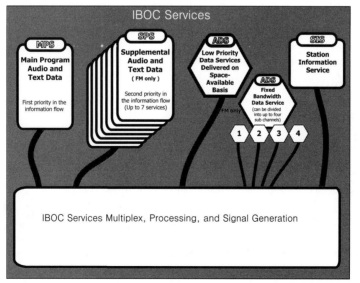

Figure 1.2 The Various Services Channeled into the IBOC Signal

Program Services

The Main Program Service (MPS) delivers the digital version of the analog main channel audio program. This is the fundamental service embedded on the IBOC digital signal. In addition to the audio, MPS can deliver Program Associated Data (PAD) to the listener. Perhaps the service that most invigorated initial IBOC deployment was the service that offers additional program choice to the listener—the Supplemental Program Service (SPS)—which enables the broadcaster to transmit more audio program channels and PAD on stations already transmitting MPS. By late 2006 there were more than 3,000 stations committed to begin IBOC broadcasting, representing more than 20% of the nearly 14,000 AM and FM stations in the U.S.A. About 1,500 had obtained their iBiquity licensing, with over 1,000 stations on the air—over 350 of which were offering additional program streams.[1]

Multicasting

Multicasting refers to the broadcasting of more than one stream of audio content simultaneously, consisting of the Main Program Service and at least one SPS channel.

Tomorrow Radio

Thanks largely to the pioneering work done under the auspices of the *"Tomorrow Radio Project,"* National Public Radio, Harris Corporation, Kenwood U.S.A. Corporation and iBiquity brought multichannel programming to FM IBOC. NPR tested the robustness of digital coverage and multicast service under varying signal propagation conditions. There were also extensive subjective listening tests done to determine acceptable bit rates for scaling of the main digital channel for multicast applications. Consequently, all post-first-generation IBOC receivers are capable of multicast reception.

The FM IBOC main program channel has a maximum bit rate of 96 kilobits per second (kbps). However, broadcasters have the option to create multiple streams by scaling the bit stream into smaller increments. Subjective listening tests have shown that 64 kbps provides an acceptable bit rate for the main channel. The available 96 kbps can be subdivided into a 64 kbps audio stream, leaving 32 kbps of capacity that can be further divided into two or more low bit rate digital audio channels. With an optional expansion of the FM IBOC signal (using Primary Extended subcarriers), up to about 150 kbps of content can be transmitted.

The HD Digital Radio Alliance

The HD Digital Radio Alliance was formed by a group of commercial radio broadcasters on December 6, 2005 to accelerate the rollout and consumer acceptance of HD Radio broadcasting. A key initiative from its inception was the promotion of the multicasting concept. The alliance also intended to promote and provide a unified vision for IBOC programming and advertising. Members of the alliance include ABC Radio, Beasley, Infinity Broadcasting (CBS Radio), Clear

---

[1] Source: HD Digital Radio Alliance, www.hdradioplaybook.com, December 2006.

Channel, Cumulus Media, Greater Media, Citadel, Entercom Communications, Emmis and Bonneville International broadcasting companies.

The alliance announced the first wave of multicast stations on January 19, 2006. There were 264 multicast stations launched in 28 markets. Clear Channel and Infinity were the leaders with 116 multicast stations and 60 multicast stations launched, respectively.

Program Service Data (PSD)

For digital radio services in general, Program Associated Data (PAD) is a term that refers to information that is transmitted with the program audio stream and is related to program on that stream. For instance, when song title and artist information is transmitted in parallel with the music in a program stream, it is considered PAD. PAD has proved to be a compelling means of attracting and retaining listeners, promoting sales of new radios, and offering added value to content providers and advertisers. PAD is used by Internet and satellite radio broadcasters as well as by the European DAB radio system; it was an attraction that was immediately embraced by early users of satellite radio. On the IBOC system the term *PAD* is an unofficial name, and should be considered a generic term for such data. The primary carrier of IBOC PAD is the Program Service Data (PSD) protocol. Advanced Data Services (see below) also have the capability of transmitting PAD, once a protocol is established for doing so. Chapter 4 includes a detailed discussion of the PSD and the PSD Transport protocols. Chapter 11 reviews Advanced Data Services and the transport protocol for them—the Advanced Application Services Transport (AAT).

The NRSC-5 protocol for PSD supports main and supplemental program channels:

1. Main Program Service (MPS) with Main Program Service Data (MPSD)

2. Supplemental Program Services (SPS's, each with SPSD)

Program Service Data (PSD) consists of a number of different fields that may be used to display text messages, including: song title, program title, artist name, album name, and music genre. Many studio automation and digital storage system manufacturers have integrated the necessary software to support PSD operation.

Station Information Service (SIS)

The Station Information Service (SIS) is delivered through a fast acquisition channel that enables the receiver to rapidly acquire basic information about the station and the signal. This is information that generally does not qualify as PAD. SIS information can tell the receiver about the station (call sign, location, station name, etc.), about time (time zone, daylight savings, etc.), and about the basics of the services offered on the station.

The Service Information Guide (SIG) is one of the messages that can be sent over the SIS. It gives more detailed information about the audio service, the service provider, authorization required for conditional access, and where to find the data in the broadcast channel. To route a service to the correct destination within a receiver, a *port number* is assigned to the service. The Service Information Guide provides the index of services and the associated ports. SIS is discussed in Chapter 10.

Advanced Data Services (ADS)

ADS is the acronym for what the NRSC-5 standard calls *Advanced Data Services*. This is the generic description of the class of data services that do not use SIS or PSD data channels on IBOC. The name ADS describes a concept. It refers to those data services that enter the NRSC-5 protocol at a certain place. Thus, ADS is the name for the capability to transmit richer data content than the basic text functions that are the primary content on SIS and PSD. ADS can be used for a variety of purposes, including PAD delivery, new program streams, and independent data services for private or public use, including conditional access services (such as subscription-based or pay-for-play services).

There is ample opportunity for confusion among the various names and acronyms in the IBOC lexicon. Consider the distinction between ADS and AAS. Where ADS represents a concept, AAS represents a realization of a technology. iBiquity offers to its licensees a technology it calls AAS, an acronym for Advanced Application Services. iBiquity's AAS technology supports the generation of several services that are inputs to the NRSC-5 protocols, including ADS, PSD, and SPS. AAS is not in the scope of the NRSC-5 protocols; however, complicating the soup of acronyms, NRSC-5 contains a transport protocol that bears the name Advanced Application Services Transport (AAT), AAT is, of course, related to AAS because AAT is one of the transports to which iBiquity's AAS technology connects.

Advanced Data Services are a key feature for differentiating digital radio from analog radio. As these are terrestrially based broadcast signals, IBOC data services also distinguish themselves from other digital audio media such as satellite radio, compact discs or MP3 players. IBOC data services can provide local, timely data to multiple users in a market area, many of which are provided for free to the end user. In 2001, a company called Impulse Radio developed some early conceptual models of data-enhanced radio broadcasting. Figure 1.3 is a still photo of a real-time simulation of dynamic text and graphics transmitted over the equivalent of 2–3 kilobits per second Advanced Data Service.

HD Radio Data Enhancements

Anticipating the deployment of new services, HD Radio receiver chipsets support functions not initially supported by the HD Radio transmission equipment. IBOC system capabilities and planned enhancements for IBOC digital radio include:

- *Multimedia Support* – This support enables HD Radio receivers to render images such as album art, artist image, logos or other graphics. The capability is supported in advanced HD Radio chipsets;

- *HD Radio Transport Protocol* – This support enables IBOC to transmit and receive nonaudio digital content wherein the radio acts as a "data pipe" for delivery of new services like real-time traffic information to in-vehicle navigation systems;

- *HD Radio Review* – This functionality is supported in advanced HD Radio ICs. It offers the ability to rewind live audio broadcasts or store fixed-length audio clips. The maximum record time of this feature was initially limited to 45 seconds.

Figure 1.3 Simulation of Consumer-oriented Data Service Synchronized to Programming (courtesy of Impulse Radio)

- *Store & Replay* – This function provides the ability to time-shift broadcast programming. Audio programs are stored in memory for later replay.

- *On-Demand Audio Services* – This capability will enable automatic storage and real-time updates of traffic, news, weather and sports programming.

- *Electronic Program Guide (EPG)* – The digital radio guide provides a listing of station programming to assist consumer selection and tuning. More than one station can be included in the guide that a station transmits.

Web-Based Possibilities

In a twist on using IBOC data to reach the listener through the receiver, technology developers are exploring ways to recover IBOC data and provide real-time and historical access to it on the Internet. For example, *Radio Sherpa* provides an online, real-time search of HD Radio stations by market, and displays instantaneous graphics regarding the digital station's on-air signal (www.radiosherpa.com). This system uses a bank of HD Radio receivers that sample and read the artist and title information of the respective stations, logging and displaying what each station is playing. Among early beta test features, listeners can search for the music of a particular artist and tune to the station that is playing that artist, receive messages when certain music plays on selected stations, and simply click online to stream the selected station.

The Digital Radio Environment

FCC First Report and Order

On the regulatory side, the Federal Communications Commission initially autho- rized use of IBOC technology for digital radio on October 11, 2002 by its *First Report and Order in the matter of Digital Audio Broadcasting Systems and Their Impact on the Terrestrial Radio Service*. In this report, the Commission selected in-band on- channel (IBOC) as the technology that will permit AM and FM radio broadcasters in the United States to introduce digital radio efficiently and rapidly. The commission also concluded that the adoption of a single IBOC transmission standard would be in the best interest of terrestrial broad- casters while deferring consideration of formal standardization of IBOC to a future proceeding.

Highlights of the *First Report and Order* (Mass Media Docket No. 99-325, FCC 02-286) are:

1. The FCC will no longer consider digital radio technologies requiring use of spectrum outside of the existing AM and FM bands (so-called new band systems) for licensing inside the United States;

2. Authorization for use of AM IBOC was limited to local daytime operations pending further evaluation of AM IBOC nighttime propagation characteristics. Pre-sunrise and post sunset operations are authorized to enable AM IBOC stations to provide digital service during rush hour drive times;

3. An interim authorization for IBOC was implemented, and all stations were directed to request STAs (special temporary authority) to operate with hybrid IBOC facilities per FCC applica- tion procedures. On March 20, 2003, the FCC's Media Bureau streamlined this procedure by announcing that AM and FM radio stations could notify the Commission by letter within 10 days of commencement of IBOC digital transmissions. On March 22, 2007, the FCC permanently authorized hybrid IBOC operations with its *Second Report and Order, First Order on Reconsideration, and Second Further Notice of Proposed Rulemaking* (FCC 07-33). It also granted full time (day and night) operation for AM IBOC; permitted FM IBOC to multicast and to operate in extended hybrid mode; and required stations that elect to transmit hybrid IBOC signals to transmit, at a minimum, the analog program on the digital signal, with at least comparable audio quality.

In contrast to the digital television (DTV) proceedings at the FCC several years earlier, the Commission does not require stations to begin hybrid IBOC operations and plans no transition to all-digital IBOC transmission. The elimination of an existing service on a certain date is called a *sunset*. There is no analog sunset for radio broadcasting, which differs from the imposition of the DTV analog sunset, intended to increase spectrum efficiency by recovering the vacated analog channels as television stations converted to DTV on separate channels. Since IBOC utilizes existing channels, there are no analog channels to recover. The conversion timeline for all-digital radio is driven by marketplace concerns, rather than by the government's desire for reclamation of spectrum (as was the case for DTV). Several features are or will be driving the adoption of IBOC in the marketplace, including increased program choice, program associated text, improved sound and reception quality, new data services, and audio-on-demand and to better serve in the public interest and compete with other digital audio media, including satellite radio.

Dissent

Overwhelmingly, the comments received by the FCC from the radio industry supported swift permanent authorization of IBOC. Some concerns were raised in particular regarding potential interference, including:

- IBOC impact on AM nighttime sky-wave service;

- Generalized concerns about interference to the reception of analog stations;

- Concerns about loss of existing coverage area near the edge of service due to increased interference.

Leonard Kahn, an innovative radio engineer is a proponent of an alternative approach to improving the performance of AM broadcasting called the CAM-D™ AM transmission system. Kahn raised concerns about nighttime IBOC performance of WLW (700 kHz) in Cincinnati, Ohio when WOR-AM (710 kHz) in New York City transmitted (under experimental authority) a hybrid IBOC signal. WOR is on the channel first-adjacent to WLW, and the WOR digital signal occupies a portion of the channel that WLW occupies. (Half the bandwidth of the WOR and WLW analog signals already overlap because of the way AM channels are assigned.) Nevertheless, Kahn claimed WOR nighttime IBOC energy causes interference to the analog reception of WLW. Kahn's concern reflected those of many domestic AM stations as well as those in neighboring Mexico and Canada who feared potential loss of secondary AM coverage if all AM stations are authorized for AM IBOC conversion on a blanket basis.[2]

iBiquity undertook AM IBOC testing and analysis to respond to interference concerns expressed by representative bodies such as the National Association of Broadcasters (NAB), the NRSC and the FCC. That information is discussed in greater detail in Chapter 12. However, based on the results of testing and analysis by a number of parties, the NAB concluded that on the whole, the benefits of AM IBOC operation, day and night, outweigh the detriments. The most that can be done to analyze the issues on a theoretical basis had been done, and the best next step was to monitor new installations and respond on a case-by-case basis to any actual interference.

Based on its review of the results of testing and analysis, the National Association of Broadcasters (NAB) filed a letter with the FCC in March 2004 endorsing nighttime AM operation, concluding:

For the foregoing reasons, NAB encourages the Commission to authorize AM broadcasters to commence nighttime IBOC broadcasts with appropriate interference resolution mechanisms. NAB further encourages the Commission to extend this authorization to all AM broadcasters licensed for nighttime analog services without the need for individual station authorizations. This will allow AM broadcasters to better understand the opportunities and challenges of IBOC and it will provide incentive for receiver manufacturers to market IBOC receivers.

In 2006, Leonard Kahn and Kahn Communications filed suit in the U.S. Southern District Court of New York charging iBiquity, Lucent Technologies, Clear Channel Communications and others with suppressing competition and monopolizing the market. Kahn's suit claimed that

---

[2] IBOC Update: A PRIMEDIA Publication, *Insight on HD Radio* from *Radio Magazine*, September 15. 2004.

the defendants boycotted Kahn's CAM-D systems and defamed CAM-D and Kahn personally. That suit was dismissed, with prejudice, in December 2006, because the "Plaintiffs have failed to state any cognizable antitrust claims against defendants and the Court lacks jurisdiction to redress plaintiffs' dissatisfaction with the FCC's regulation of digital radio."[3] The Court also found that the plaintiffs offered no basis for the defamation allegation.

The NRSC initially recommended in April 2002 that AM IBOC be used for daytime operations, only for the simple reason that the NRSC evaluation of AM IBOC had focused solely on daytime performance. Subsequently, the testing and analysis conducted by iBiquity led NAB to support nighttime operation and propose that the FCC establish resolution procedures to any special interference cases that might arise. In March 2007, the FCC authorized AM IBOC nighttime operation.

The Rise of IBOC

The IBOC rollout reached its 1,000[th] HD Radio broadcast facility in the fall of 2006. The formation of the HD Digital Radio Alliance and its promotion of multicasting has resulted in a burgeoning of new broadcast program streams available to listeners who buy HD Radio receivers.

The concept of digital radio transmission was sparked by early demonstrations of the Eureka-147 DAB digital radio technology in Europe. Eureka-147 was hailed as a digital replacement for both AM and FM analog systems. Because it required new spectrum outside the AM and FM bands, Eureka-147 DAB would be transmitted on available frequencies outside of these bands, typically within the L-Band (around 1470 MHz) either terrestrially or by satellite, or the upper VHF band. Work on In-Band On-Channel digital radio began as a response to the development of Eureka-147 DAB in the late 1980s and early 1990s, as broadcasters in the U.S.A. began to realize the benefits offered by an in-band solution.

Unfortunately, new spectrum as required for Eureka-147 is not universally available for assignment to radio services worldwide. Consequently, digital radio proponents in the United States, where L-Band use, in particular, is restricted to priority government/military applications, undertook the challenge to develop digital radio technology that would operate within the existing AM/FM bands. Following more than 10 years of development, the IBOC digital radio system was launched.

The term *Digital Audio Broadcasting (DAB)* originated in Europe and is the tradmark of the Eureka-147 system. Because of the dual role of the name DAB as a generic term and as the name for Eureka-147, the term *Digital Radio Broadcasting (DRB)* surfaced. It is employed by the FCC as the generic term. Also, the NRSC renamed its DAB Subcommittee in 2005 as the DRB Subcommittee to reflect the notion that radio broadcasting consists of more than just audio.

In 1995, the Electronic Industries Association, then-parent of the Consumer Electronics Manufacturers' Association tested several digital radio technologies, including Eureka-147 DAB, and several American digital radio systems. At that time, Eureka-147 was the dominant new band

---

[3] Kahn vs. iBiquity Digital Corp., No. 06 Civ. 1536 (NRB) (S.D.N.Y. Dec. 7, 2006).

system while IBOC (In-Band On-Channel) and IBAC (In-Band Adjacent-Channel) digital radio systems were proposed to allow AM and FM broadcasters to transmit analog and digital signals on presently assigned frequency channels.

Development of IBOC digital radio technology occurred in three stages. Leaving a more detailed history to Chapter 2, these are the three technological stages in the development of IBOC as summarized by Glynn Walden:

1. Stage I was known as Project Acorn: This was a period from 1990–1992, where USA Digital Radio's (USADR)[4] efforts were directed to a "proof of concept." This development effort was misinterpreted by the industry as an attempt at a digital radio "implementation." USADR intended to demonstrate conceptually that digital signals could be transmitted and received in the AM and FM bands with minimal interference to the analog.

   The milestones of this first period were:
   - The first FM IBOC transmissions Aug 29, 1992, on WILL, Urbana, IL;
   - The first AM IBOC transmission July 9, 1992 at 2:45 PM on 1660 kHz at Xetron Corporation, Cincinnati, Ohio (Xetron was a technology partner of USADR).

2. Stage II was USADR's creation of commercially viable AM and FM systems. This effort resulted in the fundamental digital signal characteristics that ultimately became AM and FM IBOC as it is in use today. As the following chapters of this book will show, the transmission and reception of IBOC signals is based on a very robust design that operates under the challenging conditions of the existing analog AM and FM bands.

   The milestones of this second period were:
   - Development of sufficient receiving and transmitting hardware to complete the most extensive laboratory and field testing program ever devised for a commercial radio broadcasting system;
   - The first public demonstrations of the commercial USADR FM system at the NAB Radio Show on WMMO, in Orlando, FL in September 1999.

3. "Stage III involved nearly 5 years of continuous testing on NPR member station WETA-FM in Washington, DC, on-air mobile demonstration of the AM system at the NAB 2000 in Las Vegas, NV and NRSC endorsement of AM (daytime only) and FM systems. Following the NRSC endorsement, iBiquity Digital Corporation began its commercial rollout of IBOC systems and broadcast equipment manufacturers introduced digital exciters and transmission gear. On the consumer end, 13 consumer electronics manufacturers at the Consumer Electronics Show of 2003 announced HD Radio receiver plans. The FCC's authorization of the system came in October 2002."[5]

The roles played by IBOC proponents Lucent Digital Radio (LDR) and Digital Radio Express (DRE) are absent from this very brief overview, and are discussed in more detail in the next

---

[4] USA Digital Radio (USADR) formed a research and development team in 1990 to establish an IBOC digital broadcasting system.

[5] Source: E. Glynn Walden, Senior Vice President, Engineering, Infinity Broadcasting.

chapter. The acquisition of DRE intellectual property rights and the merger of USADR with LDR by the end of December of 2000, made iBiquity Digital Corporation the only proponent of IBOC digital radio technology in the U.S.A. Broadcasters in the U.S. began converting to iBiquity's HD Radio technology in 2003.

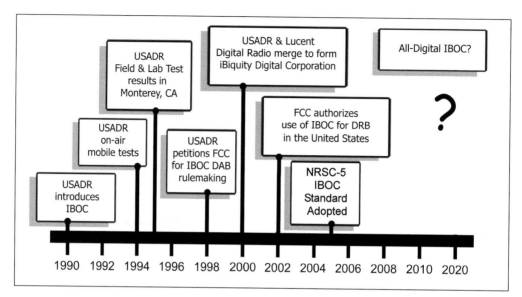

Figure 1.4 IBOC Radio Milestones

The NRSC and IBOC Development

The National Radio Systems Committee (NRSC) is jointly sponsored by the National Association of Broadcasters (NAB) and the Consumer Electronics Association (CEA). The NRSC was formed to study and make recommendations for technical standards that relate to radio broadcasting and the reception of radio broadcast signals. Through the NRSC, broadcasters and receiver manufacturers work together towards solutions to common problems in radio broadcast systems.

The NRSC became the major forum for considering, testing and evaluating proponent systems for digital radio broadcasting in the U.S. Through NRSC evaluations and literally hundreds of meetings of subcommittees, their test and evaluation working groups, and specialized task groups, the NRSC evolved into a major voice for the broadcast community on the issues surrounding IBOC development.

Through the work of the NRSC and its committees, the NRSC-5 voluntary standards were developed describing the specifications for the use of IBOC transmission. The NRSC Full Committee is the top-level committee that serves as an umbrella under which all other NRSC groups operate. Recommendations to proceed with developing technical standards usually originate within the NRSC Full Committee and are assigned to one of the NRSC Subcommittees for development and adoption.

The primary subcommittees are:

- The AM Broadcasting Subcommittee (AMB), which was formed in 2004 to review and maintain NRSC Standards relating to analog AM broadcasting;

- The Digital Radio Broadcasting Subcommittee (DRB), formerly known as the DAB Subcommittee, which has been primarily involved in the development and testing of AM IBOC and FM IBOC systems;

- The Radio Broadcast Data Standard subcommittee (RBDS), which developed the RBDS Standard (now called NRSC-4-A), the U.S. version of the European RDS standard for datacasting on analog FM radio subcarriers. In parallel with similar efforts in Europe, the RBDS subcommittee has recently engaged in harmonizing the RBDS standard with parameters required for data distribution using IBOC digital radio.

NRSC Test and Evaluation Process

With regard to IBOC and other radio technologies, the NRSC's role has been to undertake research, testing, evaluation and specification leading to the publication of technical standards. Such standards serve the public interest by enabling broadcasters, content providers and equipment manufacturers (for both transmission and reception equipment) to ensure compatibility and interoperability among hardware and systems in the same service.

NRSC testing often occurs in two stages: laboratory and field testing. In both cases, proponent demonstrations generally precede the onset of testing under the auspices of the NRSC. While the NRSC has no government standing, as it is an open consensus-based industry committee, its decisions and recommendations bear considerable weight in the public forum, including at the FCC. Leaving technology advocacy to its individual members and the committee's co-sponsors, the NRSC deliberates on the technological questions relating to the radio broadcasting industry. Throughout the development of IBOC technology, the NRSC has made significant contributions to the industry by performing and overseeing:

1. The production of radio industry open standards;

2. Documentation of the technical parameters of IBOC technology;

3. The enabling of broadcast equipment and receiver manufacturers to participate in NRSC activities who thereby develop products that are interoperable;

4. Objective and subjective evaluations of IBOC audio performance to establish whether IBOC offers improved performance and added value for consumers;

5. Examination of performance, compatibility and interference concerns, with a science-based approach to evaluation;

6. A smooth implementation and prudent transition to new technologies.

A guiding principle of the NRSC was first to determine if IBOC digital radio systems offered significant improvements over existing analog AM and FM radio services, while adequately protecting existing services from interference.

Digital Radio Transmission Technologies

In discussing digital radio technology, it is important to note that IBOC is only one of several digital transmission technologies that the U.S. could have chosen as its digital radio standard. Examining the characteristics of other digital radio technologies provides a clearer understanding of why the IBOC was selected as the best option for digital radio in the U.S.

Eureka-147 DAB

Eureka-147 DAB is a digital radio system developed in Europe by a research consortium known as the CCETT (Centre Commun d'Etudes de Telediffusion et Telecommunications). Eureka-147 is the name of the committee that developed the standard, and it is often used as a shorthand term to refer to Eureka-147 DAB technology. Eureka-147 has been deployed in Canada, several European countries including the United Kingdom and Germany, and in Asia. Eureka-147 is a broadband system that offers a minimum of five simultaneous high-quality digital audio channels, and more (perhaps of lesser quality) depending on the degree of compression employed on each channel. See Table 1.1 for an example of the manner in which the Eureka-147 bandwidth is allotted to the various channels (often called "stations" from the user's perspective). The table shows ways in which the BBC uses one radio signal (the *ensemble)* to transmit numerous program channels. To increase the number of programs available, the bit rates of individual channels are reduced, with commensurate reduction in audio quality. Eureka 147 DAB employs an early MPEG codec to digitally encode the audio (MPEG 2 Layer II), which has been the subject of debate because newer codecs would perform better at the lower bit rates now being employed on many ensembles. A new version of the technology, DAB+, employs a more efficient codec, MPEG-4 HE-AAC v2, that cannot be decoded by the existing receivers.

Eureka-147 can be received by mobile, portable and fixed receivers and may be used in a wide range of applications such as wide-area or local delivery of audio and data services for mobile, portable and fixed reception. It can be delivered terrestrially, via satellite; in a hybrid fashion (satellite with complementary terrestrial) and over cable networks. Eureka DAB systems have been implemented primarily at L-Band and at VHF frequencies. Depending on the degree of error protection employed, the system can deliver from 0.6 to 1.7 Mbps of useful information in one ensemble.

BBC "Station"	Typical data rate(s) kbps	Mode	Format
BBC Radio 1	128	Joint Stereo	Pop Music
BBC Radio 2	128	Joint Stereo	Easy Listening
BBC Radio 3	(128 –) 192	Joint Stereo/Stereo	Classical Music
BBC Radio 4	(80 –) 128	Mono/Joint Stereo	News and Speech
BBC Radio 4 (Secondary)	64	Mono	(Intermittent)
BBC Radio 5 Live	80	Mono	News and Sport
BBC 5LIVE SportX	32 – 80	Mono	Sport (Intermittent)
BBC 6 Music	128	Joint Stereo	Rock Music
BBC 7	80	Mono	
BBCAsian Network	64 (– 80)	Mono	
BBCWorld Service	64 (– 80)	Mono	
1Xtra – BBC	128	Joint Stereo	
BBC Guide	8 – 56	Packet Data	EPG

Table 1.1 BBC National DAB Ensemble Channel Allotment, 2006 (Source: *www.wohnort.org/DAB* October 2006 data)

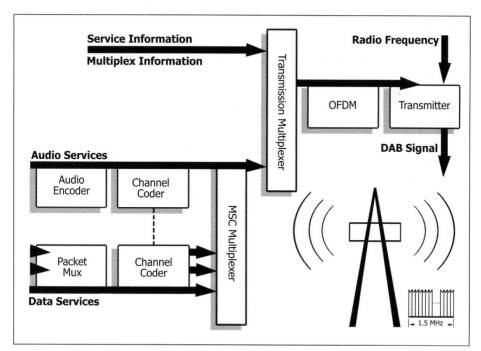

Figure 1.5 Generation of Eureka-147 DAB Signals (Source: WorldDMB)

Figure 1.5 shows how each Eureka-147 transmission is generated. A Eureka-147 signal is called an ensemble because one broadband signal carries numerous program channels and ancillary data. Each program signal is coded individually at the source level, then error protected and time interleaved in the channel coder. Eureka-147 services are multiplexed in the Main Service Channel (MSC), according to a pre-determined, but adjustable, multiplex configuration. Table 1.1 shows how the BBC varies the channel bandwidths (values in parentheses) to add temporary channels or to provide better quality to a high-value program. The multiplexer interleaves the data stream of each program channel across the width of the radio channel to obtain the benefits of frequency diversity. The multiplexer output is combined with Multiplex Control and Service information, which travel in the Fast Information Channel (FIC), to form the transmission frames in the Transmission Multiplexer. Orthogonal Frequency Division Multiplexing (OFDM) is applied to shape the DAB signal, which consists of a large number of carriers. The signal is then transposed to the appropriate radio frequency band, amplified and transmitted.

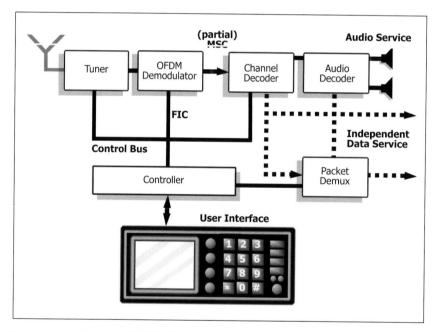

Figure 1.6 Reception of Eureka-147 DAB Signals (Source: WorldDMB)

Figure 1.6 shows a conceptual Eureka-147 DAB receiver. The DAB signal is received by the tuner section. The digital output of the tuner is fed to the OFDM demodulator and channel decoder to eliminate transmission errors. The information contained in the FIC (Fast Information Channel) is passed to the user interface for service selection and is used to set the receiver program appropriately. The MSC data is further processed in an audio decoder to produce the left and right audio signals or in a data decoder (Packet Demux) as appropriate.

Eureka DAB receivers have been on the market since the 1990s. They were very expensive initially, but prices have come down as more receivers have become available in various countries using the system. By late 2006 WorldDMB, the nongovernmental organization that now maintains and promotes the family of Eureka-147 standards, indicated that over 1,000 services had been launched in 40 nations worldwide, with signal covering territory occupied by 500 million people. The "core" DAB standards continue to be embellished, with new multimedia and IP (Internet protocol) protocols evolving that are capable of providing mobile video and data services. A Digital Multimedia Broadcasting (DMB) protocol first launched in Korea has also been adopted under the WorldDMB umbrella. This evolution prompted the WorldDAB Forum to change its name in 2006 to WorldDMB, for Digital Multimedia Broadcasting. At about the same time, the more efficient MPEG AAC was adopted as an optional audio codec for DAB technology. Countries that have not yet implemented DAB have an opportunity to employ AAC from the beginning of their operations. Countries with an installed base of DAB receivers must contemplate whether a migration to AAC that renders existing receivers obsolete is in the public interest.

Digital Radio Mondiale

DRM is an acronym for the digital audio broadcasting scheme from Digital Radio Mondiale, the name of the consortium that developed it. The DRM consortium was formed in 1998 to define a new digital audio system aimed at designing a system to facilitate conversion of analog services to digital for the bands below 30 MHz. DRM is an international standard for digital transmission on short-wave, medium-wave (which includes AM broadcasting) and long-wave frequency bands. In addition to being standardized for these bands below 30 MHz, in 2005 the DRM Consortium began the process of extending the system up to 120 MHz, with completion expected between 2007 and 2009.

Just as IBOC digital radio promises dramatic improvements for AM and FM analog radio in the U.S. broadcast bands, DRM digital radio technology provides similar advantages for worldwide transmission of programming in international bands. In addition to audio, the DRM system has the capacity to integrate data and text. This additional content can be displayed on DRM receivers to enhance the listening experience.

The DRM waveform was initially designed as a standalone waveform that would occupy vacant channels below 30 MHz. Replacing an analog signal, the DRM waveform will fit within the customary 9 or 10 kHz channels on many international broadcast bands. An enhanced version is available that occupies two adjacent channels. Since its development, several hybrid approaches have been postulated in which the DRM signal is transmitted with a companion analog signal in a pair of adjacent channels. In its most compact form, the approach would pair a 5 kHz AM single sideband signal with a 10 kHz DRM signal in a 15 kHz channel.

Many existing AM transmitters can be easily modified to carry DRM signals. Potential DRM applications include fixed and portable radios, car receivers, software receivers and Personal Digital Assistants (PDA). Several DRM receivers have been brought to market, including computer-enabled plug-in receivers, standalone receivers, and a software-based demodulator. The DRM system uses COFDM (Coded Orthogonal Frequency Division Multiplex) transmission. This means that all the data, produced from the digitally encoded audio and associated data signals, is distributed across a large number of closely spaced, relatively low bit rate carriers. All of these carriers are contained within the allotted transmission channel. The DRM system is designed so that the number of carriers can be varied, depending on factors such as the allotted channel bandwidth and degree of robustness required.

The DRM system enables the use of three variants of MPEG-4 audio compression. The high quality version with AAC coding can be replaced by a medium quality voice coder, MPEG-4 CELP (coded excited linear prediction) speech coding. For very low bit rate voice coding, HVXC (harmonic vector excitation coding) speech coding can be applied. Reducing the coder bit rate provides two benefits: decreased bandwidth and/or increased robustness. The coder rate is selected to provide the optimum balance of error protection overhead, audio quality, and channel bandwidth.

The world's first affordable DRM-capable consumer receivers, including car radios, were unveiled at the consumer electronics show IFA in Berlin, Germany, and during the International Broadcasting Convention (IBC), September 2006.[6]

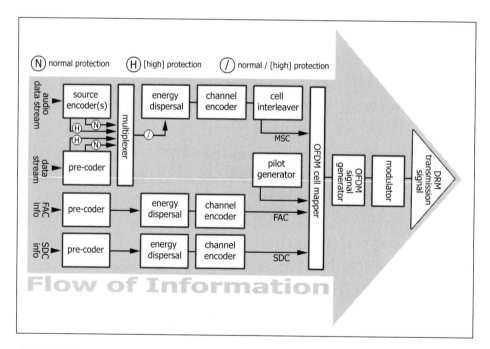

Figure 1.7 DRM Transmission System Design (Source: Digital Radio Mondiale)

---

[6] Digital Radio Mondiale, Project Office, Geneva, Switzerland.

CAM-D

CAM-D is the acronym for Compatible Amplitude Modulation-Digital, an undisclosed, nonstandardized hybrid analog/digital radio enhancement intended for AM radio broadcasting. CAM-D was developed by Leonard Kahn, who is widely known for his development of the Kahn/Hazeltine AM Stereo technology. The term *compatible* refers to the claim that CAM-D is supposed to work with most existing AM transmitters, to occupy limited sideband space in the AM mask, and to generate minimal adjacent channel interference potential. However, it is not compatible with hybrid AM IBOC operation.

There is little technical information publicly available to support the claims of CAM-D technology, despite reports that several AM stations are operating using this hybrid broadcast technology.[7] Published reports suggest that the technology increases the station's analog signal coverage area for analog radios by manipulating the analog RF signal. It has a reported analog bandwidth of ±8 kHz. A companion digital signal would provide up to 10 narrowband data channels for PAD and other services, and/or digital information that carries the high audio frequencies (8 to 15 kHz) missing from the analog signal. While the iBiquity hybrid AM HD Radio system utilizes the analog audio as a diversity backup to its complete digital copy of the audio, CAM-D is always reliant on the analog signal.

During the NRSC IBOC evaluation process, the CAM-D system was not presented to the NRSC for its consideration and therefore was not formally considered by the NRSC. Also, CAM-D is for the AM band only, and does not work in the FM band. CAM-D has not offered a migration path from a hybrid to an all-digital AM system.

Figure 1.8 Nokia World GSM Phone with DVB-H Mobile Reception (Source: Nokia USA)

---

[7] www.wrathofkahn.org

DVB-T

DVB-T (Digital Video Broadcasting – Terrestrial) is one of several digital broadcast technologies belonging to a family of related digital broadcasting systems for cable, satellite and terrestrial delivery of television services. These are known as DVB-C for DVB cable, DVB-S for DVB satellite and DVB-T for DVB television. All DVB systems were primarily designed for television broadcasting but since television transmission includes audio, DVB profiles are capable of providing audio-only broadcasts.

DVB-T proved to be inefficient for reception on mobile or portable receivers. The high data rates and wide bandwidth needed to operate the system increases power consumption and makes the design of battery-powered receivers difficult.

DVB-H

DVB-H is one of the latest standards from the DVB Project targeting handheld, battery-operated devices, such as mobile phones, PDAs, etc. Based on DVB-T, DVB-H was designed to ensure high quality, reliable mobile reception and to provide the extended battery capacity needed for mobile or handheld devices.

In a DVB-H system, formatted television content may be distributed to terrestrial DTV transmitters from satellite or another terrestrial feed (e.g., fiber or copper). Consumers then receive the content via region-specific frequencies on their mobile device from the DTV transmission or feed in their area. COFDM modulation is used in terrestrial bandwidths of 5, 6, 7 or 8 MHz.

The systems further reduce receiver power consumption through time slicing. Data is sent as "IP-datagrams" which are transmitted as data bursts in predictable time slots. The RF front-end of the mobile receiver is switched off most of the time and is only on during the selected short transmission bursts, conserving power in battery-operated devices. DVB-H has also been designed for small screen and antenna sizes to give reliable, high-speed reception.[8]

The Nokia N92 World GSM Phone with DVB-H mobile device is typical of the new generation of DVB-H devices capable of receiving TV broadcast programs. DVB-H technology enables extension of home TV services to mobile devices. Up to 50 TV channels can be delivered with low cost, over one network.

---

[8] Via satellite.

Integrated Services Digital Broadcasting for Terrestrial Sound Broadcasting (ISDB-TSB)

Integrated Services Digital Broadcasting was developed in Japan. Supported by the Digital Broadcasting Experts Group (DiBEG), formed in 1997, ISDB has obtained a foothold in the consumer marketplace. By 2006 ISDB products (mostly TV sets) were selling in Japan on the order of several millions of units per year.[9] In 2006 Brazil announced the adoption of an ISDB-based terrestrial digital broadcasting plan. The technical characteristics of ISDB-TSB offer flexibility in that it is designed for fixed, portable and mobile delivery of television and radio services and can operate in variable bandwidth channels. The ISDB-TSB system is similar to DVB-T technology.

ISDB-TSB has the capacity to provide one to seven CD quality audio channels depending on the digital audio codec bit allocation per channel as determined by the broadcast station. ISDB-TSB operates in the VHF and UHF frequency bands.

Satellite Digital Audio Radio Services (SDARS)

The era of satellite radio in the U.S. began in 1992 when the Federal Communications Commission (FCC) allotted 25 MHz of spectrum in the "S" band (2.3 GHz) for nationwide broadcasting of satellite-based Digital Audio Radio Service (SDARS). The two U.S. SDARS are both subscription-based. XM Satellite Radio was the first to launch service in the U.S., beginning in November 2001, and Sirius Satellite Radio followed in July 2002. Both services offer in excess of 100 audio channels typically programmed with a variety of music and talk content. SDARS are authorized as national services and must transmit the same signal nationwide, without local differentiation.

XM and Sirius Satellite Radio

XM and Sirius systems use complementary terrestrial transmitters known as "gap-fillers" also operating on S-Band frequencies. These gap-fillers are strategically placed to fill in coverage in tunnels, urban areas, and elsewhere on the ground where reception may be obstructed from line-of-sight satellite coverage.

XM Satellite Radio uses two Boeing HS 702 satellites, placed in parallel geostationary orbit, one at 85 degrees west longitude and the other at 115 degrees west longitude. The Geostationary Earth Orbit (GEO) is about 22,223 miles (35,764 km) above Earth. As the earth rotates, the GEO satellite revolves around the earth above the equator, maintaining a fixed position relative to receivers on the ground. The advantage of GEO satellites is the predictable position of the satellites in the sky. A disadvantage of GEO is the satellites are most directly above the equator, limiting their average elevation angle to the Northern Hemisphere. Lower elevation angles are more susceptible to terrain and building obstructions than high angles. The first XM satellite, "Rock," was launched on March 18, 2001, with "Roll" following on May 8. By 2007, Rock and Roll had been shifted to the role of in-orbit spares, and new satellites, "Rhythm" and Blues," had

---

[9] Source: Japan Electronics and Information Technology Industries Association (JEITA).

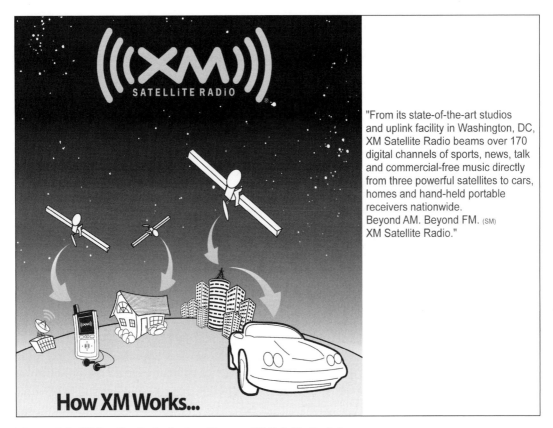

"From its state-of-the-art studios and uplink facility in Washington, DC, XM Satellite Radio beams over 170 digital channels of sports, news, talk and commercial-free music directly from three powerful satellites to cars, homes and hand-held portable receivers nationwide.
Beyond AM. Beyond FM. (SM)
XM Satellite Radio."

Figure 1.9 XM Satellite Radio System (Source: XM Satellite Radio)

taken their places. Satellite radio services became the first mobile digital radio services available to consumers in the U.S.A.

Unlike XM, Sirius does not use GEO satellites. Instead, its three SS/L-1300 satellites form a highly inclined elliptical earth orbit (HEO) satellite constellation. The satellites trace elliptical orbits that place them directly above the continental U.S. for about 16 hours a day. Because each satellite completes one orbit in 24 hours, they are said to be "geosynchronous," although they are not geostationary. Daily, each satellite follows the same path in the sky above the continental U.S.[10] Typically two satellites are above the U.S., while the third is making its slingshot run over the southern hemisphere, accelerating in its elliptical orbit, minimizing out of range time and maximizing its time over the U.S.A. At any given time, two satellites use two portions of the

---

[10] From the point of view of the ground, the satellite track is in the shape of an *analemma*—a contorted figure-eight-like shape in the sky. For more on the analemma, check out www.analemma.com. For more on the Sirius analemma, check out www.heavens-above.com/orbitdisplay.asp?satid=26390 or register as a user and use the Select Satellite option.

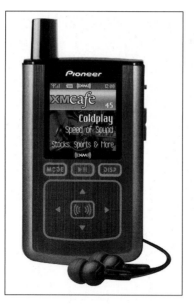

Figure 1.10 Pioneer XM2Go Portable Satellite Radio (Source: Pioneer Electronics)

frequency band to transmit their signals, while the other is silent, waiting its turn to replace the next satellite to go out of range. This design increases the complexity of the system, requiring the uplink to track the satellite, the system to handle channel hand-offs, and the like. This was a design trade-off chosen by Sirius in order to improve the average elevation angle of reception, and presumably reduce the number of terrestrial repeaters that would be necessary. Sirius completed its three-satellite constellation on November 30, 2000. A fourth satellite remains on the ground, ready to be launched if any of the three active satellites encounter transmission problems. Sirius proposed a modified system which uses a single geostationary satellite to augment the HEO satellites.

In other respects (besides satellite configuration), the Sirius system is similar to the XM system. Sirius channels are transmitted to three Sirius satellites, which then transmit the signals to the ground, where satellite radio receivers pick up one of the overlapping footprints of the satellite array. Signals are also beamed to the ground repeaters for listeners in urban areas where the satellite signal may be blocked.

To initiate their services, Sirius and XM subsidised the cost of manufacture of early car radios and home entertainment systems by the major consumer electronics manufacturers.

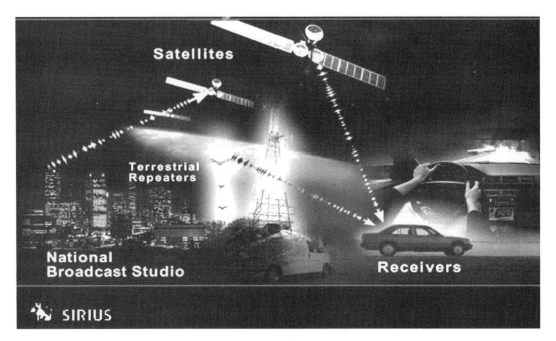

Figure 1.11 Sirius Satellite Radio Transmission (Source: Sirius Satellite Radio)

SDARS Terrestrial Repeaters

Both Sirius and XM satellite radio use complementary terrestrial repeaters operating in their licensed S-band frequencies. Repeaters rebroadcast satellite programming into hard to reach or shadowed areas where the satellite signal is blocked by tall buildings, tunnels or hard-to-reach canyons. Because of the differences in the XM and Sirius satellite system designs, more translators are required by XM to fill in coverage gaps than Sirius.

Sirius repeaters tend to be low-power covering five to 10 miles in range. XM repeaters vary from low-power up to higher powers that may emit tens of kilowatts of effective radiated power. XM-Radio alone has set up approximately 1,500 high-power terrestrial repeaters. Each XM market typically has dual repeaters operating at 2337.485 MHz and 2340.015 MHz.

There has been concern expressed by terrestrial broadcasters that these repeater networks could slip in a regulatory back door and originate local content, directly competing with local broadcasters. These repeaters, some fear, could form the basis for a third terrestrial radio service if the satellite radio business fails, or that these repeaters could be used for local origination. Without debating the benefits and detriments posed by satellite repeaters, they are an integral part of both satellite radio services and another component of the digital radio landscape.

WorldSpace Satellite

WorldSpace was originally formed to provide digital radio and data services to underserved regions of the world such as developing countries where power sources may not be readily available. Accordingly, the system was designed with regional coverage in mind using multiple satellites and whose signals were to be received by portable generator-powered receivers that were stationary. Initially, personal and mobile radios were not contemplated.

Two L-band satellite transmission systems named "Afristar" and "Asiastar" in geostationary orbit are used to cover Asia, Africa, the Middle East and parts of Europe. These satellites were launched in October 1998 and March 2000, respectively. The launch of a third satellite, named AmeriStar, was planned to cover Mexico, Central America and South America.

Each of the WorldSpace satellites' three beams can deliver over 50 channels of digital audio and multimedia programming via the 1,467- to 1,492-MHz segment of the L-Band spectrum, allocated for digital audio broadcasting.

WorldSpace was licensed as an international satellite radio service. The United States is not currently part of WorldSpace's coverage area. WorldSpace is pursuing world domination of the satellite radio market. WorldSpace's target audience is the millions of people living in Africa, Asia and the Middle East who cannot pick up a signal from a conventional radio station. WorldSpace estimates its potential audience to be about 4.6 billion people spanning five continents. World-Space is now a subscription-based service and terrestrial repeater technology is being developed to support mobile reception.

There has been some speculation that the coverage of WorldSpace's proposed AmeriStar satellite would create L-band interference in the U.S. where L-band is restricted to government and military use.[11]

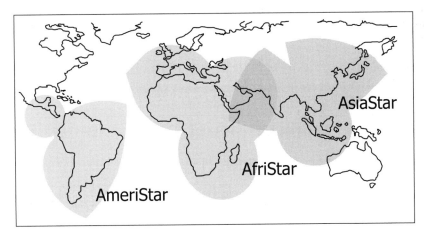

Figure 1.12 WorldSpace Satellite Radio Coverage (Source: WorldSpace Incorporated)

---

[11] How Stuff Works Inc., 1998–2006.

Figure 1.13 WorldSpace Satellite Radio Receiver (Source: WorldSpace Incorporated)

WorldSpace satellite receivers are capable of receiving data at a rate of 128 kilobits per second (kbps). The receivers use the proprietary StarMan chipset, manufactured by STMicroelectronics, to receive digital signals from the satellites.

Extended Digital Services

In addition to IBOC and other digital broadcasting technologies, several digital applications have been developed that permit broadcasters to use high capacity digital FM subcarriers for additional programming applications or eCommerce functions.

Digital Radio Express (DRE)

Proponents of digital radio broadcasting promote the ability to broadcast multiple or "multicast" channels as one of its primary advantages. The IBOC system allows the FM station to share the 96-kbit digital audio stream among the primary and multicast program channels by scaling the bit streams of each channel.

Digital Radio Express had taken this option a step further by digitizing the FM subcarrier region of the analog FM signal. The DRE system, trademarked FMeXtra™, permits analog-only FM stations as well as hybrid FM IBOC stations to transmit additional independent audio streams to provide multichannel digital content on their FM subcarriers.

DRE's FMeXtra model X1 encoder may also be used to broadcast discrete 5.1 surround sound audio channels without encoding or synthesizing. Telematic data, text messaging, and multilingual broadcast channels are also possible using this digital radio technology. Figure 1.14 shows a functional diagram of the FMeXtra encoder.

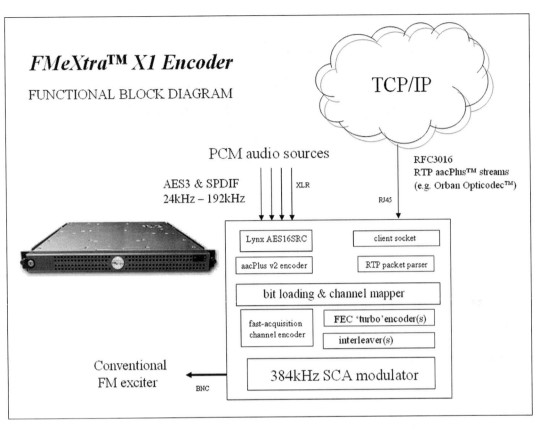

Figure 1.14 FMeXtra Model X1 Encoder (Source: DRE, Inc. U.S.A.)

The FMeXtra signal is a subcarrier that is combined with the composite baseband signal that includes the audio program. The composite baseband then frequency modulates the FM carrier. The subcarrier itself utilizes a COFDM multicarrier modulation scheme with error correction and IF equalization in the receiver to minimize multipath effects. Several different modes of operation with different data densities are available. In addition, there is flexibility in the bandwidth and number of bits allocated to each channel. This design provides the ability to tailor the FMeXtra energy to the available subcarrier spectrum on the FM station.[12]

In addition to developing chipsets and firmware necessary to build receivers, DRE developed a specialized receiver for reception of FMeXtra encoded content. According to DRE, the transmitted FMeXtra signal is at least as compatible with existing FM receivers as any other subcarrier system is, however there has been no public, independent testing or evaluation of the FMeXtra system. Existing FM subcarrier receivers cannot demodulate FMeXtra. A typical FMeXtra reference receiver is shown in Figure 1.15.

---

[12] Radio Guide, Media Magazines Inc., "Extra! Extra! FMeXtra!," October 2006.

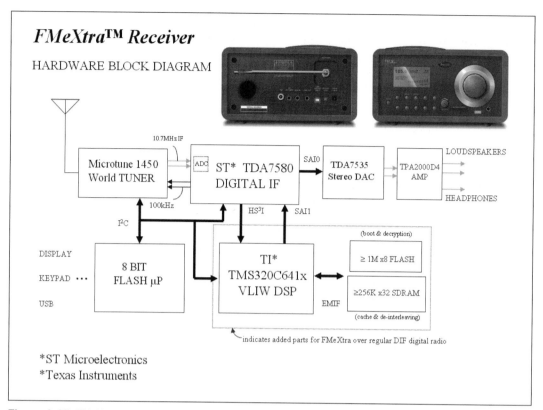

Figure 1.15 FMeXtra Aruba Model Receiver (Source: DRE, Inc. U.S.A.)

Stratos Audio Inc. and Stratos Interactive

Technology developed and patented by Stratos Audio provides radio listeners with interactivity features. Stratos highlights its "Get" button (Hit the Get[SM]) intended for consumer radios. The button provides a fundamental form of interactivity, permitting the listener to respond immediately to a call to action over the air. As with other digital radio systems, the Stratos model requires the building of broadcast infrastructure simultaneously with the introduction of consumer radios equipped with special features. Radio stations would install Stratos Audio Broadcast Management Software to support interactivity. Consumers with Stratos-equipped radios could employ four interactive segments: The Web, SMS, Interactive Automotive radios and Interactive Mobile devices such as mobile phones and MP3 players.[13] For instance, broadcasters could provide participating listeners with traffic, news or sports messages via email or their mobile phones, and advertiser interactivity on their Internet browsers.

---

[13] StratosInteractive promotional material.

With the infrastructure in place, Stratos could offer an expanding menu of extended features. Station-transmitted information could be stored at a suitably equipped receiver for later retrieval and interaction by the listener. Programming and marketing feedback could be obtained with real-time or historical monitoring of responses and interaction (behavioral aggregation), while providing "safe usage for the listener."

A Context For IBOC

It is in the context of nearly two decades of digital radio effort on all continents that IBOC came onto the scene in a uniquely American way. With the lack of a centrally controlled broadcasting environment typical of many countries where government-owned stations dominate the broadcast landscape, and instead having a diverse network of one-station, one-license, one-program broadcasts, the U.S. market was primed for an individualistic solution to the digital radio broadcasting transition. That solution, IBOC, preserves the single-station, single-frequency model and the status quo in broadcast ownership. This contrasts with the DAB model in some nations where the government operates a nationwide network of stations with one or more program channels, harboring an interest in transmitting one broadband radio signal with an *ensemble* of program channels. With a more centrally planned infrastructure, the transition to Eureka-147, a broadband signal with a large ensemble of programs on one signal, is a natural choice. In the U.S.A., radio broadcasting has always been in the context of a vigorous, diverse, competitive market of individual, privately controlled, radio stations.

The idea of consolidation of these individual stations into mere program streams on centrally controlled broadband program ensembles was anathema to the industry. Even with the broadcast ownership consolidation that began in the 1990s, the in-band solution for terrestrial digital radio fit the U.S. model of a diversely operated local radio market. In *Understanding IBOC: Digital Technology for Analog Economics*,[14] the authors describe how the "U.S. broadcasters swam against the global tide" pursuing IBOC instead of Eureka-147. Further opining that the evidence indicates Eureka-147 was technologically superior, they conclude the FCC's adoption of IBOC as the route for digital terrestrial radio in the U.S.A. reflects "the differing social, economic, and political currents in the U.S. context, and demonstrate that technological diffusion may depend largely on what causes the least disruption to existing industrial structures." Indeed, the U.S. Federal Communications Commission (FCC), among its statements on DAB and public policy said,

The Commission remains firmly committed to the related goals of "supporting a vibrant and vital terrestrial radio service for the public" and creating DAB opportunities for existing radio broadcasters. We must ensure that the introduction of DAB does not weaken the vitality of our free, over-the-air broadcast service, which provides service to virtually all Americans through a strong, independent system of privately owned and operated stations.[15]

To a broadcaster, the prospect of having to share a radio signal with a competitor, or worse, of a third party controlling access to the airwaves, did not sit well—particularly with the commercial

---

[14] Understanding IBOC: Digital Technology for Analog Economics, Journal of Radio Studies, Vol. 10, No. 1, pp. 63–79, M. Ala-Fossi, A. Stavitsky.

[15] FCC, *In the Matter of Digital Audio Broadcasting Systems and Their Impact.*

broadcasters. Adoption of a system like Eureka-147 was perceived as antithetical to the premise of local broadcasting: the U.S. broadcaster is both a programmer and a transmitter of the radio signal—a nongovernmental entity licensed to do so in the public interest. IBOC preserves licensees' individual control of each station with its specific frequency and local market place, hand-in-hand with the programming service carried on that station.

On the consumer electronics side of the equation, manufacturers need good reason to spend a few cents or dollars to add a feature to a radio product. iBiquity had its work cut out for it, having to solve the age-old chicken-and-egg problem[16] that is endemic to the broadcast industry. Why should broadcasters spend millions on a digital conversion if there are no receivers and no guarantee there will be any? Why should manufacturers spend precious pennies per receiver on a product with no service and a logo without portfolio?

iBiquity's rise required cajoling along broadcasters, manufacturers, and regulators (and of course, investors). Their effort is a case-study in navigating a very complex marketplace. Fascinating as that story will be when written, it is not the subject of this book. With the HD Radio station count up to four digits and the HD Radio logo appearing on a geometrically increasing number of radio faceplates, the technology is steadily entering the marketplace. The brand name "HD Radio" passes the lips of on-air announcers daily, gently influencing those who listen to the radio.

The technology had a strategic purpose, at first. To get radio broadcasting on the digital band-wagon and forestall eventual analog irrelevance in a digital world, IBOC seemed like the answer. The benefits of better audio quality, in the form of what digital does well—overcome the flaws of the communications channel—were subtle on the FM side and more apparent on AM, but hardly the "killer application" the industry was seeking. Some momentum was gained with the help of National Public Radio's Tomorrow Radio initiative, which, among other things, highlighted the innovation of "multicasting." This was the idea that broadcasters could do what they do best, create compelling programming, to provide the public with greater choice on the radio dial. On the commercial side, the HD Digital Radio Alliance was formed in 2005, and broadcasters committed to putting supplemental HD Radio channels on the air. The result was two eggs to solve the chicken-and-egg problem—the installation of digital transmitters and the creation of new program channels for the consumer to discover. A compelling value proposition was created for the consumer.

In the next chapter we take a look at the NRSC-process that led to the industry standard. Following that, the second section of this book dissects the technical standard known as NRSC-5.

---

[16] For those unfamiliar with the idiom, the classic question, "Which came first, the chicken or the egg?" has applied to technological initiatives in broadcasting because there are so many stakeholders in the industry with divergent objectives and needs. It all comes down to listeners who listen to the programming provided by broadcasters, and who also are the ones who buy radios, not based particularly on performance or quality, but features for a price point. Broadcasters are not inclined to invest in unproven technologies (the egg?), while receiver manufacturers must follow the fickle tastes of the consumer electronics marketplace, and need consumer demand to put the next feature in a radio (the chicken). Ultimately, the excitement for the consumer has to be there when the new radio is first turned on. Hence, it is up to the broadcaster to offer the new feature, whether it be stereo, color (TV), or digital broadcasting before the consumer will buy a device to receive it.

2 The Path to the IBOC Standard

The work of the National Radio Systems Committee (NRSC) on the IBOC project is a story of persistence and patience. In this chapter, the tale of the NRSC-5 Standard is told. First, it follows the history of IBOC technology, adding new pieces of the puzzle to the historical background given in Chapter 1. These events are then connected to the trail blazed by the NRSC.

The NRSC and its subcommittees comprise numerous volunteer member companies in broadcasting, electronics manufacturing and related fields. According to the NRSC Procedures Manual, rev 1.2, "Membership in the NRSC full committee and its subcommittees, working groups, etc., is open to organizations with a direct and material interest in a matter within the respective jurisdiction of these groups. Membership in CEA or NAB is not a requirement for participation." The member organizations volunteer the time and expertise of their representatives. These representatives spend countless hours asking, testing, proposing, and deliberating on industry technical issues. Supported by the able staff of the Consumer Electronics Association and the National Association of Broadcasters, the NRSC DAB Subcommittee[1] members' representatives ushered along the IBOC process, working in a public forum to test and evaluate IBOC technology.

The sequence of events of the entire process leading to the NRSC-5 Standard is outlined in this chapter. The regulatory role of the U.S. Federal Communications Commission (FCC) is also

---

[1] The DAB Subcommittee became the DRB Subcommittee in September 2005.

highlighted. When finished with this chapter, the reader may develop a deeper appreciation for the complexity, the diligence, the thoroughness, and the openness of the process. Some of the section titles contain acronyms for committees, working groups, or task groups highlighted in the section, to help punctuate the story with the individual roles of these groups.

IBOC Precursors

The road to IBOC has its roots in the late 1980s. To be a bit pedantic, the road to IBOC could also be said to have had its beginnings in the compact disc, which, in turn, could trace its beginnings to the 1930s. The CD, released to the marketplace in 1982, was the convergence point of decades of digital technological accomplishments and became the harbinger of digital things to come. It was the first widely adopted digital consumer medium. As digital processing became cheaper and more commonplace through the 1970s, CD technology incorporated that technology and many theoretical concepts, some dating back decades, into an affordable consumer electronics package. Among the bits of knowledge and technology that converged on the creation of the CD were analog-to-digital and digital-to-analog conversion, Reed-Solomon error correction coding from 1960, digital sampling theory (Harry Nyquist, 1928; Claude Shannon, 1948[2]), and pulse code modulation (Alec Reeves, 1937)[3]. By the late 1980s, it was clear that digital signal processing could do for wired and wireless electronic media what it did for the CD. In 1987 the Eureka-147 consortium formed, and by 1990 a Eureka-147 DAB prototype had reached the North American continent.[4]

IBOC's Beginnings

Perhaps the first official act of the IBOC era was the formation of a partnership in 1990 between CBS, Gannett, and Westinghouse to explore an in-band digital radio broadcasting solution. Not long after that, the NRSC Digital Audio Broadcasting Subcommittee was formed and began to follow developments in the field. Eureka-147 was making a lot of buzz internationally, and set the bar on what digital technology could do for DAB at the time. By 1995 the Electronic Industries Association's Subcommittee on Digital Audio Radio (DAR) and the NRSC DAB Subcommittee[5] were looking closely at the technologies. Nine DAR systems were laboratory tested, with the report published in August 1995. Field testing in San Francisco followed the next year on the Eureka-147, AT&T/Lucent IBAC, and VOA/JPL systems.[6]

---

[2] "A Mathematical Theory of Communications," Claude Shannon, 1948.

[3] *Alec Reeves: Designer of the Digital Age*, D. Robertson, Imperial College Lectures, 2006.

[4] "Digital Radio Broadcasting and CRC," Communications Research Centre Canada, 1997.

[5] The DAB Subcommittee was eventually renamed the DRB Subcommittee (for Digital Radio Broadcasting) in September 2005 to acknowledge that in the digital age, radio is not just about audio anymore, but also about other digitized broadcast information.

[6] "Field Testing of Proposed Digital Audio Radio Systems, Part 1: Mobile Data Collection System," Stanley Salek and Daniel Mansergh, Hammett an Edison, Inc, *NAB Broadcast Engineering Conference Proceedings*, 1997.

Proponent	Band (MHz)	Subgroup	Subgroup Designator
Eureka 147*	1452–1492	New Band	NB
AT&T	88–108	In-Band Adjacent-Channel	IBAC
USADR-AM	0.54–1.7	In-Band On-Channel	IBOC
AT&T/Amati*	88–108	In-Band On-Channel	IBOC
USADR-FM#1	88–108	In-Band On-Channel	IBOC
USADR-FM#2	88–108	In-Band On-Channel	IBOC
VOA/JPL	2310–2360	Direct Broadcast Satellite	DBS

These technologies each have two modes, for a total of nine systems tested.

Table 2.1 Digital Radio Test Laboratory "Table 1 System/Subgroup Designators"[7]

By September 1996 it was recognized that IBOC was not ready for prime time, and the DAB Subcommittee went on hiatus. Meanwhile Westinghouse Electric's broadcast arm, Group W, merged with CBS, and Gannett went out of the radio business. The USADR effort was now fully under the Westinghouse roof, as was sister company Westinghouse Wireless Solutions, headed by Robert Struble, President. Struble went on to become President, CEO, and Board Chairman of iBiquity Digital Corporation. In mid-1996 the new CBS decided to make IBOC a strategic objective,[8] giving Struble the nod to kick-start development. As Struble put it to Radio Ink (Sept 23, 2002), prior to 1996 the USADR effort was "a big science project...but it wasn't really a whole-hog effort."

New Technical Muscle

By the fall NAB Radio Show, 1996, Westinghouse Wireless Solutions was going whole hog with IBOC, as evidenced by its flurry of technical papers on the fundamentals of making IBOC work. Brian Kroeger, D.Sc.,[9] who became Chief Scientist at iBiquity Digital Corporation, was with Westinghouse Wireless Solutions at the time. He presented a technical paper at the 1996 Radio Show entitled, "Improved IBOC DAB technology for AM and FM Broadcasting," coauthored by A. J. Vigil, Ph.D. He presented a second paper, with a subtle title change—from "improved" to "robust"—at the 1997 NAB show, co-written with Paul Peyla, "Robust IBOC DAB AM and FM Technology for Digital Audio Broadcasting." This paper laid out the constraints within which a successful IBOC design must function, paving the way to a quantum leap in IBOC's potential for

---

[7] *Report on Digital Audio Radio Laboratory Tests; Transmission Quality, Failure Characterization, and Analog Compatibility.* Electronic Industries Association Consumer Electronics Group, Thomas B. Keller, Chairman Working Group B (Testing), August 11, 1995.

[8] "Can Radio Survive the New Millennium?" *Radio Ink*, August 30, 1999.

[9] No mention of the Herculean technical development effort of USADR and successor iBiquity, to get IBOC to work would be complete without the name of Glynn Walden, whose intricate technical understanding of the AM and FM environments in the U.S.A. helped shape the IBOC signal. Walden was called "the Godfather of IBOC" by Guy Wire, in Radio World, August 14, 2002.

success. At the 1997 NAB Radio Show that fall, Kroeger presented another paper for USADR, "Robust Modem and Coding Techniques for FM Hybrid IBOC DAB," authored with Denise Cammarata. At the same time, Xetron Corporation published an AM channel characterization and IBOC model for USADR, entitled "AM Hybrid IBOC DAB System." USADR had a relationship with Bell Laboratories/Lucent Technologies which published under the USADR logo, "An OFDM All-Digital In-Band On-Channel (IBOC) AM and FM Radio Solution Using the PAC[10] Encoder." All in all, 1996 and 1997 were watershed years in the reinvigoration of the IBOC movement.

By February of 1998, the NRSC[11] DAB Subcommittee was reactivated (Chaired by Milford Smith, of Greater Media, with the later addition of co-chair Mike Bergman of Kenwood U.S.A. Corporation). The reactivation, ironically, came at the request of Digital Radio Express (DRE), the company whose key engineer, Derek Kumar, was a transplanted IBOC player. Kumar had previously worked under contract to USADR and had filed patents on his inventions in the IBOC arena. DRE sought to have their version of an IBOC technology reviewed by NRSC. USADR, and separately, Lucent Digital Radio (LDR), quickly followed suit and rejoined the NRSC process.

NRSC Cranks It Up

Presented with a "now what?" moment, NRSC rose to the occasion and established new DAB Subcommittee objectives. The DAB Subcommittee began the process of ushering IBOC technologies down the runway for review. The key component of the subcommittee's objective at the time was to individually compare each proposed IBOC technology with the current state of analog AM and FM service, asking the question "can IBOC be better than analog?" The next question, if the answer to the first were yes, is "what is the impact of IBOC on existing analog service; can they coexist?" The rest of the objectives and goals relate to process—build a technical record, conduct and/or oversee testing, draw conclusions, be impartial. Proponents interested in participating in the NRSC process were required to have both an AM and an FM IBOC solution.

---

[10] "PAC" and "Perceptual Audio Coder" are trademarks of Lucent Technologies.

[11] The Chairman of the NRSC full committee during this period was Charlie Morgan, of Susquehanna Radio Corporation, who stepped down after more than 20 years of service, in 2007, earning the acclamation of the industry.

National Radio Systems Committee
DAB Subcommittee Goals and Objectives

(as adopted by the Subcommittee on May 14, 1998)

Objectives

(a) To study IBOC DAB systems and determine if they provide broadcasters and users with:

- A digital signal with significantly greater quality and durability than available from the AM and FM analog systems that presently exist in the United States;

- A digital service area that is at least equivalent to the host station's analog service area while simultaneously providing suitable protection in co-channel and adjacent channel situations;

- A smooth transition from analog-to-digital services.

(b) To provide broadcasters and receiver manufacturers with the information they need to make an informed decision on the future of digital audio broadcasting in the United States, and if appropriate to foster its implementation.

Goals

To meet its objectives, the Subcommittee will work towards achieving the following goals:

(a) To develop a technical record and, where applicable, draw conclusions that will be useful to the NRSC in the evaluation of IBOC systems;

(b) To provide a direct comparison between IBOC DAB and existing analog broadcasting systems, and between an IBOC signal and its host analog signal, over a wide variation of terrain and under adverse propagation conditions that could be expected to be found throughout the United States;

(c) To fully assess the impact of the IBOC DAB signal upon the existing analog broadcast signals with which they must co-exist;

(d) To develop a testing process and measurement criteria that will produce conclusive, believable and acceptable results, and be of a streamlined nature so as not to impede rapid development of this new technology;

(e) To work closely with IBOC system proponents in the development of their laboratory and field test plans, which will be used to provide the basis for the comparisons mentioned in Goals (a) and (b);

(f) To indirectly participate in the test process, by assisting in selection of (one or more) independent testing agencies, or by closely observing proponent-conducted tests, to ensure that the testing as defined under Goal (e) is executed in a thorough, fair and impartial manner.

Testing Proponents' Technologies: TGWG

The NRSC DAB Subcommittee formed a Test Guidelines Working Group (TGWG) to develop testing recommendations. At this stage, the nascent competing IBOC technologies were in various prototype stages, complicating the prospect of testing. With differing and unpredictable development schedules, there was no practicable way to have all proponents' technologies on a test bench at the same time. Further, at this stage of development, any comparisons of the technologies would have been premature. The question to answer, therefore, was not "whose technology is best?" There would be no head-to-head competition, or in culinary terms, no "bake-off" where a winner walks away with first prize. The TGWG, Chaired by Andy Laird of Journal Broadcast Group, completed Part 1—the laboratory test guidelines for AM and FM IBOC systems—and they were officially adopted by NRSC in December 1998. Part 2, the field test guidelines, were completed and adopted in March 1999. This paragraph from the Part 1 introduction reveals the tone of the TPWG's effort:

Unlike the prior DAB test program which the NRSC participated in, where multiple systems were tested simultaneously, these guidelines are designed to support independent testing of systems either by the proponents themselves (with third-party oversight, as discussed in Section 2) or by independent test contractors. In fact, the guidelines recognize that systems being designed by different organizations rarely develop according to the same schedule, and once developed, it is usually necessary to test them as quickly as possible so as to foster rapid deployment.[12]

The TGWG's system test guidelines would tell the IBOC proponents for what information the NRSC was looking, and, in a general way, how it should be accomplished. Exact test procedures were not specified. There were several dimensions to the testing. Figure 2.1 illustrates the dimensions. To begin with, there were two systems, AM and FM. Proponents were required to have a solution in both bands.

As another dimension, two fundamental issues were of interest, performance and compatibility. The performance testing sought to understand not only the audio quality and signal coverage under ideal reception conditions, but also how the system performs when conditions are imperfect, that is to say under *impairment*. The compatibility testing was focused on three components: the impact of the digital waveform of one IBOC station on the reception of other analog stations, the impact on reception of the host analog signal in the presence of the hybrid digital waveform, and the reception of one IBOC station in the presence of other IBOC stations. Tests were conducted between "desired" and "undesired" signals to determine the impact of the undesired signal on reception of the desired signal. These were the digital-to-analog and digital-to-digital compatibility tests. The other compatibility concern was how the digital signal affects analog reception of the same station (the "host" analog signal). This testing was called host compatibility testing. Not only was host compatibility testing concerned with digital interaction with analog host reception, but also in the reverse, it was concerned with the manner in which the host analog signal might interfere with its companion digital signal.

---

[12] *DAB Subcommittee In-band On-channel (IBOC) Digital Audio Broadcasting (DAB) System Test Guidelines Part I – Laboratory Tests*, National Radio Systems Committee, Adopted December 3, 1998, available at www.nscstandards.org.

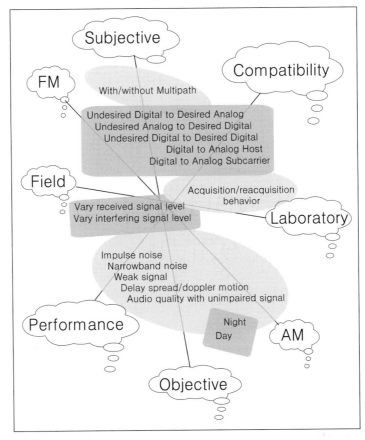

Figure 2.1 The Many Dimensions of Initial IBOC Testing

In a third dimension, testing was also divided into field and laboratory components. Tests under pristine, controlled laboratory conditions, permit precise measurements of the IBOC thresholds and characteristics, whereas the field tests determine how the systems perform in complex real-world conditions and validate the assumptions used to set up the lab tests. Signal levels, noise levels, multipath, vehicular motion, and the like were included in the lab test conditions to evaluate the system performance under signal impairments.

Two kinds of testing formed a fourth dimension to the analysis—objective and subjective testing. In addition to measurements of the system characteristics such as signal-to-noise ratio performance (objective testing), audio recordings were made under specified conditions for listening tests by expert listeners and/or consumers (subjective testing). The subjective test component provided a statistical analysis of listener reaction to the perceived quality of the received signal under the various impairment conditions. The test guidelines required subjective listener testing of the audio tracks to be conducted with members of general public as administered by qualified testing professionals.

Various parts of the testing were conducted either by qualified independent labs or by the proponents themselves. USADR submitted its system test report in December 1999, announcing almost simultaneously that it had obtained key intellectual property rights from DRE. Digital Radio Express would no longer be a proponent of a third IBOC technology. About a month later, in early 2000, LDR submitted its test report to the NRSC.

Regulatory Progress

During the same period, beginning about 1990, the U.S. Federal Communications Commission (FCC) was keeping an eye on the progress of terrestrial digital radio development. In 1990, the FCC began a Notice of Inquiry proceeding, which it subsequently described this way:

- *After opening a proceeding in 1990[13] to consider both satellite and terrestrial digital radio services, the Commission concluded that the IBOC systems under consideration for terrestrial service still were in early stages of development and that it would be premature to consider terrestrial digital audio broadcasting (DAB).[14]*

Initially the FCC showed its willingness to give the industry some latitude to perfect the IBOC technology. By 1998, the heat was on, and the industry needed to show substantive progress to the FCC. That October, USADR filed a petition for rulemaking with the FCC, which the FCC summarized in these words:[15]

- *Nature of Petition: To permit the introduction of digital audio broadcasting (DAB) in the AM and FM bands. Petition proposes the adoption of an in-band on-channel (IBOC) DAB technology that USADR contends would enable the simultaneous broadcast of analog and digital signals. Specifically, USADR requests that the Commission: determine that IBOC is the most appropriate means to transition from analog-to-digital broadcasting; establish interference criteria to ensure the compatibility of analog and digital radio stations; establish a plan to foster the transition to an all-digital environment; conclude that a Commission-adopted DAB transmission standard is necessary to ensure equipment compatibility and maintain the universal availability of domestic radio services; establish criteria and a timetable for the evaluation of IBOC systems; and select a single IBOC system and transmission standard. USADR submits substantial technical data in support of the adoption of its IBOC system as the United States DAB transmission standard.*

A year later, in the fall of 1999, the FCC issued a Notice of Proposed Rulemaking.[16] It sought public comment on what criteria should be applied to "determine which DAB model and/or system would best promote our above-stated policy objectives." While recognizing the potential of and support for the IBOC approach, the FCC kept the door open to other DAB methods. It said this was not "the start of an IBOC rulemaking," and agreed with the comments of National Public Radio that "at this time it is not possible to definitely settle this issue in favor of IBOC."

---

[13] *Amendment of the Rules with Regard to the Establishment and Regulation of New Digital Audio Radio Services*, 5 FCC Rcd 5237 (1990).

[14] Quotation from: Federal Communications Commission, *In the Matter of Digital Audio Broadcasting Systems And Their Impact on the Terrestrial Radio Broadcast Service. First Report and Order*, MM Docket No. 99-325 Adopted: October 10, 2002.

[15] FCC *Public Notice* DA 98-2244, November 6, 1998.

[16] FCC MM Docket No. 99-325, In the Matter of Digital Audio Broadcasting Systems and Their Impact on the Terrestrial Radio Broadcast Service, Adopted November 1, 1999.

The Notice concluded forcefully, on the one hand being supportive of private-sector evaluation of the technology, and on the other hand seeking a prompt and impartial process:

- *Moreover the Commission would give great weight to any industry compromise the NRSC may achieve. We plan to monitor this testing process closely for fairness, thoroughness, and timeliness. While we are encouraged by the NRSC's efforts to date, we will act promptly to provide an alternative mechanism if subsequent events undermine our confidence in the current testing process. In this regard, we expect to revisit the effectiveness and appropriateness of the NRSC approach once the Commission has reviewed the NRSC report regarding the IBOC tests..."*

The Notice included proposed criteria for evaluation of a DAB model or system (in no particular order):

1. Enhanced audio fidelity

2. Robustness to interference and other signal impairments

3. Compatibility with existing analog service

4. Spectrum efficiency

5. Flexibility

6. Auxiliary capacity

7. Extensibility

8. Accommodation for existing broadcasters

9. Coverage

10. Implementation costs/affordability of equipment

Most of these points reflect similar criteria that came out of the NRSC earlier the same year.

Evaluation Process: EWG

When the system test guidelines were completed earlier that year, in March 1999, it was then time for another group within the DAB Subcommittee—the Evaluation Working Group (EWG), chaired by Don Messer, Dr. Eng. of the U.S. International Broadcast Bureau—to establish evaluation criteria, evaluation guidelines, and an evaluation matrix; then to perform an evaluation of the results of each test. In short order, EWG had created guidelines and a ten-point set of Evaluation Criteria,[17] adopted by the DAB Subcommittee in May.

---

[17] *In-band On-channel (IBOC) Digital Audio Broadcasting (DAB) System Evaluation Guidelines*, NRSC DAB Subcommittee, May 1999.

DRB Subcommittee Evaluation Working Group

EVALUATION CRITERIA DESCRIPTIONS – IBOC RECEIVER RESULTS

- *Audio quality* – the fundamental audio quality of the IBOC system, all channel impairments aside. This assessment is to be made with respect to the audio quality of the existing analog broadcasting service as represented by the NRSC broadcast chain audio.

- *Service area* – the geographical area surrounding the transmit station which can be expected to receive a listenable (usable) radio signal. Applied separately to IBOC audio and IBOC auxiliary data capacity (i.e., degree of correlation needs to be established).

- *Durability* – characterized by an IBOC system design's ability to withstand interference from other radio signals (co-channel, 1st adjacent channel, and 2nd adjacent channel signals in particular) and to withstand the impairing effects of the RF channel. Applied separately to IBOC audio and IBOC auxiliary data capacity (i.e., degree of correlation needs to be established).

- *Acquisition performance* – the characteristics of how a receiver "locks on" to a radio signal, including acquisition time (the elapsed time between tuning to a channel and when the audio on that channel is first heard), and audio quality following acquisition. Applies to both IBOC audio and IBOC auxiliary data capacity (in the latter case, performance metric is acceptable bit and/or frame error rate).

- *Auxiliary data capacity* – characteristics of the data capacity supported by an IBOC system in excess of that needed to deliver the IBOC audio signal, including available throughput, nature of capacity (opportunistic versus continuously available), and transmission quality and durability through the channel (bit error rate and/or other relevant digital data transmission metrics as a function of impairments).

- *Behavior as signal degrades* – how an IBOC system performs as its signal degrades, in particular, how abruptly the signal becomes unusable, and how the level of quality of the signal changes as the edge of coverage is approached. Note that, due to the complexities of RF signal propagation, "edge of coverage" performance may be experienced throughout a station's service area and is not restricted simply to regions near or beyond the theoretical protected contour.

- *Stereo separation* – the amount of stereo separation present in the IBOC audio signal, and how it varies as a function of channel and received signal conditions.

- *Flexibility* – represents the potential of an IBOC system to be adapted by broadcasters and manufacturers to meet the needs of listeners and consumers, both present and future. [Primarily addressed in system description portion of submission; test results not expected to provide direct evidence of system flexibility.]

**EVALUATION CRITERIA DESCRIPTIONS –
ANALOG RECEIVER RESULTS**

- *Host analog signal impact* – changes in performance of a host analog signal (main channel audio and any subcarriers) as a result of the presence of the IBOC digital signal energy associated with that host.

- *Nonhost analog signal impact* – changes in the performance of a (desired) analog signal (main channel audio only) as a result of the presence of interfering IBOC signals. Interfering signals of interest include co-channel, 1st, and 2nd adjacent channel signals, individually and in combinations.

The dawn of the millenial year 2000 was an auspicious event for IBOC. By the time the FCC issued its notice in the fall of 1999, EWG had prepared evaluation criteria, evaluation guidelines, and an evaluation matrix. The proponents were ready to submit their reports. With the LDR and USADR submissions in hand by early 2000, the EWG performed an evaluation of each proposed IBOC system, comparing each to the current state of analog radio, but not to each other.[18] As the EWG reports concluded:

The basic conclusion: the "state-of-the-art" for IBOC technology indicates the reasonable probability of substantial improvement for broadcast listening compared to current analog performance in the AM and FM broadcasting bands.

Standardization Testing: TPWG and EWG

With the decision in April 2000 that IBOC could work, the next step was dependent on whether the industry was ready to entertain proposals for an IBOC standard. The standardization process wheels started turning. The TGWG was reformulated from its previous task of providing guidelines for proponent testing, to developing explicit test procedures for a new round of testing. The new working group was dubbed the Test Procedures Working Group (TPWG) and it began working in May. By August the NRSC Standard Project had begun, to consist of several steps, the last of which would be deliberating on a formal standard:

5.0 Standard development work plan[19]

This project will consist of the following phases (responsible party indicated in square brackets):

- *issuance of an RFP (request for proposal) for candidate technologies [NRSC sponsoring organizations];*

- *review of submitted proposal(s) and selection of system(s) to be considered [NRSC DAB Subcommittee];*

---

[18] *Evaluation of [USA Digital Radio's][Lucent Digital Radio's] Submission To The NRSC DAB Subcommittee of Selected Laboratory and Field Test Results for Its FM and AM Band IBOC System,* each document adopted by NRSC DAB Subcommittee, April 2000.

[19] *Standards setting process—NRSC Standard project initiation – IBOC DAB standards development 8/25/00.*

- *adoption of detailed laboratory and field test procedures [NRSC DAB Subcommittee];*

- *independent testing of accepted system(s) utilizing the adopted test procedures [NRSC DAB Subcommittee];*

- *evaluation of test results [NRSC DAB Subcommittee]; drafting and adoption of final report including recommendations (if any) for AM and FM IBOC standards [NRSC DAB Subcommittee];*

- *drafting and adoption of IBOC standards documents [NRSC DAB Subcommittee].*

The first step in the process was the August 2000 posting of the NRSC *Request for Proposals (RFP), In-band On-channel (IBOC) DAB Terrestrial Broadcast Systems for the AM and FM Bands.*[20] The first part of the RFP process would involve receiving all proposals, followed by testing each proposed AM and FM IBOC system.

A month before the RFP, in July 2000, the way to a standard was cleared when Lucent Digital Radio and USA Digital Radio announced their intentions to merge, eliminating the potential roadblock of two competing technologies battling for supremacy before the standards-setting body. This good news caused a minor delay as the new iBiquity Digital Corporation worked on integrating the "best of the best" technologies of the two companies. While the NRSC RFP was a public invitation open to all comers, it may come as no surprise that with all the significant technological players merged, only one IBOC technology, iBiquity's, was formally proposed to the NRSC.

In the mean time, TPWG worked on the testing details, including convening various subgroups to address specific questions—a subgroup for determining which receivers to use in compatibility testing, a subgroup to determine how to evaluate the FM subcarrier interference question, and a subgroup to select audio cuts for subjective testing of the various signal impairments. Laboratory testing would occur at the Advanced Television Technology Center (ATTC) in Alexandria, Virginia. Field testing would be done by iBiquity. Subjective testing would be done by qualified experts and laboratories. NRSC would have representatives participate in "both laboratory and field tests as a resident observer."[21] The FM test procedures were adopted in December 2000, with the adoption of the AM test procedures the following April. Within a month of the FM procedure completion, work had begun on building a "test bed" at ATTC, in early 2001.

By the end of 2001 the iBiquity FM IBOC system had undergone the rigorous NRSC testing, the EWG had conducted its evaluation, and the DAB Subcommittee had formally adopted the FM evaluation report.[22] Following the same sequence, the AM evaluation report was adopted in April 2002.[23]

---

[20] Most NRSC documents cited in this chapter are available at www.nrscstandards.org.

[21] Proposed NRSC IBOC Test Program, NRSC DAB Subcommittee Test Procedures Working Group, October 2000.

[22] *Evaluation of the iBiquity Digital Corporation IBOC System, Part 1, FM IBOC*, NRSC DAB Subcommittee, November 2001.

[23] *Evaluation of the iBiquity Digital Corporation IBOC System, Part 2, AM IBOC*, NRSC DAB Subcommittee, April 2002.

Table 2.2 lists the DAB Subcommittee Performance Goals for the testing, indicating to which evaluation categories they belong. Figure 2.2 illustrates one of the methods used to evaluate IBOC performance. It is a graph based on subjective listening tests of field-recorded audio. This graph shows the IBOC performance in the aggregate for all subjective tests of the various program audio formats. Individual graphs that provide more detail on a variety of tests are available in the evaluation reports. Other charts and tables showing signal levels, interference levels, blend-to-analog performance, and the like are included in the reports. In addition to the careful analysis of IBOC digital performance, the evaluation reports go into considerable detail regarding IBOC compatibility with analog receivers. The evaluation reports and their many appendices are available on the NRSC website, www.nrscstandards.org.

CATEGORY		IBOC PERFORMANCE GOALS
Fidelity	Frequency response and distortion	For FM: Frequency response and distortion fidelity should be comparable to or better than the best FM
		For AM: Deliver fidelity that approaches present FM analog fidelity
		To alleviate the effects of channel impairments and interference, it may be acceptable to diminish distortion and frequency response fidelity to maintain audio free of dropouts and noticeable artifacts.
	Noise	May be acceptable to compromise noise fidelity to maintain dropout- and artifact-free audio
	Stereo separation	May be acceptable to compromise in response to channel impairments
	Fidelity of digital technologies	a) Source coding should not cause artifacts that noticeably reduce fidelity throughout the service area b) Should have sufficient apparent dynamic range so that low level and dynamic content reproduce with the same fidelity as aggressively processed audio
Durability	Interference	Digital systems should reach a service area that matches or exceeds actual interference-limited service area of the analog host
	Impairments	Digital technology will be considered to be better than analog against impairments if digital multipath and fade artifacts have the following characteristics: a) They are demonstrably less objectionable, less frequent in time and less prevalent in location than those of analog services b) They maintain higher fidelity than analog for a preponderance of occurrences c) They result in fewer total losses of intelligible audio than analog, and recovery from total loss is not significantly longer than analog in similar circumstances
Flexibility	Flexibility of transmission systems (includes COMPATIBILITY with existing analog services)	A successful digital technology will: a) Reasonably protect the performance and flexibility of its analog host and adjacent channel stations (i.e., is compatible with existing analog services); b) Provide a platform that can be improved in software, firmware and hardware in a manner that is compatible with its original technology; c) Give broadcasters tools to create features to enhance the listener experience and permit the medium to remain relevant and competitive in the coming decades.

Table 2.2 NRSC IBOC Performance Goals (excerpt) (Source: Tables #8 in Parts 1 & 2 of the NRSC DAB Subcommittee Evaluation of the iBiquity Digital Corporation IBOC System)

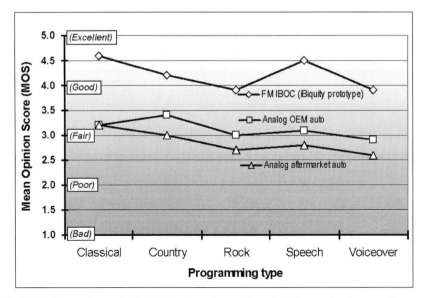

Figure 2.2 NRSC Comparison of FM IBOC and analog audio subjective evaluation results aggregating all field test conditions[24]

Response to the Testing

Based on the test results, the NRSC made a hearty recommendation that the FCC authorize the use of the iBiquity IBOC technology for the AM and FM broadcast bands. There were two reservations, one common to both systems, and one specifically for AM IBOC. The common reservation among the very positive conclusions in both reports was the fact that, in the interest of keeping up the pace in evaluating IBOC, the codec employed in the testing was not the final codec to be used in the commercial version of the system. The transition from the USADR MPEG 2 AAC audio codec to the LDR PAC codec had not yet occurred, so the substitution of the (final) PAC codec would be validated later. This was a carefully considered, pragmatic decision to avoid delays by testing the IBOC system before the PAC codec was ready.

The IBOC platform is essentially a modem that, with a little software work, is capable of carrying any coded audio source that will fit within its bandwidth. A change to a new codec after testing would not have a significant impact on the radio frequency performance of the system. However, NRSC reserved final judgment of the system until the PAC codec was integrated into the system, at which time some follow-up testing would be required.

---

[24] Source: Figure 7, NRSC FM IBOC Evaluation, as "taken from pg. 9 of main text of iBiquity Digital Corporation report to the NRSC, August 2001, with minor modification."

In addition, NRSC had not pursued the more complex question of AM nighttime performance, seeking instead to thoroughly review and document the fundamental performance of the AM IBOC system design first. Consequently, the NRSC recommended that stations desiring to operate with AM IBOC do so during daytime hours only until further study had been performed.

Within six months of the publication of the evaluation reports, the FCC issued its *First Report and Order*, finally selecting IBOC as the technology for terrestrial digital radio broadcasting:

- *By this Report and Order, we select in-band on-channel (IBOC) as the technology that will permit AM and FM radio broadcasters to introduce digital operations efficiently and rapidly. We announce notification procedures that will allow operating AM and FM stations to commence digital transmissions immediately on an interim basis using the IBOC systems developed by iBiquity Digital Corporation. We conclude that the adoption of a single IBOC transmission standard will facilitate the development and commercialization of digital services for terrestrial broadcasters, and solicit industry assistance in the development of a formal standard. We defer consideration of formal standard-setting procedures and related broadcast licensing and service rule changes to a future Further Notice of Proposed Rulemaking.*[25]

Finally, Standards-Setting: ISDWG

From October 2002, until 2005 when the NRSC-5 "core" standard and its first revision (NRSC-5-A) were adopted, the DAB Subcommittee worked on developing a set of standards documents. iBiquity asked the NRSC to initiate the drafting and adoption of a standard, which was the final step planned in the May 2000 Standard Development Work Plan cited above. At the September 2002 DAB Subcommittee meeting, the subcommittee agreed to do so and formed an IBOC Standards Development Working Group (ISDWG), co-chaired by Paul Feinberg of Sony and Don Messer of International Broadcast Bureau (previously the Chairman of the Evaluation Working Group). iBiquity supplied normative references for the draft standard and the newly formed ISDWG began the painstaking task of reviewing, validating, and editing documentation. With its 1998 objectives fulfilled, the DAB Subcommittee adopted new objectives focused on standardization.

---

[25] Federal Communications Commission, *In the Matter of Digital Audio Broadcasting Systems And Their Impact on the Terrestrial Radio Broadcast Service. First Report and Order*, MM Docket No. 99-325 Adopted: October 10, 2002.

National Radio Systems Committee
DAB Subcommittee Goals and Objectives

(as adopted by the Subcommittee on January 9, 2003)

Objectives

(a) To develop formal NRSC standards that will furnish broadcasters and manufacturers of both broadcast and receiver equipment with a complete and open transmission and reception specification of the AM and FM IBOC systems, providing a clear path for the prompt adoption of this technology and ensuring that all IBOC equipment will be suitable for the hybrid, extended hybrid and all-digital modes of the IBOC system; and

(b) to provide the FCC with an industry developed and supported standard that will aid in establishing final rules for the implementation of IBOC technology in a manner that will best serve the public interest.

Goals

To meet its objectives, the Subcommittee will work towards achieving the following goals:

(a) To produce complete and open industry standards containing all the information necessary for broadcasters and equipment manufacturers to fully understand and implement the capabilities of IBOC technology;

(b) to develop a technical record that will allow future readers to understand the technical parameters and tradeoffs upon which these standards are based;

(c) to enable manufacturers of broadcast equipment and reception equipment to produce products that are interoperable and remain functional through continuing evolution of the technology; and to enable the technology to evolve compatible new features and services;

(d) to foster a consumer experience that maintains the legacy of free over-the-air broadcasting and broadcast innovation, while enabling manufacturer flexibility to differentiate products and innovate new features; and

(e) to include the ability to interface with and support data service protocols currently being developed or that may be developed in the future to enable the broadcast of flexible and extensible data content and applications.

FM Subcarrier Compatibility: DAB Subcommittee and Others

Meanwhile, outstanding questions were addressed as well. By the end of 2002, the NRSC evaluation of the impact of IBOC on FM subcarriers[26] was supplemented by additional research and testing by National Public Radio (NPR) and the International Association of Audio Information Services (IAAIS). NPR confirmed that any interference IBOC would cause to reception of subcarrier reading services was "not a show stopper." NPR and IAAIS submitted their report, Analog SCA Compatibility with iBiquity Digital's FM-IBOC System, for the NRSC record. This report and several others on various topics were provided to the NRSC by third parties to inform the DAB Subcommittee on new information. Those reports, listed here, are available on the NRSC website, www.nrscstandardsorg.

- *FM All-Digital IBOC Field Test Report* (iBiquity, February 2002)

- *Report on FM IBOC compatibility with SCA's* (NPR/IAAIS, March 2002)

- *AM All-Digital IBOC Field Test Report* (iBiquity, April 2002)

- *AM nighttime studies* (iBiquity, May, October 2003)

- *Investigation into use of dual FM antennas* (NAB, July 2003)

- *"Tomorrow Radio" report* (NPR, January 2004)

- *Report on Perceptual Tests of IBiquity's HD Coder At Multiple Bit Rates* (NPR, October 2004)

- *Report on Perceptual Tests of Low- and Very Low-Bit Rate Codecs* (NPR, October 2004)

- *Host Compatibility Measurements for the Extended Hybrid Mode of IBOC Digital Audio Broadcasting* (NPR, November 2004)

- *Tomorrow Radio Signal Coverage Report for Hybrid IBOC DAB Booster of KCSN-FM* (NPR, January 2005)

The Path to the HDC Codec: TPWG and EWG

The transition to the final audio codec was a rocky one. The DAB Subcommittee wanted to be certain the IBOC system with the PAC audio codec, called "Gen 2" by the subcommittee, exhibited similar performance to its predecessor with the MPEG AAC codec, "Gen 1." Gen 1had been thoroughly evaluated and endorsed by the DAB subcommittee. (Gen 1 of the IBOC system was the same system as Gen 2 except for the change in audio codec.)

---

[26] The FM subcarrier is an ultrasonic signal imposed on the broadcast FM carrier along with analog audio programming. It is not receivable by users of conventional FM receivers, requiring special reception equipment to recover the signal on the subcarrier. It may carry an audio program, such as a spoken-word reading service, or it may carry digital data. Initially, these services were individually required to have FCC authorization to be transmitted, under a Subsidiary Communications Authorization (SCA), but now no such authorization is required. The name SCA has continued to be a commonly used term to identify subcarriers.

iBiquity commissioned tests on the Gen 2 system that the TPWG had specified. NRSC observed the testing. iBiquity first submitted the Gen 2 FM IBOC results to the DAB Subcommittee for EWG evaluation. In a May 2002 memorandum to the DAB Subcommittee, the EWG indicated the results of the Gen 2 FM IBOC tests were consistent with the testing already done on Gen 1. PAC audio would have been fine on FM IBOC, at least at the full 96 kbps rate.

The testing of AM IBOC Gen 2 did not go as smoothly. The AM IBOC PAC codec was still being tweaked even after the test was done, so the test was not of the most recent version. At lower bit rates, which AM IBOC uses, the PAC codec was vilified in the press—even termed "obnoxious."[27] Complicating the NRSC desire to exercise full due diligence in its evaluations, some flaws in the making of the test recordings for the subjective testing required re-recording on short notice, without an NRSC observer. Consequently, in May 2003, the DAB Subcommittee's Steering Committee suspended the standards-setting process pending resolution of the codec issues. The Steering Committee, comprising the Subcommittee leadership, other NRSC chairpersons, and co-sponsor representatives, is "empowered with the responsibility of making interim decisions for a subcommittee, between meetings of that subcommittee, or when it is otherwise necessary for decisions to be made but impractical or impossible for the subcommittee to do so."[28]

By September of 2003 the standards process had resumed. The new HDC[29] codec had been announced and demonstrated. It would replace the PAC codec, and the DAB Subcommittee would require IBOC "Gen 3" testing to verify its performance. Over the course of the next ten months, test procedures were established, testing was completed, and the test reports submitted. In July 2004 the EWG submitted its evaluation of the results, which was then formally accepted by the DAB Subcommittee. The DAB Subcommittee was satisfied that IBOC with the HDC codec met the same criteria for acceptance that IBOC with the MPEG-2 AAC codec had in the originally tested system.

AM Nighttime Performance and Compatibility: Outside-NRSC Review

The matter of AM IBOC nighttime transmissions was taken up outside the NRSC by the NAB ad hoc Technical Group on AM IBOC Nighttime Performance. In 2003, iBiquity submitted reports on the nighttime compatibility question, summarizing,

This study[30] showed that the complete conversion of the AM band to IBOC at night has minimal impact to groundwave nighttime service. The conclusions were:

- *The results assume 100% of the stations convert to IBOC in North America, which will take many years to occur – well after most receivers are able to enjoy the much upgraded digital sound.*

---

[27] Radio World, August 14, 2002.

[28] NRSC Procedures Manual, Rev 1.2.

[29] HDC™ is a trademark of iBiquity Digital Corporation.

[30] *AM Nighttime Compatibility Study Report*, iBiquity Digital Corporation, May 23, 2003.

- *The impact is restricted to the fringe areas of a station's reception area – outside the Night Interference Free (NIF) limit in the 1–3 mV/m range for most stations;*

- *IBOC has no measurable impact on local channels;*

- *IBOC has minimal impact on regional and clear channels;*

- *IBOC impacts just 5% of potential listeners near edge of coverage on average per channel using a Delphi or equivalent receiver;*

- *Directional antennas in portable and boom-box receivers help null out interference – more than compensating for lack of IF filtering which pass more adjacent channel energy than typical narrower filters in omni-directional automobile installations;*

- *The impact is limited to areas where the analog is already impaired from analog cochannel and adjacent channels.*

iBiquity completed and reported further AM nighttime field work to the NAB ad hoc group in October 2003.[31] Reassured by this data, NAB informed the FCC in March 2004 that NAB was satisfied AM IBOC could be transmitted at night with minimal negative impact. A month later the FCC issued a Further Notice of Proposed Rulemaking and Notice of Inquiry in the digital radio proceeding it started in 1999. Among the issues raised in the Further Notice was whether the FCC should permit AM IBOC nighttime broadcasting, and address interference problems on a case-by-case basis as recommended by NAB. By the time of the adoption of the NRSC-5 Standard in 2005, the FCC had not acted on the question.

Multicasting and the SIDTG

One of the key outcomes of the NPR *Tomorrow Radio*[32] project was bringing to the forefront the multichannel capability of IBOC. NPR saw the value to the public radio broadcasting community of being able to offer more than one channel of programming on an IBOC radio station. Teaming with Kenwood U.S.A. Corporation (a licensed HD Radio receiver manufacturer) and Harris Corporation (a licensed HD Radio transmitter manufacturer), and with the support of iBiquity, NPR studied the performance of a supplemental IBOC program channel in 2003. To test the concept, a supplemental broadcast mechanism had to be developed (iBiquity's Supplemental Program Service), and the results tested. The Main Program Service on IBOC has the analog program as a backup, if the digital signal drops out. A supplemental program channel is without backup, and there had been no evaluation of a digital-only program channel. NPR sought to understand how a supplemental channel would perform. The test report[33] concluded that a typical FM IBOC station's supplemental programming could provide reliable service to an area greater than that within its 70 dBμ coverage contour and less than that within the 60 dBμ contour.

[31] *Field Report: AM Nighttime Compatibility*, and *Field Report: AM IBOC Nighttime Performance*, iBiquity Digital Corporation October 2003. These reports are available on www.nrscstandards.org.

[32] Tomorrow Radio is a service mark of National Public Radio.

[33] *Tomorrow Radio[SM] Field Testing in the Washington, D.C., New York City, San Francisco, and Los Angeles (Long Beach) Radio Markets*, January 6, 2004. Available at www.nrscstandards.org.

In general terms, multicasting was found to serve an area that encompasses an FM station's city grade service area and projects toward, but does not likely extend to, the station's protected service contour.

In addition to coverage analysis, NPR studied the audio quality of the HDC codec at various bit rates.[34] IBOC remained quite acceptable to listeners at the lower bit rates necessary to transmit multiple program channels. While a small percentage of listeners could discern the difference between 48 and 96 kbps audio, in general there was not an appreciable preference for the higher rate. Speech was the audio type most sensitive to bit rate reduction, with the perceived quality slipping from good (4.0) at 96 kbps to a statistically significant reduction to the high good-to-fair range (3.7) at 48 kbps. (To connote statistical significance is simply to say that the three-tenths of a point difference is well enough resolved to say there is a difference; yet on the scale of 1–5, three tenths of a point is a minor difference.) Ironically, the classical and jazz audio cuts were least sensitive to bit-rate reduction—with good (4.0) performance down to 36 kbps, and low fair-to-good (3.2–3.7) performance at 24 kbps. Rock music fell in between speech and classical/jazz.

With encouraging results from the NPR testing, iBiquity responded to their push for multicasting by creating a protocol for the Supplemental Program Service (SPS) and incorporating it into the draft NRSC-5 standard. During the course of the ISDWG's review of SPS protocol specifications, the DAB Subcommittee also formed a task group to consider concerns about how supplemental program channels should be identified. The Supplemental Audio ID Task Group (SIDTG) found itself dealing with a human factors problem: How will people interact with supplemental channels? Will supplemental channels fundamentally change the experience of radio because of their lack of analog backup? Are there methods of tuning into a multicast station that should have recommended best practices? For instance, what happens when the radio is scanning down the band; is it good practice to treat the supplemental channel as if it were a separate station, requiring a 5-second acquisition when scanning down the dial; or should main program channel analog always come up first? Is there an opportunity to create a virtual "new band" with a new numbering scheme for all SPS channels? …or for all AM and FM main and SPS channels together?

Cox Broadcasting conducted studies to explore the questions and provided the results to the NRSC. There was significant debate within the SIDTG on whether the numbering scheme being adopted by receiver manufacturers (with supplemental audio channel indicators such as "HD2" or "2" within a circle) was indeed the best one for the industry. Ultimately, the SIDTG could not

---

[34] *Perceptual Tests of iBiquity's HD Coder at Multiple Bit Rates*, National Public Radio, October 14, 2004. Posted on www.nrscstandards.org.

reach a consensus on a specific numbering scheme recommendation however the group did agree on some recommendations for best practice:

SIDTG Recommendations to DAB Subcommittee[35]

After careful consideration of the various issues and opinions relating to the identification of supplemental audio services, the SIDTG offers the following recommendations:

- **Multicast content should be identified by a unique and simple label**

  The average consumer is nontechnical and will be easily confused by a complicated supplemental audio service ID scheme. There is a clear need to make navigation and marketing of any new content locations easy for the consumer to understand, and easy for the broadcaster to market.

- **New content identification should be easy to market**

  New content location identifiers should be easy to market to consumers by broadcasters, receiver manufacturers and consumer electronics retailers. Characteristics of easily marketed identifiers include simple construction for easy recollection, easy and consistent vocalization, an eight character limit, and clear, simple graphical presentation.

- **Identification of new content locations should not be confusing**

  Multicast services should have identifiers that are sufficiently distinct from main service identifiers to minimize confusion between them and to enable consumers to readily find multicast services. This should hold true whether or not the main and multicast services are related in a marketing and/or programmatic sense.

- **IBOC receivers should use a consistent numbering scheme for identifying main and supplemental services**

  Multicast-capable IBOC receivers should identify an FM IBOC station's audio services using the following numbering convention as a suffix to any service-identification display:

Service	Display Suffix
Analog	0 (optional)
MPS	1 (optional)
SPS1	2
SPS2	3
SPS3	4
SPS4	5
SPS5	6

---

[35] SIDTG, September 9, 2005.

| SPS6 | 7 |
| SPS7 | 8 |

- **Future technology developments should be pursued to further enhance the user experience**

  Due to the potential for additional services, two technology enhancements should be pursued:

  - Technology enhancements to minimize the delay associated with direct tuning to a supplemental service are desirable;

  - An Electronic Service Guide (ESG) and Electronic Program Guide (EPG) are recognized as valuable improvements that will help IBOC digital radio move to the next generation of features.

The key agreement in the process was one to avoid confusion—the first supplemental program channel (SPS1) would go by the number "2," permitting the Main Program Channel (MPS) to maintain sole possession of the designation "1." Broadcasters and manufacturers were given the latitude to experiment with exactly how those designations would be presented. The term *HD2*, first employed by Kenwood radios, became the familiar way to describe the first SPS channel over the air and in print. (While it is unlikely that more than two supplemental channels will be employed simultaneously, supplemental channel numbers may be assigned out of sequence, keeping open the possibility that, say, "HD8" channels could see regular use).[36]

Surround Sound: The SSATG

There are several surround sound systems vying for broadcaster and consumer acceptance with IBOC digital radio. Surround sound is not a separate "service" in the communications networking sense, because it is fundamentally an overlay of some sort on the IBOC audio service. However, surround sound is a service in the more common sense of the word—it is a feature that IBOC broadcasting can offer as a service to the listener.

A subgroup of the NRSC Digital Radio Broadcasting Subcommittee called the Surround Sound Audio Task Group (SSATG) formed in 2005 to consider how NRSC should "best handle compatible surround sound technologies on an industry-wide basis, and provide a recommendation" to the DAB Subcommittee. Deliberating through 2006 and into 2007, the SSATG settled on simply providing an informative document to educate industry participants on the characteristics of surround sound over IBOC: *Broadcasting Surround Sound Audio over IBOC Digital Radio—Issues and Resources for FM Broadcasters.*[37]

---

[36] The maximum number of audio channels supported by the Standard is 8: one main and seven supplemental.
[37] Published 2007. www.nrscstandards.org

Four system proponents participated in the SSATG process. Their systems are:

1. Dolby ProLogic II (Dolby Laboratories)

2. SRS Circle Sound (SRS Labs)

3. Neural Audio Surround (Neural Audio)

4. MPEG Surround, (Fraunhofer IIS, Telos/Omnia, Coding Technologies)

Both Dolby ProLogic II and SRS Circle Sound systems are well established in existing consumer electronics receivers worldwide. Neural Audio Surround was introduced in more recent years and had been chosen by XM Satellite Radio as its surround sound format for satellite radio receivers.

MPEG Surround is a standard developed by the ISO Moving Picture Experts Group that offers compatibility with existing MPEG audio and video standards. Unlike the other surround systems with an interest in IBOC, MPEG Surround employs a separate digital data stream, in addition to the stereo mix stream, that contains the encoded surround data (although it can support other modes discussed further below).

Composite Surround Transport

Dolby, SRS, and Neural offer *composite* surround systems that transport the surround information in composite with the two stereo channels. The composite encode-transport-decode process follows these three steps: A 5.1 surround sound source is encoded to 2-channel stereo (with the surround information embedded within) and decoded back to 5.1 surround at the receiver (using the embedded surround information). The process of making stereo (or mono) audio out of a 5.1-channel source is called downmixing. The composite system creates a stereo downmix from the multichannel source and encodes it with the additional information necessary to recover the 5.1 mix at the receiver. The encoded information and the stereo information are combined into a composite stereo stream that should be compatible with ordinary stereo receivers, while providing the necessary information to decode the multichannel information. Because composite surround is conveyed on the two channels of a stereo transmission, it is possible to broadcast surround sound on analog FM (including the analog FM host of an IBOC signal) as well as on the digital audio portion of FM IBOC. All three composite systems being used with IBOC—Dolby, Neural and SRS—have been approved by iBiquity for use with HD Radio transmissions using the full 96 kb/s data stream. By approving a system, iBiquity is not endorsing the technology, but saying that the system is compatible with nonsurround HD Radio receivers and will not negatively affect their performance. The testing at 96 kbps does not confirm compatibility with multicasting in which audio is transmitted at lower bit rates.

There has been some concern regarding the potential impact of composite surround sound systems on analog FM signal reception under conditions of multipath fading. The key element is that each of these systems alters the phase relationships between the channels as a means to identify the individual 5.1 channels within the 2-channel stereo signal. Due to the phase modifications, the resulting encoded stereo downmix contains altered levels within the L+R and the L-R signals. In many cases, the L-R RMS level is significantly increased when compared to the artistic stereo mix (the independent stereo mix offered by the artist/producer) of the same content. When composite downmixes are broadcast in FM-stereo, the L-R modulation level is significantly increased, leading to the potential for increased perception of multipath interference.[38]

There is also the issue of cross-compatibility between the type of surround encoding that is transmitted and the type of decoder in the receiver. That is to say, a receiver equipped to decode surround sound "System A" might attempt to decode a transmission containing surround audio encoded by surround sound "System B." The impact of such cross-decoding had not been studied. Look for research performed for the Audio Engineering Society (AES) regarding these unintended effects. In the HD Radio design, iBiquity has added an optional message in the Station Information Service in which a surround-enabled HD Radio receiver can be informed which surround scheme is employed on a program stream. This will prevent accidental decoding of one composite surround format by another decoder brand.

Component Surround Transport

MPEG Surround is classified as a Spatial Audio Coding[39] technique, that develops parameter information about the surround sound channels. Structurally, in a generalized sense, MPEG Surround relies on a *component* encoding format, in which a separate component (information stream) is transmitted to convey the spatial information. It does not transport surround by overlaying composite encoding on the two downmixed channels, in the manner of the composite surround encoders.[40] Rather, it "enables digital broadcasting systems to offer different audio channel configurations from stereo to 5.1 surround and beyond in one single bit stream, without simulcasting."[41] That one single bit stream carries a fully stereo-compatible MPEG stream plus the component spatial data stream. A conventional MPEG stereo decoder remains capable of decoding the stereo portion of the MPEG Surround stream.

Coding Technologies, Inc., the developer of the HDC codec, teamed with Philips to propose its surround technology to ISO/MPEG as a standard. ISO/MPEG selected a combination of two proponents' systems for the MPEG Surround Standard—Coding Technologies/Philips and Fraunhofer IIS/Agere Systems. The system can derive a downmix signal which is typically stereo (but could also be mono) from the incoming 5.1 content. A "side channel" of spatial information is embedded in the digital audio stream, consuming perhaps 5–6 kbps. The stereo channel is unencumbered by phased encoding (unless a composite encoder is also employed), leaving the most true copy of the stereo signal for non-MPEG Surround radios. An MPEG Surround receiver would use the cues in the side channel to upmix the stereo to 5.1 surround.

---

[38] *5.1 Surround Sound Compatibility Within HD Radio and the Existing FM-Stereo Environment*, Frank Foti, Omnia Audio, May. 2005.

[39] J. Breebaart, et al., *MPEG Spatia Audio Coding / MPEG Surround: Overview and Current Status*, Audio Engineering Society Convention Paper, 119th Convention, October 2005.

[40] MPEG Surround component encoding/decoding can be configured to permit a composite encode/decode process at the same time.

[41] Coding Technologies, September 2006.

Also, MPEG Surround can transmit the original artistic stereo mix instead of creating a synthetic stereo downmix. MPEG offers a solution to the purist's conundrum of wanting the 5.1 surround mix to play in 5.1 environments and the artistic stereo mix in the stereo environment. This is what they mean by transmitting two mixes "without simulcasting." In this case, it does not waste bandwidth by simulcasting an artistic stereo mix and a separate 5.1-to-stereo downmix. Instead, it uses the artistic stereo mix as the reference from which the receiver can upmix to the original 5.1 surround. It encodes the difference between the artistic stereo mix and the various 5.1 channels. For best results, the artistic stereo mix should be exactly synchronized with the 5.1 surround mix, which strangely is not always the case (the length of each mix may be different).

There are numerous subtleties in the benefits and detriments of each surround sound technology, and no broadcaster should make implementation decisions based on this brief survey. Installing the actual encoder for transmitting surround is relatively simple, however handling audio in the broadcast plant for stereo and surround, including routing and processing, will require special attention. Most stations will require audio chain upgrades to accommodate the multichannel versus stereo audio transmission. Look for the NRSC guide for more information.

Surround Sound Case Studies

Some early experiments with surround yielded promising results.

KUVO-FM, Colorado Public Radio

Under the guidance of Chief Engineer Mike Pappas, KUVO-FM is credited with having produced the first 5.1 surround sound broadcast using HD Radio technology, on September 24, 2004. The station aired a Colorado Symphony Orchestra concert with Dianne Reeves in both FM-stereo and 5.1 surround using Neural Audio's 5225 Mix-Edit Transcoder. This launched FM radio's experimentation with what could become commonplace in audio listening as surround technology is embedded in more broadcast and reception platforms.

WZLX 100.7, CBS Boston

In April 2006 WZLX and Telos/Omnia/Axia announced a joint effort to broadcast full time in MPEG Surround. The project, which was timed with a studio upgrade, took about a year to complete, launching in April 2007. WZLX reportedly had fully discrete surround recordings that amounted to about 15% of the tracks in their primary playlist. The stereo-only tracks are processed through Fraunhofer surround emulation technology until commercial releases of discrete surround versions become available. Using the MPEG Surround process, the original stereo mixes, which are stored on the station hard drives with the 5.1 versions, are broadcast. This eliminates the need to downmix the 5.1 to create the stereo mix. Telos/Omnia/Axia, a supporter of the MPEG Surround technology, joined with the Boston station because it has an opportune format for surround—classic rock—and is located at the home base of such electronics innovators as Boston Acoustics, Tivoli, Bose, Genelec and others. Supplementing the over-the-air broadcast, WXLZ streams in MPEG Surround on the Internet.

WGUC-FM 90.9, Cincinnati Public Radio

Ohio's Classical Public Radio, began broadcasting in surround sound on August 10, 2006 with the broadcast of Debussy's La Mer, performed by the Cincinnati Symphony Orchestra.[42] The surround encoding was transmitted both on the analog and digital portions of the HD Radio signal's main channel. They employed Neural Audio's 5.1 technology and claim to be the first radio station in the U.S. to broadcast commercially available recorded music in 5.1 surround.

According to Don Danko, Vice President of Engineering for Cincinnati Public Radio, WGUC approached implementation of surround sound with several criteria in mind:

*   Minimizing changes to existing infrastructure

*   No disruption of their conventional stereo listeners

*   Good surround sound imaging

*   Surround sound receiver availability

*   Objective and subjective testing of available systems

*   Affordable hardware

An NRSC standard for surround sound on IBOC was not to be. All the surround technologies come with strong pedigrees. The biggest differentiator among the technologies may be how they satisfy their customers' needs. The SSATG's answer on how to "best handle compatible surround sound technologies on an industry-wide basis," was to explore the way the technologies work and arm the industry with a guide to help inform their choices.

A Complete Standard in Two Steps: Data Put on Temporary Hold

With strong regulatory and marketplace pressure for closure on IBOC, 2004 saw considerable progress on the standards-setting work of the ISDWG. Audio quality issues had been ironed out, and the various building blocks between the audio and the radio spectrum were being worked over by the ISDWG. [These building blocks are the *protocols* that are layered on one another. The following chapters explore these *layers* of the *protocol stack*.] Missing from the core standard was the Advanced Data Service (ADS) component of the IBOC protocol stack.

The DAB Subcommittee decided that in the interest of time, it would put an advanced data service "placeholder" in the NRSC-5 standard, and move expeditiously to adopt the standard in April 2005 (calling the standard less the advanced data services portion the "core" standard). Leading up to February 2005, the subcommittee made sure all the business matters were in order. Required patent disclosures were on track. At the February 24th meeting, the DAB Subcommittee moved the proposed standard to its next phase, 14-day *comment period (pre-vote)* (CPP). In the formalities of standard-setting, the goal is to produce a standard that has been formulated and adopted with due process for all participants. Final issues and comments are formally invited during a comment period, followed by any final adjustments and responses from the DAB Subcommittee. Then the

---

[42] Neural Audio Press Release, WGUC-FM Begins 5.1 Broadcasting With Neural Surround™, August 29, 2006.

pending vote on the standard is announced, with a *14-day draft period* during which no further work is done on the standard and all participant companies have time to consider their positions and their pending votes. Figure 2.3 is the flow chart for the standard-adoption process in the NRSC Procedures Manual.

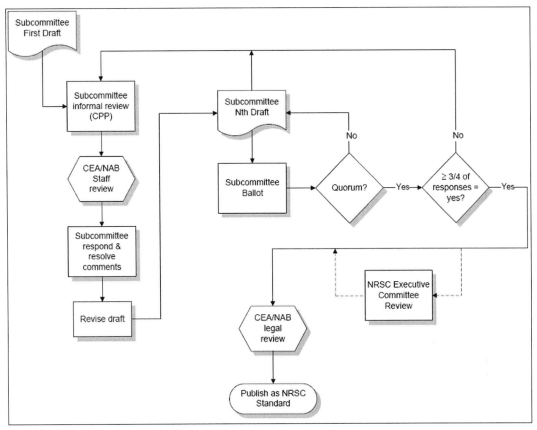

Figure 2.3 NRSC Standards Development Process (Source: NRSC)

On April 16, 2005 the NRSC-5 core standard was adopted by the DAB Subcommittee. As a *formulating committee* of the National Radio Systems Committee, the DAB Subcommittee has, under the NRSC rules, the authority to adopt the standard. A 10-day appeal period follows. In the event that an aggrieved party has an issue with the process by which the Subcommittee came to a decision, an appeal can be filed with the parent committee, the full National Radio Systems Committee. One appeal was filed and subsequently withdrawn. By mid-May, 2005 the NRSC-5 core standard had passed final review by the NRSC Sponsors—NAB and CEA—and was officially released to the public. All that remained was to replace the ADS placeholder with a protocol.

The ISDWG reviewed iBiquity's submission on the data transport and selected it as the ADS protocol.[43] It bears the iBiquity name "Advanced Application Services Transport" which is abbreviated "AAT." This transport protocol completes the technical description of the IBOC technology that transports audio and data services on IBOC transmissions. In September 2005, the DAB Subcommittee adopted a revision of the NRSC-5 core standard to include the AAT. The revised standard bears the name "NRSC-5-A."

After the Standard: DRB Subcommittee

After seven years of steady effort, the National Radio Systems Committee's Digital Audio Broadcasting Subcommittee completed its initial IBOC standardization effort on September 21, 2005—by adding the advanced data service protocol to the core standard adopted the previous April. On the same day, the NRSC changed the name of the DAB Subcommittee to the Digital Radio Broadcasting (DRB) Subcommittee, to recognize the nature of radio as including data services in addition to audio. This was driven in part by the fact that a separate NRSC Subcommittee—the Digital Data Broadcasting (DDB) Subcommittee—had formed in 2003 to address broadcast data issues, but had met only once and had since been disbanded. The renaming of DAB to DRB signaled its absorption of data broadcasting responsibilities. A year later, in 2006, the new DRB adopted new goals, in light of the completion of standards-setting and the beginning of the open-ended task of maintaining the standard and supporting IBOC developments.

DRB Subcommittee
Goals and Objectives

Adopted by the Subcommittee on September 20, 2006

In April, 2005 the Subcommittee adopted a formal standard (NRSC-5) for the implementation of in-band on-channel (IBOC) digital radio broadcasting in the U.S. utilizing the IBOC technology developed by iBiquity Digital Corporation. This standard was further modified in September, 2005 and was published as NRSC 5-A.* With this Standard in place, the Subcommittee now turns its attention to the maintenance and potential future enhancement of this Standard.

Objectives

(1) To ensure that NRSC-5 will continue to furnish broadcasters and manufacturers of both broadcast and receiver equipment with a complete, up-to-date and open transmission and reception specification of the AM and FM IBOC systems, providing a clear path for the

---

[43] Another transport protocol, proposed earlier by Impulse Radio, was called *MAT*. The MAT proposal was withdrawn when AAS was shown to be capable of supporting generic service protocols outside the NRSC-5 protocol stack. That is to say, the transport, AAT, is service-agnostic.

prompt adoption of this technology and ensuring that all IBOC equipment will be suitable for all modes of the IBOC system.

(2) To provide a cross-industry body to review new proposals for digital radio standards describing information and/or entertainment services which can be transported using a compliant NRSC-5 IBOC signal, or RF services which can co-exist with NRSC-5 IBOC transmissions, and where appropriate establish a course of action.

Goals

To meet its objective, the Subcommittee will work towards achieving the following goals:

(a) To support and maintain the existing Standard to ensure that it contains all the up-to-date information necessary for broadcasters and equipment manufacturers to fully understand and implement the capabilities of IBOC technology;

(b) To continue establishment of the technical record that will allow future readers to understand the technical parameters and tradeoffs upon which the Standard and subsequent revisions are based;

(c) To provide information that may aid manufacturers of broadcast equipment and reception equipment to produce products that are interoperable and remain functional through continuing evolution of the technology; and to enable the technology to evolve compatible new features and services;

(d) To encourage implementers and innovators of technology compatible with NRSC-5 to bring their innovations and new features to the NRSC for incorporation into the Standard;

(e) To continue to foster a consumer experience that maintains the legacy of free over-the-air broadcasting and broadcast innovation, while enabling manufacturer flexibility to differentiate products and innovate new features;

(f) To investigate and possibly evaluate the ability to interface with and support various data service protocols that may be developed to enable the broadcast of flexible and extensible data content and applications;

(g) To work with the FCC and other interested organizations and parties in order to achieve universal acceptance of the IBOC system of AM and FM broadcasting.

* Subsequent references to "NRSC 5" herein refer to the most up-to-date revision of the Standard, which at the time of adoption of this Goals and Objectives Statement was NRSC-5-A.

The work of the NRSC DRB Subcommittee continues, as does development of IBOC technologies and services by iBiquity and the many industry players. At the very least, the NRSC's rules call for periodic review (every five years) of each of its standards to ensure their relevance and timeliness. However, with continuing IBOC development comes a continuing need to evaluate and recommend best practices and potential standard revisions as they arise.

Among the continuing efforts relating to NRSC-5 was an effort to harmonize the text carried by the IBOC Program Service Data and similar text carried by the Radio Data Service (RDS) FM subcarrier. The Radio Broadcast Data Standard (NRSC-4) has some program-related and station-related text features that parallel those available through the IBOC signal. The content of corresponding fields may differ, based on how the station uses them, and based on their respective field lengths. Kenwood U.S.A. Corporation noted some awkwardness in the user experience of a radio that supported both IBOC text and RDS text.

Moving On

The work of the IBOC industry continues as receiver sales grow, IBOC stations go on line daily, and new services are developed. The NRSC monitors progress, stepping in when asked to assist with issues of interoperability. This book continues by looking back at the NRSC-5-A standard and exploring the technical details of how it works. Chapter 3 explores the structure of the standard, while Chapters 4 though 11 disassemble the layers of the IBOC protocol stack.

SECTION II

THE PROTOCOL STACK

3 Overview of NRSC-5

NRSC-5 Versions

The NRSC-5 standard, initially adopted in April 2005, is a single document supplemented by various other documents. It summarizes the structure of IBOC and refers to the "reference documents" to obtain the details. The initial version of the standard, called "NRSC-5" was considered by the NRSC to be the "core"[2] standard because it addressed the key functions of transmitting digital audio in the AM and FM bands. "NRSC-5 core" (meaning the NRSC-5 standard as originally adopted) listed nine reference documents.

The Standard and the reference documents are subject to periodic review and may be changed from time to time. In the future, changes could be made to either the Standard itself or the reference documents, and could result in the inclusion of additional reference documents, as well. For example, the first revision to the Standard was adopted in September 2005, bearing the name NRSC-5-A. It is the original NRSC-5 standard to which an "Advanced Data Services" data transport specification is added. A tenth reference document was added to provide the working details of this transport.

---

[1] Each chapter in Section II begins with this icon, showing in gray highlights those elements of the protocol stack discussed in the chapter.

[2] NRSC DAB Subcommittee, Meeting Minutes, October 8, 2004 Meeting, p. 3.

In this book, a specific version of the standard is indicated in this fashion: "NRSC-5-A" or "NRSC-5 core." When discussing the NRSC-5 standard to include any of its past, present or future incarnations, the term "NRSC-5" is used generically.

Reference Documents

In the standards community, there are two types of reference documents, normative and informative. A normative reference document contains a detailed description of a component of the standard. To be compliant with the standard, a device or system *must* satisfy not only the general criteria in the main standard document, but also the detailed criteria contained in those normative references that relate to the workings of the device. It is simply a separate document that the standard document incorporates by reference.

Normative references are a convenient way to incorporate documents from other sources into a standard. Also, by relying upon normative references, the main standard document provides a top-level description of the entire system without being burdened by the intricate details. All the normative reference documents in the NRSC-5 core standard are documents supplied by iBiquity Digital Corporation. However, as the technology matures and newcomers offer innovations to the marketplace, new normative references can come from any source, including the NRSC itself. When NRSC-5-A was adopted, the new normative reference also came from iBiquity.

The goal of the NRSC Standards development process is to create documentation that provides enough information that a person "skilled in the art"[3] could produce a working transmission system compliant with the standard. It is the role of the reference documents to provide the details. While is the NRSC-5 standard and its reference documents are available for free from the NRSC, patents may protect some of the technology it describes. Patented technology must be properly licensed before one can offer a product using the NRSC-5 recipes. Participants in the NRSC standards-setting process agree to make technology incorporated in an NRSC standard available to others on a Reasonable and Nondiscriminatory (RAND) basis.[4]

Each reference document has two numbers identifying it. NRSC-5-A numbers them sequentially, 1–10, as shown in the left column of Table 3.1. It is these numbers to which this book refers.

Included with the title of each reference document are iBiquity Digital Corporation's internal document numbers, version letters, and version dates. The specific versions indicated have been incorporated as normative references. These documents are frozen as far as the standard is concerned. If iBiquity were to make revisions to any of these documents, the revisions would have to be adopted by the NRSC to become part of NRSC-5. Similarly, if any other party were to make enhancements these would not become part of the standard unless they are adopted by NRSC.

---

[3] In the Matter of Digital Audio Broadcasting Systems MM Docket No. 99-325 And Their Impact On the Terrestrial Radio Broadcast Service, REPLY COMMENTS OF THE NATIONAL ASSOCIATION OF BROADCASTERS August 17, 2005.

[4] NRSC Procedures Manual, Adopted on September 24, 2003,Section 7.2.5.1 Patent Policy, www.nrscstandards.org, NRSC is co-sponsored by the Consumer Electronics Association and the National Association of Broadcasters.

NRSC-5 Reference Document Number	Reference Document Title	NRSC-5 Reference Document Number	Reference Document Title
1.	Doc. No. SY_IDD_1011s rev. E HD Radio™ Air Interface Design Description **Layer 1 FM** iBiquity Digital Corporation, 3/22/05	6.	Doc. No. SY_SSS_1026s rev. D HD Radio™ **FM Transmission System Specifications** iBiquity Digital Corporation, 2/18/05
2.	Doc. No. SY_IDD_1012s rev. E HD Radio™ Air Interface Design Description **Layer 1 AM** iBiquity Digital Corporation, 3/22/05	7.	Doc. No. SY_IDD_1028s rev. C HD Radio™ Air Interface Design Description **Program Service Data** iBiquity Digital Corporation, 3/31/05
3.	Doc. No. SY_IDD_1014s rev. F HD Radio™ Air Interface Design Description **Layer 2 Channel Multiplex Protocol** iBiquity Digital Corporation, 2/7/05	8.	Doc. No. SY_SSS_1082s rev. D HD Radio™ **AM Transmission System Specifications** iBiquity Digital Corporation, 2/24/05
4.	Doc. No. SY_IDD_1017s rev. E HD Radio™ Air Interface Design Description **Audio Transport** iBiquity Digital Corporation, 3/31/05	9.	Doc. No. SY_IDD_1085s rev. C HD Radio™ Air Interface Design Description **Program Service Data Transport** iBiquity Digital Corporation, 2/7/05
5.	Doc. No. SY_IDD_1020s rev. E HD Radio™ Air Interface Design Description **Station Information Service Protocol** iBiquity Digital Corporation, 2/18/05	10.	Doc. No. SY_IDD_1019s rev. E HD Radio™ Air Interface Design Description **Advanced Application Services Transport** iBiquity Digital Corporation, 8/4/05

Table 3.1 Normative Reference List, NRSC-5-A

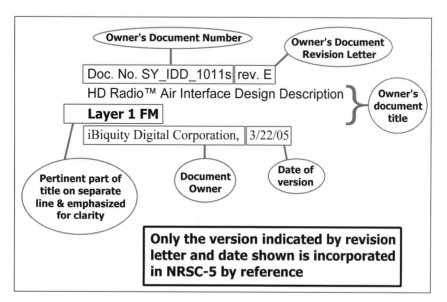

Figure 3.1 Explanation of Document References

It is extremely important that anyone who considers expanding on the standard be careful not to add features to the transmitted signal that would cause an NRSC-5 compatible radio to "break." Receiver manufacturers must rely on NRSC-5 as the "gold standard" for ensuring receiver compatibility with the IBOC signal. This assurance of compatibility with existing products is one of the purposes of a standard. Once a standard is adopted, its contents are locked down until a revision is formally adopted.

The NRSC-5 standard employs the generic term "IBOC" (for In-Band On-Channel) because the brand name "HD Radio" is reserved only for products that earn iBiquity's approval. Innovators who enter the market without the HD Radio mark may still produce NRSC-5 compliant devices. Consequently, NRSC-5 modifies the meaning of the normative references by stating,

"For the purposes of compliance with this standard, the use of the term "HD Radio" in the normative references shall be interpreted as the generic term "IBOC" for the NRSC-5 compliant system and shall not be construed as a requirement to adhere to undisclosed private specifications that are required to license the HD Radio name from its owner."[5]

In theory, a manufacturer could develop a product that is NRSC-5 compliant but that has not earned the right to use the HD Radio name and logo. In practice, the manufacturer would find it necessary to license iBiquity patents to manufacture and sell its NRSC-5 product. While doing so, the manufacturer may be enticed by iBiquity's technology to take the next step and join the HD Radio family. iBiquity's technology could be useful to a manufacturer because it is already developed, has a proven track record, and provides the developer such things as know-how, software, branded chipsets, or brand recognition that would be otherwise unavailable. In addition, access to the HD Radio brand may also provide the manufacturer with features and capabilities that are not part of NRSC-5, but are common to the brand.

Informative References

In addition to normative references, some standards include informative references. As the name suggests, an informative reference document (also called a non-normative document by some standards organizations) does not contain criteria necessary for compliance with the standard, but is provided to help the reader understand something about the standard that may not be evident by reviewing the standard and normative references. An informative reference may contain, for instance, an example of an implementation of the standard, or material that provides background information on a specification.

The initial versions of NRSC-5 contain no independent informative references. However, two of the normative references contain appendices that are informative. First, the Program Service Data normative reference document (7) describes how to label each piece of text information. These data labels, or "tags," are borrowed from another tagging protocol called ID3,[6] which is published

---

[5] National Radio Systems Committee, In-Band On-Channel Digital Radio Broadcasting Standard NRSC-5, April, 2005.

[6] Martin Nilsson, "ID3v2.3.0 Informal Standard" http://www.ID3.org.

Figure 3.2 Normative and Informative Documents

as an "informal standard."[7] for identifying MP3 audio content. The informative appendix to the normative iBiquity document contains the entire ID3 protocol, while only certain tags from the protocol are incorporated in the normative reference.

Similarly, the normative reference (10) describing the data transport contains an informative appendix. To create a data stream containing data packets requires a transport protocol, which is adapted from a protocol standardized by the Internet Engineering Task Force.[8] The informative appendix to the NRSC-5 normative reference (10) contains the entire protocol from which portions were borrowed for the data transport.

This chapter discusses the NRSC-5 standard and the normative references in a general way, providing an overview of the structure of the standard. Subsequent chapters, in Section II, describe the various layers of the NRSC-5 protocol stack in more detail. The reader is encouraged to obtain a copy of the current version of the NRSC-5 standard and the accompanying reference documents to refer to while reading this book. The NRSC website, www.nrscstandards.org, provides access to free copies of the standard and normative references.

---

[7] In the realm of data communications and software engineering, sometimes an ad hoc group will create a recommendation that is not formally endorsed by a standard-setting body, but which becomes widely adopted as a de facto standard.

[8] Network Working Group, RFC 1662 "PPP in HDLC-like Framing" STD 51, July 1994, IETF Secretariat, Reston, VA.

Chapter 3

The NRSC-5 Standard

The NRSC-5 core standard was adopted by the National Radio Systems Committee in April 2005. The NRSC *Digital Audio Broadcasting (DAB) Subcommittee* was the official standard "formulating group"[9] that formally adopted the original standard. The DAB Subcommittee was subsequently renamed the Digital Radio Broadcasting (DRB) Subcommittee in deference to the roles of both audio and data in radio broadcasting.

The standard is focused on describing how to assemble a signal for transmission. It is sometimes described as a "transmission standard."[10] NRSC-5 describes the structure of the IBOC signal in a manner that shows a transmission system developer how to create an IBOC signal. Also, with the same knowledge of the structure of the transmitted signal, a receiver manufacturer can design a receiver that will be compatible with the transmitted signal. However, there are very few receiver requirements in the standard, which leaves receiver manufacturers room to innovate and to respond to consumer preferences.

The addition of the data transport protocol in September 2005 (thus creating NRSC-5-A) filled a gap in the NRSC-5 protocol stack. The protocol stack is introduced below.

Protocol Stack

When participants on a system must communicate with one another, they need common rules of the road to communicate efficiently and reliably. Each participant must have the answer to fundamental questions about the communication. What form does the electrical signal take? How is the information packaged for carriage on the signal? What is the construction of a message or stream of information? How is the destination or purpose of any information identified? How do different messages and message types share the same channel? How is the information protected from the errors typically induced by the communications channel?

The answers to questions like these are provided in *protocols* and *specifications*. Of the ten normative reference documents in NRSC-5-A, eight are protocol related and two are performance specifications. Documents (6), FM Transmission System Specifications, and (8), AM Transmission System Specifications, describe the required characteristics of the FM and AM radio signals and do not discuss the organization of information on IBOC signals. The remaining eight documents describe the structure of the various kinds of information carried on the digital signals. These eight normative reference documents formed the NRSC-5-A protocol stack.

To understand the NRSC-5 protocol stack, it helps to start with the fundamentals of open systems interconnection. The United States federal Glossary of Telecommunications Terms, Federal

---

[9] NRSC Procedures Manual, Rev. 1/26/1006, NAB and CEA.

[10] Federal Communications Commission, Notice of Proposed Rulemaking, In the Matter of Digital Audio Broadcasting Systems and their Impact on the Terrestrial Radio Broadcast Service. FCC 99-327, November 1, 1999.

Standard 1037C (Federal Glossary),[11] contains definitions for quite a few terms relating to open systems. Fundamentally, it defines an open system:

open system: *A system with characteristics that comply with specified, publicly maintained, readily available standards and that therefore can be connected to other systems that comply with these same standards.*

NRSC-5 is a cooperatively maintained standard whose objective is to "furnish broadcasters and manufacturers of both broadcast and receiver equipment with a complete and open transmission and reception specification of the AM and FM IBOC systems, providing a clear path for the prompt adoption of this technology and ensuring that all IBOC equipment will be suitable for the hybrid, extended hybrid, and all-digital modes of the IBOC system…"[12] It creates an open system in which transmitters and receivers made by independent parties will operate compatibly with IBOC broadcasting.

The Federal Glossary further defines "open systems architecture" as a "layered hierarchical structure, configuration, or model" that allows individual layers to be implemented and modified independently of the other layers, without affecting the overall performance of the system.

The Internet is perhaps the most familiar open systems architecture. Two fundamental layers of the Internet include the TCP/IP protocols. While TCP (Transmission Control Protocol) handles the structure of data packets for transporting their contents, IP (Internet Protocol) handles the addressing and routing of those packets.[13] These protocols form two layers of the protocol stack that a device would use to communicate on the Internet.

Open Systems Model

The quintessential model for open systems protocols is described in the Open Systems Interconnection (OSI) model.[14] It describes the characteristics of each layer of interconnected systems. The Internet's TCP corresponds to the Transport layer of the OSI model. IP corresponds with the Data Link layer. Other familiar protocols reside above and below these layers. One such higher layer is HTTP (Hypertext Transfer Protocol), which enables the world wide web to exist on the Internet. Similarly, SMTP (Simple Mail Transfer Protocol) resides alongside HTTP in the protocol stack because it performs the same function for electronic mail that HTTP performs for web services. These protocols, among many others, correspond to the application layer of the OSI model.

---

[11] Federal Standard 1037C, Telecommunications: Glossary of Telecommunications Terms. Prepared by the National Communications System Technology and Standards Division Secretariat: U.S. Department of Commerce, National Telecommunications and Information Administration, Institute for Telecommunication Sciences. Published by General Services Administration Information Technology Service, August 7, 1996.

[12] NRSC DAB Subcommittee Goals and Objectives, adopted January 9, 2003.

[13] Federal Glossary.

[14] ISO/IEC 7498-1; 1994, Information Technology—Open Systems Interconnection—Basic Reference Model: The Basic Model, 2nd ed. November 15, 1994, International Organization for Standardization and International Electrotechnical Commission.

Name	Federal Glossary Description	Plain Language
Open Systems Interconnection—Reference Model (OSI—RM):	An abstract description of the digital communications between application processes running in distinct systems. The model employs a hierarchical structure of seven layers. Each layer performs value-added service at the request of the adjacent higher layer and, in turn, requests more basic services from the adjacent lower layer.	A model that classifies the individual steps in the process of getting two or more devices across a network to perform some useful task.
Application Layer: Layer 7	... the highest layer. This layer interfaces directly to and performs common application services for the application processes; it also issues requests to the Presentation Layer. The common application services provide semantic conversion between associated application processes. *Note:* Examples of common application services of general interest include the virtual file, virtual terminal, and job transfer and manipulation protocols.	An application on a computer might use such Application Layer services as FTP, MIME, SMTP, HTTP, or TELNET, among many others, to work with a corresponding application at another location on a network.
Presentation Layer: Layer 6	This layer responds to service requests from the Application Layer and issues service requests to the Session Layer. The Presentation Layer relieves the Application Layer of concern regarding syntactical differences in data representation within the end-user systems. *Note:* An example of a presentation service would be the conversion of an EBCDIC-coded text file to an ASCII-coded file.	If applications have to be translated to a common format for transport this layer would do the translation. If used, this layer might provide character conversion (as in the example to the left), encryption, data compression and similar functions as the go-between of the common network transport and the idiosyncrasies of the user's application.
Session Layer: Layer 5	This layer responds to service requests from the Presentation Layer and issues service requests to the Transport Layer. The Session Layer provides the mechanism for managing the dialogue between end-user application processes. It provides for either duplex or half-duplex operation and establishes checkpointing, adjournment, termination, and restart procedures.	Provides the logical equivalent of a handshake between participants. Logins, synchronization, connect time, reconnection services and the like are provided in this layer.
Transport Layer: Layer 4	This layer responds to service requests from the Session Layer and issues service requests to the Network Layer. The purpose of the Transport Layer is to provide transparent transfer of data between end users, thus relieving the upper layers from any concern with providing reliable and cost-effective data transfer.	If Session Layer provides the formalities, the Transport Layer does the grunt work. Data streams are chunked and packetized. Error detection/correction is applied and reviewed. Calls to replace lost or broken packets are sent back from this layer. TCP is a common example.

Table 3.2 Open Systems Interconnection Model (partly from Federal Glossary) *(continued)*

Name	Federal Glossary Description	Plain Language
Network Layer: Layer 3	This layer responds to service requests from the Transport Layer and issues service requests to the Data Link Layer. The Network Layer provides the functional and procedural means of transferring variable length data sequences from a source to a destination via one or more networks while maintaining the quality of service requested by the Transport Layer. The Network Layer performs network routing, flow control, segmentation/desegmentation, and error control functions.	This layer is the navigator. It provides the means to identify and route information to a physical location elsewhere on the network. Internet Protocol (IP) is a common example of a protocol residing at this level.
Data Link Layer: Layer 2	This layer responds to service requests from the Network Layer and issues service requests to the Physical Layer. The Data Link Layer provides the functional and procedural means to transfer data between network entities and to detect and possibly correct errors that may occur in the Physical Layer. *Note:* Examples of data link protocols are HDLC and ADCCP for point-to-point or packet-switched networks and LLC for local area networks.	This layer converts the data to (from) the format required for the data to be carried according to the "rules of the road" on the type of network being used. For instance, on an Ethernet network, the network card monitors the network and senses activity and packet collisions among different users on the net. Certain rules apply to maintain sharing of the network efficiently.
Physical Layer: Layer 1	The lowest of seven hierarchical layers. The Physical layer performs services requested by the Data Link Layer. The major functions and services performed by the physical layer are: (a) establishment and termination of a connection to a communications medium; (b) participation in the process whereby the communication resources are effectively shared among multiple users, *e.g.,* contention resolution and flow control; and, (c) conversion between the representation of digital data in user equipment and the corresponding signals transmitted over a communications channel.	This is in essence the electrical signal carried on the medium. The network electronics are designed for compatibility with this signal specification. The signal has characteristics that enable the data link layer to manage transmission and reception according to the rules of the road. It may be noted that some characteristics do not neatly fit in a single layer, as in this case where flow control is said to exist in the physical layer, but in practice flow control may have both physical characteristics (e.g. collision detection in Ethernet) and data link responsibilities (react, pause, and re-send).

Table 3.2 Open Systems Interconnection Model (partly from Federal Glossary)

While the layers of the OSI model describe important functions in a network, there is not always a one-to-one correspondence between OSI layers and the layers of an actual system. Sometimes a protocol overlaps two OSI layers and sometimes a particular OSI layer is unnecessary. For instance, in the NRSC-5-A protocol stack, there is no direct analogy to the Session Layer of the OSI model. The Session Layer typically manages a two-way communication. IBOC is a one way broadcast medium for which a Session Layer, in its most conventional sense, is not required. In a one-way medium, perhaps a session could consist of the raising of a flag or code on the channel to indicate that a certain service has become active or is presently active. Such session-like information is implicit in the IBOC transports. In the future when a return path from an IBOC receiver is implemented (via a cell phone or wireless network, for example) there could be a role for a Session Layer to administer two-way communication.

NRSC-5 As Open System

Figure 3.3 illustrates the NRSC-5 protocol stack. The role of a protocol stack is discussed in this section, and individual components of the stack are addressed in Chapters 4–11. Observe how there is a group of functional blocks stacked on one another. Each block represents a protocol for handling certain information in a certain way. Note how there are columns that involve 1) audio and data related to the audio, 2) Advanced Data Services (which was added in NRSC-5-A), and Station Information Services. The rows of the stack are called "layers." The reference document numbers associated with each block are scribed within the blocks.

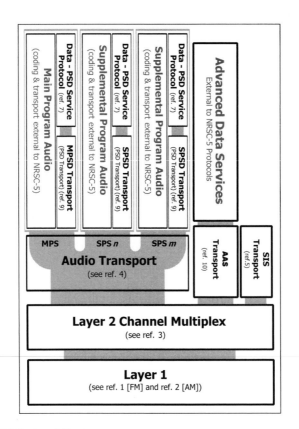

Figure 3.3 NRSC-5-A Protocol Stack

Working from the bottom, IBOC Layer 1 (NRSC-5 ref. 1 for FM and ref. 2 for AM) is closest to the actual communications medium—the electromagnetic representation of the information in the form of a radio signal. Since each radio station transmits continuously on its assigned channel, the Physical Layer does not need to manage "device contention" among multiple users on the radio channel. (Contention management is important in networks where several computers are sharing a wire or channel to carry their signals.)

Layer 1 performs the other functions of the OSI model Physical Layer and functions of the Data Link Layer. It creates a data stream comprising all the information it is fed from the higher-layer applications, plus lower-level information about the station and the signal, and the lowest-level information providing error protection, synchronization and other information necessary to lock onto the signal and decompose the data at the receiver. It describes how the information is assigned to and modulated upon the OFDM subcarriers. Chapters 6 through 9 discuss IBOC's Layer 1.

Layer 2 (NRSC-5 ref. 3) corresponds best with the OSI model Transport Layer. With several independent "services" being carried on the IBOC signal, Layer 2 functions to insert each service's data into the correct slot on the IBOC transport. Each audio program channel, with its corresponding text data, is fed into its place on each transmission frame. Information about the station and the configuration of the signal are also directed to their places in the data stream.

IBOC Layers 1 and 2 sit below the OSI Network Layer. This layer manages quality of service requirements. Quality of Service (QoS), "the performance specification of a communications channel or system,"[15] is maintained by controlling the transmission characteristics of the information being transmitted. Characteristics include the timeliness of delivery of the information, the robustness of the information as determined by error protection and channel conditions, the priority of the information over other information contending for the channel, and the like. In the IBOC system it is possible to apply differing QoS requirements to the various types of information being transmitted.

The OSI Network Layer also provides addressing and routing information. These addressing and routing functions are not placed squarely in an IBOC layer in NRSC-5.

Note how the blocks of the protocol stack in Figure 3.3 resemble the icons at the beginnings of the chapters in this section. Keep Figure 3.3 in mind when advancing to each chapter.

---

[15] Federal Glossary.

Service	Service Name	Service Description	Related Transport
MPS	Main Program Service (one service per IBOC station) [Has no independent protocol and consists of the merging of MPA and MPSD in the Audio Transport]	The provision of audio and related data	Audio Transport combines audio and related data
MPA	Main Program Audio	Audio from coder	Outside NRSC-5
MPSD*	Main Program Service Data	Data, primarily text, related to the audio	Program Service Data Transport (PSD)
SPS	Supplemental Program Service (Up to 7 services per IBOC station) [Has no independent protocol and consists of the merging of SPA and SPSD in the Audio Transport]	The provision of audio and related data	Audio Transport combines audio and related data
SPA	Supplemental Program Audio	Audio from coder	Outside NRSC-5
SPSD*	Supplemental Program Service Data	Data, primarily text, related to the audio	Program Service Data Transport (PSD)
SIS*	Station Information Service	Information about the station and the IBOC signal conveyed on OFDM referencesubcarriers	SIS also performs the transport function
ADS	Advanced Data Service	All manner of data can be transported, whether or not related to any programming on the station.	AAS Transport

* Only these Services have service protocols included in NRSC-5.

Table 3.3 IBOC "Services" Requiring Transport Protocols

In less abstract terms, consider the various services carried on an IBOC signal, as shown in Table 3.3. The Audio Transport (ref. 4) conveys any Main and Supplemental Program Services to Layer 2. Each Main and Supplemental Program service is the product of several individual transport functions that are combined into a stream of data packets. Main (or Supplemental) Program Audio packets arrive at the NRSC-5 input already packaged in a high-level coded audio transport package, not part of the NRSC-5 protocols. Program Service Data is packaged on its transport within the NRSC-5 protocols. Each pair of program audio and program data services is merged into a packet stream with the audio transport.

This packaged stream of information arrives at Layer 2 where it has bandwidth reserved for it. The quality of service for MPS is pre-ordained by design, and Layer 2 simply does as it is told by inserting the MPS packet stream in the correct places at the predetermined times. The MPS stream is essentially continuous; its priority is paramount; and error protection is fixed. Consequently, Layer 2 does not need to make decisions on the fly about timeliness or reliability. Another

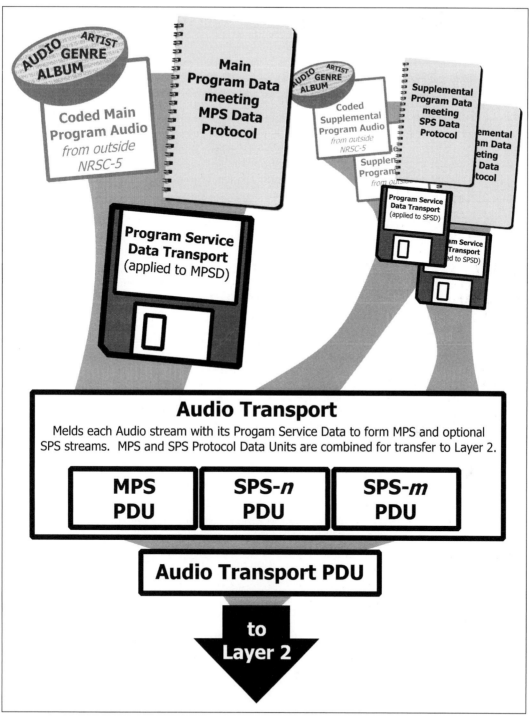

Figure 3.4 Audio Services Transport Funnel

pre-ordained characteristic of the MPS stream is that it owns a priority position within IBOC Layer 2. It is also labeled above IBOC Layer 2 with an audio port number recognized by all audio receivers.

Consequently, Main Program Audio (as well as Supplemental Program Audio) is provided with the functions of the OSI Network Layer, but without a distinct layer for the purpose.

In contrast with the Main Program and Supplemental Program Services, the Advanced Data Service (ADS, transported by the Advanced Application Services Transport NRSC-5 ref. 10) could have multiple services contending for its limited bandwidth. A QoS manager for the data services would reside above Layer 2. It would feed information to the space available for it in Layer 2. It would do so by being instructed to make decisions on what, how, and when to transmit particular pieces of information. This is addressed in more detail in Chapter 11.

To clarify some possibly confusing terminology among the data services, there is a distinction between ADS and AAS that is not self-evident. First, ADS is the generic term employed by NRSC-5 to represent the class of services that could be presented to the IBOC data transport. The IBOC data transport goes by the acronym AAT, short for Advanced Application Services Transport. We must distinguish the transport within NRSC-5, AAT, from the services that connect to it from outside NRSC-5. ADS is the generic name for the services that could be delivered to the AAT.

Complicating the picture, iBiquity has a service protocol, outside NRSC-5 that connects to AAT. It is called Advanced Application Services (AAS). iBiquity's AAS is a broad palette of services that includes access to AAT. AAS contains the iBiquity implementation of what NRSC-5 calls ADS. iBiquity's AAS technology contains the only Advanced Data Service protocol implemented with HD Radio technology.

With respect to the data services, no matter the name, the *transport protocol* is inside the NRSC-5 protocol stack; the actual *service protocols* are outside NRSC-5. Data services are discussed more fully in Chapter 11. Also, the distinction between a Service and a Transport is further discussed in this chapter.

Above IBOC Layer 2 several protocols reside; some in parallel, some in tandem. The Audio Transport (NRSC-5 ref. 4) consolidates coded audio of Main and Supplemental program streams, and bundles it with the Program Service Data (NRSC-5 ref. 7) delivered to the Audio Transport via the Program Service Data Transport (NRSC-5 ref. 9). Each program service is constrained to carry its coded audio and program data within the bandwidth assigned to it. The same is true for the AAT (NRSC-5 ref. 10) and Station Information Service (SIS) (NRSC-5 ref. 5). AAT is the way to transmit data independently of a program audio channel (although it may or may not relate to what is going on an audio channel). SIS provides information about the radio signal such as the call sign, station location, and the familiar name for the station.

Each of these services is assigned a portion of the station's bandwidth; Layer 2 pulls them all together. However, each of these services acts as an independent data channel, requiring independent assembly for transport. OSI Transport Layer functionality is therefore not only at IBOC Layer 2 for the ensemble of information streams, but also among the several protocols above Layer 2, addressing the needs of each individual service.

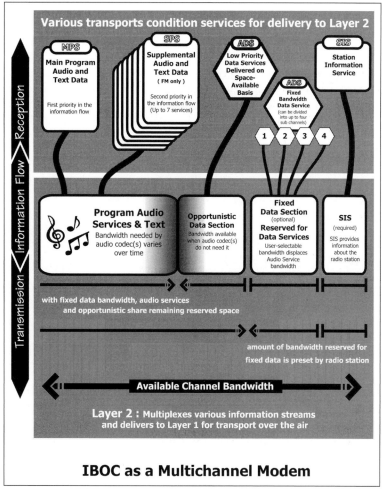

IBOC as a Multichannel Modem

Figure 3.5 IBOC as a Multichannel Modem

The structure of the MPS and each SPS is revealed in normative reference (9), Program Service Data Transport. This layer explains how the coded audio stream for each program service is merged with text information about the stream (title, artist, etc.), and the result is packaged for transfer to Layer 2.

Program audio is coded by a process not incorporated in the NRSC-5 standard. The HD Radio system employs the HDC audio codec for transmission and reception of program audio on MPS and SPS. Because of the open architecture of the standard and the lack of a codec specification in the standard, it is possible to transmit audio coded with a different system and still remain compliant with the NRSC-5 standard. However, this is a broadcasting medium for which receiver compatibility is key. There is little incentive to transmit on main and supplemental program channels audio that is encoded by a different method because existing receivers would not be able to decode it.

The Station Information Service (SIS) is described in reference (5). SIS transports information about the radio station as well as time-related information. It has a low bandwidth requirement and its messages are repeated frequently.

The two reference documents that do not contain protocols—FM Transmission System Specifications (ref. 6) and AM Transmission System Specifications (ref. 8)—instead describe characteristics of the physical medium. These documents describe such parameters as OFDM subcarrier frequencies, synchronization information, and tolerances for level, noise, and spectral occupancy.

One Standard, Several Modalities

NRSC-5 specifies the structure of IBOC on AM and FM channels as well as the structure of the IBOC waveforms when sharing the channel with the analog host (hybrid mode) or replacing the analog signal completely (all-digital mode).

NRSC-5 contains two documents specifically devoted to FM and two for AM band transmission. AM IBOC transmission is different from FM for two reasons. Most apparent is the fact that there is simply more bandwidth on the FM channel to transmit IBOC signals. The FM band is graduated into 101 channels from 87.9 to 107.9 MHz, with a channel centered every 200 kHz in the U.S.A. FM IBOC takes advantage of the bandwidth already available under the FCC radio frequency emissions mask to transmit low-level digital signals along with the analog signal. Consequently, the FM IBOC total signal bandwidth is about 400 kHz wide. This provides substantial bandwidth (in radio transmission terms) to transmit one or more information streams with good quality.

In contrast, the AM spectrum has much narrower channel spacing and signal bandwidths. Channels are allotted every 10 kHz in the U.S.A., and the FCC's AM mask is 20 kHz wide at full power, going to 40 kHz wide at reduced power level. This gives each station ±5 kHz of exclusive channel width. By narrowing the analog audio bandwidth to as little as 5 kHz, a digital signal can be inserted into the spectrum where wideband audio sidebands used to reside, between ±5 to ±10 kHz. In the hybrid mode where analog and digital signals of one station coexist, some of the digital energy extends out to ±15 kHz, beneath the FCC mask. This 30 kHz channel bandwidth offers substantially less capacity than the 400 kHz channel bandwidth of FM IBOC.

In addition to the substantial differences in available bandwidth between AM and FM, the modulation of the host analog signal has a bearing on the way the IBOC waveform is constructed. The hybrid waveform is a combination of the analog host signal and a compatible digital signal. On FM, the hybrid waveform steers as clear as possible of the bulk of the power spectral density of the analog host. Because the frequency-modulated waveform contains the analog program audio, there is no practicable way to place IBOC digital subcarriers where there is substantial analog information in the channel.[16] The digital Primary Main signal occupies about 70 kHz on each side

---

[16] The term "subcarrier" has two meanings not to be confused. The IBOC digital signal consists of a spectrum of many digital subcarriers that in the aggregate form the orthogonal frequency division multiplexing (OFDM) digital signal. Meanwhile, the traditional FM signal can carry subcarriers such as those generated by RDS, radio reading services, or the Digital Radio Express, Inc. FMeXtra technology. When employed, FM subcarriers are an integral component of the FM signal. OFDM subcarriers are generated and received independently of the FM signal.

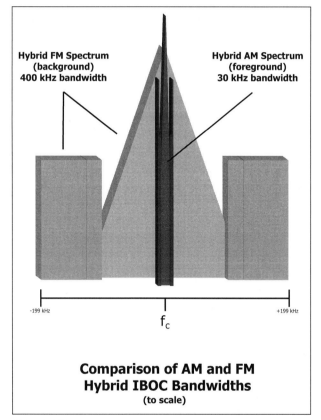

Hybrid FM Spectrum
(background)
400 kHz bandwidth

Hybrid AM Spectrum
(foreground)
30 kHz bandwidth

-199 kHz

f_c

+199 kHz

**Comparison of AM and FM
Hybrid IBOC Bandwidths**
(to scale)

Figure 3.6 IBOC Signal Bandwidths

of the analog FM signal. Pushing the envelope, the digital signal in hybrid can be squeezed closer to the analog with the Primary Extended subcarriers, at a minor cost in analog performance. This is called Hybrid Extended mode. With the extended subcarriers in operation, the digital signal occupies about 97 kHz on each side of the analog.

In contrast to the hybrid FM signal, in which the digital signal has to exist outside the occupied spectrum of the analog, AM can be exploited to hide some digital information within the analog sidebands. Hybrid AM operation maintains Primary, Secondary and Tertiary digital subcarrier groups. The hybrid AM Primary subcarriers are well removed from the analog host, at ±10–15 kHz offset. The Secondary subcarriers operate at reduced levels in the audio sideband range of ±5–10 kHz. A set of Tertiary subcarriers and a pair of reference subcarriers coexist with the analog host in the range from about 0 to ±5 kHz.

The bandwidth and unique waveform constraints of AM and FM IBOC operations require separate documentation of the protocol layer (Layer 1). Layer 1 describes how to assemble the frames of digital information and encode them on OFDM subcarriers. Hence, there are separate normative references for Layer 1 AM (ref. 2) and Layer 1 FM (ref. 1) IBOC. Likewise, the spectral characteristics of AM and FM IBOC signals require independent transmission specifications, found in reference documents (8) and (6), respectively.

The remaining layers provide protocols common to AM and FM systems. The packaging and transport of audio, program service data, and other information follows the same rules for both the AM and FM systems. The remaining reference documents describe these functions generically so they may be applied to both AM and FM IBOC. Some of the flexibility FM can afford is not available in the AM IBOC system. For instance, the manner in which the Audio Transport protocol is described suggests that it is technically possible to transmit Supplemental Program Services on AM as well as on FM IBOC. As a practical matter, the limited bandwidth of AM IBOC is not conducive to multiple audio channel transmissions, so it is not presently implemented.

Initially, hybrid operation is necessary to support continued analog listening. Anticipating a time when the vast majority of consumer radios in use are NRSC-5 complaint devices, the standard provides the structure of the all-digital IBOC signals. While all-digital operation has not been tested under the auspices of the NRSC and it has not been authorized by the FCC, the standard provides a migration path to all-digital operation. Since all IBOC receivers are compatible with all-digital modes, the consumer's transition to hybrid is also the transition to all-digital.

"Services" Versus "Transports"

Some components of the NRSC-5 standard describe services while others are describe transports. The Program Service Data (7) protocol is the only one that exclusively describes a service without describing an accompanying transport. Other protocols describe only transport functions, including Audio Transport (4), Program Service Data Transport (9), and Advanced Application Service Transport (10). One protocol blends service description with transport functions—Station Information Service (5). Layer 2 Channel Multiplex Protocol (3) describes a transport function by providing the framework for integrating the outputs of the various transports for unified delivery to Layer 1. The Layer 1 documents contain the ultimate transport description, as well as the recipe for creating the waveforms.

To illustrate a service protocol in connection with its transport protocol, consider this analogy with a business letter. The Business Letter Forum decides to create protocols for creating and sending business letters to provide a more uniform environment for business communications. The Business Letter Service protocol describes how a letter is constructed. The Business Letter Transport protocol describes how a letter is prepared for transmission to the recipient. These imaginary protocols are presented in Table 3.4.

Attributes	Assigned values
Business Letter Service Protocol	
Letter segment size	8.5 × 11 inches (U.S.A.)
Extensibility	Letter segments may be appended to first.
Format:	
Top of page	Sender logo
Upper left	Recipient name and address
Upper right	Date
Start of message	Salutation: "Dear NAME"
Message	Alphanumeric characters in language of recipient
End of message	Closing: "Yours truly, SENDER NAME"
Authentication	Signature; preceding SENDER NAME
End of all but last letter segment	Page number
End of last letter segment	Sender address
Business Letter Transport Protocol	
Transport package size	#10 Business envelope
Number of letter segments per transport package	5 letter segments maximum, in sequence, folded in thirds as a group. If message is greater than 5 segments, do not split into multiple transport packages; use Business Document Transport Protocol
Format:	
Upper left	Sender address
Center	Recipient address
Upper right	Postal fee impression
Security	Moisture-actuated security seal

Table 3.4 Business Letter Forum Protocols

The NRSC-5 reference documents contain tables that are similar in nature to the two shown in Table 3.4. For instance, Table 4-1 of Reference Document 5, the Station Information Service protocol, provides a message identifier for the SIS transport. It is a table with a message ID code, a payload size for each message type, a description of the message, and comments, shown in abbreviated form in Table 3.5.

MSG ID (binary)	Payload (bits)	Description	Comments
0000	32	Station ID Number	...Consists of Country Code and FCC facility ID
0001	22	Station Name (short)	...call sign plus optional extension
0010	58	Station Name (long)	...call sign or other identifying information...
Etc.	...	...	...

Table 3.5 SIS Message ID Definitions Example (from NRSC-5-A reference document 5)

The definitions of each message collectively are the service protocol portion of the SIS. The format of each message in SIS differs from the others. Each message has a subsidiary table describing how the information is tailored for that message. These are presented in bitmap form. For example, Table 3.6 is the bitmap of SIS MSG 0000, Station ID Number.

Station ID Number

10 bits	3 bits	19 bits
Country Code	Reserved	Facility ID Number

Table 3.6 SIS MSG ID Bitmap for Station ID Number

The format of each block of bits is further explained in the reference document. For instance, the Facility ID Number field is defined as "Binary representation of unique facility ID assigned by the FCC..."

With information structured according to its service definitions, as in the preceding example, it is ready to be inserted onto a transport. The structure of a transport is given in similar fashion. There are bitmaps of the headers with which the service data are transported. For example, the SIS messages (above) are packaged in a common transport format (below). Table 3.7 shows the bitmap of the SIS transport, taken from Figure 4-1 of the SIS document.

1 bit	1	4	Variable (see MSG ID Table)	4	Variable (see MSG ID Table)	1	1	2	12
Type	Ext	MSG ID1	Message Payload	MSG ID 2	Message Payload	Resv	Time-Locked	ALFN	CRC

The total count of bits in the two message payloads may not exceed 54 bits.

If total is less than 54 bits, second payload is padded with zeros.

Table 3.7 SIS Transport Bitmap

While the tables describing the structure of messages, headers, fields, and the like are important components of a protocol, it is necessary to supplement them with a written narrative explaining relationships, conditions, exceptions, examples and other information. For instance, the SIS protocol document is about evenly split between descriptive text and graphical presentations including tables and figures.

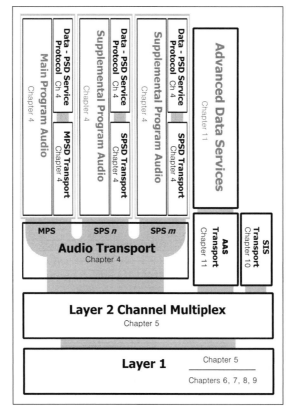

Figure 3.7 IBOC Protocol Stack with Chapter Sequence

Structure of Section II

The remander of Section II in this book—Chapters 4–11—delves into the details of the services and transports in the IBOC protocol stack. The descriptions follow a "top-down" sequence. That is to say, the reader can follow the journey of a frame of information as it travels from its inception through third-layer transports, into Layer 2 to Layer 1 and onto the air. The exposition begins with a discussion of audio coding, even though no audio codec is specified by NRSC-5. Since radio is traditionally an audio service, it is fitting to start a journey through the IBOC transmission chain with a little background on the audio source.

Following the chapter on audio coding and transport, the path of the "PDU" is followed into the Audio Transport and on to Layers 2 and 1. The term PDU stands for Protocol Data Unit. Each block in the protocol stack takes information in, performs work on it, and puts the newly structured information out the other side. The inputs and outputs of each layer are called *PDUs*. As will become apparent in the following chapters, the "work" performed by a layer may consist of synthesizing a new PDU from content data, combining or processing incoming PDUs, or a little of both.

4 From the Top Down: Program Services

This chapter covers the process of assembling the program audio and program related text into a monolithic package to hand off to lower layers of the NRSC-5 protocol. It begins with a discussion of audio codecs, despite the lack of a specified codec in NRSC-5. This will provide the necessary background in the role of the codec to create context for the discussion of the program service protocols. This chapter discusses the Audio Transport Protocol, as well as two protocols that supply program related data to the audio transport—the Program Service Data protocol and the Program Service Data Transport protocol. These are shown in Table 4.1.

NRSC-5 Reference Document Number	Reference Document Title	NRSC-5 Reference Document Number	Reference Document Title
1.	Doc. No. SY_IDD_1011s rev. E HD Radio™ Air Interface Design Description **Layer 1 FM** iBiquity Digital Corporation, 3/22/05	6.	Doc. No. SY_SSS_1026s rev. D HD Radio™ **FM Transmission System Specifications** iBiquity Digital Corporation, 2/18/05
2.	Doc. No. SY_IDD_1012s rev. E HD Radio™ Air Interface Design Description **Layer 1 AM** iBiquity Digital Corporation, 3/22/05	7.	Doc. No. SY_IDD_1028s rev. C HD Radio™ Air Interface Design Description **Program Service Data** iBiquity Digital Corporation, 3/31/05
3.	Doc. No. SY_IDD_1014s rev. F HD Radio™ Air Interface Design Description **Layer 2 Channel Multiplex Protocol** iBiquity Digital Corporation, 2/7/05	8.	Doc. No. SY_SSS_1082s rev. D HD Radio™ **AM Transmission System Specifications** iBiquity Digital Corporation, 2/24/05
4.	Doc. No. SY_IDD_1017s rev. E HD Radio™ Air Interface Design Description **Audio Transport** iBiquity Digital Corporation, 3/31/05	9.	Doc. No. SY_IDD_1085s rev. C HD Radio™ Air Interface Design Description **Program Service Data Transport** iBiquity Digital Corporation, 2/7/05
5.	Doc. No. SY_IDD_1020s rev. E HD Radio™ Air Interface Design Description **Station Information Service Protocol** iBiquity Digital Corporation, 2/18/05	10.	Doc. No. SY_IDD_1019s rev. E HD Radio™ Air Interface Design Description **Advanced Application Services Transport** iBiquity Digital Corporation, 8/4/05

Table 4.1 Protocols Addressed in Chapter 4

Program audio is melded with program related text to create each of the program services. The Main Program Service (MPS), and on FM IBOC, the optional Supplemental Program Service(s) (SPS), are assembled by the Audio Transport. NRSC-5-A Reference Document (4), Audio Transport describes the process of preparing the program services for Layer 2.

If any supplemental program streams are being transmitted, the Audio Transport processes them in the same fashion as the main program. The reference document titled Program Service Data applies to Main and to Supplemental Program Service Data. The data related to each program audio channel is transported with that program's audio.

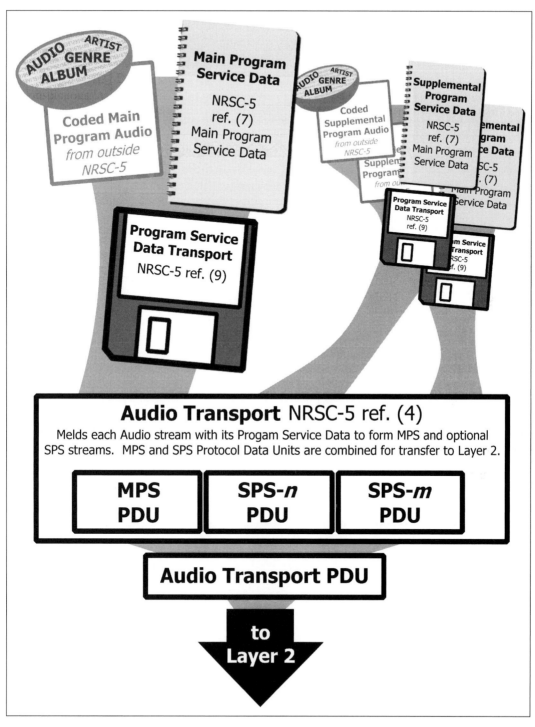

Figure 4.1 Audio Services Transport Funnel

Audio Codec

The term "codec" is a contraction of the term "coder/decoder," which describes the function of encoding data for transmission or storage, and decoding it upon reception or playback. NRSC-5 specifies no audio codec for main and supplemental audio services. All of the HD Radio-branded transmission and reception products utilize the proprietary HDC codec by iBiquity. HDC is a trademark of iBiquity Digital Corporation.

People involved in the technical side of the electronic media are likely to be familiar with the characteristics and purposes of so-called lossy coding/decoding schemes. HDC is one among an evolving marketplace of lossy codecs designed to optimize the use of transmission bandwidth and storage capacity by "losing" information about the audio that is considered inaudible or tolerable in its absence. As a result of lossy coding, the number of bytes of data required to transmit or store a given amount of audio is substantially less than that with the uncompressed audio data or a nonlossy form of data compression.

A codec selected for operation on IBOC broadcasting has upper limits on the bandwidth available to it. Nominally the hybrid FM IBOC channel has capacity for up to 96 kilobits per second (kbps) of Main Program Audio. The limit for AM is a little more complicated, due to the use of two layers of audio coding, referred to in the standard as "streams." The streams are hierarchical, bearing the names "core" and "enhanced." (Core audio is not related to the term "core" as it applies to the initial version of the NRSC-5 standard, discussed in the previous chapter). Hybrid AM IBOC is set up with about 20 kbps core audio and 16 kbps enhanced audio. In the Audio Transport reference document (6), iBiquity calls this a "multistream codec" that is used to "provide robust coverage and fast tuning times." Core audio data is transmitted with a greater degree of error protection, making it more "robust" than the enhanced audio stream. It may also be transmitted in smaller blocks of data to provide more rapid acquisition. Core audio stands on its own, providing enough information to reproduce an audio output at the decoder. Enhanced audio, on the other hand, is only useful in the presence of core audio. As the name suggests, enhanced audio data, when it is available, provides an enhancement to the perceived quality of the core audio.

IBOC Frames

IBOC continuously transmits a series of "frames" of data. Each frame has a duration of approximately 1.49 seconds. This is true for both AM and FM IBOC signals. The frame is the basic building block of the IBOC transport. The characteristics of the framing of IBOC signals are discussed in Chapter 6.

Coded Audio Payload

The maximum audio codec rates on AM and FM IBOC are directly related to the payload capacities of the AM and FM IBOC transports. On the FM side, the 1.49-second frame has a capacity of 146.176 kilobits (Table 7-3, reference document (1)). Dividing the frame's payload capacity by the duration of the frame, the available data rate is computed:

$$146.176 \text{ kb} / 1.49 \text{ s} = 98.1 \text{ kbps (approximately)} \qquad \text{Eq. 4.1}$$

On AM IBOC, the frame payload for core audio data can be as great as 30 kb and the enhanced audio as great as 24 kb. Dividing by the 1.49-second frame duration, the hybrid AM audio data rates are revealed—20 and 16 kbps, core and enhanced.

As the following development reveals, the frame rate is not exactly 1.49 seconds per frame, due to rounding. The exact frame rate is precisely defined by ratios of certain characteristics of the signal structure, just as the tempo of a song is defined by the rate of a metronome and the number of beats per measure. One key characteristic is the sampling rate of the audio program source delivered to the coder (and output by the decoder). The relationship between the program audio data rate and the frame rate is explained below. This information scratches the surface of the structure and timing of the IBOC data stream. Chapter 6 fully decomposes the IBOC frame structure and timing.

Main Program Audio Carried on:	Logical Channel Payload Capacity per Frame	Logical Channel Payload Capacity per Second
Hybrid FM Primary Main (core only)	146176 bits	98 kb
Hybrid AM Core	30000	20
Hybrid AM Enhanced	24000	16

Table 4.2 Nominal Maximum Coder Rates

Logical Channels

Logical Channels are exposed in detail in Chapters 5 and 6. In short, Logical Channels subdivide the IBOC data stream in a fashion that permits information to be segregated. The segregation of information in logical channels allows information to flow independently on different parts of the IBOC digital signal. The digital signal is composed of digital subcarrier groups to which one or more logical channels are assigned. This permits information to be segregated in two ways. First, to obtain frequency diversity, related information is transmitted on separate logical channels on different subcarrier groups. Second, more than one logical channel can be interleaved on the same subcarrier group, permitting their delivery and acquisition at different rates—block-pair, block, or frame. For the purposes of this discussion, it is useful to know that core and enhanced audio streams, for example, are carried on independent Logical Channels that are transmitted on separate portions of the channel spectrum.

While the AM core and enhanced audio are transported on separate logical channels, a logical channel can also carry more than one service. For instance, the same FM IBOC Logical Channel carrying a Main Program Service audio stream may also be subdivided to carry Supplemental Program Service(s) and/or Advanced Data Services. Doing so reduces the capacity available to each service, and the maximum values shown in Table 4.2 would be reduced accordingly.

Based on the capacity limitations of the AM and FM IBOC communications channels, the MPS codec must function adequately at the rates shown in Table 4.2. In the FM case, channel partitioning to allow the transmission of additional program audio channels or data means the codec must deliver credible audio performance at lower data rates.

After the HDC coder encodes the audio to the desired bit rate, the information is in the form of mathematical representations of the audio waveform. To convert these encoded samples to a coded audio stream, the audio information must be packetized by a transport. As with the HDC coder, the HDC packet transport is out of the scope of NRSC-5. It delivers a packet of data to the Audio Transport for each 2048-sample segment of the source audio, running at 44.1 kSa/s (kilo-samples per second).

Reference document (4), Audio Transport, indicates that, on the average, 32 packets of coded audio data will be transmitted per frame. For dual-stream transmissions such as hybrid AM IBOC, there are 32 packets for core and 32 for enhanced audio data. The codec may employ variable size packets for conveying the coded audio data to the Audio Transport, which explains why the figure is an average. This is called a variable bit rate encoding process. Some segments of source audio data have more complex waveforms than others, requiring more data to describe them in their coded form. For a simplistic example, a coder can describe succinctly a segment of silence or a simple sine wave. Meanwhile, sounds with complex waveforms will demand more coding resources and produce a larger packet of code.

To feed the coder at a steady rate, program audio is delivered to it at 44.1 kSa/s. The coder breaks each audio channel into segments of 2048 samples. The coder processes each segment and the resulting numerical representations of the audio are passed on to the Audio Transport in a series of variable-size audio packets. These packets are also called Audio Frames.

Each 2048-sample segment at 44.1 kSa/s represents 2048/44100 = 46.4 milliseconds of audio. 32 samples, therefore, represent about one and a half seconds of audio. Table 4.3 shows the exact relationship between the number of source audio samples represented by each packet and the IBOC frame rate.

Amount of Source Audio Coded Per Frame				
Packets per frame (average)		Source audio samples represented by each packet (exact)		Source audio samples represented per frame (average)
32	X	2048	=	65336

Frame Duration Required				
Source audio samples represented per frame (average)		Source audio samples per second (exact)		Seconds per frame (fixed value, to three decimal places)
65336	/	44100	=	~1.486

Table 4.3 Derivation of IBOC Frame Rate from Source Audio Rate

The 44.1 kSa/s data rate is not used anywhere within the NRSC-5 IBOC system, yet it plays a key role in the design of the IBOC structure. To be certain the source data rate of 44.1 kSa/s will compress, pass through the transmission system, and ultimately come out the receiver decoder at exactly 44.1 kSa/s without any glitches, the frame rate is computed with a precise ratio to the 44.1 kSa/s rate. Table 4.3 shows how the 1.49-second frame duration is based on the 44.1 kSa/s source audio rate, and the thirty-two packets representing 2048 audio samples each. This ratio appears prominently in the Layer 1 documents where the frame rate influences the structure of the radio signal.

The power of using a lossy codec is evident in the compression of a 44.1 kSa/s audio source to fit audio into a data channel with no more than 96 kbps capacity. Table 4.4 compares the source rate with the coded rate. The Source column employs the integer values that define the system operation. The Coded column is based on the nominal bit rate of 96 kbps, yielding the compression ratio and the approximate payload consumed per segment

	Source before Coding	Transported after Coding
Sample Rate	44.1 kSa/s per channel	Not applicable
Bits per sample	16 left + 16 right = 32	Not applicable
Samples per coding segment	2048	Not applicable
Bits per coding segment	65,536	4,458 (approx)
Bits per frame duration	2,097,152	142,663 (approx)
Frame rate	44100/65536 fps	
Bits per second	1,411,200	96,000 (nominal)
Compression ratio	15:1 (approx)	

Table 4.4 Comparison of Source and Coded Audio

For instance, with the 96 kbps rate for FM hybrid audio transmission, each packet, representing 46.4 milliseconds of audio, would contain on average 4.5 kb of coded audio. This is a nearly fifteen-fold reduction from the 65.5 kb of stereo audio information arriving at the coder in that period.

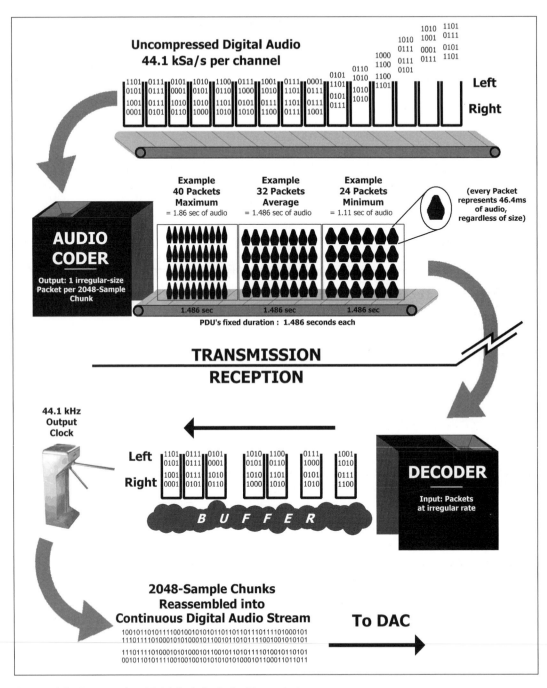

Figure 4.2 Compressing 44.1 kSa/s Audio for Transmission

Side Processes: The Configuration Administrator

The audio coder must receive some key information from the IBOC transport system. It must be told how much payload capacity has been reserved for the audio so it will code to the correct transmission rate. If there are supplemental channels, it must be aware of the capacity assigned to each audio service. Likewise, the audio coder has a duty to inform other layers in the stack if there is any unused space in the codec transport that could be utilized by other protocols.

A process alongside the protocol stack handles this communication to and from the audio codec protocols. The side processes are not described by protocols in NRSC-5. NRSC-5 symbolically presents a vertical bridge on one side of the protocol stack interconnecting all of its horizontal layers.[1] This is called the Configuration Administrator. The Configuration Administrator is the conduit for passing status information and settings up and down the stack.

In the case of the audio coder and coder transport, whose protocols are outside NRSC-5, the Configuration Administrator is the symbolic point of contact between the NRSC-5 protocols and the external coder protocols. While PDUs[2] carrying chunks of information are passed from one layer to another, this virtual conduit (the Configuration Administrator) conveys such things as bandwidth requirements, data rate settings, numbers and type of services assigned, and transmission modes.

Audio Transport

NRSC-5 Reference Document 4, Audio Transport, briefly mentions the role of the Audio Encoder and the Audio [Encoder] Transport in its sections 4.2 and 4.3 to provide a top-level understanding of these coder functions residing outside NRSC-5.

The 32 audio packets per frame, per audio stream (core and enhanced) are delivered to the Audio Transport for preparing program service PDUs. Because of the variability of the packet size, upper and lower limits are established for the actual packet count in a frame. The reference document gives an example of a setting in which as many as 40 and as few as 24 may be delivered to the Audio Transport per stream per frame, as long as the average is 32.

The Audio Transport handles each stream independently, producing PDUs for each stream. Core and enhanced PDUs are transmitted on independent "Logical Channels," which are handled in Layers 2 and 1. Because of their variable size, the number of packets per PDU is variable. However, to maintain data flow like clockwork, the number of PDUs per frame is fixed for the particular logical carrying an audio stream.

In the simplest case, hybrid FM IBOC MPS consists of only one audio stream, with no segregation into a core and enhanced pair. One Main Program Service PDU is sent per frame, with the 32-packet average per PDU.

---

[1] (NRSC-5, Figures 2 and 12).

[2] Recall from Chapter 3 that the Protocol Data Unit (PDU) is the building block assembled by a protocol layer and output to the next layer.

Core and enhanced audio streams are always transmitted in the other IBOC transmission modes: AM hybrid mode, AM all-digital mode, and FM all-digital mode. In these dual-stream modes, core audio packets are grouped 4 (average) per PDU, with 8 PDUs per frame (fixed). This provides the receiver with a faster-arriving, smaller PDU to disassemble, to more rapidly recover the core audio. Enhanced packets are always transmitted 32 per PDU (average), one PDU per frame (fixed).

IBOC Service Mode	Logical Channel	PDU Capacity (bits)	PDUs per Frame	Frame Capacity (bits)	Effective Bit Rate of Payload (kbps)	Audio stream transported
FM Hybrid Mode MP1	P1	146176	1	146176	96	Core*
FM All-digital	P1	9216 or 4608	8	73728 or 36864	48 or 24	Core
Mode MP5 or MP6	P3	72448 or 109312	1	72448 or 109312	48 or 72	Enhanced
AM Hybrid	P1	3750	8	30000	20	Core
Mode MA1	P3	24000	1	24000	16	Enhanced
AM All-digital	P1	3750	8	30000	20	Core
Mode MA3	P3	30000	1	30000	20	Enhanced

Notes: The Effective Bit Rate of Payload column shows the nominal maximum rate of an MPS stream if the entire Logical Channel were employed for MPS. This table does not address all possible service modes of FM IBOC signals. Also, FM All-digital modes have additional RF channel capacity in the center of the channel that can provide full redundancy to the figures shown for MP5 and MP6 modes; this increases the robustness of the All-digital signal.

*The Audio Transport specification refers to the single audio stream of hybrid FM IBOC as "core," which has full fidelity, with no companion enhanced stream.

Table 4.5 Derivation of Maximum Effective Bit Rates of Primary Logical Channels

In addition to preparing for transport the MPS core and MPS enhanced audio streams, the Audio Transport prepares SPS audio in the same manner. Once the Audio Transport has received a batch of MPS audio coder packets and SPS audio coder packets, intended for the next frame, it groups each audio stream (core or enhanced) of each service (MPS or SPS) into its own PDUs. These PDUs of each service/stream are then grouped into the larger Audio Transport PDUs by the Logical Channels to which they belong. An SPS PDU can be transported alongside an MPS PDU in the same Logical Channel, but a core and an enhanced PDU of the same service cannot. (See Figure 4.6 for an example.)

The system operator allocates bandwidth for each MPS and SPS, the total of which cannot exceed the capacity of the Logical Channels to which they are assigned. The Audio Coder must be aware of this setting in order to pass 32 correctly sized audio packets for each service/stream to the Audio Transport. The Audio Transport assembles the packets into the PDUs, and must be aware of the bandwidth settings for each service and for each Logical Channel. It passes an Audio Transport PDU, consisting of MPS and SPS PDUs, down to Layer 2.

The Audio Transport performs an additional function for the MPS before sending MPS PDUs to Layer 2. Since the MPS audio is backed up by the analog audio, the Audio Transport must synchronize analog audio and Main Program Service audio. Supplemental services do not have an analog backup in NRSC-5.

Program Service Data (PSD)

In addition to collecting the 32, more or less, audio packets per frame for each audio stream, the Audio Transport handles text-based information that is related to the audio program service on which it is transported. This is sometimes referred to as program-associated data or "PAD." In NRSC-5 and the iBiquity reference documents the technical term for the text transmitted with the audio is Program Service Data (PSD). Keep in mind that there are several ways to deliver PAD to the listener, PSD being one of them. At the option of the broadcaster, its FM analog broadcasts continue to be supported by an RDS FM subcarrier, which can include PAD. Additionally, PAD is not limited to the PSD Transport on the IBOC signal; Advanced Data Services can be configured to provide a substantially richer PAD experience than the limited capabilities of the PSD Transport.

However it is named, the PSD arrives at the Audio Transport for insertion into the appropriate MPS (or SPS) PDU. It is called *Main (or Supplemental) Program Service Data (MPSD or SPSD)*. The data arrives at the Audio Transport as a data stream that the Audio Transport trickles into available space in the MPS and SPS PDUs. See Figure 4.1. The structure of PSD and its path to the Audio Transport are explored following this discussion of the Audio Transport.

MPS and SPS PDUs

Starting with a simple example in which an FM IBOC station is transmitting only Main Program Service audio in the full available bandwidth, the Audio Transport buffers a series of Main Program Audio packets arriving from the coder. The packets are variable size, and the coder is informed how much variability is permitted. This is referred to as the elasticity of the packet stream. The Configuration Administrator informs the audio coder and the Audio Transport of the required elasticity for the station's transmission mode. It is the Audio Transport that informs the receiver how much buffering is required to manage the elasticity.

In this example, there will be from 24 to 40 variable-size packets per MPS PDU, with an average of 32. (See Figure 4.2.) A value called "latency" is inserted in the MPS PDU to communicate the elasticity to the receiver. The receiver uses this information to maintain the necessary output delay time to allow a buffer to accumulate. The buffer permits the packets of varying sizes to arrive at their uneven pace, enabling the receiver to decode one every 46.4 milliseconds, like clockwork.

The Audio Transport is also aware of the analog-to-digital delay settings in the hybrid mode and informs the receiver how to buffer the digital audio stream to ensure time alignment with the analog audio. This is transmitted as the "post-decoded common delay" value. It is transmitted as a 6-bit number that, when multiplied by 4, indicates how many 46.4-millisecond audio frame periods to delay the digital audio to synchronize it with the analog audio. When the digital signal is not available because it has yet to be acquired or has fallen below a receiver-defined quality threshold, the receiver plays analog audio. When this "blend to (from) analog" function is occurring, the analog audio should be in synch with the digital audio to provide a smooth transition between the two. It is a "common" delay because the core and the enhanced streams have this delay in common to ensure both synchronize with the analog audio.

Time Alignment: Not Only Good Form, But Also Required

People generally understand the value of a first impression, yet stations sometimes turn on their new IBOC signals without having the analog/digital audio time alignment in place. The result is certain annoyance to HD Radio listeners. Consumers hearing a blend to analog for the first time on an unaligned station are likely to think their IBOC receiver is broken, or that IBOC is not all it is cracked up to be. To enforce this critical factor of station performance, the iBiquity broadcaster license (2006 version, www.iBiquity.com) has the following requirement:

9.2 Time Synchronization. *Licensee agrees to use commercially reasonable efforts to operate the Licensed Station with time synchronization of the analog audio and Main Channel Audio signals to support the blend feature of the IBOC system.*

In addition to transmitting the common delay alignment value in hybrid mode, there is the digital equivalent of an on-off switch for the blend-to-analog function. The Audio Transport informs the receiver when analog delay is engaged for blending or when it is not being used, requiring no blending to occur. This switch is called the "blend control" flag. When analog delay is turned off at a station, it is intended to allow analog listeners to hear live events as near as real-time as possible. This is sometimes called "ball game mode" because people observing such events while listening to the radio would otherwise hear a disconcerting delay between the event and the radio broadcast. When considering whether to engage ball game mode, the relative benefits to some listeners of the near-real time analog audio must be weighed against the detriments of taking away seamless blend-to-analog for IBOC listeners.

Another header value is the "TX Digital Audio Gain Control." This is transmitted only with each core audio stream "to equalize the subjective loudness of the digital and analog audio." It represents sixteen values in whole dB, from –8 to +7.

Figure 4.3 shows on the left these key facts being communicated to the Audio Transport via the Configuration Administrator. The transport places this information into a header for passage to the receiver. Each fact is placed in its respective *header field.*

The Audio Transport not only passes on configuration information, but also generates its own information for passage to the receiver. Figure 4.3 shows the names of these header fields. The information generated is almost entirely structural, giving the receiver pointers, literally and figuratively, on how to read the MPS PDU. The Audio Transport tells the receiver how many audio packets are in the PDU, whether the first packet is continued from the previous PDU or starts anew, and whether the last packet is continued to the next PDU. The ability to split an audio packet across two PDUs, and therefore across frames, makes sure that when there is heavy demand on the coder and larger than average packets are being sent, every available byte in the PDU is utilized.

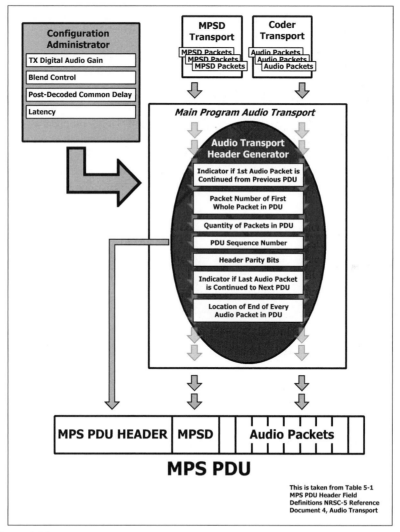

Figure 4.3 Basic MPS PDU Functions

In the event that part of the body of the PDU is corrupted, there are pointers giving the address of the last byte of each packet in the PDU. These are called the packet locator fields. To ensure these pointers, and other header information, are well protected from corruption, an extra level of error protection is applied to the header. See sidebar and Figure 4.4. Also given a locator byte is the PSD packet. Since the Main Program Service Data is inserted in the MPS PDU after the header and before the first audio packet, it is important to tell the receiver where it is located. Even if the MPSD packet were corrupted, the receiver could find the beginning of the first audio packet.

Error Protection

Reed-Solomon coding for the Program Service PDU Header

Layer 1 provides a level of error detection/correction that covers the entire transmitted data stream. It is in the form of *convolutional coding*, which is treated in detail in Chapter 5. To further protect the audio payload, the headers of the MPS and SPS PDUs (Figure 4.4) are protected by a Reed-Solomon (RS) code. First described in 1960,[3] the theory of this coding scheme became practical reality when computer processing became powerful enough to implement it. The specifications for Compact Discs, created in the late 1970s, included RS coding to protect from "burst errors" in reading the data from a disc. Burst errors can obliterate an entire byte or several bytes in sequence. The nature of the RS code is that it requires no more effort to correct a byte that has many bit errors than it does to correct a byte with one bit error. Depending on the depth of the code, one or more such bytes can be identified and corrected. In the case of the MPS PDU header, which is 96 bytes or less in length, the RS coding protects from the failure of any four incorrect bytes.

The nomenclature, for those familiar with RS codes, is RS(96, 88) using a 2^8 Galois Field shortened to 96 bytes, which results in (96–88)/2 correctable bytes. The 96 value represents the length of the "codeword," which is the term for the block of data resulting from the Reed-Solomon encoding process. In this case, it includes both the header data and the parity symbols (bytes). Within those 96 symbols, the data being protected consists of 88 symbols. The correctable number of bytes is half the difference between the two.

Error Protection

Cyclic Redundancy Checks for Audio Coder Packets

In addition to RS coding to protect the header, each audio packet in the MPS PDU (Figure 4.4) is tagged with a Cyclic Redundancy Check value (CRC-8). This 8-bit figure gives the receiver the ability to check the integrity of the packet. It is a value that represents the remainder of a mathematical operation performed on the contents of the packet. The entire contents of the header are treated as one large binary number. This large number is divided

---

[3] Irving S. Reed and Gustave Solomon. *Polynomial codes over certain finite fields*. Journal of the Society of Industrial and Applied Mathematics, 8(10):300–304, 1960.

at the transmitter side by a 9-bit divisor known to transmitters and receivers, published in the Audio Transport document. The remainder of this operation is transmitted as the CRC-8 value. The receiver performs the same function on the received packet of audio data and compares its remainder with the one in the CRC-8 field to determine if there is an error.

Unlike the RS coder's protection of entire bytes, CRC's provide bitwise error detection and even a little error correction capability. This is possible because it is highly unlikely that a header received with a few random errors will produce the same CRC-8 remainder as the original header. If the transmitted CRC-8 remainder differs from the receiver-computed CRC-8, an error is indicated. With a little mathematical horsepower, the correct audio coder packet value can be inferred from the corrupt packet and the transmitted CRC-8 value, as long as the errors are not too pervasive.

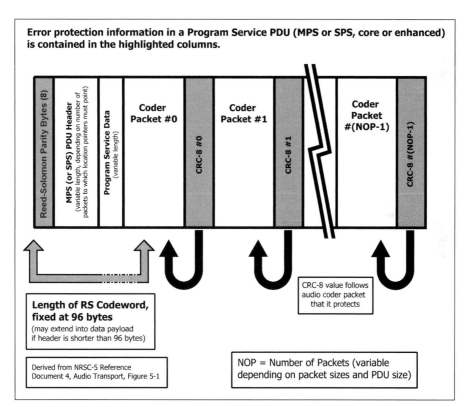

Figure 4.4 Error Protection in Audio Transport

Figure 4.3 shows how three groups of things are inserted into the MPS PDU—the coded audio packets and PSD delivered from higher layers, the information provided via the Configuration Administrator, and the information generated internally by the Audio Transport. The MPS PDU consists of a header containing the header fields, followed by any Program Service Data to be delivered, on a space-available basis, followed by the 32, more or less, audio packets.

Each MPS PDU transmits the "Starting Sequence Number," from 0 to 63, of the first full packet in the PDU. The sequence number of each subsequent packet in the PDU is inferred from this value. This provides the receiver a way to be certain it is reading the PDUs from the receiver memory in the proper sequence. When core and enhanced streams are being transmitted, each stream has independent PDUs, with independent sequence numbers assigned to each stream. However, the streams are synchronized by assigning matching sequence numbers to corresponding core and enhanced audio packets.

Figure 4.3 and the discussion above address the basic functions of the Audio Transport in handling MPS. When a Supplemental Program Service is added, or there are core and enhanced streams for a particular Main or Supplemental service, the Audio Transport has a few more housekeeping chores, as shown in Figure 4.5.

While it may be inferred from the Logical Channel carrying the Program Service PDUs whether the PDUs represent core or enhanced audio, the Stream ID provides an unambiguous indication that rides with the audio stream. As mentioned above, only on Hybrid FM IBOC does the Main Program Service transmit core audio without a companion enhanced stream. Hybrid AM and all-digital AM and FM transmissions carry both core and enhanced. In all-digital mode, the core stream serves as the faster-access channel to compensate for the lack of a backup analog audio channel. To indicate whether a stream is core or enhanced, it is assigned a "Stream ID" in the MPS PDU header. The same is true for SPS PDUs. The value "00" indicates core and "11" indicates enhanced. Values "10" and "11" are reserved for future use.

To distinguish among the MPS PDU and one or more SPS PDUs on the same Logical Channel, two methods are applied. First, the MPS PDUs always appear first in the Audio Transport PDU, before any SPS PDUs or other data. Second, each PDUs header can contain an optional header expansion field that indicates the Program Number associated with the PDU. If the expansion field is not used, the PDU is assumed to carry an MPS stream. If the expansion field is activated, a simple Program Number scheme is employed.

To avert confusion in identifying channels by number, NRSC came to a consensus in 2005 on channel numbering for receiver displays. Since the first SPS program on a station would be the second audio program available on the IBOC station, it makes sense to refer to the first SPS as number 2. MPS channels need no number at all, or can be assigned the number 1, in harmony with the SPS channel numbering. Table 4.6 shows the value in the Program Number header field for each Program. This value suits a machine (transmitter or receiver) well, but having a program with the number "0" is not intuitive. The last column of the table shows the Human-Machine Interface (HMI) value that is customarily used to identify Program Numbers.

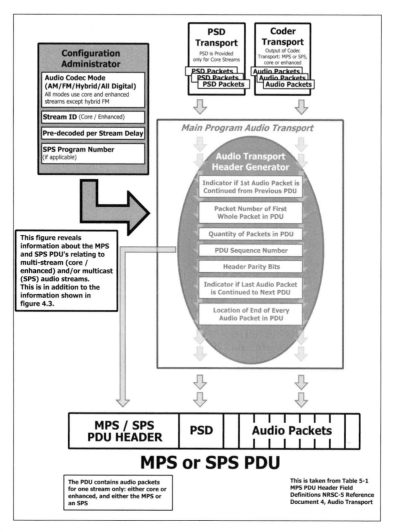

Figure 4.5 Additional MPS/SPS PDU Functions

	Program Number Field, Binary	Decimal Equivalent	Receiver HMI Presentation
Main Program Service	000	0	1 (optional)
Supplemental Program Services	001	1	2
	010	2	3
	011	3	4
	100	4	5
	101	5	6
	110	6	7
	111	7	8

Note: The names SPS-n and SPS-m are employed in this book to represent two Supplemental Program Services bearing any Program Number from 1–7. When displayed on a radio, the numbering is increased by one, spanning the values 2–8, as shown in the HMI column of the Table. For example, if n = 1 and m = 5, these would be SPS-1 and SPS-5, represented on the IBOC system by the binary values 001 and 101, respectively; meanwhile, they would display on a radio as, for instance, 96.9 HD2 and 96.9 HD6, or 96.9-2 and 96.9-6.

Table 4.6 Program Services Numbering Scheme

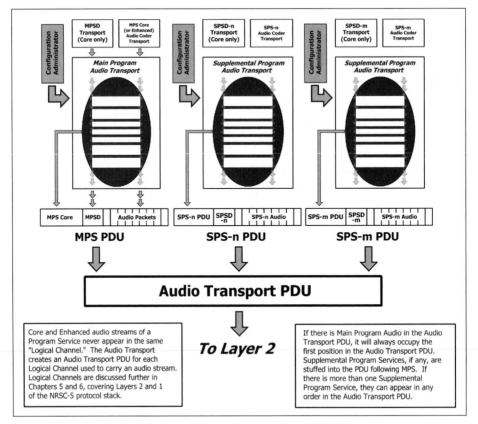

Figure 4.6 Multiple Streams and Services Processed by the Audio Transport

Kenwood U.S.A. Corporation, manufacturer of aftermarket automotive radios capable of receiving IBOC, was one of the companies that participated with National Public Radio in early implementation of the Supplemental Program Service feature. Kenwood led the way in developing an SPS-capable receiver, using the "HD2" nomenclature for identifying supplemental channels on their car radios. The NRSC consensus gives receiver manufacturers guidance on the use of the Supplemental Program Service numbering, and supports the underlying approach that led to Kenwood's implementation. Other implementations are possible, even welcome in a competitive market, with the proviso that when the station announces a channel by the number "two," the radio should show it as a "two," whether it be "HD2," <callsign>dash-2, <circle-2> or some other designator.

It may seem excessive to have potentially seven simultaneous supplemental channels, which indeed would be difficult to squeeze into the FM IBOC bandwidth, whether in hybrid or, to a lesser extent, all-digital modes. However, the higher numbers could be used to identify Program Services by skipping the assignment of lower numbers. NRSC-5 does not require the numbers to be assigned in sequence. In other words, if a transmitter can be instructed to do so, it is NRSC-5 compliant to transmit, say, an MPS program, an SPS-3 program, and an SPS-7 program. This gives broadcasters flexibility to create memorable program identities or even to daypart Supplemental Programs with different numbers to indicate different formats or content.

The Role of Header Expansion

A key element of transport design is to leave room to add new functions to a service or transport protocol. Because all devices (receivers in this case) already in use in an open system must continue to work in the presence of an enhancement to the transmitted information, the new information must not, in a manner of speaking, "break" an existing device. A header expansion scheme allows the system to inject new information that is meaningless to existing devices without confusing those devices.

For example, at the inception of the MPS delivery system, SPS was not yet implemented. No program numbering scheme was necessary with a single program service. The addition of SPS required a new way to identify the independent program services. Both a numbering scheme and a program type identification scheme would have to be transported with each program service. New fields for carrying this information would have to be inserted into the Program Service PDU. It would have to be done without confusing receivers already on the market. Since all receivers are aware of the rules for expanding the header, even if some do not know the meaning of the contents in the expanded fields, they are able to skip over them and find additional useful information in the PDU. They can do so by using the header expansion flags as pointers to find the end of the unfamiliar expansion content.

If a header expansion scheme is in place at the inception of a protocol's design, as was the case for the Audio Transport, enhancements can be implemented safely later on. See Figure 4.7 for details.

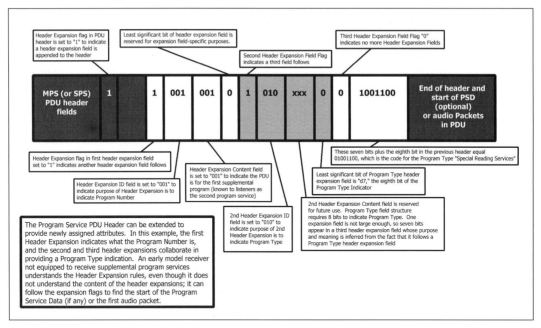

Figure 4.7 Program Service Header Expansion

When transmitting Supplemental Program Services, certain requirements are stipulated in the standard. With SPS there is a Program Number assigned to each Service, it is required to appear in the first Header Expansion Field of the Program Service PDU. Program Type is optional, but if used it should appear in at least one of the Program Service's PDUs per frame. That is at least once every 1.49 seconds. This facilitates rapid receiver acquisition of all program types being transmitted on a station. In an attempt to simplify receiver requirements, the first 32 of the 256 MPS/SPS Program Types are identical to the RDS Program Types (PTY).

Opportunistic Data

With variable-size audio coder packets populating the Program Service PDUs, it is possible to have a little extra space in the PDU when the packets are smaller than average. Any spare capacity in a Program Service PDU is set aside at the end of the Audio Transport PDU. If more than one Program Service is carried on an Audio Transport PDU, the spare capacity (if any) on each Program Service is consolidated into a single block of bytes at the end of the Audio Transport PDU. See Table 4.7. This block is available for the provision of other data services. As the name "opportunistic" implies, the availability and rate of flow of data transmitted in this manner is variable and not guaranteed.

Opportunistic data relies on the Advanced Application Service Transport (AAT) protocol to transport data in this portion of the Audio Transport. This is discussed in detail in Chapters 5 and 11, relating to the Layer 2 channel multiplex protocol and the AAT protocol, respectively.

Header, HEFs*, MPSD, Coder Packets	Header, HEFs, MPSD, Coder Packets	Header, HEFs, MPSD, Coder Packets	Opportunistic Data
MPS PDU	**SPS-n PDU**	**SPS-m PDU**	
Audio Transport PDU Passes Down to Layer 2			

*HEFs – Header Expansion Fields. While these are considered part of the header, to make room for them, they encroach on PSD space, if any, and if necessary, displace coded audio packets.

Table 4.7 Components of an Audio Transport PDU Showing Three Program Services and Opportunistic Data Capacity

Program Service Data

Program Service Data (PSD) may be transmitted with each Program Service.[4] As described above, PSD is a subset of the family of data that is considered Program Associated Data, because PSD is one way of transporting information about an audio program service. In NRSC-5, PSD is strictly a text-transmission protocol conveying information such as Artist and Title.

Each Program Service (MPS, SPS-2, etc.) conveys its own PSD within its Program Service PDUs. Like Opportunistic Data, PSD opportunistically relies on the likelihood that there will be space for it in the Program Service PDU. Source audio that is more complex to encode will leave less room for PSD and Opportunistic Data.

Table 4.8 provides an estimate of the typical rates of transmission of PSD. It is based on the assumption that only MPS is being transmitted at the full capacity of the IBOC signal. When multiple services are transported on the same Logical Channel, each service is operating at a fraction of the total available rate of transfer. If this were the case, the typical PSD rates shown in Table 4.8 could diminish for each Program Service.

IBOC Service Mode	Logical Channel	Estimated Typical PSD Bytes Per Program Service PDU	Program Service PDUs per Frame	Estimated Typical PSD Bytes Per Frame	Audio stream transported
FM Hybrid *Mode MP1*	P1	128	1	128	Core*
FM All-digital *Mode MP5 or MP6*	P1	7	8	56	Core
	P3	0	1	-	Enhanced
AM Hybrid *Mode MA1*	P1	7	8	56	Core
	P3	0	1	-	Enhanced
AM All-digital *Mode MA3*	P1	7	8	56	Core
	P3	0	1	-	Enhanced

*Hybrid FM operation conveys the full fidelity of the audio in one stream, called "Core."
Note: The Estimated Typical PSD Bytes columns show approximate rates of an MPSD stream if the entire Logical Channel were employed for MPS.

Table 4.8 Typical Program Service Data Capacity

---

[4] There is one exception to this generalization. According to NRSC-5 Reference Document (4), Audio Transport, section 5.2.2, if Supplemental Services are offered on AM IBOC, they cannot carry any SPS Data.

PSD Protocol and Transport

Program Service Data is prepared for transmission in two steps. First, NRSC-5 Reference Document (7), Program Service Data, describes the manner in which the content of PSD transmissions is formatted. Reference Document (9), Program Service Data Transport, describes the rules for encapsulating blocks of PSD into packets and transmitting them as a stream.

PSD ID3 Tags

PSD consists of various types of text information that describe program content. These pieces of information can be transported together in the form of "Tags." The Tags are based on the ID3 format, which is discussed further below. The transported information in a Tag is classified among several types: Title, Artist, Album, Genre, Comment, and Commercial. The types are called Attributes. Each Attribute is given a Frame ID, which is an alpha-numeric code that is transported with each piece of information to inform the receiver what the Attribute of the information is.

Each Frame ID is associated with a frame structure. In the cases of Title, Artist Album and Genre, the structure is as simple as can be. For example, a Title frame is labeled with a "TIT2" Frame ID and contains one field with the title of the song being played.

The Comment and Commercial frames are more complex. The Comment frame, identified by the Frame ID "COMM," has a field for a short description of the comment and a field for the comment itself. The Comment can be anything. It could be used for contact information, with "contact" in the description field and the comment could contain an address, phone number and web address. It could contain a headline in the description and news or information in the comment. The ways to use this field are up to the imagination of the broadcaster, with one caveat. The field is only useful if receiver manufacturers find the field is consistently used in a manner that they can design receivers to utilize.

Higher in complexity is the Commercial frame. It is structured rather like a classified advertisement with fields available for a Price, "Valid Until" expiration field, Seller Name, Contact URL (website), "Received As" method by which the goods are delivered, and Description of the advertised item. While the emphasis of the IBOC ID-3 protocol is text fields, there are a couple of exceptions. The Commercial frame is capable of conveying two possible image fields. One, the Picture, is of the product and the other is a "Seller Logo." These two fields are binary files. If implemented on IBOC transmitters and receivers, they risk being particularly demanding on the limited PSD capacity on the Audio Transport. Small bit-mapped logos would be easier to transmit than a full picture of a product. Early generations of IBOC transmission and reception products had not supported these images.

Attribute	Frame ID	Field(s)
Title	TIT2	Information
Artist	TPE1	Information
Album	TALB	Information
Genre	TCON	Information
Comment	COMM	Short Description, Comment
Commercial	COMR	Price, Valid Until, Seller Name, Contact URL, Received As, Description, Picture, Seller Logo
Reference Identifier	UFID	Owner Identifier, Identifier

Table 4.9 ID3 Frames Permitted in PSD (NRSC-5-A)

One additional frame, Reference Identifier, is a housekeeping frame. It enables a Tag to be associated with another carrying the same Identification Number. In this case, the Owner Identifier is assigned the value "PADLINK," indicating the Identification Number serves as a common identifier of more than one batch of PSD. This permits the system to break up the PSD Tags into smaller packets that the receiver can recognize as needing to be strung together when decoding.

The ID3 format is a protocol called an "informal standard" by its author, Martin Nilsson.[5] ID3 was created to provide a universal format for providing a plethora of data about stored audio files such as MP3 files. The seven Frames incorporated in the NRSC-5 system only scratch the surface of what the ID3 protocol can do. However, much of the information that ID3 can transmit with an MP3 file is irrelevant in a broadcast medium, such as equalization, reverb, play counter, tempo, relative volume setting, media type, among many others. Other information such as composer, lead performer/soloists, band/orchestra, or lyricist, might be useful in some program formats, but with limited bandwidth for the information, and increased complexity in displaying or interacting with richer information, the NRSC-5-A standard limits the use of the ID3 tag to those attributes in Table 4.9.

The ID3 standard contains a listing of Genre code numbers for 126 music styles, from the familiar pop, oldies, rock, symphony, and hip-hop, to such specialties as samba, grunge, industrial, trance, Christian rap, and porn groove. While a station already transmits the format of each of its services on the Audio Transport, the ID3 tag permits the broadcaster to use this field as it chooses, if at all, as long as a supported Genre ID is indicated. More than one genre can be indicated in an ID3 Tag.

It is the value to the users of the various ID3 attributes that will determine if and how these attributes will evolve on consumer radios. This is particularly so for the less-utilized attributes, such as Genre, Commercial, and Comment. The initial selection of the attributes is expressed in the PSD reference document, with the evolution of new attributes possible. While ID3 tags were intended for recorded music and sound tracks, it was apparent to the IBOC developers that broadcast audio not only consists of music but also "talk" and "announcement." The PSD reference document suggests that Title could convey a talk show topic or the name or title of an announcement or advertisement. The Artist attribute could be used to name a program host or the author or

---

[5] www.id3.org

sponsor of an announcement. The Album name attribute could be the place for the name of a show or sponsor. Genre 101 is "speech" and might apply to nonmusic programming, if the Genre attribute were to be used.

The PSD reference document contains a pair of informative appendices. Appendix A contains the entire ID3 informal standard. Appendix A-1 contains the ID3 informal standard as implemented for NRSC-5, with all irrelevant sections excised.

In addition to the tags, frames, and fields described in the ID3 standard, the structure of an ID3 tag is outlined. Since an ID3 tag is a self-sufficient package of information, it must be packetized for handling. It contains a header identifying the tag and its size, with the obligatory backward compatible header expansion field to protect against obsolescence. It can contain an optional CRC-32 error protection value computed on the frame data.

While an ID3 tag can be up to 256 MB long, large ID3 PSD tags would be counterproductive in a broadcasting medium. The ID3 PSD tag is limited to 1024 bytes. When a tag is created and set up for transmission, it is "looped." That is, as long as the information in the tag is not updated, the same tag is transmitted repeatedly. This provides two valuable benefits. Erroneous tags are quickly replaced by a new copy. Also, no matter when an individual tunes in, new tag will soon begin to populate the listener's display. Shorter tags will take less time to be captured after tune in.

Individual Frames within an ID3 Tag are given individual headers. In the Frame header, the frame is identified by the four-character Frame ID. The length of the frame is indicated in the Frame header, enabling an existing receiver to skip over an unrecognized frame type, if one were to be added to the ID3 PSD protocol later on.

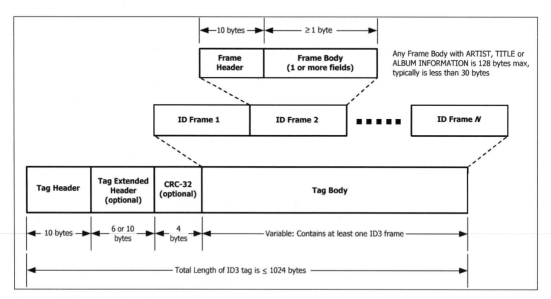

Figure 4.8 ID3 PSD Tag Structure

To provide more certainty to the receiver manufacturer and keep the text information from being too unwieldy, the PSD reference document indicates the Artist text field should not exceed 128 characters, and "typically" should be 30 characters or less.

PSD Etiquette

The PSD reference document is adamant about one thing, "Broadcasters providing PSD must, at a minimum, transmit the Title and Artist information." This helps give receiver manufacturers an expectation that if they provide Title and Artist displays, broadcasters who transmit PSD will provide data at least for these two attributes. Indeed, most HD Radio receivers on the 2007 Consumer Electronics Show floor had Title and Artist display capability (with the exception of some add-on adapters that are forced to rely on the existing radio to display information). Some models offered Title only. Meanwhile, IBOC broadcasters were doing the best they could, populating at least the title display with information as it was available via the stations' automation systems. One field available on a very limited number of radio models displayed Album name. This field was the most neglected by the IBOC broadcasters in the market, appearing as an empty field on the receivers. Electronics manufacturers express concern that when a field is consistently blank, consumers tend to think the radio is broken.

Since receivers may not be equipped to display all PSD fields, it suggests that some coordination between broadcasters and electronics manufacturers is in order to determine which fields are most useful to consumers and are most practicable for the broadcaster to populate with data. (This discussion does not include Station Information Service data, such as the short and long station names that many receivers also display, which is discussed in Chapter 10.)

Improper use of text fields can give IBOC a bad reputation and can have a chilling effect on the addition of features to new radio models. On the one hand, the ID3 protocol sensibly prevents the wasting of channel capacity on empty frames—only the desired frames and fields are filled with information and transmitted in a Tag; empty fields are not transmitted. On the other hand, some IBOC radios offer very limited selections of text fields, and if they are not given something to display, an opportunity to enrich the user experience is wasted. For instance, some IBOC radios make only the SIS station name and PSD title available, and with a limited number of characters. If the title is not sent, the user may feel deprived.

Another thing some IBOC broadcasters do is to "push" more information than what is intended in a field. For instance, rather than transmitting just the title over the PSD title field, some broadcasters add other information to be certain listeners with limited text displays can see it. It is tempting to break protocol by including specious information on tags with specific purposes. If a station is intent on pushing extra information in an ID3 field, the first characters should be the information expected for that field. For instance, if using the title field to transmit extra information there may be a temptation to transmit "Now playing on KDAB, Stairway to Heaven by Led Zeppelin." After the full text scrolls by, it may freeze on the first characters, revealing useless information for the radio user, on, say, a 16-character display, "Now playing on K..." The user then must interact with the receiver to obtain the title (and it looks rather goofy, too). Alternatively, if information must be pushed, it most honors the intent of the PSD fields to put the most relevant information first, "Stairway to Heaven by Led Zeppelin Now Playing on KXYZ."

Despite the fact that some radios display a limited selection of fields, it is advisable that broadcasters consistently populate as many PSD fields as practicable, so that receiver manufacturers may be more likely to incorporate broader features in their products. Consumers can be confused by text fields that are not populated or are populated with truncated or wrong information. At the same time, receiver manufacturers should consider giving consumers as much text display capability as possible, including the ability to select and deselect which fields are to be displayed.

PSD Harmonization with RDS

With the development of IBOC radios that also could receive RDS[6] transmissions in the U.S.A., manufacturers sought a way to harmonize the program associated data coming via RDS and MPSD. It was observed that when a radio was in a blending zone where the hybrid IBOC signal was blending back and forth between digital and analog reception, the PSD would be inelegantly replaced by RDS data that was formatted differently or had different content. When the receiver makes a transition from IBOC reception to analog reception with RDS (or vice versa), it repopulates the IBOC text display with RDS text (or vice versa). When the text elements differ between the two transmission formats, the transition causes disconcerting changes in the displayed text.

The RDS Open Data Application for Program Associated Data (ODA PAD) was adopted in April 2005 to address this problem. It is Annex U of the NRSC-4-A standard. The ODA PAD specification intended to let stations continue to transmit their RDS Radiotext (RT) to conventional RDS-equipped receivers, while providing a separate "map" indicating what parts of the RT can be matched to PSD. A station might program its RT to say: "Now Playing… <title> by <artist> on the Best Mix Station," in which the title and artist name are inserted in the text string for transmission. In this example, the separately transmitted text map indicates to the ODA PAD-equipped receiver which part of the RT character string is the title and which is the artist. This was an ingenious proposition to create a backward compatible protocol, and was incorporated into the NRSC-4 standard. It would use the Radiotext on RDS to harmonize IBOC and RDS text in the same receiver. However, internationally, other events caught up with this idea.

The RDS Forum adopted a feature called Radiotext-Plus (RT+) in late 2006. It included some prospective harmonization for RT+ with IBOC PSD and SIS data. RT+ employs a mapping protocol similar to the NRSC-4 ODA protocol. RT+ contains a richer mapping of text attributes to make Radiotext more useful to a new generation of RDS receivers. Kenwood proposed a harmonization scheme to provide uniform treatment of RT+ and IBOC text. Table 4.10 shows how Kenwood suggested the IBOC PSD and RDS RT+ fields can be paired. Broadcasters may wish to consider the length of the RDS fields when populating their IBOC PSD fields. Check www.nrscstandards.org for the latest RDS harmonization recommendations from the NRSC. (Also, see Chapter 10 for more on Station Information Service (SIS) data).

---

[6] RDS is standardized in the U.S. as RBDS,the Radio Broadcast Data System that transmits information on an FM subcarrier, including program associated text. *NRSC-4-A, United States RBDS Standard, Specification of the Radio Broadcast Data System (RBDS), April 2005.* It is available at www.nrscstanards.org.

Item	Information	How Sent		Kenwood Suggestions
		NRSC-5-A IBOC Fields	Suggested RDS RT+ (consult standard)	
1	Title	TIT2 via PSD	ITEM.TITLE	Length limited to 32–36 characters in many receivers
2	Artist	TPE1 via PSD	ITEM.ARTIST	Length limited to 32–36 characters in many receivers.
3	Program Type	PSD header expansion 010	RDS PTY	
4	Call Letters	Station Name (Short)-SIS Message 0001	STATIONNAME.SHORT	Consider differences between IBOC and RBDS versions of the Program Type tables.
5	Commercial	COMR via PSD	Not Supported	
6	Station Slogan	Station Name (Long)-SIS Message 0010	STATIONNAME.LONG	
7	Program Service Information		PS field	
8	Station Text Message	Station Message- SIS Message 0101	RBDS RT (per NRSC-4-A)	Note length of RT is limited to 64 characters. Avoid nulls (0x00) in transmission.
9	Subtitle/ Movement	Not an NRSC-5-A field- proposed new field	ITEM. MOVEMENT	

Table 4.10 Suggested Harmonization of PSD with RT+
(Source: Kenwood U.S.A. Corporation; edited for presentation here)

PSD Transport

Once PSD ID3 tags have been generated, they are fed to the next layer of the protocol stack, the Program Service Data Transport. This transport is described in NRSC-5 Reference Document (9). It makes reference to "PPP in HDLC-like framing" as the source of the transport's structure. Attached to the document is an informative Appendix from the Internet Engineering Task Force that discusses this concept. The goal of the transport is to transmit a continuing series of packets in a manner that enables the recipient to enter the stream at any time and recognize when the next whole packet begins to arrive.

The Internet Point-to-Point Protocol (PPP) provides content-agnostic methods for transporting packets of data over point to point serial data links. A technique for framing information from a PPP protocol was outlined in the IETF Network Working Group's Request For Comments 1662, *PPP in HDLC-like Framing*. This is the informative reference attached to the PSD Transport document. HDLC stands for High-level Data-Link Control, which is a link frame structure standardized by the International Organization for Standardization (ISO).

The long and the short of this soup of acronyms is that the authors of the PSD Transport relied on the accumulated knowledge of two standards bodies to come up with a tried and true way to transport PSD packets. HDLC-like framing is a method of sending a stream of placeholders, null characters, until a packet is ready to send. The packet is encapsulated in some transport information. In the case of PSD, the packet is preceded by a Protocol Field. This field tells the receiver that the packet is formatted as a PSD packet. If in the future other information is to be sent over the PSD transport, requiring a different packet protocol, the value of this field would be changed, and existing receivers should be smart enough to ignore the contained packet.

The protocol field is followed by a port number indicating a logical port to which the receiver should be open for the data. There is a sequence number (two bytes) to ensure the order of the packets is maintained in the buffer. This is followed by the actual PSD packet, which is up to 1024 bytes long.

The HDLC-like framing wraps up the encapsulation with a 16-bit Frame Check Sequence for error detection. This a CRC-16 value computed on the entire encapsulation, from the Protocol Field to the end of the PSD packet.

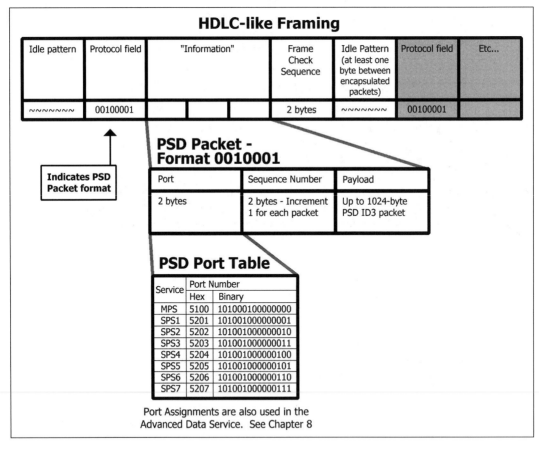

Figure 4.9 PSD in HDLC-like Framed Stream

Following the Frame Check Sequence, one or more null characters are transmitted until the next encapsulated PSD data begins with its protocol field. The null characters are called Flags. The Flag has the binary value equal to an ASCII tilde character (~). The transmission of a series of Flags is called an Idle Pattern, indicating that the stream is still coming in but no new data is being transmitted. Unlike other protocols discussed in this chapter, this protocol has no file size indicator or end pointer. At the receiver, this information is fed serially into the PSD Transport layer, where data between Flags is steered off to a buffer. If a packet is no good, it is discarded and the receiver waits for the next data following a flag to begin to arrive.

How A Tilde Can Be a Flag and a Character

If a tilde character were embedded in the PSD as part of the message, the PSD Transport would see it as a null character indicating a break between two packets. This would cause the packet to fail. An escape mechanism is used to permit the tilde to be represented as text within PSD. A Control Escape byte is defined as the binary value for right curly bracket "}". When tilde must be placed in the PSD, it is transported as the binary value for the two characters " } ^ ". Right bracket indicates the character to follow has a newly defined meaning.

But what then of the right curly bracket? If it is a Control Escape character, how is a right curly bracket sent? It is also used in a control escape sequence of two characters to represent itself; " }] ".

This type of pattern recognition is the legacy of serial communications by modem. The underlying medium might use special control characters in the ASCII table to provide control of the modems and links. That left higher layer applications to rely on printable but less common ASCII characters as control or null values. It is simple because it eliminates end-of-file pointers and other header structures and allows the serial stream to be unaware of the framing occurring in the Audio Transport. It is efficient because the amount of byte-doubling caused by the infrequent use of tilde and right curly bracket in most PSD content is inconsequential.

The flow of data at this level of the PSD protocol is not unlike the flow of patrons into a theater. Each patron is a package of data encapsulated for transport. The sizes of the packages vary. The contents of the package are of no interest to the usher. The usher is only interested in where the patron is expected to sit and looks at the ticket for direction. The patrons may be lined up one after the other, or may be trickling in with gaps between them. The usher must recognize when the next patron has arrived. To extend the analogy, perhaps to the absurd, the patron removes his encapsulation (his coat) after entering the theater and proceeds as directed to the correct port in the auditorium. The seat number serves as the patron's sequence number, ensuring proper placement in relation to the others arriving for the show. The transport protocol doesn't have any ticket to check, but it does look for the Protocol Field, Port, and Sequence Number to properly strip and direct the PSD packet to its destination.

One key to this use of "PPP in HDLC-like Framing" is the movement of a PSD ID3 packet through a serial data transport with no consideration for the underlying 1.49-second transmission frames of the IBOC system. An Audio Transport frame could be filled and only have room for, say, the first few bytes of the next PSD packet. The system will not be deterred by incomplete PSD packets in an audio Transport frame. The HDLC-like stream is taken in by the transmitter and stuffed into space available without regard for ends or beginnings of packets. The receiver takes the data as it arrives and buffers it; when the terminating Flag character indicates the packet is done, the packet is stripped of its encapsulation and sent to its proper port.

PSD Metadata

While the structures of the Program Service Data protocols are outlined in the relevant NRSC-5 reference documents, as discussed in this chapter, there is a movement to enhance the service for public radio broadcasting. Public radio broadcasting tends to have more complex program content taxonomy than would be associated with a typical commercial music broadcasting format. Recall that the PSD protocol borrows from the ID3 tag protocol. ID3 is a metadata tag originally intended for MP3 audio files. It defines tag fields that would normally be associated with MP3 files, and in particular, music files. Title, artist, genre, and album are the fundamental ID3 frames supported by PSD. PSD also supports commercial information about the audio file and a comment space.

The ID3 tag has limited utility when a public radio station's programming may have several layers of information to convey. The variety show model, such as the Prairie Home Companion, and the news and information program model, such as All Things Considered, each present a deeper metadata challenge than the music broadcast model. On stations broadcasting a music format, the meaning of the ID3 tags can be stretched to provide information about an advertiser during a commercial or about a program element such as a newscast. However, when the title display says "Eat at Joe's" during a restaurant commercial, it is a case of deviating from the metadata definition (title) to push other information to a receiver display. To reach receivers with one PSD display element (such as title) it is tempting to use a field off-type in this fashion.

Public broadcasters see the opportunity to convey richer and more purposeful data to the radio (and television) audience. For instance, a Series data element would describe information about a program at the highest level, relating information about the program series, independently of any individual program episode. Program elements would provide information specifically about the individual program. Within the program, specific program events—monologue, music, drama or comedy performance, dialogue, news, etc.—also deserve their own metadata.

A number of public broadcasting stakeholders convened under the leadership of Public Radio International to promote orderly use of PSD by public radio stations. It is called the PRI PSD Consortium. With funding from the U.S. Corporation for Public Broadcasting, the consortium formed an initiative called the PSD Standards Project and pursued the PSD metadata question.[7] Public

---

[7] psd.publicbroadcasting.net

broadcasting has evolved a fairly sophisticated distribution structure for which metadata is key. The Public Radio Satellite System, managed by an entity of National Public Radio called NPR Distribution, developed Content Depot, a next-generation content distribution system. Content Depot relies on metadata to provide all participants with a common structure for communicating about the program materials handled by the service. Metadata is most effective when it is harmonized among the various layers of production and distribution. This minimizes the need for hands-on translation of information from one distribution layer or media platform and another, which increases efficiency and reduces errors in content translation and management. Meanwhile, public television broadcasting in the U.S. is focused on similar objectives, with the launch of the Public Broadcasting Service's Next Generation Interconnection System and the broadcast television industry work on the U.S. over-the-air television Program and System Information Protocol (PSIP).

The PSD Standards Project has roots in international metadata management practice. The most direct progenitor is PBCore, the CPB Public Broadcasting Metadata Dictionary Project. In 2005 PBCore Version 1 listed 48 metadata elements for public broadcasting content. In 2006, the project released an initial XML schema for marking the metadata elements. PBCore's progenitor is the work of various metadata efforts and principally of the Dublin Core Metadata Initiative, which created a Metadata Element Set that is ISO standard 15836.

In 2006, the PSD Standards Project published sets of suggested metadata elements in three categories– Series, Program, and Segment/Song. (Table 4.11) A fourth-level category called "Pieces" is contemplated for further breaking down parts of a segment or song. Each field within the categories is accompanied by a definition containing purpose, usage, and structural information. For example, this is the definition of the Program Title element:

Element name: PgmTitle

Available for display? Yes

Element description: Name of an episode in an ongoing series

Encoding: ASCII text, 64 characters

Obligation: Optional (Mandatory if SeriesIsSeries is set to "N")

Discussion: Many public radio shows have episode names associated with them, e.g., This American Life "Holiday Spectacular" or "David and Goliath," or Fresh Air "Recalling the Iranian Hostage Crisis."

Series Elements	Program Elements	Segment/Song Elements
<SeriesTitle>	<PgmTitle>	<SegTitle>
<SeriesDescription>	<PgmDescription>	<SegDescription>
<SeriesHost>	<PgmHost>	<SegHost>
<SeriesGenre>	<PgmGenre>	<SegGuest>
<SeriesComment1>	<PgmComment1>	<SegComment1>
<SeriesComment2>	<PgmComment2>	<SegComment2>
<SeriesUnderwriterName1>	<PgmUnderwriterName1>	<SegUnderwriterName>
<SeriesUnderwriterTag1>	<PgmUnderwriterTag1>	<SegUnderwriterTag>
<SeriesUnderwriterName2>	<PgmUnderwriterName2>	<SongTitle>
<SeriesUnderwriterTag2>	<PgmUnderwriterTag2>	<SongTitleLong1>
<SeriesUnderwriterName3>	<PgmUnderwriterName3>	<SongTitleLong2>
<SeriesUnderwriterTag3>	<PgmUnderwriterTag3>	<SongArtist>
----Housekeeping tags----	----Housekeeping tags----	<SongAlbum>
<SeriesID>	<PgmID>	<SongConductor>
<SeriesHasPgmInfo>	<PgmNumber>	<SongComposer>
<SeriesIsSeries>	<PgmHasSegInfo>	<SongSoloist>
	<PgmAudioFile>	----Housekeeping tags----
	<PgmAudioFileLocation>	<SegID>
		<SegNumber>
		<SegType>
		<SegAudioFile>
		<SegAudioFileLocation>

Table 4.11 PRI PSD Consortium, PSD Standards Project, Suggested PSD Field Descriptions

The project is intended to take industry input and provide guidance on the evolving nature of PSD data services. The various data elements must be mapped to the limited PSD fields based on what features are available on the installed base of receivers in the marketplace. In the long run, the creation of a suggested metadata format for content destined to be PSD is only the beginning. To make effective use of PSD radio stations, content providers, radio station automation and traffic management systems developers, transmitter manufacturers, and receiver manufacturers all must be influenced by the possibilities of PSD and other broadcast data. Initiatives such as the

PSD Standards Project help provide structure for evolution and innovation among the various stakeholders, with the common objective of providing compelling benefits to the consumer.

Audio Transport to Channel Multiplex

This chapter started at the top of the NRSC-5 protocol stack and followed the path of broadcast audio and program associated data to a point where one or more Program Services and their Program Service Data have been merged into an Audio Transport PDU. Other services parallel to the Audio Services include opportunistic and fixed-data, and the Station Information Service (SIS)—addressed in the Data Services Chapters 10 and 11. One or more Audio Transport PDUs are sent once every transmission frame period to Layer 2. Layer 2 is responsible for setting up logical channels and populating them with the correct Audio Transport PDU sections as well as AAT PDUs.

5 From the Top Down: Channel Multiplex to Interleaver–Layer 2 and Part of Layer 1

As these chapters progress down the NRSC-5 protocol stack, the relationship between the information content and the protocol structure becomes more abstract. Coded Program Service Audio and Program Service Data were merged and encapsulated via the Audio Transport protocol. Parallel to these processes are other processes that will be addressed in Chapters 10 and 11—Station Information Service (SIS) and Advanced Data Service (ADS). The next step down in the stack is the Channel Multiplex, known as Layer 2 for the simple reason that it is the second layer above the transmission medium or physical layer.

The NRSC-5 Reference Document for this layer is number 3, *Layer 2 Channel Multiplex Protocol*, highlighted in Table 5.1. This layer of the protocol stack, like the layers above it, is has a single document common to both the AM and FM IBOC signals. The protocols split below Layer 2, where separate documents describe Layer 1 for AM and FM IBOC. See sidebar for an explanation of the role Layer 1 plays in this chapter.

NRSC-5 Reference Document Number	Reference Document Title	NRSC-5 Reference Document Number	Reference Document Title
1.	Doc. No. SY_IDD_1011s rev. E HD Radio™ Air Interface Design Description **Layer 1 FM** iBiquity Digital Corporation, 3/22/05	6.	Doc. No. SY_SSS_1026s rev. D HD Radio™ FM Transmission System Specifications iBiquity Digital Corporation, 2/18/05
2.	Doc. No. SY_IDD_1012s rev. E HD Radio™ Air Interface Design Description **Layer 1 AM** iBiquity Digital Corporation, 3/22/05	7.	Doc. No. SY_IDD_1028s rev. C HD Radio™ Air Interface Design Description Program Service Data iBiquity Digital Corporation, 3/31/05
3.	Doc. No. SY_IDD_1014s rev. F HD Radio™ Air Interface Design Description **Layer 2 Channel Multiplex Protocol** iBiquity Digital Corporation, 2/7/05	8.	Doc. No. SY_SSS_1082s rev. D HD Radio™ AM Transmission System Specifications iBiquity Digital Corporation, 2/24/05
4.	Doc. No. SY_IDD_1017s rev. E HD Radio™ Air Interface Design Description Audio Transport iBiquity Digital Corporation, 3/31/05	9.	Doc. No. SY_IDD_1085s rev. C HD Radio™ Air Interface Design Description Program Service Data Transport iBiquity Digital Corporation, 2/7/05
5.	Doc. No. SY_IDD_1020s rev. E HD Radio™ Air Interface Design Description Station Information Service Protocol iBiquity Digital Corporation, 2/18/05	10.	Doc. No. SY_IDD_1019s rev. E HD Radio™ Air Interface Design Description Advanced Application Services Transport iBiquity Digital Corporation, 8/4/05

Table 5.1 Protocols Addressed in Chapter 5

At 11 pages, the Layer 2 document is the thinnest of the NRSC-5 protocol documents, rivaled in brevity only by the AM and FM transmission system specification documents. Nevertheless, the Layer 2 document contains some key components of the structure of the digital information flow on IBOC signals. It addresses Logical Channels, content-based PDU structures, and "Protocol Control Information" embedded in its PDUs.

Forging Ahead into Layer 1

This chapter begins with Layer 2 and drills part way into Layer 1. When information is processed through Layer 2, it exits Layer 2 organized into Logical Channels. Layer 1 receives Layer 2 output and maintains the Logical Channel structure. The concept of the Logical Channel infuses both layers. Meanwhile, the Layer 1 Reference Documents, one for AM and one for FM, are as large as Layer 2 documentation is small. These circumstances make it convenient to forge ahead into Layer 1 in this chapter. Those processes in Layer 1 that AM and FM have in common, including the basics of Logical Channels, are addressed in this chapter. Chapters 6 through 9 delve into the specifics of the AM and FM systems at the lowest levels of Layer 1.

Unlike previous layers, Layer 2 adds no fields of data for headers, header expansion, or error protection. There is a 24-bit sequence, called the Protocol Control Information (PCI), that is dispersed across each Layer 2 PDU (L2 PDU). The PCI provides a header-like function that is discussed further below. Other than that, the role of Layer 2 is as a traffic cop. Information coming in the top must be directed to the correct outputs at the correct times.

Layer 2 is called the *Channel Multiplex* because it brings together information from several sources (services) and passes it along to Layer 1, organized in Layer 2 PDUs. It might as well have been called the Service Multiplex, as the different streams of content entering Layer 2 are classified as services. While a number of inputs are multiplexed into Layer 2—MPS, SPS, ADS, SIS—the output of Layer 2 is also channelized into the Logical Channels that propagate to Layer 1.

Logical Channels

Layer 1 expects the incoming information from Layer 2 to be organized in the various Logical Channels. Why Layer 1 uses Logical Channels is worth an overview here. Segregating information by Logical Channels gives the system the ability to control independently the robustness and PDU rates of each channel.

Logical Channels and the Frequency Domain

Consider the IBOC Radio Frequency (RF) channel as having the characteristic of a comb (Figure 5.1). Each tine of the comb is an RF subcarrier modulated with a series of symbols of information. Sections of the comb may operate at different levels (Figure 5.2). With the presence of an analog host signal, some parts of the comb may be more susceptible to interference from the analog sidebands. (Figure 5.3)

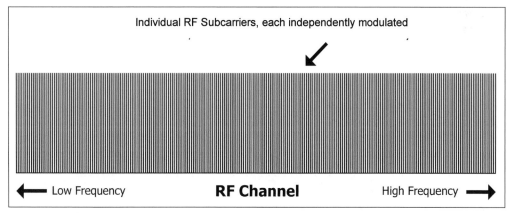

Figure 5.1 RF Channel as a Comb

Orthogonal Frequency-Division Multiplexing (OFDM) is the waveform chosen for IBOC transmissions. Consisting of hundreds of closely spaced RF subcarriers, each modulated at very low rates, the OFDM channel spectrum can be segmented in a fashion that single-carrier waveforms cannot accommodate. The single-carrier waveform is modulated in a serial fashion at a high bit rate. In contrast, OFDM's individual subcarriers are modulated simultaneously, creating a parallel bitstream operating at a lower bit rate per subcarrier. More important information can be placed on higher-level OFDM subcarriers to take advantage of their higher signal to noise ratios. OFDM subcarriers that are more likely to interfere with OFDM subcarriers on other stations in the all-digital mode can be reduced in level. Figure 5.2 illustrates an OFDM spectrum with frequency-dependent levels.

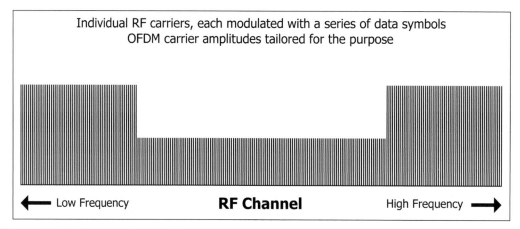

Figure 5.2 RF Comb with Tailored Signal Levels

IBOC digital subcarrier signals have been designed to co-exist with analog signals. "Hybrid" is the term for the simultaneous transmission of digital IBOC subcarriers with an analog host. The compatibility of the analog and digital portions of the IBOC signal in the AM and FM bands is a key component of the hybrid IBOC waveform design. The sidebands of the host analog signal fall near and beneath some of the OFDM carriers. Upon reception, these carriers may have a poorer signal to noise ratio than carriers more removed from the host energy. An illustration of analog sideband stress on the OFDM spectrum is given in Figure 5.3.

It is beneficial to segregate OFDM subcarriers that are more susceptible to interference. On hybrid FM IBOC for instance, the region closest to the analog part of the signal is segregated where reception of OFDM subcarriers is most challenged by the analog host energy. These subcarriers are transmitted at the same level as others in the "Primary" segment. They are called the *Primary Extended (PX)* subcarriers. PX subcarriers are optional, while their neighbors, the Primary Main (PM) subcarriers are required in FM IBOC transmission. Figure 5.4 illustrates the manner in which the Main and Extended subcarriers fit in the overall scheme of the FM IBOC waveform.

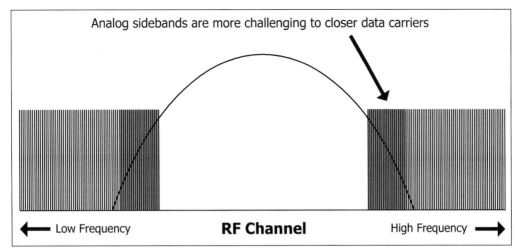

Figure 5.3 RF Comb with Analog Signal Interference

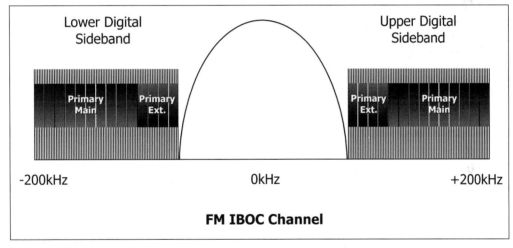

Figure 5.4 FM Logical Groupings at RF

When the analog signal is switched off in all-digital operation, the analog host is replaced with a lower level group of OFDM subcarriers, described as the "Secondary" subcarriers on FM IBOC. They are transmitted with less power to reduce their interference potential with adjacent channel signals. This is illustrated in Figure 5.5, which shows how the OFDM energy related to adjacent-channel stations is tailored to prevent mutual interference in the fringe areas between stations.

The all-digital FM band interlaces the blocks of Primary subcarriers on adjacent stations. After analog is turned off, rather than filling the hole left in the FM channel with high power digital energy, the gap is retained to allow the adjacent channel digital signals to propagate farther without

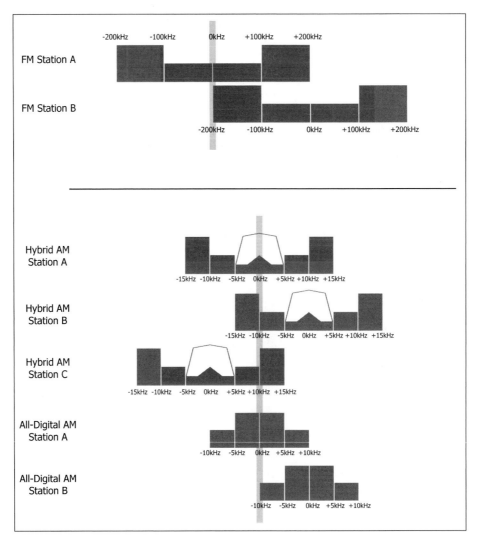

Figure 5.5 Spectral Interlace of IBOC Signals

interference. Each station benefits from the gap left by the removal of the adjacent channel analog signal. To preserve this benefit on analog turn-off, only a low-level secondary set of subcarriers is inserted.

AM IBOC spectral interlacing is more complex than FM. The FM IBOC Primary subcarriers stay put when switching from hybrid to all-digital. Hybrid AM IBOC occupies 30 kHz of spectrum, with the highest power subcarriers, the Primary subcarriers, as far removed from the analog host as possible. All-digital AM transmission repositions the primary subcarriers and narrows the bandwidth occupied by the IBOC signal. (Figure 5.6)

The second plot in Figure 5.5 shows how the interlacing of OFDM spectra takes advantage of the ability to tailor OFDM subcarrier levels to manage interference among stations.

The extension of a station's occupied bandwidth with a digital waveform is made possible by the ability to tailor the OFDM waveform for best results. Several competing interests are balanced in the signal level structure. The OFDM subcarriers must be strong enough and robust enough to provide practical service, with each subcarrier requiring an adequate signal-to-noise ratio for the type of modulation employed on it. The OFDM signal must be reasonably compatible with continued reception of the analog host. and be low enough in level to avoid significant interference to adjacent channel stations. Chapter 9 contains a discussion of the occupied bandwidth of hybrid and all-digital IBOC signals.

In a nutshell, the ability to tailor OFDM spectral occupancy permits optimum spectrum utilization. With spectral optimization comes a hierarchy of more and less valuable RF "real estate" in the channel. This encourages the segregation of RF subcarriers into logical groupings with similar performance characteristics.

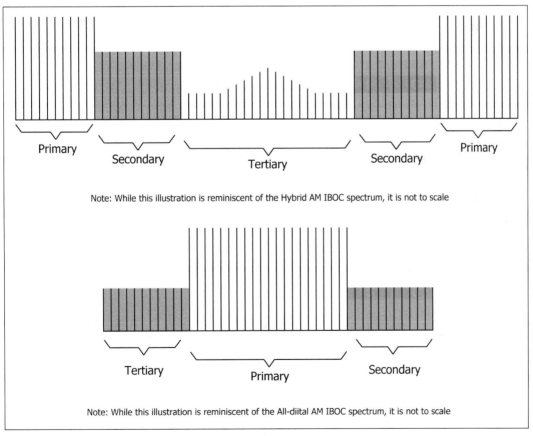

Figure 5.6 AM Logical Groupings at RF

Logical Channels in the Time Domain

It is not enough to segregate data streams into sections of the radio spectrum. Sometimes two information streams will deserve same-quality RF subcarriers, sharing the same part of the channel spectrum, but they will have different delivery characteristics. A single logical channel could convey core audio, enhanced audio, or Station Information Service (SIS) PDUs. (Data services can be conveyed on logical channels with or without audio.) On a given portion of the FM IBOC OFDM spectrum, there may be more than one logical channel. (See Table 5.2)

While the frame rate is constant, the PDUs of various logical channels may pass at different clock rates. Enhanced audio is clocked through with one PDU per 1.49-second frame. Core audio is clocked through with eight PDUs per frame (except for hybrid FM, which has one audio PDU per frame). Similarly, but not identically, the logical channel that carries station information from the SIS is clocked at the fastest rate available—8 PDUs per AM IBOC frame and 16 PDUs per FM IBOC frame. On the FM IBOC signal, SIS information (called *PIDS* and *SIDS*) is transmitted on the same OFDM spectra as core and enhanced audio.

Discussed further below, Layer 1 performs independent operations on each logical channel, tailored to the PDU rate, RF robustness, desired error protection level, and size of the PDUs. FM IBOC has a smorgasbord of spectral and logical channel configurations available. AM is much simpler, at least from the perspective of Logical Channels. Table 5.2 lays out the options.

Band and Modes		Spectrum to which Logical Channels are Assigned				
FM IBOC	Service Mode	Primary Main -PM-	Primary Extended -PX-	Secondary Main -SM-	Secondary Extended -SX-	Secondary Protected -SP-
Hybrid Modes	MP1	P1 & PIDS	-			
	MP2, MP3, or MP4	P1 & PIDS	P3			
Used with All-digital Modes	MP5	P1, P2 & PIDS	P3 & P1'			
	MP6	P1, P2 & PIDS	P1'			
All-digital Modes	MS1			S4 & SIDS		S5
	MS2			S1, S2 & SIDS	S3 & S1'	S5
	MS3			S1, S2 & SIDS	S1'	S5
	MS4			S2 & SIDS	S3 & S1'	S5

AM IBOC	Service Mode	Primary	Secondary	Tertiary	Individually Assigned Subcarriers
Hybrid	MA1	P1	P3	P3	PIDS
All-digital	MA2	P1	P3	P3	PIDS

Note: P1' is pronounced "P1 prime"

Table 5.2 Logical Channels, Service Modes, and OFDM Spectra

Logical Channel Types and Rates

Of primary interest are the hybrid service modes, which for AM provide paths for core and enhanced audio (Logical Channels P1 and P3, respectively). For hybrid FM, Logical Channel P1 carries the audio Program Services; there is no enhanced stream. When extended OFDM subcarrier spectrum is added, Logical Channel P3 can carry expanded audio services. As discussed further below, these Logical Channels can also be subdivided to carry data services as well.

The PIDS and SIDS Logical Channels are the Primary and Secondary IBOC Data Services. Only all-digital FM IBOC uses the SIDS Logical Channel. PIDS and SIDS carry the basic station information provided by the SIS protocol, discussed in Chapter 10. The Logical Channels served by Layer 2 fall into two categories, the dedicated functions of PIDS and SIDS, and the content delivery capability of the others, P1–P3 and S1–S5. Layer 2 passes "Layer 2 PDUs" to Layer 1, with PDU sizes matching the requirements of each Logical Channel. Table 5.3 shows key L2 PDU capacities for hybrid operations.

Hybrid Logical Channel	AM			FM		
	P1	P3	PIDS	P1	P3*	PIDS
L2 PDU size (bits)	3750	24000	80	146176	9216	80
L2 PDUs per Frame	8	1	1	1	8	16
Logical Channel bits per frame	30000	24000	80	146176	73728	1280
Effective bits/s @ 1.486 frames/s	20188	16151	54	98369	49615	861

PDU size shown for FM P3 is based on Service Mode MP4, which utilizes entire Primary Extended bandwidth.

Table 5.3 Hybrid IBOC PDU Capacities per Logical Channel

Layer 2 PDU Structure

With a foundation in the reasons and roles for Logical Channels, attention can turn to the Layer 2 PDU structure. Each Logical Channel receives independent Layer 2 processing, in which one Layer 2 PDU (L2 PDU) is generated for each Logical Channel. The resulting set of L2 PDUs is clocked into Layer 1 once each frame period.

Folding in Data

Ignoring PIDS and SIDS Logical Channels for the moment, the L2 PDU capacities can be devoted completely to Audio Transport PDUs. However, it is in Layer 2 that any Advanced Data Services are folded into these PDUs. There are two methods for making room for ADS—"fixed" and "opportunistic." The station operator selects how much bandwidth the Program Services will occupy, how much bandwidth is "fixed" (set aside) for Advanced Data Services. In addition, sometimes the Audio Transport has an opportunity to give up a little unused capacity for data transmission. This occurs when the codec is not working hard and does not require all the capacity reserved for it. The IBOC operator can instruct the transmission system to utilize opportunistic data capacity.

The side process called the Configuration Administrator informs the Audio Transport, the Advanced Data Services transport, and Layer 2 what the station's settings are. Layer 2 calls for audio and/or data PDUs from the layers above it to fit into the L2 PDUs for each Logical Channel.

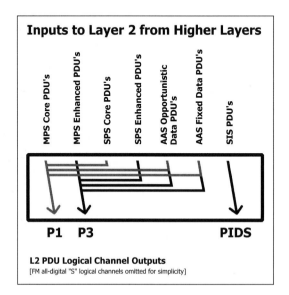

Figure 5.7 Layer 2 Inputs and Outputs

As described in the previous chapter, the Audio Transport exploits the variations in Program Audio PDU size to squeeze Program Service Data into the resulting Program Service PDU. This same mechanism is used to provide Opportunistic Data capacity. First, PSD is given priority. If there is any space remaining after PSD insertion, it can be made available for Opportunistic Data.

When more than one Program Service is transmitted on a logical channel, the Audio Transport consolidates the opportunistic capacity of each service and places it after the Audio Transport PDU. Enhanced audio streams lack PSD, and any excess capacity due to variations in Program Audio coding is fully available for Opportunistic Data delivery. On the opposite side of the coin, if a Logical Channel has no Program Service on it, there is no opportunistic capacity.

L2 PDU Types

An L2 PDU falls into one of several classes, depending on the logical channel with which it is associated and the manner in which the Logical Channel is configured. Table 5.4 displays the combinations of L2 PDU content. A rule for Audio Transport PDUs applies to L2 PDUs as well—

when there is MPS in the PDU, MPS always takes first position. SPS, if any, always follows. Opportunistic Data capacity, when employed, follows the program services. Fixed-data, when employed, is always at the end of the L2 PDU. Table 5.4 honors the relative position of each component. The relative width of each component is not to scale because that is pre-selectable by the operator, or in the case of Opportunistic Data capacity, the space available varies from PDU to PDU.

Contents of L2 PDU	MPS/SPS
Binary 'Header' Seq. CW$_0$	1 1 0 0 1 0 1 1 0 0 0 1 1 0 1 1 0 0 0 1 1 1 0 0

Contents of L2 PDU	MPS/SPS	Opportunistic
Binary 'Header' Seq. CW$_1$	0 0 1 0 1 1 0 0 0 1 1 0 1 1 0 0 0 1 1 1 0 0 1 1	

Contents of L2 PDU	MPS/SPS	Fixed
Binary 'Header' Seq. CW$_2$	0 0 1 1 0 0 1 0 1 1 0 0 0 1 1 0 1 1 0 0 0 1 1 1	

Contents of L2 PDU	MPS/SPS	Opportunistic	Fixed
Binary 'Header' Seq. CW$_3$	1 1 0 0 1 1 0 0 1 0 1 1 0 0 0 1 1 0 1 1 0 0 0 1		

Contents of L2 PDU	Fixed
Binary 'Header' Seq. CW$_4$	0 1 1 1 0 0 1 1 0 0 1 0 1 1 0 0 0 1 1 0 1 1 0 0

Table 5.4 Layer 2 PDU Formats

Each PDU format is indicated by the position of a string of bits. The second line for each L2 PDU configuration in Table 5.4 is labeled "Binary Header Sequence CW$_n$," where "n" represents a number 0–7 that uniquely identifies a header sequence code word. (CW$_5$ – CW$_7$ are defined but are designated "Reserved" and are not shown here.) Each L2 PDU contains a code word string of 24 bits. The bits are spread evenly across the L2 PDU width, regardless of the width, based on algorithms contained in the Layer 2 document.

The binary code words in Table 5.4 are shown spread across the length of the L2 PDU to symbolize the manner in which they are spaced throughout the L2 PDU, leaving the remaining space for Services to be inserted. Since the bits are placed at known intervals across the L2 PDU, the payload information can be distributed within the remaining space.

This bit string is called a header; although in the traditional bit-mapping sense, it is not a header, which one would expect to be at the head of the PDU. The Layer 2 Reference Document also calls this string Protocol Control Information (PCI) consisting of "one of eight cyclic permutations." No matter how it is named, the stated purpose of the string is to identify the type of PDU.

The five code words shown in Table 5.4 reveal the structure of a cyclic permutation. The same string of bits is employed for each 24-bit code word. It is just the starting point in the string that differs. For the reader's convenience, the starting point of the CW$_0$ sequence is marked by an underscored numeral 1 on each of the sequences. Starting at the underscore, the pattern of ones and zeroes is identical among the five versions. The receiver can look at this string and determine the format of the L2 PDU. Even if there are corrupted bits in the received code word, there may be enough remaining good bits to infer the correct code word and determine the type of PDU. This is a characteristic of using a carefully chosen cyclic permutation that lends itself to use in error protection schemes. The PCI is an extra way to determine the nature of the PDU. Other information is provided via the Audio Transport and the Advanced Data Service transport from which the receiver can determine where in th PDU structure information begins and ends.

With a PCI code word embedded in the L2 PDUs for each Logical Channel, each L2 PDU is then stuffed with its payload and transferred to Layer 1. Layer 2 completes its traffic cop task of multiplexing several services into several Logical Channels.

Layer 1—Processes Common to AM and FM

Digital radio systems are designed for the characteristics of the radio channel with which they will be used. In this context, the radio channel is described not only by the place in the radio spectrum reserved for the signal (the frequency and bandwidth), but also by the characteristics of the propagation and interference environment likely to be encountered by the radio signal on its way from the transmitter to the receiver. The radio channel is like an imaginary pipe between the source and the destination. In a manner characteristic of that pipe, it has limited capacity and attenuates, distorts, and adds noise to the desired digital signal.

The most obvious condition of the AM and FM IBOC radio channels is the presence of analog signals. The proper design of a signal deals with the capacity of the signal to cause interference to other users of the spectrum, as well as its ability to resist interference from other sources. One way to control interference to other users of the spectrum is to tailor the signal's power spectral density and bandwidth. Constriction of power and bandwidth must be balanced against meeting the capacity and robustness requirements of the signal.

IBOC signals strive to make the necessary compromises between minimizing interference to the reception of other stations' signals (analog and digital) and providing sufficient bandwidth and coverage area to provide beneficial service.

Meanwhile, the digital portion of the received IBOC signal must contend with interference from spectral background noise, the analog host signal (in hybrid mode), analog adjacency signals, new digital signals in the spectrum, and characteristics of the communications channel. These are sources of noise that can interfere with reception of the desired IBOC signal. One characteristic of the radio channel is the mobility of the radio receiver. Depending on the motion of the receiver, the rate at which the signal peaks and fades varies. Bursty, impulsive noise results from short term variations in signal and/or noise. Longer fades may occur, caused by phenomena such as structural obstructions or stoplight fades.

One other factor key to the design of the digital portion of the IBOC signal is power efficiency. It is beneficial from several perspectives to maintain as low a peak-to-average power ratio as possible.

Transmitters must be sized to handle the peak power levels to be emitted. With higher peak-to-average ratios, larger components are necessary to handle the peak power dissipation while maintaining the desired average power; amplifiers may need higher gain or more gain stages. To handle a signal with a higher peak-to-average ratio while maintaining an adequate noise floor, the Digital-to-Analog Converter (DAC) that generates the radio signal must have a higher bit resolution and dynamic range. Over the air, higher energy peaks can provoke more interference to reception of other signals; lowering power to control interference sacrifices the signal-to-noise ratio of the desired signal.

On the receiving side, the same issues that affect transmitter components affect receiver components. Noise levels, dynamic range, and ADC (Analog-to-Digital Converter) characteristics in the receiver must accommodate the peak signal power while maintaining adequate signal-to-noise ratios.

For the AM and FM IBOC channels, good digital system design must handle the noisy spectrum, tolerate bursty interference, tolerate longer fade durations, and have a minimal peak to average power ratio. To achieve these objectives, Layer 1 scrambles, encodes, interleaves, and maps the information on the Logical Channels to the OFDM subcarriers.

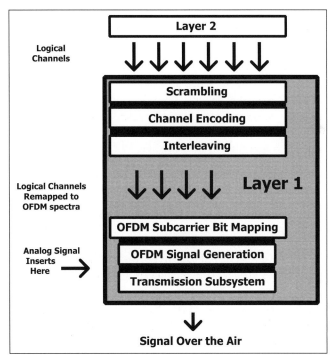

Figure 5.8 Layer 1 Structure (Generic)

Scrambling a stream of bits pseudo-randomizes the stream to eliminate any repetitive patterns over time, called periodicities, which may be present. This makes the spectral occupancy of the data stream more "white" noise-like, which minimizes the peak-to-average ratio.[1]

Channel encoding is a means of applying error protection to the bit stream. It employs mathematical techniques to create a degree of redundancy to the information being transmitted. However, rather than transmitting the same information more than once—a very crude form of redundancy—the information is encoded in a fashion that enables the reconstruction of missing data from the available data. This permits the receiver to recover useful information under moderate and in some cases severe noise and interference conditions.

Interleaving gives the channel encoding further leverage in the presence of bursty errors. Interleaving reorganizes a sequence of bits, with the result that the eight bits of any byte of information are distributed in time across the transmitted frame and are interleaved among the bits of many other bytes. A burst of noise will not damage entire bytes of information, but individual bits belonging to various bytes. The act of interleaving effectively spreads a brief burst of noise into background noise on the information. The channel encoding is better equipped to handle a white noise-like distribution of errors in the data than a catastrophic loss of several entire bytes.

These three processes, scrambling, channel encoding, and interleaving are discussed in more detail in this chapter. Once Layer 1 has produced interleaved data, its mapping to OFDM subcarriers is specific to the AM or FM IBOC system. Spectral mapping of the interleaved Layer 1 information to OFDM subcarriers is addressed in Chapters 7 and 8.

Once into Layer 1, the processing of Logical Channel PDUs is described by the Reference Documents under the term "transfer frame." Because Logical Channels may clock information through the channel at one of several rates (frame, block, block-pair), the terms "transfer frame rate," "...modulus," "...multiplexer," "...number," and "...size" are coined and supported by information in tables in the Layer 1 documents. The transfer frame is a concept distinct from the 1.49-second transmission "frame" that structures the transmitted signal. Numerous transfer frames are processed in Layer 1 to occupy the transmission frame.

PDUs and Transfer Frames

The early evolution of the iBiquity specifications is visible in the Layer 1 reference documents by the overlapping use of the terms "PDU" and "transfer frame." As the specifications were developed, the wording of different authors was harmonized with careful alignment of terminology among the documents. The only vestige of this process is in the fact that Layer 2 PDUs are alternately described *as* transfer frames and described as being conducted *by* transfer frames. Meanwhile, the Layer 1 glossary treats the two terms separately, but it is hard to glean any real difference between the terms' definitions. The terms are used interchangeably in this book.

---

[1] White noise is characterized by a uniform spectral density over the frequency range of interest.

Scrambling

Scrambling helps maintain a randomness to the datastream that is beneficial to the operation of transmitters and receivers. Counter-balancing all the advantages of OFDM is the disadvantage presented by high peak-to-average envelope power of the signal. Each OFDM subcarrier is a continuous wave signal of constant amplitude (except during transitions from one symbol to the next, when the power is ramped down briefly to permit a phase shift of the subcarrier). When summing two or more sine waves of different frequencies, a complex waveform is produced. When the peaks of the waves align, the amplitude of the waveform is higher than when the peak of one wave aligns with the trough of another. This section describes how scrambling helps avoid peak alignment, and how it works.

The Spectral Challenge of OFDM

The combining of hundreds of OFDM subcarriers produces a complex signal with a crest factor greater than that of a single sine wave. The crest factor is the ratio of the peak voltage to the RMS voltage of the waveform. High crest factor signals are more difficult to amplify because the amplifier must have greater headroom above its average power to handle the peaks. Chapter 13 contains a detailed discussion of the crest factor in the context of the FM signal.

OFDM subcarriers are members of a class called "harmonically related carriers" (HRC), being spaced at regular intervals on the spectrum (see sidebar). On the FM IBOC system, OFDM subcarriers are spaced at 363.4 Hz intervals; while on AM they are at 181.7 Hz spacing. These values are rounded approximations of the "OFDM Subcarrier Spacing" indicated by the symbol Δf in the NRSC-5 standard. In Chapters 7 and 8, these characteristics are discussed in relation to the structure of the OFDM signals.

The Harmonic Relationship of OFDM Subcarriers

For the moment, consider a radio channel with a center frequency, f_c, and a set of N OFDM subcarriers above f_c, spaced at Δf intervals. (Let's ignore the subcarriers below f_c for now.) Each subcarrier is spaced by Δf in sequence starting with $f_c + \Delta f$ as shown in Figure 5.9.

Transpose the center frequency to 0 Hz. This is called "zero IF," indicating an intermediate frequency at which the center frequency of the channel has been converted to 0 Hz. At zero IF, the OFDM subcarriers are harmonics (multiples) of the lowest frequency OFDM subcarrier. This arrangement makes it a relatively easy task for a signal processor to extract the phase of each subcarrier. In the frequency domain, the sidebands of each modulated subcarrier have nulls on the adjacent subcarrier frequencies, which is a characteristic of the property of orthogonality.

(continued on following page)

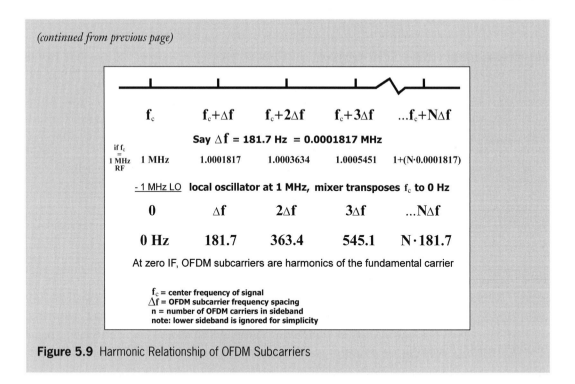

(continued from previous page)

Figure 5.9 Harmonic Relationship of OFDM Subcarriers

Figure 5.10 shows nine harmonically related subcarriers of equal amplitude and starting phase. The sum of the amplitudes of the subcarriers is also shown. For this illustration, the subcarriers are cosine functions, each started at the peak level of +1 amplitude units. With N subcarriers, the peak amplitude of the composite waveform is N times the peak amplitude of the individual subcarriers. The example shows the highest peak level possible for this nine-subcarrier signal—a value of +9 units. Since peak power is proportional to peak amplitude squared, in a resistive medium, peak power is 81 units in this example.

The RMS amplitude of each sinusoidal subcarrier is 0.707 units. The average power of each subcarrier, then, would be proportional to the RMS amplitude squared, or 0.5 units. Multiplied by nine subcarriers of equal amplitude, the average power of the 9-subcarrier waveform is 4.5 units. The Peak-to-Average Power Ratio (PAPR) is:

$$10 \, Log(81/4.5) = 12.55 \ dB.$$

Generalizing, the worst-case PAPR of an N-subcarrier OFDM symbol occurs when it has simultaneous peaks on all subcarriers, with a peak amplitude that is N times the unit amplitude of a single subcarrier:

$$PAPR_{worst\text{-}case} = 10 \, Log \, (N^2/(0.5N)) = 10 \, Log \, (2N)$$

For example, the 382 Primary Main OFDM subcarriers on the hybrid FM IBOC signal have a theoretical PAPR of $10 \, Log \, (2 \cdot 382) = 29$ dB. As a practical matter, the probability of all the subcarriers

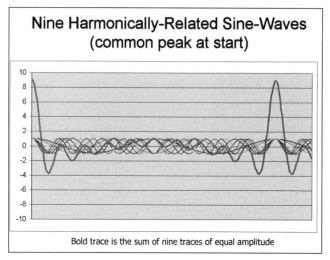

Figure 5.10 Peaks generated by nine harmonically related cosine subcarriers (common positive peak)

being assigned the same phase for one symbol period is vanishingly small. Systems do not have to be designed around this high peak figure. On the extremely rare occasions such a peak might occur, it would be clipped by the system and a small burst error could result.

Figure 5.11 shows a slight reduction in peak amplitude is obtained with the nine OFDM subcarriers as sine functions, each in quadrature with their counterparts in Figure 5.10. Now they have a common zero crossing. The peak amplitude has declined from 9 to 7.38 units for this nine-subcarrier example. Its PAPR is 10 Log $(7.38^2/4.5) = 11$ dB

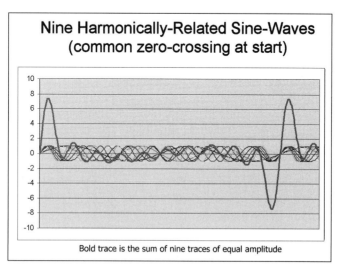

Figure 5.11 Peaks generated by nine harmonically related sine subcarriers (common zero crossing)

These extreme cases require all subcarriers to be in phase. However, conditions in which a large majority of the subcarriers have phase alignment also can produce high PAPR's. These events have greater probabilities than full peak alignment does because they can be produced by more than one combination of modulated OFDM subcarriers. It is helpful to design the system to minimize the probability of these higher peak levels.

In the next example, Figure 5.12, the phases of about half the subcarriers, randomly selected, have been inverted (comparable to a BPSK symbol with two possible phase states for each subcarrier). The peak amplitude has declined to 4.96. This yields a PAPR of 7.4 dB, a much more manageable figure.

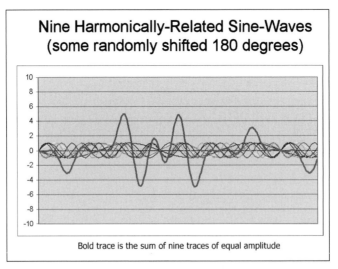

Figure 5.12 Peaks generated by nine harmonically related subcarriers (four, randomly selected, set 180 degrees out of phase)

How Scrambling Works

Scrambling ensures the OFDM symbol data are random and noise-like without periodicities. A mechanism must be implemented to make scrambled data that are readily descramble-able. This is accomplished by using a shift register to create a pseudo-random binary sequence. This sequence is combined with the incoming data from Layer 2. The same shift register is used in the receiver to recover the information.

Figure 5.13 shows the structure of the scrambler as a shift register and adders. The same scrambler design is employed in AM and FM IBOC systems. Because each Logical Channel has independent PDUs passing from Layer 2 to Layer 1, each Logical Channel has an independent scrambler.

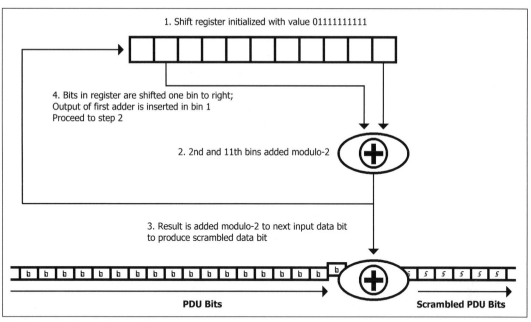

Figure 5.13 Scrambler Design

There are two adders in the scrambler—one to generate the scrambling sequence and one to apply that sequence to the information bits. A modulo-2 adder sums the values of the bits input to the adder, divides by two and reports the remainder. In the IBOC scrambler, the second and eleventh bits in the shift register are added, modulo-2. If both input bits are ones, their sum is binary 10. Dividing by two (which is binary 10) there is no remainder and the output is 0. Similarly, if both values are zero, the sum is zero and the remainder is zero. If one value is a one and the other is a zero, the adder outputs a remainder of 1.

First Input	Second Input	Modulo-2 Output
0	0	0
1	0	1
0	1	1
1	1	0

Table 5.5 Modulo-2 addition of two bits

The first adder creates the scrambling bit, which is used for two purposes. It is the value that is used to produce an output by scrambling the next bit in the PDU. It also is placed in the first shift register after the other registers are shifted one step to the right. In Table 5.6, this sequence is shown for six data bits (d) from the PDU.

Shift Register Position	1	2	3	4	5	6	7	8	9	10	11	Scrambler output	Sum MOD-2 with input data (d)
Initial State	0	1	1	1	1	1	1	1	1	1	1		
Scrambler value computed				Position 2 added to Position 11, Modulo-2								0	$0 \oplus d_1$
Data shifted right one position. Prior scrambler output inserted in Position 1	0	0	1	1	1	1	1	1	1	1	1		
Compute				Position 2 added to Position 11, Modulo-2								1	$1 \oplus d_2$
Data shifted right one position. Prior scrambler output inserted in Position 1	1	0	0	1	1	1	1	1	1	1	1		
Compute												1	$1 \oplus d_3$
Shift, Insert	1	1	0	0	1	1	1	1	1	1	1		
Compute												0	$0 \oplus d_4$
Shift, Insert	0	1	1	0	0	1	1	1	1	1	1		
Compute												0	$0 \oplus d_5$
Shift, Insert	0	0	1	1	0	0	1	1	1	1	1		
Compute												1	$1 \oplus d_6$

Table 5.6 Scrambling of First Six Bits ($d_1 \ldots d_6$) in an L2 PDU

As Figure 5.13 shows, the scrambler itself is not dependent upon the Layer 2 input data. The scrambler's output is deterministic; in other words, every time the scrambler is run, it produces the same sequence of bits. The nth bit of the scrambling sequence is always the same. It is determined by the initialization of the shift register and the feedback of bins 2 and 11, modulo-2, to the first register. A lookup table of scrambling bits could just as well be used to scramble the PDU data as the scrambler modeled in Figure 5.13.

When the scrambler output is added to the information in the Layer 2 PDU, the PDU contents are scrambled. The first six scrambling bits, written left to right 011001, are always produced by the scrambler, as shown in Table 5.5. If the first six bits of a PDU in a logical channel were, say,

111111, they would be combined one bit at a time with the corresponding bit of the scrambler, resulting in the sequence 100110. Modulo-2 addition is identical to the "exclusive-or" operation, sometimes indicated by the $\oplus$ symbol or the term XOR.

Upon reception, the same scrambler is used to unscramble the data in the PDU. This is possible due to the involutional property of the exclusive-or operation; that is to say, the operation, applied once at transmission and applied a second time at the receiver, returns the original data sequence. In the example, exclusive OR-ing the output sequence 100110 with the original scrambler sequence 011001 returns the input sequence 111111.

The scrambler produces an open-ended pseudorandom scrambling word. No matter how much data is contained in a Logical Channel's PDU, the scrambler outputs a sequence long enough to scramble the PDU bits. The scrambler's pseudorandomness not only breaks up long sequences of a single digit (1 or 0), but also ensures that repetitive patterns of bits are scrambled. It helps maintain a noise-like and periodicity-free OFDM waveform.

Convolutional Coding

The next step in preparing the logical channel PDUs for transmission is the encoding stage. This process is often referred to as Forward Error Correction (FEC) because it actively forwards information that can be used by the receiver to detect and correct errors. At this point, Layer 1 has scrambled the bits in the PDUs in a reversible manner. Scrambling added no overhead to the data stream; meaning the number of bits input to the scrambler equals the number put out. The encoding stage, on the other hand, develops redundant information to improve the reliability of the information flow. Redundant information requires additional bandwidth.

To discuss convolutional encoding, several concepts must be developed. The information in each Layer 1 PDU (transfer frame) is manipulated in *vector* and *matrix* forms. The encoder has a *memory* that it uses to incorporate a quantity of bits in each computation. The redundancy provided by the encoder is represented in its *rate*. Shift registers and adders, such as those that proved so useful in scrambling, are employed to convolve the information in the encoder.

Convolution is a mathematical process that combines the effects of two functions. The technical meaning of the term convolution arises out of the dictionary definition of convolve, which means to coil or twist together. With fields of data in vector or matrix form, two fields of data are convolved to produce a third. While convolution is employed as encoding in this instance, it is also employed for other purposes. Those familiar with image processing may recall convolutional techniques are employed to sharpen or blur images. In the world of digital signal processing, a filter representing, say, a channel impulse response, can be convolved with a signal to produce a modified waveform; or, in reverse, a known channel response can be employed as a convolutional filter to clear up channel impairments and restore an original signal.

In the application of convolution, a relationship is established between each data point in a set and certain nearby data points. Convolution employs two functions, one of which is often called a filter or a kernel. The other function is that which generates the primary information destined for convolution with the filter function. For example, the vector of data in a scrambled PDU (one function) is convolved with a polynomial filter (the other function) to produce a new, longer data vector.

Vectors and Matrices

A linear string of data is called a vector, while a block of information with two dimensions is called a matrix. Commonly, vectors are identified by a variable name with a single underline, such as $\underline{V}$, while matrices use a double underline, $\underline{\underline{M}}$. This convention is employed in the NRSC-5 reference documents.

To illustrate convolution, consider a binary vector $\underline{V}$ and a kernel $\underline{I}$:

$\underline{V}$ = 1011010001

$\underline{I}$ = 1001

Vector $\underline{V}$ consists of i elements. In this case i = 10 (ten). Kernel $\underline{I}$ has K elements; in this case, four. Let's use $\underline{U}$ as a map that indicates how to process the data in $\underline{V}$. When there is a 1 in $\underline{I}$, the corresponding values in $\underline{V}$ are XOR-ed. $\underline{I}$ is best represented as a shift register through which $\underline{I}$ is passed (Figure 5.14).

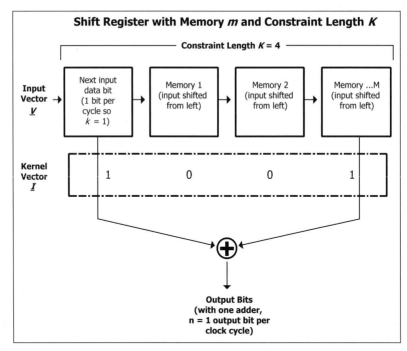

Figure 5.14 Convolution of a Data Field with a Kernel

This first example shows the key building blocks of a convolutional encoder. There are three shift registers in this one. These are the memory elements of the encoder. m = 3. The length of the "word" processed by the encoder in each cycle is the constraint length, which contains three memory bits and one input bit. Constraint length K = 4. In this example, and throughout the IBOC system, only one input bit is taken at a time. This is represented by the number of input

Input / Output Table													
Output G	Memory (initialized at 0)				Input Vector V								
	3	2	1	Input Bit									
1	0	0	0	1	0	1	1	0	1	0	0	0	1
0	0	0	1	0	1	1	0	1	0	0	0	1	←
1	0	1	0	1	1	0	1	0	0	0	1	←	
0	1	0	1	1	0	1	0	0	0	1	←		
0	0	1	1	0	1	0	0	0	1	←			
0	1	1	0	1	0	0	0	1	←				
1	1	0	1	0	0	0	1	←					
0	0	1	0	0	0	1	←						
1	1	0	0	0	1	←	XOR-ed fields (by row) are in highlighted columns						
1	0	0	0	1	←	To preserve the order of V as shown in the text, this table processes right to left; Fig. 5.14 is left to right							
0	0	0	1	←									
0	0	1	←										
1	1	←											
	Alternatve: Memory initialized with final input bits												
1	0	0	1	1	0	1	1	0	1	0	-	-	-
0	0	1	1	0	1	1	0	1	0	←			
0	1	1	0	1	1	0	1	0	←				
0	1	0	1	1	0	1	0	←					
Etc.													

Table 5.7 Input/output table of the convolution of a data field with a kernel

bits per cycle, $k = 1$. (In other applications, more complex convolutions can use $k > 1$, with parallel inputs to parallel shift register chains.)

A function having i elements convolved with a function having K elements produces an output with $i + K - 1$ elements. The example in Figure 5.14 has a ten-element input word and a constraint length of 4. The shift registers are initialized with zeros. Consequently, the output column in Table 5.7 contains $10 + 4 - 1 = 13$ elements. This increase is a result of the extra cycles required to flush the final input bit through the shift register. To avoid this extra overhead, the end of the input vector can be wrapped around to the beginning. This is accomplished by taking the final m elements of the input word to initialize the shift registers, as shown in the latter portion of the Input/Output Table 5.7.

The coding rate, r, is the ratio of the number of input bits to output bits per cycle: $r = k/n$. The coding rate is indicative of the redundancy applied to the data stream. Figure 5.14 shows an unrealistic convolutional encoder because it has only one modulo-2 adder. This would produce the ineffectual coding rate of 1/1. IBOC logical channels use "mother code rates" of 1/3 or 1/4. For every input bit, an encoder produces three, or four, output bits. These are called mother code rates because they are the parent coding rates from which other rates are derived. A method called "puncturing" is applied to the mother code rate to create punctured code rates such as 2/7, 2/5, or 1/2. Puncturing is discussed below.

The number of adders in the encoder determines the denominator of the mother rate, n. The encoder of Figure 5.14 is converted to a rate 1/3 encoder by incorporating three adders in Figure 5.15. The three adders produce a set of three output bits for each input bit. Each adder is assigned a kernel vector, $\underline{I}_n$, mapping the modulo-2 addition for that adder. These vectors are called "generator polynomials."

Generator polynomials are a shorthand means of describing the adder inputs. In the Figure 5.15 example, the three generator polynomials are 1001, 1011, and 0110. These can be applied to a truth

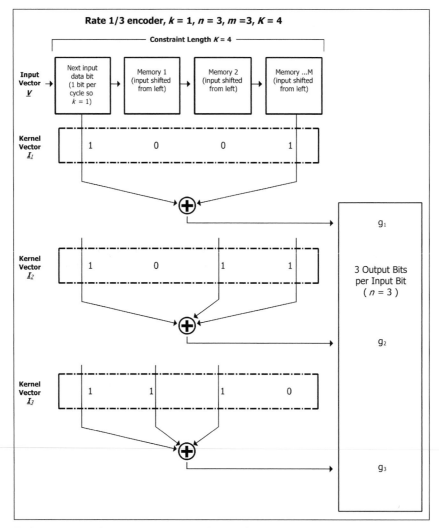

Figure 5.15 Simple rate 1/3 Encoder, k = 1, n = 3, m = 3, K = 4

table representing a binary polynomial. Table 5.8 shows the relationship between the generator polynomial and the registers that feed each adder. A value of 1 in the table represents a "true" condition, which indicates the shift register corresponding to that exponent is connected to the adder.

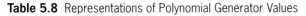

Adder	Shift register polynomial				Polynomial	Hex	Octal
	x	x^2	x^3	x^4			
G1	1	0	0	1	$x+x^4$	0x9	11
G2	1	0	1	1	$x+x^3+x^4$	0xB	13
G3	0	1	1	0	x^2+x^4	0x6	6

Table 5.8 Representations of Polynomial Generator Values

Not all polynomials are alike. Much research has been done to identify the most effective polynomials for various encoding circumstances. An early effort on polynomial selection was documented by W. W. Peterson and E. J. Weldon, Jr. in "Error Correcting Codes, 2 nd ed.," Cambridge, MA: The MIT Press, 1972.

FM IBOC Rate 2/5 Encoder Example

For illustration, consider the PDUs of two different FM IBOC Logical Channels—P1 and PIDS. Each PDU contains data destined for the next 1.49-second frame. The P1 PDU is processed with a rate 1/3 mother code and punctured to rate 2/5. Puncturing is explained later in this illustration. In a separate process, the PIDS logical channel is also processed with a rate 1/3 mother code and punctured to rate 2/5. A constraint length $K = 7$ is selected. The number of modulo-2 adders is $n = 3$. There are three corresponding polynomials for the adders, octal 133, 171, and 165.

Characteristic	Designation	Value
Constraint	K	7
Input bits per cycle	k	1
Output bits per cycle	n	3
Memory	m = K – 1	6
Polymonial 1	octal	133
	binary	1011011
Polymonial 2	octal	171
	binary	1111001
Polymonial 3	octal	165
	binary	1110101
Mother code rate	r = k/n	1/3
Punctured to rate	r (punctured)	2/5

Note, there is a variety of conventions for describing convolutional encoders. The convention depicted in this table is in harmony with the terminology in the Layer 1 Reference Documents.

Table 5.9 FM IBOC Rate 2/5 Encoder Characteristics

The structure of the mother code generator, shown in Figure 5.16, is based on the constraint length and the rate. Table 5.9 shows that there are seven places in the binary representation of the generator polynomials. This corresponds to the constraint length. There are seven corresponding points on the generator in Figure 5.16, consisting of the current input bit and six shift register memory places. Tapped off these points are inputs to the three modulo-2 adders. The taps feeding the adders are defined by the generator polynomials.

The leftmost position on the generator is the current input bit. This value is tapped for all three adders. Moving from left to right on Figure 5.16 and on the binary polynomials in Table 5.9, the polynomial exponents increase: x, x^2, x^3...x^7. Each adder is fed from the memory positions that correspond to the adder's polynomial. The first adder, octal 133, binary 1011011, is represented by the polynomial

$$\mathbf{x} \oplus \mathbf{x^3} \oplus \mathbf{x^4} \oplus \mathbf{x^6} \oplus \mathbf{x^7}$$

indicating that the first, third, fourth, sixth, and seventh memory positions in the shift register are XOR-ed to produce one of the output bits.

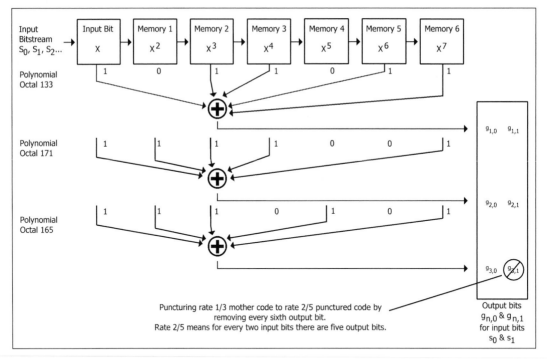

Figure 5.16 FM IBOC Rate 1/3 Mother Code Generator with Rate 2/5 Puncture

Puncturing

Figure 5.16 also illustrates puncturing, in which one or more output bits are discarded. In this rate 1/3 other code generator, a single input bit results in a three-bit output vector, $\underline{G}$. The next input bit produces a new three-bit vector. The input vector from the scrambler, $\underline{S}$, consists of bits $s_0, s_1...s_{N-1}$, where N is the length of the vector. Treating the outputs as a parallel port, over the duration of the frame a matrix $\underline{G}$ is produced.

In the case of the rate 2/5 puncturing, two columns of the output vector $\underline{G}$ are paired. This is a pair of rate 1/3 vectors, equivalent to a rate 2/6 output—six output bits for every two input bits. To conserve bandwidth, one of the output bits is discarded, resulting in the rate 2/5 product. Even with the absence of the punctured element(s), the encoded matrix retains enough of its redundancy to remain a worthwhile investment in extra bandwidth for error protection. There is an art to selecting the optimum puncture pattern for a given convolutional coder. The goal is to identify the pattern that is least detrimental to the encoder's error correction capability.

How Convolutional Encoding Helps

The convolution of data bits works in a causal fashion, enabling the receiver to rely on the causal relationships among convolved input bits and their predecessors to reconstruct the original input sequence. In other words, a history of $(K-1)$ data bits already in the register determine the two possible output vectors, depending on the value of the next input bit. A decoder relies on the causality of the code generator to decide correctly the value of an output bit, even in the presence of errors (noise) in the data flow.

To illustrate the guidance an encoder offers, consider the example encoder shown in Figure 5.15. It is a rate 1/3 encoder with constraint $K = 4$. There are $2^K = 16$ possible input sequences in the shift registers. The output is dependent on the polynomials of the three modulo-2 adders, so there are $2^3 = 8$ possible output combinations. (The larger constraints of IBOC encoders, such as $K = 7$, are impracticably large to use in an example; hence the more manageable $K = 4$ was chosen for illustration.)

Table 5.10 shows each of sixteen possible current states of the polynomial generator register (left, column 1). The second column indicates the three-bit output of the generator's adders for the corresponding state of the generator. Because there are twice as many shift register states (1st column) as there are polynomial generator output values (column 2), each polynomial value is representative of two input states; each value in the second column appears in two places. It may be ambiguous to a receiver which of the two 4-bit input states of the shift register is represented by a certain 3-bit output. This possible ambiguity is relieved by the fact that it is not only the current polynomial generator output value, but the sequence of polynomial generator output values preceding the current one that indicates the value of the current bit in the input vector.

Current state is		If next bit is 0		If next bit is 1	
Register	**Output $\underline{G}_0$**	**Register becomes**	**Output $\underline{G}_1$**	**Register becomes**	**Output $\underline{G}_1$**
Column 1	Column 2	Column 3	Column 4	Column 5	Column 6
$s_0, m1_0, m2_0, m3_0$	$g1_0, g2_0, g3_0$	$0, m1_1, m2_1, m3_1$	$g1_1, g2_1, g3_1$	$1, m1_1, m2_1, m3_1$	$g1_1, g2_1, g3_1$
a,b,c,d,e 0000	000	0000	a_0,b_0,c_0,d_0 000	1000	a_1,b_1,c_1,d_1 111
e 0001	110				
d 0010	011	0001	d_0 110	1001	d_1 001
e 0011	101				
c 0100	001	0010	c_0 011	1010	c_1 100
e 0101	111				
d 0110	010	0011	d_0 101	1011	d_1 010
e 0111	100				
b 1000	111	0100	b_0 001	1100	b_1 110
e 1001	001				
d 1010	100	0101	d_0 111	1101	d_1 000
e 1011	010				
d 1100	110	0110	c_0 010	1110	c_1 101
e 1101	000				
d 1110	101	0111	d_0 100	1111	d_1 011
e 1111	011				
Step 1 – Start at initial state a. in this column	Step 2 – Output shown in this column	Step 3 – If next input is 0, this is new state	Step 4 – if next input is 0, this is new output	Step 3 – If next input is 1, this is new state	Step 4 – if next input is 1, this is new output
Step 6 – Repeat Steps 3–6 until all input bits are encoded		Step 5 – look for this state and output pair in columns 1 and 2. The letter designation here (e.g., "d") will increment upon returning to column 1 (e.g., "e")		Step 5 – look for this state and output pair in columns 1 and 2. The letter designation here (e.g. "d") will increment upon returning to column 1 (e.g., "e")	
Outputs based on adder kernel/polynomials 1001, 1011, 1110 Letters a–e mark recursive paths through the table. See text.					

Table 5.10 Sequential Outputs for a K = 4, rate 1/3 Polynomial Generator

Table 5.10 can be used to follow a sequence of bits in the input vector. Starting with the current state in column 1, anticipate the next clock cycle, in which the register shifts its contents to the right and introduces the next data bit to the generator. Look to column 3 for a new state with the input bit of value 0. Look to column 5 for a new state with the input bit of value 1. The adjacent columns, 4 and 6, show the output of the generator for the corresponding states in 3 and 5.

The general impression Table 5.10 should make is the fact that each new input bit is mapped to one of $2^n = 8$ output words depending on the history contained in the generator's memory. For instance, if the generator were initialized at 0000 (column 1), its initial output state would be 000 (column 2). Applying the first bit of the input data to the generator, which of course is either a one or a zero, only two of the eight output states are possible. Table 5.10 (columns 4 and 6) show that the next output state of this polynomial generator will be either 000 or 111, depending on the value of the new input bit.

Following the trail of any series of input bits, the letter "a" in the left column is the starting point. With the addition of a 0 or a 1 as the next bit in the input vector, the new register value is given as 0000 (column 3) or 1000 (column 5). The corresponding output of the generator is shown in the fourth and sixth columns of the same row, as marked with a_0 (000) or a_1 (111). Once these output values are recorded, it is time to move to step b.

To prepare for processing the next input bit, the new register value in column 3 or 5 (0000 or 1000) is then looked up in the first column, and marked with a "b". The new input bit is applied (column 3 or 5) resulting in output b_0 or b_1. There were two possible a outputs, and now four possible b outputs. Recording the selected b output, it is time to return to the first column and find the register state corresponding with that in column 3 or 5 of the selected b output. These four states are marked by the letter "c" in the first column. As each choice is made, a branch in the possible paths occurs. For illustration, the recursion through the table stops at the beginning of step "e", at which point all possible branches have been connected from the starting value. The recursion of an input vector may continue indefinitely, until all bits of the input vector have been fully flushed through the registers. All polynomial generator outputs are dependent on which of the sixteen states of column 1 is the current state.

A Diagram Is Worth a Thousand Words

There are several ways to show the behavior of a convolutional encoder, among which is the popular trellis diagram. Scuba divers familiar with reading repetitive dive tables may quickly grasp the recursive nature of Table 5.10; however the table is not intuitively parsed. Instead, Figure 5.17 presents the situation graphically with a trellis. Where Table 5.10 uses the letters a-e to illustrate the branching paths of the encoder, Figure 5.17 shows the branching as a map.

Figure 5.17 creates a visual interpretation of the relationship between the polynomial generator output and the possible series of input bits from the input vector. In Figure 5.17, the vertical axis represents the $2^K = 16$ polynomial generator states, and shows the corresponding $2^n = 8$ possible three-bit outputs of the polynomial generator for each state. Each output value appears twice in this version of a trellis diagram because there are twice as many generator states as output bits.

Starting from the reference point in the upper left, the trellis maps a sequence of input bits by following a unique path through the trellis. From a single starting point, the number of valid possible paths is determined by the fact that there is a simple binary branch at each step of the input clock (horizontally). Considering the first N bits of the input vector, there will be 2^N possible valid paths on the trellis. In, say, four steps, there are 2^4 possible valid paths. In contrast, if the received sequence were fully compromised by noise, there would be no correlation between the current state of the register (with corresponding output bit) and the next states in time. In such a random environment, there would be n^N possible sequences; in this case that is 8^4 possible paths, both valid and invalid.

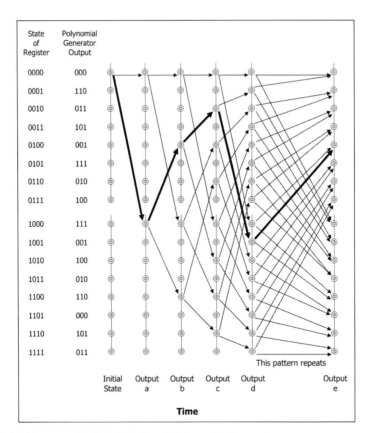

Figure 5.17 Trellis Diagram of a Rate 1/3, K = 4 Polynomial Generator

Because of the manner in which the valid paths are spread among all possible path combinations, convolutional coding is most effective as protection against random errors, or as it is put more technically, most effective in an AWGN environment (additive white Gaussian noise). The use of interleaving, careful spectral assignment of information, and other methods, including iBiquity's patented complementary pattern-mapped coding, helps overcome non-noise-like impairments by spreading the impairments across the received data in a manner that is more white noise-like and conducive to decoding.

In the receiver, a maximum likelihood decoder takes advantage of the fact that there are significantly fewer valid trellis paths than there are possible received paths, seeking the most likely valid path in the presence of erroneous information. The decoder can correct a quantity of errors by making a mathematical determination as to which valid path is closest to the received path. This technique was pioneered by A. J. Viterbi as presented in "Error Bounds for Convolutional Codes and an Asymptotically Optimum Decoding Algorithm," *IEEE Transactions on Information Theory*, vol. IT-13, April, 1967, pp. 260–269. Numerous refinements and enhancement have been contributed by others since then.

This section on convolutional encoding provides a superficial conceptual introduction. For more in-depth discussion of decoding techniques, readers might start by looking into coding-related terms such as Viterbi decoding, trellis, Hamming distance, free distance/Euclidian distance, soft and hard decision. The iBiquity patent, number 7043681, *Digital audio broadcasting method and apparatus using complementary pattern-mapped convolutional codes*, contains in its Background of the Invention section an overview of the strengths and weaknesses of traditional convolutional encoding techniques in the IBOC environment that led to this coding invention for AM IBOC.

Inferring Polynomial Generator State from Output Value

The path marked with bold arrows in Figure 5.17 is the result of the input vector 10010. The input value 1 is indicated by downward movement of the path (or the path stays at the bottom of the trellis). Upward movement (or horizontal movement at the top) represents a 0 input value. For instance, in the right column, the upward arrow ends at the row with the polynomial generator input 0100. The left digit, 0, in the polynomial generator is the current input bit. The output of the polynomial generator, 001, is transmitted.

A receiver decoding the 001 value in the fifth row of the right-hand column has limited choices for interpreting the value. That point shows two possible predecessor states, indicated by the two incoming arrows from the left. One is our intended value (bold arrow) which began at the output value 001 representing register state 1001. Because there are half a many output words as there are generator states, the output value 001 appears in the tenth row as well as the fifth row.

This walk through one step of the trellis shows that, with only two successive correct output words, one can infer the current state of the polynomial generator. Knowing the state of the polynomial generator at any given time reduces the possible valid paths from that point by half.

Puncturing

One wrinkle in the simplicity of the encoding technique is the puncturing to reduce the information redundancy slightly. Recall that the puncturing of the rate 1/3 encoder eliminates an output every other cycle to produce a rate 2/5—five output bits for each two input bits. In the trellis diagram, one bit is eliminated in the output word in every other column. The resulting pattern is shown in Figure 5.18.

In the odd columns there are eight possible output words for sixteen register states. In the even, punctured, columns the ambiguity increases with four output words for the sixteen states. The valid paths depicted in Figure 5.17 remain the same with the punctured code in Figure 5.18. While there is one bit less every other output cycle, there is still information allowing the decoder to seek the most likely valid path in the presence of errors.

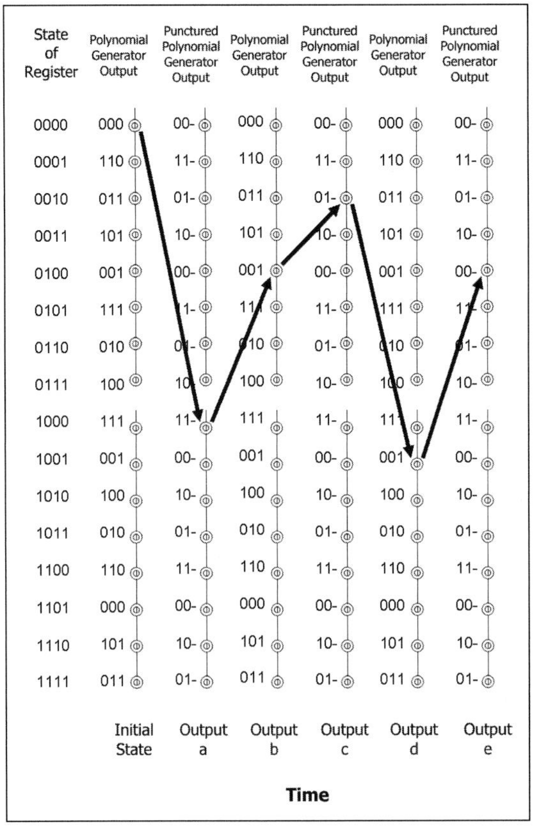

State of Register	Polynomial Generator Output	Punctured Polynomial Generator Output	Polynomial Generator Output	Punctured Polynomial Generator Output	Polynomial Generator Output	Punctured Polynomial Generator Output	Polynomial Generator Output	Punctured Polynomial Generator Output
0000	000	00-	000	00-	000	00-		
0001	110	11-	110	11-	110	11-		
0010	011	01-	011	01-	011	01-		
0011	101	10-	101	10-	101	10-		
0100	001	00-	001	00-	001	00-		
0101	111	11-	111	11-	111	11-		
0110	010	01-	010	01-	010	01-		
0111	100	10-	100	10-	100	10-		
1000	111	11-	111	11-	111	11-		
1001	001	00-	001	00-	001	00-		
1010	100	10-	100	10-	100	10-		
1011	010	01-	010	01-	010	01-		
1100	110	11-	110	11-	110	11-		
1101	000	00-	000	00-	000	00-		
1110	101	10-	101	10-	101	10-		
1111	011	01-	011	01-	011	01-		

Initial State / Output a / Output b / Output c / Output d / Output e

Time

Figure 5.18 Trellis Diagram with Punctured Rate 2/5 Encoding

The convolutional encoder spreads each information bit out in time to increase its resistance to error. Convolution accomplishes this by spreading each bit through a filter with a known impulse response—the polynomial generator. Under perfect channel conditions the coding is unnecessary. Under the anticipated channel conditions the bandwidth overhead required to carry the additional coded bits is counterbalanced by the power of the coding technique, resulting in a net gain in efficiency of the system.

Once the Logical Channels are encoded, they are ready for the next step, interleaving.

Interleaving

The role of scrambling was to pseudo-randomize the bitstream, while the role of convolutional encoding was to add error protection against a noisy channel. Interleaving is intended to complement the convolutional encoding by handling another common channel impairment, bursty noise. Interleaving takes the sequential output of the convolutional encoder and places it out of sequence in the transmission frame.

This is a transmitted message without interleaving and with a noise burst in the middle represented by the "#" symbol:

```
bytes_are_####t_in_time
```

Here is the message with every 5th character interleaved, then transmitted and exposed to the noise burst:

```
b_s_itrlne####yapimeei_
```

Here is the de-interleaved message, with the noise burst spread across the message.

```
b#te#_are#split_in_#ime
```

It is easier to infer what the correct message is when the interleaver has distributed the burst's damage across the message.

Interleaving serves to disperse a concentrated burst of noise whose duration is a fraction of the 1.49-second transmission frame into lower level background noise across the data in the frame or a portion of the frame. (One exception is the FM Logical Channel P3, which optionally can be interleaved across two frames.) Interleaving helps the convolutional encoder because it is better able to recover from a larger number of small errors in the data stream than from a single large burst, which could leave a large uncorrectable hole in the data.

The Layer 1 reference documents contain algorithms for interleaving the bits of the encoded PDUs—see section 10 of both Layer 1 reference documents, 1 and 2. Interleaving is performed across the entire frame for those PDUs transmitted one frame at a time. Some Logical Channels convey PDUs in blocks or block pairs, with multiple blocks per frame. The interleavers for these PDUs interleave the information within the bounds of the blocks or block pairs. Blocks are subdivisions of the 1.49-second transmission frame. Upon reception, information that was scrambled, encoded, and interleaved over the entire frame must be buffered for the duration of the frame before it can be processed. Information that is processed on a block-wise basis can be recovered in the receiver block by block without waiting for the entire frame to buffer. Block-wise processing provides faster access to program audio and data at the expense of robustness.

The interleavers also function to combine and/or divide the incoming Logical Channels into new Logical Channels that are ready for mapping onto the OFDM spectrum. IBOC interleavers, therefore, not only perform a time-spreading function within the frame or block, but also prepare the information for frequency diversity on the OFDM spectrum.

Input to the interleavers is described in the form of vectors whose length are those of the PDUs passed from the encoding process above. Output is described in matrix form. Matrices are employed to facilitate mapping the information directly to the OFDM subcarriers. The AM hybrid interleavers produce matrices that are 25 columns wide, one matrix each for the upper Primary subcarriers, lower Primary subcarriers, Secondary subcarriers, and Tertiary subcarriers. Each column maps to one OFDM subcarrier, such that each row represents one OFDM symbol period. The entire matrix represents one 1.49-second frame period with the number of symbols per frame corresponding to the number of rows of the matrix.

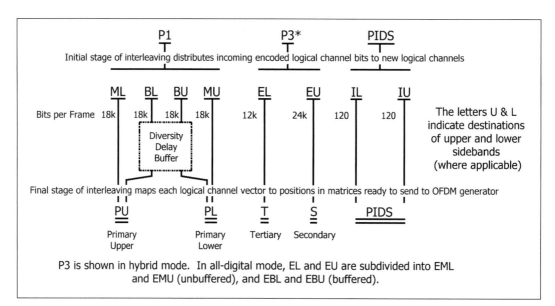

Figure 5.19 AM IBOC Interleavers and Logical Channels

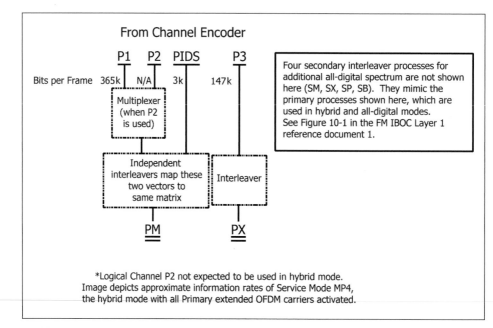

Figure 5.20 FM IBOC Interleavers and Logical Channels

Likewise, the FM interleavers produce matrices that have columns corresponding to the OFDM subcarriers. FM IBOC primarily utilizes QPSK modulation, with two bits per symbol. Each column in the FM interleaver matrices represents one bit; thus there will be two columns for each QPSK subcarrier. (See Figures 5.21 and 5.22.) In contrast, the AM interleavers store "elements" containing more than one bit. In this way, each matrix column maps to a specific subcarrier. AM IBOC primarily utilizes a combination of 64 QAM, 16 QAM, and QPSK modulation of the OFDM subcarriers. Six-bit elements go in matrices corresponding to 64 QAM subcarriers; four-bit for 16 QAM; two-bit for QPSK.

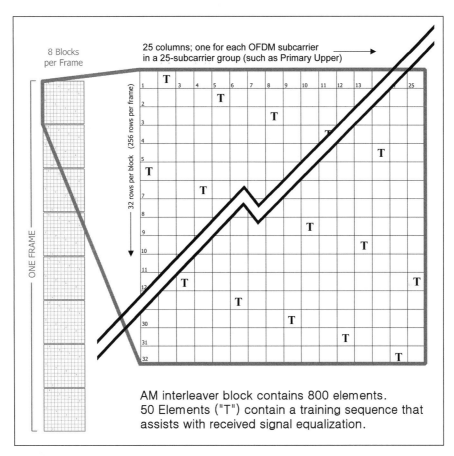

Figure 5.21 Structure of AM Interleaver Matrix

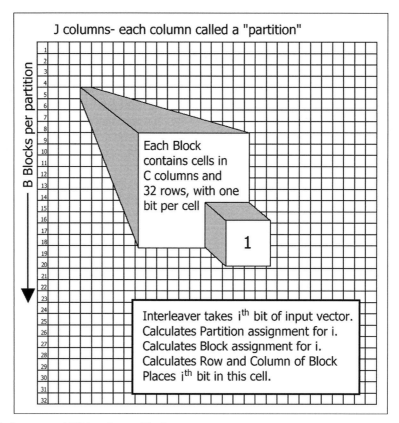

Figure 5.22 Structure of FM Interleaver Matrix

The FM Primary Main interleaver, for example, has J = 20 partitions, B = 16 blocks, C = 36 columns per block, and 32 rows per block. The total capacity of the PM matrix is J·C·B·32 = 368640 bits per frame. Figure 5.20 shows that PM is stuffed with the output of two interleavers. Recall that the size of the hybrid mode P1 vector entering its interleaver is 365440 bits. The interleaver output to PM is the same size. That leaves room in PM for 3200 PIDS bits to be inserted by the PIDS interleaver (365440 + 3200 = 368640). In a single frame there are sixteen blocks of 200 PIDS bits. Each block is separately interleaved and inserted in a portion of the available space in the PM matrix.

Where scrambling and convolutional coding are executed quickly, requiring buffers only as large as the depth of the shift register polynomial, interleaving requires a buffer that is as large as the size of the frame or block over which the interleaving occurs. Thus, the processing delay of the interleaving process is substantially greater than that of scrambling or convolutional coding. The latency of a full-frame interleaver, such as the 365440-bit PM interleaver, is sixteen times that of the PIDS interleaver, which operates in one block at a time.

AM interleaving adds a time diversity element. The AM interleaving process, like the FM process, provides the interleaved time-spreading within the frame or block and sets up the matrices for frequency diversity across the OFDM spectra. Unlike the FM interleaving process, the AM process also divides the interleaved data stream and delays a portion of it. While interleaving within the frame or block "spreads" the data in time by smearing sequential bits throughout the duration of the frame or block, the delay buffer shown in Figure 5.19 withholds bits across the frame boundary. The diversity delay time, T_{dd}, is specified as three frames, a duration of about four and a half seconds. The P1 vector, which carries the AM core audio, is divided in half, with one half directed to the interleaver buffers. This delay improves the robustness of the core audio against long fades.

Layer 1 Continues

This chapter addressed the multiplexing function of Layer 2 and the first three processes in Layer 1—scrambling, encoding, and interleaving. The interleaving process sets the scene for generation of the OFDM subcarriers. Where this chapter has focused primarily on the features common to AM and FM IBOC, the next chapter highlights the unique characteristics of each system.

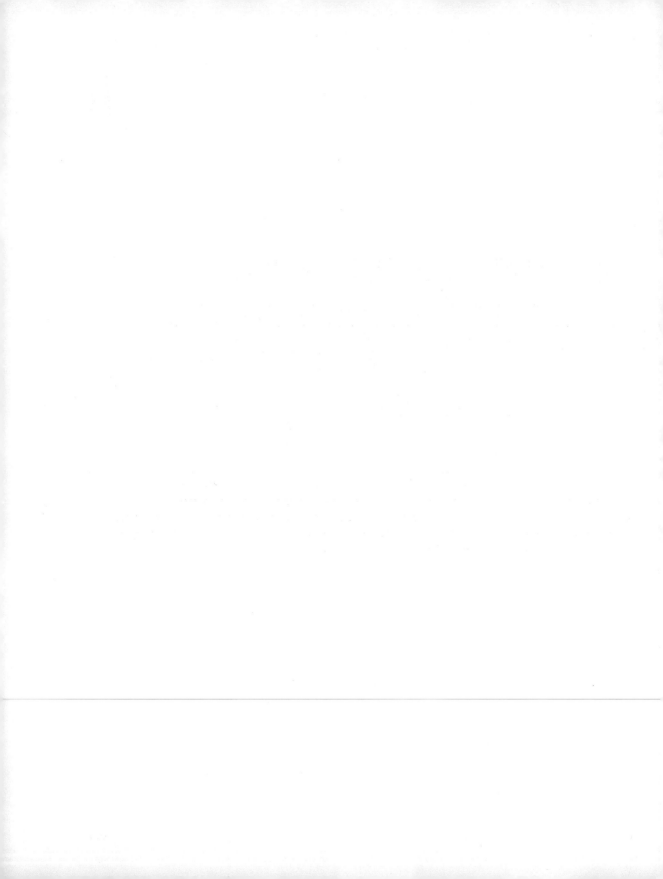

6 From the Top Down: Layer 1–Populating the OFDM Waveform with Information

Layer 1 sits at the bottom of the IBOC protocol stack. On the transmission side, all information must go through this layer to get on the air. Program audio, data services, station information, and system control information are funneled through this layer. On the reception side, the Layer 1 protocol informs the design of the receiver. This is the layer in which the electrical characteristics of the received signal are converted to matrices and vectors of structured information. Layer 1 lets the receiver make sense out of the IBOC radio spectrum.

NRSC-5 Reference Document Number	Reference Document Title	NRSC-5 Reference Document Number	Reference Document Title
1.	Doc. No. SY_IDD_1011s rev. E HD Radio™ Air Interface Design Description **Layer 1 FM** iBiquity Digital Corporation, 3/22/05	6.	Doc. No. SY_SSS_1026s rev. D HD Radio™ FM Transmission System Specifications iBiquity Digital Corporation, 2/18/05
2.	Doc. No. SY_IDD_1012s rev. E HD Radio™ Air Interface Design Description **Layer 1 AM** iBiquity Digital Corporation, 3/22/05	7.	Doc. No. SY_IDD_1028s rev. C HD Radio™ Air Interface Design Description Program Service Data iBiquity Digital Corporation, 3/31/05
3.	Doc. No. SY_IDD_1014s rev. F HD Radio™ Air Interface Design Description Layer 2 Channel Multiplex Protocol iBiquity Digital Corporation, 2/7/05	8.	Doc. No. SY_SSS_1082s rev. D HD Radio™ AM Transmission System Specifications iBiquity Digital Corporation, 2/24/05
4.	Doc. No. SY_IDD_1017s rev. E HD Radio™ Air Interface Design Description Audio Transport iBiquity Digital Corporation, 3/31/05	9.	Doc. No. SY_IDD_1085s rev. C HD Radio™ Air Interface Design Description Program Service Data Transport iBiquity Digital Corporation, 2/7/05
5.	Doc. No. SY_IDD_1020s rev. E HD Radio™ Air Interface Design Description Station Information Service Protocol iBiquity Digital Corporation, 2/18/05	10.	Doc. No. SY_IDD_1019s rev. E HD Radio™ Air Interface Design Description Advanced Application Services Transport iBiquity Digital Corporation, 8/4/05

Table 6.1 Protocols Addressed in Chapter 6

This chapter explores the structure of the OFDM signals of AM and FM IBOC, and explains the System Control functions that form the IBOC skeletal system. The previous chapter delved deeply into workings of Layer 1, addressing the upper level subsystems—scrambling, channel encoding, and interleaving. It was shown how the interleaving process sets the information up in matrices that are ready for mapping to the OFDM subcarriers. This chapter picks up at this point, drilling into the basement of the IBOC protocol stack. This lowest level of the logical structure of Layer 1 is discussed, leaving the spectral and electrical characteristics of the IBOC signal to Chapters 7, 8 and 9.

For starters, the structure of Layer 1 is reviewed in depth. The information flow, in the form of data vectors and matrices, is related to the Logical Channels and Layer 1 processes. Information cannot flow without an effective system control structure. The role of the System Control Channel is explained.

This chapter continues with a look at the time domain characteristics of the logical structure. The fundamental role of the 44.1 kSa/s audio sampling rate is explored. Each frame and block of data is pumped through the IBOC channel at their respective rates. Layer 1 manages analog and digital diversity delay, which are discussed along with the latencies of the system. An introduction to the smallest time element of the logical structure, the symbol, is given.

As the logical structure has time domain components, the IBOC signal must convey information that allows the receiver to synchronize to the data flow. This chapter explains the role of Layer 1 in providing the basics in the form of differentially encoded Reference Subcarriers with synchronization sequences. Each frame's reference to Universal Time is described.

Layer 1 also communicates to the receiver the structural characteristics of the transmitted IBOC signal. This chapter focuses on the logical side, in which structural information is transmitted as the Service Mode, indicating which OFDM subcarrier groups and corresponding Logical Channels are active. Electrical characteristics are reserved for the next chapters. Finally, the role of backward compatibility is addressed. The Service Modes are designed for future improvements, while maintaining at least basic functionality of existing receivers.

Layer 1 Structure

Figures 6.1 and 6.2 are the NRSC-5 block diagrams of Layer 1 for AM and FM. Consistent with the fact that NRSC-5 is primarily a transmission standard, the information flow through the diagrams is from the top down, toward the ultimate transmission of the radio signal. Each processing stage is represented as a block with a functional label. Between each stage are indications of the Logical Channels through which information is conveyed. One- to four-character labels indicate Logical Channels with a single underscore for vectors and double underscore for matrices. The previous chapter introduced the role of Logical Channels and the function of vectors and matrices in maintaining orderly description and processing of the information.

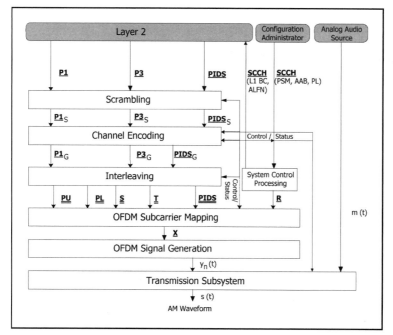

Figure 6.1 AM Layer 1 (Source: NRSC-5-A)

Because of the AM IBOC system's narrow bandwidth, the Logical Channel structure is fairly flat. When converting from hybrid to all-digital modes, the Logical Channel Structure remains intact while the OFDM spectrum is restructured. Vectors P1 (carries core audio and Program Service Data), P3 (enhanced audio), and PIDS (carries Station Information Service data) represent the three logical channels used in hybrid and all-digital modes. As discussed in the previous chapter and shown in Figure 6.1, the information in these Logical Channels flows through the upper process of Layer 1 until the interleaver processes reorganize the flow into Logical Channels better suited to populating the OFDM waveform. The subscript, such as $P1_s$, indicates a vector that has completed a Layer 1 process—"S" for scrambling and " G" for channel encoding.

Once through the interleaver, the information is organized in matrices whose rows represent the contents of one OFDM symbol and whose columns represent the particular OFDM subcarrier to which the information is assigned. An entire matrix contains enough information to last for an entire 1.49-second frame. Figure 6.3 illustrates how each frame is divided into blocks, and each block contains vectors of data, in which each vector is employed to create a set of OFDM subcarriers lasting for one symbol period. Each vector of data contains bits belonging to Logical Channels P1, P3, and PIDS. Additional processing of primary, secondary, and tertiary matrices is performed prior to OFDM subcarrier mapping. The creation of these final matrices is depicted in Figure 5.19. This step divides the data into various upper and lower sideband groupings.

One row of all of the matrices is peeled off to form the OFDM symbol vector $\underline{X}$. $\underline{X}$ then contains the information necessary to modulate each OFDM subcarrier for one symbol period. As that symbol is transmitted, the next row on the matrices is formed into a new vector $\underline{X}$ ready for conversion into the next OFDM symbol. This continues until all rows of the matrices are exhausted, indicating the end of the frame. The next frame's matrices are brought down from the interleaver for processing in the same fashion, and so on.

The generation of the actual OFDM waveform at the OFDM Signal Generation block is a function, $y_n(t)$, that modulates the nth OFDM subcarrier over a period of time (t) based on the nth element in the vector $\underline{X}$. More on the OFDM waveform math appears in the next chapter. At this point just recognize that OFDM Signal Generation is where strings of ones and zeros are converted to analog electrical signals.

System Control

To the right of the Logical Channels in Figure 6.1 are the System Control Channel (SCCH) paths. Two fundamental types of information are carried on the SCCH. First, the station's desired settings must be communicated to the protocol stack, including Layer 1. Three facts to be communicated are identified as PSM (Primary Service Mode), AAB (Analog Audio Bandwidth) and PL (Power Level). These are settings of the AM IBOC system that inform Layer 1 how it is expected to operate. They also are transmitted so receivers know what to expect. Let us call SCCH information of this type "static" because it is set and does not change until the operator intervenes.

Protocol Versus Implementation

The role of a standard is to provide a description of how a system works, independent of any particular hardware or software implementation. A person skilled in the art should be able to use the information in the standard to build a system from scratch. That system, by virtue of following the standard, should be compatible with devices employed by other implementers of the same standard.

Being a transmission standard, NRSC-5 is primarily concerned about the inputs and output at each end of the protocol stack: digitally coded audio and data as inputs, radio signal as output. A transmission system built to the standard should produce a waveform that any receiver built to the standard can receive and demodulate.

NRSC-5 does not prescribe how the internal workings of a device should function. Some features described in the standard, such as the Configuration Administrator and System Control Channel (SCCH), are not required structures; they are merely logical representations of control and status information that must be passed among layers to enable each layer to perform its tasks. For instance, an actual "control channel" may not be evident in the architecture of a transmitter, but the control functions it represents are implemented in some fashion.

If operator-set SCCH information can be considered static, then let us use the term "dynamic" to describe information that is passed between layers of the protocol stack to maintain the flow. In Figure 6.1 the AM SCCH shows two dynamic values are communicated between Layer 1 and Layer 2—L1 BC (Layer 1 Block Count) and ALFN (Absolute Layer 1 Frame Number). This information synchronizes Layer 2 to Layer 1, providing Layer 2 what are in effect the current time and the rate at which to clock information through to Layer 1.

The static and dynamic elements of SCCH are discussed in more detail later in this chapter.

Like the NRSC-5 AM Layer 1 diagram (Figure 6.1), the FM diagram (Figure 6.2) shows the Logical Channels flowing through functional blocks that are supported on the side by the interchange of SCCH information. Also similar to the AM diagram, the FM Logical Channel vectors input to the Interleavers come out regrouped into matrices bearing new Logical Channel names. Again, these matrices are stepped through the OFDM Subcarrier Mapping stage to produce a series of OFDM symbol vectors $\underline{X}$. Each vector $\underline{X}$ is passed to the OFDM Signal Generation task to be transformed from bits to phase and amplitude components.

FM IBOC Layer 1 differs slightly from AM. Where AM uses only the Primary Logical Channel designation in both the hybrid and all-digital modes, FM all-digital mode retains the Primary designation used in hybrid mode and adds Secondary OFDM energy. A menagerie of Secondary Logical Channels beginning with the letter "S" appears in the FM IBOC Layer 1 diagram. When the spectral structure is discussed later on, the location of these Secondary Logical Channels in all-digital mode will be explored.

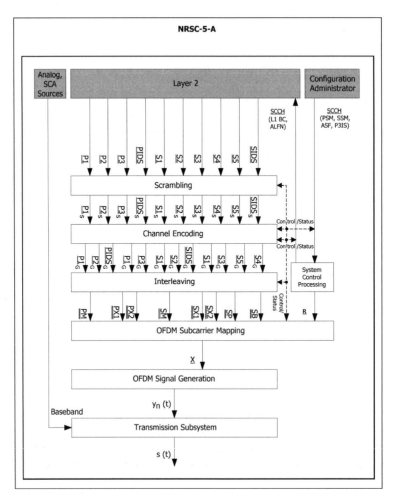

Figure 6.2 FM Layer 1 (From NRSC-5-A with permission)

FM IBOC conveys the same dynamic SCCH information to Layer 2 as the AM does—block counts and frame numbers. The one static value used by both the AM and FM IBOC systems is the Primary Service Mode. This informs Layer 1 how the Primary Logical Channels are employed. FM IBOC has 6 defined Primary Service Modes, MP1–MP6, with future expansion capability to 64. In contrast, AM has two, MP1 and MP3.

Unlike AM IBOC, FM does not adjust analog audio bandwidth (AAB) and does not have a two-position OFDM power switch (PL). Instead, FM IBOC has Secondary Service Mode settings when in all-digital mode, and has the ability to set Secondary OFDM subcarriers to one of four amplitudes. These appear on Figure 6.2 as SSM (Secondary Service Mode) and ASF (Amplitude Scale Factor). The other SCCH information is an optional increase in interleaver depth on the

Primary Extended (PX) subcarriers identified as P3IS (P3 Interleaver Select). This increases the robustness of PX information by interleaving it across two frames' duration.

Finally, the vector $\underline{R}$ appears in both figures (6.1 and 6.2). This is information that is mapped to specialized OFDM subcarriers, the Reference Subcarriers. The information on Reference Subcarriers provides basic structural information about the IBOC signal by indicating the Service Modes to the receiver. Reference Subcarriers also provide synchronization patterns to assist the receiver in locking onto the block and frame sequence. With its limited bandwidth, AM IBOC has two Reference Subcarriers to convey to the receiver critical information necessary to lock onto and parse the IBOC signal. The FM IBOC system employs 30 Reference Subcarriers in hybrid mode and 61 in all-digital. In addition to the timing and structural information these Reference Subcarriers provide, the large number of Reference Subcarriers distributed across the FM IBOC channel allows a receiver to use them to equalize distortions across the channel. The spectral characteristics of these carriers are discussed in the next chapters.

IBOC in the Time Domain

The structure of the IBOC information stream was determined by a number of constraints. In Chapter 4 the imposition of a framing structure on the coded audio was discussed. The 44.1 kSa/s base audio sampling rate is a constraint on the IBOC information flow. Also, the available bandwidth in the AM and FM bands, the characteristics of short and long term channel impairments, and the nature of expected signal to noise and interference ratio, are considerations in designing the structure of the information flow.

Units			Time Duration in Seconds		Rate Units per Second		Units per Frame
FM IBOC							
Frame	T_f	$512\ T_s$	$\frac{65536}{44100}$	1.49	R_f	0.67	1
Block pair	T_p	$64\ T_s$		0.19	R_p	5.4	8
Block	T_b	$32\ T_s$		0.1	R_b	10.8	16
Symbol	T_s	$(1+\alpha)\cdot\frac{1}{\Delta f}$	$\frac{135}{128}\cdot\frac{4096}{1488375}$	$\frac{1}{344.5}$	R_s	344.5	512
AM IBOC							
Frame	T_f	$256\ T_s$	$\frac{65536}{44100}$	1.49	R_f	0.67	1
Block	T_b	$32\ T_s$		0.19	R_b	5.4	8
Symbol	T_s	$(1+\alpha)\cdot\frac{1}{\Delta f}$	$\frac{135}{128}\cdot\frac{8192}{1488375}$	$\frac{1}{172.3}$	R_s	172.3	256

Table 6.2 IBOC Timing Structure

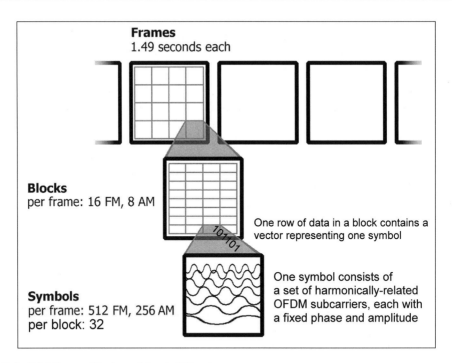

Frames
1.49 seconds each

Blocks
per frame: 16 FM, 8 AM

One row of data in a block contains a
vector representing one symbol

Symbols
per frame: 512 FM, 256 AM
per block: 32

One symbol consists of
a set of harmonically-related
OFDM subcarriers, each with
a fixed phase and amplitude

Figure 6.3 IBOC Frame, Block, and Symbol Structure

Audio Sampling Rate Implications

As mentioned in Chapter 4, IBOC-delivered encoded digital audio is not transmitted on IBOC at
44.1 kSa/s because the encoding is a perceptual compression scheme with a variable packet size.
However, to maintain synchronization between the source audio at 44.1 kSa/s and the receiver-
played audio at the same rate, it helps to maintain a frame rate that is proportional to the audio
sampling rate. A discrete number of audio samples is processed by the audio encoder (and decoder)
for each variable-size packet. While the system can tolerate brief delays in the transport of larger
than normal audio packets, ultimately the average rate of audio packet delivery must correspond
to the audio sampling rate.

Table 6.2 shows the timing and rates of the key components of the IBOC information stream.
Note how the frame duration T_f is defined by a rational number whose denominator is 44,100.
The frame rate R_f is therefore proportional to 44.1 kHz. This is perhaps the first constraint in the
design of the IBOC information flow.

Frame and Block Duration

The duration of a frame is chosen to allow the interleaver to handle likely channel impairments
while avoiding excessive latency required by buffering and processing the frame on both the transmission and reception sides of the system. iBiquity settled on the nearly one-and-a-half-second

frame duration as the optimum for both the AM and FM IBOC systems. Bursty channel impairments are likely to be relatively short compared to the frame duration, enabling interleaving to distribute the burst noise across the frame of information.

Some information is intended to be received and processed faster than at the frame rate. For this information, the block rate R_b, or block pair rate R_p, is employed to reduce latency. System Control Channel (SCCH) information is conveyed on the Reference Subcarriers at block rates to enable receivers to lock onto the signal rapidly. The Station Information Service (SIS) is carried on the PIDS and SIDS logical channels at block rates. This enables the receiver to acquire rapidly the key information about the station. Core audio on AM IBOC is transmitted at block rates. Some FM IBOC modes transmit core audio at block pair rates. This helps receivers acquire (and reacquire upon interruption) audio more quickly than is possible with the usually more robust frame-by-frame audio information.

Latency

According to the Layer 1 reference documents, in the IBOC system latency is the inherent delay in transmission of a PDU resulting from the interleaver depth and any diversity delay applied to the information. The term "latency" does not officially describe the processing delays that occur as information is manipulated and transferred within and among layers. For instance the (very short) time required to scramble and convolutionally encode an information stream is a delay that is not latency. While latency is a fixed value implicit in the definitions of the logical channels, other delays may vary among various implementations of transmitter (or receiver).

There are six latencies in the IBOC system: block (T_b), block pair (T_p), frame (T_f), frame pair $(2 \cdot T_f)$, and diversity delay (T_{dd}) added either to T_p or T_f. Information interleaved across an entire frame has latency equal to the frame duration T_f. The framewise interleaver must have processed a full 1.49 seconds of information before the frame can be passed to OFDM generation. The blockwise interleaver, meanwhile, only must accumulate the information intended for one block, latency T_b, before interleaving it into the correct block area of the frame. Then it accumulates the information for the next block, interleaving it into the next block region of the frame, and so on. For transmission, all blocks (8 AM or 16 FM) must be interleaved into their spaces in the frame, one at a time, along with the framewise data.

Once the frame is full of information from interleavers for all logical channels, the trigger is pulled, sending it to OFDM generation and transmission. However, upon reception, as soon as the first block of information comes through (a partial frame) the blockwise logical channels can be de-interleaved and processed. The framewise information must be accumulated in a buffer until the entire frame has been received. The system designer must take latencies into account to ensure related information on different logical channels arrives at the expected times.

Diversity Delay

In addition to the realizing the benefits of interleaving information across the duration of one frame, block, or block pair, the IBOC system employs diversity delay techniques to improve the robustness of some Logical Channels. Diversity delay is the method of transmitting a delayed copy of the current information being transmitted. This provides a degree of time diversity that spans beyond the frame boundary. For instance, it might take at least one and a half seconds for an AM receiver in a car to pass under a grounded conductive structure (e.g., an overpass). The duration of the information loss might exceed the capability of the interleaver and convolutional decoder to recover. In this instance, a diversity delay capability may be the only remaining means of maintaining an intelligible program.

The Layer 1 Reference Documents define T_{dd} as the diversity delay time of a delayed Logical Channel. Diversity delay time is a whole number of frames, 3, resulting in an approximately 4.5-second diversity delay between undelayed and delayed Logical Channels.

AM Time Diversity

AM hybrid operations apply diversity delay time T_{dd} to half of the core audio signal by delaying half of the information carried on the P1 logical channel (Figure 6.4). In all-digital mode, the AM IBOC system also applies diversity delay in the same manner to the enhanced audio data stream on P3.

The AM diversity delay method is reflected in an iBiquity patent, U.S. patent number 7043681, *Digital audio broadcasting method and apparatus using complementary pattern-mapped convolutional codes.* This method gives AM IBOC flexibility to resist two types of channel impairments—longer fades and adjacent channel interference. Figure 6.4 shows the encoded data is divided into four components. The upper and lower Primary sidebands carry half of the information each. Meanwhile each sideband is half populated by undelayed data and half by delayed data. The patent refers to the delayed data as backup data.

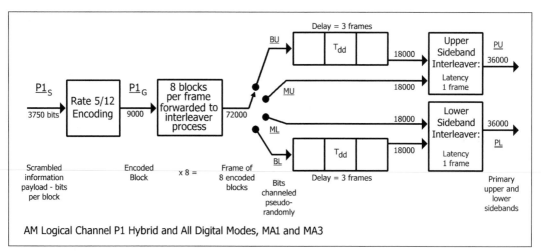

Figure 6.4 Information Flow on AM Logical Channel P1

Counting PU or PL Data Bits in the Frame

As a quick thought exercise to test our understanding of the relationship between Logical Channel PU (or PL) and the OFDM spectrum, consider this. There are 25 OFDM subcarriers in each Primary sideband. They are modulated 64 QAM (6 bits per subcarrier symbol), and there are 256 symbols in a 1.49-second frame. Multiplying the three, the OFDM frame transmits 38,400 bits on PU (or PL). Note in Figure 6.4 that Logical Channel PU (or PL)only conveys 36,000 bits. It turns out that for every 16 bits in each symbol, one is a "training bit." These bits (transmitted in groups of six bits called elements) are a predetermined pattern of bits for which the receiver can search as it reads the incoming symbols. Since the receiver knows what the training pattern is, it can correct for errors in the training pattern by applying equalization to the signal. With the signal equalized, the desired information on the Logical Channels will be significantly more reliable. Taking 15/16 of the 38,400-bit frame yields the 36,000-bit PU (or PL) payload.

If the channel is compromised by a long fade or noise event, the time diversity data provided by the backup vectors BL and BU contain enough data from which to recover the program service. Alternatively, if half the channel is compromised by an adjacent channel interferer, the combination of the one undelayed and one delayed component on the good sideband contains enough data to recover the program service. For example, with an upper adjacent interferer, the main and backup vectors on the lower sideband, ML and BL, are combined to recover the program. Of course, in either scenario half of the data is compromised or unusable, thus lessening the robustness of the data from the recovered vector pair.

Early HD Radio receivers would select all four matrices (ML, MU, BL and BU) in a complementary mode discussed further in Chapter 8, or switch to selecting the best sideband (ML and BL, or MU and BU), an independent sideband mode, depending on which method is performing best. Later HD Radio receiver versions employ maximum ratio combining to eke extra performance out of the fact that there is gain to be obtained from combining the weighted results of both decoding methods.

All-digital AM operation retains the diversity delay on the core audio Logical Channel P1, and adds the same feature to the enhanced audio Logical Channel P3. In hybrid operation, 36,000 enhanced bits per frame are encoded, interleaved and conveyed in dual-redundant versions on upper and lower sidebands; analog energy rides on top of much of the enhanced digital sidebands. In all-digital operation, the interference from the analog carrier is eliminated, leaving the encoder and interleaver to more robustly encode 72,000 bits per frame, and add the diversity delay to the P3 information.

FM Time Diversity

Only all-digital operation of FM IBOC uses digital diversity delay. The FM diversity delay process develops redundant information with a second Logical Channel, while the AM diversity delay process merely delays half of the encoded information within the Logical Channel. FM IBOC in all-digital mode may transmit a fully redundant copy of the P1-delivered audio stream by delaying it and transmitting it on the Logical Channel P1′ (P1 prime). FM hybrid operations do not employ digital diversity, relying solely on the time diversity provided by the analog transmission.

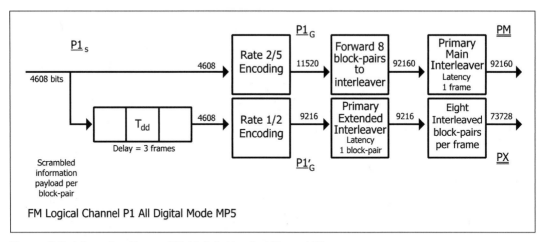

Figure 6.5 Information Flow on FM All-digital Logical Channel P1

Note in Figure 6.5 how the FM P1 Logical Channel is split prior to channel encoding, with two full copies of the information being separately encoded, one at rate 2/5 and one delayed and encoded at rate 1/2. In contrast, the AM diversity delay is an extension of the interleaving function, in which the Logical Channel is encoded and its contents divided among interleaver paths. One-half of the encoded information is delayed going into the interleaver stage.

The diversity delay with which most IBOC radio station operators are familiar is the diversity delay between analog and digital audio in the hybrid transmission mode. The diversity delay between analog and digital audio is also indicated in the Layer 1 documents as T_{dd}. However, in addition to the diversity delay component of analog audio delay, the specifications anticipate further delay adjustment "to account for processing delays in the analog and digital audio chains." (§14.2.3 Diversity Delay, in both Layer 1 documents) See sidebar.

The Layer 1 documents refer to a "time alignment" or "transmit alignment" variable T_{T1a} in conjunction with the diversity delay time T_{dd}. T_{T1a} is an implementation-specific adjustment to ensure that after information is processed for the various Logical Channels, the delayed information is delayed exactly T_{dd} upon transmission.

Estimating Analog Audio Delay

Performing a brief thought exercise, consider an analog transmitter with analog audio fed directly to it, with a variable delay control at the analog transmitter input. Say the analog audio is also fed to a parallel digital transmitter's input. Let us estimate the delays in the digital transmission path to determine the analog delay setting. The audio is almost instantaneously digitized by the analog-to-digital converter. Then the HDC coder must buffer 2048 audio samples (see Chapter 4 for more detail) and compute the first packet's worth of coded audio information—at least 46 milliseconds delay. 32 packets are queued for Layer 2 processing— one frame delay, 1.486 seconds. However, because of the elastic buffer that permits variable audio packet sizes to spill into an adjacent transmission frame, another latency is incorporated. Table 5-1 of the Audio Transport Reference Document allows the operator to set up to 10/32 of one frame, about 1/3 second.

Layer 2 then accumulates one frame of audio packets for passage to Layer 1. Layer 1 scrambles, convolutionally encodes, and interleaves the incoming Layer 2 frame—assume a very small delay with a very fast processor. The OFDM waveform is created, transmitted, and propagates to the receiver nearly instantly.

The receiver buffers the incoming frame (1.486 seconds), then de-interleaves, decodes, and descrambles the information very quickly. On the hybrid AM IBOC system, the core audio information is split between the current frame and one that will arrive three frames after the start of the current frame—in 4.5 seconds, buffering two additional frames before the rest of the information begins to arrive. The delayed information was interleaved block-by-block, adding 1/8 frame delay to recover the first block. Assume decoding happens quickly. The delays are at least four whole frames, plus potentially 1/3, plus 1/8—a total of more than 6.6 seconds. This overlooks any of the processing times in the transmitter and receiver. Therefore the analog transmitter must have its input delayed not only the three-frame diversity delay time T_{dd}, but also the time required to overcome interleaving and processing delays.

The Symbol

The symbol is the shortest element, in time, of the IBOC information structure. The OFDM symbol is the waveform that is the composite of each OFDM subcarrier modulated with a particular phase and amplitude. Its duration is the period T_s. A series of symbols forms a block; a series of blocks forms the frame.

The output of the Layer 1 interleaver processes is an amalgam of all the logical channels, ready to be vector-mapped, one symbol at a time, to the ensemble of OFDM subcarriers. Some logical channels are interleaved frame by frame, some block by block, and some (on FM IBOC) block-pair by block-pair. The OFDM Subcarrier Mapping stage generates a vector $\underline{X}$ that represents the next OFDM symbol, defining the value to be assigned to each OFDM subcarrier. With AM IBOC, 256 of these vectors describe one frame of information. 512 vectors describe the contents of an FM IBOC frame.

Since the OFDM symbol is the building block of blocks and frames, each block and each frame must contain a whole number of symbols (Figure 6.3). Thus, if the frame rate must be proportional to the 44.1 kSa/s audio sampling rate (Chapter 4), the symbol rate also will be so. While the symbol rate therefore is constrained on the one hand by the audio sampling rate, it is on the other hand constrained by the radio frequency characteristics of the symbols.

OFDM symbols are modulated at a rate that is determined by the OFDM subcarrier frequency spacing (Δf) and the length of time required to protect from multipath interference (given as the ratio α, called the "cyclic prefix"). This relationship is discussed further in the next chapter. Note for now that Table 6.2 shows the modulation rate for each OFDM symbol, approximately 344.5 symbols per second on FM IBOC and 172.3 on AM. These rates are derived from the precise ratios in Table 6.2. Dividing, for instance, the FM IBOC frame time T_f by the number of symbols per frame, the result is a rational number defining the symbol time T_s. This ratio preserves the relationship between the 44.1 kSa/s audio clock and the IBOC OFDM symbol rate.

$$T_f \cdot \frac{1}{\text{symbols per frame}} = T_s$$

$$\frac{65536}{44100} \cdot \frac{1}{512} = \frac{128}{44100}$$

The OFDM process formulates a symbol, ramps it up to desired power, holds it for a period and ramps power back to zero. Then it repeats for each successive symbol. The next chapter discusses this process in detail. In addition to processing and transmitting information received from Layer 2, Layer 1 is also responsible for creating symbols that contain cues to help a receiver latch onto an IBOC signal and decompose it.

Syncing Up

Layer 1 must incorporate structural information about the transmitted IBOC signal. This role falls to the Reference Subcarriers. Blocks and frames must be identified so the receiver can track and decode them. Even before the receiver begins to draw out blockwise and framewise information for de-interleaving, it must establish a reference point for the signal's center frequency and a phase reference for discerning the information on the signal. The positions of the Reference Subcarriers in the IBOC channel act as guideposts for aligning the receiver with the signal. The information in the Reference Subcarriers provides block and frame synchronization information.

System Control Processing

The System Control Processing function of Layer 1 (see Figures 6.1 and 6.2) creates a matrix $\underline{R}$ for modulating the Reference Subcarriers. In Chapters 7, 8, and 9, the radio frequency characteristics of the Reference Subcarriers for AM and FM IBOC are discussed. As there are 32 symbols per block on both the AM and FM IBOC signals, the Reference Subcarriers are configured to act as a 32-symbol "heartbeat." With one bit per symbol, the Reference Subcarriers can convey 32 bits of information with every block.

For the most part, the information on each Reference Carrier duplicates the information on the other Reference Subcarriers. Table 6.3 lists the key information conveyed by Reference Subcarriers. At the start of each block, Reference Subcarriers transmit a synchronization sequence, 0110010, in unison. Receivers can hone in on this sequence, synchronize to the block rate, and read the rest of the Reference Carrier information.

With only the two Reference Subcarriers on AM IBOC, the center frequency of the AM signal is easily inferred as being halfway between them. With the wideband nature of the FM signal and up to 61 Reference Subcarriers, there is a potential for the receiver to be off frequency, locking onto the Reference Subcarriers but offset from center frequency. To help the receiver center on the signal, the FM Reference Carrier ID distinguishes each Reference Carrier from its three nearest neighbors on each side.

The 32 bits of System Control Data that constitute one block of Reference Carrier information are described in the bitmap Table 6.4. Table 6.4 shows where the System Control Data is mapped into the 32-bit control word. Additional tables in Sections 11 of the Layer 1 reference documents provide the actual binary values represented by each component of System Control Data. Once the receiver acquires the System Control Data, it can discern the frame synchronization from the Block Count, the OFDM structure from the Service Mode Indicator, and other characteristics of the signal.

System Control Data	AM	FM Primary (Used in hybrid and all-digital modes)	FM Secondary (Used in all-digital modes)
Sync	7-bit sequence beginning with first symbol of block. 4 additional bits placed in fixed positions within block.		
Power Level Indicator (PLI)	Indicates PIDS and Secondary carriers are set to one of two optional levels		
Analog Audio Bandwidth Indicator (AABI)	Indicates 5 or 8 kHz analog bandwidth		
Block Count (BC)	Counts blocks 0–7. Counts through all blocks in same frame	Counts blocks 0–15	
Service Mode Indicators (SMI, PSMI, SSMI)	MA1 hybrid or MA3 all-digital MA4–32 reserved	Primary Modes MP1–4 hybrid MP5–6 all-digital MP7–63 reserved	Secondary Modes MS1–4
Reference Subcarrier ID (RSID)		Each Reference Carrier marked sequentially 0–3, starting from center frequency and counting out from center both ways	
Secondary Channel Indicator (SCI)		Indicates presence of Secondary carriers	
P3 Interleaver Select Indicator (P3ISI)		Indicates short or long interleaver on Primary Extended subcarriers	

Table 6.3 System Control Data on OFDM Reference Subcarriers

Symbol #	AM	FM Primary	FM Secondary
1		sync	
2		sync	
3		sync	
4		sync	
5		sync	
6		sync	
7		sync	
8	PLI	r	r
9		p	
10		sync	
11	r	RSID	RSID
12	r	RSID	RSID
13	AABI	SCI	r
14		p	
15		sync	
16	r	r	r
17	r	BC	BC
18	BC	BC	BC
19	BC	BC	BC
20	BC	BC	BC
21		p	
22		sync	
23		sync	
24	r	P3ISI	r
25	r	r	r
26	r	PSMI	r
27	SMI	PSMI	SSMI
28	SMI	PSMI	SSMI
29	SMI	PSMI	SSMI
30	SMI	PSMI	SSMI
31	SMI	PSMI	SSMI
32		p	
		p = parity r = reserved	

Table 6.4 Reference Carrier System Control Data Bitmaps

The bitmaps for AM, FM Primary, and FM Secondary Reference Subcarriers are understandably similar. They use a common synchronization format, simplifying receiver architecture with the need for only one common synchronization algorithm. Each parity bit indicates even parity for the data bits in the light areas on Table 6.4, between the parity bit and the sync bit above it. Parity bits provide a most basic form of error protection in which the parity bit is a zero if the number of 1-bits in the preceding data is even, and is a one if the number of 1-bits in the preceding data is odd.

Reserved bits are not further described in the Reference Documents, except that any reserved bit shall remain unchanged for the duration of an entire frame. Block Counts and Service Mode

Indicators occupy the same spaces in each Reference Carrier model. Other System Control Data values are assigned to available positions in the 32-bit control word.

Differential Encoding

The manner in which the Reference Subcarriers convey their information is designed to aid the receiver in acquiring the IBOC signal and the System Control Data. They utilize differential encoding. Differential encoding is a familiar technique for conveying information by utilizing the *transition* between states rather than in the *values* of the states themselves. When a receiver is acquiring a signal that has no pilot from which to obtain a phase reference, differential encoding eliminates phase ambiguity.

For instance, while the first seven synchronization bits are 0110010, they, and the remaining bits of the 32-bit control word, are passed through an XOR gate comparing the present input bit with the previous output bit. The result is a change in state whenever a 1 is read into the gate, and no change in state whenever a 0 is read in. The receiver, seeing the Reference Carrier in a phase state whose reference value is unknown to the receiver, waits for the next symbol. If the next symbol has changed phase, the next bit is a 1; and if no phase change occurs, the bit is a zero. The first seven synchronization bits would be transmitted as shown in Table 6.5.

Differential Encoder Operation		Time (top to bottom left to right)...						
1	Input: sync string 0110010	0	1	1	0	0	1	0
2	XOR (read vertically)	⊕	⊕	⊕	⊕	⊕	⊕	⊕
3	Previous output of encoder (row 5 shifted right) (*First value assumed)	0*	0	1	0	0	0	1
4	Equals	=	=	=	=	=	=	=
5	New output of encoder- transmitted	0	1	0	0	0	1	1
Differential Decoder								
6	Received bits (same as row 5)	0	1	0	0	0	1	1
7	XOR upon reception	⊕	⊕	⊕	⊕	⊕	⊕	⊕
8	Previously received bits (row 7 shifted right one position)	0*	0	1	0	0	0	1
9	Equals	=	=	=	=	=	=	=
10	Received sync string	0	1	1	0	0	1	0
Differential Decoder, if receiver flips incoming phase...								
11	Received bits, if receiver inverts phase (from row 6)	1	0	1	1	1	0	0
12	XOR	⊕	⊕	⊕	⊕	⊕	⊕	⊕
13	Previously received output of encoder with phase flip (row 11 shifted right one position)	1*	1	0	1	1	1	0
14	Equals	=	=	=	=	=	=	=
15	Received sync string	0	1	1	0	0	1	0

Table 6.5 Example of Differentially Encoded Sync Word

Table 6.5 illustrates how the absolute phase of the received differentially encoded signal is irrelevant for recovering sync and other System Control Data. After the encoding process is illustrated in the first five rows of the table, the decoding process is shown next with correct received phase and separately with inverted phase. The sync string comes out correctly in both cases (highlighted data). Once the block synchronization is obtained through differential decoding, the receiver can go to work on establishing correct framing.

As with many of the specialized components of IBOC, the features of the synchronization scheme and the Reference Subcarriers are incorporated in iBiquity patents. See sidebar for an example.

iBiquity Patent

Reference Subcarriers, Sync-words, and Differential Encoding on FM IBOC

United States Patent	6,982,948
Kroeger, et al.	January 3, 2006

Method and apparatus for transmission and reception of FM in-band on-channel digital audio broadcasting

Abstract

A transmitter for transmitting data in a digital audio broadcasting system includes a signal generator for providing a plurality of orthogonal frequency division multiplexed subcarriers, with the subcarriers including data subcarriers and reference subcarriers, and a modulator for modulating the data subcarriers with a digital signal representative of information to be transmitted. The reference subcarriers are modulated with a sequence of timing bits, wherein the sequence of timing bits includes an unambiguous block synchronization word, and the number of bits comprising the block synchronization word is less than one half of the number of bits in said timing sequence. The orthogonal frequency division multiplexed subcarriers are transmitted to receivers that differentially detect the block synchronization word and use the block synchronization word to coherently detect the digital signal representative of information to be transmitted are also included.

Universal Time

To ensure consistency of each station's IBOC transmissions over time, the frame rate T_f is synchronized with a reference master clock. That clock is provided by the Global Positioning System (GPS). The GPS satellite transmits precise frequency and timing information, enabling not only accurate determinations of geographic position, but also precise coordination of disparate electronic systems and networks.

IBOC frames are assigned a frame number, called the Absolute Layer 1 Frame Number (ALFN). The hypothetical first frame, ALFN 0, started at the GPS epoch, which occurred at 0000 Universal

Time (UT) on January 6, 1980. Each subsequent frame is launched at a time that is a whole number of frames after that reference time. This is computed by multiplying the ALFN (a whole number) times the frame duration T_f in seconds and adding to 0000 UT January 6, 1980. The manner in which ALFN is utilized is discussed further in the Station Information Service section of Chapter 10.

Service Modes

One of the characteristics communicated to the receiver by the Reference Subcarriers is the Service Mode of the transmitted signal. AM IBOC has two Service Modes, one for hybrid operation and one for all-digital. With the far greater bandwidth of the FM IBOC system, the configuration of the signal can be flexible, both spectrally and logically. Spectrally, in addition to the basic hybrid OFDM subcarrier configuration, FM IBOC offers three extended hybrid configurations. Logically, the various FM spectral configurations—hybrid and all-digital—offer an assortment of Logical Channel arrangements.

AM Service Modes

The hybrid AM IBOC Service Mode MA1 is symmetrical around the AM channel center frequency. OFDM subcarrier positions are numbered from –81 to +81, with number 0 at channel center frequency. As Table 6.6 shows, there are upper and lower sideband appearances of each subcarrier group—Primary, Secondary, and Tertiary. Spectral characteristics are discussed in detail in Chapter 9. In logical terms, the upper and lower sideband Primary subcarriers are each fed one half of the convolutionally encoded P1 data stream containing core audio. In contrast, the Secondary Lower Sideband (LSB) contains an exact copy of the information in the Secondary Upper Sideband (USB). Likewise, the Tertiary LSB and USB contain identical information. Among them, the Secondary and Tertiary LSB's and USB's convey two complete copies of Logical Channel P3, containing enhanced audio. To compensate for the lower levels of the Secondary and Tertiary subcarriers, and their proximity to the modulated analog host's energy, this doubling of the information on USB and LSB provides further redundancy beyond the convolutional encoding and interleaving already applied to the P3 logical channel.

Table 6.6 represents the sequence of OFDM subcarriers from LSB, to the left, to center channel, center, to USB, on the right. The top row provides the name of each OFDM subcarrier or subcarrier group. The next row, OFDM Subcarrier #'s, indicates the official number or range of numbers assigned to the subcarrier(s) represented in each column. OFDM subcarrier number 0 is at center frequency, and is never activated. Subcarriers #1 and #–1 are the Reference Subcarriers. The Tertiary subcarrier groups include subcarriers #–26 through #–2 and #2 through #26; and so on. The individual Reference Subcarriers and the individual PIDS subcarriers are shown at their relative positions across the channel. Alternating among these singular subcarriers are groupings of subcarriers that form the Tertiary, Secondary, and Primary LSB and USB groups. The second row indicates how any subcarriers are in each group. Since a single column of the table may represent one or many OFDM subcarriers, the table is not scaled by frequency.

Each subcarrier or subcarrier group is associated with a Logical Channel (listed in the next row). One or more Logical Channels are then associated with an Interleaver Matrix (the following row). Finally at the bottom row, the amount of data delivered by each subcarrier group per 1.49-second frame is indicated in bits.

← Lower Sideband   Upper Sideband →

Hybrid Subcarrier Groups

	Primary	Gap*	PIDS	Secondary	PIDS	Tertiary	Reference	Gap*	Reference	Tertiary	PIDS	Secondary	PIDS	Gap*	Primary
OFDM Sub-Carrier #'s	-81 / -57	-56 / -54	-53	-52 / -28	-27	-26 / -2	-1	0	1	2 / 26	27	28 / 52	53	54 / 56	57 / 81
Quantity	25	3	1	25	1	25	1	1	1	25	1	25	1	3	25
Logical Channel	P1		PIDS	P3	PIDS	P3	R		R	P3	PIDS	P3	PIDS		P1
Interleaver Matrix	PL		PIDS	S	PIDS	T	R**		R**	T	PIDS	S	PIDS		PU
Logical Ch. Bits/Frame	36k		960	24k	960	12k	256		256	12k	960	24k	960		36k

* No OFDM Subcarriers occupy these gaps
**R is not interleaved

Table 6.6 Hybrid AM IBOC OFDM Subcarrier Groups

← Lower Sideband   Upper Sideband →

All-Digital Subcarrier Groups

	Tertiary	PIDS	Primary	Reference	Gap*	Reference	Primary	PIDS	Secondary
OFDM Subcarrier #'s	-52 / -28	-27	-26 / -2	-1	0	1	2 / 26	27	28 / 52
Quantity	25	1	25	1	1	1	25	1	25
Logical Channel	P3	PIDS	P1	R		R	P1	PIDS	P3
Interleaver Matrix	T	PIDS	PL	R**		R**	PU	PIDS	S
Logical Ch. Bits/Frame	36k	960	36k	256		256	36k	960	36k

* No OFDM Subcarrier occupies this gap
**R is not interleaved

Table 6.7 All-Digital AM IBOC OFDM Subcarrier Groups

Switched to the MA3 all-digital Service Mode, the configuration of AM IBOC changes substantially (Table 6.7). It no longer has the symmetry provided by redundant Secondary and Tertiary information in both sidebands. Instead, with the removal of the analog host, self-interference is eliminated, and the Secondary and Tertiary OFDM subcarrier groups are segregated, with Secondary to the USB and Tertiary to the LSB. Since Secondary and Tertiary are now on opposite sides of center frequency, each carries half of the convolutionally encoded P3. This is analogous to how P1 is split across center frequency by the Primary USB and LSB.

Note also that with the removal of the analog host, the Primary groups are moved from outer sidebands to innermost position by the channel center. With only one Secondary group and one Tertiary group, the bandwidth of the signal is reduced, from ±81 OFDM subcarrier positions, to ±52, yet the total throughput of the hybrid and all-digital signals is 144 kb per frame; more on bandwidth is in the next chapters.

In hybrid mode MA1, four PIDS subcarriers convey two copies of the PIDS information. In all-digital mode MA3, only two PIDS subcarriers remain, splitting the PIDS information between them. In both Service Modes, a pair of Reference Subcarriers straddles the center frequency, which remains vacant. To protect the Reference Subcarriers of stations on adjacent channels, hybrid mode leaves a three-subcarrier-wide gap centered at ±10 kHz offset, on OFDM subcarrier positions ±54, 55, and 56. In all-digital mode, PIDS subcarriers ±53 are also dropped, providing an additional one-subcarrier-position guard band between the all-digital signal and the Reference Subcarriers of adjacent channel stations.

FM Service Modes

With substantially more bandwidth available to FM IBOC than AM, there is more flexibility in the shared use of its Logical Channels for multicasting and/or data services. FM Service Mode Tables 6.8 and 6.9 are similar to AM Tables 6.6 and 6.7, with some distinctions. Horizontally, the subcarrier groupings are similarly represented, but to save room in the Table, the upper sideband is condensed, leaving the center frequency to appear offset to the right. The structure of the upper sideband of the FM IBOC signal is the mirror image of the lower sideband. Because of this condensation of the USB on the table, the bit-related data shown in the LSB side of the table are the sums of USB and LSB bit-counts per frame per Logical Channel. For instance, in Service Mode MP1 Logical Channel P1 conveys 365,440 bits per frame, divided equally between upper and lower Primary Main sidebands.

The fine structure of the FM IBOC signal contains sets of OFDM subcarriers grouped into partitions of 18 information subcarriers each. The partitions are separated each by a single Reference Carrier. For legibility, the Reference Subcarriers are given their own space at the bottoms of the tables, with the OFDM subcarrier number and the Reference Carrier number assignments shown for each Reference Carrier. In Primary FM Table 6.6, the vital information about the Primary Reference Subcarriers is shown in the two columns expanded to reveal the information—at OFDM subcarriers –280 and +280. Their characteristics remain the same in all Service Modes. Since each Primary Reference Carrier is nearly a carbon copy of the next, the 512-bit payload shown represents the per-frame payload of each Reference Carrier.

Lower Sidebands ← → Upper Sidebands

OFDM Subcarrier group headers (diagonal labels, left to right): Primary Main (×10), Primary Extended (×4), Reference, Gap*, Reference, Primary Extended, Etcetera..., Primary Main

	Partitions															Reference	Gap*	Reference			Primary Main
Service Mode	OFDM Sub-Carrier #'s	-545 -528	-526 -509	-507 -490	-488 -471	-469 -452	-450 -433	-431 -414	-412 -395	-393 -376	-374 -357	-355 -338	-336 -319	-317 -300	-298 -281	-280	-279 279	280	298 281	545 528
	Quantity	18	18	18	18	18	18	18	18	18	18	18	18	18	18	1	559	1	18	18
MP1	Log. Chan.	P1, PIDS															R		R	
	Intlv. Matrix	PM															R**		R	
	Bits/Frame	P1 = 365440 , PIDS = 3200 (USB & LSB totals)															512			
MP2	L.C.	P1, PIDS										P3					R		R	
	I.M.	PM										PX1					R		R	
	B/F	P1 = 365440 , PIDS = 3200										36864					512			
MP3	L.C.	P1, PIDS										P3					R		R	
	I.M.	PM										PX1					R		R	
	B/F	P1 = 365440 , PIDS = 3200										73728					512			
MP4	L.C.	P1, PIDS										P3					R		R	
	I.M.	PM										PX1					R		R	
	B/F	P1 = 365440 , PIDS = 3200										147456					512			
MP5	L.C.	P1, P2, PIDS										P3		P1'			R		R	
	I.M.	PM										PX1		PX2			R		R	
	B/F	P1 = 92160, P2 = 273280, PIDS = 3200										73728		73728			512			
MP6	L.C.	P1, P2, PIDS										P1'					R		R	
	I.M.	PM										PX2					R		R	
	B/F	P1 = 184320, P2 = 181120, PIDS = 3200										147456					512			

(Right margin labels: "Secondary subcarriers inserted for all-digital"; "Upper Sideband Mirrors Lower")

Subcarrier #'s of Reference Subcarriers	-546	-527	-508	-489	-470	-451	-432	-413	-394	-375	-356	-337	-318	-299	-280		280	299	... 527	546
Ref. Sub. #'s	0	1	2	3	4	5	6	7	8	9	10	11	12	13	14		46	47	... 59	60

One Reference Subcarrier is inserted between each partition of 18 information subs. R Matrix applies. 512 bits per frame per subcarrier
Two of the 30 Primary Reference Subs , #14 and #46, are shown for illustration at OFDM carrier positions -280 and +280.

*This gap used for analog signal or Secondary subcarriers
**R is not interleaved

Table 6.8 Primary FM IBOC OFDM Subcarrier Groups

Hybrid Service Modes MP1 – MP4 reveal the hybrid FM's optional feature. The Primary Extended partitions may be left deactivated, or they may be turned on as one, two, or four partitions. The NRSC-5 Reference documents indicate Service Modes MP2 – MP4 activate the extended hybrid waveform. The extended hybrid waveform always includes the Primary Main subcarriers, plus one of the three combinations of Primary Extended subcarriers.

Meanwhile, Service Modes MP5 and MP6 are listed in the Reference Documents as being either extended hybrid or all-digital modes. In practice these two modes have been dedicated to all-digital operation. In all-digital operation, all Primary Main and Primary Extended subcarriers (Table 6.8) are employed simultaneously with the Secondary Main and Secondary Extended subcarriers (Table 6.9).

This entire ensemble of partitions resides in the space marked "Gap" in Table 6.8

◄——— Lower Sideband   Upper Sideband ———►

Partition labels (diagonal, left to right): Secondary Protected, Secondary Extended, Secondary Extended, Secondary Extended, Secondary Extended, Secondary Main, Secondary Main, Secondary Main, Secondary Main, Secondary Main, Secondary Main, Secondary Main, Secondary Main, Secondary Main, Secondary Main, Reference, Secondary Main, Etcetera..., Secondary Extended, Secondary Protected

Service Mode	Partitions																			
	OFDM Sub-Carrier #'s	-278 / -267	-265 / -248	-246 / -229	-227 / -210	-208 / -191	-189 / -172	-170 / -153	-151 / -134	-132 / -115	-113 / -96	-94 / -77	-75 / -58	-56 / -37	-37 / -20	-18 / -1	0	1 / 18	248 / 265	267 / 278
	Quantity	12	18	18	18	18	18	18	18	18	18	18	18	18	18	18	1	18	18	12
MS1	Log. Chan.	S5	S4, SIDS															R		
	Intlv. Matrix	SP	SB															R**		
	Bits/Frame	24576	S4 = 511616, SIDS = 4480															512		
MS2	L.C.	S5	S1'		S3		S1, S2, SIDS											R		
	I.M.	SP	SX2		SX1		SM											R		
	B/F	24576	73728		73728		S1 = 184320, S2 = 181120, SIDS = 3200											512		
MS3	L.C.	S5	S1'				S1, S2, SIDS											R		
	I.M.	PM	SX2				SM											R		
	B/F	24576	147456				S1 = 92160, S2 = 273280, SIDS = 3200											512		
MS4	L.C.	S5	S1'		S3		S2, SIDS											R		
	I.M.	SP	SX2		SX1		SM											R		
	B/F	24576	73728		73728		S2 = 365440, SIDS = 3200											512		

Upper Sideband Mirrors Lower

#'s of Reference Subcarriers	-279	-266	-247	-228	-209	-190	-171	-152	133	-114	-95	-76	-57	-38	-19	0	19	... 247 ...		279
Ref. Sub. #'s	15	16	17	18	19	20	21	22	23	24	25	26	27	28	29	30	31	... 43	44	45

One Reference Sub. is inserted between each partition of 18 information subs. R Matrix applies. 512 bits per frame per subcarrier
The center-frequency Secondary Reference Sub. , #30 is shown at OFDM subcarrier position 0.

**R is not interleaved

Table 6.9 Secondary FM IBOC OFDM Subcarrier Groups

The logical channel structure shows how two or more logical channels, on the Primary Main partitions, are combined through a common interleaver matrix to be transmitted on the same partitions. Each of these Logical Channels has its own convolutional coding scheme and operates at its native transfer rate—block, block-pair, or frame. The interleaver matrix ensures that block-wise information is interleaved across the correct 1/16th of the frame, block-pair-wise information occupies the correct 1/8th of the frame and framewise information is interleaved across the entire frame. In the process, none of the data interleaved at one transfer rate collides in the matrix with data interleaved at other rates. Interleaver function is discussed in the previous chapter.

Each Logical Channel's characteristics determine its robustness. Each of the following contributes to the robustness: the rate of the convolutional coder, the depth of the interleaver (related to the transfer rate), the quality of the OFDM subcarrier partition, and the presence or absence of time diversity. Table 6.10, derived from Tables in Section 7 of the Layer 1 documents, summarizes the transfer rate and relative robustness of each Logical Channel. The characteristics of some Logical Channels change with operating settings. These differences are shown in the table.

Logical Channel (Service Mode)	Frame, Block or Block-Pair rate	iBiquity Relative Robustness	Note
Hybrid AM			
P1 (MA1)	B	5	Tdd Diversity
P3 (MA1)	F	6, 8	Hi, Low Power Level Setting
PIDS (MA1)	B	3, 7	Hi, Low Power Level Setting
All-Digital AM			
P1 (MA2)	B	1	Tdd Diversity
P3 (MA2)	F	4	Tdd Diversity
PIDS (MA2)	B	2	
Hybrid FM			
P1 (MP1–4)	F	2	Only P1 available
P3 P3IS = 0	P	4	Single-frame interleaver
P3 P3IS = 1	P	3	Interleaves across 2 frames
PIDS	B	3	
All-Digital FM			
P1 (MP5, MP6)	P	1	Uses P1 and P1′ Diversity
P2 (MP5, MP6)	F	2	
P3 (MP5)	P	4	P3IS = 0 Single-frame interleaver
P3 (MP5)	P	3	P3IS = 1 Interleaves across 2 frames
PIDS	B	3	
S1 (MS1–3)	P	5	Uses S1 and S1′ Diversity
S1 (MS4)	P	11	Only S1′ available
S2 (MS2–4)	F	9	
S3 (MS2, MS4)	P	11	
S4 (MS1)	P	7	
S5	B	6	
SIDS	B	10	

1 is most robust; 11 is least robust.

Table 6.10 Logical Channel Frame Rates and Robustness

Backward Compatibility

One of the principal strengths of free over-the-air broadcasting is its ubiquity. Every radio tuning into the AM or FM band is capable of receiving the default program service of each station. For instance, an FM radio made in 1950 can still receive today's FM broadcasts. The default program source, monophonic audio, is still available on FM receivers of all vintages. Looking forward, as long as hybrid IBOC is the norm, the default program audio of AM and FM broadcasts remains accessible to legacy analog radios.

Some day, all-digital IBOC transmissions may be authorized by the FCC, breaking the uninterrupted chain of receiver backward compatibility. (We overlook the discontinuity in FM broadcasting when at the end of World War II the fledgling 42–50 MHz FM band in the U.S.A. was officially abandoned in favor of the 88–108 MHz band, leaving the early FM receiver owners high and dry). At present there is no timetable either within the industry or at the FCC for authorization of all-digital IBOC.

The focus of this section however, is backward compatibility—how to improve IBOC transmissions with new features while protecting the basic functionality of IBOC receivers already in use. Two backward compatibility issues are addressed. First, if all-digital operation is authorized and broadcasters begin transmitting all-digital signals, it is wise to ensure that all receivers that are capable of receiving an NRSC-5-compliant transmission can do so for all-digital as well as analog. Second, if enhancements such as codec improvements, become available, it is wise to continue to provide a default program service that continues to serve incumbent receivers already in use but at the same time allows the industry to take advantage (in some fashion) of new enhancements.

On the first point, NRSC-5 is a transmission standard; there is no requirement that IBOC receivers be able to handle all-digital operation. Because of agreements between iBiquity and its receiver licensees, all-digital capability is built into every HD Radio receiver, ensuring that if all-digital transmissions are authorized and commence, all-digital transmission is backward compatible with existing HD Radio receivers. (In this context, it might be better said that HD Radio receivers are forward compatible with a possible change in transmission to all-digital, because the receivers are equipped with an unutilized all-digital reception feature.)

The assignment of new Service Modes provides a backward compatibility path if new features are added to NRSC-5 transmissions (regardless whether they are hybrid or all-digital). The default program is that which is carried on Logical Channel P1 (AM and FM IBOC). Program content on P1 must continue to be transmitted to support at least "medium quality digital audio." (NRSC-5 Reference Documents (1) and (2), Sections 6.2.1 in each.) The housekeeping that occurs on Reference Subcarriers and PIDS also must be preserved.

"Free to be redefined," in the words of the standard, are Logical channels P3 and P2, on FM IBOC, and P3 on AM. In FM all-digital mode, and in both hybrid and all-digital on AM, core audio would be on P1 and enhanced could be on P2 or P3. (Hybrid FM has no "multistream" core/enhanced audio structure, providing a single quality of audio service on P1.) Table 6.11 illustrates the IBOC backward compatibility scheme. Each reserved Service Mode is assigned a backward compatibility characteristic.

IBOC Mode	Default Service Mode	Reserved Expansion Service Modes	Retain for Backward Compatibility	Free to be Redefined
FM Hybrid	MP1	MP9, 17, 25, 33, 41, 49, 57	P1, PIDS, R, analog	None
	MP2	MP10, 18, 26, 34, 42, 50, 58	P1, PIDS, R, analog	P3
	MP3	MP11, 19, 27, 35, 43, 51, 59	P1, PIDS, R, analog	P3
	MP4	MP12, 20, 28, 36, 44, 52, 60	P1, PIDS, R, analog	P3
FM All-Digital	MP5	MP13, 21, 29, 37, 45, 53, 61	P1, P1′, PIDS, R	P2, P3
		MP7, 15, 23, 31, 39, 47, 55, 63	P1′, PIDS, R	P1, P2, P3
	MP6	MP14, 22, 30, 38, 46, 54, 62	P1, P1′, PIDS, R	P2
		MP8, 16, 24, 32, 40, 48, 56	P1′, PIDS, R	P1, P2
AM Hybrid	MA1	MA6, 10, 14, 18, 22, 26, 30	P1, PIDS, R, analog	P3
AM All-Digital	MA3	MA7, 11, 15, 19, 23 27, 31	P1, PIDS, R	P3
Reserved (see text)	Reserved	MA4, 5, 9, 13, 17, 21, 25, 29	N/A	N/A
		MA8, 12, 16, 20, 24, 28, 32	P1, P2, PIDS, R, analog	N/A

Table 6.11 Backward Compatibility Default Service Modes for Reserved Expansion Service Modes (Source: From NRSC-5 Reference Document (1), Table 6-4 and Reference Document (2), Table 6-3.)

Each of the initially assigned Service Modes is the default mode for seven or eight reserved Service Modes. In FM hybrid mode, Logical Channel P3, which resides on the Primary Extended OFDM subcarriers, is available for future assignment as an enhancement to Service Modes MP2–4. P1 remains the source of backward compatible "medium quality" audio. FM All-digital operation has two options. P1 and the delayed P1′ can be retained for backward compatibility, releasing P2 and/or P3 for nonbackward-compatible enhancements. Alternatively, in the event that significant improvement in service can be obtained by releasing P1 to a new audio enhancement, only P1′ need be retained for backward compatibility.

AM IBOC, being more limited in scope, can only release its enhanced audio stream on P3 to nonbackward-compatible purposes. This applies to both transmission modes—hybrid and all-digital.

Evolution of IBOC in the Fossil Record

Table 6.11 shows the only NRSC-5 reference to an AM IBOC logical channel P2. It is the last vestige in the AM Layer 1 document of a Logical Channel now purged from the specification. Conspicuous by its absence in the AM IBOC protocol, P2's former existence is evidenced in the continuing use of Logical Channels P1 and P3. A similar discontinuity between Service Mode MA1 and MA3 belies the former existence of MA2. The history of IBOC's evolution includes the merging of two competitors' technologies during the development, and the transition among several codecs before HDC was settled upon. Like a biological adaptation no longer needed for survival, P2 and MA2 have withered out of the AM IBOC DNA.

The IBOC specifications prudently provide these Reserved Service Modes in anticipation of future improvements. Such improvements might warrant limiting the functionality of incumbent IBOC radios to medium quality audio on a default Logical Channel. This occurs at the very lowest layer of the IBOC protocol stack. Other tools are available at higher layers to manipulate the IBOC information while retaining functionality for incumbent receivers. Foremost, Layer 2 has the capability of partitioning any Logical Channel (excluding PIDS, SIDS, and R) to provide capacity for data services, which could include audio services. The information rate of the codec must be reduced to provide this capacity and retain main program compatibility with receivers. Similarly, the advent of multicasting saw the partitioning of the audio portion of the Logical Channel into two or more simultaneous broadcasts, while retaining functionality of nonmulticast radios. In addition, expansion of multicasting to include Logical Channel P3 on FM IBOC was accomplished by repurposing Audio Codec Mode 13 (b1101) to indicate a split-across-logical-channels codec mode. It was employed after the Audio Transport document was finalized (see Table 5-2 in the Audio Transport Reference Document (4)). Similarly, FM mode MP11 was activated to support multicasting into the Primary Extended partitions.

From Logical to Physical

This chapter picked up where Chapter 6 left off, with the passage of the interleaver outputs to the OFDM Subcarrier Mapping process. The logical structure of the IBOC OFDM waveforms is based on the capacity, bandwidth, and interference susceptibility of the various functional groups of OFDM subcarriers. With this background in the function and purpose of the OFDM spectral parts, the next chapters can focus on the physical and electrical characteristics of the IBOC signal.

7 From the Top Down: The Physical Layer– FM OFDM

Taking our trip down the IBOC protocol stack, it has taken the better part of two chapters to drill into Layer 1. Chapter 5 covered the thin Layer 2 and burrowed into the upper-level processes of Layer 1—scrambling, channel encoding, and interleaving. Chapter 6 continued the journey, pursuing logical connection to the OFDM IBOC signal. The Logical Channels were linked to the IBOC signal structure, with symbols, blocks and frames in the time domain, and interleaver matrices assigned to OFDM subcarrier groups in the frequency domain. What remain to be discussed about the FM and AM IBOC Layer 1 documents (NRSC-5 Reference Documents 1 and 2) are their electrical characteristics.

NRSC-5 Reference Document Number	Reference Document Title	NRSC-5 Reference Document Number	Reference Document Title
1.	Doc. No. SY_IDD_1011s rev. E HD Radio™ Air Interface Design Description **Layer 1 FM** iBiquity Digital Corporation, 3/22/05	6.	Doc. No. SY_SSS_1026s rev. D HD Radio™ FM Transmission System Specifications iBiquity Digital Corporation, 2/18/05
2.	Doc. No. SY_IDD_1012s rev. E HD Radio™ Air Interface Design Description Layer 1 AM iBiquity Digital Corporation, 3/22/05	7.	Doc. No. SY_IDD_1028s rev. C HD Radio™ Air Interface Design Description Program Service Data iBiquity Digital Corporation, 3/31/05
3.	Doc. No. SY_IDD_1014s rev. F HD Radio™ Air Interface Design Description Layer 2 Channel Multiplex Protocol iBiquity Digital Corporation, 2/7/05	8.	Doc. No. SY_SSS_1082s rev. D HD Radio™ AM Transmission System Specifications iBiquity Digital Corporation, 2/24/05
4.	Doc. No. SY_IDD_1017s rev. E HD Radio™ Air Interface Design Description Audio Transport iBiquity Digital Corporation, 3/31/05	9.	Doc. No. SY_IDD_1085s rev. C HD Radio™ Air Interface Design Description Program Service Data Transport iBiquity Digital Corporation, 2/7/05
5.	Doc. No. SY_IDD_1020s rev. E HD Radio™ Air Interface Design Description Station Information Service Protocol iBiquity Digital Corporation, 2/18/05	10.	Doc. No. SY_IDD_1019s rev. E HD Radio™ Air Interface Design Description Advanced Application Services Transport iBiquity Digital Corporation, 8/4/05

Table 7.1 Protocols Addressed in Chapter 7

This chapter and the next discuss characteristics such as the phase, amplitude, modulation, frequencies, and pulse shaping of the IBOC signal, relating the logical flow in the previous chapter to the electromagnetic spectrum. This discussion is essentially about the physical layer as defined in the classic Open Systems Interconnection Reference Model. Sections 12, 13, and 14 of the AM and FM Layer 1 Reference Documents relate to the OFDM characteristics.

This chapter, 7, speaks to OFDM basics and applies the knowledge to the FM IBOC physical layer. Chapter 8 follows with discussion of OFDM in the AM IBOC physical layer. Finally, Chapter 9 considers the two Reference Documents that are not components of the protocol stack—AM and FM Transmission System specifications—outlining performance specifications of the IBOC signal. These are NRSC-5 Reference Documents (6) and (8).

It may be helpful to open NRSC-5 Reference Document 1 (see Table 7.1) to sections 11, 12, 13, and 14 while reading this chapter. Section 11 of the NRSC-5 FM Layer 1 Reference Document, the System Control Processing section, provides the entrée into the physical layer discussion. System Control, covered in the previous chapter, addresses how transmitters and receivers are informed what the configuration of the IBOC signal is. The Service Mode is the primary structural indication for the receiver.

Section 12 of the FM Layer 1 Reference Document defines the OFDM Subcarrier Mapping Process. Here, the various interleaver matrices are mapped to the OFDM subcarrier groupings.

The previous chapter developed the logical relationship of the interleaver matrices, such as FM Primary Main (PM), to the symbol vector $\underline{X}$ that maps to specific subcarrier numbers within the OFDM subcarrier groups. This chapter discusses the frequencies, amplitudes, and modulation of the FM IBOC OFDM subcarriers. Section 5 of the FM Layer 1 Reference Document, titled Waveforms and Spectra, also informs this discussion.

Sections 13 and 14 of the FM Layer 1 Reference Document describe the algorithms that create the OFDM waveform. Section 13, OFDM Signal Generation, describes the manner in which a single symbol pulse is created, while Section 14, Transmission Subsystem, describes the assembly of the transmitted stream of pulses, and the insertion of the analog source for hybrid operation.

FM IBOC OFDM Spectrum

In Chapter 6 the interleaver matrices were mapped to groups of OFDM subcarriers. The mapping for FM hybrid and all-digital operation was tabulated in tables 6.8 and 6.9, respectively. OFDM subcarriers are assigned unique subcarrier numbers. The same numbering scheme applies to hybrid, extended hybrid and all-digital configurations. Recall that the frequency spacing of the OFDM subcarriers, Δf, is the ratio 1488375/4096, or about 363.4 Hz. OFDM subcarrier #546 is most remote from center frequency. Its frequency offset from the center of the FM channel is $546 \times \Delta f =$ 198,401.55 Hz.

FM IBOC OFDM Frequency Plan

Figure 7.1 shows the OFDM subcarrier number and frequency of the first and last OFDM subcarrier in each logical subcarrier group. Note that Figure 7.1 shows only the upper sideband; the lower sideband is just a mirror image of the upper. The frequencies in Figure 7.1 are the center frequencies of the OFDM subcarriers. The frequency of subcarrier #546 is rounded in the figure to 198,402 Hz.

Figure 7.1 combines the hybrid, extended hybrid, and all-digital OFDM subcarrier groupings in one image. The Primary subcarriers remain in the same position in hybrid and all-digital modes. When changing from hybrid to all-digital operation, the Secondary subcarriers replace the analog FM signal at center band. The three extended hybrid modes employ one, two, or four extended frequency partitions.

The FM IBOC model employs Reference Subcarriers throughout the channel, with one Reference Subcarrier for every 18 information subcarriers. Each set consisting of one Reference Subcarrier and 18 information subcarriers is called a partition. The Primary Main (PM) group has ten partitions on each sideband, incorporating 180 information subcarriers and 10 Reference Subcarriers per sideband. Like bookends around the outermost partitions, an eleventh PM Reference Subcarrier is added at each end of the IBOC spectrum—at subcarriers #546 and #-546.

The Primary Extended (PX) group has four partitions, employed in extended hybrid modes at the discretion of the operator. Each fully extended sideband hosts 72 information subcarriers and 4 Reference Subcarriers. In total, there are 15 Reference Subcarriers per Primary sideband.

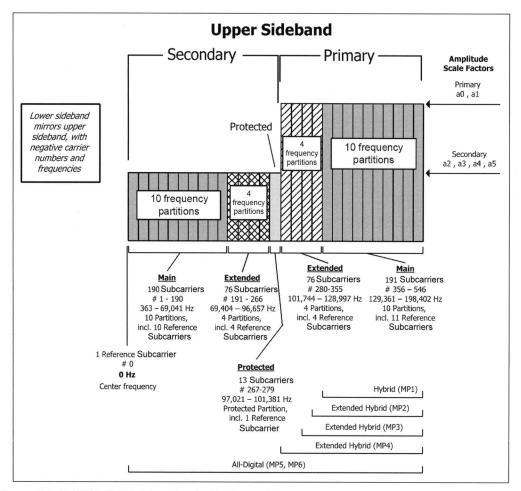

Figure 7.1 FM IBOC OFDM Subcarriers by Number and Frequency

In all-digital operation, all PM and PX partitions are activated, as well as the Secondary Main (SM) and Secondary Extended (SX) partitions. As Figure 7.1 shows, the structure of SM and SX is symmetrical with the structure of PM and PX, having ten and four partitions, respectively. These fourteen partitions per sideband include fourteen Secondary Reference Subcarriers. Recall from Chapter 6 the fact that some of the information on the Secondary Reference Subcarriers is different from that of the Primary Reference Subcarriers. An additional Secondary Reference Subcarrier is placed at center frequency between the two sidebands. The total Reference Subcarrier count discussed so far is 29 in the Secondary sidebands and 30 in the Primary.

There are two more Reference Subcarriers in the ensemble. Between the highest SX subcarrier (Secondary Reference Subcarrier at #266 or 96,657 Hz) and the lowest PX subcarrier (Primary Reference Subcarrier at #280 or 101,744 Hz) falls a curious grouping called Secondary Protected

(SP) (#267–279). One of the subcarriers, #279, is the last Reference Subcarrier in the Secondary spectrum, abutting the first Reference Subcarrier in the Primary spectrum (#280). The remaining 12 subcarriers form the abbreviated partition of SP subcarriers. The FM Layer 1 Reference Document points out that this region is the least likely to suffer from interference caused by other stations' signals (analog or digital), although it remains silent on how this feature might be exploited in all-digital operation. These subcarriers straddle the 100 kHz mark, which is equidistant from the center frequencies of adjacent channels ($f_c \pm 100$ kHz). The 100 kHz channel offset is most removed from any analog modulation. It also is a region, spectrally, where there is a gap between some of the SP subcarriers and a first-adjacent station's higher power Primary subcarriers.

With one Secondary Reference Subcarrier in each SP partition (USB and LSB), the count of Secondary Reference Subcarriers climbs to 31. Added to the 30 Primary Reference Subcarriers, the total count of FM IBOC Reference Subcarriers is 61. At first blush, this may seem like a large number of subcarriers devoted to communicating synchronization and structural information about the IBOC waveform. Indeed, it is a large number; only two subcarriers in AM IBOC provide the necessary synchronization and center frequency references. However, those 61 Reference Subcarriers stand like sentinels across the broader FM IBOC channel. Through the Reference Subcarrier numbering, they help the receiver resolve the receive frequency clock error. They also permit the receiver to monitor the phase and amplitude distortions across the IBOC channel. Channel conditions affecting the 400 kHz-wide signal are frequency variant. Receivers can utilize the known characteristics of the Reference Subcarriers to equalize independently each partition of data for best reception.

The Many Tasks of FM IBOC Reference Subcarriers

Imagine an FM IBOC receiver that has just been told to tune in a new channel. To keep parts cost down, the local oscillator in the receiver may not be particularly accurate; the IBOC system design must help the radio get the signal correctly. Initial tuning of the station might be off by, say, an unintentional 10–20 kHz local oscillator offset.

Symbol Sync. The pulse train of OFDM symbols is discernable in the time domain, and the receiver finds a coarse symbol sync—enough to differentially detect all subcarriers, looking for the differentially encoded Reference Subcarriers. A cross correlation is performed on the subcarriers to identify the sync string in the Reference Subcarriers, with a "majority logic vote" employed to maximize detection of the Reference Subcarriers in a less than perfect channel.

Frequency Sync. The Reference Subcarrier numbers on the individual Reference Subcarriers are examined to determine how far off center frequency the receiver is. Appearing every 19th subcarrier, the Reference Subcarriers are spaced 6.9 kHz apart. If the receiver is mistuned by an offset of, say, 10–20 kHz, that's an offset of perhaps one or two Reference Subcarrier spacings. The modulo four numbering scheme of the Reference Subcarriers (Chapter 6) gives the receiver enough leeway to identify the frequency offset and correct for it. A corresponding correction is made to the receiver frequency clock.

Coherent Detection. With the job of the differential detection done, the differential encoding is in effect stripped off the Reference Subcarriers, leaving the receiver to examine the phases and amplitudes of each subcarrier. The intended phase and amplitude states of the Reference Subcarriers are known because the contents of the Reference Subcarriers are predictable. The intended states become a reference for coherent detection of the entire OFDM waveform. That is to say, the known correct phase and amplitude states of the Reference Subcarriers are subtracted from the received values, leaving a set of channel state metrics for each Reference Subcarrier—gain error, phase error, and noise. These metrics are employed to equalize the received signal across the channel, and to inform the statistical process of the Viterbi decoder.

Block & and Frame Sync. The sync symbols of the Reference Subcarriers indicate the starting point of each block. The block numbers, transmitted on the Reference Subcarriers, indicate the beginning of each frame. With block and frame synchronization complete, the task of demodulating the information on the Logical Channels begins.

FM IBOC OFDM Modulation: Symbols

The spectral characteristics of OFDM signals were touched upon in Chapter 5, in the section The Spectral Challenge of OFDM. Figure 7.2 illustrates the conversion of a series of output vectors to OFDM subcarrier symbols. On the left the figure symbolizes the passage of a continuing series of blocks and frames containing matrices of information. Each row of the matrices is clocked into the OFDM Signal Generation stage for conversion from a vector, $\underline{X}$, to an OFDM symbol consisting of many modulated subcarriers.

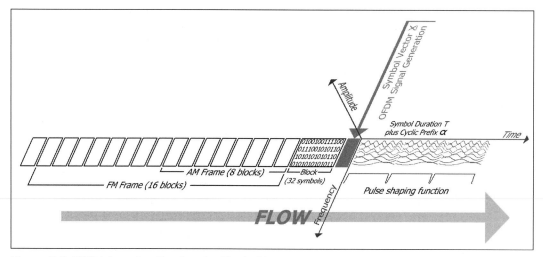

Figure 7.2 IBOC Information Flow into the Physical Layer

Each FM IBOC OFDM subcarrier is modulated in one of two ways—either with one bit per symbol or with two. The phase of the subcarrier conveys the information. The Reference Subcarriers (every 19th OFDM subcarrier, plus some others) are modulated in a simple manner to make them as robust as possible. The modulation is binary phase shift keying (BPSK). As the term "binary" suggests, a reference subcarrier has two states representing binary one (1) and binary zero (0). It is said that a BPSK subcarrier conveys a symbol representing one bit. Table 7.2 representing the two states is simple.

0
1

Table 7.2 BPSK Symbol Values

The remaining OFDM subcarriers are modulated with a more complex waveform—quadrature phase shift keying (QPSK), also called quarternary phase shift keying. QPSK has four states, which requires two bits to represent. Hence, there are two bits per QPSK symbol.

00
01
10
11

Table 7.3 QPSK Symbol Values

To create a BPSK symbol, one need only modulate the subcarrier by setting it to one of two phase states, 180 degrees apart. The QPSK modulated subcarrier requires four states, 90 degrees apart. To generate the symbol and subsequently recover the information from it, the subcarrier is treated as the sum of a real and an imaginary component. The real, or "in-phase," component is represented by a cosine while the imaginary, or "quadrature," component by a sine.

Constellation

Representing the states of BPSK and QPSK symbols in grid form, the symbols and their corresponding bits are shown in Tables 7.4 and 7.5. The in-phase (I) and quadrature (Q) components of the subcarrier are represented in the two axes. The I and Q values have two possible states each. They are indicated by the multipliers that have the scalar value, 1, and a positive or negative sign. Since the only scalar value is one, there is no variation in amplitude of the various I and Q sinusoids. This indicates phase-only modulation. The real component, I, is a cosine function that has unity amplitude and a positive or negative phase (zero or 180 degrees). The same is true for the imaginary component, Q, a sine function, except the sine wave is 90 degrees out of phase with the cosine (that is, they are in quadrature). Hence the sum or (difference) of the two quadrature waves will have unity amplitude and will be at 45, 135, 225, or 315 degrees, depending on the phases of I and Q. Below, these relationships will be explored using units of radians—$\pi/4$, $3\pi/4$, $5\pi/4$, $7\pi/4$.

		I	
		–1	1
Q	j1	–	1
	–j1	0	–

Table 7.4 Bitmap of FM IBOC BPSK Constellation

		I	
		–1	1
Q	j1	01	11
	–j1	00	10

Table 7.5 Bitmap of FM IBOC QPSK Constellation

Tables 7.4 and 7.5 show how each I-Q pair is quantized as one of four symbols. Each table is analogous to a complex plane—a plane with a real and an imaginary axis. The phase and amplitude of the ideal symbols are indicated by a point at the center of each quadrant. In the physical layer, the symbols are affected by noise and distortion, causing each received symbol to miss the ideal phase and amplitude values. Figure 7.3 shows the measured values of 100 FM IBOC subcarrier symbols. This display, called a "constellation" for the resemblance to its astronomical namesake, records the I and Q values of each OFDM symbol as a dot on the complex plane. The symbols shown are from an actual FM IBOC transmission line sample. The figure depicts the constellations of five OFDM subcarriers. These are at the outer end of the lower sideband—numbers -546 to -542. Note how # -546, a Reference Subcarrier, has the two states of a BPSK signal, while the others have the four QPSK states.

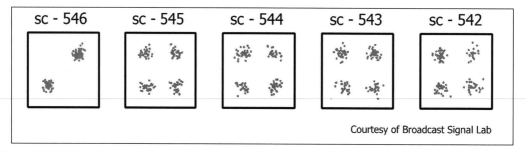

Figure 7.3 Constellations of five OFDM subcarriers

When a point in the constellation is plotted on the complex plane, the result is a constellation diagram. Figure 7.4 reveals the structure of a constellation diagram. A QPSK-modulated subcarrier has four possible ideal phase and amplitude points, one for each value of the symbol. Note how, ideally, these points target four positions that are at odd multiples of 45 degrees or $\pi/4$ radians with respect to the I and Q axes. This is the result of the combining of the various pairs of quadrature signals shown in Tables 7.4 and 7.5.

An incoming signal has phase and amplitude errors that cause a symbol point to miss its ideal mark. As long as the point is unambiguously within the intended quadrant, the decoder may interpret it correctly. The closer to another quadrant that a symbol point appears, the greater the probability it is in the wrong place. It may actually be an errant point that belongs in the adjacent quadrant.

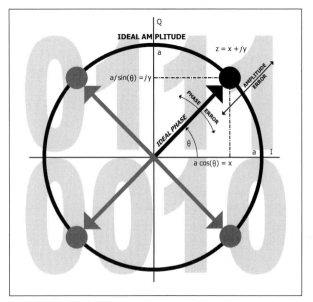

Figure 7.4 Constellation Diagram

The arrangement of the two-bit symbols in the QPSK constellation employs a Gray code to minimize bit errors. If a symbol error occurs, in which a point on the constellation is mistaken for an adjacent symbol, the symbol error results in only one bit error. A Gray code is a sequence of codewords in which there is only a one-bit difference between a codeword and the adjacent codeword. Each QPSK symbol is placed between two symbols whose values differ from it by only one bit. For example, in Figure 7.4 symbol 00 is adjacent to 01 and 10. It is much less likely that a symbol error in demodulating 00 would result in the two-bit error 11 and more likely that the symbol error would result in either 01 or 10. Examination of the other three symbols will reveal the same Gray code relationships with their neighbors.

Meanwhile, the FM IBOC Reference Subcarriers employ BPSK symbols to maximize their robustness. The phase "distance" (in degrees of arc) between the two possible BPSK symbols is twice the distance between two QPSK symbols. This provides less phase ambiguity in the presence of noise, at the expense of one bit per symbol. The use of BPSK maximizes the Reference Subcarriers' resistance to noise, helping the Reference Subcarriers perform their critical mission of providing timing and synchronization information to the receiver.

FM IBOC OFDM Modulation: Computational Basis

Transmission and reception of OFDM signals was made possible by the genesis of mass-produced Digital Signal Processing (DSP) technology. OFDM is one technology for which it would be impracticable to create an analog generator or demodulator. The complexity of an analog circuit board with filters for hundreds of subcarriers within a few hundred hertz of one another would boggle the mind. DSP employs the power of computing to do away with discrete electronic components.

Of course, the radio signal is an electrical representation of phase and amplitude states—an analog signal. That's the physical part of the physical layer. At each end of the analog RF pipeline, the OFDM signal is transposed to and from the digital domain by Digital-to-Analog (DAC) and Analog-to-Digital (ADC) converters. Some conditioning of the signal may occur in either the digital or analog domains. Frequency conversion, filtering and I-Q processing can occur on either side of the digital/analog fence. Amplification, on the other hand, is fundamentally an analog affair, compensating for the power limitations of the DACs and ADCs.

Even with digital signal transmissions, frequency conversion to/from the RF channel frequency is often done with analog mixers. High speed DACs and ADCs that run fast enough to operate directly in the desired FM channel have practical limitations. Cost, speed, precision and dynamic range are competing variables in the design of digital converter circuits. On the transmission side, there may be less price sensitivity than performance sensitivity in the system design. Transmitter design favors DACs with high precision, such as 16-bit, high speed, and good noise and distortion performance. While analog mixing can be performed to bring an Intermediate Frequency signal up to the channel frequency, "direct-to-channel" transmission equipment performs all conversions in the digital domain, until the DAC generates the RF signal directly at the assigned frequency of the station. If analog filtration is necessary, it is to protect the radio spectrum from spurious products that result from imperfect mixing and amplification processes. Sophisticated "pre-correction" algorithms are employed in the digital domain to pre-distort the signal in a manner that corrects for the distortion subsequently induced by the amplification process.

In the receivers, analog filtration may be necessary to reduce out-of-channel signal power being fed to the mixers and ultimately to the ADCs. Classic Intermediate Frequency (IF) design (10.7 MHz for FM reception and 455 kHz for AM) provides a time-tested way to inexpensively filter the incoming signal. Digital broadcasting receiver designs frequently incorporate the classic IF topology—with analog local oscillator, mixer and IF filter, which simplifies the performance requirements of the ADC. For example, the Texas Instruments mixed-signal integrated circuit chip, AFEDRI8201, converts the IF output of the tuner circuit to digitized samples using a precision IF analog-to-digital converter (ADC) running an 80 MHz sampling rate with 12-bit sampling. Then it passes the digitized samples to another chip for HD Radio signal decoding.

In the digital domain it is straightforward to process a waveform to combine or separate the I and Q components. Similarly, to shift the OFDM subcarriers to their fundamental harmonic relationships, the digital signal processing can perform the final adjustment of the frequency of the received signal down to "zero IF" where center frequency becomes zero Hz. The role of the Reference Subcarriers, as mentioned above, includes supplying information for adjustment of the "frequency clock" for this purpose. Note the terminology is digital in nature; it is not a local oscillator that is fine tuned in the analog domain, but a frequency clock tweaked in the digital domain. (Alternatively, a "zero-IF" receiver design directly converts the radio signal to baseband with no intermediate stage, losing the benefits of IF filtering to exclude unwanted energy; this places higher demands on the performance of the mixer and baseband filtering).

The DSP at the transmitter must take each input vector $\underline{X}$ and convert it into a multifrequency OFDM symbol. To do so there are certain OFDM waveform characteristics of which the DSP must be aware. Table 7.6 is taken from the FM System Parameters table, Section 3.5 of the NRSC-5 FM Layer 1 Reference Document (1). It describes the relationship between the FM IBOC OFDM subcarrier frequencies and the symbol rate. The critical ratios were discussed briefly in Chapter 6, relating the 44.1 kHz source audio sampling rate to the rational numbers in the OFDM parameters.

Parameter Name	Symbol	Units	Exact Value (rational)	Rounded Value (4 significant figures)
OFDM Subcarrier Spacing	Δf	Hz	$\dfrac{1488375}{4096}$	363.4
Cyclic Prefix Width	α	none	$\dfrac{7}{128}$	5.469×10^{-2}
OFDM Symbol Duration	T_s	s	$\dfrac{1+\alpha}{\Delta f} = \dfrac{135}{128}\dfrac{8192}{1488375}$	2.902×10^{-3}
OFDM Symbol Rate	R_s	Hz	$1/T_s$	344.5
OFDM Frame Duration	T_f	s	$512\,T_s = \dfrac{65536}{44100}$	1.486

Table 7.6 FM System Parameters

How the subcarrier frequency spacing, Δf, was derived may not be readily apparent. It is described by the ratio between two numbers with no obvious purpose, 1,488,375 and 4,096. To understand the ratio, it is necessary to visit the concept of the cyclic prefix and develop the relationship between Δf and the symbol rate R_s.

In a perfect communications channel, the symbol rate could be simply the inverse of the subcarrier frequency spacing, in other words, $1/\Delta f$. If Δf were, say, 363 Hz, and we were creating a baseband OFDM waveform, the first OFDM subcarrier would be 363 Hz. If $1/\Delta f$ were the symbol rate, then one full cycle of the first subcarrier would contain the phase information of the subcarrier for one symbol. The second subcarrier, at $2 \times 363 = 726$ Hz would have two complete cycles per symbol, and so on. The harmonic relationships of OFDM subcarriers are part of what makes OFDM an elegant scheme.

A cyclic prefix is added (discussed further below) to make the symbol period slightly longer than $1/\Delta f$. This provides protection from delayed multipath reflections and gives the signal processor time to ramp up and down the pulse-like symbol power gracefully.

To delve into the nature of the OFDM waveform, the subjects of convolution and discrete Fourier transformation must be introduced. Convolution, discussed in a different context in Chapter 5, enables the marrying of information characterized by an impulse response to provide practical results. The Discrete Fourier Transform (DFT) enables the shifting between time domain and frequency domain representations of a digitized signal. The convolution of two functions in the time domain is equivalent to the multiplication of those functions in the frequency domain, and vice versa. This powerful relationship, when applied to harmonically related OFDM subcarriers, provides the system designer with a tool kit to transmit hundreds of bits simultaneously (in parallel, so to speak) and recover them reliably.

Convolution

In Chapter 5, convolution was introduced in the process of convolutionally encoding a string of data bits. The information, consisting of i input elements was convolved with a kernel with K memory points. The kernel "smeared" each information bit across K elements of the output word. If, instead of being a vector of data as in Chapter 5, the i information bits describe a sinusoidal wave, and if the K memory points are not a coding algorithm as in Chapter 5, but an impulse response of a signal channel, we would have two functions to convolve in OFDM generation.

The following sections describe the two functions to be convolved in OFDM generation. After that, we turn to the role of the Discrete Fourier Transform before pulling all the pieces together.

OFDM Sinusoidal Subcarriers

A set of OFDM subcarriers is to be encoded with phase information. There is a phase and amplitude characteristic for each sinusoidal OFDM subcarrier. These characteristics are assembled in the data vector $\underline{X}$, which is the output of the Layer 1 digital process driving the OFDM generator. This vector is essentially a spectral map describing in the frequency domain the characteristics of each OFDM subcarrier. In OFDM generation, this vector is convolved with another component to produce the OFDM symbol pulse. Although the role of this convolution in the physical layer differs from the error correction role of the convolutional coding, the processes are analogous.

Like the vector of i data bits in our Chapter 5 convolution, the OFDM data vector $\underline{X}$ is convolved with a kernel that has a characteristic impulse response. For $\underline{X}$, that kernel is the OFDM pulse shaper discussed below. In addition to being convolved, the frequency domain information represented by $\underline{X}$ must be translated to a time domain signal voltage. $\underline{X}$ represents phases and amplitudes of L subcarriers of the OFDM waveform for the period of one symbol, T_s. To convert the binary representations of $\underline{X}$ into an ensemble of OFDM sinusoidal signals, $\underline{X}$ is processed with an algorithm. (See section 13.2 of the FM Layer 1 Reference Document.)

The OFDM symbol waveform is generated by a summation algorithm that is executed for each of the L subcarriers. For FM IBOC, the maximum number of OFDM subcarriers available is

$L = 1093$. The OFDM subcarriers are indexed by their subcarrier numbers, $-546, -545, ...,0,$ $1, ...,545, 546$. To generate each subcarrier from the correct data in vector $\underline{X}$, a function $\underline{X}[l]$ is defined where the index $l = -546, ...,546$.[1] Each indexed value of $\underline{X}[l]$ represents a scaled constellation point for one OFDM subcarrier.

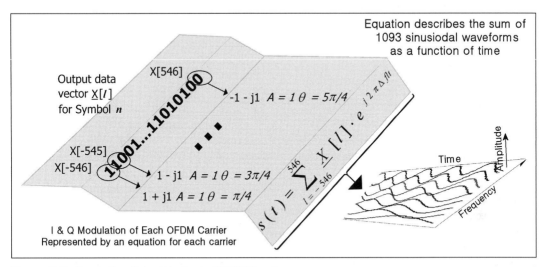

Figure 7.5 Converting Output Vector to OFDM Waveform

Figure 7.5 illustrates how the individual bits (for BPSK subcarriers) and pairs of bits (for QPSK subcarriers) are converted to scaled constellation values with real and imaginary components, I & Q. These values were shown in Tables 7.4 and 7.5 above. Equation 7.1 describes the individual OFDM subcarrier in terms of I and Q, where f is the frequency of the subcarrier, in Hz, and t is time.

$$x(t) = I \cos (2\pi ft) - Q \sin (2\pi ft)$$ **Eq. 7.1**

Solving for the correct phase angle θ, a pair of phase shifts can be substituted for the I and Q components: (An amplitude component is left out of these equations for simplicity, as BPSK and QPSK employ phase modulation only.)

$$x(t) = \cos (2\pi ft) \cos \theta - \sin (2\pi ft) \sin \theta$$ **Eq. 7.2**

The constellation phase θ has two possible states for BPSK and four for QPSK. Equation 7.2 can be manipulated by the following trigonometric identity:

$$\cos(a + b) = \cos(a) \cos(b) - \sin(a) \sin(b)$$ **Eq. 7.3**

---

[1] Readers may observe that the index k is employed in the algorithm in the Reference Document; we have chosen to simplify our algorithm by pre-processing $k = 0, 1, ..., L-1$ into a new index l.

To produce a conventional representation of a phase modulated subcarrier with phase θ: (amplitude A has been restored in this equation.)

$$x(t) = A \cos(2\pi f t + \theta) \qquad \text{Eq. 7.4}$$

Equation 7.4 describes any individual phase modulated OFDM subcarrier over a period of time t, with a frequency f, amplitude A, and phase θ. Computationally there is a more elegant way to represent the OFDM subcarrier. It involves Euler's identity, in which the formation of a sinusoidal wave is described using the natural exponential function. In plainer language, instead of using trigonometric functions (sin and cos), exponents of e are employed. Euler's identity connects these two mathematical forms:

$$e^{jy} = \cos(y) + j \sin(y) \qquad \text{Eq. 7.5}$$

The FM IBOC OFDM equation capitalizes on this relationship. Implicitly, e^{jy} has both a real and an imaginary component, designated $\text{Re}\{A\, e^{j2\pi ft + \theta}\}$ and $\text{Im}\{A\, e^{j2\pi ft + \theta}\}$. Since our next task is to create a real waveform from formula 7.4, we can neglect the imaginary $j \sin(y)$ part of Euler's identity. The value $(2\pi ft + \theta)$ from Equation 7.4 is substituted for the variable y in Equation 7.5, the amplitude factor is inserted, and attention is given only to the real component of the exponential function,

$$x(t) = A \cos(2\pi ft + \theta) = \text{Re}\left\{A\, e^{j2\pi ft + \theta}\right\}$$
$$= \text{Re}\left\{A\, e^{j\theta}\, e^{j2\pi ft}\right\} \qquad \text{Eq. 7.6}$$

Equation 7.6 describes a phase modulated sinusoidal wave in natural exponent form. For notational convenience, the real number indication and brackets are dropped, and the amplitude-phase component is restored to its original form, using the symbol for the scaled constellation points, $\underline{X}[l]$

$$x(t) = \underline{X}[l] e^{j2\pi ft} \qquad \text{Eq. 7.7}$$

So far, we have the makings of one OFDM subcarrier with this form. Let us further generalize the equation to represent the sum of L OFDM subcarriers indexed by the variable l. Since l is an index, let us also multiply it by the subcarrier frequency spacing Δf to establish each frequency.

$$x(t) = \sum_{l=546}^{546} \underline{X}[l] \cdot e^{j2\pi \Delta f l t} \qquad \text{Eq. 7.8}$$

This is a general form of the equation for generating one OFDM symbol consisting of

- L subcarriers

- indexed by l,

- spaced by frequency Δf,

- modulated by the appropriate values in vector $\underline{X}$,

- for a period of time $T_0 \ldots T_s$,

- indexed by time increment t.

At last, Equation 7.8 is the time domain version of the first of two algorithms that must be convolved in the communications channel. It is a time domain description of the ensemble of 1093 potential OFDM subcarriers. There is more work to be done to prepare the symbol(s) for transmission.

Gaps in the OFDM Subcarrier Ensemble

What happens to the subcarriers that are not used in hybrid mode? They are simply represented by null phase values and multiplied by zero amplitude. Hence no subcarriers appear on frequencies that are to be left unpopulated. Since the digital signal processing processes the full bandwidth of the channel, it may be convenient to multiply unused subcarriers by zero amplitude rather than to reconfigure the transmitter or receiver act only upon certain subcarrier frequencies for each mode of operation. Similarly, when the FM IBOC secondary subcarriers are activated in all-digital mode, their amplitudes are set by the use of an amplitude scale factor that treats the secondary independently of the primaries. The amplitude scale factors are presented in the Reference documents in the form a_n. Reference Document (1), the FM Layer 1 document, identifies the amplitude scale factor for each grouping of subcarriers (PM, PX, SM, SX, SP) in hybrid and all-digital modes. Reference Document (6), the FM Transmission System Specifications, indicates the power spectral densities associated with each amplitude scale factor. These are discussed in more detail in Chapter 9.

OFDM Symbol Pulses

Having developed the algorithm for generating a composite signal of modulated OFDM subcarriers, the next step is to transmit the symbol for a fixed period of time—the symbol period. Following that, each symbol must be conditioned before it can be concatenated with the symbols that precede and follow it. The conditioning consists of applying a pulse shaping function to reduce the discontinuities between symbols, thereby controlling the bandwidth of the signal.

The symbol period simply could have been $1/\Delta f$, providing the highest possible throughput rate while maintaining the orthogonality of the subcarriers. Let's call this version of a symbol period $T = 1/\Delta f$, because the IBOC symbol period, T_s, is slightly different, as is explained below. In this simplified case, the symbol rate R_s would equal the frequency spacing, Δf. While this avoids Intercarrier Interference (ICI), which protects all subcarriers of one symbol from each other, it does not provide any protection from Intersymbol Interference (ISI), which occurs when each successive symbol, in time, pollutes the symbol that precedes or follows it.

ICI is caused by the spectral energy of one subcarrier stepping on the frequency of another subcarrier. It is a frequency domain problem. The OFDM subcarriers retain their orthogonality by being modulated in a fashion that each subcarrier's sidebands have zero energy at the center frequencies of the other subcarriers. This phenomenon is further explored in the DFT discussion below.

In OFDM waveforms, ISI can be caused by time-delayed reflections (with multipath propagation) putting unwanted energy from an adjacent symbol period into the current symbol period. See

Figure 7.6. The communication channel has a range of possible delays, called the delay spread, that are likely to occur. As the reflected signal paths are longer than the most direct signal path, the reflected energy of a symbol arrives later than that on the most direct path. The late-arriving copies of the symbol end after the initial symbol period has ended. The tail ends of these late copies bleed into the time slot of the next symbol, corrupting the beginning of of the next symbol. To combat this cause of ISI, the duration of the symbol period can be extended by the anticipated delay spread. (Figure 7.7.)

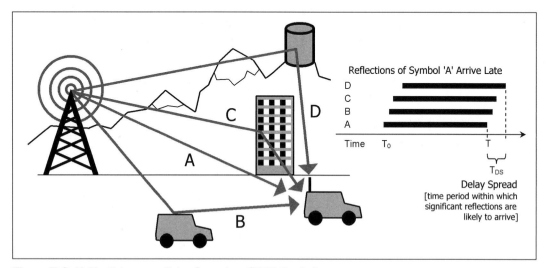

Figure 7.6 Multipath Imposes Delay Spread on OFDM Symbols

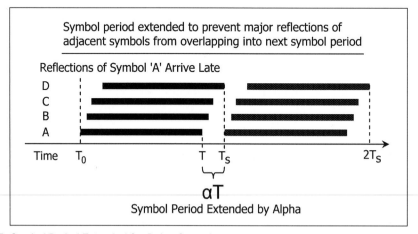

Figure 7.7 Symbol Period Extended for Delay Spread

Guard Interval

The addition of a guard interval to the symbol period protects against ISI caused by the delay spread of the channel, although doing so creates a new problem—what to do during the guard interval? Transmitting nothing in the guard interval creates a series of gaps in the transmitted signal, resulting in a pulse train of symbols. (Illustrated by the gaps in Figure 7.7.) Sharp pulses have wide bandwidths and high peak-to-average ratios. These characteristics do not bode well for transmitting a clean signal with a narrow spectrum.

Figure 7.8 illustrates the time domain representation of a single subcarrier transmitted for one symbol period, incorporating a whole number of cycles, plus a guard time with the subcarrier turned off. The initial subcarrier is the light line appearing as a sinusoid starting on the left and ending at the beginning of the guard time.

Also shown is a delayed copy of the subcarrier, a dotted line, starting late and ending in the guard interval, after the initial subcarrier ends. The reflection ends before the beginning of the next symbol, thereby preventing ISI. (The delay and the guard interval are exaggerated to illustrate the effect.) The third trace, a bold line, is the sum of the initial and the delayed subcarrier as might be received under multipath conditions.

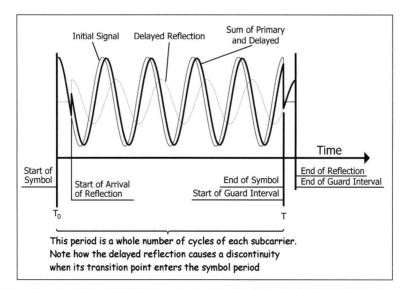

Figure 7.8 Time Domain of One OFDM Subcarrier for One Symbol, with Multipath Reflection

Without any signal being transmitted during the guard interval, each symbol begins and ends abruptly. Likewise, as reflections arrive, their starts and ends are also abrupt. These steeply sloped symbol pulses contain broadband spectral energy and are likely to cause individual OFDM subcarriers to spread energy onto their neighbors, resulting in ICI. The sum of the initial subcarrier's energy and the delayed signal's energy reveals several points of possible discontinuities. The addition of other reflections with various delays would exacerbate the spectral chaos.

Cyclic Prefix

To solve the problem of a signal gap during the guard interval, a simple and extraordinarily effective feature called the cyclic prefix extends the transmission of the symbol into the guard interval. Figures 7.9 and 7.10 illustrate this. The initial subcarrier is extended through the guard interval. It is no longer a whole number multiple of cycles long and therefore contains redundant information. The reflection is identical to the initially received signal, but delayed, with energy extending into the next symbol time. Note, however, that the addition of the cyclic prefix forces all discontinuities to appear in a period of time equal to the guard interval. The time assigned to be the guard interval is positioned at the beginning of each symbol period to allow the unwanted energy from reflections of the previous symbol to end. The receiver is still able to look for an uncorrupted symbol-sampling interval that is a whole number of cycles long, a critical element for recovering the information.

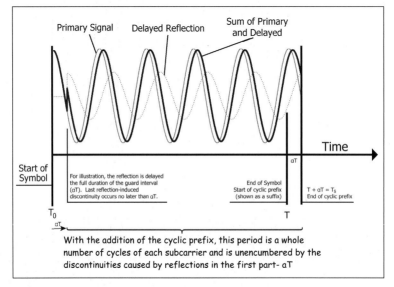

Primary Signal   Delayed Reflection   Sum of Primary and Delayed

Time

αT

Start of Symbol

For illustration, the reflection is delayed the full duration of the guard interval (αT). Last reflection-induced discontinuity occurs no later than αT.

End of Symbol
Start of cyclic prefix (shown as a suffix)

$T + \alpha T = T_S$
End of cyclic prefix

T_0

αT

T

With the addition of the cyclic prefix, this period is a whole number of cycles of each subcarrier and is unencumbered by the discontinuities caused by reflections in the first part- αT

Figure 7.9 Time Domain of One OFDM Subcarrier for One Symbol Plus Cyclic Prefix, with Delayed Reflection

Traditionally, the cyclic prefix is placed in front of the symbol to occupy the guard interval. Close examination of the FM IBOC equation reveals that the cyclic prefix is actually computed as a suffix, in which the symbol a) starts at its initial phase state, b) continues for the period $1/\Delta f$, in which it completes a whole number of cycles of each subcarrier, and c) continues further for a period of α times $1/\Delta f$. As will be seen in the DFT discussion, whether it is a prefix or suffix, α provides the necessary computational breathing room.

While the guard interval protects the symbol from ISI caused by delayed components of the previous symbol, the cyclic prefix is also the first step in spectrally shaping the signal to avoid ICI. The cyclic prefix provides extra time in which the symbol pulse can be ramped smoothly up and down in amplitude to ease the transition between symbols and to give the DSP a periodic waveform with which to work.

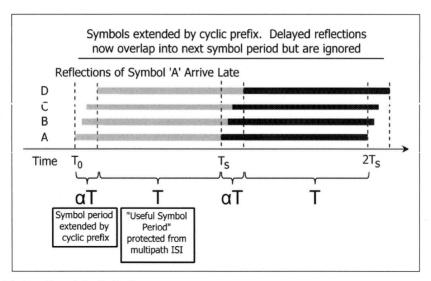

Figure 7.10 Insertion of Cyclic Prefix

The FM IBOC waveform employs a guard interval, α, that is 7/128 of the basic OFDM symbol. The basic OFDM symbol duration, often called the useful symbol period, is $1/\Delta f$, in which time each OFDM subcarrier has a whole number of cycles. This is called T in Figures 7.6 – 7.10. The guard interval, αT is added to T to define the full symbol period, T_s. (See Table 7.6 and Equation 7.9.)

$$T_s = \frac{1+\alpha}{\Delta f} = \frac{135}{128} \cdot \frac{4096}{1488375} \approx 2.9ms$$

Eq. 7.9

Multipath's Impact on the Useful Symbol Period

ISI from delayed reflections bleeding into the next symbol period is addressed by the guard interval. Often overlooked is another question: how is the useful symbol period immune to multipath? The subcarrier-symbol in Figure 7.9 is corrupted by a fairly high level reflection of itself. In the useful symbol period, the sum of the initial signal and a reflection of the same signal produces a phase shift and amplitude change in the subcarrier. No new frequency sidebands are created from this superposition of two copies of the same sinusoid, so there is no ICI. However, since information is incorporated in the phase of a subcarrier, a reflection-induced phase/amplitude shift is a potential source of error for that subcarrier. The multipath-induced phase shift of OFDM subcarriers increases with increasing OFDM subcarrier frequency, because for a given time delay, the higher frequency OFDM subcarrier sees more phase shift. It is the role of the channel estimator in the receiver to equalize the OFDM channel. It relies on known information populated across the OFDM bandwidth. In FM IBOC, this is carried on the Reference Subcarriers, enabling the phase and amplitude corrections to be interpolated between every nineteenth reference. Only those subcarriers that are deeply nulled into the background noise by selective fading are unrecoverable by the channel estimator.

Despite the isolation of delay-induced discontinuities to the guard interval, it is still undesirable to generate unnecessary sidebands as the amplitudes of adjacent symbols jump from the ending value of one symbol to the starting value of the next symbol during the guard interval. This is where the second function, the pulse shaper, comes into play. In the simplest sense, the pulse shaper rolls the power up at the start of each symbol and rolls it off toward the end. Timed correctly, this pinches off the ends of the symbol at zero amplitude, allowing it to make a continuous connection to the zero amplitude start of the next symbol. Nevertheless, the roll-offs in the time domain at each side of the symbol are modulation that creates spectral sidebands. The goal is to create a roll-off function and apply it in such a way that it avoids ICI and facilitates the use of digital signal processing to recover the symbol without ISI.

Pulse Shaping Function

To see how the pulse shaping function works, we look at it in the time domain first. The artful nature of the function will become more apparent as its relationship to the DFT is explored. As described above, the pulse shaping function in effect fades in and fades out each symbol to provide a smooth transition between symbols. It is based on a raised cosine (RC) function, designed to create a nearly rectangular pulse of the symbol, but with rounded corners.

Application of the raised cosine shape is a classic method of rounding off a pulse. A cosine has positive amplitude half the time, and negative the other half. It splits its time above and below the horizontal time axis. To make a raised cosine envelope, the cosine curve is "raised" so that its lowest point rests on the horizontal axis (see Figure 7.11-a). This creates a smooth pulse envelope, starting at zero amplitude, ramping up to unity and back down again. The fundamental raised cosine equation is:

$$f(x) = (1 + \cos(x))/2$$

Eq. 7.10

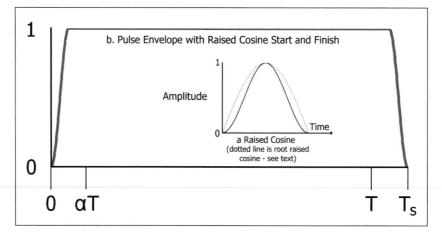

Figure 7.11 Raised Cosine Pulses

Our pulse, however, must be more square, holding a flat top at its specified amplitude for a period of time. (Figure 7.11-b) To accomplish this, the pulse shaper is designed to rise with a raised cosine curve during the period 0 to αT, hold steady at full level (nominally = 1) for the period αT to T, and ramp back to zero with the down side of a raised cosine curve from T to (T + αT). α takes on the role of the slope or roll-off factor. It determines that the first and last 7/135ths of the symbol are in the roll-off region.

Thus the raised cosine filter's smooth roll-off curve shapes the pulse in time, controlling the spectral shape of the energy in the frequency domain. The goal of the shaping is to minimize ICI by protecting each OFDM subcarrier from the frequency sidelobes of the other subcarriers. The IBOC raised cosine pulse shaper is also acting as a filter, but in the time domain. To see how, we must visit the world of the Fourier Transform. Following the Fourier discussion, we'll split the raised cosine into two filters, called matched filters, and explain how and why the transmitter and receiver each execute half the raised cosine filter.

Discrete Fourier Transform

Fourier transforms enable the translation of a time domain representation of a signal into the frequency domain. The "discrete" in Discrete Fourier Transform (DFT) refers to the fact that it works with a digitized signal with a finite number of samples, N. DFT is used in the receiver to recover phase and amplitude of each OFDM subcarrier from the sampled waveform. The inverse of the DFT is the IDFT, which converts a frequency domain representation to the time domain. IDFT is employed to generate the waveform at the transmitter by converting the frequency domain information about the symbol to a time domain signal. The Fast Fourier Transform (FFT) is an efficient means of computing a DFT and has helped make DSP-based communications hardware possible.

Anyone who has observed a continuous audio tone or unmodulated radio carrier on a spectrum analyzer has seen an embodiment of the Fourier transform from time to frequency domain. The time domain signal is a continuous sinusoid, that for our purposes is infinite in duration. The time domain signal is translated by the transform into a "pulse" on the analyzer's frequency display. This spike indicates the frequency and signal power of the continuous wave being monitored. A more sophisticated analyzer could evaluate the phase of the signal as well, because for the time that the continuous wave signal is sampled there is no change in frequency or phase of the signal.

Windowing

The DFT must sample the signal for a period of time in order to obtain the information needed to parse its spectral components into a frequency domain representation. As far as the DFT is concerned, the sample is a snapshot of a periodic waveform of infinite duration. Imagine looking through a window at a passing freight train. (The train is illustrated in Figure 7.12A; Figure 7.12B shows the effect of the window.) Three whole cars are visible, representing the contents of one symbol. The information at the end of the window is a perfect match to its beginning (each car coupling is the complement of the other). The symbol could be repeated infinitely without discontinuity. Looking at it another way, the symbol could be rolled up on itself and the beginning married with the end. These characteristics of periodicity or circularity are key elements of DFT. The DFT uses a window in a similar fashion to view a full cycle of what it assumes to be a periodic signal.

The DFT looks at the OFDM pulse in the window and assumes the pattern repeats. If the window is set at the correct width, it can frame the time domain information to enable the DFT to do its job. If the window is not the correct width (Figure 7.12C), the pattern we see may not appear periodic—the breakpoints will include fractional cars, and opposite ends of the window will not match. If the window is offset in time (Figure 7.12D), we may see some of one information symbol and the rest from another, giving a false impression of the information being conveyed, and producing serious discontinuities at the match points of an otherwise repetitive pattern.

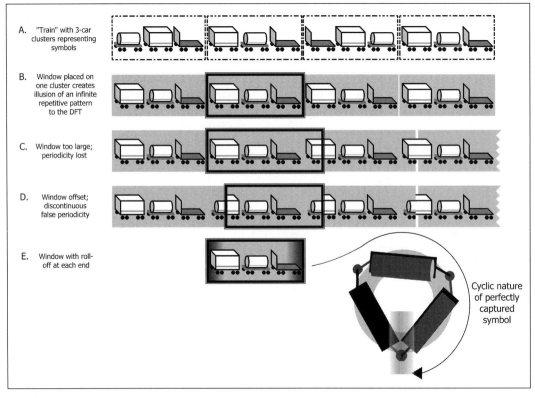

Figure 7.12 Looking at Train of Symbols though a Window

Carrying the analogy one step further, the DFT window has the roll-off function at each end, depicted as curtains that dim the view of the window edges. (Figure 7.12E) This allows us to take advantage of the roll-off as a part of the periodic signal by overlapping the two ends and forming a (mathematically) circular sample. As described above, the delay spread in the channel can distort the beginning of the symbol and the window's curtains help mask the effect. The shape of the roll-off at the window edges can be manipulated to shape the frequency spectrum of the DFT.

Functions in Frequency and Time Domains

For those familiar with filters in the frequency domain (bandpass, low-pass, high-pass, notch, etc), a little backtracking is in order to set the stage. Imagine a bandpass filter with steep but rounded roll-offs on each side. Let's say its slopes have an RC shape. This is an *RC transfer function* in the frequency domain. When the bandpass filter is excited with an impulse, the transfer function in the frequency domain has an *impulse response* in the time domain—the filter's output will "ring" in the time domain. The shape of the frequency domain filter determines the characteristic of the ripples that occur in the time domain.

However, with our OFDM signal, we are applying the RC shape in the opposite direction. The RC pulse shaper is in the time domain, and the resulting ripple pattern is in the frequency domain. The roles are reversed: the ripple pattern becomes the transfer function in the frequency domain, and the RC pulse shape in the time domain is the impulse response.

The OFDM symbol pulse is shaped in the time domain by an RC roll-off (Figure 7.11). This produces slopes on the time-domain envelope for the symbol that are similar to a square wave. A square wave in the time domain, transforms to a sin(x)/x function in the frequency domain, also known as a sinc(x) function. The sinc function has sidelobes with a characteristic ripple that rolls off from the central spike (see Figure 7.13). Our square-wave-like RC pulse-shaper (time domain) produces sinc-like frequency sidelobes (frequency domain) that are beneficial to OFDM.

The zero energy points of the sinc-like pulse are what make it so valuable in OFDM processing. They appear at multiples of Δf. This places the zero energy points of each subcarrier's spectrum on the center frequencies of the other subcarriers. This is the orthogonality that puts the "O" in OFDM. To maintain orthogonality, the receiver must obtain a good synch to the symbol rate, a good lock on the start time of each symbol, and a good frequency clock with which to sample the symbol.

Just like the true sinc spectrum, our sinc-like frequency spectrum has convenient zero energy points and a similarly infinite theoretical bandwidth. The only difference is that the ripples of the sinc-like pulse of the raised cosine function are not as pronounced as those of the sinc pulse shown in Figure 7.13, indicating less energy in raised cosine sidebands than in those of a square wave.

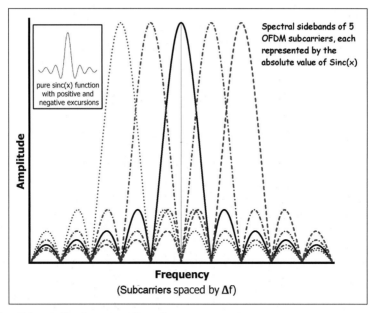

Figure 7.13 Sinc Pulses in the Frequency Domain

Doppler, too!

The structure of the IBOC waveform is based on channel-specific constraints that lead to the selection of: OFDM channel bandwidth; frequency spacing, Δf, that has an inverse relationship to the symbol rate; carrier modulation, such as BPSK and QPSK, balancing the bit rate against robustness; and multipath delay spread, that affects the symbol rate. One other factor in OFDM design for a mobile environment is the speed of the mobile receiver with respect to the various incoming reflections of the signal. The variations in the apparent speeds of the received reflections are called the "Doppler spread." Where the delay spread is the variation in times of arrival of the signal, the Doppler spread is the range of apparent speeds, as indicated by the apparent frequencies of the received reflections.

The resulting Doppler frequency shifts of the reflections impinge on the orthogonality of the OFDM subcarriers. If the spectrum of the received direct signal is similar to Figure 7.13, then the spectrum of a Doppler-shifted reflection would be a frequency-shifted version of Figure 7.13 superimposed on Figure 7.13. Given a large enough frequency shift of the reflected signal, the unwanted sideband energy could be excessive at the underlying Δf zero crossings. Thus, Doppler spread contributes to ICI. Consider two signal paths and a moving vehicle such that the two versions of the signal at the receiver have an apparent speed differential of about 80 mph (say 36 m/sec, 130 km/hr). With a wavelength of 3 m at 100 MHz, the speed differential divided by the wavelength yields a frequency differential of about 12 Hz. This is a very modest proportion of the frequency spacing Δf, indicating that even an extreme Doppler spread in FM IBOC would only be a minor source of ICI.

DFT Computation

The DFT process produces a received signal in the frequency domain that consists of a series of overlapping sinc-like spectral footprints, one for each OFDM subcarrier, similar to those shown in Figure 7.13. To see how these sinc spectra result from the process, first a look at the DFT equations is in order, followed by the incorporation of the pulse function in the equations.

Since the DFT is set up to analyze specific frequency steps, it is looking at the L individual frequencies of the OFDM subcarriers. In the FM IBOC OFDM ensemble there are 1093 possible subcarriers, indexed from –546 to +546 (including 0). To create a one-for-one correspondence between OFDM subcarrier complex data points (frequency domain) and complex data points of the waveform (time domain), assume there are L individual time domain data points, indexed by time t. Vector $\underline{x}(t)$ is a set of digital samples of one symbol arriving at the receiver. The following DFT equation transforms these time domain samples into the frequency domain representation of the OFDM subcarriers' amplitudes and phases, with real (in-phase) and imaginary (quadrature) components. Frequency domain functions are generally capitalized, as is $X(l)$ on the left.

$$X(l) = \sum_{t=-546}^{546} \underline{x}[t] \cdot e^{-j2\pi\Delta flt} \qquad \text{Eq. 7.11}$$

On the right, two functions appear. The vector $\underline{x}(t)$ should now be recognizable as the time domain representation of the symbol. It was the result of Equation 7.8. With a lower case function name indicating this is a time domain function, $\underline{x}(t)$ is the representation of the OFDM symbol waveform amplitude that is received by the receiver (in a perfect world, without any channel impairments). For each subcarrier frequency l, the DFT multiplies each time element of the time domain vector by the natural exponential function (e), and sums the results. This draws out the I and Q components of each frequency of interest, represented by $X(l)$, enabling phase and amplitude to be determined for each subcarrier. (The finer points of complex DFT versus real DFT are overlooked to keep the explanations at a top level.)

The IDFT function that initially generates the time domain waveform $x(t)$ is in fact an equation already developed above—Equation 7.8, repeated as Equation 7.12 for convenience:

$$x(t) = \sum_{l=-546}^{546} X[l] \cdot e^{j2\pi\Delta flt} \qquad \text{Eq. 7.12}$$

Compare Equations 7.11 and 7.12. The visible differences between the DFT and the IDFT are the change of sign of the exponential function's exponent, the reversal of the positions of the time domain and frequency domain functions, $x(t)$ and $X(l)$, and switching the increment l or t of the summation process. To maintain simplicity, a scale factor, 1/L, that is applied either to one equation or the other to make them balanced, has been omitted.

The IDFT and DFT are implemented in transmitters and receivers, respectively, using the FFT to reduce the number of computations necessary to process the data.

Insert Pulse Shaping Function

To process the signal for transmission, the expression in Equation 7.12 is multiplied by a pulse-shaping function—$h(t)$. That is to say, the time domain representation of the symbol without rounded edges $(x(t))$, is multiplied by the time domain representation of the pulse shape $(h(t))$.

$$h(t) = \begin{cases} \cos\left(\pi \dfrac{\alpha T - t}{2\alpha T}\right) & \text{if } 0 < t < \alpha T \\[2mm] & \text{if } \alpha T \leq t \leq T \\[2mm] 1 & \\[2mm] \cos\left(\pi \dfrac{T - t}{2\alpha T}\right) & \text{if } T < t < T(1+\alpha) \\[2mm] 0 & \text{otherwise} \end{cases}$$

Eq. 7.13

Time t extends from the beginning of the symbol period, through the useful symbol time T, and ends after the addition of the guard time, $T \times (1+\alpha)$, also known as T_s. If α is 7/128ths of the useful symbol time, T, then it is 7/135ths of the total symbol period, T_s. As equation 7.13 shows, the function ramps up during the first 7/135ths of T_s, which is αT. Then the pulse is unchanged for most of its duration, where it is multiplied by 1. The ramp down at the end of the symbol period also lasts 7/135ths of T_s.

The shape of the pulse, in the time domain, is depicted by the wide flat trace in Figure 7.14. On inspection, the pulse shape does not have the characteristic shape of a cosine curve. (See the inset for better detail.) It lacks the finer structure of the characteristic "s" shape of the cosine (also part of the inset). The reason for this condition is that the pulse shaping curve is the really the square root of a raised cosine. This is called square root raised cosine, or simply Root Raised Cosine (RRC). The RRC pulse shaper has a slope similar to the Raised Cosine (RC), and therefore has similar bandwidth controlling characteristics, although the RRC is slightly less effective in this regard. Using the RRC on transmission enables the use of a second RRC at the receiver.

Identical RRC filters are placed at the transmitter and receiver; this is called a matched filter. (In practice, the filter at the receiver is the complex conjugate of the transmitter's filter, with matching amplitude and complementary phase characteristics.) If the goal of the filtering were simply to control spectrum occupancy, the RC filter would be placed entirely at the transmitter. However, on its way to the receiver, the signal picks up delayed reflection energy in the guard times, and realizes a general increase in noise. To better control the spectral energy in the pulse arriving at the receiver, and maximize the likelihood of recovering the waveform now compromised by the propagation channel, it is valuable to have a pulse shaping filter at the receiver as well(as long as it is also synchronized in the time domain to correctly shape the incoming flow of symbols). Recall that the raised cosine shaped pulse provides an ideal sinc-like function for OFDM orthogonality. It stands to reason that placing the two RRC filters in the path between transmitter and receiver is like placing one RC filter somewhere in the path. In the time domain, the matched pulse shapers multiply the passing signal by their characteristic impulse responses. Thus, the effect of the first RRC filter at the transmitter is multiplied by the second RRC filter at the receiver. RRC × RRC = RRC^2 = RC. The second trace on the inset of Figure 7.14 is the multiplication of two RRC pulse shapes in the time domain—an RC pulse shaper. The receiver's RRC pulse shaper helps reform the pulse shape in the presence of noise, providing the DFT the window it requires to demodulate the symbol.

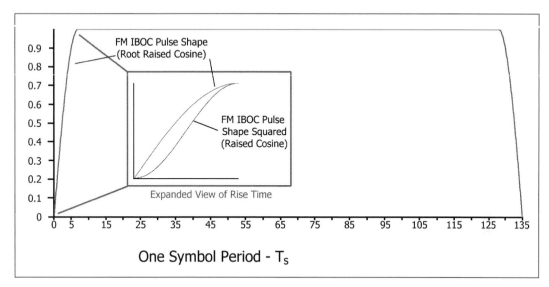

Figure 7.14 FM IBOC Pulse Shape and Matched Filter Shape

A Stream of Symbols

Equation 7.13 is the pulse shaping function that is multiplied with the time domain symbol, Equation 7.12. To combine the equations and generalize them to the nth symbol, time t is extended from representing the duration of one symbol (T_0 to T_s) to represent all time, encompassing an infinite continuum of symbols. In this case, nT_s then represents the duration of n symbols, and $t = 0\ldots\infty$.

For calculating each OFDM pulse, the time during any given symbol is computed by subtracting the n previous symbols, from the current time: $t - nT_s$. Also, to duplicate the FM time domain equation in section 13.2 of the Layer 1 Reference Document (1), we restore the index l from –546 to +546 numbered OFDM subcarriers to the index k from 0 to 1093 indexed subcarriers.

$$y_n(t) = h(t - nT_s) \cdot \sum_{k=0}^{L-1} \underline{X}_n[k] \cdot e^{j2\pi\Delta f\left(k - \frac{L-1}{2}\right)(t - nT_s)}$$

Eq. 7.14

By its lower case designation, "y_n", this equation is known to be a time domain function. It indexes individual symbols with n, OFDM subcarriers per symbol with k, and time t is indexed by an undefined quantization rate to be employed by the transmitter's DSP. Figure 7.15 is an actual FM IBOC signal captured from the digital transmitter of hybrid IBOC station. Evident in the waveform are the steep shoulders of the pulses leading to zero amplitude pinch-offs between symbols. In the time domain this is the only recognizable structure of the digital signal. Even if one were to zoom in to fractional symbol times or zoom out to encompass blocks or frames of symbols, no other patterns emerge. The sample for this signal was taken from the digital exciter sampling port of a station with high-level combining. This sample has no analog FM component.

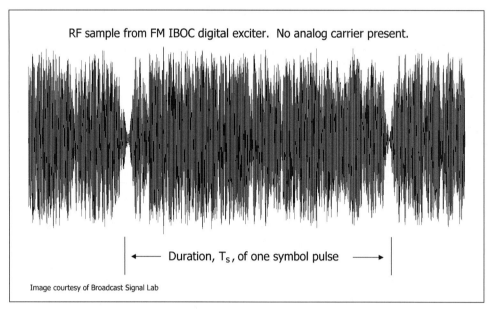

RF sample from FM IBOC digital exciter. No analog carrier present.

◄── Duration, T_s, of one symbol pulse ──►

Image courtesy of Broadcast Signal Lab

Figure 7.15 FM IBOC Waveform

Convolution Revisited

At the outset of this discussion, two functions were described as being key elements of a convolution in the transmit-receive process. The two functions, appearing in Equation 7.14, are connected to the convolution. However, Equation 7.14 consists of the multiplication of two time domain waveforms. No convolution is shown. What's the story?

Convolution is represented by the symbol " $\star$ ", not to be confused with the multiplication symbol, "·". Recall from Chapter 5 that convolution of the data stream involved a vector of finite length (N points) and kernel, or impulse response, of finite length (M points). The full length of the kernel was employed to process each individual data point of the vector, to "smear" the information of each data point across M points of the output vector. The net length of the convolved data would be $N+M-1$ points. This is true, unless the last $M-1$ points are wrapped around to the front of the data vector and convolved with it. When this is performed, the output vector becomes a circular function with a cyclical characteristic.

The cyclic nature of a circularly convolved data vector is illustrated in Figure 7.12. It shows a cyclical representation of the OFDM symbol in the time domain, in which the front and back ends of the symbol are overlapped to form a complete circle. The frequency domain transform of this cyclical OFDM waveform is likewise circular in nature (but more difficult to represent graphically). In the frequency domain it is the frequency spectrum that in effect "wraps around" on itself. This is the "aliasing" that occurs when an input frequency exceeds one half the sampling rate of the DFT, appearing on a frequency alias within the DFT spectrum. It is important, then, to ensure the time domain sample of the waveform has high frequencies filtered out before executing the DFT.

A useful fact about Fourier Transforms is that multiplication on one side of the transform is equivalent to convolution on the other side, and vice versa. Thus, if the time domain pulse shaper $h(t)$ is multiplied with the time domain OFDM symbol, $x(t)$, then the frequency domain versions of these functions are convolved. In other words, the impulse response of the pulse shaper (in the time domain) is multiplied with the time domain representation of the symbol. In the frequency domain, the equivalent would be to convolve the sinc-like transfer function with the individual OFDM subcarriers to achieve the same result—minimize ICI. From a processing perspective, in the IBOC case it is less cumbersome to perform this multiplication in the time domain than it is to convolve in the frequency domain.

$$F[h(t) \cdot x(t)] = H(t) * X(t)$$

Eq. 7.15

where $H(t) * X(t)$ denotes the convolution of the frequency domain forms of the pulse filter impulse response and the OFDM frequency spectrum.

Equation 7.15 states that impulse response multiplication and taking the Fourier Transform (F) on the time domain side is the same as convolving the transfer function of the pulse shaper with the frequency domain representation of the OFDM waveform on the frequency domain side. To reiterate, the impulse response of the pulse shaper in the time domain results in a sinc-like transfer function in the frequency domain. It has infinite bandwidth, and through convolution, spreads each individual OFDM subcarrier's energy across the entire bandwidth of the channel. Figure 7.13 illustrates this convolution by showing how the sinc-like pulse is convolved with each OFDM subcarrier. The convolution in the frequency domain "smears" each subcarrier across the frequency spectrum in sinc-like spectral pulses. The spectral energy of all the subcarriers overlaps, yet at each Δf point the spectra leave no extraneous energy to cause ICI.

Processing Efficiencies across the Convolution/Multiplication Divide

Convolution is a far more processing-intensive activity than multiplication, particularly for complex waveforms. The DFT benefits from time domain multiplication of the pulse shaping function to achieve convolution in the frequency domain. Multiplication in the time domain is an efficient means of performing convolution in the frequency domain, earning the benefits of frequency domain orthogonality with the simplicity of time domain multiplication. Interestingly, the reverse is also true; multiplication in the frequency domain is an efficient means of performing convolution in the time domain. This comes into play in channel equalization. Channel impairments caused by propagation conditions convolve the signal with the channel conditions, in the time domain as the signal propagates. Rather than design an equalizer that adapts to phase and amplitude shifts using convolution in the time domain, it is much simpler to perform the equalization as multiplication in the frequency domain. The signal is processed by the DFT to produce an array of phase/amplitude values for each subcarrier frequency. Using the known information in the Reference Subcarriers, the errors are computed. Each subcarrier can be equalized for the error using ordinary multiplication in the frequency domain.

We have come full circle, so to speak, with our convolution process in the radio channel. The time domain OFDM subcarriers are multiplied by a RRC pulse shaper, which is the same as convolving them with the filter in the frequency domain. Then they are transmitted as a time domain waveform. Upon reception, the time domain waveform is filtered again by being multiplied in time with a RRC filter. Therefore, for a second time the frequency domain is convolved with a RRC. The net of the two filters' actions is an RC filter that produces, in the received frequency domain, the convolution of the sinc-like spectrum with the OFDM frequency spectrum, which maintains orthogonality among OFDM subcarriers.

What a journey the development of practicable OFDM has taken. From the early 1800s when Fourier developed the transform concept, until now, the subtleties of DFT, FFT and other aspects of the transform were steadily exposed like the proverbial peeling of the onion. Practical computer application of DFT resulted in the rediscovery of the FFT method in the 1960s. The subsequent evolution of the computer first, then DSP hardware, brought this powerful tool to the masses. The genius of OFDM was realized by the incredibly clever use of FFT to efficiently create virtual periodic waveforms (OFDM symbols) modulated with window functions to maintain orthogonality and minimize interference. These waveforms could be readily configured, generated, transmitted and received with inexpensive technology.

The FM IBOC waveform is based on these OFDM fundamentals, using the constraints of the communications channel to obtain optimum performance from the system. Those constraints include the presence of analog FM carriers (both host and adjacent), the presence of adjacent-channel IBOC signals, the noise characteristics of the spectrum, the coverage areas of the host analog signals, the reliability and information rates required for the service, and so on. The design of IBOC OFDM is innovative because this is a service that had to be modeled for a complex environment. Not only did it have to ensure compatibility with other like OFDM signals in the band, but also had to be compatible with the existing infrastructure of high power analog transmitters and legacy analog receivers.

In the next chapter section we divert to AM IBOC, discussing those characteristics that differ from FM IBOC. In the subsequent chapter, attention is given to the performance characteristics of the AM and FM IBOC systems.

8 From the Top Down: The Physical Layer– AM OFDM

Continuing our trip down the IBOC protocol stack, this time on the AM IBOC signal, it took the better part of two chapters to drill into Layer1. Chapter 5 covered the thin Layer 2 and burrowed into the upper-level processes of Layer 1—scrambling, channel encoding, and interleaving. Chapter 6 continued the journey, pursuing logical connection to the OFDM IBOC signal. The Logical Channels were linked to the IBOC signal structure, with symbols, blocks and frames in the time domain, and interleaver matrices assigned to OFDM subcarrier groups in the frequency domain. What remain to be discussed about the AM IBOC Layer 1 document (NRSC-5 Reference Document 2) are its electrical characteristics.

NRSC-5 Reference Document Number	Reference Document Title	NRSC-5 Reference Document Number	Reference Document Title
1.	Doc. No. SY_IDD_1011s rev. E HD Radio™ Air Interface Design Description **Layer 1 FM** iBiquity Digital Corporation, 3/22/05	6.	Doc. No. SY_SSS_1026s rev. D HD Radio™ **FM Transmission System Specifications** iBiquity Digital Corporation, 2/18/05
2.	Doc. No. SY_IDD_1012s rev. E HD Radio™ Air Interface Design Description **Layer 1 AM** iBiquity Digital Corporation, 3/22/05	7.	Doc. No. SY_IDD_1028s rev. C HD Radio™ Air Interface Design Description **Program Service Data** iBiquity Digital Corporation, 3/31/05
3.	Doc. No. SY_IDD_1014s rev. F HD Radio™ Air Interface Design Description **Layer 2 Channel Multiplex Protocol** iBiquity Digital Corporation, 2/7/05	8.	Doc. No. SY_SSS_1082s rev. D HD Radio™ **AM Transmission System Specifications** iBiquity Digital Corporation, 2/24/05
4.	Doc. No. SY_IDD_1017s rev. E HD Radio™ Air Interface Design Description **Audio Transport** iBiquity Digital Corporation, 3/31/05	9.	Doc. No. SY_IDD_1085s rev. C HD Radio™ Air Interface Design Description **Program Service Data Transport** iBiquity Digital Corporation, 2/7/05
5.	Doc. No. SY_IDD_1020s rev. E HD Radio™ Air Interface Design Description **Station Information Service Protocol** iBiquity Digital Corporation, 2/18/05	10.	Doc. No. SY_IDD_1019s rev. E HD Radio™ Air Interface Design Description **Advanced Application Services Transport** iBiquity Digital Corporation, 8/4/05

Table 8.1 Protocols Addressed in Chapter 8

The previous chapter provided an introduction to OFDM, which will not be repeated here. This chapter focuses on AM IBOC-specific characteristics such as the phase, amplitude, modulation, frequencies, and pulse shaping of the IBOC signal, relating the logical flow in Chapter 6 to the electromagnetic spectrum. This discussion is essentially about the physical layer as defined in the classic Open Systems Interconnection Reference Model. Sections 12, 13, and 14 of the AM Layer 1 Reference Document relate to the OFDM characteristics. In addition, the two Reference Documents that are not components of the protocol stack—AM and FM Transmission System specifications—outline performance specifications of the IBOC signal. These are NRSC-5 Reference Documents (6) and (8). They are discussed in Chapter 9.

It may be helpful to open NRSC-5 Reference Document 2 (see Table 8.1) to sections 11, 12, 13, and 14 while reading this chapter. Sections 11 of the AM and FM Layer 1 Reference Documents, the System Control Processing sections, provide the entrée into the physical layer discussion. System Control, covered in Chapter 6, addresses how transmitters and receivers are informed what the configuration of the IBOC signal is. The Service Mode is the primary structural indication to the receiver. In addition, on the AM side, some other indicators convey the selected analog audio bandwidth and the selected hybrid OFDM scale factors.

Section 12 of the AM Layer 1 Reference Document defines the OFDM Subcarrier Mapping Process. Here, the various interleaver matrices are mapped to the OFDM subcarrier groupings. Chapter 6 developed the logical relationship of the interleaver matrices, such as AM Primary Upper or Lower ($\underline{PU}$, $\underline{PL}$), to the symbol vector $\underline{X}$ that maps to specific subcarrier numbers within the OFDM subcarrier groups. This chapter discusses the frequencies, amplitudes, and modulation of those OFDM subcarriers. Section 5 of the Layer 1 Reference Document, titled Waveforms and Spectra, also informs this discussion.

Sections 13 and 14 of the AM and FM Layer 1 Reference Documents describe the algorithms that create the OFDM waveform. Section 13, OFDM Signal Generation, describes the manner in which a single symbol pulse is created, while Section 14, Transmission Subsystem, describes the assembly of the transmitted stream of pulses, and the insertion of the analog source for hybrid operation.

AM IBOC OFDM System

Turning to the AM Layer 1 Reference Document (2) of NRSC-5, we can rely heavily on the similarities between AM and FM IBOC to describe AM IBOC. The fundamental timing and rate parameters are close kin. Modulation on AM includes basic BPSK and QPSK as on FM, but expands to higher order waveforms. AM takes advantage of the ability to apply varying amplitude scale factors to each sideband of OFDM subcarriers, tailoring the power spectral density of the digital signal to optimize performance and compatibility. FM uses OFDM scaling only to distinguish between primary and secondary subcarriers in all-digital operation.

AM Parameters

AM Table 8.2 contains the same kinds of parameters as FM Table 7.6. The key difference in the values of the parameters begins with the frequency spacing, Δf, of the subcarriers. AM IBOC subcarriers have half the frequency spacing of FM, about 181 Hz versus 363. Correspondingly, AM has twice the symbol duration and half the symbol rate. Achieving equilibrium with the FM scheme, AM IBOC transmits 256 symbols per frame while FM does 512. This permits both systems to have the same one-and-a-half-second frame rate. Recall that the frame rate is based on that ratio to the source audio sampling rate, 44.1 kSa/s—a characteristic just as critical for audio clocking on AM as on FM IBOC. ($T_f = 65536/44100$) This symmetry in frame rates also simplifies receiver design.

Parameter Name	Symbol	Units	Exact Value (rational)	Rounded Value (4 significant figures)
OFDM Subcarrier Spacing	Δf	Hz	$\dfrac{1488375}{8192}$	181.7
Cyclic Prefix Width	α	none	$\dfrac{7}{128}$	5.469×10^{-2}
OFDM Symbol Duration	T_s	s	$\dfrac{1+\alpha}{\Delta f} = \dfrac{135}{128}\dfrac{8192}{1488375}$	5.805×10^{-3}
OFDM Symbol Rate	R_s	Hz	$1/T_s$	172.3
OFDM Frame Duration	T_f	s	$512\,T_s = \dfrac{65536}{44100}$	1.486

Table 8.2 AM System Parameters

Modulation

To pack as much information as possible in the AM IBOC channel, higher-order modulation schemes are required. Figure 8.1 labels the AM IBOC spectrum with the modulation types in each sideband. The two Reference Subcarriers are modulated with BPSK, the most noise-resistant modulation because it has the fewest bits per symbol (one).

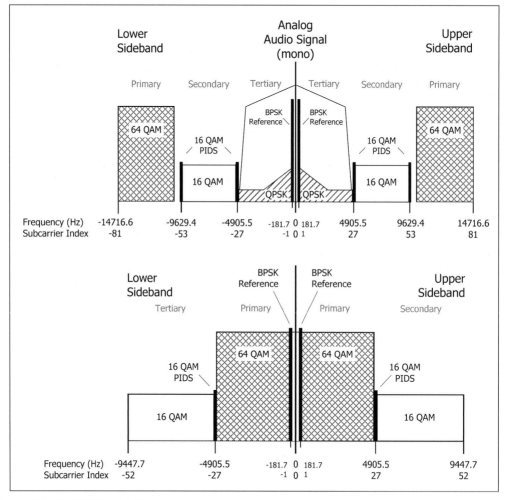

Figure 8.1 AM IBOC Modulation

Like BPSK, QPSK is constructed of phase shifts, and no information is conveyed in the amplitude of the waveform. QPSK has two phase-states for In-Phase and two for Quadrature components of the signal, netting two bits per symbol. QPSK is employed on the hybrid Tertiary subcarriers riding beneath the analog signal. On the constellation diagram, the four possible data words are 90 degrees apart and share the same amplitude (See Figure 7.4). To obtain more bits per symbol, the number of phase states can be increased, and also the amplitude of the signal can be used to convey information. Without using amplitude, 16-PSK would employ 22.5-degree phase shifts on the circle in Figure 7.4. 64-PSK would employ 5.6-degree phase shifts. In the presence of noise, and with minor imperfections in obtaining a phase reference, symbols with such narrow phase resolutions would be difficult to recover reliably. Conveying information in both phase and amplitude reduces the ambiguity between adjacent states on the constellation, permitting higher-order modulation.

Quadrature Amplitude Modulation "QAM" is the term for this family of methods using amplitude and phase states to convey information. The two types of QAM employed in AM IBOC transmission are 16-QAM and 64-QAM. 16-QAM is always employed on the PIDS subcarriers. In hybrid mode, 16-QAM is also employed on the Secondary sideband subcarriers, while the Primary subcarriers are the only ones with 64-QAM. Note how in hybrid mode the complexity of the modulation increases as the distance from center frequency increases. Subcarriers closer to the host analog signal's sidebands must be more robust in the presence of more interference from the analog host. In all-digital mode, the Secondary and Tertiary subcarriers are pushed up to 64-QAM, taking advantage of the lack of analog host interference and offsetting the reduction in IBOC channel bandwidth.

Table 8.3 shows four-bit words are defined by each of the 16 points on the 16-QAM constellation. Phase is defined by the combination of a pair of I and Q components. The amplitude units of the constellation are established with two possible amplitude states for I and for Q. For instance, the codeword 1111 is conveyed with the quadrature modulation 0.5 + j0.5. Notice how the codewords are set up in Gray code fashion where each codeword abuts horizontally and vertically with codewords that differ by only one bit. An error in reading a codeword is most likely to result in a one-cell offset, which produces one bit-error out of the four bits.

		I			
		–1.5	–0.5	0.5	1.5
	1.5	0001	1001	1101	0101
	0.5	0011	1011	1111	0111
Q	–0.5	0010	1010	1110	0110
	–1.5	0000	1000	1100	0100

Table 8.3 AM IBOC 16-QAM Bitmap

A bitmap for 64-QAM would be a larger rendition of Table 8.3, consisting of an eight by eight matrix with each cell containing a six-bit codeword. The eight quantization levels are defined as ±0.5, ±1.5, ±2.5, ±3.5. These levels are relative values. The actual transmitted levels of the QAM signals are dependent on the Amplitude Scale Factors assigned to each subcarrier. Figure 8.2 illustrates constellations of 64 QAM and 16 QAM modulation.

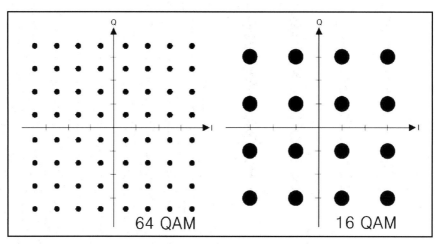

Figure 8.2 64 QAM and 16 QAM Constellation Diagrams

Amplitude Scaling

Level Reference	Hybrid			All-Digital		
	Unmodulated analog power, dBc per...			Licensed analog power, dBc per...		
Sideband Subcarriers	OFDM subcarrier	300 Hz	Sideband (25 subcarriers, upper or lower)	OFDM subcarrier	300 Hz	Sideband (25 subcarriers)
Reference	−26	Single subcarriers		−15	Single subcarriers	
Primary	−30	−27.8	−16	−15	−12.8	−1
	Low Power Option					
Secondary	−43	−40.8	−29	-30	−27.8	−16
Tertiary*	−44 to −50	47.8 and up	−33.9	-30	−27.8	−16
PIDS	−43	Single subcarriers		-30	Single subcarriers	
	High Power Option					
Secondary	−37	−34.8	−23			
Tertiary	−44	−41.8	−30			
PIDS	−37	Single subcarriers				

Hybrid Tertiary in Low Power Level mode has a slope. (Figure 8.1) Starting near center frequency and counting out, the first Tertiary subcarrier on each side begins at −44 dBc. Each adjacent subcarrier is 1/2 dB less, ending with the thirteenth at −50. The remaining twelve subcarriers are at −50. The power level in the Sideband column is the power sum of all 25 subcarriers in one Tertiary sideband.

Table 8.4 AM IBOC Power Levels

Table 8.4 is a compilation of the Amplitude Scale Factors referenced in the AM Layer 1 Reference Document (2), and whose numerical values are specified in the AM Transmission System Specifications Reference Document (8). The power reference for both the hybrid and all-digital modes is the power level of the analog AM signal. In hybrid mode, the actual unmodulated power of the analog is the reference. In all-digital, there is no analog signal to reference, so it must be the licensed power that becomes the reference.

The power level for each OFDM subcarrier is specified in the OFDM column. Sidebands with multiple subcarriers can be measured with a spectrum analyzer set to 300 Hz resolution bandwidth. These target values are given in the 300 Hz column. The total power of each sideband could be measured using a channel power measurement feature available on some spectrum analyzers, in which the instrument integrates the total power in a user-specified bandwidth. The target values for each sideband are given in the Sideband column.

These values are the target values of the OFDM generation process and should not be mistaken for the spectrum masks that establish upper bounds on these levels. Measurement methods and the spectral masks are covered in Chapter 9. Note that the singleton subcarriers, PIDS and Reference, will not have useful 300 Hz bandwidth values because each is in a nominally 181.7-Hz space among subcarriers of other types.

The Negated Complex Conjugate

Simultaneously transmitting energy for analog and digital signals on the same frequencies presents some compatibility challenges. Compatibility of the digital signal with existing analog radios is paramount—analog radios must remain as unaffected as possible by the host station's digital subcarriers. This is where an innovative technique is employed to help isolate the digital and analog energy in AM receivers. It utilizes the principles of *conjugation* and *negation* of complex functions. The goal of this method is to create upper and lower digital sidebands that are *complementary*, such that when they are added in an analog demodulator they cancel each other.

As mentioned above, in anticipation of host analog interference to digital reception, the hybrid AM Secondary and Tertiary subcarriers are modulated with lower-order constellations (16-QAM and QPSK, respectively). This improves digital robustness in the presence of the host analog "noise." The information rate of the constellation is selected to optimize the information rate versus the interference from the host analog signal. The choice of a given constellation size does not provide any benefit to analog receivers.

Analog Channel

To develop an appreciation for the way in which some digital sidebands are made to appear complementary to an analog receiver, let us first review the structure of the AM IBOC signal. The recommended bandwidth for the analog signal is ±5 kHz. This encompasses the Tertiary sidebands. An optional analog mode is available that permits analog bandwidth to ±8 kHz, placing additional energy on the Secondary sidebands. With a total Level 1 power of –33.9 dBc for each Tertiary sideband, upper and lower, the digital energy beneath the passband of a 5 kHz analog radio therefore totals about –31 dBc. If both Tertiary sidebands were simply noise-like, they would contribute to a fairly high, noise floor in the received analog audio, about –31 dB-S/N. If, instead, the Tertiary sidebands were phase mirror images of each other—complementary—the analog AM radio would effectively sum the two sidebands in the demodulation process, canceling out the unwanted tertiary energy with a net zero sum.

AM detection commonly employs either synchronous or envelope detection. In synchronous detection the received signal is divided by a phase-locked copy of the raw, unmodulated carrier, producing the audio baseband. The synchronous detector obtains the real (In-phase) component of the AM signal. Upper and lower sideband energy is combined. If the underlying digital energy on one sideband were complementary to that on the other sideband (identical to, but inverted in phase) a perfect synchronous detector would be immune to the digital energy.

Meanwhile envelope detection rectifies the envelope through a diode or diode bridge and smoothes out the result with a low pass filter to produce baseband audio. The envelope detector takes the shape of the waveform, including the contribution of any quadrature components, and detects it as audio. It is important, therefore, to create digital sidebands that are complementary not only in the real plane, but also in the imaginary. As is developed further below, even analog radios with envelope detection obtain some advantage when unwanted digital energy symmetrical about center frequency is complementary.

Another key observation, particularly for synchronous detection, is that the digital energy's in-phase component should be synchronous with the analog signal's in-phase component. This ensures a perfect phase cancellation on the digital sidebands by an analog radio phase-locked to the analog signal.

Here, the plot thickens. The real and imaginary sideband components behave differently. The phase of the real component (I) of an AM analog signal is identical on the upper and lower sidebands. To make the real components of our digital USB and LSB energy cancel in the analog receiver, it is a simple matter of reversing the phase of the real component on the digital LSB. The result is that when the analog receiver sums the upper and lower sideband energy, the analog signal is recovered as usual, and the digital USB and LSB energy cancels out. The imaginary (Q) component is another story.

Complex Conjugate

On the USB, the imaginary components of an AM signal are +90 degrees phase with respect to the real component, while they are –90 degrees on the LSB. There is an intuitive rationale for this phenomenon—the LSB begins at center frequency and counts down and away from center, while the USB counts up. While the USB and LSB real components remain in-phase with each other, the imaginary components must rotate in opposite directions. This reverse rotation in the imaginary plane accounts for the frequency reversal of the LSB. Hence, as a natural consequence of the modulation process the LSB imaginary component has a negative phase. In other words, the modulation process creates an LSB that is the "complex conjugate" of the USB. The analog demodulation process is the reverse of the modulation process, so it expects the analog LSB to be the complex conjugate of the USB. To reverse complex conjugation, one executes a second complex conjugation, in the same manner that a double negative is a positive. The receiver inherently complex conjugates the LSB again in the detection process, summing the energy with USB and producing the analog audio.

The complex conjugate is a sign reversal of the imaginary component. Complex conjugation is often represented by an asterisk (*) or a caret (^). The IBOC Reference Documents use the asterisk, which is used here. In this text the conjugation symbol * is distinguished from the convolution symbol ⋆ by its smaller size and superscript position. Stripped of its subtleties, the basic function for a complex signal is Equation 8.1. Negating the phase component creates the complex conjugate, as in the lower right quarter of Figure 8.3. The negation of the phase has no effect on the real component. Equation 8.2 is complex conjugation, showing how mathematically it can be reduced to negating the imaginary component, $j \sin \theta$. Figure 8.3 shows how this results in rotating the constellation point in the opposite direction from the real axis. If Equation 8.1 represents the modulated AM USB, Equation 8.2 describes the AM LSB.

$$z = a(\cos \theta + j \sin \theta) \qquad \text{Eq. 8.1}$$

$$z^* = a(\cos -\theta + \sin -\theta) = a(\cos \theta - j \sin \theta) \qquad \text{Eq. 8.2}$$

$$-z = a(\cos(\theta+\pi) + \sin(\theta+\pi)) = a(-\cos \theta - j \sin \theta) \qquad \text{Eq. 8.3}$$

$$-z^* = a(-\cos \theta + j \sin \theta) \qquad \text{Eq. 8.4}$$

Negation is the inversion of the phase of both the real and the imaginary components, as shown in Equation 8.3 and illustrated in the lower left quarter of Figure 8.3. Phase inversion is represented by a 180-degree (π radians) shift in the phase angle of the signal. It can also be described as the negation of both the real and imaginary components.

The analog USB is described by z. The demodulator is expecting the analog LSB as described by z^*. To render the analog LSB out of phase with what the demodulator expects, z^* must be negated. Equation 8.4 is the combination of negation and complex conjugation that is necessary to have the In-phase and Quadrature components of the digital signal cancel themselves in analog radios. In the complex plane, the negated complex conjugate is represented in the upper left corner of Figure 8.3.

Figure 8.4 shows in graphical form how the digital and analog sidebands are manipulated in the complex plane to achieve the intended purposes. Positive and negative I and Q values are represented by arrows indicating their directions on the complex plane. The analog AM sidebands are represented by solid black arrows, while the digital sidebands have light dashed arrows. Each time a complex conjugation and/or negation occurs, the orientation of the I and/or Q vector changes accordingly.

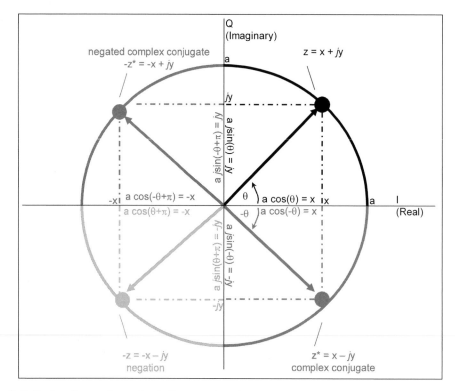

Figure 8.3 Conjugation and negation in the complex plane

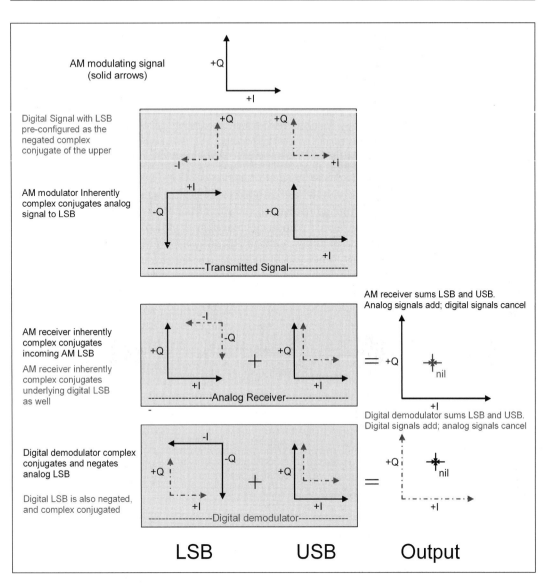

Figure 8.4 Modulating and Demodulating Analog and Digital IBOC Sidebands Illustrated on the Complex Plane

Interference Protection

In AM IBOC transmission, negated complex conjugation is applied to all LSB OFDM subcarriers, in both hybrid and all-digital modes. This is done across the board primarily to simplify receiver design. The real benefits come from the hybrid secondary and tertiary subcarriers having this feature. In hybrid operation, identical information is carried simultaneously on the Tertiary upper and lower sidebands; likewise the information on upper and lower Secondary sidebands is the same (see discussion in Chapter 6, AM Service Modes). An AM receiver with a bandwidth as wide as ±10 kHz– the bandwidth of the hybrid secondary and tertiary sidebands– is presented with pairs of complementary digital sidebands.

The negated complex conjugate transmission of Secondary and Tertiary lower sidebands practically eliminates digital interference to reception of the analog host. While the synchronous demodulation process constructively sums the analog USB and LSB energy, it is destructively summing the unwanted digital energy in the passband. iBiquity informally reports that its experience with AM radios with synchronous detection is as close to ideal as practicable. With a good incoming signal, noise pickup of the Secondary and Tertiary sidebands on a synchronous analog receiver is trivial. (Antenna and propagation distortions to the signal complicate reception of the analog and rejection of the digital.) Similarly, while envelope detection is less robust than synchronous in this instance, iBiquity's experience with analog receivers suggests that the received noise level of the Secondary and Tertiary subcarriers on an envelope-detected radio is about twice as low, in dB-S/N, as the digital energy is in dBc. That is, if total sideband power (Secondary and Tertiary) were, say, 26 dB down at RF, the envelope-detected noise from these sidebands can be expected to be 52 dB down.

This protection applies to reception of the host radio station's analog signal because the digital sidebands are symmetrical to the desired analog signal. In deliberating on IBOC technology, NRSC referred to the tendency of an IBOC signal to interfere (or not) with reception of the host analog signal as "host compatibility." Host compatibility was tested in the subjective testing submitted to NRSC in which human subjects listened to various recorded audio samples and scored them.[1]

In addition to providing good analog host compatibility, the design of the hybrid IBOC system must provide similar compatibility between unwanted host analog modulation and desired digital modulation in a digital receiver. Conveniently, the negated complex conjugate of the LSB digital signal provides the digital receiver with the same capability to null the analog signal as the analog receiver has in nulling the digital signal. Figure 8.4 shows the manner in which the sign of the I and Q values of the LSB are manipulated to cancel out the digital signal in an analog receiver. The figure also shows, on the bottom row, how the same LSB can be manipulated to null the analog signal in favor of the digital. An extra step of LSB negation is applied to bring the digital USB and LSB in phase on both axes, and simultaneously bringing the analog USB and LSB out of phase. These two sidebands are summed in the digital receiver, providing some gain to the received digital signal while canceling the analog interferer.

---

[1] *Evaluation of the iBiquity Digital Corporation IBOC System, Part 2 – AM IBOC,* NRSC DRB Subcommittee, Evaluation Working Group, Dr. H. Donald Messer, Chairman, 2002.

Diversity Technique inside AM HD Radio

Initial releases of the iBiquity HD Radio receiver architecture relied on picking the best of two methods to demodulate Secondary sidebands. These receivers looked at the combined output of the complementary sidebands and nulled the digital interference, as described above. Also, they looked at each Secondary sideband independently. If adjacent channel interference was causing more harm to the quality of the reception than was the host digital noise, the receiver could opt to use the better independent sideband and ignore the complementary combining approach. The availability of two independent sidebands and one combined complementary combination of the sidebands was, and still is, employed as a form of reception diversity. By picking the best signal at any given moment, this method is called *selection diversity*.

Beginning in products released in about 2007, an improved HD Radio receiver architecture enables the receiver to perform a more sophisticated form of diversity called *maximum ratio combining*. This technique is common in wireless communications where it improves diversity gain with, for instance, two receiving antennas, or two phase delay taps on a receiver front end. Applied in the AM HD Radio receiver, maximum ratio combining permits the receiver to merge the three signal sources—the two sideband signals decoded independently, plus the combined complementary signal. The receiver makes rapid adjustments to the three-way mix based on their signal-to-noise ratios. Even a noisy signal, when mixed with a less noisy one in the right proportions, will tend to reinforce the signal more than the combined noise, because the signals are correlated while the noise is not. Thus, the signals are combined to obtain the maximum signal-to-noise ratio under the current channel conditions.

The use of complementary digital sidebands is effective in controlling interference to the reception of a hybrid IBOC digital signal caused by its analog host, and vice versa. Complementary digital sidebands provide no advantage for interference caused by the presence of a strong adjacent channel station. Such interference to analog reception is not diminished by the negated conjugate because it does not affect both sidebands symmetrically.

AM Pulse Shaping

Sharing the band with amplitude modulation communications is particularly challenging for digital waveforms. In addition to the use of the complementary sidebands to improve digital compatibility with analog, the symbol pulse shaping function is also adapted specifically to the AM band. Looking back at the FM IBOC waveform, Figure 7.15, it is clear that pulse-shaping function produces a series of pulses running at a 344-hertz rate. This type of pulse, were it used in the AM band, would run at the AM IBOC rate of 172 Hz and would likely be audible on an AM detector. The clear periodicity of the symbol pulses needs to be "smeared" out of the AM IBOC signal to further protect analog radios from an annoying low frequency artifact. To accomplish this, the pulse must be convolved with something that will soften the periodicity to protect analog radios and still leave the symbol stream accessible to the digital radio.

As with FM IBOC, AM IBOC utilizes a raised cosine function to create the pulse envelope. AM IBOC goes a step further, using a Gaussian function to spread the envelope slightly into the adjacent symbol periods. Equation 8.5 is the raised cosine function (see Figure 7.11 for an illustration of a raised cosine pulse shape). Increments of time are substituted for the variable ξ (Xi). During the symbol time $T_s = T(1+\alpha)$, the pulse rises, holds, and falls. Outside of the symbol time the function returns zero amplitude for that symbol. Each successive symbol is discrete from the next.

$$h(\xi) = \begin{cases} 0.5 \cdot \left[1 + \cos\left(\pi \dfrac{\alpha T - \xi}{\alpha T}\right)\right] & \text{if } 0 < \xi \leq \alpha T \\ 1 & \text{if } \alpha T < \xi \leq T \\ 0.5 \cdot \left(\pi \dfrac{T - t}{2\alpha T}\right) & \text{if } T \leq \xi \leq T(1+\alpha) \\ 0 & \text{otherwise} \end{cases}$$

Eq. 8.5

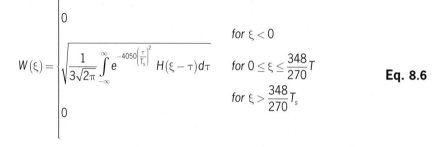

$$W(\xi) = \begin{cases} 0 & \text{for } \xi < 0 \\ \sqrt{\dfrac{1}{3\sqrt{2\pi}} \displaystyle\int_{-\infty}^{\infty} e^{-4050\left(\frac{\tau}{T_s}\right)^2} H(\xi - \tau)\,d\tau} & \text{for } 0 \leq \xi \leq \dfrac{348}{270}T \\ 0 & \text{for } \xi > \dfrac{348}{270}T_s \end{cases}$$

Eq. 8.6

Next, the pulse envelope is convolved with a Gaussian function. Notice, in Equation 8.6, how the time interval over which the pulse is convolved is greater than the symbol time—$(348/270)T_s$. The 5.8-millisecond time allotted for each symbol is exceeded by a factor of 348/270 = 1.29, resulting in a 7.5-millisecond window. As shown in Figure 8.5, there are flat, nearly zero-amplitude feet at the beginning and end of the convolved pulse window. The actual width of the pulse at its base is about 6.2 ms. A portion of each slope of the pulse falls within the period of the adjacent symbol.

The AM IBOC pulses gently overlap in the time domain, softening the transition from one symbol to the next. However, this smearing of the symbols comes at some cost. First, the lack of a highly defined transition between pulses is a challenge for the receiver designer. iBiquity developed a technique where the receiver hones in on the symbol by peaking the demodulated symbol, targeting the zero point of the FFT on the middle of the symbol. Second, the signal-to-noise ratio is slightly diminished by the overlap of the symbols, a small price to pay for significantly improved compatibility with analog receivers.

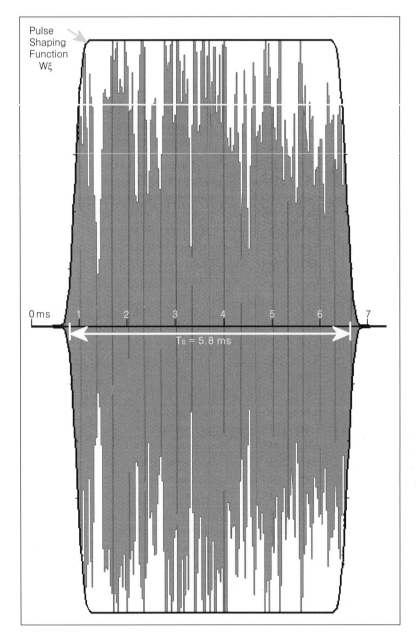

Figure 8.5 AM IBOC Pulse Shape–Raised Cosine Convolved with Gaussian Function (simulated waveform inserted for illustration)

To produce the transmitted waveform $y_n(t)$, the pulse shape, $W(\xi)$, is multiplied with the time domain representation of the OFDM symbol. This is structured in the same manner as the process of creating the FM symbol—converting from its frequency domain description to the time domain pulse (Equation 7.14), then mutiplying. Equation 8.7 incorporates n symbols, with L OFDM subcarriers indexed by k, sampled in time intervals t. The equation begins with the new pulse shaping function $W(\xi)$, which is multiplied with the IDFT for the AM OFDM subcarriers.

$$y_n(t) = W(t - nT_s) \cdot \sum_{k=0}^{L-1} \underline{X}_n[k] \cdot e^{j2\pi\Delta f\left(k - \frac{L-1}{2}\right)(t - nT_s)}$$

Eq. 8.7

Finally, in hybrid operation the analog signal is modulated in phase with the real component of the OFDM waveform and the two signals are combined. With substantially narrower channel bandwidth than FM, plus the sensitivity of AM radios to AM noise in band, the design of the AM IBOC waveform is significantly more constrained than FM. The use of many special tools collectively contributes to the viability of IBOC transmission in the AM band, including: half the OFDM subcarrier spacing of FM, complementary sidebands, reduced analog bandwidth, OFDM subcarrier amplitude scaling, coherent transmission of analog and digital, higher-order constellations, and a two-layered pulse-shaping function.

In the next chapter, the Transmission System Specifications for AM and FM IBOC are discussed. These specifications cover such topics as gain and phase flatness, and frequency accuracy and stability. This is where the theoretical performance of the preceding two chapters is related to boundaries on the performance of physical systems.

9 From the Top Down: The Physical Layer–Transmission System Specifications

We have completed our trip to the bottom of the IBOC protocol stack, Chapters 5 through 8 addressed the logical, spectral and timing characteristics of the ideal IBOC signal. Supplementing the documents describing the protocol stack are two Transmission System Specifications documents, one each for AM and FM IBOC. The Logical Channels were linked to the IBOC signal structure, with symbols, blocks and frames in the time domain, and interleaver matrices assigned to OFDM subcarrier groups in the frequency domain. Phase and timing relationships have been explored.

NRSC-5 Reference Document Number	Reference Document Title	NRSC-5 Reference Document Number	Reference Document Title
1.	Doc. No. SY_IDD_1011s rev. E HD Radio™ Air Interface Design Description **Layer 1 FM** iBiquity Digital Corporation, 3/22/05	6.	Doc. No. SY_SSS_1026s rev. D HD Radio™ **FM Transmission System Specifications** iBiquity Digital Corporation, 2/18/05
2.	Doc. No. SY_IDD_1012s rev. E HD Radio™ Air Interface Design Description **Layer 1 AM** iBiquity Digital Corporation, 3/22/05	7.	Doc. No. SY_IDD_1028s rev. C HD Radio™ Air Interface Design Description **Program Service Data** iBiquity Digital Corporation, 3/31/05
3.	Doc. No. SY_IDD_1014s rev. F HD Radio™ Air Interface Design Description **Layer 2 Channel Multiplex Protocol** iBiquity Digital Corporation, 2/7/05	8.	Doc. No. SY_SSS_1082s rev. D HD Radio™ **AM Transmission System Specifications** iBiquity Digital Corporation, 2/24/05
4.	Doc. No. SY_IDD_1017s rev. E HD Radio™ Air Interface Design Description **Audio Transport** iBiquity Digital Corporation, 3/31/05	9.	Doc. No. SY_IDD_1085s rev. C HD Radio™ Air Interface Design Description **Program Service Data Transport** iBiquity Digital Corporation, 2/7/05
5.	Doc. No. SY_IDD_1020s rev. E HD Radio™ Air Interface Design Description **Station Information Service Protocol** iBiquity Digital Corporation, 2/18/05	10.	Doc. No. SY_IDD_1019s rev. E HD Radio™ Air Interface Design Description **Advanced Application Services Transport** iBiquity Digital Corporation, 8/4/05

Table 9.1 Protocols Addressed in this chapter

AM and FM Transmission System Specifications

When it comes to transmitting a signal that will operate compatibly with receivers, the transmitted signal must have some boundaries placed on its performance. In the upper layers of the IBOC protocol stack, logical relationships are described, requiring no hardware performance specifications. Meanwhile in the bottom of Layer 1, the physical characteristics of the IBOC signal require not only functional description, but also a set of system specifications.

The physical layer is the interface between independent devices—transmitters and receivers. To maintain interoperability, devices on each side of the physical layer must be aware of how much the signal is allowed to deviate from ideal. These requirements are published in NRSC-5 Reference documents (6) FM Transmission System Specifications and (8) AM Transmission System Specifications (see Table 9.1).

These Reference Documents contain criteria for the following characteristics:

Timing Issues:

- Clock Synchronization Tolerances.

- Time and Frequency Accuracy and Stability.

- Analog Diversity Delay Tolerances.

Signal Quality Issues:

- Spectral Emissions Limits (RF Masks).

- Amplitude Scaling of various OFDM subcarrier sidebands.

- Phase Noise Specification.

- Error Vector Magnitude.

- Gain Flatness.

- Group Delay Flatness.

Timing Issues

Timing related issues are for the most part identical in the AM and FM IBOC transmission specifications. These are summarized in Table 9.2. The frequency tolerances may appear not to be the same, where the permissible errors, given in Hertz, are different for AM and FM IBOC. However, when the tolerances are considered as ratios to their center frequencies, the FM frequency tolerances are about the same order of magnitude as AM. For example, the FM specification is 12 to 15 parts per billion (ppb) Level I frequency error across the U.S. FM band—88 to 108 MHz. The IBOC frequency tolerance across the U.S. AM band—0.52 to 1.7 MHz—is 12 to 37 ppb. See Table 9.2 for each band's frequency tolerances.

Characteristic	Comment	Specification
Level I Synchronization	GPS-Locked	
Symbol Clock Error		± 0.01 ppm
Digital Subcarrier Frequency Error		±1.3 Hz (FM) ±0.02 Hz (AM)
Layer 1 Frame Timing	Time of Start of ALFN	±1 µs
Level II Synchronization	Not GPS-Locked	
Symbol Clock Error		±1.0 ppm
Digital Subcarrier Frequency Error		±130 Hz (FM) ±2.0 Hz (AM)
Layer 1 Frame Timing		no spec.
Analog Audio Diversity Delay	Tdd = 3 • 65536/44100 sec	±68 µs

Table 9.2 IBOC Timing and Frequency Specifications

A GPS-locked transmission facility is defined as being in Level I synchronization. In the case of a transmitter facility that has no GPS reference—Level II synchronization—the transmission is expected to free-run within more relaxed limits. For the most part, a GPS-locked transmitter will simply function as ordered, requiring no further intervention than typing in the correct station frequency upon setup. Transmitter product lines bearing the HD Radio mark were tested and approved by iBiquity as meeting these and other performance specifications to the degree that the manufacturer's design has control over the performance. Obviously, once installed and in operation, component failures that affect performance are out of the control of the manufacturer of the transmitter. It is then the responsibility of the station operator to maintain performance to specification.

Of all the timing and frequency specifications, the one most under the control of the broadcast facility is the Analog Audio Diversity Delay, so long as the IBOC transmitter is very stable. To maintain high stability in the transmitter, a tight 68-microsecond tolerance is imposed on the T_{dd} to ensure a high degree of uniformity of performance among all makes and model of transmitter. From the listener's perspective, a 68 μs offset is essentially imperceptible.

How was the 68 μs maximum analog-to-digital audio delay tolerance in the transmission specifications established? It is rooted in the simple idea that a transmitter can keep the offset with ±3 audio samples of perfect synchronization. (Recall the discussion in Chapter 4 regarding the elasticity of the digital audio transport stream and the need to have a buffer to handle the elasticity—a little variation in analog-to-digital synchronization is understandable.) At the 44.1 kHz audio sampling rate, each sample represents 22.68 μs; three samples therefore occupy 68 μs. IBOC signal monitors offer analog/digital audio delay error measurements, offering the option of viewing the results in milli- or micro-seconds of time or in the number of 44.1 kHz samples.

The human threshold for perceiving an echo as an independent sound occurs in the vicinity of a few milliseconds of delay. Echo perception disappears where the precedence effect takes over. This occurs in the delay range of 50 to 3 ms. The precedence effect is a psycho-acoustic phenomenon in which a listener cannot distinguish an echo from the initial sound if the delay is brief enough, resulting in a perceived difference in sound quality or location, but not as an echo. Delays less than 3 ms will not be perceived as echoes, and have diminishing impact on the perception of the audio.

The 68 μs tolerance, then, appears to be more oriented to the design of stable transmission equipment than it is in providing latitude for satisfactory blend performance. iBiquity suggests on its website that a 400-sample alignment error, or about 9 ms, "will be inaudible to most listeners."[1] It may not be possible to achieve a 3-sample or less offset (68 μs) between digital and analog audio, due to the differences in the way each audio stream is processed and transported. The 68 μs tolerance is substantially more restrictive than the few-millisecond threshold of echo perception and precedence effects.

Could there be other effects besides echo and stereo platform motion at delays between a few milliseconds and 68 μs? Theoretically, very close delays can produce comb-filtering effects. With

---

[1] Proper Time and Level Alignment, www.iBiquity.com.

a 68-μs $T_{dd\ offset}$ certain audio frequencies will cancel while others reinforce. A 68-μs delay represents the period of one cycle at 14.7 kHz; a half-cycle at 7.4 kHz. A half-cycle delay creates a phase cancellation at that half-cycle frequency and its odd-harmonics (in this case, 7.4, 22, 37, etc. kHz). Therefore, the delay error between analog and digital audio during the blending period will be manifested in a subtle comb filtering effect. With a 9-ms delay, the half-cycle frequency is 55 Hz. A lower-frequency comb filtering effect is potentially audible at odd multiples of 55 Hz, until the number of cycles of a particular frequency are so delayed that the precedence effect diminishes to a perceived spatial or echo effect.

Mitigating the impact of alignment error is the fact that the experience of the alignment error is transient as the analog and digital audio briefly crossfade from one to the other. There is little time to experience the comb effect, if it is audible at all. Second, the sonic differences between the analog and digital audio caused by the differences in audio processing of each (and by the subtle effects of the audio coding on the digital source) will probably be more apparent to the listener during the crossfade than the effects of a short, in-spec, time delay error.

Diversity Delay Alignment

To monitor a hybrid station's analog and digital audio simultaneously, a variety of HD Radio receivers have made available a "Split Mode" capability. Certain Kenwood car radios were the first to have the feature, which requires a series of special keystrokes to replace right channel digital audio with left channel analog audio. Other consumer radios offer the split mode feature, including Boston Acoustics Receptor tabletop models and JVC dashboard radios. iBiquity maintains an application note called *HD Radio Transmission Side Analog Diversity Delay Alignment*. This and other documents relating to time alignment and split mode may be found on the www.broadcastsignallab.com/splitmode web page. Also look on the iBiquity website for the latest advice.

Michael LeClair reports in Radio World Engineering Extra that alignment with an oscilloscope and program audio is not a sure thing, but transmitting test tones in the wee hours will work. A more convenient alternative uses the power of digital signal processing to provide an alignment metric on demand. Professional-grade broadcast monitors employ a sophisticated cross-correlation technique. Time samples of digital and analog audio are compared as one sample is shifted in time against the other. The alignment error is calculated by successively applying offsets to the samples until the correlation peaks. The time offset between the two samples is reported on the monitor's display as the alignment error. It is typically reported in milliseconds and number of audio samples. IBOC broadcast monitor manufacturers include Audemat-Aztec, Belar, Day Sequerra, and Inovonics. Also, look for work by NPR Labs evaluating the best methods of obtaining a good time alignment.

iBiquity recommends that broadcasters who have lost the initial factory settings use the following settings to start their alignment process: For FM, set the diversity delay to 7.9215 sec or 349,341 samples. For AM, start with 8.403 sec or 370,575 samples. This gets the alignment close to start, requiring only minor adjustments to synchronize.

Signal Quality Issues

In addition to the time/frequency specifications common to AM and FM IBOC, some of the spectral specifications also apply to both bands. These specifications are phase noise, error vector magnitude (EVM), gain flatness and group delay flatness, shown in Table 9.3.

Characteristic	Specification
Error Vector Magnitude: Individual Subcarrier	20%
Error Vector Magnitude: All Subcarriers Combined	10%
Gain Flatness	AM: ±0.5 dB 0–10kHz* ±1 dB 10–15 kHz*
	FM: ±0.5 dB
Group Delay Flatness	AM: 3 µs max. differential
	FM: 600 ns max. differential
Phase Noise	Table 7.11
Amplitude and Phase Symmetry	AM only: Table 7.13

In the NAB Engineering Handbook, 10th Edition, iBiquity recommends gain flatness ±0.5 dB to 5 kHz, and ±4 dB to 15 kHz, and group delay flatness 5 µs to 15 kHz.

Table 9.3 Spectral Characteristics Specifications Common to AM and FM IBOC

Error Vector Magnitude

The characteristic that most qualifies as a quality metric of the IBOC signal is Error Vector Magnitude (EVM). While phase noise and flatness characterize the performance of components of the IBOC transmission system, EVM measures a characteristic of the individual OFDM subcarriers. EVM is a collective measure of how far off the mark a series of constellation points is. Recalling the constellation diagram (Figure 7.4), an individual data point on the constellation is described by a vector with a real (I) and a complex (Q) component. The vector also can be described by its phase and magnitude, as in Figure 8.2. The error vector marks the difference between an actual constellation point and the point on the ideal phase and magnitude vector. Each error vector has a phase and a magnitude independent of the underlying symbol's phase and magnitude.

Over time a series of error vectors is accumulated from a series of constellation points. If they have a random, noise-like distribution, the phase of each error vector will be random, and the magnitude of each error vector will fall within some range from the ideal. Figure 9.2 illustrates a short series of error vectors and the computation of their EVM. The error vectors in all the quadrants of the constellation are combined to produce one EVM value for each OFDM subcarrier. Individual error vector magnitudes are combined in a root-mean-square fashion to produce the EVM value per subcarrier. The error vectors of an entire set of OFDM subcarriers can be combined (RMS) to characterize the set with one EVM figure. NRSC-5 specifies an individual OFDM subcarrier EVM limit of 20%, and a combined EVM limit across the channel of 10%.

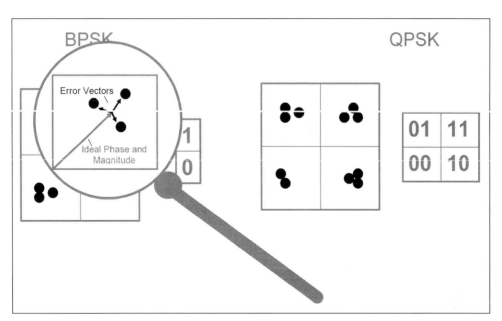

Figure 9.1 Error Vectors on a Constellation

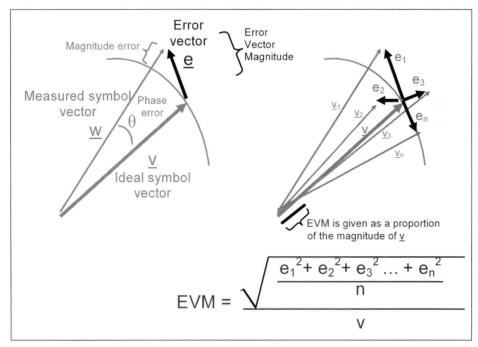

Figure 9.2 Error Vector Magnitude

Phase Noise

One measure of the quality of a transmitter's or receiver's frequency reference is its phase noise. The AM and FM Reference Documents specify phase noise tolerances. Phase noise is the spectral spreading of a signal due to minute variations in the instantaneous phase of the signal. It is most easily characterized by looking at such things as an unmodulated carrier or the output of an oscillator. On a spectral display, phase noise is seen as a low base straddling the narrow single-frequency peak of the signal. Lower phase noise is indicated by lower-level, and narrower bandwidth sidebands. Phase noise is quantified as a power spectral density at one or more specified frequency offsets. (dBc/Hz @ n-kHz offset) On phase-modulated signals, phase noise is one potential source of phase error in the time domain, and a potential contributor to intercarrier interference in the frequency domain. Phase noise is implicit in the design and construction of the RF device, leaving the operator little to do to address phase noise problems after a transmitter is purchased, other than replacing bad components, or modifying circuitry.

Frequency Offset (F) from Single OFDM Subcarrier	AM IBOC Phase Noise Limits		FM IBOC Phase Noise Limits	
	dBc/Hz Equation	dBc/Hz (rounded) at breakpoint in curve	dBc/Hz Equation	dBc/Hz (rounded) at breakpoint in curve
1 to 10 Hz	$-1.1 \cdot F - 38.9$	-40 @ 1 Hz	no specification	
10 to 100 Hz	$-4.44 \cdot 10^{-1} \cdot F - 45.6$	-50 @ 10 Hz	$-2.78 \cdot 10^{-1} \cdot F - 39.2$	-42 @ 10 Hz
100 to 1000 Hz	$-5.56 \cdot 10^{-3} \cdot F - 89.4$	-90 @ 100 Hz	$-1.11 \cdot 10^{-2} \cdot F - 65.9$	-67 @ 100 Hz
1 to 10 kHz	$-1.67 \cdot 10^{-3} \cdot F - 93.3$	-94 @ 1 kHz	$-1.11 \cdot 10^{-3} \cdot F - 75.9$	-77 @ 1 kHz
10 to 100 kHz	$-1.11 \cdot 10^{-4} \cdot F - 108.9$	-110 @ 10 kHz	$-2.22 \cdot 10^{-4} \cdot F - 84.8$	-87 @ 10 kHz
> 100 kHz	-120	-120 @ 100 kHz	-107	-107 @ 100 kHz

Table 9.4 AM and FM IBOC Phase Noise Specifications

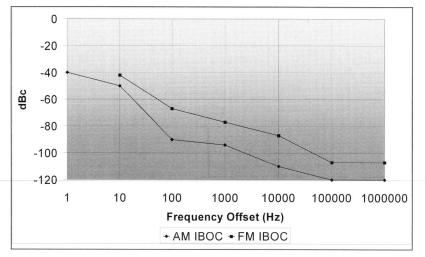

Figure 9.3 AM and FM IBOC Phase Noise Specifications

Table 9.4 shows the AM and FM IBOC phase noise specifications. The limits that form the phase noise masks are presented in dBc per hertz. The masks apply to an individual OFDM subcarrier, with the unmodulated subcarrier level as the reference for 0 dBc. The masks consist of a series of line segments defined for each decade of the adjacent frequency spectrum. Together, these line segments produce the masks' limit lines shown in Figure 9.3. Figure 9.3 shows the masks as they would appear for the upper sidebands of an AM and an FM OFDM subcarrier. For convenience, Table 9.4 also shows the nominal limit values at the breakpoints between line segments (1, 10, 100, etc. Hz).

In evaluating phase noise within the IBOC channels, the specifications give some latitude to in-band phase noise components to exceed the phase noise mask. AM IBOC phase noise between ±15 kHz may be measured at 100-Hz bandwidth, while FM IBOC may be measured at 300-Hz bandwidth between ±200 kHz. These are defined as the "Discrete Phase Noise" specifications, permitting some 1-Hz values to exceed the limits as long as the discrete 100 or 300-Hz values remain compliant.

Phase noise is measured by setting the IBOC transmitter to a special mode that transmits only one OFDM subcarrier and no analog signal. In addition, the AM IBOC phase noise specification calls for independently verifying the phase noise of the unmodulated AM carrier. The device measuring phase noise must have excellent phase noise performance to eliminate ambiguity in the measurement.

Flatness

Gain Flatness and Group Delay Flatness describe the amplitude and phase response of the system across its pass band. Filter effects in the signal chain affect gain flatness and group delay. Filtering occurs in devices such as hybrids, combiners, filters, and antennas whose characteristics in the pass band may be imperfect. Also, power amplifiers may have tuned circuits or impedance characteristics that affect the amplified signal.

Filters typically used in FM transmission systems do not exceed the IBOC Gain and Group Delay Flatness requirements, unless they have steep slopes that are close-in to the Necessary Bandwidth. Filters originally installed for analog systems should be evaluated as part of the IBOC system design process to ensure that they are compatible with the digital waveform.

AM transmission systems, on the other hand, employ antennas with restrictive bandwidths. The AM antenna system is a significant filter. Careful attention to system design and adjustment is necessary to create favorable flatness. The peculiarities of AM system adjustment are discussed further in Chapter 12.

AM Amplitude and Phase Symmetry

In addition to the limits on gain and phase flatness across the band, the ideal AM IBOC system is also endowed with a characteristic called "Hermitian symmetry." The upper and lower sideband responses should reflect each other, but in a special way. Gain response should be as close as possible to a mirror image above and below center frequency. Phase response should be a negated mirror image above and below center frequency. A Hermitian transposition is also known as a conjugate transposition. By transposing the complex conjugate of the response on one sideband to the other sideband, Hermitian symmetry is created. Complex conjugates play an important role in the AM IBOC scheme, as discussed in Chapter 7 (see the section: Negated Complex Conjugate). Consequently, Hermitian symmetry of the AM passband helps maintain the noise-rejecting aspects of the AM IBOC signal.

Hermitian symmetry has always been beneficial to analog AM broadcasting, although it has been easily set aside for other priorities. By maintaining identical amplitude flatness characteristics above and below center frequency, as well as complementary phase characteristics above and below, the symmetry of the AM envelope is preserved. This eliminates the distortions caused by the differences of the upper and lower sidebands in the AM detector. Thus, even though the imperfect flatness may color the detected audio, maintaining sideband Hermitian symmetry prevents further distortion of the received analog signal. However, in analog-only broadcasting, this symmetry has been readily sacrificed to simplify the design of directional arrays.

In hybrid IBOC transmission, the role of Hermitian symmetry is amplified by the need to maintain precise phase relationships that prevent the host station's IBOC and analog signals from interfering with each other. Recall that in hybrid mode, the upper and lower sidebands of the Secondary and Tertiary subcarrier groups are negated complex conjugates. These IBOC sidebands effectively cancel out in analog AM detectors. Similarly, IBOC receivers can invert the detection process on one sideband and cancel out the analog AM sidebands to better recover the IBOC sidebands.

Hermitian symmetry helps preserve the benefits of the negated complex conjugate IBOC sidebands. Since there is going to be some phase and amplitude deviation across the band, the goal is to warp the amplitude response in a like manner on both sides of center frequency. The phase response must be warped in a negative direction on one side of center frequency with respect to the other.

Figure 9.4 illustrates a Hermitian symmetry. The curve, shaped like a smile in this example, is representative of an amplitude response curve (indicating Gain Flatness). Its symmetry is about the center frequency, where the amplitude at $F_c + n$ is the same as the amplitude at $F_c - n$. In this example, the amplitude rises with increasing offset from center frequency.

The phase response of the Figure 9.4 Hermitian symmetry illustration is also symmetrical about the center frequency, if one observes the absolute value of the curve. This example has a positive-going curve above F_c, and a complementary negative-going curve below. The amplitude at $F_c + n$ is the same, but negated, at $F_c - n$.

Together, the two response curves form a Hermitian symmetry. Even though phase and amplitude are not flat across the channel, Hermitian symmetry preserves the constructive relationships of the I and Q components of the upper and lower sidebands when passed through an analog demodulator. Chapter 12 includes further discussion of Hermitian symmetry with respect to AM antenna design.

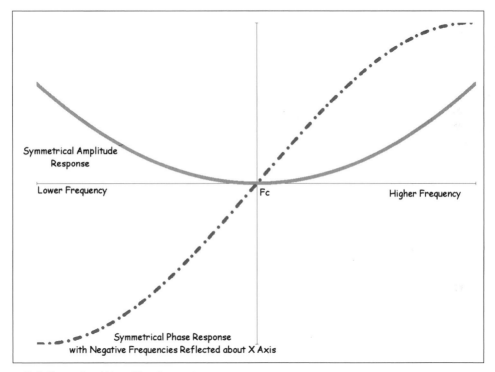

Figure 9.4 Example of Hermitian Symmetry

Where to Measure AM and FM IBOC Specs

The transmission specifications speak to transmitter performance as well as to the performance of the radiated signal. Table 9.5 lists the manner in which each characteristic is to be measured according to NRSC-5 Transmission System Specifications. Several AM system measurements are described specifically as transmitter characterizations, complete with termination into 50-ohm resistive loads.

Specification	Point of Measurement	
	AM	FM
Gain Flatness	Transmitter RF output into nonreactive 50-ohm load	"as verified at the antenna output" (Elsewhere in the spec. this appears to mean an output to the antenna.)
Group Delay Flatness	Transmitter RF output into nonreactive 50-ohm load	Includes "entire transmission signal path (excluding the RF channel)"
Phase Noise	Transmitter RF output	Transmitter RF output.
Error Vector Magnitude	Transmitter RF output	Transmitter RF output
Spectral Emissions Limits (discussed in next section)	None specified	Hybrid: "measurements of the combined analog and digital signals" All-digital: "at the input of the broadcast antenna"
Amplitude and Phase Symmetry	Transmitter output into nonreactive 50-ohm load. Also recommends entire transmission system, including antenna, "adhere as closely as is practicable" to this criterion, with suggestion to use sample loop on main tower.	None specified

Table 9.5 Locations Where NRSC-5 Transmission Characteristics Are Measured

With the complexities of impedance matching, phasing, and/or combining filters potentially affecting the final output of the broadcast system, it is helpful to break up the system analysis into segments. First, determine whether the transmitter itself is capable of compliant performance. With AM IBOC, this testing is performed after the transmitter output network and is discussed in more detail in Chapter 12. Second, the subsequent stages of the transmission system (the antenna system) may affect the IBOC signal. For AM IBOC, this is also discussed further in Chapter 12. FM is discussed in Chapter 13. Also, be aware of the presence of any pre-correction or pre-distortion functions that might affect the results. If these functions are employed to compensate for imperfections in later stages of the transmission system than the point of measurement, they may make the signal in earlier stages look worse than it is over the air. Pre-correction can create the appearance of noncompliance at the transmitter output because it has been adjusted to mirror the errors introduced by the later stages.

It is important to understand the nature of the signal being sampled before comparing it with the specifications. An AM transmitter, for instance, would be placed on a 50-ohm load and operated only with any pre-distortion intended to compensate for its amplifier nonlinearities. When the transmitter is operated into a complex load, the AM system as a whole should be evaluated from a point in the field. Similarly, an FM exciter may have pre-correction tables, or adaptive pre-correction feedback inputs that will cause the exciter output to look bad. Out of the transmitter, any exciter pre-correction intended to compensate for power amplifier distortions will result in a cleaner PA output than without the pre-correction. However, if there are adaptive pre-correction samples farther up the line, such as after combiners or filters, even the transmitter output will not be representative of the IBOC signal leaving the transmission plant.

Spectral Emissions

The final transmission system specifications to consider are the spectral emissions limits. These include the AM and FM IBOC spectral masks. The following sections address these specifications.

Spectral Emissions Limits

Existing Analog Masks

The only Transmission System Specifications that directly affect other stations on the AM and FM bands are the Spectral Emissions Limits. These are specified in section 4.4 of the NRSC-5 FM Transmission System Specifications reference document and in sections 4.4 and 4.5 of the AM Transmission System Specifications reference document. Historically, the U.S. Federal Communications Commission has maintained spectral masks for analog transmissions. The FM spectral mask is codified in 47 C.F.R. 73.317. The AM mask can be found in 47 C.F.R. 73.44. They are summarized in tables 9.6 and 9.7.

Offset from Carrier	Attenuation below Carrier
120 to 240 kHz	25 dB
240 to 600 kHz	35 dB
> 600 kHz	80 dB, or 43 +10 log (power in W) whichever is the lesser attenuation
Measurement method not specified	

Table 9.6 Analog FM Spectral Mask—47 CFR 73.317

Offset from Carrier	Attenuation below Carrier
10.2 to 20 kHz	25 dB
20 to 30	35 dB
30 to 60	5 + 1dB/kHz
60 to 75	65 dB
> 75 kHz	80 dB, or 43 +10 log (power in W) whichever is the lesser attenuation [but no less than 65 dB attenuation at 158 W or less].
Measurement method involves spectrum analyzer set to 300 Hz resolution bandwidth, no video filter, monitoring with peak hold over 10-minute period. RBW may be increased for measurements at offsets greater than 11.5 kHz.	

Table 9.7 Analog AM Spectral Mask—47 CFR 73.44

Using spectrum analyzers in peak hold mode, the analog masks ensured against even fleeting instances of an excessive spurious emission that would be recorded as a peak. Decades after the inception of the analog emissions criteria, the advent of digital transmissions brings along new approaches. First, digital signals have characteristically wide, flat, dense spectral characteristics. The total power of the digital waveform is dispersed quite evenly across its channel, leaving no tell-tale peak density at center frequency the way analog signals do. Spurious emissions involving digital signals are likely to have similar broad, dense characteristics. Second, spectrum analyzers and other measurement instruments have evolved. Analyzers with the capability of examining average power spectral densities have become quite affordable. In combination, these two aspects of the state of the art lead to the manner in which NRSC-5 expects spectral occupancy to be evaluated.

IBOC spectral occupancy is constrained by masks that are much tighter than the FCC analog masks. Under the IBOC masks, analog and digital emissions must be reigned in to protect stations' low-level digital signals. To protect reception of the host station's digital signals, the host's analog emissions should not stray beyond what is necessary to convey the broadcast program. To minimize interference to the reception of other digital and analog signals, each IBOC station must limit out-of-band emissions as well. Intermodulation products of the upper and lower digital sidebands and the analog host signal fall on adjacent channels. Because of the density of the digital waveform, intermodulation products that appear quite low-level on a spectral density display may pack a powerful punch, due to their wide bandwidths.

Considering the nature of digital waveforms, and the measurement methods, the IBOC spectral masks must be more restrictive outside the IBOC channel than the analog masks are. For instance, from 250 to 600 kHz offset from the FM center frequency, the FM IBOC mask is nearly 40 dB more stringent than the analog mask. On the AM band, the IBOC mask is already 65 dB down at 16 kHz offset, while the analog mask is 25 dB down. The analog mask finally ramps down to 65 dBc at 60 kHz offset. Even after accounting for the difference between the analog peak-hold measurement and the IBOC power averaging measurement methods, the hybrid IBOC spectrum has a substantially more restrictive mask.

IBOC Masks

The NRSC evaluated the performance of analog radios with IBOC signals present in the spectrum, but it did not specifically evaluate the impact of IBOC spurious emissions. The current masks are the product of the collaboration of the manufacturing industry with iBiquity to develop restrictive, but practicable emissions limits. The masks contained in the NRSC-5 reference documents are annotated with the following disclaimer:

• *The requirements for noise and spurious emission limits defined in this subsection reflect acceptable performance criteria. In certain circumstances, additional measures may be needed to reduce the spectral emissions below the limits given in this subsection in order to reduce mutual interference between broadcast stations."*

The NRSC disclaimer parallels the general interference clauses of 47 C.F.R. 73.317 "…should harmful interference to other authorized stations occur, the licensee shall correct the problem promptly or cease operation," and 73.44, "Should harmful interference be caused to the reception of other broadcast or nonbroadcast stations by out-of-band emissions, the licensee may be directed to achieve a greater degree of attenuation than specified." In some circumstances, stations have added filtering to further attenuate IBOC spurious emissions that were close to the mask limits. While these spurs are low with respect to the power of the primary signal, they may fall on a channel that is occupied by another station some distance away. When the receiver is close to the source of the spur, the spur may be strong enough to interfere with reception of the more distant signal. Broadcasters should keep this in mind when firing up new IBOC facilities.

Emissions Taxonomy

With the masks, our primary interest is in the regulation of spurious emissions to maintain good RF hygiene in the broadcast band. The International Telecommunications Union defines various types of emissions, which help organize the discussion when considering the sources and impacts of each type.

• *Necessary bandwidth*

The width of the frequency band which is just sufficient to ensure the transmission of information at the rate and with the quality required under specified conditions.

(continued on following page)

(continued from previous page)

- *Occupied bandwidth*

  Bandwidth occupied by 99% of the signal power

- *Out-of-band emission*

  The part of an emission which is outside the necessary bandwidth and which results from the modulation process, with the exception of spurious emissions.

- *Spurious emission*

  Emission ... outside the necessary bandwidth and the level of which may be reduced without affecting the corresponding transmission of information. Includes harmonics, parasitics, intermodulation, frequency conversion products, etc. Excludes Out-of-Band Emissions.

- Unwanted emissions

  Spurious emissions and out-of-band emissions.

Paraphrased from 47 CFR 2.1 Terms and Definitions, and RECOMMENDATION ITU-R SM.328-10, SPECTRA AND BANDWIDTH OF EMISSIONS

Spectral Density

The IBOC masks are based on the power spectral density (PSD) of the emissions. In evaluating emissions one can measure the total power of a signal, such as within the signal's Occupied Bandwidth or Necessary Bandwidth. The spectrum analyzer, however, provides an opportunity to reveal the characteristic spectral shape of the signal and compare it to an RF mask tailored to optimize compatibility in the band. PSD is reported as power per unit bandwidth. Using, say, a 1 kHz resolution bandwidth and a reference level set to the host station total carrier power, the spectrum analyzer presents PSD in units of dBc/kHz—decibels, with respect to carrier, per kilohertz.

PSD and Spectrum Analyzer Settings

According to iBiquity and NRSC-5, FM IBOC measurements employ 1-kHz unit bandwidths while AM IBOC is measured with 300-Hz units. The Transmission System Specifications simply call for averaging the PSD over a 30-second period. When it comes to setting up a spectrum analyzer, this criterion is open to interpretation. First of all, the sweep time is dependent on the sweep rate and the displayed bandwidth on the analyzer. Thirty seconds of averaging results in some indeterminate number of sweeps to be averaged.

Experience has shown that the averaging produces diminishing benefits after sweeping about 25 to 40 times. To be certain the average is representative, iBiquity recommends 100 sweeps. Spectrum analyzers can be left in automatic modes to permit the analyzer to self-select the sweep rate based on the resolution bandwidth setting and the frequency span of the display. It is helpful to be aware of the number of data points on a digital in the spectrum analyzer's memory and be certain the number of data points times the resolution bandwidth is equal to or greater than the span of the display. If not, there will be gaps of unmeasured energy between the data points. For instance, a span of 800 kHz collected with a 501-point register covers 1.6 kHz per display "bin." At 1 kHz resolution bandwidth, there are 600-Hz gaps between bins. While the display will still have the appearance of an accurate 1-kHz PSD plot, there remains a (small) possibility that something will be missed. Digital spectrum analyzers often have an indication when the span/RBW relationship is not ideal.

Spectrum Analyzer Detectors and Averaging

An average power level per frequency bin represents the PSD, requiring the use of certain detectors available in digital analyzers. To obtain an average power level, the instrument should not be detecting peaks. Averaging a series of traces that display peak-detected energy produces an average of the peaks in each bin, not an average of the power.

The earliest spectrum analyzers equipped with PSD capabilities employed a *sample detector*. The sample detector essentially takes a random sample of the instantaneous power in each frequency bin to create the trace. By averaging traces, one could develop a trace that approximates the PSD spectrum.

The use of a sample detector and trace averaging is a method of post-detection processing. There is a likely 2.5-dB understatement of the PSD with sample detection. If the energy in the 1 kHz or 300 Hz frequency bin is more noise-like than sinusoidal, then the average of a series of random samples in the bin may be about 1 dB below the RMS value. In addition, in log detection mode, the log is taken first, and the averaging is done in post detection processing, resulting in an average of the logs, rather than the log of the average, which produces a further 1.5-dB understatement if the energy in the bin is noise-like.[2]

Newer models of digital spectrum analyzers are equipped with more sophisticated detector algorithms, average and RMS detection. Figure 9.5 illustrates the time period during which a spectrum analyzer dwells in one frequency "bin" collecting data on the envelope of the selected resolution bandwidth. The peak and pit detectors (also called max and min) simply seek the highest and lowest level appearing during the bin's sample time. These are not useful for PSD work. The sample detector is illustrated as taking the last data point in the bin period. In most cases, the sample is effectively a random sample from one sweep to the next. One sweep will produce a series of sample points for each bin. This is one trace. The average of multiple traces provides a close estimate of the PSD in each bin.

---

[2] Sources: IBOC Spectrum Occupancy Measurements, David Maxson, National Association of Broadcasters Broadcast Engineering Conference, April 2005; Application notes by Agilent and Tektronix.

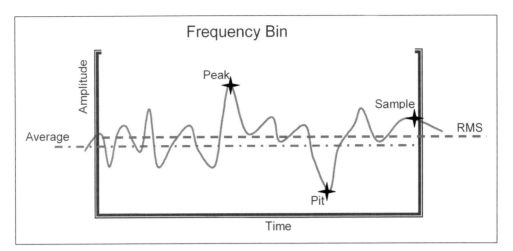

Figure 9.5 Spectrum Analyzer Detection Illustrated by the Detected Envelope over the Analyzer Dwell Period in One Frequency Bin

The averaging detector and the RMS detector process data points taken during the dwell time in the frequency bin. The averaging detector should not be confused with trace averaging; promotional literature, and even operation instructions, sometimes fail to make a clear distinction as to what averaging features a certain analyzer model has. Succinctly, if averaging appears in a detector list, it is the averaging illustrated in Figure 9.5. If an averaging function has a selectable number of sweeps, it is trace averaging.

The RMS and averaging detector functions increase the number of data points that go into the final averaged trace. Instead of one data point—the sample detection point—per bin per sweep, the RMS and averaging detectors utilize all the data points in each sweep through the bin. If the sweep is run slowly enough there is no need to average separate sweeps; the RMS or average detector will have done it during the dwell time in each bin.

Setting Reference Levels

To set the reference level for FM IBOC spectrum analyzer measurements, the unmodulated carrier could be observed at 1 kHz resolution bandwidth or less. To avoid interrupting modulation, a 300 kHz resolution bandwidth may be employed to integrate the total power of the modulated FM signal into the center frequency bin on the analyzer. The presence of the IBOC sidebands (~1% of the FM analog power) will not appreciably affect the reference level setting with 300 kHz RBW because it introduces no more than a 0.04 dB error.

If not using an unmodulated carrier for AM carrier level reference, simply averaging at 300 Hz resolution bandwidth should be sufficient. The average power in the 300-Hz span from −150 to +150 Hz provides an accurate representation of the unmodulated AM carrier power.

In terms of which detection/averaging method is correct or most accurate, the Transmission System Specifications reference documents are silent. In fact, since the iBiquity reference method is described in a manner that implies a trace-averaging function, then the greater accuracy of the RMS detector is irrelevant. In general, the three methods—trace averaging of sample detection, average detection with or without trace averaging, RMS detection with or without trace averaging—produce results that are very close and likely within the measurement error of the setup. Only peak detection should be avoided, as it will artificially inflate the results, causing the transmitter to be set with a level that is several dB lower than that which is allowed.

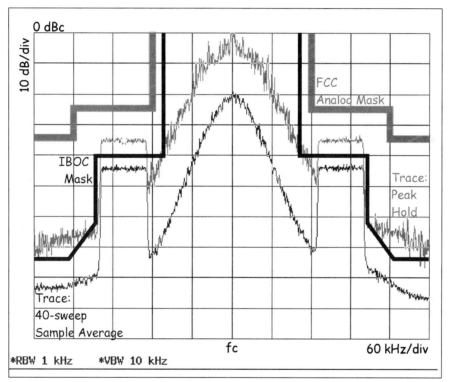

Figure 9.6 Spectrum Analyzer Traces (FM IBOC)

FM Mask

The hybrid FM mask is tailored to the spurious emissions that are characteristic of the signal. The hybrid FM IBOC transmission has the three components, the analog carrier at center frequency and the upper and lower IBOC sidebands. The lower trace of Figure 9.6 shows the 1-kHz average PSD of such a signal. Considering these three components as separate signals, they have the potential to intermodulate with one another as they pass through the transmit signal path (up to and including the antenna), producing *spectral regrowth* emissions outside the necessary bandwidth of the hybrid IBOC signal. Spectral regrowth is a spurious emission resulting from densely modulated digital waveforms that intermodulate.

Digital-to-Digital Intermodulation

The upper and lower Primary Main sidebands appear as A and B in Figure 9.7. They are centered at about 164-kHz offset from the analog carrier frequency. In the upper image of Figure 9.7, the digital-to-digital third-order intermodulation appears as spectral regrowth products at 2A-B and 2B-A, which fall at 492-kHz offsets from center frequency. This is halfway between second and third-adjacent channels.

Analog/Digital Intermodulation

When the analog signal joins the digital signal in the transmission path, additional third-order intermodulation products appear between the digital products. These appear as spectral regrowth at 328-kHz offsets (lower image of Figure 9.7, products 2A-C and 2B-C). Another product is worth noting—analog/digital third-order products also fall directly on the digital sidebands because they symmetrically straddle the analog host. Note how the 2C-B and 2C-A products coexist with the A and B PM sidebands. This suggests that preventing intermodulation is better than filtering it after it happens, because these IM products corrupt the digital sidebands and cannot be filtered.

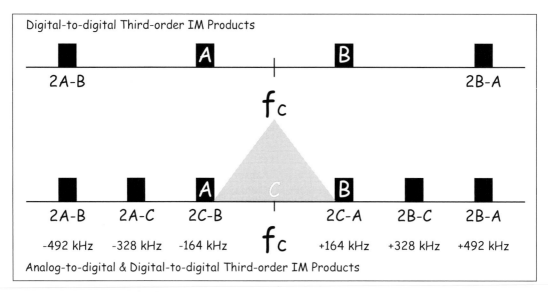

Figure 9.7 Hybrid FM IBOC Third-order Intermodulation Product Frequencies

NRSC-5-A Mask (Hybrid FM IBOC)

The spectral regrowth products take on the bandwidths of the source components. They spread out in what appear as rounded bumps with 100 to 200 kHz bandwidths. The 492-kHz product rolls off to about 600 kHz (Figure 9.9). The hybrid FM IBOC mask anticipates these components by rolling off between the 540 and 600 kHz offset. Table 9.8 describes the NRSC-5-A mask limit-line, including the slope at these offsets. Figure 9.8 shows the NRSC-5-A hybrid FM IBOC mask with the FCC analog mask. Figure 9.9 shows how the mask is tailored to wrap around the 492-kHz product, dropping to –80 dBc at 600 kHz. Spectral regrowth also appears under and alongside the OFDM subcarriers; the FM IBOC mask accommodates the "shoulders" of these products as they extend outside the Necessary Bandwidth of the OFDM subcarriers. After NRSC-5-A was adopted, a slight relaxation of the mask out to 250 kHz was proposed to better accommodate the shoulders—discussed in the following text.

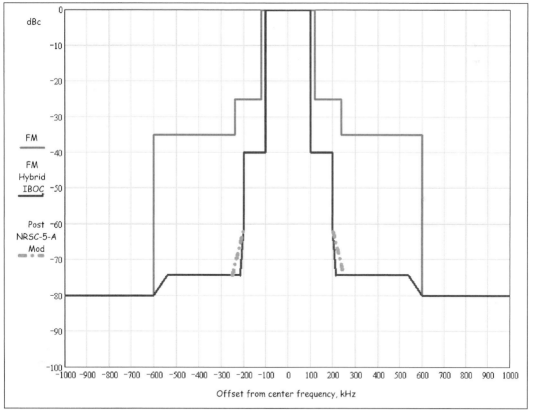

Figure 9.8 Hybrid FM IBOC and Analog Masks

Frequency Offset, F kHz, from Center	Mask Limit, dBc/kHz
NRSC-5-A	
100–200	–40
200–215	–61.4 – ((|F|-200)·0.867)
215–540	–74.4
540–600	–74.4 – ((|F|-200)·0.093)
>600	–80
Post-NRSC-5-A Revision	
100–200	–40
200–250	–61.4 – ((|F|-200)·0.260)
250–540	–74.4
540–600	–74.4 – ((|F|-200)·0.093)
>600	–80

Table 9.8 Hybrid FM IBOC Masks

The hybrid FM IBOC mask also covers the Primary sidebands. While the target value of the Primaries is –41.4 dBc/kHz, the mask allows a little room for error, riding at the slightly higher level of –40 dBc/kHz.

Digital Sideband Self-Intermodulation

Each FM IBOC Primary Main sideband consists of 191 simultaneously transmitted OFDM subcarriers. When intermodulation occurs, each subcarrier also intermodulates with the others in the same sideband. The result is a spectral regrowth product directly beneath the sideband. As Figure 9.9 suggests, the bandwidth of the spectral regrowth directly beneath each PM sideband spreads about 70 kHz beyond the last OFDM subcarrier frequency. The NRSC-5-A mask maintains a plateau between 215 and 540 kHz in anticipation of these products as well as their neighbors centered at 368 and 492 kHz.

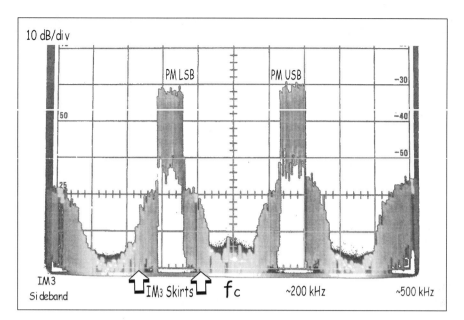

Figure 9.9 Digital-to-Digital Spectral Regrowth Products

Hybrid Mask Fine Tuning

The IBOC spectrum masks are the products of matching the ideal with reality. In the R&D world, with laboratory grade equipment and emphasis on building a working test platform over designing product efficiency, extremely clean performance is possible. Once the realities of manufacturing, sales, and operations must be faced, the pristine linear amplifier with plenty of headroom is left at the test bench. Product cost and operational efficiency become design constraints. The practicalities create opportunities for the hybrid IBOC signal to be distorted, such as running high power amplifiers, installing separate or common amplification of digital and analog, using multitransmitter sites, retrofitting existing transmitters, driving directional antennas, and using combiners, filters and the like.

The original hybrid FM mask that iBiquity filed with the FCC in 2002 did not benefit from experience in practical transmitter manufacture and installation. This mask is described in Table 9.9. It shows the emissions limits with respect to the Primary Main subcarrier PSD. Understanding that the PM sidebands are ideally –41.4 dBc/kHz with respect to the analog FM power, a column has been added to the original table to adjust the mask to reference analog carrier power. Note how the original specification required emissions outside the necessary bandwidth to very rapidly drop to –101.4 dBc/kHz. In contrast, the NRSC-5-A mask is more practicable, leveling out at –74.4 dBc/kHz before dropping to the final –80 dBc/kHz at the 600-kHz offset. With the benefit of manufacturer experience, iBiquity submitted transmission system specifications to the NRSC in 2004 that contained the more practicable mask.

Frequency, F kHz, Offset from Channel Center	Level, dB/kHz relative to OFDM Sideband, 1 kHz PSD		Level, dBc/kHz Relative to Analog Carrier Power (values are derived from iBiquity information in second column)
	Equation	Range	Range
200–205	–20 – ((|F|-200) * 4.0)	–20 to –40	–61.4 to –81.4
205–270	–40 – ((|F|-205) * 0.3077)	–40 to –60	–81.4 to –101.4
>270	–60	–60	–101.4

Table 9.9 Early 2001 Hybrid FM IBOC Mask Referenced by FCC (Source: IBOC FM Transmission Specification, August 2001, iBiquity Digital Corporation—filed with the FCC and referenced as Appendix B in the First Report and Order, in the matter of Digital Audio Broadcasting Systems And Their Impact on the Terrestrial Radio Broadcast Service, MM Docket No. 99-325, adopted October 10, 2002)

After NRSC-5-A was adopted, it became apparent that there remained a minor difficulty with the Hybrid FM IBOC mask. Some transmitters could not quite meet the mask on the slopes of the PM sidebands. The NRSC-5-A mask has a slope from 200 to 215 kHz that anticipates a little noise alongside the PM sideband. As figure 9.9 shows, the spectral regrowth appears as a mound-like spectrum beneath the mask (at least with the particular transmitter depicted). Careful inspection of the nearly vertical sides of the PM sidebands reveals a slight spreading above the spectral regrowth.

To accommodate the slightly broader PM sideband emissions of some transmitters, iBiquity revised the mask adopted in NRSC-5-A and submitted the revision to the FCC in July 2006. The skirts sloping from 200 to 215 kHz were spread, sloping from 200 to 250 kHz. These are listed in Table 9.8 and depicted in Figure 9.8. The NRSC is expected to incorporate this latest mask revision into the next version of NRSC-5.

NRSC-5-A Mask (All-Digital FM IBOC)

Since there is no analog host in the all-digital case, the all-digital mask uses the PM sidebands as the level reference. Mask compliance is measured with respect to the 1-kHz PSD of the PM sidebands. The mask slopes out from the PM sidebands to accommodate regrowth, hitting a –70 dBc plateau at 300 kHz. In place of the analog signal, a low-level set of Secondary OFDM sidebands is inserted.

Frequency Offset, F kHz, from Center	Mask Limit, dBc/kHz
NRSC-5-A	
200–207.5	–20 – ((|F|-200)·1.733)
207.5–250	–33 – ((|F|-207.5)·0.2118)
250–300	–42 – ((|F|-250)·0.56)
300–600	–70
>600	–80

Table 9.10 NRSC-5-A All-Digital FM IBOC Mask

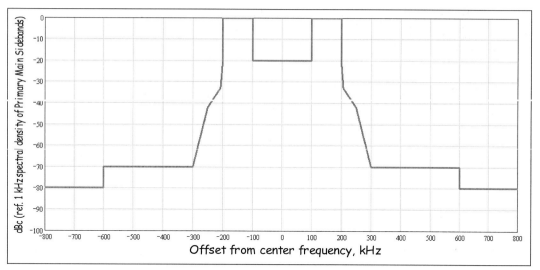

Figure 9.10 NRSC-5-A All-Digital FM IBOC Mask

OFDM Subcarrier Scaling

Implicit in the masks are the expected levels of the OFDM subcarrier groups. These levels are set by the Amplitude Scale Factor, discussed tangentially in Chapters 6 through 8. Amplitude Scale Factor a_0 (see Table 9.11) assigns the level of the Primary and Primary Extended subcarriers in hybrid FM operation. It is set with respect to the analog carrier power. The –48.5 dBc per subcarrier value is set to have the Primary Main sidebands total 1% of the analog power: –45.8 dBc/subcarrier times 382 Primary Main subcarriers (a factor of 25.8 dB) equals –20 dBc, or 1%. The Amplitude Scale Factor remains unchanged when one to four partitions of Extended Hybrid subcarriers are added to the signal. Adding all four Primary Extended partitions increases the total digital power by 1.4 dB, to –18.6 dBc.

Computation of the all-digital subcarrier power levels differs from hybrid. Without an analog host as a power reference, the specification anticipates each all-digital station will operate under a licensed all-digital power level.[3] Amplitude Scale Factors a_1 through a_5 apply to all-digital operation and reference the total authorized digital power of all Primary sidebands. Factor a_1 sets the level of the Primary subcarriers, and the other four are optional levels for the Secondary subcarriers.

Multiplying factor a_1 (–27.3 dBc) by the 534 Primary subcarriers, an increase of 27.3 dB, nets the 0 dBc reference level. The Secondary all-digital subcarriers are set to a common level that is selected from one of the four choices, a_2–a_5. These factors permit the Secondary power, per subcarrier and per kilohertz, to be set 5, 10, 15, or 20 dB below the corresponding measure of Primary power. Since there is nearly the same quantity of Secondary subcarriers as Primary, the total power of the Secondary subcarriers will closely track the selected 5, 10, 15, or, 20, dB per-subcarrier attenuation below total Primary power.

---

[3] The FCC's interim authorization of IBOC does not address, nor does it allow, all-digital operation.

Sidebands	Configuration	Service Mode(s)	Amplitude Scale Factor	Specified PSD		Total Power (of Primary or Secondary)
				dBc per OFDM subcarrier	dBc/kHz	
Primary	Hybrid	MP1	a0	−45.8	−41.4	−20 dBcFM
	Extended Hybrid	MP2–6				
Secondary	All-Digital	MP5–6	a1	−27.3	−22.9	0 dBcPM
		MS1–4	a2	−32.3	−27.9	−4.8 dBcPM
			a3	−37.3	−32.9	−9.8 dBcPM
			a4	−42.3	−37.9	−14.8 dBcPM
			a5	−47.3	−42.9	−19.8 dBcPM

Table 9.11 FM IBOC OFDM Subcarrier Scaling (Derived from FM Transmission System Specifications NRSC-5-A reference document (6), Table 4-3.)

NRSC-5-A does not contemplate a relationship between licensed analog power and the power of all-digital operation. That is something that deserves further assessment when the time comes. By establishing a power level for all-digital operation at, say, 10 dB below that of the (currently) licensed analog power, it would be 10 dB above the current hybrid digital power level. The resulting 10-dB increase in all-digital power would increase reliability as well as the reach of the digital signal. For this example, total power would remain substantially less than in the current analog arrangement, perhaps conferring an interference reduction benefit on all stations. Power consumption and transmitter size would be reduced, as well.

AM Mask

Just as with the FM mask, the hybrid AM mask is tailored to the spurious emissions that are characteristic of the signal. The hybrid AM IBOC transmission has a continuous span of digital energy across the IBOC channel, varying in level and modulation complexity among the Primary, Secondary and Tertiary digital sidebands. Laid on top, the modulated analog signal has a selectable bandwidth—±5 or ±8 kHz. The higher-PSD regions are the analog signal at center frequency, and the Primary sidebands at 10–15 kHz offsets.

Analog-to-Digital and Digital-to-Digital Intermodulation

Figure 9.11 is a spectrum analyzer image of an AM signal showing spectral regrowth right where it is expected, on the third-order product of the analog carrier and each Primary digital sideband. With the Primary sidebands at 10–15 kHz offsets, the products fall in the 20–30 kHz offsets. The hybrid AM IBOC mask is overlaid on the trace, revealing how the mask neatly wraps around the spectral regrowth (at least in this example).

The digital-to-digital intermodulation in Figure 9.11 is much less pronounced at the 37 kHz offsets than the analog-to-digital products at 25 kHz. The ever-present AM carrier is the most potent contributor to intermodulation products. Also, to the extent that spurious emissions are created in the transmitter, the bandwidth of the antenna system will act as a bandpass filter (however, the antenna system is a potential source of distortion as well). The Hybrid AM IBOC mask places limits at practicable levels.

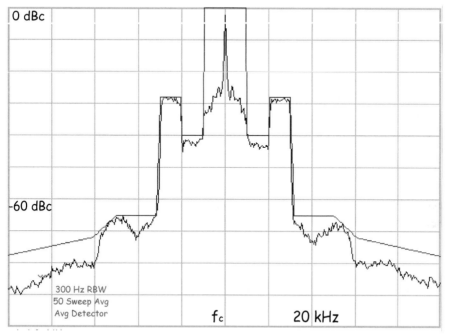

Figure 9.11 Hybrid AM IBOC Spectral Regrowth under Mask

NRSC-5-A Mask (Hybrid AM IBOC)

As seen in the FM IBOC examples, so also the bandwidths of the AM IBOC spectral regrowth products take on the bandwidths of the source components. They spread out to as much as 10 kHz widths. The hybrid AM IBOC mask anticipates this with its short roll-off from 25 to 30.5 kHz, followed by the steadily descending slope out to 75 kHz. Table 9.12 describes the NRSC-5-A mask limit-line, including the slope at these offsets. Figure 9.12 shows the NRSC-5-A hybrid AM IBOC mask with the current FCC analog mask.

The hybrid AM IBOC RF Mask outside the Necessary Bandwidth is depicted on Figure 9.12 as the dark portion of the outline, and in Table 9.12. Levels for the interior portions of the spectrum are also shown in the figure and in Table 9.12 for reference. Hybrid AM IBOC has two optional levels, Level 1 and Level 2, depicted by the dotted line and the gray line, as labeled. This is discussed further in OFDM Subcarrier Scaling.

The analog RF bandwidth for 5- and 8-kHz audio bandwidths also appears in Figure 9.12. The overlap of both with the Tertiary energy is apparent, as is the overlap of the 8 kHz analog energy with the Secondary OFDM subcarriers.

The AM IBOC mask is based on 300-Hz power spectral density. Spectrum analyzers should be set to the 300-Hz resolution bandwidth when measuring compliance with the mask.

According to Table 9.12, the interior of the AM IBOC mask, including the Secondary and Tertiary sucbarriers shows a limit only for the Secondary subcarriers because the Tertiaries are beneath the analog modulation sidebands and need no mask for spectral occupancy purposes. For the purpose of maintaining proper scaling of a station's OFDM subcarrier levels and gain flatness, it is still helpful to have a target level when operating well below the mask. The upper portion of the table lists the target levels.

The RF mask for the hybrid Secondary subcarriers is based on the higher-level OFDM subcarrier scaling—Level 2—and is not particularly useful for validating performance because it is some 6 dB higher than the Level 1 OFDM subcarrier settings that are commonly employed by AM broadcasters. For testing amplitude scale settings, transmitter manufacturers are relying on a tolerance of about 1/2-dB with respect to the nominal Level 1 values (dashed line on center of Figure 9.12, labeled Level 1). For comparison, the hybrid FM IBOC mask specified for the OFDM subcarriers is −40 dBc/kHz, which gives a 1.4-dB tolerance above the nominal −41.4 dBc/kHz operating level.

The Tertiary subcarriers have no RF mask at all, and for performance testing a target value is still desirable. Manufacturers also employ the 1/2-dB tolerance with respect to the ideal Tertiary scale factor values.

Frequency Offset, F kHz, from Center	Mask Limit, dBc/300 Hz
OFDM Spectrum Nominal Levels	
0 – 5 (Tertiary)	−41.8 sloping to −47.8 [Level 1] & -41.8 [Level 2]
5 – 10 (Secondary)	−40.8 [Level 1] & -34.8 [Level 2]
10 – 15 (Primary)	−27.8
NRSC-5-A RF Mask	
5 – 10 [8 – 10]*	−34.3
10 – 15	−26.8
15 – 15.2	−28
15.2 – 15.8	$−39 − ((|F|-15.2)\cdot43.3)$
15.8 – 25	−65
25 – 30.5	$−65 − ((|F|-25)\cdot1.273)$
30.5 – 75	$−72 − ((|F|-30.5)\cdot0.292)$
>75	−85

Table 9.12 Hybrid AM IBOC Masks

For best digital performance, analog audio bandwidth is limited to 5 kHz. An optional 8 kHz analog mode is provided in the specifications. The starting point of the mask is shifted from 5 kHz to 8 kHz offset to allow analog sidebands to overlap the Secondary sideband. The AM Transmission System Specifications caution that reception of the digital signal may be compromised with the wider analog bandwidth. However, the impact of an 8-kHz host signal audio bandwidth on reception of the host's digital signal may only be subtle, due to the ability of the IBOC receiver to perform host analog cancellation to recover the digital signal.

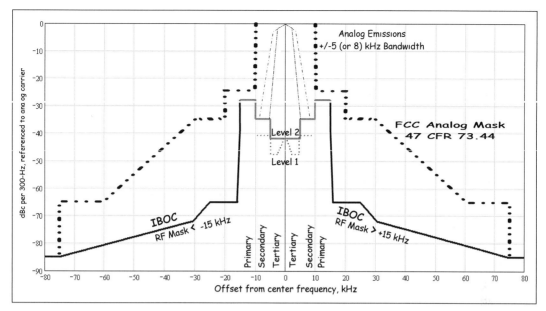

Figure 9.12 Hybrid AM IBOC and Analog Masks

Why not 8 kHz?

• *Minor impairment to digital reception*: At 5 kHz, the analog sidebands do not fall on the Secondary digital sidebands, which occupy the 5–10 kHz offset. The receiver can detect each Secondary sideband independently, even if one sideband is corrupted by adjacent channel interference. With 8 kHz analog bandwidth, analog energy is imposed on the Secondary sidebands, which appears as noise on each sideband, making it more difficult to detect either sideband independently. This forces the receiver to rely on dual detection of the complementary sidebands. If there is also adjacent channel interference to one Secondary sideband, the receiver has no options left for recovering the information on the Secondary sideband. In the limited circumstances where the 8 kHz bandwidth provokes the loss of the host Secondary sideband, the consequence is only the loss of enhanced audio. The core audio, carried on the Primary sidebands, may continue unaffected.

• *Little benefit to analog reception*: The results of a 2005 AM receiver study conducted by the NRSC's AM Broadcasting Subcommittee confirm the narrow bandwidths of consumer AM radios. The study was incorporated in a 2006 report prepared for the Subcommittee by NPR Labs.[4] Various receiver categories were analyzed for analog AM audio bandwidth

(continued on following page)

---

[4] Consumer Testing of AM Broadcast Transmission Bandwidth and Audio Performance Measurements of Broadcast AM receivers, September 8, 2006, NPR Labs.

(continued from previous page)

(no operation using IBOC was included in this study). The combined –10 dB audio bandwidth of each class was reported: home stereos—3.8 kHz, portable/boom box—4.7 kHz; clock radios—5.5 kHz; OEM car—4.6 kHz; HD Radio car—4.7 kHz; aftermarket car—4.2 kHz. On its subjective listener testing of analog AM audio bandwidth, the report concludes, "overall, although there was some variation in preference between genres, the data strongly suggest that in general consumers preferred lower bandwidths (between 5 and 7 kHz) to higher bandwidths." This is due in part to the AM sidebands of adjacent-channel stations, when transmitting at greater than 5 kHz audio bandwidth, that overlap the desired signal's sidebands. The minimal benefits to perceived audio quality obtained by increasing analog bandwidth from 5 to 8 kHz are offset by the increased interference to adjacent stations.

- *Increased IBOC susceptibility to 2nd-adjacent interference*: The impact of the 8-kHz bandwidth may be more profound when considering the potential for second-adjacent channel interference. As long as both sidebands of the desired hybrid AM IBOC signal are unencumbered by second-adjacent interferers, the IBOC receiver can use host analog cancellation techniques to recover the secondary digital sidebands. In the presence of second-adjacent interference, the receiver must rely on one secondary sideband, which sees the 8-kH analog signal as an inteferer. More discussion of the channelization of the AM broadcast band and AM IBOC emissions is found in Chapter 12.

Like the original FM mask presented to the FCC in 2002, the original hybrid AM mask did not benefit from experience in practical transmitter manufacture and installation. This mask is described in Table 9.13. Note how the original specification required emissions outside the necessary bandwidth to very rapidly drop to –100 dBc/300-Hz at 20.5 kHz. In contrast, the NRSC-5-A mask is more practicable, tapering down to –85 dBc/300-Hz at 75 kHz offset.

Frequency, F kHz, Offset from Channel Center	Level, dBc/300-Hz
5 – 10	–39
10 – 15	–25
15 – 20.5	$-78 - ((|F|-15)\cdot4)$
>20.5	–100

Table 9.13 Early 2001 Hybrid AM IBOC Mask Referenced by FCC (Source: IBOC AM Transmission Specification, November 2001, iBiquity Digital Corporation—filed with the FCC and referenced as Appendix C in the First Report and Order, in the matter of Digital Audio Broadcasting Systems And Their Impact on the Terrestrial Radio Broadcast Service, MM Docket No. 99-325, adopted October 10, 2002.)

Analog Host Performance with Hybrid

The AM Transmission System Specifications require the analog signal to meet performance criteria to protect the digital component of the hybrid signal. Disabling the hybrid digital subcarriers, the modulated analog carrier with 5 kHz audio bandwidth must not have emissions in the 5–20 kHz offset greater than a mask at –65 dBc per 300-Hz. With 8 kHz audio bandwidth, the analog mask extends from 8 to 20 kHz.

NRSC-5-A Mask (All-Digital AM IBOC)

Since there is no analog host in the all-digital case, the all-digital mask uses the licensed AM carrier power level as the reference. The necessary bandwidth of the all-digital AM IBOC signal is reduced from the hybrid ±15 kHz to the all-digital ±10 kHz. The mask is narrowed corresponding to the reduced bandwidth.

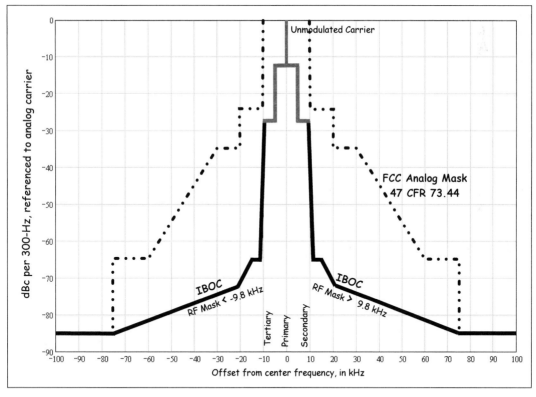

Figure 9.13 NRSC-5-A All-Digital AM IBOC Mask

Frequency Offset, F kHz, from Center	Mask Limit, dBc/300-Hz
OFDM Spectrum	
0.1817 – 4.81465	–12.8 Nominal OFDM Level
4.81465 – 9.8	–27.8 Nominal OFDM Level
NRSC-5-A RF Mask	
9.8 – 10.5	–28– ((|F|-9.8)·42.86)
10.5 – 11.5	–58– ((|F|-10.5)·7.0)
11.5 – 15	–65
15 – 20.5	–65 – ((|F|-15)·1.273)
20.5 – 75	–72 – ((|F|-20.5)·0.239)
>75	–85

Table 9.14 NRSC-5-A All-Digital AM IBOC Mask

Discrete Components Exception

The AM IBOC spectral masks (hybrid 5 & 8 kHz, and all-digital) have an exception for what are termed "discrete components." While this term is undefined, it is reasonable to anticipate that an occasional noise spike might ascend above the mask when taking measurements, or that an oscillator or switching spur might be resident in the measured spectrum. Such components would be perhaps no more than a few display bins wide. A portion of an entire spectral regrowth curve ought not to qualify as a discrete component.

Discrete components between ±75 kHz of center frequency:

• No more than two exceeding the mask by no more than 10 dB each, or

Discrete components outside ±75 kHz of center frequency:

• No more than four exceeding the mask by no more than 5 dB each.

OFDM Subcarrier Scaling

The Amplitude Scale Factors for AM IBOC are considerably more intricate than for FM IBOC (Table 9.15). In particular, hybrid AM IBOC operation involves three sets of sideband groups —Primary, Secondary and Tertiary—transmitted at different levels. In addition, the Tertiary sidebands beneath the analog signal may be shaped with a polygon that reflects the analog power spectral density. This applies in power level setting #1. The alternate power level setting, #2, flattens the spectrum of the Tertiary sidebands, increasing the total Tertiary power by 4 dB per sideband. Also, power level setting #2 increases each Secondary sideband by 6 dB. Power level setting #2 makes the Secondary and Tertiary sidebands more robust against analog interference, at the possible expense of the quality of analog reception.

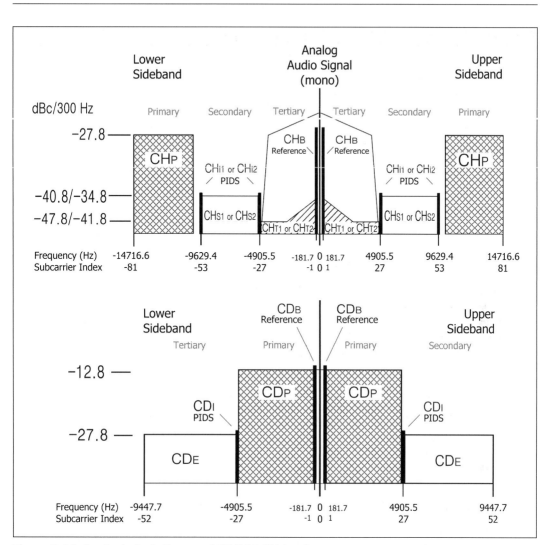

Figure 9.14 Amplitude Scale Factors of AM IBOC Sidebands

RF Mode	Sideband Group	Subcarrier Numbers	Subcarriers Per Side-band Group	dBc Per Sideband Group Per AM Sideband	Amplitude Scale Factor		
					ID	dBc/subcarrier	dBc/300-Hz
Hybrid	Primary	57 to 81 −57 to −81	25 USB, 25 LSB	−16	CHP	−30	−27.8
	Secondary (Level 1)	28 to 52 −28 to −52	25 USB, 25 LSB	−29	CHS1	−43	−40.8
	Tertiary (Level 1 slope)	2 to 13 −2 to −13	12 USB, 12 LSB	−34	CHT1	−44 to −49.5 in half-dB steps per subcarrier	−41.8 to −47.3 (approx)
	Tertiary (Level 1 flat)	14 to 26 −14 to −26	13 USB, 13 LSB			−50	−47.8
	PIDS	27, 53, −27, −53	2 USB 2 LSB	na	CHI1	−43	na
	Alternate Power Levels for PIDS, Tertiary and Secondary						
	Secondary (Level 2)	28 to 52 −28 to −52	25 USB, 25 LSB	−23	CHS2	−37	−34.8
	Tertiary (Level 2)	2 to 26 −2 to −26	25 USB, 25 LSB	−30	CHT2	−44	−41.8
	PIDS (Level 2)	27, 53, −27, −53	2 USB 2 LSB	na	CHI2	−37	na
	Reference	1 and −1	1 each	na	CHB	−26	na
	Analog carrier	0		0 dBc reference		0	
All-Digital	Primary	2 to 26 −2 to −26	25 USB, 25 LSB	−1	CDP	−15	−12.8
	Secondary	28 to 52	25 USB	−16	CDE	−30	−27.8
	Tertiary	−28 to −52	25 LSB	−16	CDE	−30	−27.8
	PIDS	27, −27	1 each	−30	CDI	−30	na
	Reference	1 and −1	1 each	−15	CDB	−15	na
	Pilot	0		0 dBc reference		0	

Table 9.15 AM IBOC OFDM Subcarrier Scaling (Derived from Table 5-1 NRSC-5-A Reference Document (2)—AM Layer 1, and Table 4-4 NRSC-5-A Reference Document (8)—AM Transmission System Specifications.)

Computation of the all-digital OFDM subcarrier power levels is based on the same reference as hybrid—the analog carrier power. At the station's licensed power, the former analog carrier is transmitted without modulation as a part of the all-digital signal. It serves as a pilot conveying frequency and phase information to the receiver. Amplitude Scale Factors CD$_{subscript}$ apply to all-digital operation.

The combined power of one 25-subcarrier all-digital AM Primary sideband is nearly the same as the licensed analog power (–1 dBc each). The Secondary sideband is now placed only in the upper sideband and the Tertiary is placed only in the lower sideband. Core audio now resides on the Primary sidebands at channel center, where it is best protected from interference. The less critical enhanced audio on the Secondary and Tertiary sidebands is conveyed at lower levels, occupying the 5–10 kHz channel offset where adjacent channel interference is more likely to have an impact.

IBOC or IBAC?

There is a misguided idea put forth by IBOC detractors[5] that the technology is not really In-Band On-Channel, but In-Band Adjacent-Channel (IBAC), because the bandwidth of the hybrid IBOC signals is broader than what is perceived as the "channel." The argument seems intended to imply that IBAC technology inherently causes interference. This is a misrepresentation for two reasons. First, the fundamental characteristics of IBAC technology are different than IBOC, so the term is misused. Second, the concept of a "channel" as an immutable protective boundary is mistaken, because the channel is a more complex concept than simply a fixed bandwidth reserved for the exclusive use of one transmission. By the detractors' definition, even existing analog services are "IBAC," rendering the term meaningless. IBOC aligns itself with the structure of adjacent-channel protections, IBAC does not.

IBAC Characteristics Differ From IBOC

What is IBAC, really? IBAC is an asymmetrical digital transmission scheme for broadcast radio bands already occupied by analog services, in which an independent channel frequency is assigned to the digital signal. It is asymmetrical because the digital signal is paired with an adjacent channel analog signal and resides on one side of the analog signal. It is centered on the adjacent channel frequency and occupies substantial bandwidth within the adjacent channel. Typically, the IBAC signal would be assigned to the second- or third-adjacent channel of the analog host.

The symmetry of IBOC around the center frequency of the analog host provides a number of benefits over the IBAC concept. First, IBOC provides an uncomplicated one-to-one relationship between analog hosts and hybrid digital operation. In doing so it provides 100% parity such that all radio stations are able to transmit a hybrid digital signal.

The allotment scheme for IBAC offers no such implicit guarantee. Collisions will occur where the digital signals of a pair of, say, fourth-adjacent stations would be forced to occupy the same second-adjacent channel,[6] requiring either a complex frequency-assignment rubric, complementary power reductions, and/or interference overlap zones that reduce the effectiveness of the

---

[5] See, for instance, Guy Wire's article in *Radio World*, April 25, 2002, "A Bumpy Ride for iBiquity at NAB 2002" and related articles on www.rwonline.com.

[6] Even if the technology were able to utilize first-adjacent channels for the IBAC signals, the same assignment conflicts seen in the example of fourth-adjacent stations and their second-adjacent IBAC signals would occur between second-adjacent stations and their first-adjacent IBAC signals.

digital signals with respect to their analog hosts. This precludes the IBAC digital signal, in some circumstances, from replicating the coverage of the analog host.

Furthermore, the IBAC signal lacks the frequency diversity offered by the IBOC signal, which could also result in reduced coverage with respect to the analog host. When an IBOC signal is confronted with first-adjacent channel interference on the fringe of its coverage area, it can continue to rely on the opposite sideband to maintain service. An IBAC signal will fail if it is compromised by a first-adjacent analog signal on the edge of the host station's coverage area. As well, frequency-selective fading over the IBAC channel may be more destructive because it lacks IBOC's diversity of upper and lower sidebands separated by an analog host.

By occupying a full adjacent channel, the IBAC signal will impinge on the reception of a second-adjacent analog signal in a way that IBOC does not. Also, if the power levels required to make the IBAC signal work are greater than that of the IBOC signal, IBAC may potentially interfere with first-adjacent reception within the protected area of the first-adjacent station.

All-in all, IBAC is not the most effective way to achieve hybrid digital operation in the AM and FM bands, but not for the reasons implied by those who misuse the term "IBAC." By no stretch of the name "IBAC" is IBOC technology an adjacent-channel-centric technology. It simply expands on the principles of Desired-to-Undesired ratio protection of stations sharing the spectrum, with each IBOC digital signal employing the same center frequency as the analog host.

The Radio "Channel"

Let us look at the idea of a channel. Radio channels are fundamentally assigned on a specified channel spacing. The energy in adjacent channels may or may not overlap, depending on the allotment scheme. To ensure maximum spectrum efficiency, the allotment scheme for a particular service takes into account several factors. One of them is the channel spacing assigned to a particular service (200 kHz on-center for FM in the U.S., 100 kHz in some other parts of the world; 10 kHz on-center for AM in the U.S., 9 kHz in some other parts of the world). But that's not enough.

Part of the equation for broadcast services, among others, is geographic diversity. Analog AM broadcasting relies on geographic diversity to interleave signals that overlap in the radio spectrum to help minimize potential interference. The channel, then, is defined in part by the spectrum required by the signal, and in part by the manner in which the spectral overlap of other signals is managed.

With geographic diversity comes the *near-far* problem. A user might be near an undesired signal source and far from the desired signal source. The filtering, if any, in the receiver must resolve the difference between two signals close in frequency. Thus, even if the energy of two signals does not overlap in the radio spectrum, it can cause interference to the reception of one when the strength of the other is too great. This characteristic is evaluated with the use of *desired-to-undesired ratios* (D/U). For example, in the U.S. FM band a receiver might be able to resolve two first-adjacent channel signals, but only if the undesired signal is at least about 6 dB weaker than the desired (D/U ≥ 6 dB). The signals do not overlap spectrally, in a literal sense, but they do overlap practically, if the D/U is not right.

While it is convenient to think of the FM "channel" in the U.S.A. as a simple 200 kHz-wide slot reserved for the exclusive use of a station, the idea of a "channel" has a richer context. The communications channel between a transmitter and one listener's receiver is characterized by a host of conditions.

The Radio Channel

The following characteristics define the channel available between a particular station in a radio service and its recipient:

- The frequency spacing of the service;
- The bandwidth of the signals, including:
  - the necessary bandwidth, and
  - the out-of-band emissions, and
  - possible spurious emissions;
- The nature of undesired signals on the same and nearby frequencies (determined by geographic allotment of frequencies and power levels, and the modulation characteristics);
- The characteristics of the receiver (which in U.S. broadcasting are established in the marketplace, not the regulatory environment);
- The radio noise environment;
- The radio propagation environment (such as multipath).

The simplistic interpretation of "IBAC," in which the energy of two signals on adjacent channels is allowed to overlap spectrally, is not meaningful, because it applies just as well to the analog services as it would to IBOC technology. Any analog radio channelization scheme that overlaps energy on adjacent channels is just as entitled to be branded by the pejorative use of the term "IBAC." That would be the AM band worldwide, a well as the FM band in some parts of the world. In addition, since the receiver bandwidth also defines the channel, even the more conservatively spaced U.S. FM band potentially overlaps adjacent channel energy, from the perspective of the receiver. FM radios are susceptible to first- and second-adjacent channel interference just as if the signals were overlapping in the spectrum.

Based on the foregoing, the concept of IBAC is misused by IBOC detractors. IBAC is an asymmetrical allotment of spectrum that does not provide one-to-one correspondence between digital and host analog stations, assigns a new channel to the digital signal, increases the potential for inter-station interference, does not marry the spectral occupancy of the digital signal with the host analog signal, and fails to exploit the implicit protections already established in the D/U ratios of existing station allotments. IBOC honors the existing allotment schemes, enabling a compatible, symmetrical, universal, single-channel way to deliver a hybrid digital signal.

10 From the Top Down: Other Input to the Protocol Stack–The SIS Data Services

In Chapters 4 through 9 we journeyed down the main trail of the IBOC protocol stack. Coded audio (entering from above the stack) percolates down the stack, as Program Service Data (PSD) marries with its flow toward the physical layer at the bottom. In addition to the PSD text information, structural information about the transmission, and forward error protection information also meld with the Audio information as it progresses into Layers 2 and 1. This chapter focuses on the first of two other data inputs to the NRSC-5 protocol stack.

In Chapter 4, we laid out the audio program services, MPS and SPS, and explained the process of embedding the PSD into these program streams. In subsequent chapters we drilled down the stack until the data becomes a radio signal. To the side of this main portion of the protocol stack reside additional information paths for other data services.

There are two data services that are not embedded in the program streams: Station Information Service (SIS) and Advanced Data Service (ADS). Being services, SIS and ADS each require two levels of protocol to function. First, they must have a layer that packages the information so it will be ready to transport. This is described by a service protocol. Second, to embed the service on the IBOC signal, the services must be processed through a transport protocol.

Recall, for instance, how the PSD has a protocol defined in reference document (7) in which the ID3 formatting is invoked; it is followed by a companion PSD Transport described in reference document (9) where HDLC-like packet encapsulation is applied. These complementary service-and-transport descriptions are discussed in detail in Chapter 4. Similarly, SIS also must have a service protocol and a transport protocol. The same is true for ADS.

In the case of the SIS and its transport, both are described in a single NRSC-5 reference document. That is document (5) listed in Table 10.1. See the right hand side of Figure 10.1 for the position of SIS Transport within the protocol stack. The ADS service protocol and transport, residing alongside SIS, are the subjects of Chapter 11.

NRSC-5 Reference Document Number	Reference Document Title	NRSC-5 Reference Document Number	Reference Document Title
1.	Doc. No. SY_IDD_1011s rev. E HD Radio™ Air Interface Design Description **Layer 1 FM** iBiquity Digital Corporation, 3/22/05	6.	Doc. No. SY_SSS_1026s rev. D HD Radio™ **FM Transmission System Specifications** iBiquity Digital Corporation, 2/18/05
2.	Doc. No. SY_IDD_1012s rev. E HD Radio™ Air Interface Design Description **Layer 1 AM** iBiquity Digital Corporation, 3/22/05	7.	Doc. No. SY_IDD_1028s rev. C HD Radio™ Air Interface Design Description **Program Service Data** iBiquity Digital Corporation, 3/31/05
3.	Doc. No. SY_IDD_1014s rev. F HD Radio™ Air Interface Design Description **Layer 2 Channel Multiplex Protocol** iBiquity Digital Corporation, 2/7/05	8.	Doc. No. SY_SSS_1082s rev. D HD Radio™ **AM Transmission System Specifications** iBiquity Digital Corporation, 2/24/05
4.	Doc. No. SY_IDD_1017s rev. E HD Radio™ Air Interface Design Description **Audio Transport** iBiquity Digital Corporation, 3/31/05	9.	Doc. No. SY_IDD_1085s rev. C HD Radio™ Air Interface Design Description **Program Service Data Transport** iBiquity Digital Corporation, 2/7/05
5.	Doc. No. SY_IDD_1020s rev. E HD Radio™ Air Interface Design Description **Station Information Service Protocol** iBiquity Digital Corporation, 2/18/05	10.	Doc. No. SY_IDD_1019s rev. E HD Radio™ Air Interface Design Description **Advanced Application Services Transport** iBiquity Digital Corporation, 8/4/05

Table 10.1 Protocols Addressed in Chapter 10

The Station Information Service is a mélange of data fields relating to the station transmitting the IBOC signal. Because this information is station-related, SIS data is not in the class of what is known by the familiar term of Program Associated Data (PAD). PAD is generally considered to be data that has a direct relationship to a program stream of main or supplemental audio. SIS data is a notch above PAD in the information hierarchy. Both may be considered metadata, with PAD being data about the digital audio program and SIS being data about the source of the signal being received, describing things such as station name, station location, and local time

Among the many things the AAS transport (AAT) might do, it can also be a bearer of PAD content. PAD is not an NRSC-5-defined term. In Chapter 4, we explained how Program Service Data is the fundamental source of PAD. It is embedded with the audio stream. New services could deliver richer PAD experiences via ADS. To do so would require a standard protocol that broadcasters could use for transmission and receiver makers could employ in new models.

This chapter examines the SIS protocol. Chapter 11 looks into the AAS Transport (also called "AAT"), introducing concepts that underlie advanced data services, putting them in perspective in the datacasting marketplace.

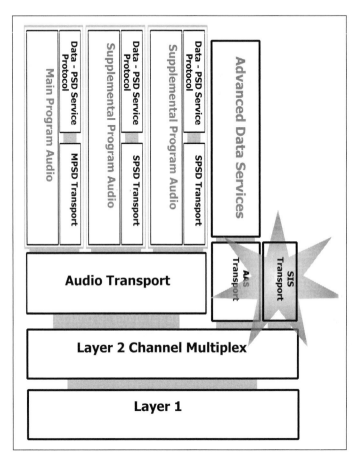

Figure 10.1 NRSC-5 Protocol Stack with SIS and ADS

Station Information Service Protocol

The SIS Protocol contains two layers described as one. First, it describes the transport function utilizing an 80-bit PDU. In addition to some housekeeping and error protection, the PDU has space for one or two message payloads. If the PDU is considered the transport, then the messages are the service. The SIS protocol describes seven message types, leaving spare numbering for future types. Let's talk about the messaging first, then fold in the transport function.

The seven SIS messages are shown in Table 10.2. Nine message ID's are reserved for future use. Post NRSC-5-A additions to the message list are appended to Table 10.2. Each message is assigned an ID number. Among the seven assigned in NRSC-5-A, three convey text that a receiver could display—Station names (long and short) and Station Message. The other four contain information a receiver might use for display or processing purposes.

Several SIS messages are extendable, permitting the *message content* to be distributed among more than one *message frame* bearing the same Message ID. The reference document lacks consistent nomenclature, so we make this distinction. The message frame is the carrier of a finite set of information bearing a Message ID number and in some cases a (message) Frame Number. The message frame is the product of the Station Information Service the way an audio packet is a product of the Program Service (Chapter 4). Such frames are then coupled with a transport. The SIS message frame is inserted into the SIS Transport.

Message content is the largest component of a message frame, consisting of a string of text or a set of numbers such as latitude, longitude and altitude. Message content may require more than one message frame to be completely transmitted. With the term *message*, we refer to the arrangement that gets the entire message content across—a group of one or more message frames under the same Message ID number that bear a complete set of message content.

Message ID	Multi-Frame?*	# of Bits	Contents	Name	Description
0000	No	32	Bitmap values	Station ID	Country Code and Facility ID
0001	No	22	Text plus flag	Station Name (short)	4-character call sign plus extension
0010	Optional 8 max.	58	Text, multiple frames, 56 character max.	Station Name (long)	Station identity
0011	No	32	Binary number	ALFN	IBOC Frame Number
0100	2	27	Bitmapped values	Station Location	Geographic coordinates and elevation
0101	Optional 24 max	58	Text,124 characters max	Station Message	Text message
0110	-	27	-	Reserved	No indication of purpose
0111	2 max.	22	Bitmapped values	SIS Parameter Message	Time information
1000–1111	-	-	-	Reserved	Future use
Lower section of table contains messages devised after NRSC-5-A.					
Unpublished	Optional		Text, 11 characters max	Call Sign Universal	Improved Station Name (short)
Unpublished	Optional		Text, 95 characters max	Station Slogan Universal	Improved Station Name (long)
Unpublished	no	27	Bitmapped values	Service Information Message	Service discovery – see discussion at end of Chapter 11

Multiframe indicates whether more than one message frame is necessary (or optional) to convey the message content. Optional means the number of frames is content-dependent.

Table 10.2 SIS Transport Message ID's

Station Name (Short Format) a.k.a. Call Sign Standard

The Station Name (short) is intended to convey conventional radio broadcast call signs in the U.S.A. These consist of three- or four-alpha-character words. For FM stations officially designated with the "–FM" suffix, to distinguish from other broadcast services with the same call, a two-bit extension selects the suffix. The specification suggests stations with three-letter calls place a space character in the fourth (right) character position.

Bit position	0...4	5...9	10...14	15...19	20,21
Value	1st character (left)	2nd character	3rd character	4th character (right)	00= none 01= -FM 10,11 spare

Table 10.3 Bitmap of SIS Station Name, Short Form
(Source: From Table 4-3, NRSC-5 reference document (5).)

The Station Name (short) has a compact 5-bit alphabet, in which A = 0000 through Z =11001. Extra characters <space>, ?, –, *, and $ are available as 11010 through 11110, respectively—although only the space seems applicable to this purpose. Transmission equipment manufacturers provide the user interface for inputting the Station Name (short) and other user-defined messages.

At the time the SIS was developed, it overlooked the more complex call signs for special types of licenses in the broadcast band. Translators in the U.S.A. employ a letter-number-letter format such as W243AI. Travelers Information Service (TIS) call signs take the form WPVQ743. Neither is accommodated by the Station Name (short) format. In time, these types of stations might join the IBOC family. A new station ID format could be created or the current format extended, but initial IBOC receivers would continue to rely on the limited capability of the SIS Station Name (short) field. (See Call Sign Universal, below.)

Translators are a special case. Translators may simply retransmit the radio frequency signal of the primary stations they are translating, making no changes to the incoming IBOC signal. When translators evolve to generating their own IBOC signals, it is sensible to continue to transmit the call signs of their primary stations and provide some alterative way of identifying the translator itself. (The same might apply to on-frequency boosters)

A different bureau of the FCC, than the one that licenses broadcasters, licenses TIS facilities in the U.S.A. A single call sign may be assigned to multiple TIS facilities. (These stations have no FCC Facility ID numbers, either; Facility ID's are discussed in a following section.) It may be a long time before TIS stations switch to IBOC, if ever. The consequences of having no official place for a TIS call sign on the SIS transport may not be significant. However, if all radio transmissions offer a consistent presentation of richer information, then radio users will enjoy a smarter, more user-friendly radio experience.

U.S. Low Power FM (LPFM) stations operate with an –LP suffix which could be seamlessly accommodated on the SIS Station Name (short) by adding –LP to the extension list. (Such as assigning it to Extension 10).

Call Sign Universal

Addressing the just-mentioned difficulties with Station Name (short) after the adoption of NRSC-5-A, iBiquity added an SIS message called Call Sign Universal. Instead of relying on a custom character set, as does Station Name (short), the Call Sign Universal message is an ISO 8859 (Latin) character-set-based message, in keeping with other SIS text messages. It supports 11 character bytes. iBiquity's exciter firmware version IRSS 2.3.3 was the first to incorporate the new message.

Station Name (Long) a.k.a. Station Slogan Standard

In contrast to the Station Name (short), the Station Name (long) offers some tantalizing database and menu-oriented capabilities. If stations were to consistently transmit their familiar identity at the beginning of the Station Name (long) field, applications developers would be encouraged to employ the information in an alphabetical or voice-activated look-up table in receivers. Imagine the convenience of looking for "Magic," "Kiss," or "Mike" without having to resort to the traditional tuning/scan control.

Because it can be long, the Station Name (long) field has a more complex structure than the short. Up to eight Station Name (long) message frames can be tied together, for a maximum of 56 characters in the whole Station Name (long). At its simplest implementation, each Station Name (long) message frame can carry seven U.S. ASCII characters. Concatenating eight message frames yields the potential 56 characters.

In defining the character set for Station Name (long), NRSC-5 reference document (5) anticipates the use of writing systems employed throughout the world. The 7-Bit Unicode Transformation Format (UTF-7) character format earned the responsibility of encoding and providing multilingual support on the Station Name (long) message. The SIS reference document cites the UTF-7 protocol.[1]

To understand UTF-7, the role of Unicode deserves brief attention. The Unicode Consortium (www.unicode.org) explains that their mission is to maintain a universal code set that provides a unique "number for every character" in every language. There are about 100,000 characters, ideographs, and symbols in the Unicode code set. The Unicode set starts with the basic Latin characters and symbols of the U.S. ASCII[2] set, and extends the numbering to include all character sets worldwide. All Unicode character numbers fit within a 32-bit word. To encourage more compactness, the most heavily used characters of the world are encoded in 16-bit space. Still, when transmitting mostly ASCII characters it is inefficient to send a 16-bit word for every character, when only 7 bits are necessary. Unicode also endorses an 8-bit transformation that delivers the frequently used U.S. ASCII characters efficiently, in raw 7-bit ASCII form. The 8th bit is toggled to the value 0 when an ASCII character is present, and to 1 when the numbering is extended to further octets for characters with eight bits or more. This is called Unicode Transformation Format 8 (UTF-8) and is an Official Internet Protocol Standard (www.ietf.org).

---

[1] D. Goldsmith and M. Davis, "UTF-7 A Mail-Safe Transformation Format of Unicode," Internet Engineering Task Force RFC2152, May 1997.

[2] American Standard Code for Information Interchange.

This brings us around to a different Unicode transformation format, UTF-7, employed for Station Name (long) messages. Forgoing the eighth bit, UTF-7 provides a Unicode-capable protocol. This protocol is not an official standard, but a published informative document at ietf.org. Rather than using an eighth bit as a flag indicating higher-order characters, the plus-sign character (+) plays the role of a shift character indicating higher-order characters follow. Each 7-bit word is read as an ASCII character unless the plus sign appears in a text string, meaning the characters after the plus sign are encoded Unicode characters. UTF-7 uses a special variable-length format for the shifted Unicode characters, averaging 16 to 24 bits per non-ASCII character.

It is safe to assume that receivers with text displays are equipped with basic ASCII display capability. Of course, to go beyond the fundamental ASCII character set requires both the transmitter and the receiver to be equipped with matching Unicode language subsets. Considering the size of the entire Unicode set, it would not be economical for receiver manufacturers to embed full Unicode capability into their products just to support the Station Name (long) message. It would require cooperation among iBiquity, broadcasters and receiver manufacturers to establish expectations for which Unicode language subsets should be supported in receivers intended for the international market.

UTC-7 provides the SIS Transport with the most economical bit count for ASCII text. Each 58-bit Station Name (Long) message frame contains 9 housekeeping bits and 49 message content bits (see Table 10.4). At 7 bits per character, the 49 message content bits represent 7 whole U.S. ASCII characters. By concatenating 7 message frames, 56 U.S. ASCII characters can be transmitted as one Station Name (long). If higher-order Unicode characters are activated with the shift character, the 56-character maximum could diminish to 20 or 30, depending on the number of extra octets (bytes) needed per character. The efficiency of 7-bit U.S. ASCII characters in some circumstances may be offset by the inefficiency of shifting to provide other, larger, character codes.

Anticipating the need to support text in other languages with Latin-based characters, iBiquity enables the Latin-1 character set to be employed in HD Radio devices. Latin-1, described by the ISO/IEC 8859-1 standard, is a one-byte, 256-character set that is one of a suite of similar sets (Latin-1, Latin-2, Latin-3, etc as ISO 8859-1, 8859-2, 8859-3, etc). Each 8859 standard begins with the U.S. ASCII set, and assigns higher-level code numbers 160–255 to special characters. These higher-order character codes each contain a different set of many diacritical marks and special characters not common to the English language. Conveniently, all Latin-1 characters use the same numerical values in Unicode as in the ISO/IEC standard that defines Latin-1. See Table 10.4. Perhaps less conveniently, other ISO 8859 single-byte Latin character sets require additional bits to be represented in Unicode.

The SIS message architecture makes a design choice between two approaches. The Unicode approach provides a fully extensible character set. However, this may be cumbersome due to the limitations on how much of the Unicode is stored in the receiver. Computer users familiar with loading new character sets have experienced the challenge of supporting different languages. Consumer electronics, such as radios, are not typically built or networked like computers and are unlikely to support such open-ended character sets. The other approach is to identify to the receiver a single character set based on the most common languages in a region. The 8-bit ISO

8859-1 Latin-1 character set will suffice on parts or all of several continents. In places where other ISO 8859 character sets would be more appropriate, transmitters and receivers can be equipped to support those sets. In the worst case, a receiver equipped with say, only Latin-1, would present some wrong characters or no characters if confronted with a Latin-2 message. Thus, it may be more efficient to use limited 8859 character sets regionally than to try to support Unicode worldwide.

While Table 10.4 shows the full Latin-1 character set (nonprintable characters and graphics characters are not included), the manufacturer implementation (transmitter or receiver) may limit the characters that can be displayed. With the use of ISO 8859 character sets on other SIS text messages, it may be a design burden to have the receiver rely separately on Unicode in the Station Name (long) message.

Dec	Hex	Char. Name	Dec	Hex	Char. Name	Dec	Hex	Char. Name
32	0020	Space	96	0060	Grave accent	192	00C0	L. cap ltr a with grave
33	0021	Excl. mark	97	0061	L. sm ltr a	193	00C1	L. cap ltr a with acute
34	0022	Quotation mark	98	0062	L. sm ltr b	194	00C2	L. cap ltr a with circumflex
35	0023	Number sign	99	0063	L. sm ltr c	195	00C3	L. cap ltr a with tilde
36	0024	Dollar sign	100	0064	L. sm ltr d	196	00C4	L. cap ltr a with dieresis
37	0025	Percent sign	101	0065	L. sm ltr e	197	00C5	L. cap ltr a with ring above
38	0026	Ampersand	102	0066	L. sm ltr f	198	00C6	L. cap ltr ae
39	0027	Apostrophe	103	0067	L. sm ltr g	199	00C7	L. cap ltr c with cedilla
40	0028	Left paren.	104	0068	L. sm ltr h	200	00C8	L. cap ltr e with grave
41	0029	Right paren.	105	0069	L. sm ltr I	201	00C9	L. cap ltr e with acute
42	002A	Asterisk	106	006A	L. sm ltr j	202	00CA	L. cap ltr e with circumflex
43	002B	Plus sign	107	006B	L. sm ltr k	203	00CB	L. cap ltr e with dieresis
44	002C	Comma	108	006C	L. sm ltr l	204	00CC	L. cap ltr i with grave
45	002D	Hyphen-minus	109	006D	L. sm ltr m	205	00CD	L. cap ltr i with acute
46	002E	Full stop	110	006E	L. sm ltr n	206	00CE	L. cap ltr i with circumflex
47	002F	Solidus	111	006F	L. sm ltr o	207	00CF	L. cap ltr i with dieresis
48	0030	Digit zero	112	0070	L. sm ltr p	208	00D0	L. cap ltr eth (icelandic)
49	0031	Digit one	113	0071	L. sm ltr q	209	00D1	L. cap ltr n with tilde
50	0032	Digit two	114	0072	L. sm ltr r	210	00D2	L. cap ltr o with grave
51	0033	Digit three	115	0073	L. sm ltr s	211	00D3	L. cap ltr o with acute
52	0034	Digit four	116	0074	L. sm ltr t	212	00D4	L. cap ltr o with circumflex
53	0035	Digit five	117	0075	L. sm ltr u	213	00D5	L. cap ltr o with tilde
54	0036	Digit six	118	0076	L. sm ltr v	214	00D6	L. cap ltr o with dieresis
55	0037	Digit seven	119	0077	L. sm ltr w	215	00D7	Multiplication sign
56	0038	Digit eight	120	0078	L. sm ltr x	216	00D8	L. cap ltr o with stroke
57	0039	Digit nine	121	0079	L. sm ltr y	217	00D9	L. cap ltr u with grave
58	003A	Colon	122	007A	L. sm ltr z	218	00DA	L. cap ltr u with acute
59	003B	Semicolon	123	007B	Left curly bracket	219	00DB	L. cap ltr u with circumflex
60	003C	Less-than sign	124	007C	Vertical line	220	00DC	L. cap ltr u with dieresis

Table 10.4 Latin-1 Character Set

Dec	Hex	Char. Name	Dec	Hex	Char. Name	Dec	Hex	Char. Name
61	003D	Equals sign	125	007D	Right curly bracket	221	00DD	L. cap ltr y with acute
62	003D	Greater-than	126	007E	Tilde	222	00DE	L. cap ltr thorn (icelandic)
63	003F	Question mark			–End U.S. ASCII –	223	00DF	L. sm ltr sharp s (german)
64	0040	Commercial at	160	00A0	No-break space	224	00E0	L. sm ltr a with grave
65	0041	L. cap ltr a	161	00A1	Inv. excl. mark	225	00E1	L. sm ltr a with acute
66	0042	L. cap ltr b	162	00A2	Cent sign	226	00E2	L. sm ltr a with circumflex
67	0043	L. cap ltr c	163	00A3	Pound sign	227	00E3	L. sm ltr a with tilde
68	0044	L. cap ltr d	164	00A4	Currency sign	228	00E4	L. sm ltr a with dieresis
69	0045	L. cap ltr e	165	00A5	Yen sign	229	00E5	L. sm ltr a with ring above
70	0046	L. cap ltr f	166	00A6	Broken bar	230	00E6	L. sm ltr ae
71	0047	L. cap ltr g	167	00A7	Section sign	231	00E7	L. sm ltr c with cedilla
72	0048	L. cap ltr h	168	00A8	Dieresis	232	00E8	L. sm ltr e with grave
73	0049	L. cap ltr I	169	00A9	Copyright sign	233	00E9	L. sm ltr e with acute
74	004A	L. cap ltr j	170	00AA	Fem. ordinal ind.	234	00EA	L. sm ltr e with circumflex
75	004B	L. cap ltr k	171	00AB	Left double angle quotation mark	235	00EB	L. sm ltr e with dieresis
76	004C	L. cap ltr l	172	00AC	Not sign	236	00EC	L. sm ltr i with grave
77	004D	L. cap ltr m	173	00AD	Soft hyphen	237	00ED	L. sm ltr i with acute
78	004E	L. cap ltr n	174	00AE	Registered sign	238	00EE	L. sm ltr i with circumflex
79	004F	L. cap ltr o	175	00AF	Macron	239	00EF	L. sm ltr i with dieresis
80	0050	L. cap ltr p	176	00B0	Degree sign	240	00F0	L. sm ltr eth (icelandic)
81	0051	L. cap ltr q	177	00B1	Plus-minus sign	241	00F1	L. sm ltr n with tilde
82	0052	L. cap ltr r	178	00B2	Superscript two	242	00F2	L. sm ltr o with grave
83	0053	L. cap ltr s	179	00B3	Superscript three	243	00F3	L. sm ltr o with acute
84	0054	L. cap ltr t	180	00B4	Acute accent	244	00F4	L. sm ltr o with circumflex
85	0055	L. cap ltr u	181	00B5	Micro sign	245	00F5	L. sm ltr o with tilde
86	0056	L. cap ltr v	182	00B6	Pilcrow sign	246	00F6	L. sm ltr o with dieresis
87	0057	L. cap ltr w	183	00B7	Middle dot	247	00F7	Division sign
88	0058	L. cap ltr x	184	00B8	Cedilla	248	00F8	L. sm ltr o with stroke
89	0059	L. cap ltr y	185	00B9	Superscript one	249	00F9	L. sm ltr u with grave
90	005A	L. cap ltr z	186	00BA	Masc. ordinal ind.	250	00FA	L. sm ltr u with acute
91	005B	Left sq bracket	187	00BB	Right double angle quotation mark	251	00FB	L. sm ltr u with circumflex
92	005C	Rev. solidus	188	00BC	Vulg. Frac. one qtr.	252	00FC	L. sm ltr u with dieresis
93	005D	Rt sq bracket	189	00BD	V.F. one half	253	00FD	L. sm ltr y with acute
94	005E	Circumflex acc.	190	00BE	V. F. three quarters	254	00FE	L. sm ltr thorn (icelandic)
95	005F	Low line	191	00BF	Inv. question mk	255	00FF	L. sm ltr y with dieresis

Hex values are the code numbers in both Unicode (four digits) and ISO 8859-1 (2 least significant digits).
Table sources: Unicode and ISO/IEC 8859-1.

Table 10.4 Latin-1 Character Set *(continued)*

To tell the receiver how to concatenate several Station Name (long) message frames, the message frame uses three bits to indicate the current message frame number (called a Frame Number) and three bits to indicate the number of the last frame in the sequence.

3-bit	3-bit	49-bit	3-bit
Last Frame No.	Current Frame No.	Message Content (or portion)	Sequence No.

Table 10.5 Bitmap of SIS Station Name, Long Form

The message frame(s) that carry the station name are transmitted repeatedly, based on the transmission schedule established at the IBOC transmitter. All the frames that compose a message share one sequence number. When the content of the Station Name (long) changes, the sequence number is incremented by one. This tells the receiver to store and refresh the display with the new message text. Unused characters at the end of the last 7-character message frame are assigned the ASCII NUL value, decimal 0.

Station Slogan Universal

The Station Slogan Universal message is capable of carrying 95 character bytes. Four character-encoding methods are available. iBiquity has settled on ISO 8859-1 (Latin) as the primary character encoding. Addressing the cumbersome arrangement of the early choice of the Station Name (long) format for SIS, iBiquity added a new message after NRSC-5-A was adopted. It is Station Slogan Universal. iBiquity's exciter firmware version IRSS 2.3.3 was the first to incorporate the new message.

iBiquity reminds station operators that the Station Name (Long) and Station Slogan Universal can appear on an HD Radio receiver tuned either to the main or supplemental audio channels. Consequently, the station name should be oriented to station identity and not solely to one program service. Also, iBiquity suggests that names longer than 20 characters may not be visible on some receivers.

Station ID Number

The Station ID Number message is designed to indicate the country and Facility ID number of the station broadcasting the IBOC signal. The Country Code is a 10-bit word intended to correspond to a country identifier (10 bits = 1024 possible values). In an oversight, the ITU Country Codes for telephone numbering were referenced – ITU E.164. Unfortunately this means that the code for the U.S.A.—the number 1—also represents Canada and the Caribbean nations, among others. To make this field more useful, the Country Code should be a value that uniquely identifies the jurisdiction of the Facility ID.

Possible Overlay (Just Thinking...)

To provide a Facility ID service that might be more useful to applications and receivers, the Country Code could be redefined. With ten bits available, the numbering could be restructured into two 5-bit characters. ISO 3166 defines two-letter country codes—US (United States), CA (Canada), BR (Brazil), KY (Cayman Islands), and so on. Using the custom character set from SIS Station Name (short) where A = 00000 and Z = 11001, two character codes are represented by one ten-bit number. US would be 10100,10010 = 658 decimal. CA = 00010,00000 = 64. BR = 00001,10001 = 49. No modifications are required to implement this overlay, so long as receivers haven't started expecting the ITU telephone country code for an application.

The Facility ID field is a 19-bit field containing the identifying number of the IBOC radio station. (19 bits = 524,288 possible values) In the U.S.A., that is the FCC Facility ID number. Three bits in the 32-bit message frame are reserved for future use.

10-bit	3-bit	19-bit
Country Code	Reserved	Facility ID

Table 10.6 Bitmap of SIS Station ID Number

A consistent and well-working official station naming protocol would support receiver features that are menu-oriented, automatic, and/or database driven. In broadcasting, call signs are fungible and do not make the most reliable long-term database keys. In the late 1900s, the U.S. FCC recognized that the broadcast industry was reliant on the call sign for its market identity and adapted its database management to include a new key. The FCC assigned radio (and TV) stations a Facility ID number. The Facility ID remains fixed to a broadcast assignment through changes in call sign, location, ownership and even frequency. There is a one-to-one correspondence between stations (on the air or in process) and Facility ID numbers. For program guides and other database-oriented services, this number uniquely identifies broadcast facilities. It may be a better choice than the Station Name (short) for identifying each radio station for enhanced radio features. The Station Name (short) then remains relegated to the simple task of populating an optional text display on receivers.

Station Location

Station latitude and longitude are split over a pair of SIS message frames. FCC license coordinates are based on the 1927 horizontal control datum, NAD27. To encourage their use by navigation applications, IBOC station coordinates should be converted to the GPS-native WGS84 format. It may be easiest to convert from NAD27 to WGS84 with a GPS unit in hand. Enter the antenna coordinates and use the GPS unit to do the conversion. Alternatively, if the GPS unit is more accurate than the coordinates on the license, take a GPS reading of the antenna location.

Each message frame of the lat/long pair of SIS message frames also contains half of the bits representing the antenna altitude. Antenna elevation is stored in 16-meter increments (elevation in meters above mean sea level divided by 16). The user interface at the transmitter conveniently takes the elevation in meters and performs the conversion internally.

The Station Location coordinates have a precision of 2^{-13} degrees. That amounts to quantization steps of 0.439 seconds of arc. The Station Location coordinates, therefore, will be transmitted at a value that is within ±0.22 seconds of the values that are entered into the IBOC transmitter. The coordinates are signed integers, using the convention in which the most significant digit is the sign indicator, and the remaining digits represent the value. (Negative values are represented as the two's complement of the corresponding positive values; see Table 10.10 for an illustration of binary signed integers in the context of time zone offsets). West longitude, for example is a negative value.

Field Size	1-bit	1-bit	21-bit (8 integer, 13 decimal)	4-bit
Latitude Message	1	0=N 1=S	Latitude decimal degrees	Altitude MSB's
Longitude Message	0	0=E 1=W	Longitude decimal degrees	Altitude LSB's

Table 10.7 Bitmap of SIS Station Location Message Frame

Station Message

The Station Message is the largest defined SIS message. It has selectable character encoding formats. It can carry up to 95 16-bit Unicode characters in a maximum 32 frames, or up to 124 ASCII characters in a maximum of 24 frames using 8-bit encoding. Like the Station Name (long), Station Message has housekeeping functions for handling the message split across multiple frames. Frames continuing the same message are numbered in order with the Frame Count; Length indicates how long the message is; and Sequence Number indicates when a message content has changed. There is also a checksum to help ensure corrupt character strings do not make it to the receiver display. Naturally, all this text is dependent on the receiver having the ability to display Station Messages, and store its message content as long as 124 characters, in potentially a plethora of languages.

Initial Frame		Subsequent Frames of the Set	
Field	Bits	Field	Bits
Frame Count	5 (Value = 00000)	Frame Count	5 -Increment through set (00001–11111 max.)
Sequence	2	Sequence	2 -Same value as initial frame
Priority	1	Reserved	3
Text Encoding Format	3		
Length	8		
Checksum	7		
Text Payload	32 [4 8-bit characters] or [2 16-bit characters]	Text Payload	48 [6 8-bit characters] or [3 16-bit characters]

Text Encoding Format Number	Encoding Type
000 (default –UTF-7), 001, 010	ISO-646 Repertoires E.1, E.2, E.3
100	Unicode
Others	Reserved for future use

Table 10.8 Bitmap of SIS Station Message Frame

If stations and receivers become so sophisticated that numerous messages are queued, the priority flag indicates a message that should be directly promoted to the top of the queue.

Time—ALFN and Time Parameters

The IBOC receiver can keep time by reading the Absolute Layer 1 Frame Number (ALFN) that is assigned to each 1.49-second Layer 1 frame. To account for variations between local time and GPS time, SIS transmits a number of parameters. This section describes how the ALFN transmission works, then looks into the SIS Parameter Message frame structure.

ALFN

The Layer 1 frames are the heartbeat of the IBOC signal. For marking time, the initial ALFN Frame, 0, is defined as the frame that would have been transmitted at the beginning of the GPS epoch, if there had been IBOC then. The start time for the GPS epoch, and the IBOC clock, was 00:00:00 Coordinated Universal Time (UTC) on 6 January 1980. Exactly 500 million IBOC heartbeats later, the time was 23 July 2003 at 23:35:47 GPS time. Since ALFN is transmitted as a 32-bit number, the clock rolls around to zero again about 202 years after 1980. So, in about 150 years receiver manufacturers should start to think about whether their IBOC receivers will roll over without hiccupping.

ALFN is transmitted in two ways. The required method is to transmit two bits on each SIS PDU, so all 32 bits trickle in across the period of the Layer 1 frame. This is embedded in the SIS Transport, which is discussed in the next section. Some applications might benefit from a faster, more sporadic delivery of ALFN. One of the optional SIS message formats carries the 32-bit ALFN in a single message frame on a single SIS PDU.

ALFN is referenced to GPS time. If the next ALFN to transmit is n, multiply n by the frame rate R_f, and add that to the start time of midnight, 6 January 1980. Recall that the Layer 1 frame rate is 65536/44100 seconds per frame, or about 1.49 seconds each. This accounts for the half-billion ALFN frame numbers that preceded 23 July 2003.

Leap Seconds

Since the beginning in 1980, the GPS timebase has been synchronized to the timebase of International Atomic Time (IAT).[3] In other words, the "pendulums" of both clocks swing at the same rate (with a miniscule tolerance for error); the real difference between IAT and GPS time is that the clock "dials" are set to different numbers. UTC also runs on the same timebase. Thus, UTC, GPS and IAT tick away at the same rate. On 6 January 1980, GPS and UTC were perfectly synchronized by timebase and by the times on their clocks.

Meanwhile, the time authorities mess with the time UTC reports to us, for very good reason. Another timebase, UT1, is not locked to an atomic clock. This is the time according to the earth, whose rotation rate over the millennia varies. To keep the "civil time," as indicated by UTC, within 0.9 seconds of earth time, UT1, it requires the occasional adjustment of UTC. Those adjustments have come in the form of the insertion of "leap seconds" in UTC. For instance, as of 1 January 2006, 33 leap seconds were inserted in UTC timekeeping to keep it in synch with earth time, putting it 33 seconds behind IAT. When GPS started in 1980, it was set to UTC at that time, which was already 19 seconds off IAT. Between 1980 and 2006, the other 14 leap seconds were progressively inserted in UTC, leaving GPS ahead of UTC by that much. Leap seconds are added to UTC when necessary, not on any schedule.

SIS Parameter Messages

To get accurate time from an IBOC signal, not only must the GPS time be known, but also the number of leap seconds since the GPS epoch. IBOC transmits an SIS Parameter Message indicating the present leap-second correction for GPS time. For a clock device to anticipate upcoming leap seconds, it must be aware of when the next leap second is scheduled. This information is also transmitted on SIS Parameter Messages.[4]

---

[3] Source material for this discussion includes the U.S. Naval Observatory, tycho.usno.navy.mil.

[4] The U.S. National Institute of Standards and Technology (NIST) was a participant in the NRSC IBOC standards process and responsible for proposing these time-oriented parameter messages.

SIS Parameter Number (Index)	Parameter (16 bits)
000000	Leap second offset Pending = 8 MSB, Current = 8 LSB
000001, 000010	GPS Time of pending adjustment 16 LSB, 16 MSB, respectively
000011	Local Time Data
000100–111111	Reserved

Table 10.9 SIS Parameter Message Content Types

Leap Second Offsets

Each SIS Parameter Message frame is 22 bits long, starting with a 6-bit identifier, called the Index. The remaining 16 bits contain the Parameter value itself. (Table 10.9) The first Station Parameter message type, Leap Second Offset, describes two values: the accumulated leap seconds since 1980 (the Current Offset) and the sum of the Current Offset plus the next planned change in the offset (Pending Offset). Leap seconds have been positive. In other words, the atomic "pendulum" for UTC (and GPS) swings a little faster than the earth's "pendulum." Every couple of years or so, an extra second has been added to UTC time to slow the advance of the UTC clock and keep it within the required 0.9 seconds of earth time.

The Leap Second Offset values are 8-bit signed values (decimal -128 to +127). Negative leap second offsets are permitted. Allowing for the possibility that the earth's astronomical clock might run faster than the atomic clock, a leap second could be subtracted from UTC to let UTC catch up to earth time. If enough negative leap seconds accumulate to counter the positive ones, the Current Offset could go negative. However, if the trend continues, at a rate of 14 positive leap seconds in 26 years, it will take 68 years to hit the +127-second Current Offset value, in the year 2048. That should be plenty of time to make adjustments to the protocol, if necessary.

Giving a clock the opportunity to anticipate the next leap second, the SIS Parameter Message types also include a pair of message type formats with the GPS time of the next leap second event. As a 32-bit time code, it must be split over two 16-bit parameter message frames.

Local Time Data

Once the receiver has managed to derive UTC, the next order of business is to compute the local time. Local time is computed from transmitted time zone offsets, daylight savings flags and schedule. A boundary problem challenges the receiver manufacturer. Radio stations operating at time zone boundaries have figured out how to announce to their audience on two schedules. Now, with the possibility of automated IBOC time updates on consumer receivers and other devices, electronics manufacturers must make hard choices on how to implement time features for consumers. Receivers that balk, switch times, or consistently give the "wrong" time from the user's perspective, are radios the consumer feels are broken. Receiver-driven clocks will have to be simple, user-friendly and reliable.

To assist receivers with local time adjustments, a Station Parameter Message carries time zone offsets from UTC and local Daylight Saving Time (DST) information. The time zone offsets are given in minutes, using an 11-bit signed binary integer. Because the time zone offsets are reported in minutes, even those locations in the world with fractional-hour time zone offsets will be accommodated by the system.

Signed Integers

Signed integers use the two's complement for the negative magnitudes, as illustrated in Table 10.10. This is a common method employed for its computational efficiency. Like an odometer set to 0000, positive values normally count 0001, 0002, etc. Rolling the odometer backwards to negative 1 produces 1111, the one's complement of zero (the value of each bit is inverted). More useful to the computer is the relationship between −1 (at 1111) and +1 (at 0001). To take the two's complement of 0001, we invert the values of each digit and add one: 1110 + 1 = 1111. Thus, the negative value of each signed integer is the two's complement of the positive value, and vice versa. Roll the odometer back to negative two (1110) and take its two's complement (0001 + 1 = 0010) to obtain positive two.

Time Zone	Time Zone Offset	UTC Offset in Parameter Message		Modulo 2 calc: Value$_{Mod\ 1}$ +1 (for negative sign Values)	Time Zone Offset (Minutes)
		Sign	Value		
Atlantic	UTC-4 hr	1 (−)	1100010000	0011101111 + 1	= −240
Newfoundland	UTC-3.5 hr	1 (−)	1100101110	0011010001 + 1	= −210
Chamorro	UTC+10 hr	0 (+)	1001011000	N/A	= +600

Table 10.10 Examples of Time Zone Offset Values

Local Standard Time (ST), and its variant, Daylight Saving Time (DST), are most challenging to communicate in a broadcast environment. Broadcast signals do not conveniently observe time zone boundaries. Keep in mind that while IBOC radio stations may transmit time information, it is up to the receiver manufacturer to decide how best to implement time and DST features in its IBOC products.

In a nutshell, the receiver looks for either a preprogrammed schedule or a real-time indicator to know whether it is currently Daylight Saving Time according to the national plan (Answering the question: is DST In-Season?). Second, the receiver looks for permission to invoke DST as a locally observed practice (Answering the question: is DST Locally Observed?). This two-step process gives the receiver manufacturer more options in designing the receiver. Receiver users might have a reason to override either the schedule or the local-observance flag.

There are two basic ways to trigger an IBOC receiver to adjust for DST:

1. Lacking any official terminology for the two methods of informing receivers about DST, let's call this first method the *Pre-Ordained Schedule Method*. The IBOC station tells the receiver that a pre-ordained schedule applies to the national area of the IBOC signal and lets the receiver recall the schedule from its firmware, or

2. Call this the *Real-Time Indicator Method*: The IBOC station tells the receiver whether DST is presently in effect.

To support the Pre-Ordained Schedule Method, three Daylight Saving Time Schedules have been defined in the SIS Parameter Message, Local Time protocol. The first (000) is the default value for nations with no daylight savings, with irregular schedules, or with no schedule listed. The second schedule (001) refers to the U.S./Canada schedule that was in effect at the time of NRSC-5-A adoption in 2005 (First Sunday, April; last Sunday, October – 2 AM). The third (010) is the European Union schedule in effect at that time (last Sunday, March; last Sunday, October – 1AM). Five unassigned schedule ID's remain. (We'll get to the 2007 U.S. DST schedule change in a moment.)

If the receiver has a calendar (which can be discerned from the GPS time), it can rely on the schedule number to look up a schedule in its internal memory and apply DST at will. It would cross reference the time zone with the pre-programmed DST schedule to produce the time. In some instances, the receiver might be in an area where DST does not apply, even though most of the time zone in that region or nation does observe DST. NRSC-5 SIS reference document (5) employs Indiana as a case study because it observes several DST variations.

The DST Schedule code is applicable to the country or region of the broadcast, such as U.S./Canada or Europe. A second indicator provides a confirmation, telling the receiver whether the locality observes DST. This, the DST Local Deployment Indicator, is a 1-bit flag that indicates the receiver may rely on the schedule to automatically invoke DST on schedule. A more descriptive term for the DST Local Deployment Indicator might be the *DST Observed Locally Flag*, because it tells the receiver that DST is observed by the locality. This flag may stay on year round, permitting the receiver to read the schedule and plan ahead. With the Pre-Ordained Schedule Method, the flag gives the receiver permission to plan to change its clock to/from DST on schedule. With advanced knowledge of the change, the receiver can adjust its clock at the instant of the DST change, even if the receiver section of the radio were turned off.

In areas of the U.S. and Canada that do not practice DST, the DST Local Deployment Indicator flag would remain set to zero, even though the station might still transmit the applicable national schedule identifier.

To support the Real-Time Indicator Method, the DST Local Deployment Indicator, and another indicator are employed together. The other is the DST Regional Deployment Indicator, which is another 1-bit flag. This flag indicates that the daylight saving time season is currently in effect in the nation or region. It provides instantaneously what the DST Schedule provides in advance, an indication of when the DST Season is in effect. In winter the DST Regional Deployment Indicator would be off (= 0) and during DST season it would be on (= 1). A more descriptive name for this flag might be *DST In-Season Flag*, because it provides a real-time indication whether DST season is in effect regardless whether it is employed locally.

Table 10.11 summarizes how a receiver can implement DST from the SIS Parameter Message.

DST Schedule	Local Deployment Indicator — Functions as: "DST Observed Locally Flag" (This bit is fixed year-round, per 4.6.1.3)	Regional Deployment Indicator — Functions as: "DST In-Season Flag" (Receivers should "Honor this bit in preference to any predetermined schedule" per 4.6.1.4)*	Example	Receiver Implementation — Pre-Ordained Schedule Method	Real-Time Indicator Method
000 No schedule specified	= 1 Observed	=1 Nationally in season	Most of U.S. and Canada	Receiver must offer user-programmed schedule	DST
		= 0 Nationally out of season			ST
	= 0 Not Observed	=1 Nationally in season	Indianapolis	Receiver ignores user-programmed schedule	ST
		= 0 Nationally out of season			ST
= 001 2005 U.S./Canada Schedule, [Obsolete as of 11 March 2007]** or =010 2005 European Schedule,	= 1 Observed	=1 Nationally in season	Europe	Receiver relies on IBOC station to transmit schedule code that has not gone out of date	DST
		= 0 Nationally out of season		Receiver ignores schedule	ST
	= 0 Not Observed	=1 Nationally in season	Iceland***	Receiver ignores schedule	ST
		= 0 Nationally out of season			ST

*This directive seems to render the schedule indicators moot. It might be more useful to create a protocol to transmit the date and time of the next DST transition much like the time utility can transmit the scheduled occurrence of the next leap second. This obviates the need for any embedded look-up schedule in the receiver, while allowing the receiver to "plan ahead" for the next DST change.

**If, as it appears to be the case, no receivers have implemented this code, the definition could be changed to represent the 2007 schedule change: 2nd Sunday in March until 1st Sunday in November.

***Iceland's situation can be interpreted another way. It observes the standard time of the adjacent time zone, and might therefore be characterized instead as observing DST year round, with respect to its own time zone.

Table 10.11 Implementing Daylight Saving Adjustments

The SIS local time feature raises a host of user interaction issues in areas where the radio station is close to two time zones. Even if one station is reliably giving the time for time zone A, the user tuning among stations might happen across the station while in time zone B. The receiver should not react unpredictably. On a road trip it may be convenient for the receiver to update with the local time as a new station is selected. Buzzing around town, automatic time adjustment may be desirable if the only adjustment occurs twice a year at the appropriate times. But near a time zone boundary, or an area with both DST and non-DST practice, automatic time selection may become a hassle. Receiver manufacturers must decide whether to incorporate user selected setups and user interfaces for smart clock features. They must be easy to understand and employ easy to set-and-forget functions. Nevertheless, as with many IBOC features available to broadcasters, if the broadcast community fails to manage the time features well, receiver makers will not be encouraged to try using them. Stations should set aside SIS messaging space for local time transmissions and be sure to configure the messages properly for their markets.

Station Information Service Transport

So far, we have exposed the service side of the Station Information Service Transport. Seven message frame formats ranging from 22 to 58 bits convey information about the station and the time. The transport component of the SIS protocol carries these messages on the SIS portion of the radio channel. The transport consists of an 80-bit SIS transport PDU. (Table 10.12) This PDU carries one or two message frames, depending on their sizes. With a 58-bit space for the message payload, the PDU transports one message frame up to 58 bits. To carry two message frames on the PDU, a second-message frame header occupies 4 of the 58 bits, leaving the remaining 54 bits to be divided between the two message frames. For example, a 22-bit Station Parameter message frame (Local Time) could be paired with a second one (GPS Leap Offset), totaling 44 bits, leaving 10 unused null bits. Alternatively, the 22-bit Station Parameter message frame and the 32-bit ALFN message frame could be paired on the SIS PDU, with no wasted bits. How the station operator can plan the SIS schedule for most effective throughput is discussed in a following section.

Single Message Frame Payload	Two Message Frame Payload	
Type (1 bit) Default = 0 Reserved = 1		
EXT (1 bit) Single = 0 Two message frames = 1		
1st MSG ID (4 bits) See Table 10.2		
Single message frame payload (58 bits)	First message frame payload (54 bits – 2nd payload)	
	2nd MSG ID (4 bits)	
	Second message frame payload (54 bits – 1st payload)	
	Unused message bits padded with zeroes	
Unused message bits padded with zeroes		
Reserved (1 bit) Default = 0 Reserved = 1		
Time Locked (1 bit) Level I: GPS locked = 1 Level II: unlocked = 0		
Adv ALFN (2 bits)		
CRC (12 bits)		

Table 10.12 SIS Transport PDU Structure (Derived from NRSC-5-A Reference document (5) Figure 4-1.)

Each message frame is preceded by the 4-bit Message ID number (Table 10.2). When the total number of message bits is fewer than the 58-bit message space on the PDU, the remaining bits are zeroed. After the message space, the remaining space on the 80-bit PDU is employed for two basic purposes – dedicated GPS time data and PDU housekeeping.

Dedicated GPS Time Data

While Station Messages can carry leap second and local time data, as well as an occasional full ALFN if desired, the SIS Transport reserves three bits for dedicated, required time information. The FM Layer 1 frame has 16 blocks. Each SIS PDU is transmitted during one block period. Each FM SIS PDU carries two bits of the 32-bit ALFN. This ensures that a full copy of the ALFN always accompanies each FM Layer 1 frame.

The AM Layer 1 frame requires a time-sharing feature to squeeze the entire ALFN on the AM Layer 1 frame. It has only 8 blocks, allowing only 8 SIS PDUs, and only 16 ALFN bits. The 16 least significant bits are transmitted most of the time. Once every four Layer 1 frames, the 16 most significant bits are transmitted. The MSB substitution is made in the Layer 1 frame when the ALFN's two least bits equal 00. The FM ALFN is fully transmitted in one Layer 1 frame, while it may take up to four Layer 1 frames and about 6 seconds to recover the full ALFN on AM IBOC.

The Time Locked flag on the SIS Transport PDU indicates which synchronization state the station is operating under. When the station is operating at Level I synchronization (GPS-locked) the Time Locked flag is raised to 1. The flag is set to 0 when in Level II non-GPS operation.

SIS PDU Housekeeping

The SIS PDU begins with a Type flag that remains at 0. If in the future a new SIS PDU format were created, the flag would change to 1. Existing receivers should recognize that when the flag is not at the expected value of 0, they should ignore the contents of the PDU. (See sidebar.) The second bit in the SIS PDU, called "Extension," indicates whether there are one or two message frames within the SIS PDU. Each message frame is preceded by its 4-bit Message ID, from which the receiver can infer the length of the message frame. By knowing where the end of the first message frame is, the receiver can look for the Message ID of the optional second message frame.

After the message payload on the SIS PDU, come the following: a reserved bit with no present purpose, the Time Locked and ALFN bits just discussed, and a Cyclic Redundancy Check word (12 bits). The CRC performs a division operation on the first 68 bits of the SIS PDU. The divisor is a polynomial whose value is $x^{12} + x^{11} + x^3 + x + 1$, representing a binary number with ones at each exponent of the polynomial: 1100000001011. The polynomial is selected to provide the greatest error detection power. Once the 68 bit PDU word is divided by the polynomial, the remainder is posted in the 12-bit CRC space of the PDU. The receiver divides the arriving PDU by the same polynomial and compares the new remainder with the transmitted remainder. Most errors will be detected with this technique.

Reserved Attributes and Interoperability

As a cautionary note, there are numerous reserved fields and values throughout the NRSC-5 standard to be reckoned with. System and product designers should anticipate the potential use of reserved values and design and test accordingly. Reserved values, such as the SIS PDU Type flag 1, are clearly intended for possible future expansion. Other reserved values, such as Audio Codec Mode 1111 (Table 5-4, Audio Transport reference document (4)), have no intended expansion purpose. Receivers confronted with a new field value that they were not designed to use, should be able to ignore the unrecognized value and continue to function. For instance, when asked whether a reserved codec mode could be utilized for another purpose, iBiquity rigorously tested the concept on receivers then in production and determined that the proposed use was not compatible with several models. With the number of receiver models on the market increasing annually, it will become more difficult to test the implementation of reserved values on the installed base of receivers. The work of designing a receiver should include paying attention to the possible use of currently reserved values.

Table 10.13 shows the relationship between the 80-bit SIS Transport PDU and the AM and FM IBOC signals that transmit it. The table shows how convolutional coding expands the 80-bit PDU. For example, a rate 1/3 code increases the 80 bits of information to 240 bits of coded data. Layer 1 routes the SIS information through the proper logical channel (PIDS, SIDS) on its way to OFDM carrier mapping. The AM IBOC signal reserves specific OFDM carriers for the SIS information. FM IBOC interleaves the SIS information with the program services on the main OFDM carrier groups.

RF Mode	Service Mode	Bits per SIS PDU	Coding rate	Coded bits per SIS PDU	PDUs per 1.49-second frame	Info rate, bps	Text rate, @ 6 char per PDU, char/s	Logical Channel	OFDM Spectrum
FM Hybrid	All MP's	80	2/5	200	16	861	65	PIDS	Primary Main
FM All-Digital	MS1	80	2/7	280	16	861	65	SIDS	Secondary Main & Extended
	MS2–MS4		2/5	200					Secondary Main
AM Hybrid	MA1	80	1/3	240	8	431	32	PIDS	4 PIDS carriers @ 4.9 & 9.6 kHz offsets
AM All-Digital	MA2								2 PIDS carriers @ 4.9 kHz offsets

Table 10.13 Station Information Service Characteristics

The information rate is the effective bit rate of the 80-bit SIS PDU, excluding coding overhead. We also calculated an overall SIS text rate that assumes a text-intensive SIS message schedule with an average of about 6 character bytes per PDU. To estimate the maximum possible SIS character rate, consider the Station Message fully stuffed with 124 characters in 21 message frames across 21 SIS Transport PDUs, which represents nearly 6 characters per PDU. Assume also that all 16 SIS PDUs in the FM frame, and all 8 in the AM frame, are stuffed exclusively with Station Message message frames, to the exclusion of other text messages and nontext messages—ALFN, Location, and SIS Parameter. With about 6 characters per SIS PDU and 16 SIS PDUs per Layer 1 frame (FM), the total, 96 characters per frame, divides out to about 64 characters per second (32 on AM). The practical SIS text rate diminishes with the insertion of nontext messages in the SIS message schedule. The SIS messages are short, meaning the 64 cps maximum rate is not so much a real throughput rate as just a benchmark for how little text in the aggregate is available on SIS. It reinforces the idea that when it comes to SIS text, brevity is a virtue.

When setting up an SIS message rotation, the HD Radio transmission equipment presents the operator with a schedule form. It allows the operator to select the pattern of SIS message types to be transmitted. Longer messages can be scheduled more often. For instance, message frames with long, multiframe text messages might deserve a higher rotation rate to ensure timely delivery of each complete long message. If Station Name (long) requires four blocks to be transmitted and only two Station Name (long) messages are scheduled in one frame, it will take the time of two frames for the entire message to come across.

SIS Scheduling Strategy

There are strategies to consider in the creation of the SIS rotation schedule. Recall that the FM IBOC Layer 1 frame has 16 blocks while the AM IBOC frame has 8. Each frame's duration is 1.49 seconds. Since information is delivered block by block on the PIDS logical channel, it does not require the buffering of a full frame to begin to recover messages. Each SIS block is decoded as it is received. Acquisition time of SIS information may not be critical, but there might be a preference for getting certain messages faster to a newly tuned receiver.

- *Priority by repetition.* The receiver starts receiving blocks at the point the first receivable block is deciphered. It does not require a full frame to be received, so the first block might as likely be the third or the sixteenth, as the first. If acquisition of any message should be delayed, say, no more than half an L1 frame, then repeating the same message twice within the frame may help with consistently more rapid acquisition. A twice-scheduled message will transmit once every 3/4 second. (That's 2 slots out of 16 on FM IBOC, and 4 slots out of 16 on AM.) There may not much benefit in scheduling a full message more than twice a frame.

- *Intersperse or clump?* Based on the "more is faster" concept in the preceding point, a message has priority, on the average, if it is repeated most often within the frame. By clumping too many entries for long multiblock messages, one might obstruct the scheduling of short-turn-around information. Allow shorter and more important messages to be interspersed within the schedules of longer messages.

- *Machines before humans?* Information that is to be displayed for the user might not be missed for a few extra tenths of a second, when deferred by a few blocks or rotated across multiple frames. Information used by receivers to seek or recognize the station or a service may be more time-critical. A receiver scanning the band, for instance for a particular Service Message or the Facility ID, is delayed at each radio signal by the time it takes to acquire the necessary message block. Placing the machine-searched information in high-priority rotation will speed up the average reaction time of a receiver on tune-in (assuming the receiver is equipped to make such snap decisions.)

- *Match clump size to the contents.* Plan the length of the long messages and schedule accordingly. If a multiblock message is clumped in a group of four on the schedule and takes 5 blocks to come across, the full message will not make it across until the second clump finishes it, defeating the purpose of the clumping.

- *Keep in mind carousel message types.* Some message types can convey different content in subsequent messages. One message type posted into the schedule might represent several messages that are rotated. For instance, as services are added to the station, the Service Message type may be associated with several different messages. The HD Radio system rotates different messages of the same type. If only one block per frame were scheduled for the Service Message type, it will take several frames to convey several different messages of that type. Similarly, the Station Location message alternates latitude and longitude, requiring two Station Location message events in the schedule to complete the message. With one Station Location event per 16 blocks, it will take two frames to be received on FM IBOC and three or frames on AM IBOC. While location data is probably not a hot item in need of fast acquisition, it illustrates the point that the scheduling of a multimessage-frame message type helps determine the latency of a full message.

- *Stretch out less important long messages.* The Station Message might some day find a higher purpose, so populating it with a low priority placeholder message might be sufficient until then. If it only appears once in the rotation, it might take several L1 frames to deliver the information. As long as using the Station Message once in the rotation does not detract from the timely delivery of messages more frequently accessed by consumer receivers and their owners, there is no harm in putting something up such as, "If u cn read ths, call 800-zzz-zzzz for a free CD."

In general, identify all the information that is truly needed to be transmitted twice in a 1.49-second Layer 1 frame. Keep in mind the number of message-frames needed to convey long messages. Also keep in mind the message types that rotate different messages under the same schedule name. Schedule the high priority items and squeeze in the rest. Err in favor of putting out more types of information messages to encourage innovation in receiver applications.

When filling out an SIS schedule, the system will lock out the second message space in the block if the first message requires the full message space. Any message whose size exceeds 54 bits requires the full block. Table 10.14 illustrates an example SIS schedule. It illustrates the use of the two Payload columns for shorter messages, and the manner in which multiple-block messages might be scheduled.

Block #	Payload 1	Payload 2
0	Service Message	Service Message
1	Station ID	Call Sign Standard
2	Call Sign Universal	-
3	Slogan Universal	-
4	Slogan Universal	-
5	Slogan Universal	-
6	Slogan Standard	-
7	Slogan Standard	-
8	Station ID	Call Sign Standard
9	Call Sign Universal	-
...	...	...
14	Station Message	-
15	Local Time	Station Location

Table 10.14 Illustration of SIS Schedule Form

SIS Recap

The Station Information Service operates on the Primary and Secondary ID Service (PIDS and SIDS) logical channels. On FM IBOC this is woven into the Layer 1 frame while on AM IBOC it is carried on up to four individual OFDM carriers. SIS can carry several message types. Some message types provide text for receiver displays while others carry time, location, or service information. Not all defined message types are available to transmit in various versions of HD Radio exciter firmware. Likewise, not all message types are supported by various receivers. To encourage innovation in the development of consumer receivers, it is incumbent on broadcasters to populate SIS with as much useful and accurate information as is practicable. Set latitude, longitude, elevation, local time, DST, GPS/UTC offsets, country, and facility ID information and arrange them in the SIS schedule. There will be no receivers to take advantage of the information unless first the broadcasters consistently provide the information.

11 From the Top Down: Other Input to the Protocol Stack– Advanced Data Services

In Chapter 10 we introduced the data services side of the NRSC-5 protocol stack and ventured into the Station Information Service. In parallel with the SIS protocols for both the service and its transport is the protocol for transporting Advanced Data Services. This chapter focuses on the Advanced Data Services component of the NRSC-5 protocol stack.

As previously described about SIS and PSD, ADS requires two levels of protocol to function. First, it must have a layer that packages the information so it will be ready to transport. This is described by a service protocol. Second, to embed the service on the IBOC signal, the services must be processed through a transport protocol.

We explained how, for instance, the Program Service Data has a protocol defined in reference document (7) in which the ID3 formatting is invoked; it is followed by a companion Program Service Data Transport described in reference document (9) where HDLC-like packet encapsulation is applied. These complementary service-and-transport descriptions are discussed in detail in Chapter 4. Similarly, ADS also must have service protocols and a transport protocol.

Unlike SIS and PSD, for which NRSC-5 describes both service and transport protocols, NRSC-5 describes only the transport for carrying Advanced Data Services. The corresponding service protocols are not part of NRSC-5. The transport protocol is described in NRSC-5 reference document (10), called Advanced Application Services Transport (Table 11.1). iBiquity also uses the name "Advanced Application Services" to describe a technology it offers to licensees.

iBiquity's AAS technology provides a suite of services, including SPS, SPSD, and ADS functionality.[1] To differentiate the iBiquity services suite from the transport, the acronym AAS stands for iBiquity's service protocols outside NRSC-5; AAT indicates the transport protocol within NRSC-5.

See the right hand side of Figure 11.1 for the position of SIS Transport and Advanced Application Services Transport (AAT) within the protocol stack. The conceptual ADS service protocol sits above the NRSC-5 stack, as shown.

NRSC-5 Reference Document Number	Reference Document Title	NRSC-5 Reference Document Number	Reference Document Title
1.	Doc. No. SY_IDD_1011s rev. E HD Radio™ Air Interface Design Description **Layer 1 FM** iBiquity Digital Corporation, 3/22/05	6.	Doc. No. SY_SSS_1026s rev. D HD Radio™ **FM Transmission System Specifications** iBiquity Digital Corporation, 2/18/05
2.	Doc. No. SY_IDD_1012s rev. E HD Radio™ Air Interface Design Description **Layer 1 AM** iBiquity Digital Corporation, 3/22/05	7.	Doc. No. SY_IDD_1028s rev. C HD Radio™ Air Interface Design Description **Program Service Data** iBiquity Digital Corporation, 3/31/05
3.	Doc. No. SY_IDD_1014s rev. F HD Radio™ Air Interface Design Description **Layer 2 Channel Multiplex Protocol** iBiquity Digital Corporation, 2/7/05	8.	Doc. No. SY_SSS_1082s rev. D HD Radio™ **AM Transmission System Specifications** iBiquity Digital Corporation, 2/24/05
4.	Doc. No. SY_IDD_1017s rev. E HD Radio™ Air Interface Design Description **Audio Transport** iBiquity Digital Corporation, 3/31/05	9.	Doc. No. SY_IDD_1085s rev. C HD Radio™ Air Interface Design Description **Program Service Data Transport** iBiquity Digital Corporation, 2/7/05
5.	Doc. No. SY_IDD_1020s rev. E HD Radio™ Air Interface Design Description **Station Information Service Protocol** iBiquity Digital Corporation, 2/18/05	10.	Doc. No. SY_IDD_1019s rev. E HD Radio™ Air Interface Design Description **Advanced Application Services Transport** iBiquity Digital Corporation, 8/4/05

Table 11.1 Protocols Addressed in Chapter 11

Among the many things the AAT might do, it could be a bearer of program associated data content (PAD). PAD is not an NRSC-5-defined term. In Chapter 4, we explained how Program Service Data is the fundamental source of PAD. In Chapter 10 the nonpad nature of (most) SIS information was discussed. New services could deliver richer PAD experiences via ADS. To do so would require a standard protocol that broadcasters could use for transmission and receiver makers could employ in new models. One such protocol would be in the form of a service discovery feature. We briefly touched on this in the previous chapter with the addition of the Service Message to the SIS message portfolio. With greater bandwidth than SIS, ADS could offer a richer service discovery

---

[1] iBiquity promotional materials, and sales materials of major transmission equipment manufacturers.

feature. iBiquity calls this concept the Service Information Guide (SIG). The last section of this chapter discusses the possibilities of service discovery.

ADS also offers the potential of providing richer PAD content and interactivity, as well as providing new services unrelated to station program streams.

This chapter examines first the transport, AAT. Following discussion of the mechanics of the AAT, the chapter introduces the concepts that underlie advanced data services, putting them in perspective in the datacasting marketplace.

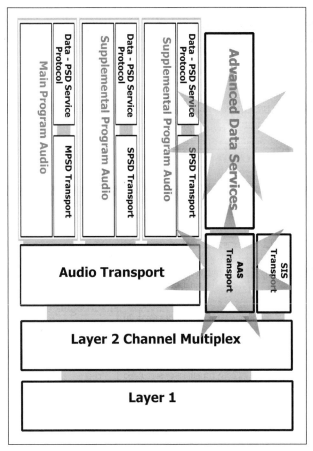

Figure 11.1 NRSC-5 Protocol Stack with SIS and ADS

Advanced Applications Services Transport (AAT)

While the SIS Protocol contains a service function as well as the transport function, Advanced Data Service protocols are external to NRSC-5, feeding into the NRSC-5 AAT (NRSC-5 reference document (10)). The AAT protocol is capable of conveying any form of data for which a party chooses to develop a service interface. This section of the chapter breaks out the components of AAT, revealing its configurability and flexibility.

Unfortunately, AM IBOC does not implement AAT because of the platform's limited bandwidth. Conceivably, a low-grade AAT functionality could be added in the all-digital mode when the channel width narrows by 1/3, station IBOC power goes up, and signal-to-noise-and-interference ratios improve.

Logical channels convey streams of ADS data using the AAT protocol. On the FM IBOC channel, there are logical channels P1 and P3 in Hybrid and Extended Hybrid modes. P1 occupies the Primary Main OFDM subcarrier group and P3 resides in the optional Primary Extended group. In all-digital modes, secondary FM IBOC subcarriers can convey logical channels S1 through S4, depending on the operating mode. Recall from Chapter 5 that each logical channel's Layer 2 PDU can be configured to handle this data as opportunistic and fixed bandwidth. Figure 11.1 reviews the relationship of the various services to Layer 2. Note how the fixed portion of the PDU is set to the desired capacity, reserving the bandwidth away from the audio program(s). The audio data rate must be reduced to accommodate AAT. For instance, to reserve, say, 4 kbps for AAT, the 96 kbps logical channel P1 can be set to carry 92 kbps for audio. The loss is minor, even with a multicast of, say, a 60 kbps audio program and a 32 kbps program. The fixed-data capacity remains reserved whether or not there is data to be transmitted.

The opportunistic data capacity breathes with the audio coder. As the audio coding demands more or less space for its packets on the L2 frame, a small gap occurs between the last audio coder packet and the end of the L2 audio space. Opportunistic data is allowed to fill this gap, which varies in size from L2 frame to frame.

L2 PDU CW_0 Structure	MPS/SPS		
L2 PDU CW_1 Structure	MPS/SPS		Opportunistic
L2 PDU CW_2 Structure	MPS/SPS		Fixed
L2 PDU CW_3 Structure	MPS/SPS	Opportunistic	Fixed
L2 PDU CW_4 Structure	Fixed		

Elements are not proportionally sized. Only their position from left to right is meaningful.

Table 11.2 Layer 2 PDU Formats

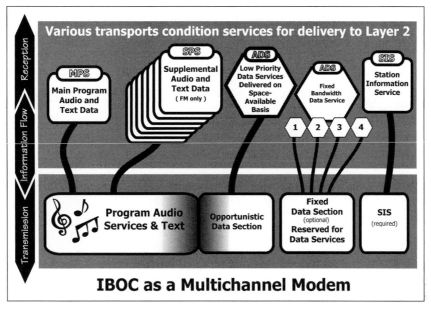

Figure 11.2 IBOC as a Multichannel Modem

The transport of advanced data services over IBOC is a complicated affair. It parallels the design of the program audio process, with its own quirks. Upper layers produce information packets that have to be massaged and transported in lower layers to enable reliable recovery upon receipt. As a comparable model, the audio process handles multiple program streams and marries audio data with program related data. The irregular, but incessant, pace of the audio packets requires buffering. Packets must be counted and directed to the correct program outputs.

The AAT takes about a half-dozen steps to get an advanced data service transmission just to Layer 2. The steps are summarized in the following paragraphs. Follow along on Figure 11.3.

Data Transport Packet

Incoming ADS data originates from one or more services. The information has to be identified with its service (marked by a Port Number). If it is large or a stream of information, it must be segmented to fit into variable-sized Data Transport Packets. At the service level (above the transport) the information is already packaged in the format required by the service. The transport then packetizes that information, sometimes breaking the information from the service into a series of smaller packets. Individual packets requiring reassembly are marked with a sequential count.

AAT PDU

Each Data Transport Packet is "encapsulated" in a PDU that identifies the format of the packet (as of NRSC-5-A, there was only one such format), and provides an error detection Frame Check Sequence.

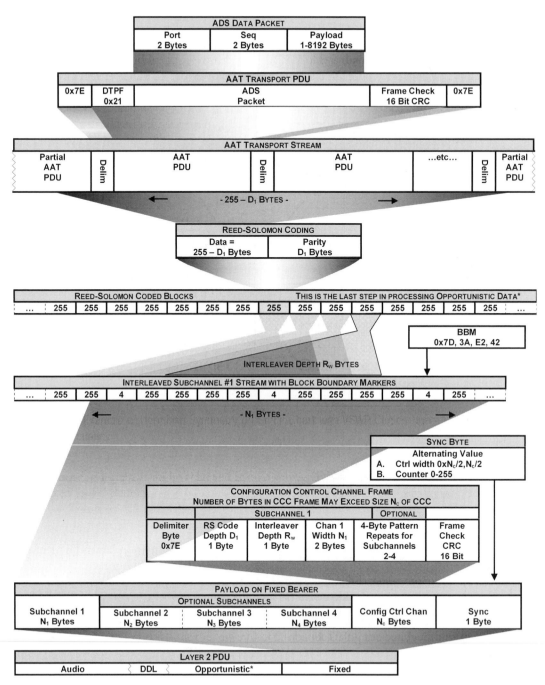

Figure 11.3 Steps in Packaging Information on the Advanced Application Services Transport (AAT)

AAT PDU Stream

AAT PDUs are assembled into a stream. Each PDU is separated from the next by a delimiter word. Adjacent PDUs may belong to different incoming services.

Reed-Solomon FEC

Reed-Solomon (RS) forward error correction is applied. A fixed number of bytes is accumulated from the PDU stream. The number depends on the setting for the depth of the RS coding. Say the coding is set to produce 32 parity bytes. Then 223 data bytes are taken from the AAT PDU stream and RS-processed for a total of 255 bytes per RS block.

Interleaving

The interleaver takes the contents of a 255-byte RS block and interleaves it across a number of 255-byte FEC blocks. The selected number of FEC blocks is the interleaver depth, R_w, ranging from 1 to 64 FEC blocks. Thus the individual bytes of one RS block are spread across the next R_w FEC blocks to be transmitted. Because the FEC block stream is continuous, each FEC block contains some bytes from the most recent RS blocks. A receiver can randomly jump into the stream, buffer R_w FEC blocks, and de-interleave the first full RS block available across the buffer. With the arrival of each new FEC block in the buffer, there is enough information to de-interleave the next RS block.

Block Boundaries

If strung together, the 255-byte FEC blocks would have nothing to distinguish the first byte in each block from any other byte. A four-byte pattern is inserted to provide a rhythmic pattern of block boundaries. The AAT byte stream is ready for insertion into the Layer 2 PDU.

These are the steps that data elements go through to get to Layer 2. However, with the variety of ways to configure the AAT, an exploration of the AAT channel structure is necessary.

Bearer Channels

The AAT reference document defines three IBOC "bearer channels." They are PSD, Fixed and Opportunistic. Recall from Chapter 4 that the Program Service Data is transmitted to the Audio Transport using "HDLC-like framing" borrowed from IETF RFC-1662. This is the process that begins with packetizing the information, encapsulating the packets for transport, and joining the packets with a delimiter word to form a data stream. A receiver can begin to pick up the data stream at any time and start looking for packets that correspond to its desired service. The preceding description of AAT begins with the same three steps. Thus, AAT also employs "HDLC-like framing" to generate a continuous information stream carrying a variety of advanced data services.

Data Transport Packet Format

The advanced data service supplying the data would deliver a file or stream to a transport mechanism that would handle the creation of packets. The default Data Transport Packet Format (DTPF) can carry from 1 to 8192 bytes of data. When breaking a file into packets, there is a happy medium in the size. Packets that are too small waste the overhead required to encapsulate the information. Packets could be too large if they take so long to transmit that they obstruct the flow of other data or are more prone to error. The bandwidth available on the bearer channel and the amount of forward error protection applied to the channel may help determine the optimal packet size.

Port Number

On all three bearer channels the framing process includes adding a Port Number to the data packet. Port numbering is independent of the bearer channel. In other words, it does not matter over what channel the information is transmitted, the Port Number has the same meaning. There are 65,536 possible Port Numbers.

Main Program Service Data has the dedicated Port Number, in hexadecimal notation, 0x5100. Officially, MPSD is only carried over the PSD bearer channel. However, if a receiver were designed to look for it, a packet on another bearer channel with the 0x5100 Port Number would be a valid MPSD packet.

NRSC-5-A only defines PSD ports. These include the MPSD Port Number, and seven SPSD numbers. The series of port numbers 0x5201 through 0x5207 are assigned to the first through seventh Supplemental Program Services' PSD. All other port numbers were reserved as of NRSC-5-A. The most significant byte of every Port Number is considered a "Service ID" that helps a receiver ignore entire groups of port numbers, conserving receiver processing for useful tasks. Service ID's 0x51 and 0x52 represent MPSD and SPSD, respectively. Ports 0x5100–51FF and 0x5200-52FF are associated with these services, even though only eight of these ports were assigned in NRSC-5-A.

Mirroring a concept employed by the Internet Assigned Numbers Authority (iana.org), the AAT reference document indicates that the system does not define the mapping of applications to ports. Instead, AAT "uses a combination of 'well known' and 'station defined' ports." (Reference document (10)) For illustration of the concepts, consider IANA, which registers the port numbers used in Internet communications. It maintains the first 1024 port numbers as "well-known" ports. IANA also speaks of a port "providing services to unknown callers as a service contact port," in which the service contact port is defined as a well-known port– in Star Trek terms, a sort of "hailing frequency" from which communications are transferred to another port once the link is established. Originally, well-known ports were intended for use at the system level, leaving their access to qualified system administrators. With the passage of time, access to port numbers on networked devices has become more universal and the role of well-known ports has been challenged.

IANA requires registration of well-known ports. Above the range of well-known ports on the IANA list are Registered ports, then Dynamic and Private Ports. AAT's "well-known" ports would parallel the IANA approach—they are common, publicly disclosed numbers that are well-known to the community, but essentially accessible to system developers. Well-known ports must not be reassigned for other purposes, because receivers may be preprogrammed to look at a well-known port for a specific service.

"Station-defined" ports, on the other hand, would parallel IANA private ports in which an application or user chooses a port outside the registered port number range. With AAT applications in their infancy, no private port range was mentioned in NRSC-5-A. As applications evolve, individual stations might assign station-defined ports on a case-by-case basis. There will be no concern with port conflicts, so long as the station can tell the receiver on what port to find a particular application's data.[2]

The process of assigning AAT port numbers was the subject of a discussion in the NRSC DRB Subcommittee in 2006. AAT Port Numbering is a subset of the larger class of IBOC "reserved bit assignments" considered by NRSC. A suggestion was made to place these assignments under NRSC purview to ensure equitable, public assignment and deployment of IBOC numbering (not unlike the role of IANA). The NRSC accepted an offer by iBiquity to administer such assignments and make them publicly available on iBiquity's website.

Sequence Number

One unit of information transmitted by an application is segmented into as many as 65,536 packets. Those packets bear a common Port Number. To keep track of them, identify lost packets, and ensure reassembly in the proper order, the transport assigns each packet on the port an individual Sequence Number. The system manages each Port Number with its own sequence numbering.

HDLC-Like Framing

Discussed further in Chapter 4, HDLC refers to High Level Data Link Control methodology adopted by ISO/IEC and adapted as "HDLC-like" in IETF RFC-1662 (see the informative reference RFC-1662 appended to PSD Transport reference document (9)). With the Data Transport Packets ported, sequenced, and stuffed, they must be assembled into a stream that a receiver can parse. (Table 11.3)

Packets are encapsulated in the HDLC-like transport wrapper. This is the AAT PDU, which identifies the format of the encapsulated packet (DTPF) and supplies an error-detecting Frame Check Sequence (FCS). Recall that before the packets are put in the PDUs, the packets already contain a Port Number, Sequence Number, and data payload. To distinguish each PDU in the data stream from the next, the PDUs are bounded by delimiter markers, called flags.

---

[2] This task is the role of a services discovery protocol, which iBiquity calls *Service Information Guide (SIG)*. As of this writing, iBiquity has only presented SIG conceptually to the NRSC. More discussion of service discovery appears further in this chapter.

Flag	DTPF	Port	Seq	Data	FCS	Flag
0x7E	0x21	0x0000–FFFF	0x0000–FFFF	1–8192 Bytes	16-Bit CRC	0x7E

Table 11.3 AAT PDU Format (Source: From Table 6-1, NRSC-5 AAT reference document (11))

The reserved value for the delimiter is 0x7E, which in a file editor would appear as the ASCII tilde. To ensure the 0x7E delimiter flags appear only between PDUs and not within them, any appearance of 0x7E within the PDU must be replaced with some other value. All other values of the 8-bit byte have their own meanings and cannot substitute for 0x7E on the transport PDU. A 2-byte code—0x7D, 0x5E—becomes the replacement for the value 0x7E. The starting byte of the pair, 0x7D (equivalent to the ASCII right curly bracket), is reserved as the "escape" byte assigned to indicate a two-byte word. Now the value 0x7D also has a special meaning and is unable to represent itself. A second two-byte escaped code is assigned to represent the 0x7D byte: 0x7D, 0x5D. The result is a code set where there are 256 binary values and one delimiter byte represented by 255 one-byte words and 2 two-byte words. (The escape byte never appears alone, only in byte-pairs).

The code set represents 256 binary values and one delimiter character with a total of 259 bytes. The slight drop in efficiency resulting from having double bytes represent individual bytes is the ratio of the 257 information "words" (including the delimiter) conveyed by 259 bytes (255 one-byte words and two 2-byte words). Assuming the stream uses all byte values equally, the average information word is 101% of a byte. This method provides an efficient way to synchronize to the stream and to do so with variable-size PDUs.

Reed-Solomon Coding and Interleaving

As discussed in more detail in Chapter 4, Reed-Solomon coding is a block coding method that appends error-correcting data to a block of information. The form of the coding on the AAT transport is RS(255, k), where 255 represents the size of the coder's output block in bytes. The variable k represents the number of input bytes processed by the coder for each output block. This is shown as a variable for the AAT transport because the operator can set the depth of the RS encoder on each data channel. The AAT Configuration Control Channel conveys this setting and is further discussed below. A common setting for RS coders is RS(255, 223) which provides 32 bytes of error protection, which can correct up to 16 bad bytes at unknown locations or 32 bad bytes at known locations in the block. Of course, a higher degree of error protection, produced by reducing the data bytes and increasing the parity bytes, decreases the throughput of the AAT channel. When setting the RS coding for an AAT channel, an optimum balance must be struck between rate of throughput and robustness, keeping in mind the requirements of the various applications services that are using the channel.

The RS coding process takes the next k bytes of the AAT data stream and encodes it into the next 255-byte RS-coded block. The result is a series of RS-encoded blocks representing the AAT stream. The interleaver buffers a number of these blocks to provide byte-wise interleaving. Like the RS coding depth, the setting for the interleaver is a variable that is chosen for the AAT channel and communicated over the Configuration Control Channel. The contents of as many as 64 255-byte blocks may be interleaved. The latency caused by the interleaving process is dependent on the interleaver depth and the bandwidth allocated to the AAT channel (e.g., the number of blocks per L1 frame).

The interleaver puts out a series of 255-byte FEC blocks. To enable the receiver to recover each block, a synchronization scheme is necessary. A Block Boundary Marker (BBM) is inserted in the AAT block stream, separating the beginning of one block from the end of another. The BBM is a four-byte sequence whose periodic appearance in the AAT data stream is recognizable and unambiguous, even if the sequence occasionally appears elsewhere in the stream.

Bearer Channels and Blocks

The description of Reed-Solomon block coding and interleaving is most applicable to the AAT transport on Fixed bearer channels. The Fixed bearer has selectable coding and interleaving, with one block boundary marker between every fourth block. In contrast, the Opportunistic bearer channel employs a fixed RS coding depth (255,223) and no interleaving; each 255-byte block is paired with a block boundary marker. Meanwhile, the PSD bearer channel does not employ block encoding or interleaving.

iBiquity estimates a packet error rate with the unprotected PSD at about 0.01%, while the RS encoding assigned to opportunistic data would improve its performance about tenfold.

Insertion into Bearer Channel

The processed byte stream is ready for insertion into the bearer channel.

Opportunistic Bearer

In the case of Opportunistic data, it is simply inserted as space is available on the bearer channel. In the Layer 2 PDU, a Data Delimiter (DDL) separates the Opportunistic data from the end of the Program Services. The DDL is a five-byte sequence. The DDL provides confirmation of the location of the start of the Opportunistic data. Recall that the Program Service portion of the L2 PDU (Chapter 5) contains Audio Transport material that is already marked with location pointers (Chapter 4, packet locators, MPS and SPS PDU). These pointers tell the receiver where to find each audio packet on the L2 PDU. The receiver can also use the pointer information to determine where the end of the program material is in the L2 PDU, inferring where the beginning of the Opportunistic data's DDL is.

Fixed Bearer

The Fixed bearer channel is more complex than the Opportunistic. The Fixed bearer is last on the L2 PDU. Layer 2 is capable of indicating that a Fixed bearer exists on the L2 PDU, but without offering any details (Table 11.2). To find the beginning of the Fixed bearer, the receiver must start by looking at the most certain location, the final byte of the L2 PDU. Here it can discover where to look for more information. The final byte of the L2 PDU is called Sync byte. It alternates between being a synchronization counter and an indicator of the size of the Configuration Control Channel (CCC). By learning the size of the CCC, the receiver can read the CCC for information on the size of the Fixed bearer channel.

Standing before the Sync byte, the CCC is the second-to-last information in the L2 PDU.

The CCC contains the information that maps out the contents of the Fixed bearer. The Fixed bearer can support as many as four subchannels on the L2 PDU. By reading the CCC, the receiver figures out how many subchannels are in use, and where each begins within the Fixed bearer channel space on the L2 PDU.

The CCC is structured with the same HDLC-like arrangement as the AAT streams. There is a delimiter byte (0x7E) that indicates the beginning of the block of CCC information. For each of the four possible subchannels assigned within the Fixed bearer, the CCC provides the Reed-Solomon depth (1 byte), the interleaver depth (1 byte), and the number of bytes of data in the L2 PDU that are assigned to the subchannel (2 bytes). This is repeated for each active subchannel, followed by a 16-bit CRC Frame Check to detect errors.

AAT Data Tunneling

AAT streams "tunnel" through the lower IBOC layers. "Serial tunneling allows… High-level Data-Link Control (HDLC) devices to connect to one another through a multiprotocol internetwork rather than through a direct serial link." This definition of tunneling from cisco.com seems to apply neatly to the IBOC AAT. Each AAT channel is a stream of packetized data with boundary markers and delimiters that are by definition "HDLC-like." The AAT channels are serial streams that flow into the IBOC Layer 2 without regard for the L2 framing. No frame synchronization is necessary. When the allotted space in the Layer 2 PDU is full, the AAT stream continues by filling the allotted space in the next L2 PDU. On the receiving end, the AAT information is pulled off the L2 PDUs and reassembled into serial streams for passage onto the AAT transport layer for disassembly.

Stretching for an analogy, consider a continuous pour of concrete at a large construction site, where truck after truck arrives from the plant and pours out its load into the project's foundation. The trucks are like packets traveling down the highway with a multitude of other services. However, at the job site, the trucks are queued up so a steady stream of material is delivered down the chute to the foundation. The workers at the bottom of the chute see a continuous flow of concrete, even though it was delivered in large packets via a "multiprotocol internetwork," the public highways. The continuous pour of material was "tunneled" through the public road network and reconstructed as a stream at the job site.

The settings for CCC and Fixed subchannels should not be changed frequently. iBiquity suggests that broadcasters think in time periods no smaller than broadcast dayparts (morning drive, midday, etc.) when considering how often to change the Fixed configuration, if at all. A change in Fixed configuration results in a "transmission gap" when the AAT interleaving has to be restarted following the change. The duration of the gap is determined by the time it takes to transmit one interleaver's-worth of the new information, which is a combination of the interleaver size and the bandwidth allotted to the subchannel.

Regarding AAT latency, iBiquity has indicated that after the receiver locks onto the Layer 1 frame (approximately 1/2 to 2 1/2 seconds from tuning the channel) the first full frame has to be buffered (1.49 seconds). This enables the logical channel P1 de-interleaver to function, bringing the frame up to Layer 2. This is the first frame of latency. Begin here to follow Figure 11.3 from the bottom up.

The buffered frame has the necessary configuration information, requiring no appreciable extra time to find the data stream in the L2 PDU. The next component of the latency is the time required to sync up with a BBM to find the start of a block (a period of up to four 255-byte blocks on the Fixed subchannel). The next component of the latency is computed by multiplying the interleaver depth (in 255-byte blocks) times 255 bytes per block times 8 bits per byte to obtain the number of bits per interleaver. (The perfectionist would account for the extra 4-byte BBM's as well.) Then divide the bits per interleaver by the subchannel information rate in bits per second. The result is the number of blocks required to get the first block off the interleaver.

A 64-block interleaver holds 132.5 kilobits. Round up to 140 kb to account for the BBM sync time. With a 10 kbps information rate it would take 14 seconds to load the interleaver. A 5-block interleaver would require about 1 second to begin recovering data at 10 kbps. At 2kbps, a one-block interleaver requires 1 second. With fairly light interleaving, the latency of the AAT subchannel can be kept near that of the program audio channels. Once the HDLC-like data stream is recovered, it will require additional time to find the next whole data packet in the stream. This is dependent on packet size. If the payload packets are small with respect to the 255-byte block size, final data acquisition time will not be burdened. Particularly large payloads may tend to clog the channel and create widely varying acquisition times.

Above AAT—What Happens Outside NRSC-5?

The AAT protocol provides IBOC broadcasting a way to extend the value of its broadcast service. It is capable of serving the market in several ways:

- *Program Associated Data*
  The limited capabilities of PSD (primarily text) can be enhanced using AAT to deliver richer program associated data.

- *Broadcast Medium in its Own Right*
  As a tunneled serial stream, AAT can be configured to deliver streaming services (audio and very low bit rate video) in addition to file-based services. AAT is also capable of transporting multimedia content designed for a world-wide-web-like experience.

- *Niche Services Unrelated to Radio Programming*
  AAT can support targeted services serving private or public users. Such services may include the traditional subjects, such as those that have used analog FM subcarriers for disseminating utility load management commands, paging, private data networks, and the like. AAT is also open to innovation, such as services providing information updates and traffic information to in-vehicle navigation systems via the in-vehicle IBOC radio.

In the AAT, broadcasters have the opportunity to create a marketplace for delivering advanced broadcast data services. The successful ADS market relies on two key components—aggregation and delivery. On the aggregation side, broadcasters must build a server infrastructure that enables the interconnection and administration of a multitude of services to a multitude of radio stations. On the delivery side, a set of common, low-cost receiver architectures must be available to support the range of services that can be offered.

The components on the aggregation side belong in a layer above the NRSC-5 stack, connecting to the AAT transport. Impulse Radio, Inc. pioneered the approach to using IBOC as a multiprotocol data transport. From 1999 to 2004, during the height of the NRSC standardization process, Impulse Radio developed the first technology to manage the flow of data through an IBOC transport.

With their prototype Datacast Server™, Impulse Radio showed how effective datacasting on FM IBOC could be, even with only a few kilobits per second. In 2002 David Maxson co-authored with Impulse Radio a paper titled *How Data Transmitted over an IBOC Station Will Be Managed: Using A Gateway To Generate Data Revenue.*[3] The next section of this chapter works with information originally presented in that paper. Impulse Radio's seminal work on a proposed structure for Advanced Data Services still stands as a model for making the highest and best use of IBOC data capacity. Regardless of how applications services roll out to market, developers would be wise to pursue a common system of classifying services and receiver types.

Impulse Radio developed its data content management gateway, called the Datacast Server, as a model for dynamically managing the data capacity available on IBOC. With the prospect of numerous services being offered to numerous end-users over numerous radio receiver platforms via numerous radio stations, Impulse Radio recognized the importance of developing a common hierarchy of service classifications and receiver classifications. The objective is to maintain an efficient and interoperable advanced data service architecture. The successful architecture would support just about any kind of service in the presence of other services being transmitted on the same data pipe. The approach to developing an architecture relies on using network engineering best practices.

The work done by Impulse Radio transcends individual applications, developing the principles upon which to develop an ADS protocol stack layer. Their development of Use Cases, Service Classification, and Receiver Classification provides a structure for the thought processes behind the creation of an advanced data service protocol.

---

[3] "How Data Transmitted over an IBOC Station Will Be Managed: Using A Gateway To Generate Data Revenue," *2002 NAB Broadcast Engineering Conference Proceedings, David Maxson, Paul Signorelli.*

Learning from History

To set the context for the data gateway discussion, we begin with a discussion of traditional radio data broadcasting architectures and business models and how they differ from a contemporary network model. Broadcasters familiar with the FM subcarrier economic model may recognize that ADS over IBOC offers a more bandwidth-efficient service model. FM subcarriers are traditionally leased in a tenant/landlord fashion. The radio station locks in a long-term agreement to provide a fixed bandwidth to a service provider. It falls on the service provider to determine how efficiently his bandwidth is utilized.

AAT can be configured to provide the equivalent of four subcarrier-like subchannels per logical channel. Each might be leased to a different tenant. There is risk, however, in partitioning the limited fixed-data bandwidth for permanent use by individual clients. A tenant leasing a Fixed subchannel as if it were a traditional subcarrier, with a permanently reserved amount of band-width, might not fully utilize the bandwidth. Also, the tenant may control his leased bandwidth for the duration of a several-year agreement, diminishing the opportunity for new uses of the bandwidth to take hold. The leased-capacity business model prevents the station from maximizing the use of any bandwidth already dedicated exclusively for a particular user. Tenant partitioning of the AAT channel structure may perpetuate the old subcarrier paradigm at the expense of a flexible multiparty data delivery system.

A Better Reason to Use AAT Subchannels

To optimize throughput, the use of AAT subchannels is best applied, if at all, for Quality of Service (QoS) management, rather than as a tenant partition. Services are already partitioned on a packet basis with the use of Port Numbering, leaving a service scheduler to manage delivery of data on schedule. Instead, AAT subchannels offer segregation of data content by QoS because they are designed to enable different degrees of error protection on each subchannel. The Reed-Solomon coding and interleaving is customized for the subchannel. However, only if there is a real performance gain for certain advanced data services should the partitioning of an additional subchannel be considered. Each subchannel offers less bandwidth than the whole, narrowing the peak traffic rate available to each channel and potentially preventing the ability of one service on a busy channel to exploit unused capacity on another underutilized subchannel. It may be more efficient to employ a single AAT subchannel with a selected optimum level of error protection.

The Radio Broadcasting Model for Advanced Data Services

AAT can support a business model more like the radio business model than the subcarrier model. Radio sells time by the spot while subcarriers are leased full time to third parties. In radio broad-casting, the traffic manager maintains the flow of paid content, prioritizing each item on the schedule, and establishing rotations for certain items on the schedule. With an effective data traffic management system above the IBOC protocol stack (the gateway), the AAT can be directed to carry data content on a prioritized, scheduled basis. Services utilizing the transport can be configured to pay for data by the byte and by the QoS offered. Quality of service characteristics include robustness of the service, timeliness of delivery, repetition rate of delivery, priority of delivery over other data contending for the bandwidth, and the like.

Revenue Comparisons

To illustrate how the subcarrier business model is not one to emulate with IBOC advanced data services, consider this analysis of the value of a subcarrier compared to audience-related station income. Subcarrier tenant revenue is often viewed as found money, with little cost or risk to obtain. Subcarriers are low-overhead enhancements to a station's portfolio. Aside from occasional contract administration matters and routine or emergency maintenance by station personnel, the third-party subcarrier has no cost associated with its operation (except to those who feel the loss of main channel modulation with each subcarrier is a penalty). In contrast, the main channel audio attracts a large audience whose desire for free entertainment drives revenue generation. Of course, as the core business of the radio stations, the main channel program has a substantial cost to produce and transmit.

For a quick value comparison between pre-IBOC earnings for radio and subcarrier operations, we looked at 2001 figures from the Boston market. With an annual market revenue figure of just over one third of a billion dollars, and sixty-five stations listed in the revenue count, the average station revenue was about $5 million. Assuming a 40% broadcast cash flow, the per-station revenue is adjusted in Table 11.4 to obtain an earnings figure. This annual earnings figure is weighted for the 53 kHz that the stereo audio occupies in the composite spectrum. This is an average estimate for all Boston radio.

Next, assume a subcarrier on an FM station in Boston generates $10,000 per month revenue with a 100% margin. A typical subcarrier will occupy an assigned channel of 67 or 92 kHz and require 25 kHz of the composite baseband. The results of each per-hertz-per-year earnings calculation are placed in a ratio to illustrate how much more the audio portion of the broadcast is worth to the station owner. In this example, the main channel audio is 9 times more productive per hertz of composite spectrum. Using the same calculations for New York, San Francisco, and Los Angeles, with an estimated 50% higher subcarrier revenue in NYC and LA, the per hertz earnings ratios are even more bleak for the best earning subcarriers, with average radio earnings up to twelve times more productive than subcarrier. This shirtsleeve analysis selects middling radio revenue and high subcarrier income, erring in favor of the subcarrier income.

	Market Radio Revenue (000)	Stations per Market	Average Station Annual Radio Revenue (000)	High Subcarrier Annual Revenue	Cash Flow Margin	Earnings BITDA (000)	Hertz Composite Bandwidth	Annual Earnings per Hertz
Main Channel Boston Market	$362,100	65	$5,571		40%	$2,228	53,000	$42.04
Subcarrier Major Market				$120,000	100%	$120	25,000	$4.76
Broadcast to Subcarrier Earnings Value Ratio								9:1

Table 11.4 Coarse Estimate of Subcarrier Value

If the hypothesis holds that subcarriers can be expected to be about ten times less productive per unit bandwidth than the analog program, then it is clear that auxiliary services need a larger audience and greater purpose to generate full value from the use of the bandwidth. The NAB Subcarrier Report,[4] last published in 1997, reported that subcarriers were utilized on less than half of FM stations, and two subcarriers or more are employed on only 8% of stations. This further confirms that, industry-wide, subcarriers are underutilized because the market is small and their value is unrealized. Low utilization and low per-hertz earnings reinforce the notion that the potential public benefit of auxiliary services is not fully achieved with the traditional subcarrier business model. The legacy of multiple subcarrier formats, proprietary applications and protocols, extra component costs in receiver design, and the resulting low utilization, contributes to the inefficiencies of the subcarrier-based auxiliary data and audio services industry.

Network Design Modeling

The IBOC Advanced Data Service lends itself to a dynamic data management protocol, serving both the program content with program-related data and any auxiliary data being transmitted. The basic architecture of a data gateway provides an ideal way to schedule, control, prioritize, transmit and charge for multiple advanced data services.

The Impulse Radio Datacast Server is one data gateway concept. Other implementations are possible. The gateway architecture would be the ADS interface to the NRSC-5 protocol stack, residing just above the AAT transport. The use of a gateway architecture has implications in the manner in which data is routed and received. Impulse Radio, in considering the implications of this, developed a set of Use Cases. Use Cases, examples of which are shown in Table 11.5, are descriptions of ways the system could be employed to provide a service. For example, a Use Case might be characterized as "provide audio cut of recent traffic report" or "broadcaster provides visual weather map for receiver display, triggered with weather report."

The Use Cases illustrate the types of service capabilities the gateway can push through the IBOC channel. The Use Cases permit system designers to define classes of receiver and classes of service that enable radios to be functional for a variety of services. By relying on the classifications, the market benefits with lowered receiver cost, receiver interoperability among various services, and innovation among competitors targeting new services to specific receiver and service classes.

In broadcasting, where the entire market chain consists of independent interests, including service providers, broadcasters, transmitter makers, receiver makers, and consumers, it may be difficult to develop standard use classifications. Receiver and service classification is a fairly straightforward process in a closed proprietary system where the transmission and reception processes are centrally planned and controlled. Satellite radio services, for example, have the ability to control the deployment of new services from the service end to the user end. However, the benefits of cooperative, structured classifications for the delivery of advanced radio data services should not be overlooked by the broadcast industry. Receiver and service classifications provide a uniform

---

[4] *FM Subcarrier Report/ Technology Guide*, National Association of Broadcasters, 1997.

transmission and reception environment that lowers the cost of entry both for service providers and service users/subscribers, setting the stage for a robust market of advanced broadcast data services.

The Flow of IBOC Transmissions

IBOC broadcasting enables a change to the traditional subcarrier data paradigm. The IBOC platform delivers main channel audio at bit rates selectable by the broadcaster. Based on the preceding discussion of the value of broadcast audio programming per unit bandwidth, multicasting of Supplemental Program Services may present the highest and best use of most of the FM IBOC spectrum. However, in the longer run, radio broadcasting may be able to exploit IBOC's data features to provide the marketplace with unique, rich, innovative, consumer-oriented benefits that are worth the bandwidth they occupy.

Because the IBOC system brings data together with audio programming at Layer 2, the cost of implementing advanced data services in an IBOC receiver is minimal. IBOC receiver chipsets receive frame by frame all the "bits" of information that are transmitted. Basic audio receivers need only focus on decoding the audio portion of the Layer 2 PDU and the corresponding PSD. Because the remaining AAT data is already demodulated and recovered within the frame, it is a fairly simple matter to push this Fixed and Opportunistic data to another process in the receiver. No additional demodulation work is necessary. In contrast, analog and digital subcarriers have required side circuits to separate and demodulate them.

The provision of advanced data services over the IBOC medium is layers above the physical layer, providing access to the services entirely in the logical domain without concern for the radio frequency section of the receiver. The radio's firmware determines what services it can offer, and the receiver class determines how those services are rendered. For IBOC data there is no direct analogy to the SCA jack on the back of an FM exciter. Advanced data services must flow through a gateway to obtain their rightful position on the IBOC bit stream.

Figure 11.4 illustrates the logical relationships between the sources that might feed an IBOC transmitter. Fundamentally, where an auxiliary service would have "leased a jack" on the rear of the FM exciter, the IBOC model permits a more complex system of allocating data flow.

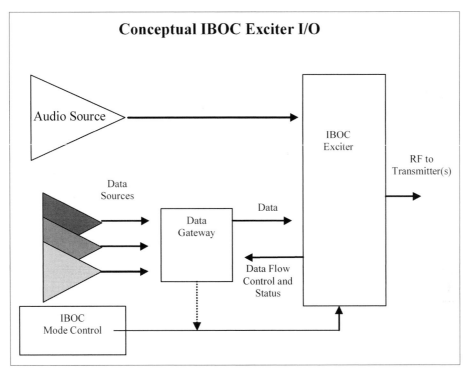

Figure 11.4 Conceptual IBOC Exciter Inputs/Outputs

The Concept of Multiple Services Sharing the Pipe

In the analog broadcasting world of subcarriers, each service would hire a subcarrier and try to fill it with revenue-generating content that relates to its core business. Unused data blocks or unprogrammed audio time represents bandwidth time that is lost to the subcarrier user and to the broadcaster. In the IBOC data model, a data gateway can be inserted in the data path to administer the prioritization and flow of data over the air.

A paging service may hire a certain number of bits, with a certain maximum delay time between system receipt and IBOC transmission. This service may be willing to pay extra for priority service on some or all messages. Meanwhile, the radio station may be offering a stored audio file to those with radios enabled to save and play it. Perhaps the audio has to have arrived by the time a program begins. And a financial data service may simply wish to obtain a certain number of bits per hour, with no other constraints on their delivery.

The principles of data flow management have a surprising similarity to the principles of managing radio programming. Programming is scheduled typically in time blocks with a set of rules for filling those blocks—a certain number of spots per hour, music rotations, station promo announcement rotations, spot schedules and rotations. Spots are scheduled on a priority scheme, which allows a computer to determine which spots to shift in time or "bump" in favor of others. Program content

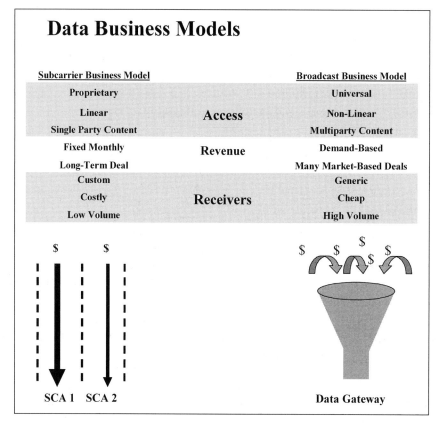

Figure 11.5 Comparison of Leased Model with Spot Model for Data Services

flow is managed by preset rules and billable events are tracked, verified and billed. The data gateway performs these same types of functions in orchestrating the data flow.

The gateway can look ahead in the schedule and determine what it must accomplish. Perhaps some program related data must get to radios in a timely fashion—not too soon that late tuners-in will miss it, but not too late that it will fail to synchronize with the programming. Perhaps the data has a looping rule that it must be sent three times over the course of five minutes to be sure that people tuning in can "catch up" with a full set of data related to the programming. Meanwhile, the messaging service deposits a message with a delivery latency time attached to it. The gateway will have a set of rules that inform it how to prioritize the message delivery according to the contract with the service provider. In this example, the financial service comes closest to the old subcarrier model because they have paid for a fixed number of bits every hour. The gateway will look at all these scheduled and instantaneous events while referring to the rules it has been given for each service. The gateway will also communicate with the IBOC exciter. It has to know that the station has decided to operate the IBOC audio streams at, say, a total of 80 kbps for the next hour. This leaves the gateway to determine what to do with the remaining approximately 18 kbps, based on all the data that is scheduled and arriving at the queue.

If the gateway can obtain information about the opportunistic data from the audio chain or the exciter, it would be able to modulate the amount of data it is sending based on the amount of opportunistic data capacity available. The gateway provides the flow control process that prioritizes and maximizes the data throughput.

Use Cases and Service and Receiver Classifications

The flow control process requires a framework within which it can make decisions about data formatting, prioritization and flow. This framework is based on the anticipated ways in which the data delivery system will be used. To create a universal data standard that can be employed by broadcasters and third parties to transmit data, and by receiver manufacturers and consumers to receive data, one must build a protocol that anticipates general ways that the system might be used. Does the system need to synchronize data events? Is there a need for security on data that is private or fee-based? If access is controlled to certain data, how should a universal standard be created so that receiver and chip manufacturers do not give the data away to enterprising users and individual service providers have the confidence that their authorizations to their clients are not in conflict with someone else's authorizations? What are the needs for authentication of communications and transactions? The list goes on.

System programmers study how a system will be used in order to identify the connections it must make with the outside world and the internal processes required to accomplish each task. The preceding questions arise from considering ways that the system could be used. Other questions that arise in the Use Case process may relate to human interface or peripheral interface issues. For instance, if a radio is going to deliver program related graphics, what are the display, memory, and processing demands? What are the receiver design implications about auxiliary audio files or streams? What are the limits to a display and controls on the dashboard of a car? How does one format data to send to it? Use Case Analysis defines the problem in terms of how people will use the system. "People" in this case are broadcasters, service providers (anyone from the local broadcaster to international vendors such as Yahoo, Microsoft, Google, CNN, ESPN, Navteq, and the like) and IBOC radio end users.

The problem to solve is "what will people do with this IBOC data pipe, that not only allows streaming audio and data, but the sending of any ASCII or binary data for a multitude of purposes?" To define the problem one must

- Examine the characteristics of both IBOC and radio:
  - Broadcasting medium
  - Free, ubiquitous
  - One-way point-to-multipoint
  - No impact to the network on adding users
  - Long-range data transmission at low power (low cost)
  - Good mobile reception at high speeds and in difficult conditions

- – Limited data bandwidth
- Examine the way a digital pipe enhances radio broadcasting (beyond digital audio):
  - – Radio broadcasting in a nonlinear mode
  - – Brand new, adjunct business models
- Examine user preferences:
  - – Entertaining and informative information
  - – Personalized content flexibility

This leads to the identification of the types of applications that would be well suited for IBOC and the types of features that the IBOC system would need to enable them. Here are some features and applications examples:

Applications Examples

- Program Associated Data
- On-demand programming
- Time-shifting
- Telematics
- Commerce
- Listener Interaction
- Subscription
- Supplemental Audio
- Messaging
- Electronic Program Guide
- Emergency Alert System

Features Examples

Location-Based Programming

Audio or data customized to the location of the vehicle

Time Associated

Audio or data customized to the time

Data Caching

Storage of audio and data on the receiver for later use

External System Interface

> Using IBOC data to interact with another system such as a navigation system or an Internet application

Transactions

> Using IBOC data to initiate response back to the data source via another channel such as the Internet or wireless web

Security

> Protects access to data as well as protects the data itself for transaction based activities and subscription services

User Personalization

> Data that is customized based upon user preferences

A list of possible Use Cases was assembled by Impulse Radio in the summer of 2001. Examples from the list are contained in Table 11.5. From studying the Use Cases, a pattern of classifications emerges. Two major classifications describe characteristics of categories of advanced data services. Service Classes describe how groups of Use Cases are employed to provide a service, from a data transport perspective. Receiver Classes describe what a receiver has to do to handle the processing, rendering and delivery of data for particular services and applications. The Service Classes are functional groups of services that are likely to share common applications, features, users, and receiver characteristics. The Applications examples bear a strong resemblance to the Service Classes. The distinction between the two is that the Service Classes are more transport-related, involving the common transport and flow control issues of groups of Use Cases, while the Applications categories are more user-related, focusing on the manner in which one or more Use Cases are implemented to provide useful functionality.

Each Service Class has implications on the design of receivers, for characteristics such as human and data interfacing, memory, processing power, and the like. To simplify the receiver and chip design process, and to foster a family of interoperable receivers, a set of Receiver Classes must be defined as well.

Service Classes

The Use Case examination develops an understanding for the structure of advanced data services, which are divided into Service Classes. At the base layer there is a general definition of a Data Service, and above that are application-specific rules that must be applied to the services. The Data Service Definition identifies the physical attributes of the data service in the system. This answers questions such as: How is the data transported– is it streamed; is it file based? How much bandwidth does the service get? What type of error correction is associated with the data? Is the data encrypted? Is it binary data or ASCII data? Does the file have a time-to-live associated with it? Is it application specific data? Does it require authentication to use? Is the data synchronized (with audio, time, or location)? This definition creates an environment where unrelated data can readily coexist on the same channel.

Beyond the Data Service Definition are the application-specific rules that must be applied to services. These rules help establish the expectations for the consumer, the broadcaster (and their customers), and the hardware and service providers. For example, the treatment of information intended for display would have basic guidelines for its rendering. This might dictate, for instance, that text never scrolls to avoid driver distraction, or that an image must be rendered at or above a minimum resolution to satisfy an advertiser or an artist.

A Service Class, such as Program Associated Data (PAD), could benefit from the ability to synchronize with events on the audio channel, or with other PAD coming down the AAT channel or down the PSD channel. In contrast, a remote control service, such as load management, has nothing to do with the main program and would not require program synchronization. Instead, the load management application would fall into a Service Class that might include location-based or time of day functions in the radio and a standard Input/Output port for connecting to remote devices under control.

Service Classes are therefore groups of Use Cases that serve similar applications. Applications are associated with a family of features. Features are clustered into groups identified with Receiver Classes.

Use Mapping

In Figure 11.6, the relationship between these groupings is shown as a functional map. For example, a series of Use Cases might involve providing content related to the station's main program channel (PAD) beginning on the left. Some Use Cases might involve content that are graphics and text, some might provide audio, and some might involve listener response or interactivity. Together, these Use Cases are grouped into a Service Class, moving to the right. However, this Service Class may feed several applications—processes that in this example are Program Associated, but have various purposes. One PAD application may simply be to play the main channel audio and display artist and title text. Another could involve feeding graphics to an interactive display that permits the radio listener to toggle into the stats of the pitcher on the mound.

On another path in the Use Map is the example of a set of Use Cases revolving around On Demand Programming content (ODP). Together, they compose the ODP Service Class. ODP applications may be program independent, or they may be related to the activity on the main audio program. In either case, ODP applications require capabilities that are distinct from PAD functions. ODP audio must be cached for later retrieval. Memory capacity and cache management features would be among the functions tied to the ODP Service Class. Meanwhile, the PAD Service Class chosen above might only involve temporary real time buffering and display rendering of text or graphical data, requiring a different but overlapping set of functions compared to the ODP Service Class.

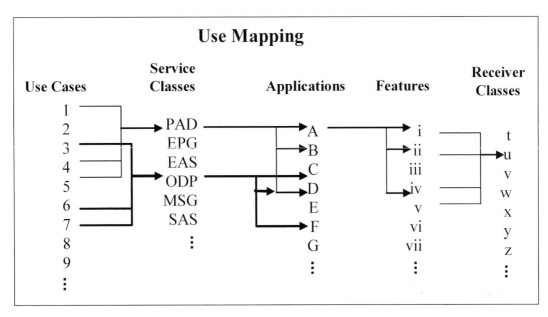

Figure 11.6 Use Map Illustrating Relationships among Classifications

Moving along the map from applications to features, the applications for which people will buy radios will have to have certain features to enable those applications. Menu buttons, memory, hooks to an automobile data bus, a navigation system or a back-channel communications device, and the like will be required of a radio that enables certain applications. Some applications may share common features with other applications. Features are grouped into sets that are common to applications or similar groups of applications. These are mapped to one or more receiver classes. For example, a receiver in a dashboard of a car will require certain display features and display management features for in-vehicle safety. This same radio may be a no-additional-frills model that maintains lowest cost. One receiver class could be defined for this type of radio. To satisfy an additional Use Case another dashboard radio may have all of the above, and may require hooks to the automobile clock, the navigation system, and the concierge phone (e.g., OnStar®). This could define another Receiver Class. Meanwhile, a home stereo, a portable boombox, a PDA radio module, or a personal computer peripheral, or an application specific load management controller may each fall into one or more other Receiver Classes.

Receiver Classes

As illustrated by the preceding discussion, a Receiver Class is a blueprint that must be followed for any receiver that wishes to enable specific Use Cases. Practically, enabling a Use Case equates to enabling the group of IBOC functions that are required by the Use Case. A receiver class is not a recipe that must be strictly followed. In fact, a well-defined receiver class would be devoid of any implementation details. This is best illustrated by example.

Take the Use Case that a broadcaster sends an on-demand traffic report audio cut to the listener. The Service Class to which this Use Case belongs will be described by a Data Service Definition that dictates the on-demand audio would be a file of a particular format. It could give guidelines for transport of the file; is it a stream or a file transfer? In this case it would probably be a file transfer. The receiver class for on-demand audio would set some minimum space requirement for supporting on-demand audio. For instance, it might be that at a minimum, a receiver supporting on-demand audio must be able to store at least 30 seconds of audio files at one time. Receiver manufacturers could choose to put more memory in the device. That might make the receiver more attractive to consumers who want the device to retain information for longer periods of time or when they tuned off of the station.

Still, in this example the receiver class is implementation agnostic. The form and exact amount of memory is up to the individual electronics manufacturer, provided it meets the base requirement that broadcasters and other advanced data service providers are expecting to support certain Service Classes and applications.

Classes Are the Key to Interoperability

With broadcasters, content providers and receiver manufacturers sharing the same hierarchy of classifications, any content transmitted by an IBOC radio station will be receivable by any radio designed to function under the Service Class of the content being transmitted. This permits broadcasters the flexibility to develop applications that people find useful while giving receiver manufacturers the latitude to implement those uses in their own ways.

Data Service Definitions associated with each Service Class describe the characteristics of the Class that make it unique and the means to organize, transport, identify and render the data in that class. In addition to the specifics of such things as file formats supported, rendering or markup rules, storage expectations, interactivity expectations and the like, the Data Service Definitions relate to global features required by the Class.

Global features are features that are not specific to a single service class or application and are available to be applied to any class that requires them. Synchronization to programming or location or time is one set of global features that may be required to implement a Service Class. The Authentication and Encryption features embrace secure access to subscription music, financial data, or copy-protected music, text or graphics. The Transaction feature enables back channel communication to be established to make a purchase, enter information or make a request. The Transaction feature is not a definition of a particular means of communication (e.g., wireless phone, 802.11, Bluetooth, Smart Card, etc.). Rather, it describes the information required and input and output required to initiate and complete a transaction. The choice of transaction medium remains in the hands of the service provider in conjunction with the radio designer. This way, three automobile electronics companies could design two back channel methods each and they would all work with their Transaction-capable IBOC radio. The broadcaster and service provider would know that when they design a new service to the specifications of the appropriate Service Class, it will work on any radio built to function within the relevant Receiver Class.

In addition to creating an assurance of interoperability between many receiver brands and types, this classification hierarchy will give content and service providers assurance that their valuable content and services will be available only to those whom are authorized and used only in the manner allowed. Data could be permitted for one-time use, no-recording, pay per use, free use, or no-exporting to other devices, among others.

Use Cases Lead to Protocols

Overall, the Use Mapping hierarchy developed by Impulse Radio creates an environment in which broadcasters and receiver manufacturers can create applications that attract consumer interest and revenue. Gateways like the original prototype Impulse Radio Datacast Server control the flow of numerous data services sharing the same "data pipe." Receiver manufacturers can implement the available broadcast data services while retaining the ability to differentiate their products from others.

Based on the results of the Use Case analysis, Impulse Radio created a data protocol called eXtensible Data Service (XDS), to support IBOC advanced data services. XDS is discussed further in the next section of this chapter. Impulse Radio has offered this protocol for the industry to freely utilize. It creates the necessary bridge between those who produce content and services and those who produce the hardware to offer a rich array of opportunities to serve the public and obtain their business. The protocol harbors no specific application for data broadcasting, leaving the industry to create the applications. The data protocol offers the hooks necessary to create applications that do anything imaginable on this point-to-multipoint data service. Companies developing services that can take advantage of IBOC data capacity and would benefit by keeping these global principles and concepts in mind, rather than focusing narrowly on how to tunnel their specific service through their own custom service hierarchy and custom receiver characteristics.

Table 11.5 Selected Use Cases identified in the Impulse Radio analysis

Use Case Code	Category	Function Description
PAD001	PAD	Advertiser places visual advertisements An advertiser places an ad during regular programming that is viewed on the screen of on a receiver by a user.
PAD002	PAD	Advertiser places supplemental audio advertisement with on-demand audio An advertiser places an audio ad at the beginning and/or end of a piece of audio that is stored on the receiver and played by the request of the user.
PAD003	PAD	Advertiser enhances main program audio ad with visual data An advertiser has data related to the information conveyed in the audio portion of an advertisement appear on the visual display of the receiver as the ad is heard by the user.
PAD004	PAD	Advertiser enhances program audio ad with supplemental audio data An advertiser has supplemental audio data stored on a receiver for a period of time after an ad is aired to allow the user to retrieve pertinent information (such as prices, locations, phone numbers, etc.) related to the ad at a later time.
PAD005	PAD	Broadcaster enhances music programming with supplemental data A broadcaster has data related to a song being aired appear on the visual display of the receiver.

Table 11.5 Selected Use Cases identified in the Impulse Radio analysis *(continued)*

Use Case Code	Category	Function Description
PAD006	PAD	Broadcaster enhances music programming with supplemental audio data A broadcaster has audio information related to a song stored on the receiver for a period of time it has aired to be played back upon request of the user.
PAD007	PAD	Broadcaster triggers visual traffic report on receiver A broadcaster sends visual traffic information that is displayed on the receiver and viewed by the user.
PAD008	PAD	Broadcaster triggers visual weather report on receiver A broadcaster sends visual weather information that is displayed on the receiver and viewed by the user.
PAD009	PAD	Broadcaster triggers visual news report on receiver A broadcaster sends visual news information that is displayed on the receiver and viewed by the user.
DLS001	DLS	Broadcaster sends a music download to a device. The broadcaster sends a special music service that consists of music that users can purchase by subscribing to the service.
DLS002	DLS	Device uses profile to select downloaded music The device uses a profile to determine if the user is entitled to the music.
DLS003	DLS	Device writes downloaded music to a permanent storage device Device selects music by profile from a download service and stores the information on a permanent storage unit on the device.
DLS006	DLS	Device plays music from a download service User selects option to play download music and the device reads selections from the storage device, whether it is a CD, permanent storage, removable flash memory, etc., and plays them.
DLS008	DLS	Broadcaster sends a news download to a device The broadcaster sends a special news service that consists of news that users can purchase by subscribing to the service.
DLS011	DLS	Service provider transmits an electronic version of a periodical Service provider transmits an electronic version of a magazine or a newspaper that the device will then record for later viewing or hearing by the user.
DLS013	DLS	Service provider transmits an electronic version of a book Service provider transmits an electronic version of a magazine or a newspaper that the device will then record if the user has subscribed for it, for later viewing or hearing by the user.
EAS001	EAS	User receives a warning about an emergency situation. An emergency service provider alerts the community at large via one more IBOC stations.
EAS002	EAS	Send a weather alert A weather alert is sent to a car alerting the driver to an impending weather event.
EPG001	EPG	Broadcaster transmits an electronic program guide of channel services The broadcaster transmits a special service that indicates all of the services available on the channel and gives a description for each, and the user views them on the receiver.
EPG002	EPG	Receiver displays program guide information based upon device capability The receiver scans the information in the electronic program guide and only displays the services that the device is capable of handling.
EPG003	EPG	Receiver displays program guide information based upon profile The receiver scans the information in the electronic program guide and only displays the services that the user has indicated they are interested in by their profile. EPG004 EPG User selects a service from the electronic program guide The user chooses a service from the electronic program guide and the device starts rendering that service.
FLM001	FLM	Fleet Management Schedule Distribution A set of schedules and objectives for a specific fleet of vehicles is broadcast via the IBOC network.
FLM002	FLM	Request for mission status A request for a status update from a specific fleet of vehicles is broadcast via the IBOC network.

Table 11.5 Selected Use Cases identified in the Impulse Radio analysis *(continued)*

Use Case Code	Category	Function Description
LBP001	LBP	Broadcaster sends location encoded traffic information to be integrated with on-board GPS A broadcaster sends traffic information encoded by zone and the user sees the traffic that is effecting their current zone and surrounding zones where the zone information is supplied by the on-board navigation system of the vehicle.
LBP003	LBP	Broadcaster sends location encoded ad information to be integrated with on-board GPS A broadcaster sends an ad for a chain of stores or restaurants in a city encoded by zone and the user sees the information for a store or restaurant in their zone where the zone information is supplied by the on-board navigation system of the vehicle.
MSG001	MSG	Service provider sends a numeric page Service Provider broadcasts a numeric page to an addressable device and the device with the matching address receives the message and displays it.
MSG002	MSG	Service provider sends a text page Service Provider broadcasts a text page to an addressable device and the device with the matching address receives the message and displays it.
MSG003	MSG	Service provider sends updated stock quotes Service provider sends updated stock quotes to addressable devices and the devices with appropriate addresses receive the messages and display them.
MSG004	MSG	Service provider sends updated financial information Service provider sends updated financial news to addressable devices and the devices with appropriate addresses receive the messages and display the news.
MSG005	MSG	Service provider sends updated news information Service provider sends news headlines to addressable devices and the devices with appropriate addresses receive the messages and display them.
MSG006	MSG	Service provider sends updated sports information Service provider sends sports scores to addressable devices and the devices with appropriate addresses receive the messages and display them.
MSG007	MSG	Device uses profile information to customize messaging service Device receives message service data encode by areas of interest and the device uses a service profile to display only the area of interest to the user.
LBP002	LBP	Broadcaster sends location encoded traffic information to be integrated with IBOC GPS A broadcaster sends traffic information encoded by zone and the user sees the traffic that is effecting their current zone and surrounding zones where the zone information is supplied by an IBOC based GPS calculation.
MSG008	MSG	User receives a page and responds on a two-way network The device receives a page via the IBOC network and displays it to the user, the user responds on a two-way network to the entity originating the page with the source address information included in the message.
LBP004	LBP	Broadcaster sends location encoded ad information to be integrated with IBOC GPS A broadcaster sends an ad for a chain of stores or restaurants in a city encoded by zone and the user sees the information for a store or restaurant in their zone where the zone information is supplied by an IBOC based GPS calculation.
GPS001	GPS	User uses IBOC data to calculate global position User uses IBOC broadcast data from three locations to triangulate global position. ODP001 ODP Broadcaster supplies on-demand visual traffic reports A broadcaster sends visual traffic information that is
PER001	PER	Service provider personalization request to the user A service provider sends a request using the IBOC network to users asking the user to personalize the service using criteria particular to that service.

Table 11.5 Selected Use Cases identified in the Impulse Radio analysis *(continued)*

Use Case Code	Category	Function Description
PER002	PER	User receives customized services A broadcaster sends a data service with information that is customized by areas of interest to the user, the receiver uses on-board profile to only display information of interest to the user as indicated by the user.
PER003	PER	User enters profile information into the device manually A user enters profile information for a service using the input of a receiver device.
PER004	PER	User enters profile information on a web server A user enters profile information for a service at a website and the receiver uses a two-way network connection to retrieve the profile.
PER005	PER	Service profile is permanently stored on the receiver The device receives profile information and that profile is stored on a permanent storage unit on the device.
PER006	PER	Service profile is stored on a website. The device receives profile information and the information is posted to a website using a two-way network connection.
PER007	PER	Service profile is stored on a removable flash memory card. The device receives profile information and the information is stored on a flash memory card that can be removed from the device.
PER008	PER	Service profile is stored on a CD. The device profile is written to a CD and the receiver reads the profile information from the CD.
PER009	PER	Service profile is stored on a tape. The device profile is written to a tape and the receiver reads the profile information from the tape.
RCM001	RCM	Radio station conducts a contest Radio station sends data eliciting a response to a contest from one or more users in order to win something where the user responds to the contest via a two-way connection on the device.
RCM002	RCM	Radio station conducts a poll Radio station sends data eliciting a response to a poll question from one or more users where the users responds to the contest via a two-way connection on the device.
RCM003	RCM	Radio station conducts a poll integrated with profile information Radio station sends data eliciting a response to a poll question from one or more users where the users responds to the contest via a two-way connection on the device and the device transmits profile information back to the station.
RCO001	RCO	Service provider sells pre-recorded audio The service provider transmits data that allows the user to purchase pre-recorded audio that is associated with the song or artist being played by the radio.
RCO002	RCO	Service provider sells concert tickets The service provider transmits data that allows the user to purchase concert tickets that are associated with artist being played by the radio.
RCO003	RCO	Guest author sells a book The broadcaster transmits data that allows the user to purchase a book by a guest being interviewed by the on-air personality.
RCO004	RCO	Radio station conducts promotion on behalf of a guest The broadcaster transmits data promoting events on behalf of an artist whose song is being aired, or who is being interviewed by on-air personality.
RCO005	RCO	Retailer sells advertised merchandise A retailer transmits data that allows the user to purchase merchandise related to the advertisement is being played on the radio.
RCO006	RCO	User conducts purchase via the device The user interacts directly with the device to engage a commerce transaction.
RCO007	RCO	User manually inputs commerce instructions on the device The user uses buttons on the receiver to initiate the commerce transactions.
RCO008	RCO	User uses voice response to initiate a commerce transactions The user uses a voice response capability of a device to initiate a transaction.

Table 11.5 Selected Use Cases identified in the Impulse Radio analysis *(continued)*

Use Case Code	Category	Function Description
RCO009	RCO	Device conducts transaction via a two-way connection The device transmits the purchase instructions to an appropriate service provider using a two-way network connection and responds back to the user as to the result.
RCO010	RCO	Device conducts transaction via a flash memory card The device records the purchase instructions to an appropriate service provider using a removable flash memory card which is later placed in a machine with a twoway network connection to transmit the information to the service provider.
RCO011	RCO	Device conducts a sale via bluetooth The device transmits the purchase instructions to a machine with a two-way network connection using bluetooth. The purchase instructions are sent by the machine to the service provider.
RCO013	RCO	User requests more information on a product The user interacts with the device to request more information about a portion of the broadcast such as an ad, a song, a guest, a station promotion, etc.
SAS001	SAS	Broadcaster transmits a free supplementary music program A broadcaster sends secondary audio program consisting of a different selection of music than the main audio programming that the user can optionally choose to listen to.
SAS002	SAS	Broadcaster transmits a for-fee supplementary music program A broadcaster sends a secondary audio program consisting of music that the user can subscribe to by entering an authorization code into the listening device.
SAS003	SAS	Broadcaster transmits a free supplementary news program A broadcaster sends a secondary audio news program that the user can optionally choose to listen to.
SAS004	SAS	Broadcaster transmits a for-fee supplementary news program A broadcaster sends a secondary audio news program that the user can subscribe to by entering an authorization code into the listening device.
SAS005	SAS	Broadcaster transmits a free supplementary weather program A broadcaster sends a secondary audio weather program that the user can optionally choose to listen to.
SAS006	SAS	Broadcaster transmits a for-fee supplementary weather program A broadcaster sends a secondary audio weather program that the user can subscribe to by entering an authorization code into the listening device.
SAS007	SAS	Broadcaster transmits a free supplementary traffic program A broadcaster sends a secondary audio traffic program that the user can optionally choose to listen to.
SAS008	SAS	Broadcaster transmits a for-fee supplementary traffic program A broadcaster sends a secondary audio traffic program that the user can subscribe to by entering an authorization code into the listening device.
SAS009	SAS	Broadcaster transmits a supplementary location-based traffic program. A broadcaster sends a secondary traffic program than is encoded with zone information and the user will hear the traffic information that effects the zone they are in and surrounding zones.
SDS001	SDS	Broadcaster transmits a free data news program A broadcaster sends a data news program that the user can optionally choose to view on the receiver.
SDS002	SDS	Broadcaster transmits a for-fee data news program A broadcaster sends a data news program that the user can subscribe to by entering an authorization code into the receiving device.
SDS003	SDS	Broadcaster transmits a free a data weather program A broadcaster sends a weather program that the user can optionally view.
SDS004	SDS	Broadcaster transmits a for-fee data weather program A broadcaster sends a data weather program that the user can subscribe to by entering an authorization code into the receiving device.

Table 11.5 Selected Use Cases identified in the Impulse Radio analysis *(continued)*

Use Case Code	Category	Function Description
SDS005	SDS	Broadcaster transmits a free data traffic program A broadcaster sends a data traffic program that the user can optionally view.
SDS006	SDS	Broadcaster transmits a for-fee data traffic program A broadcaster sends a data traffic program that the user can subscribe to by entering an authorization code into the receiving device.
SDS007	SDS	Broadcaster transmits a location-based traffic program. A broadcaster sends a data traffic program than is encoded with zone information and the user will see the traffic information that effects the zone they are in and surrounding zones.
TEL001	TEL	Update service station information The on-board service station information for the city or region a car is traveling in is updated via an IBOC network.
TEL002	TEL	Send a telematics weather alert A telematics weather alert is sent to a car's telematics weather system on the IBOC network.
TEL003	TEL	Update point-of-interest information The on-board point-of-interest information for the city or region a car is traveling in is updated via the IBOC network. This information includes names, locations, phone numbers, and even menus.
TEL006	TEL	Stolen car retrieval A telematics message is sent via the IBOC network to cars in a city or region asking for a specific car to report its location via its two-way network where the car or cars being asked to respond have been stolen.
TEL009	TEL	Request traffic pattern information from vehicles by zone A message is broadcast via the IBOC network asking vehicles to respond with location information via their twoway connection if they are in the zone indicated in the message.
TEL011	TEL	Update navigation information Updates to the on-board guidance database for a region a car is traveling in are made via the IBOC network.
TEL012	TEL	Update traffic information for on-board navigation system Traffic information is broadcast via the IBOC network that is coded by zone so that the on-board guidance system of the car can help a vehicle avoid potential traffic jams.
TEL014	TEL	Vehicle theft countermeasures initiation A user notifies the police vehicle was stolen and a message is sent to the vehicle via an IBOC network to initiate the onboard theft countermeasures.
TSS001	TSS	Service provider encodes a portion of the broadcast for recording purposes Service provider encodes a portion of a broadcast so that a device can determine the beginning and end of a program so that the device may record and label the program.

Advanced Data Service Protocols (Not in NRSC-5)

Riding above the AAT protocol, Advanced Data Services must be structured for insertion into the AAT packet scheme. The Port Number feature in AAT performs a very basic addressing function, telling the receiver the general purpose of the content by relating it to a port. However, additional information about the data must be included with it. This role belongs to the application generating the data, and to the service interface between the application and the transport.

To be more concrete, consider an analogy to two computers on a network. A file on computer "A" has a file name composed from a limited character set, with a point separating file name and suffix. The suffix, such as ".doc," ".jpg," ".htm" and so on, identifies the file format so the computer can associate the file with a program that can read it. When that file is transferred across the network to computer "B," it may need to be associated with other files or actions. Computer B may know the file is, say, an image based on its suffix, but it does not know what to do with it. This is where a markup language comes into play.

A markup language, such as the familiar hypertext markup language (HTML) used on the World Wide Web, provides the computer at the other end of the link with instructions on how to present or utilize the files coming its way. Also, to reliably move the files across the network, a transfer protocol is required. While it can serve other purposes as well, the familiar hypertext transfer protocol (HTTP) is the basis for the transfer of HTML content, which includes HTML files and the various other files the HTML marks up for presentation. Because networks are typically two-way links, HTTP employs a request-response method to transfer information. HTML and HTTP stack above the link and network functions provided by lower layers, such as TCP/IP.

In comparison, IBOC Layers 1 and 2 handle the mechanics of moving information across the channel, and AAT provides a way to tunnel data through the IBOC channel. The functions that are the equivalents of HTTP and HTML would reside above AAT, outside the scope of the NRSC-5 protocol stack. To provide for the markup and orderly transfer of IBOC data, two methods have been proposed—the previously mentioned XDS protocol (developed by Impulse Radio) including an XML-based markup, and a markup called HD Broadcast Multimedia Language (HD BML™, developed by iBiquity).

HD BML is based on SMIL, the Synchronized Multimedia Integration Language, which is XML-based. Where Impulse Radio started with a blank slate, employing the use cases to guide its creation of an extensible markup, iBiquity chose the path of tuning an established multimedia language for the expected use cases of the IBOC medium.

The iBiquity model for gateway management of data services employs an Ensemble Operations Center (EOC). The EOC acts as the traffic cop managing the flow of various data services. In this sense, the EOC plays the same role as was intended for the Impulse Radio Datacast Server. iBiquity's implementation with EOC, however, incorporates a number of service management issues, beyond the role of the gateway.

As a data gateway, the EOC takes from the station operator a number of inputs to determine how to manage the information flow. Among these inputs are settings for new services, new service providers, and service parameters called service provider contracts. The EOC Logistics Processor handles the taking in of the services and administering their transmission, including attending to meeting QoS requirements for each service. The EOC Connection Manager manages the connections with the services, including performing authentication of the connections. The Contract Management process gives the station a means to link the business side of the operation with the EOC.

In addition to its role as a data gateway, the EOC provides management of the IBOC channelization, channel bandwidth and the like. In particular, both the SPS channel management and AAS management are conducted through the EOC. These combined functions are classified under the umbrella of iBiquity's Advanced Applications Services. The EOC also manages the permissions iBiquity's license provides to the broadcaster.

Service Discovery

With all this consideration of transmitting data services on IBOC, the question arises, how does the receiver know a service is available on a particular station? Service discovery for Program Services can occur in the first frame acquired by the receiver. For advanced data services, the situation is different.

When it comes to Main Program audio and Supplemental Program audio, the receiver looks at a relatively high layer in the program audio protocol stack to discover the SPS program number(s). MPS is either numbered or, without a number, is MPS by default. The program stream number is described in reference document (4), Audio Transport (see chapter 4). Every Layer 2 frame contains audio program service headers within which the program stream PDUs each have a stream number.

Advanced data services on IBOC may be discontinuous. That is, a particular service may be idle for seconds or for hours. Information passes when it is available and scheduled to transmit. There is no beacon to inform the receiver of the presence of the service. In contrast, FM subcarriers act as beacons identifying their presence. If the receiver senses the subcarrier energy and is able to detect and make sense of the information stream, the service is discovered. No matter when a receiver tunes in, it can immediately discover the subcarrier service.

To address this concern, iBiquity revealed a conceptual plan for service discovery that qualifies as a service outside the NRSC-5 standard. It consists of a new SIS message for rapid service identification as well as a Service Information Guide conveyed by iBiquity's AAS.

Recall that the SIS messages are carried on the PIDS logical channel and are rotated among several different message types in a rotation selected by the station operator. The idea behind the Service Information Message (SIM) is to communicate information about the audio programs, such as the program type and special information about the audio. The type of surround sound encoding could be indicated in the SIM. Similarly, the SIM could communicate information about each advanced data service that is "open" on the data channels. A receiver seeking a particular advanced data service would quickly learn whether it can monitor the chosen station and expect to see the service when information is finally transmitted.

The concept for the Service Information Guide (SIG) involves using the greater capacity of the AAT channel to provide richer information about the services open on the channel. In addition to service identification by name and ID number, it can communicate service parameters, such as the assigned port number, content formatting (e.g., MIME), conditional access parameters, pointers to alternative sources (e.g., other stations), and such. A service schedule could be transmitted to enable receivers to conserve power between successive transmissions of a periodic service.

SIG is envisioned as having a low-volume "basic" format that is looped frequently for rapid discovery, and a larger format "enhanced" guide structure that is looped less often. The basic SIG files would use Port Number 0x0020. Enhanced files could be mapped to other ports, as indicated in the service's basic file.

Telematics

iBiquity promotes the first generation of advanced data services under the heading of *telematics*. According to globaltelematics.com, the term telematics comes from a French contraction of the words for telecommunication and computing—*telematique*. Within the class of telematics, iBiquity includes traffic, navigation and automotive services. These three subsets fall within the more recent context of telematics, which the automotive industry employs to more narrowly describe the application of computing and telecommunications to improve highway transportation. In addition, iBiquity includes in the class of telematics other services that are not necessarily automotive in nature, such as subscription audio, mobile entertainment, and specialized data targeted to specific groups of users.

Traffic Message Channel

iBiquity has created an automotive telematics service that delivers traffic information to the vehicle dashboard. The Traffic Message Channel (TMC) is a generic service that supports traffic messaging information from a variety of service providers to a variety of mobile products. By the end of 2006, Traffic information provider Clear Channel Traffic had launched the HD Radio version of its service in 48 markets in the U.S., paralleling the almost 20 times slower RDS TMC already in use. Consumer electronics manufacturers, including Audiovox, TomTom, Garmin, and Cobra, were already offering TMC-capable navigation products for RDS receivers and began offering HD Radio TMC devices.[5] In addition to providing up-to-the-minute traffic information, the TMC can deliver timely weather forecasts and provide updates to the data contained in navigation systems. For instance, navigation systems contain data describing points of interest, including such things as restaurants stores and services. Point of Interest (POI) data transmitted over the TMC keeps subscribers' navigation system maps up-to-date. In addition to Clear Channel Traffic, other traffic and mapping service providers partnering with iBiquity include Traffic.com, TrafficCast, SmartRoute Systems, Shadow Broadcast Services, Navteq, and TeleAtlas.

iBiquity offers service providers further expansion of the traffic and navigation features as consumer devices are developed to take advantage of them.

- *Traffic text-based streaming data service that provides text-based reports of accident information, flow information as well as traffic notices.*

- *Traffic data in objects files with graphics/JPEG images representing traffic incident and flow information delivery to in-vehicle multimedia display screens on non-navigation systems.*

- *Traffic database update service for mobile delivery of large files to on-board navigation system.*

- *POI updates for mobile delivery of local/regional points of interest information. Tremendous commercial opportunity for database and service providers—to provide a rotation of sponsored business.*

---

[5] *This Week in Consumer Electronics*, June 5, 2006, Reed Business Information.

- *Automotive-based services including customer relationship management to deliver targeted messages to classes of vehicles on a regional basis.*

- *Customer retention programs to deliver targeted messages and incentives to targeted vehicles (such as new vehicles or classes of vehicles, like all leased vehicles).*

- *Fleet-specific services or private label service to deliver premium information to targeted vehicle platforms or fleets.*[6]

End of the IBOC Stack

In this chapter and the previous one, we covered the data path on the side of the IBOC protocol stack, SIS and AAT. As new applications are developed, the workings and implementations of Advanced Data Services will be threshed out in the marketplace. This chapter concludes the second section of the IBOC Handbook, discussing the NRSC-5 IBOC standard and its protocol stack from the top layer down.

---

[6] Source: *ibiquity.com/automotive/new_mobile_service_providers.*

SECTION III

IMPLEMENTATION

12 AM Considerations

With the end of the previous chapter, we have completed our detailed tour of the NRSC-5 protocol stack. As shown, the theory of operation of In-Band On-Channel transmission is a complex yet elegant solution to the challenging problem of working within the existing AM and FM bands. The next section of this book is devoted to more practical issues. To put an IBOC signal on the air there are several considerations to which the broadcast engineer must attend. First, AM and FM transmission facilities each have specific design constraints that affect the quality of the IBOC digital signal. This chapter discusses the AM broadcast facility considerations. Chapter 13 follows with a discussion of FM considerations. Second, the station's program sources must be connected to the transmission facilities. Chapter 14 discusses the topology of the broadcast facility and how it connects with the IBOC transmitter.

AM IBOC

IBOC for AM is similar in many respects to its FM counterpart, but has several subtle, yet significant differences. All of these distinctive characteristics are direct responses to the unique characteristics of the AM channel. A good understanding of the requirements for acceptable AM IBOC performance requires consideration of several phenomena that may not appear to be related at first glance. We try to present each of these subjects in an orderly fashion and ask you, the reader, to "hold that thought" more than once in this chapter. If we are successful, we will have woven it all together by the end.

This chapter borrows much information from the earlier, pioneering research of many engineers and engineering firms, including contemporary published works of Clark Communications, duTreil, Lundin & Rackley and Hatfield & Dawson. A list of all those deserving credit could fill the pages of this book. Also, the first draft of this chapter was penned by Grady Moates, of Loud and Clean Broadcast Science, who collaborated with the author, David Maxson. David hails the collaboration in the Acknowledgements section at the front of the book. However, it is the accumulated work of generations of AM broadcast facility designers that makes AM IBOC possible and upon which this chapter relies.

In this chapter we touch on these issues:

- Analog audio bandwidth

- Antenna impedance and bandwidth

- Antenna improvements

- AM nighttime operations

Our AM Legacy

The term "legacy" is often used in technology circles to describe an old technology that has been eclipsed by modernity, but is still widely used. In "legacy" AM broadcasting, the information to be transmitted is simply a single audio-frequency waveform (0 to 10 kHz audio spectrum). Amplitude Modulation (AM) is a means of varying the power (amplitude) of a radio frequency carrier in order to transmit information while maintaining the frequency of the carrier constant.

To transmit an AM broadcast signal, the amplitude of the radio frequency (RF) carrier is caused to vary as a linear function of the audio waveform being transmitted. In this simplest form of wireless transmission of audio, observation of the signal in the time domain on an oscilloscope allows us to actually see the audio waveform impressed upon the RF carrier—the *RF envelope*. This form of transmission is relatively spectrum-efficient, utilizing only twice as much RF bandwidth as the highest frequency being transmitted.

In the reception of such an AM broadcast signal, a simple legacy receiver "detects" the carrier envelope using a diode that only responds to one excursion of the RF carrier, either positive or negative. By low-pass-filtering the resulting RF pulse train, a good copy of the original audio waveform can be recovered. The simplicity of this concept allows schoolchildren to build receivers using rocks out of the back yard and coils of wire wrapped around cardboard toilet-tissue rolls. Easy access to these crystal radio sets helped fuel the dawn of the broadcast industry. Advances in receiver technology have produced newer methods of demodulating an analog AM carrier, but the hybrid IBOC signal was designed to not render obsolete any legacy analog receiver topologies, including these early crystal radio receivers. This characteristic of a new technology protecting the continued performance of an old technology is "backward compatibility."

Backward Compatibility

Paralleling the history of aviation, we might equate the crystal radio with the primitive bi-plane. By the 1980s, technology had advanced, more quickly for aviation than for AM broadcasting. AM receivers had entered the jet age, abandoning the crystal detector, for the most part, for more sophisticated integrated circuit (IC) -based detection. Envelope detection of the crystal radio, while still fully compatible with AM reception, took a back seat to IC-based synchronous detection. The capability of cheap ICs prompted AM broadcasters to attempt a leap into the jet age to be more competitive with FM, through the introduction of AM stereo. All of the schemes for AM stereo attempted to be 100% backward compatible with crystal radio sets. The stereo separation information was modulated onto the AM carrier utilizing phase modulation. Three of the four systems effectively increased the channel bandwidth required for successful reception by a factor of two or so. To operate with a greater bandwidth, AM facilities required more careful design and adjustment. Many trees gave their lives to dissemination of information about AM antenna system bandwidth improvement to enhance the accuracy of the received stereophonic sound-stage and reduce distortion of the received audio.

In addition to the legacy monaural audio channel, AM stereo transmits a second channel of intelligence—the left-minus-right (L-R) stereo difference component. AM stereo utilized FM techniques (phase modulation) to transmit the L-R, which do not readily crosstalk into the reception of legacy AM mono audio. The practical results of inadequate bandwidth in AM stereo systems is primarily very poor stereo performance, and secondarily some added audio distortion of the mono audio.

What is Bandwidth, and What Does It Mean to Us?

To discuss AM bandwidth issues, there are a number of different bandwidth concepts which must be considered, including:

- Necessary bandwidth,
- Regulatory bandwidth,[1]
- Bandwidth Ratio,
- Transmitter Output-match bandwidth, and
- Pattern bandwidth.

Let's review their definitions now, and then we'll return to the concepts later to see how they affect AM IBOC performance.

---

[1] "Regulatory" bandwidth is a term of convenience employed to make the point in this chapter, having no official definition.

Necessary Bandwidth

This is a term defined by the ITU as (paraphrasing) the minimum bandwidth required to convey the transmitted information at the prescribed quality. The ITU defines bandwidth in two ways: 1. "Necessary," as just explained, and 2. "Occupied," which is the 99% power bandwidth.[2] Emissions other than within the necessary bandwidth are either "out-of-band" emissions that are a consequence of the modulation process but are not necessary, and "spurious" emissions outside the out-of-band emissions whose elimination has no impact on the quality of the transmission.

It is important to recognize that the Necessary Bandwidth of a signal may or may not overlap the necessary bandwidth of another signal sharing the spectrum, as is explained further in this discussion.

Regulatory Bandwidth

In order to maximize the number of wireless broadcast services while minimizing interference to any channel from any other, the spectrum must be allocated efficiently. Consider for example the U.S. FM band. Each channel is spaced 200 kHz from the center of one to the centers of its nearest neighbors. Each station within a channel transmits a signal whose necessary bandwidth is conveniently approximated by Carson's rule: bandwidth of a signal frequency modulated with a broad spectrum of frequencies equals two times the sum of the maximum frequency deviation (75 kHz) and the maximum modulating frequency (say, 20 kHz for monaural). Thus, the bandwidth of the initially authorized FM signal is estimated at about 190 kHz, extending some energy leaving an approximately 20 kHz wide guard-band between adjacent signals. With stereo modulation, as well as with higher-frequency subcarriers, Carson's rule suggests the bandwidth could exceed 200 kHz. (See Figure 12.1 for the power spectral density of two adjacent stereo FM signals.) The

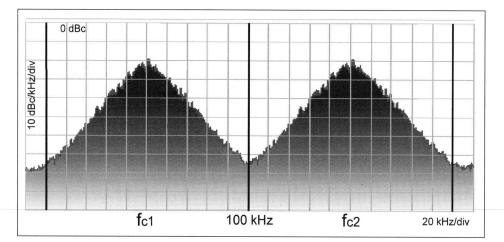

Figure 12.1 Necessary Bandwidth of FM Signal

[2] *Recommendation ITU-R SM.328.10 Spectra and Bandwidth of Emissions (Question ITU-R 76/1)*, International Telecommunications Union, 1999.

FM mask permits substantial out-of-band and spurious emissions to occur within the necessary bandwidth of adjacent channels, but the necessary bandwidth of the mono FM signal does not overlap the necessary bandwidth of adjacent channel signals. Transmitting stereo and subcarrier signals in the baseband expands the tails of the FM spectrum to where they will overlap with a first-adjacent channel station's signal. However, due to the spacing of first-adjacent stations geographically, and to the low levels of each station's far sidebands, the potential for interference is minimized. Effectively, each adjacent-channel station occupies independent spectrum.

In the AM band, a similar allocation system is utilized, except that each channel center in the U.S.A. is spaced 10 kHz from its nearest neighbors, while each analog station on a channel transmits a signal that is effectively 20 kHz wide. Figure 12.2 shows the power spectral density (per 300 Hz) of AM signals at two audio bandwidths. On the left is an NRSC-2 compliant AM signal occupying ±10 kHz of spectrum, corresponding to its 10 kHz audio bandwidth. A stylized outline, shown in the circle on the left plot, is utilized in subsequent figures to make them clearer. The right-hand plot of Figure 12.2 shows an actual power spectral density (per 300 Hz) measurement of an AM station running 5 kHz audio bandwidth, for comparison. This is the bandwidth employed in the 5-kHz hybrid IBOC mode, shown without the digital signals present.

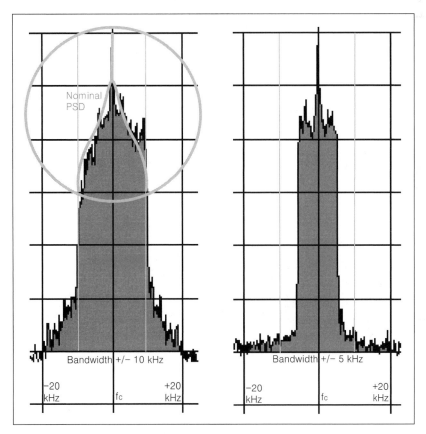

Figure 12.2 Necessary Bandwidth of AM Signal

Rather than having an inherent guard-band between channels as in mono FM, or slight overlap with FM stereo, the entire upper sideband necessary bandwidth of one AM signal overlaps the entire lower-sideband necessary bandwidth of the next higher channel. The same is true for the lower sideband of the signal and the upper-sideband of a signal in the next lower channel. (See Figure 12.3) Even second adjacent stations have no FM-mono-like guard-band between them. (See Figure 12.4)

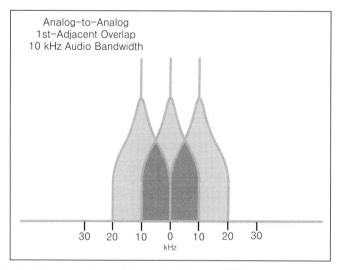

Figure 12.3 Overlapping Necessary Bandwidths of 1st-Adjacent AM Signals

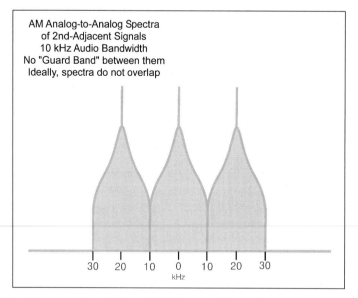

Figure 12.4 Abutting Necessary Bandwidths of 2nd-Adjacent AM signals

Bandwidth Ratio

Bandwidth Ratio is a term used to define the relationship between the carrier frequency and the spectrum needed for modulation. Bandwidth Ratio is the quotient of the Necessary Bandwidth over the carrier frequency expressed as a percentage. It turns out that the higher this percentage, the more difficult it is to achieve maximum power transfer and minimize phase and amplitude distortion across the Necessary Bandwidth.

Once again, let's consider the FM band first. Assuming a 150 kHz Necessary Bandwidth, the bandwidth of each station expressed as a percentage of its frequency is 0.153 % at 98 MHz, the center of the band. While this value varies with frequency, from 0.139% at 108 MHz to 0.17% at 88 MHz, it never exceeds 0.2% anywhere in the FM band.

The bandwidth of analog AM transmissions with a 10 kHz frequency response is effectively 20 kHz. The bandwidth of an AM station at 1120 kHz (the center of the band) is 1.79%. This value varies substantially with frequency, from 1.18% at 1700 kHz to 3.7% at 540 kHz! Not only are these values an order of magnitude higher than those in the FM band, but the variation across the AM band is much greater than with FM.

The useful bandwidth of an antenna is determined by its physical characteristics. As the bandwidth ratio of a signal rises, it becomes more challenging to achieve uniform antenna performance across the Necessary Bandwidth of the signal. Thus, the practical consequence of these high AM bandwidth ratios is that it is much more difficult to achieve a good impedance match between a transmitter and an antenna system across the span of the Necessary Bandwidth.

Transmitter Load Bandwidth

Transmitter Load Bandwidth is the bandwidth at which the load impedance presented to a transmitter by the antenna system remains within a chosen tolerance. Because the antenna impedance varies with the frequency being transmitted, the load it presents to the transmitter varies with the modulation of the transmitted signal. A perfect match that provides maximum power transfer is generally only achievable at the exact carrier center frequency. The resistance and reactance variations presented by a typical antenna system will distort the relationships in amplitude and phase of the carrier and the energy in the modulation sidebands.

Pattern Bandwidth

This is the bandwidth at which the pattern of a directional antenna remains the same as the pattern at center frequency, within a specified tolerance. Pattern Bandwidth restrictions introduce phase errors and amplitude errors in the AM signal that vary geographically with respect to the antenna. The pattern of a directional AM multitower array varies with the instantaneous frequency that is being transmitted. Since the modulated carrier of a legacy AM station occupies a range of spectrum that is 20 kHz wide, the pattern of the station is inadvertently modulated by the energy in the modulation sidebands. This effect can be minimal with some antenna systems, and quite unacceptable with others. Reception of a legacy analog signal, and particularly analog stereo, can be affected by Pattern Bandwidth limitations. Likewise, as an IBOC receiver is moved through the coverage area of a station, reception of an AM IBOC signal can be inconsistent and unpredictable due to Pattern Bandwidth shortcomings.

Propelled from the Jet Age to the Space Age

AM stereo was not the great success that many had hoped it would be. With all the new digital media delivery systems inundating the marketplace, our oldest wireless broadcasting service needed another technological retrofit to help it maintain its relevance. In the eyes of the crystal radio builder from the 1920s, today's digital signal processing capability provides the AM broadcast service with tremendous power that would have been the stuff of science fiction. In sci-fi terms, replacing analog AM stereo with the introduction of AM IBOC technology could be analogous to replacing a jet engine with a futuristic space propulsion system. The level of sophistication required of the facility manager makes a quantum leap along with the level of sophistication of the technology.

Use of the AM band, however, presents two major challenges– backward compatibility and bandwidth. As we have seen, the AM channel allocation scheme severely imposes restrictions upon how wide necessary bandwidth can be and remain useful on a crowded band. Meanwhile, the laws of physics greatly stress transmitter load bandwidth and pattern bandwidth. The IBOC hybrid system is quite elegant in the way that it deals with these limitations, so much so that it borders on the magical.

Invisible IBOC

The IBOC system uses many OFDM subcarriers, which in the aggregate appear to behave like an amplitude-modulated signal. Unlike the AM stereo system, which used phase modulation to convey the left-minus-right stereophonic information, the hybrid AM IBOC system comprises 156 OFDM subcarriers that are independently and rapidly switched in phase, and in some cases, amplitude. These subcarriers coexist in the same spectrum as, and immediately adjacent to, the host analog signal. Since, in the composite, the AM IBOC waveform is amplitude variant, one would expect that a legacy AM receiver would detect the IBOC energy along with the legacy analog signal, adding noise to the derived audio. This is where the first bit of design magic comes in.

As discussed in Chapter 8, the hybrid AM IBOC system is designed with symmetrical, redundant, opposing subcarrier pairs within the host channel, which are designed to perfectly cancel in an analog detector. It works superbly when an engineer connects a transmitter to a good dummy load. Unfortunately, not many folks can receive a signal that is not radiated from an antenna. Hence, to preserve the noise-canceling characteristic of the IBOC digital signal, the AM antenna bandwidth must be optimized.

Antenna System Effects on the AM IBOC Signal

As with many things in life, the hybrid AM IBOC signal can be degraded in more than one way. Impairments can cause less reliable digital performance and degrade analog reception of the analog host signal. They also can contribute to the generation of spurious emissions.

Transmission impairments can cause the IBOC receiver to work harder to decode the digital signal. Such impairments can effectively waste error-correction overhead on correcting problems caused at the transmitter site. When the distortions caused by the transmission of the signal force the receiver to utilize more error correction to overcome them, there is less room for errors caused by signal path problems, noise, or interference. With a higher error rate comes a higher probability that the IBOC receiver will "fall back" to analog more often.

Transmission impairments affecting the digital IBOC signal also can contribute to interference with reception of the analog host and interference with the reception of stations on other channels. A distorted digital signal can impose an irritating noise in the received program material of the analog host. Impairments can also increase out-of-band and spurious emissions, creating what may appear as "adjacent-channel interference" to other stations, when it is in fact unwanted emissions falling on the necessary bandwidth of another signal.

All of these results can degrade the listener's experience in one way or another. Listeners using analog receivers can become fatigued and seek out alternative sources of entertainment if noise is added to the programming by a poorly tuned AM IBOC system. Listeners trying out a new AM IBOC receiver might be unimpressed if their first listening experiences include frequent fall-back to the analog signal. This experience could be exacerbated if the fall-back to the analog signal is also compromised by noise caused by distorted IBOC subcarriers. Careful attention to system bandwidth issues is the key to ensuring good listener experiences with both IBOC and analog receivers.

A rigorous description of the AM IBOC system at the physical layer is provided in Chapter 8. Here is a simplified recap of the information found there. The hybrid AM IBOC signal is composed of three groups of digital subcarriers. Each subcarrier group comprises two sets of subcarriers, arranged as mirror images of each other above and below the carrier center frequency. These are referred to as upper sideband (USB) and lower sideband (LSB) subcarriers. To make these discussions easier to visualize, (See Figure 12.5) we'll refer to the areas within 5 kHz of a channel center as the "inner" sideband area (officially called the Tertiary sidebands). We'll call the areas between 5 and 10 kHz removed from the channel center as the "outer" sideband area (officially, the Secondary sidebands), and the areas between 10 and 15 kHz removed from the channel center as "outermost" sideband area (officially, the Primary sidebands).

Outermost, or Primary, Sidebands

The Primary group of IBOC subcarriers extends from –10,356.1 Hz to –14,716.6 Hz and from +10,356.1 Hz to +14,716.6 Hz, occupying the outermost sideband area of the desired signal. For comparison, the desired outermost subcarriers fall on the inner sideband area of the first adjacent channels. (Figure 12.5) Note how these fall between the first and second adjacent channel frequency. The outermost subcarriers therefore also fall on the second adjacent channel's outer sideband area. The outermost subcarrier group is composed of 25 discrete subcarriers in each sideband—USB and LSB. These subcarriers convey the "core" audio data, which is described further in Chapter 4. Being farthest removed from the desired center frequency, the outermost subcarriers may be most affected by antenna system problems. Consequently, to best protect the core audio information from transmission problems, the antenna system must be operating optimally all the way out to the Primary subcarriers. The outermost subcarriers are sufficiently removed from the analog host signal that they do not cause interference to reception of the analog host (which we'll call "self-interference"). In contrast, there is the potential that the outermost subcarriers of one station may affect the quality of reception of another station. This effect has been minimized by the careful selection of the power level of the Primary sidebands, which falls below the FCC and NRSC-2 emissions limitations.

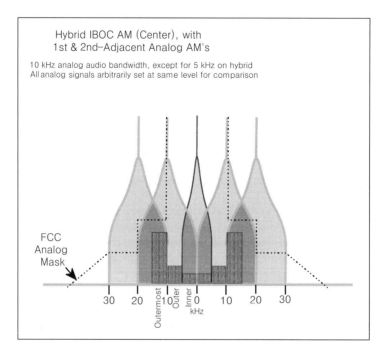

Figure 12.5 AM IBOC 1st and 2nd-Adjacent Sidebands in U.S. Frequency Assignments

Outer or Secondary Sidebands

The Secondary subcarrier group, our "outer" group, extends from –5,087.2 Hz to –9,447.7 Hz and from +5,087.2 Hz to +9,447.7 Hz. The USB and LSB groups consist of 25 discrete subcarriers each. These subcarriers convey a portion of the "enhanced audio" data. Being between 5 and 10 kHz offset from the desired center frequency, the outer subcarrier group may fall within the passband of an analog receiver tuned to the host. In a poorly adjusted transmission system, they could be picked up as self-interference to analog receivers. Analog detection in IBOC receivers may be more immune to such noise because it can sharply filter the high frequency noise caused by distorted Secondary sidebands (>5 kHz).[3] Also, in an IBOC receiver, analog detection of distorted

---

[3] As discussed elsewhere in this book, analog AM radios typically roll audio off beyond 5 kHz anyway, so the risk of interference to analog reception from misadjusted Secondary bandwidth is less than one might expect with the rare wideband analog radio.

IBOC subcarrier energy is further minimized by the nature of a digital receiver—it can equalize the incoming signal to minimize the effects of distortion across the Necessary Bandwidth.

Inner or Tertiary Sidebands

The Tertiary sideband group, our inner sideband area, extends from the −4,723.8 Hz to −363.4 Hz and from +363.4 Hz to +4,723.8 Hz. It also consists of 50 discrete subcarriers, 25 in the lower sideband and 25 in the upper sideband. These subcarriers convey the remainder of the enhanced audio data. In a poorly adjusted transmission system, this subcarrier group can cause serious self-interference to reception of the analog signal on both analog and digital receivers because it falls within the ±5-kHz analog signal bandwidth. However, in the IBOC receiver, analog detection of the distorted IBOC subcarrier energy is further minimized by the nature of a digital receiver—it can equalize the incoming signal to minimize the effects of distortion across the Necessary Bandwidth.

The pair of Reference subcarriers at ±181.7 Hz, and the two pairs of PIDS (Primary Identification Service) data subcarriers at ±4,905.5 Hz and ±9,629.4 Hz complete the IBOC digital signal.

Self-Canceling Sidebands

We return to the virtual IBOC magic mentioned earlier. The reference subcarriers and the Secondary and Tertiary subcarrier groups are transmitted in symmetrical pairs about the channel center frequency.[4] Each lower sideband subcarrier and its mirror-image upper sideband subcarrier transmit the same information, with equal amplitude signals that are instantaneously 180 degrees out of phase. There are three benefits to this scheme:

- 100% data redundancy under impaired reception conditions gives the IBOC receiver two complete, identical copies of the enhanced audio, in different portions of the channel. An asymmetrical interferer may only affect one sideband, leaving the other unscathed for recovering enhanced audio data.

- An analog receiver acquiring a perfect hybrid IBOC signal will exhibit no additional noise in the analog audio, because each subcarrier pair will sum to zero amplitude in the analog detector.

- An IBOC receiver acquiring a perfect hybrid IBOC signal sees the analog energy as an interferer to the inner digital sidebands. With some mathematical sleight of hand, the IBOC receiver can cancel the analog AM energy and recover perfect copies of the enhanced audio data on the Tertiary and Secondary sidebands.

That's 53 subcarrier pairs each dancing in lock-step—53 separate and simultaneous perfect energy cancellations, 173.2 times each second, like matter and anti-matter quietly combining and leaving nothing behind. Absolute magic!

---

[4] See also Chapter 8 for a deeper discussion of complex conjugates and noise cancellation.

Unfortunately, the moment the IBOC signal leaves the AM transmitter, it has already been subjected to imperfections and distortions. Asymmetrical antenna system loads within the host channel will increase the noise level on analog receivers by altering the symmetrical, out-of-phase behavior of each subcarrier pair so that they do not fully cancel in the analog receiver. The residual energy that does not cancel is then detected and adds noise into the analog audio. For this reason, antenna system behavior within the Necessary Bandwidth of the analog signal must be carefully controlled for best performance. Likewise, the IBOC digital receiver must work harder to recover the digital in the presence of the analog and other sources of interference. Optimizing system bandwidth out to ±10 kHz takes maximum advantage of the symmetrical properties of the Secondary and Tertiary sidebands. Optimizing out to ±15 kHz also benefits the recovery of the Primary sidebands, but to a lesser degree, since they are not symmetrically modulated.

Transmitter Loading and System Bandwidth

In order for the IBOC subcarriers in the Secondary and Tertiary groups to properly cancel upon detection in the receiver, the antenna system must preserve their symmetry as it passes the IBOC signal. Hence, even if the antenna bandwidth distorts the passband, there are benefits to ensuring the distortion to the USB and the LSB subcarriers is symmetrical. Because of the nature of the creation and detection of double-sideband signals, preserving the amplitude and phase relationships of the USB and LSB requires a peculiar form of symmetry.

Hermitian Symmetry

The term used to describe the necessary antenna system characteristics is *Hermitian Symmetry*, which gets its name from Charles Hermite, a brilliant French mathematician. Hermitian Symmetry occurs when the complex impedance at each frequency in the upper sideband is equal to the complex impedance at the corresponding lower sideband frequency, but with a reversal of the sign of the imaginary component.[5] Table 12.1 shows a perfect Hermitian Symmetry for a hypothetical ±5 kHz AM passband. Note how the values at ±2.5 kHz match, with the only difference being the sign on the imaginary (j) components. Likewise, the ±5 kHz values are similarly symmetrical. To be symmetrical, the actual values in the table are irrelevant, as long as USB and LSB retain their symmetry. [Of course, it pays to keep the real and imaginary components (the resistance and reactance) as close to the ideal as possible, so the resulting Voltage Standing Wave ratio (VSWR) is not too high.]

Table 12.1 has four rows. The first indicates the center frequency and two pairs of frequency offsets from center frequency. The second row contains a set of (simulated) impedance values for each frequency. For a Smith chart, the center frequency is normalized to unity, and the other frequencies are normalized to the center frequency—appearing in the third row. The final row presents the resultant VSWR at each frequency offset, with respect to center frequency.

---

[5] The reversal of sign of the imaginary component is referred to as complex conjugation. This is discussed in more detail in Chapter 8.

It may not be practicable to obtain a perfect Hermitian match between all USB frequencies and their corresponding LSB frequencies. Consequently, a Hermitian Symmetry tolerance must be established so the broadcast engineer can determine whether the results are "close enough" to be considered Hermitian symmetrical. Rackley and Dawson have suggested[6] that adequate Hermitian symmetry has been achieved when the VSWR of one sideband load impedance does not exceed 1.035:1 when normalized to the complex conjugate of the corresponding sideband load impedance on the other side of the carrier frequency. What does this mean? It is best visualized on a Smith chart, which comes a little further on in this discussion. (Figure 12.7, bottom image) Basically, for any data point on the chart, there is another point that is its complex conjugate. If we measure and plot the complex impedance at a certain frequency in the USB and at the same frequency in the LSB, we want the data point in the LSB to be within a certain distance of the complex conjugate of the USB data point, that is, within a certain distance of perfect Hermitian Symmetry. That distance is the recommended tolerance of 1.035:1 VSWR. This is one of those places where we'll ask you to "hold that that thought." We'll get back to the chart as we discuss making measurements.

When the load impedance conforms to the symmetry specification across the bandwidth, each OFDM subcarrier in the lower portion of the Secondary and Tertiary subcarrier groups will, upon AM detection, satisfactorily cancel with its counterpart in the upper portion of the subcarrier groups. This is because each corresponding USB and LSB subcarrier pair has been subjected to nearly equal amplitude change and nearly equal but opposite phase shift. The Hermitian Symmetry tolerance is a much more stringent requirement than was necessary during the AM stereo era, and can be a challenge to achieve in many real-world antenna systems.

While Hermitian Symmetry is desirable throughout the IBOC passband, it is most critical where the analog and digital energy co-exist—the inner-sideband area ±5 kHz about the channel center frequency.[7] Asymmetry in the outer-sideband area of the channel (±5–10 kHz) might affect an analog receiver with unrestrained audio bandwidth (a rare commodity in the world of consumer electronics). Most analog receivers attenuate the information in this range quite severely, either in the Intermediate Frequency stage of the receiver, if the receiver has one, or in the audio section of the receiver.

Frequency	–5 kHz	–2.5 kHz	f_c	+2.5 kHz	+ 5 kHz
Impedance	40.0 –j 9.0	46.0 –j5.0	50.0 ±j0.0	46.0 +j5.0	40.0 +j9.0
Normalized to 50 ohms	0.8 –j0.18	0.92 –j0.1	1.0 ±j0.0	0.92 +j0.1	0.8 +j0.18
VSWR	1.35:1	1.15:1	1.0:1	1.15:1	1.35:1

Table 12.1 Example of Perfect Hermitian Symmetry within a ±5 kHz AM Passband

[6] "AM IBOC Ascertainment Project" NAB Broadcast Engineering Conference, slides, CPB_IBOC_NAB_2005.pdf, duTreil, Lundin & Rackley/Hatfield & Dawson joint venture.

[7] For the purposes of this discussion we are overlooking the optional 8-kHz audio bandwidth mode available on AM IBOC. The logic applied to the analog 5-kHz bandwidth can be extended to 8 kHz, if the 8-kHz mode is selected.

Measurement

Another important factor is *where* the system bandwidth measurements are made. The symmetrical load required for best performance is the load presented *at the output of the RF Power Amplifier* within the transmitter, not at the output connector of the transmitter. Unfortunately, it is not generally convenient to make these measurements directly at the RF PA output. Tube-type transmitters generally exhibit very high impedances at the anode of the tube, and solid-state transmitters generally exhibit very low impedances at the power combiner summing point, making them difficult to measure with RF bridges designed to work in the 20- to 600-ohm range. For this reason, transmitter manufacturers provide phase shift information for the output network design used in each model of transmitter, so that measurements may be made where the output of the transmitter connects to the transmission line. The results are then corrected for the known phase shift of the transmitter's output network. By disconnecting the transmission line from the transmitter output connector one can measure the impedance at the input of the line. (See Figure 12.6)

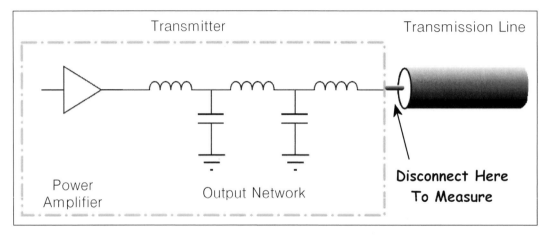

Figure 12.6 Breakpoint for Impedance Measurement of AM Transmission System

The analog and IBOC signals from the RF Power Amplifier(s) are phase shifted when traveling through the output networks of the transmitter, as well as the RF transmission line between the transmitter output connector and the antenna system input. Because of this phase shift, measurements made at any other point in the antenna system are difficult to evaluate. Fortunately, Phillip Smith developed a visual tool in the mid-20th century that makes such evaluation simple at any point in the system. In his honor we call it the "Smith chart."

The antenna system impedance across the signal bandwidth is plotted on the Smith chart. A plot that conforms to the Hermitian symmetry specification resembles an arc, nearly a semi-circle, that is positioned in a certain way. First, the Smith chart has a central axis that represents a resistive, nonreactive load (horizontal line, Figure 12.7). Resistance increases from left to right, with the center point representing a normalized unit resistance. The ideal Hermitian arc is centered on, and symmetrically straddles, the resistance axis. (See left image of Figure 12.7) With the resistance line as the axis of symmetry, each point on the arc above the axis has a corresponding point at the same distance and reverse angle below the axis. The below-axis curve mirrors the above-axis curve.

Armed with the output network phase shift information from the transmitter manufacturer, the load impedance may be rotated about the reference point so that it is not symmetrical about the resistance axis. (right image of Figure 12.7) In this example, the arc has been rotated 135 degrees toward the source to represent the 135-degree phase shift away from the power amplifier caused by the transmitter output network.

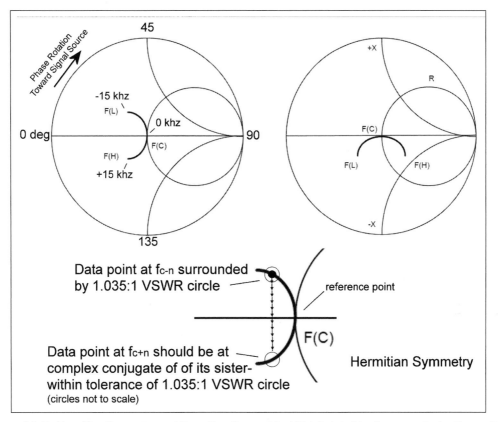

Figure 12.7 Hermitian Symmetry and Hermitian Symmetrical Plot Rotated to Compensate for Transmitter Matching Network. (Based on material by duTreil, Lundin & Rackley, Inc.[8])

[8] Rackley, *BEC Proceedings 2004*.

In addition to managing Hermitian symmetry with a 1.035:1 tolerance between conjugate pairs, Rackley and Dawson further suggest limiting the passband VSWR relative to that of the center frequency. Within ±10 kHz they recommend a VSWR of less than 1.20:1, and inside ±15 kHz, less than 1.40:1, as reasonable objectives to provide adequate performance.[9] Figure 12.8 illustrates the relationship between the impedances at frequency offsets from carrier frequency and the impedance at center frequency. This figure uses the Smith chart to show the center frequency impedance as the normalized reference value. The radial distance from center frequency impedance to the impedance at another frequency is the VSWR with respect to center frequency.

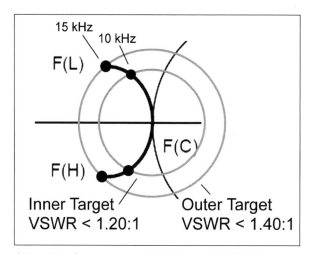

Figure 12.8 Example of Hermitian Symmetry on Smith Chart with VSWR Circles Normalized to Impedance at Center Frequency.

Furthermore, symmetry can be achieved in two ways—Table 12.1 shows one way, with sideband resistances lower than center-frequency resistance. This produces the left-facing "smile" curve shown in Figures 12.7 and 12.8. Alternatively, the sideband resistances could be higher than center-frequency resistance, flipping the smile to the right. Field experience has confirmed that most present-day transmitters provide better performance with sideband resistances lower than the center frequency resistance.[10]

As mentioned earlier, channels in the AM band occupy a much larger segment of spectrum than in the FM band when expressed as a percentage of the center frequency.

Acceptable antenna performance for legacy monaural AM signals occupying the 20 kHz channel is problematic enough, especially at the low end of the band. Using the bandwidth ratio calculation,

---

[9] Recall from Chapter 9 that there are also specifications for gain and group delay flatness of the AM IBOC passband.

[10] For a related discussion see "Evaluation and Improvement of AM Antenna Characteristics for Optimal Digital Performance," *NAB Broadcasting Engineering Conference Proceedings 2004*, Ronald Rackley, 2004

the 30 kHz-wide hybrid IBOC signal occupies a bandwidth that is 5.6% of the channel center frequency at 540 kHz. Achieving the more stringent performance specifications required for acceptable IBOC signal transmission over a 30 kHz passband is challenging for a number of reasons. Here are a few examples:

- Real-world vertical radiators exhibit resistance and reactance changes with frequency that are not symmetrical about the center frequency over a range of electrical heights.

- Real-world arrays of vertical radiators exhibit mutual impedances among the towers which multiply the asymmetries of the individual radiators.

- Real-world matching networks, comprising coils and capacitors connected with tubing within metal enclosures, introduce irregularities in the impedance-vs.-frequency transfer curve due to open turns or shorted turns in coils, stray capacitance between components and the enclosure, undesired inductance in tubing connections, transformer-like coupling between nearby coils, and the like.

- Real-world trap circuits designed to mitigate intermodulation between nearby antenna systems, as well as multiplexing networks at multistation sites, introduce asymmetrical impedance "lumps" in the transfer curve.

The dark arts of AM antenna design are thoroughly understood by a few wizards in the broadcast industry. The AM broadcaster would be wise to seek expert advice on making the most of IBOC on his AM facility.

Analog's Regulatory Vicious Cycle

In addition to their impact on antenna design and tuning, the impedance/bandwidth issues also create challenges with respect to spectral occupancy and the regulatory environment. A little history may clarify. The channel allocation scheme within which the AM industry operates was devised at a time when audio processing technology was in its infancy; audio peak limiting to prevent over-modulation was the only technique in widespread use, and no pre-emphasis of high frequencies was used. Because the energy distribution of typical program material at the time exhibited a rapid fall-off in amplitude as audio frequency increased, channels 20 kHz wide were spaced 10 kHz apart, with each channel sharing spectrum with its first-adjacent upper and lower channels. By geographically separating first-adjacent channel station assignments based on the expected power spectral density of the AM sidebands, the potential for first-adjacent channel interference was minimized. This would work quite nicely if radio signals would conform to governmental regulation, tidily filling but not exceeding the appropriate coverage area and keeping the spectral occupancy to 1930s expectations. As the number of stations increased, interference between first-adjacent stations also increased. With the growth in the number of AM stations, an AM station's coverage steadily evolved from being defined by signal strength (signal-strength-limited coverage) to being defined by interference boundaries (interference-limited coverage).

Stations attempted to increase their usable coverage area with more aggressive audio processing techniques, which increased the density and intensity of sideband energy, further increasing the potential interference between first-adjacent stations. When receiver manufacturers attempted to mitigate interference by reducing the bandwidth of receivers, broadcasters attempted to regain the resultant high-frequency response loss with pre-emphasis.[11] Over time, aggressive audio processing and extreme pre-emphasis of high frequencies changed the power spectral density of the AM waveform in a way that conflicted with the scheme of station allotments and channel spacing. The resulting cacophony in the AM band may have helped to fuel the mass exodus of listeners to FM stations beginning in the 1970s.

In 1987, the NRSC adopted its NRSC-1 standard, *NRSC AM Preemphasis/De-emphasis and Broadcast Audio Transmission Bandwidth Specification.*[12] This was the industry's attempt to end this tug-of-war between receiver manufacturers and broadcasters—between the interests of interference management and audio fidelity protection—through standardization of pre-emphasis and audio bandwidth constraints. Then the National Radio Systems Committee developed and promulgated the NRSC-2 Standard, *NRSC-2 Emission Limitation for AM Broadcast Transmission*, which created an "RF Mask", because even after applying the audio mask of NRSC-1, there remained "characteristics of the AM transmission process that may cause the RF occupied bandwidth to exceed a nominal 20 kHz."

NRSC-1 Purpose

"The purpose of the NRSC[-1]voluntary standard is to create a transmission/reception system where (1) AM broadcast stations will know, with certainty, the likely audio response characteristics of AM receivers, and (2) AM receiver manufacturers will know, with certainty, the likely audio response characteristics of AM broadcasts. A "matching" of preemphasis and de-emphasis is expected to improve the consumer's overall satisfaction with the technical quality of listening to AM radio... This document also describes a specification for the maximum audio bandwidth transmitted by AM broadcast stations... [which will] reduce second-adjacent channel interference and thereby lead to (1) a significant reduction of second-adjacent channel interference as perceived on "wideband" receivers; (2)a corresponding increase in the interference-free service areas of AM stations; and (3)an incentive for the further building of dual bandwidth AM "wideband" receivers...(First Adjacent channel interference considerations may continue to discourage the building of single bandwidth "wideband" receivers; however, the extent and nature of this form of interference has not been fully studied by the NRSC.)"

---

[11] This is a classic example of a positive feedback mechanism, the likes of which are postulated in the global warming debate and from which equally dire predictions of total catastrophe are predicted. The appearance of IBOC may provide the revolutionary technological shift that chokes off the feedback loop and provides a way out for the medium.

[12] Available at www.nrscstandards.org.

Even in 1987, the NRSC acknowledged the difficulties posed by the first-adjacent channel problem (sidebar). If we knew a half-century ago what we know now, things might have been different, but it is obviously far too late to make wholesale changes to the station assignment scheme, and the laws of physics are quite immutable.

IBOC transmissions literally take this process to a new level. Continuing with the historical review, when the National Radio Systems Committee was developing the NRSC-1 audio mask, it anticipated nonlinear RF products that would not be corrected by the imposition of an audio mask: "It should be noted that the operation of nonlinear AM Stereo systems theoretically may produce phase modulation components outside the desired RF bandwidth. The NRSC will examine this phenomenon with the goal of determining whether such components exist and, if they do exist, whether they are objectionable."[13] The ultimate RF mask published in NRSC-2 "accommodates these transmission characteristics."[14] The mask effectively grandfathered certain transmitters' characteristics by adding the "shoulders" on either side of the channel that are 35 dB lower than the unmodulated carrier, and extend outward to ±30 kHz. This area beneath the "stop-band" was not intended to be part of the Necessary Bandwidth, rather, to be occupied, if needed, by out-of-band or spurious emissions. The stop-band is the area outside and above the mask within which no emissions are permitted. Although not part of the Necessary Bandwidth, if the energy between 10 and 30 kHz remained below the −25 to −35 dBc steps, it remained below the stop-band threshold and was permissible.

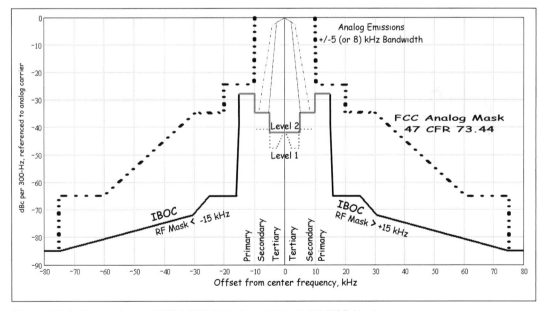

Figure 12.9 Comparison of FCC/NRSC-2 Mask and Hybrid AM IBOC Mask

---

[13] Footnote #3, NRSC-1.

[14] NRSC-2.

The Primary hybrid IBOC subcarriers occupy just some of the –25 dBc region of the NRSC-2 RF mask. (Figure 12.9) This places one station's Primary IBOC subcarriers in the region shared by the first and second-adjacent channels. (Figure 12.10) It falls within part of the inner sideband of the first-adjacent channel, which is also part of the outer sideband of the second-adjacent channel. Also, the Primary sideband is only 5 kHz removed from the edge of the third adjacent channel signal. This was a challenging design constraint—minimize the power of the Primary sidebands to eliminate or limit interference to fringe areas as much as possible, while having sufficient power to provide useful IBOC service for the host station.

Intermodulation Products

The intermodulation products between the Primary IBOC subcarriers and the host analog carrier with its analog modulation sidebands appear as a cluster of energy about 15 kHz wide that falls between the center frequencies of the second- and third-adjacent channel. (Figure 12.10) Because of the way that all these signals must coexist in the tightly packed AM band, minimizing corruption of the hybrid IBOC signal is essential to robust digital reception and minimum interference to reception of adjacent-channel signals.

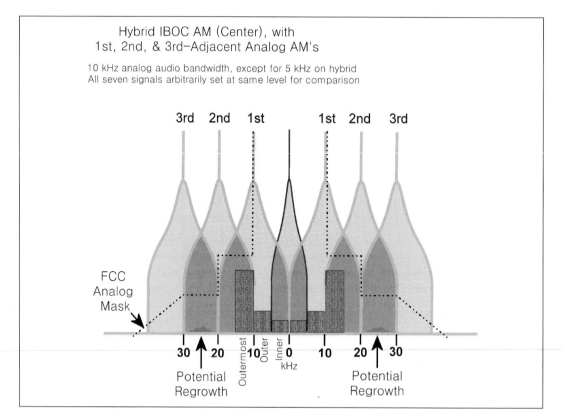

Figure 12.10 AM IBOC 1st, 2nd and 3rd-Adjacent Sidebands in U.S. Frequency Assignments

AM IBOC Transmitter/Exciter Alignment

This chapter is focused on performance issues arising from imperfect systems "outside the box," meaning external to, and downstream from, the transmitter. First-generation AM IBOC systems have an additional alignment procedure that is critical to good performance, because those AM transmitters are not capable of generating the IBOC subcarriers internally.

First-generation AM IBOC exciters create the hybrid AM IBOC signal at low level, and then decompose it into amplitude and phase components. These two components are connected to the transmitter at two inputs called "magnitude" (applied to the audio input of the transmitter) and "phase" (an RF signal applied in place of the RF oscillator stage of the transmitter). Precise alignment of these two signals at the power amplifier output must be achieved for proper system performance. Variations in the magnitude and phase signal paths within each transmitter require that each system be aligned in the field. In this procedure, the amplitude and the delay of the magnitude signal are trimmed to match the phase signal. As the adjustments approach optimum, the engineer will note that the digital/analog intermodulation products centered at ±25 kHz from the channel center will drop sharply in level. Because both the amplitudes and the phases of the two signal components must be aligned, these adjustments can be time-consuming.

Second-generation techniques generate the hybrid IBOC RF signal in the transmitter, eliminating the need for these adjustments. An outboard IBOC signal generator may deliver a Low Voltage Data Signal (LVDS), representing the IBOC waveform digitally, to digital processing circuits internal to the transmitter; digital-to-analog conversion within the transmitter creates the waveform. Ultimately, a fully integrated analog/IBOC transmitter may have inputs for the analog and digital audio program streams, and perform all IBOC signal generation internally.

Pattern Bandwidth

Finally, the shape of the coverage pattern emitted from a directional AM array of antennas changes with frequency. Such an antenna system has two or more antennas, spaced some distance(s) apart. Each antenna receives a portion of the power output from the transmitter, and the phase and amplitude of the signal applied to each of the towers is manipulated to achieve an interference pattern such that the signals from all the towers add in some directions and subtract in others. It works precisely as planned, at the center frequency of the channel.

However, radio frequency energy, being of the same stuff as visible light, travels at the same speed, about 300,000 kilometers per second. Consider a single cycle of an AM radio signal at 1000 kHz. It is almost exactly 300 meters in length as it travels through space. However, at 985 kHz this wavelength is 304.5 meters, and at 1015 kHz it's 295.6 meters. If one divides the 300-meter wavelength by 360 degrees, each degree of this wave occupies about 833 millimeters. The wavelength of the whole spectrum of a hybrid IBOC signal varies more than ±5 electrical degrees between the ±15 kHz edges of Necessary Bandwidth.

Because the antennas of the array are separated by a fixed physical distance, the electrical spacing, in degrees, varies across the Necessary Bandwidth. The array is tuned to provide the optimal directional pattern at center frequency, but the pattern will vary, depending upon the instantaneous frequencies being emitted. Moreover, the transmission lines, which carry the hybrid signal to each antenna, have a physical length, which translates into an electrical length, which also varies with frequency—introducing more deviation from the ideal. As if that were not enough, the components in the phasing and branching networks which divide the power to each antenna and control the phase of the signal in each tower also vary with frequency—introducing still more error. The further in frequency an emission is removed from the center frequency of the channel, the greater the deviation from the desired phase and amplitude values. This causes phase and gain offsets, depending on frequency, and depending on orientation with respect to the antenna array. Figure 12.11[15] illustrates the change in a peanut-shaped AM pattern between center frequency and the ±15 kHz edges of the Necessary Bandwidth. It shows how, at some azimuths from the array, one 15-kHz edge may be rolled off to a level less than that of the center frequency, while the opposite 15-kHz edge of the signal might see an increase over the level of the center frequency. Such a plot shows how much the "frequency response" of the hybrid IBOC signal will vary depending on location, but it does not characterize any phase shifts that also occur in the process.

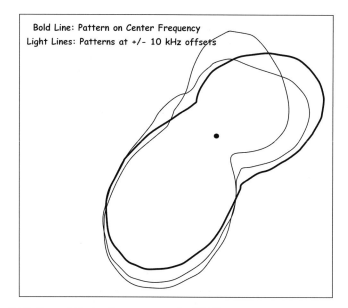

Figure 12.11 An AM Pattern at Center Frequency and ±15 kHz

---

[15] The plot is derived from a pattern shown in slides *AM IBOC Ascertainment Project*, prepared by the duTreil-Rackley/Hatfield-Dawson Joint Venture, April 2005, presented at the NAB Broadcast Engineering Conference and posted at www.hatdaw.com.

These pattern bandwidth errors have two kinds of detrimental effects upon the hybrid IBOC signal. First, the digital signals in the Primary subcarrier group can be so disturbed in phase and amplitude within the primary coverage area of the pattern that the receiver cannot decode them as reliably, if at all. Fortunately there are cues within the digital signal that enable the receiver to perform channel equalization to compensate for phase and amplitude distortions, but these will only do so much before the signal is compromised beyond repair. Second, interference to reception of adjacent channels can increase dramatically; in particular, the amplitude of the Primary IBOC subcarriers, removed from the center frequency by ±10 to ±15 kHz can be orders of magnitude higher than the pattern design calls for in the "null" areas of the pattern, which are designed to protect other co- and adjacent-channel stations.

To provide guidance on setting a station's pattern bandwidth, iBiquity recommends two tolerance specifications.[16] The pattern bandwidth tolerances describe how much the pattern at a 15-kHz offset is permitted to deviate from the pattern at center frequency—in amplitude terms and phase terms. It is recommended that at any point on the ground, the amplitude at ±15 kHz should be within ±2 dB of the amplitude of the center frequency. This is the pattern bandwidth amplitude flatness tolerance. The pattern bandwidth phase flatness tolerance is recommended to be limited to a ±5 μs variation in group delay to ±15 kHz.

Rackley and Dawson's AM study produced some observations about the challenges of AM antennas. Among them are the cautions that with nondirectional antennas, "poor performance may result from electrically short antennas, poor skirt-feed design, and odd vertical geometry or other antenna mounting or structural geometry." With respect to directional antennas, they suggest, "poor performance may result from high RSS/RMS ratio, nonoptimum feed system, possible parameter inversion, unfortunate choice of system geometry."

To summarize, impedance/bandwidth issues make it extremely difficult to control interference to second- and third-adjacent channels because of the nature of regulatory bandwidth and station assignment. For this reason, extreme measures may be called for to ensure that good performance is achieved throughout the passband of the IBOC signal, to prevent interference and to maximize useful coverage of the IBOC signal.

High-Performance, Precision Antenna Systems

Evaluation and adjustment of AM antenna systems has traditionally been accomplished with little more than an RF bridge and a tunable RF generator. While time-consuming, and labor-intensive, these traditional methods can be used to fine-tune an existing system for IBOC operation. However, the work will go much more quickly and smoothly if a network analyzer is available. As each network component is changed, the network analyzer provides a complete visual representation of impedance throughout the 30-kHz-wide passband of interest, a task that requires at least ten discrete measurements with an RF bridge and generator set.

[16] Rackley, 2004.

To re-state the IBOC bandwidth performance goals mentioned earlier:

Suggested Bandwidth Performance For All AM Stations[17]		
Frequency Range with reference channel center	Hybrid IBOC spectrum component	Desired performance
−15 kHz to −10 kHz	Primary subcarriers	VSWR below 1.40:1
+15 kHz to +10 kHz		
−10 kHz to −5 kHz	Secondary subcarriers PIDS subcarriers	VSWR below 1.20:1
+10 kHz to +5 kHz		
−5 kHz to +5 kHz	Tertiary subcarriers Analog sidebands Reference subcarriers	Hermitian Symmetry Impedance at any frequency must be within 1.035:1 of the complex conjugate of the impedance at the mirror image frequency
Suggested Bandwidth Performance For Directional AM Stations[18]		
Pattern bandwidth performance such that, throughout the major coverage areas of the pattern(s), amplitude response is within ±2 dB and phase response is within 5µs (or ±27°)[19] across the entire 30-kHz-wide passband.		

Table 12.2 Recommended AM Bandwidth Performance Goals

The last requirement (suggested by Rackley and Dawson) is far beyond the scope of this chapter to address. Directional systems that do not conform to the ±2 dB, ±27° specification can be expected to tax the ability of the IBOC receiver to decode the digital signal throughout much of the protected coverage contour of the station. Owners and operators of complex directional AM antenna systems are encouraged to contact their consulting engineering firm for assistance. However, it is likely that there are existing directional AM antenna systems that cannot be adjusted to provide adequate performance as built and licensed.

Real-world antenna systems will probably fall into six general categories:

- *Adjustment*
  Most omni-directional facilities and some simple directional systems will require only simple adjustments to existing matching networks (low expense),

- *New Components*
  Some omni-directional facilities and directional systems will require additional networks (low to moderate expense),

---

[17] Rackley, 2004.

[18] Rackley 2004.

[19] *So, What Have We Learned, or What to Do about IBOC*, Stephen S, Lockwood, slides, May 26, 2005, Hatfield and Dawson, www.hatdaw.com.

- *Redesign and Replace Subsystems*
  Some directional systems will require redesign of the phasing and branching systems (moderate to substantial expense),

- *Modify Licensed Pattern*
  Some directional systems will require re-licensing with modified patterns using the same geometric antenna arrangement (substantial expense), and

- *New Array*
  A few directional systems may require a different geometric arrangement of antennas, modified patterns and a new phasing and branching system (great expense).

- *Multiplexing*
  Each channel transmitted through a multiplexed antenna system must be considered separately; depending upon the spacing of the channels within the band and the design of the networks, each of the channels served could fall into any of the first five categories.

Improvements to facilities in the first three categories can usually be accomplished quickly and at moderate expense by making simple adjustments to existing matching networks or by adding impedance-sloping and phase-rotation networks to the existing systems. Dramatic improvement in performance can sometimes be achieved by simply altering the phase shift of a matching network by as little as 20°. Phase shifts of more than 50° will usually require an additional network. Frequently, an additional network is desirable to alter the curvature of the impedance plot on the Smith chart to achieve Hermitian symmetry. In some cases, an additional network also allows the impedance plot to be shifted so that a "high-Q" resonant circuit can be added to reduce the reactance spread at passband extremes, or to correct narrow-band "lumps" in the impedance plot.

Directional antenna systems sometimes provide unexpected opportunities for improvement within the phasing and branching system. Design techniques that were acceptable in the early days of the industry can sometimes be updated at nominal cost to make dramatic improvements in performance with the new, wider hybrid IBOC signal. Each antenna system is unique, and requires a custom-designed solution.

AM Nighttime Operations

The ionosphere was a good friend to the AM band at the dawn of broadcasting, providing service at night to citizens in far-away towns, villages and wildernesses who had no local service. Reflection of Medium Wave signals from the ionosphere back to earth, referred to as "skip" or "skywave" reception, is more of a mixed blessing in the 21st century. With local AM service available in nearly every nook and cranny of the United States, as well as much of the world, skip reception causes unexpected interference to local service from distant signals on co- or adjacent-channels.

The advent of hybrid AM IBOC has complicated this picture because the new Primary IBOC subcarrier energy in the outermost-sideband has the potential to cause interference in several modes:

- Additional groundwave interference to desired skywave reception of distant signals.

- Additional skywave interference to local co- and adjacent-channel groundwave signals caused by the IBOC subcarriers of the skywave interferer.

- Additional skywave interference to adjacent-channel skywave signals.

Many comments were received by the FCC, but by the end of 2004 the National Association of Broadcasters (NAB) and most major broadcasting companies had endorsed nighttime operation with IBOC. The FCC authorized nighttime hybrid AM IBOC operation in 2007.

Nighttime AM Testing and Analysis

Among the evidence used by those who endorsed AM nighttime operation were several rigorous tests conducted by iBiquity. These tests were presented to the NAB's Ad Hoc Committee on Nighttime AM IBOC, which after careful review, recommended that NAB endorse nighttime operation of AM IBOC, with the stipulation that the FCC agree to handle on a case-by-case basis any instances of unexpected interference. The test methodology, analysis and conclusions were published by iBiquity in 2003, and are available at the NRSC website. These tests include:

1. "AM Nighttime Compatibility Report" (May 23, 2003), in which audio recordings were made in a laboratory of several receivers' audio outputs under carefully controlled conditions designed to simulate various Desired-to-Undesired (D/U) signal ratios. These recordings were then played in a carefully controlled listening environment to panels of listeners who scored each recording according to its perceived quality. Simultaneously, studies were conducted analyzing the D/U ratios of AM and hybrid IBOC signals, based upon computer-generated contours of field intensity based upon the FCC M3 metric curve groundwave data and the FCC 50/50 skywave field strength curves. To estimate the proportion of the listening population affected, the subjective listening test results were applied to the D/U coverage patterns of existing radio stations that might be expected to receive additional interference from first-adjacent skywave IBOC signals.

2. "Field Report – AM IBOC Nighttime Performance" (October 20, 2003), in which nighttime IBOC-to-IBOC interference between two first-adjacent Class "A" clear channel stations was evaluated. The two stations used identical transmission facilities. Interference tests were conducted in both summer and winter, using driving tests over fixed routes, using automated data gathering equipment and software to log the field intensity of the desired signal as well as on the upper and lower first adjacent channels, GPS location of the vehicle and its distance from the transmitter location of the desired signal, and the digital/analog mode status of the IBOC receiver. Graphs of all these parameters were then created, and maps were created showing the locations at which the IBOC receiver lost lock on the digital signal.

3. "Field Report – AM IBOC Nighttime Compatibility" (October 31, 2003), in which nighttime IBOC-to-Analog interference between two first-adjacent Class "A" clear channel stations was evaluated. The two stations used identical transmission facilities. Interference tests were conducted in both summer and winter. Audio recordings were made of several receivers' audio outputs while toggling the IBOC transmissions of the two stations on and off on a predetermined schedule. Recordings were made in many locations grouped into five geographic areas, allowing characterization of first-adjacent skywave IBOC interference to groundwave analog reception, first-adjacent groundwave IBOC interference to skywave analog reception and first-adjacent skywave IBOC interference to skywave analog reception. The selection of the five geographic areas also allowed testing of the interference rejection capability of typical AM receiver ferrite-loop antennas, which exhibit significant directionality. 262 audio recordings gathered from these tests were then played for several groups of listeners, who graded each listening experience.

These tests produced a great volume of data, and distilling this data into useful information was a daunting task for the researchers. A careful reading of all three reports shows that the tests were well-conceived and completed, and the results of all three tests, when considered together, supported approval of nighttime AM IBOC operation.

Tests 1 and 3 show that listener perception of skywave first-adjacent IBOC interference to analog reception appears to be limited to fringe ground-wave coverage areas that already exhibit high levels of co-channel interference. Nearly all of these areas are outside the Nighttime Interference-Free (NIF) contour of the desired station. The worst cases revealed by Test 1 are regional stations on channels that are first-adjacent to crowded regional or local channels; even so, most of this interference is outside their NIF contour.

Test 2 shows that IBOC reception of a desired station is minimally affected by an interfering first-adjacent skywave IBOC signal. The maps provided show the locations at which the IBOC receiver could not decode the digital signal. There are two maps for each vehicle route—one with and one without the undesired skywave IBOC signal. It can be seen from a comparison of the two maps for each route that the IBOC receivers behave almost identically throughout the desired station's 5 mV/m contour, and that digital reception becomes less consistent outside this contour whether or not a first-adjacent IBOC interferer is present.

These and other reported results lead the authors of the reports to state, "The performance tests established [that], although digital coverage will not extend to all areas currently able to receive analog signals, the digital signal will cover the primary service areas of these stations. These performance tests also demonstrate that the first adjacent digital skywave interference will not materially impact nighttime digital coverage." Furthermore, "Overall, the complete conversion to IBOC at night will not noticeably degrade primary groundwave service in a vast majority of listening areas."

All of these tests were performed using the complete hybrid AM IBOC signals in all cases, both for desired and undesired signals. Because the hybrid AM IBOC system was designed to allow independent control of the energy in the upper and lower primary subcarrier groups, substantial amelioration of those few interference issues is possible.

Clark & Associates Engineering provided an extensive analysis of the various factors having an impact upon the potential for interference with nighttime IBOC, and suggested that about 80% of existing stations could operate with normal-power hybrid AM IBOC at night without increasing interference to distant first-adjacent stations. Clark also states that half of the remaining stations (10% of all AM stations) might reduce the transmitted power in one or both primary sideband groups allowing these stations to operate at night without increasing interference to distant stations. Finally, Clark also suggested a simple means of determining which stations were eligible to begin IBOC operation at night, and an orderly regulatory process to employ at the onset of such operation.

Conclusion

AM IBOC broadcasting has several disadvantages compared with FM IBOC. Its narrower bandwidth reduces the data capacity of the IBOC signal. The AM channelization scheme creates overlapping channel assignments, already a problem for analog service. The high bandwidth ratio creates an impedance/bandwidth problem that distorts the signal across its bandwidth.

iBiquity's design of the hybrid AM IBOC system ingeniously makes the most of an awkward communications channel, employing complementary Secondary and Tertiary upper and lower sidebands to maximize compatibility and performance. This design also utilizes carefully selected digital power levels that conform not only to the analog AM mask, but also to the spirit of protecting service within each station's protected contour. The AM broadcaster must take maximum advantage of the features hybrid AM IBOC has to offer by ensuring the antenna system is well-tuned and optimized for the hybrid signal. The directional antenna pattern should be examined by a qualified professional to optimize its pattern bandwidth.

13 FM Considerations

In this chapter we discuss the implications of hybrid[1] IBOC operation on FM transmission facilities. The goal of hybrid FM IBOC signal generation and amplification is to radiate analog and digital signals that are as undistorted as possible and are in proper power relationship to each other. As discussed in Chapter 9, the emissions of the hybrid FM IBOC signal must also protect the FM band from excessive out-of-band emissions. In this chapter, we examine the various forms of hybrid combining for FM IBOC signals.

Antennas and Combining

Unlike AM antenna systems, the FM antenna does not have such a significant impact on hybrid IBOC operation. The bandwidth ratio of the FM signal makes the process of emitting hybrid IBOC signals fairly simple, at least from the standpoint of antenna design. Where the AM IBOC signal bandwidth is about 2–6% of the frequency, the FM IBOC bandwidth is only about 0.4% of its frequency. In contrast to the AM antenna discussion in the previous chapter, its smaller bandwidth-to-frequency ratio enables the FM antenna to maintain reasonably constant performance across the bandwidth of the FM IBOC signal.

---

[1] In this chapter, the term *hybrid* refers to the combined analog and digital waveforms of the IBOC signal in hybrid operation. A distinction is made between the analog-only signal, the digital-only signal, and the hybrid signal as they appear in various stages of the combining process.

Since the process of generating a hybrid FM IBOC signal is not so constrained by the antenna design, there is considerable flexibility in how the hybrid signal is transmitted. Fundamentally, the digital signal can be generated either separately from, or in composite with, the analog host signal. If the analog and digital signals that form the hybrid FM IBOC signal are created separately, they are *combined* at some stage in the transmission process. This approach allows older analog equipment to work in concert with newer digital gear. Alternatively, to synthesize the composite hybrid signal in one device, a broadcaster must acquire a new exciter with hybrid IBOC capability, sometimes referred to as FM+HD or FM/HD capability by manufacturers. Let's give this capability the name *co-generation*, meaning a common digital-to-analog converter jointly generates the analog and digital signals in a common digital-to-analog converter. With co-generation, there is no point in the signal chain where the analog and digital signals are separate waveforms; therefore they do not require some form of combining. The term applied to the amplification of a co-generated source is *common amplification*. This refers to the fact that the digital and analog components of the hybrid signal are amplified together in the same amplifier. Common amplification also applies to *low-level combining*—the combining of a separately generated digital and analog signal at a low level in the early stage of amplification.

The main distinction between the IBOC digital signal and its analog host is how the modulation places constraints on the amplification process. The classic analog FM signal operates at a continuous power level while its frequency is *modulated* to convey information. It has a *constant envelope*, meaning the amplitude of the signal is essentially invariant when modulated. In contrast, the OFDM multicarrier modulation scheme has a degree of amplitude variation in its waveform.

Analog FM Signals

In its most basic form, the FM *carrier* signal is modulated only by the electrical representation of the analog monophonic audio channel (designated left-plus-right, L+R, in a stereo FM signal). Increasing its complexity, the FM signal is permitted to carry 2-channel stereo information and *subcarriers* along with the L+R audio. The stereo information is conveyed with a stereo *pilot* signal and a left-minus-right (L-R) audio signal component. For the purposes of this discussion, the stereo pilot and the 38-kHz L-R component are not considered FM subcarriers. FM subcarriers carry special audio programs or data in a manner that is not received by normal mono or stereo FM radios. Together, the L+R, pilot, L-R, and any subcarriers are combined into a single *composite baseband* signal.

To be put on the composite baseband, the L-R and the subcarriers are converted to ultrasonic electrical signals that appear in the baseband above the audio frequencies occupied by the L+R audio. (The stereo pilot appears at 19 kHz, which is in what is conventionally considered the high end of the audible spectrum; however, as a practical matter it is inaudible to the FM listener.) Figure 13.1 illustrates the spectrum of the composite baseband.

So far, this information would be familiar to the FM enthusiast and the broadcast engineer. The modulation process, in which the frequency modulated signal is generated from the composite baseband signal is also familiar to the FM engineer. Figure 13.2 shows functionally how the baseband is converted to an FM radio signal. The carrier is a signal that, when it is not modulated, resides on the center of the radio station's channel (center frequency, or f_c). When modulated, the

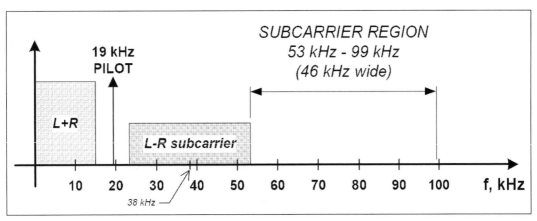

Figure 13.1 Composite Baseband (Source: NAB)

frequency of the carrier varies in proportion to the voltage of the baseband signal. In the time domain, this appears as the stretching and compressing of the carrier's sinusoidal wave (depicted in exaggerated form on upper right of Figure 13.2). The perfect sine wave of the quiescent FM carrier gets distorted as the carrier is slewed up and down in frequency. Recalling the discussion

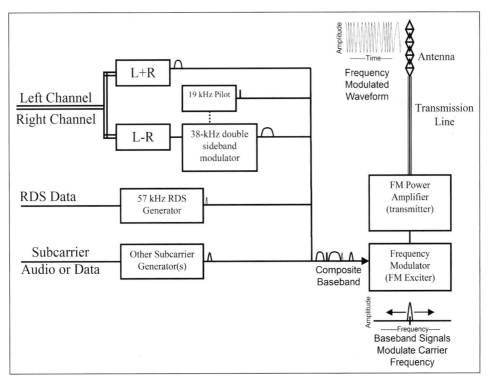

Figure 13.2 Creation of an FM Signal

of complex waveforms and the FFT in Chapter 7, a nonsinusoidal signal in the time domain can be described as the sum of a set of sinusoidal components, observable in the frequency domain. In other words, the spectrum of the modulated FM waveform is composed of energy in various frequency bins—its sidebands—depending on the nature of the baseband signal modulating the carrier and the deviation of the carrier frequency.

Mathematically, the FM spectrum has infinite sidebands.[2] Practically, only the most significant sidebands are necessary to recover a low distortion copy of the original baseband signal. Figure 13.3 shows the spectra of two FM signals. One contains a heavily modulated program source, showing the triangular power spectral density. The carrier reference is preset to the top of the display, not the top of the trace. At 60 kHz offset from carrier frequency, the level is about 55 dB below the carrier reference (–55 dBc/kHz). At 120 kHz offset, the power spectral density level[3] is about –80 dBc/kHz or lower. This is typical of an FM broadcast signal under heavy modulation, but can vary due to the spectral characteristics of the baseband signal modulating the FM carrier and the amount of modulation (frequency deviation) of the carrier.

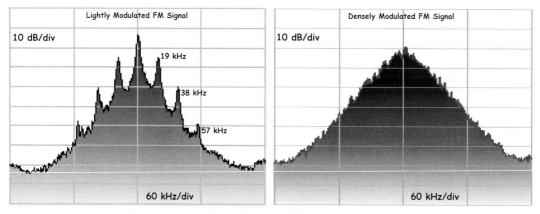

Figure 13.3 Spectra of Frequency Modulated Broadcast Signals

The other spectrum plot in Figure 13.3 shows the spectrum of a signal lightly modulated by voice or low-level program material. The baseband signal's spectrum is dominated by the 19 kHz stereo pilot. Consequently, the modulated FM spectrum is dominated by energy at 19 kHz and its multiples—38 and 57 kHz are evident, with a slight rise also visible at 76 kHz. This illustrates relationship between the modulating frequency and the theoretically infinite sidebands.

---

[2] T. Rappaport, *Wireless Communications Principles and Practice*, 2nd Ed., Prentice Hall, 2002; Agilent Application Note *Spectrum Analysis 150-1 Amplitude and Frequency Modulation*, and a multitude of other texts treating the basics of the FM waveform.

[3] When describing spectral density, the bandwidth of the measurement must be identified. For FM IBOC measurements, the specified bandwidth is 1 kHz. Hence, spectral density levels are reported in decibels, with respect to the carrier reference power, per kHz of spectrum—dBc/kHz.

Recalling the discussion of Necessary Bandwidth in the previous chapter, sidebands that are not critical to the recovery of the baseband signal may be present in the spectrum, and they are deemed to be outside the Necessary Bandwidth. These are called the out-of-band emissions because they are a product of normal modulation, but are not necessary to recover the baseband in reasonable quality. The Necessary Bandwidth of an FM broadcast signal is at least 190 kHz wide. In addition to out-of-band emissions, there are spurious emissions, which are emissions that are not inherently part of the modulation process but may be generated by unintended mechanisms in the transmission process. Harmonics and intermodulation products, among others, are spurious emissions.

Historically, FM transmitters were quite capable of producing substantial out-of-band and spurious emissions, which required the imposition of an RF mask to ensure the emissions' compatibility with other stations allotted a place in the band. Contemporary broadcast equipment can generate very clean signals; however, the rules for station allotment and spectral occupancy still anticipate substantial out-of-band emissions.

To transmit an FM signal is a fairly simple process. A transmitter and an antenna are connected by a length of transmission line (Figure 13.2). Because of the small bandwidth ratio, the antenna is readily constructed as a broadband device, easily passing the Necessary Bandwidth of the station with, at most, nothing more than an initial tune-up. The antenna size is manageable, with its one or more *bays* mounted on a tower. Stand-alone FM systems are typically "plug-and-play" affairs, with no extraordinary attention necessary to impedance/bandwidth issues.

The process is made more complex when additional hardware is inserted in the transmission chain. Notch or wide bandpass filters intended to protect the transmitter from ingress of unwanted signals are typically so far removed from the Necessary Bandwidth that their impact on the analog signal is of no concern. Combining systems designed to radiate multiple FM stations from a common antenna can be a little more complicated.

Multistation Combining

The two common methods of combining multiple FM stations are the branch and the balanced combiner. The branch combiner, also called star or starpoint, simply passes each transmitter through its own bandpass filter (or notch filters) and joins the outputs of each transmitter's filters at one point. (Figure 13.4) Attention is paid to the lengths of the branches that connect each transmitter-filter pair to the starpoint. A quarter-wavelength branch improves the match with the starpoint. This combiner is inexpensive, compact, and often good enough for combining a few stations.

The balanced, also called constant impedance, combiner provides a more uniform, higher-isolation combining environment. (Figure 13.5) The balanced combiner is typically used with a larger number of stations than the branch combiner and in circumstances where the isolation characteristics of the balanced combiner are desired. It employs 90-degree hybrids and bandpass filters—one set for each signal to be injected into the stream. The fundamental building block of the injector is the 90-degree four-port hybrid, also called a *quadrature hybrid*, which has peculiar characteristics that RF engineers exploit. (Figure 13.6) One input to a quadrature hybrid yields two outputs, with one output in quadrature (shifted 90 degrees) with respect to the other. This hybrid is symmetrical in both axes; one input to any port yields two outputs from a pair of opposite ports.

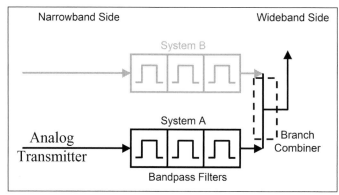

Figure 13.4 Branch Combiner

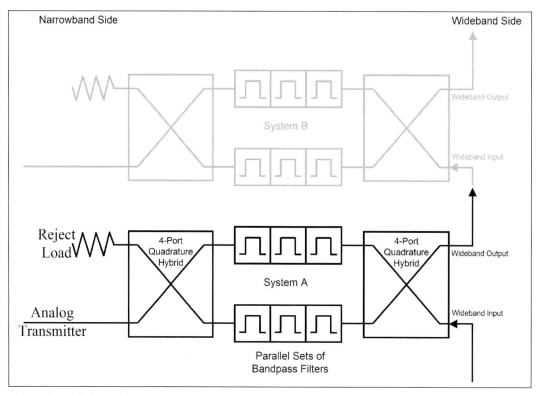

Figure 13.5 Balanced Combiner

In reverse, two identical inputs to two corresponding ports results in one output to an opposite port. (See right half of Figure 13.6) Because of the phase-shifting, phase-canceling effects of the hybrid, any reflected energy resulting from load mismatch or reverse path signals does not reflect back to the input port, but passes to the fourth port, where a load may be placed to absorb the unwanted energy. This is called the isolated port. The load on this port isolates the input port from outside influences, creating the conditions from which the name "constant impedance" derives. With a good load on the isolated port, the single-port input sees it as the hybrid's impedance, despite any variations in the loads on the two output ports.

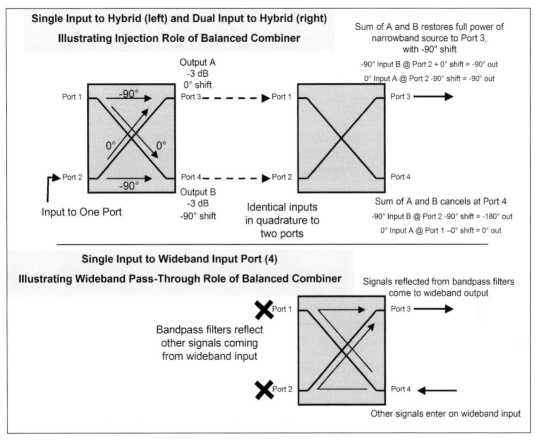

Figure 13.6 90-degree Hybrid

The quadrature hybrid plays a role in three IBOC combining schemes, so it is worthwhile to explore it a little more before opening up the discussion on FM IBOC hybrid combing.

In the multistation balanced combiner, the combiner unit that directs a single signal into the combined signal flow is sometimes called an *injector*. The *narrowband* side of the injector takes in a single station's transmitter output. The first element of the injector is a hybrid that splits the transmitter output in two. (Figure 13.5) The resulting two outputs are fed into parallel bandpass filters. The two bandpass filters pass duplicate copies of the signal, with one in quadrature with the other, to another hybrid. By using these two filter outputs as inputs to the second hybrid, the second hybrid reverses the process that split the signal in the first hybrid. The second hybrid takes the two identical inputs, which are still in quadrature, and combines them into a single output. Why bother? Here is where the cleverness of the balanced combiner is revealed.

The output of the second hybrid is connected to a cascade of these injectors, each adding one station's signal to the transmission line. This is the *wideband* end of the injector, because it will pass the signals of all stations driving the antenna. The combined output of the second hybrid is emitted through one port, downstream toward the antenna. At this point in the description, the injector has done nothing useful. It has simply split, filtered, and recombined the signal, delivering it to the output port of the injector. Three ports of each hybrid are utilized for the injected station. The fourth port plays a crucial role on the injector's second hybrid.

Recall that when a single port on a hybrid is driven by a signal, it splits the signal out to two ports. Consider the hybrid on the wideband side of the injector. What if we drive the fourth port with the signals of other stations in the combiner cascade? If the fourth port were driven with the signals of other stations on the combiner, the energy into that one port would be directed to the two opposing output ports. These output ports would be the filter ports on the hybrid, ports 1 and 2. (Figure 12.6, wideband side hybrid) The filters, however, block the incoming signals from port 4 because they are outside the filters' passband. The filters reflect the incoming energy back to the hybrid, which dumps the energy out the downstream port (3).

In summary, the balanced combiner injector uses two ports on the second hybrid to pass the injected station on toward the antenna, while the fourth port takes in the other signals on the wideband side and routes them also toward the antenna. There is also a convenient symmetry to the injector that is exploited as an IBOC combining method. Our FM signal driving the narrowband input to hybrid port 2 passes through the injector and comes out port 3 on the wideband-side hybrid. This sequence is mirrored if a signal is applied to the opposite narrowband input (1); it comes out the opposite wideband output (4) and travels in the reverse direction on the wideband transmission line. Further on in the chapter, we'll get back to this as a means of injecting the IBOC digital signal in a multistation situation.

Combining Digital Signals in the FM Band

Because FM antennas typically have substantially wider bandwidths than the FM signals require, they are not as problematic as AM antenna systems. However, as part of the due diligence required to develop an IBOC conversion plan, the FM engineer should review the specifications and any performance tests of the antenna system to ensure that it is optimally tuned for IBOC operation. It may be prudent to perform a field tune-up of the antenna to ensure it is performing as well as possible. Review the gain flatness and phase flatness requirements of the FM IBOC signal, discussed in Chapter 9 (Table 9.3). For the most part, it is easy to radiate a hybrid IBOC signal from an FM antenna. Getting the digital and analog signals to coexist elsewhere in the transmission plant is another matter.

In the following sections we'll look at common amplification with co-generation and low-level combining, plus split-level, and high-level combining. Also, we'll discuss dual-feed antennas, interleaved antennas, and separate antennas as combining techniques.

Common Amplification

Co-generation

The simplest method of combining the analog and digital components of the hybrid FM IBOC signal is not to combine separate signals, but to co-generate them so they always exist as a single RF signal. As mentioned above, we have invented the term to distinguish between signals combined at RF and signals jointly synthesized in a digital-to-analog converter. Co-generation simply means that the exciter generates the analog and the digital signals at once in its digital signal processor, putting out a single RF waveform that is the combination of both.

By purchasing and installing a new transmitter (or linearizing an old one), the broadcaster can sidestep the rigmarole of installing extra hardware, lines, and/or antennas. For a new full power transmitter, this may require an extra financial commitment that the station is not prepared to make. Technologically, the new transmitter must have the capacity to handle the licensed analog power, plus the licensed digital power, plus the headroom necessary to carry the peaks of the digital waveform. Of course, the average digital power is only about 1% (–20 dBc) of the analog power, so the addition of the IBOC signal imposes a very modest average power increase. However, this translates to a headroom demand of about 1.3 dB (about a 35% increase in peak power) because of the peak-to-average power demand of the OFDM waveform. To avoid interrupting the flow here, a section at the end of this chapter explores the math of this peak-to-average relationship, for those curious enough to follow the calculations.

In addition, the transmitter, by being linearized, no longer operates in Class C, and becomes substantially less efficient. A Class C transmitter linearized for combined analog-digital amplification can be expected to fall from about 60–67% efficiency to about 45–55%. Transmitting digital-only, the efficiency falls to about 30%. Running 10 kW analog and 100 W digital output in common amplification, the transmitter consumes 18,364 to 22,222 W of electrical power. We'll keep these figures in mind as we work on the other approaches to combining.

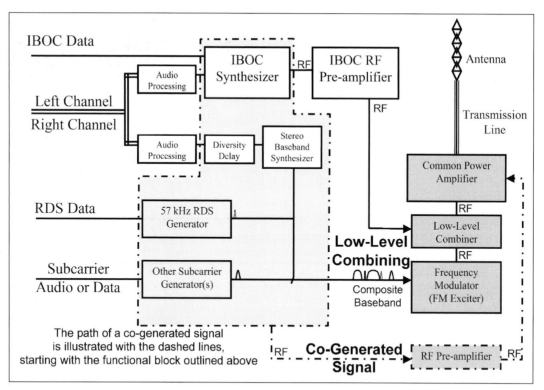

Figure 13.7 Co-generation and Low-Level Combining

Low-Level Combining

Like the other combining terminology, the term "low-level combining" has no formal definition. It evokes the image of two separate signals being combined at low power levels prior to high power amplification. Low-level combining is often included in the category of common amplification, because the final stages of amplification are in common. What matters most about the designation is that a low-level combined signal drives a high power amplifier. With the power amplification stages of a transmitter suitably linearized for the entire hybrid IBOC signal, one could invest in a separate exciter for the IBOC digital signal, and combine the analog and digital exciters' RF at the input to the transmitter. With the first generation of IBOC exciters, this would have been a prudent approach. In the event of a problem with the first-generation IBOC exciter, the analog exciter would continue to operate, protecting the prime analog service. Also, when combining the two signals at low power levels prior to final amplification, the inefficiencies of the combiner result in relatively small power losses. However, IBOC exciters are evolving from being personal computers in fancy boxes to fully implemented embedded systems. Embedded systems tend to be more reliable and faster-starting than their PC-based counterparts. Consequently there is not necessarily an advantage to low-level combining over co-generation.

Either co-generation or low-level combining can be employed in common amplification with an existing transmitter, so long as the transmitter can be linearized, and has enough power headroom to handle the higher power output and the lower efficiency.

High-Level Combining

While low-level combining occurs at the initial stage of RF transmission, high-level combining occurs after the final active stage. (Figure 13.8) The IBOC and analog waveforms are generated in separate exciters and fed to separate transmitters. The analog transmitter still runs at maximum efficiency, as a Class C amplifier. The digital transmitter operates at lower power levels than the analog transmitter, so the amount of power wasted on analog transmitter inefficiency is minimized by leaving the analog transmitter alone. Using very round figures, to generate, say, a 10 kW analog signal on a dedicated transmitter consumes 16,667 W of power (60% efficiency). Say the analog signal loses 12 percentage points of efficiency when the analog signal is moved to an analog-digital hybrid transmitter. If run through a combined amplifier, the analog portion is responsible for 20,833 W power consumption (48% efficiency). Hence, an additional 4 kilowatts are lost to FM generation in the new hybrid transmitter. However, by keeping the analog signal on its dedicated transmitter and performing high-level combining, we must instead tolerate the power loss of the combining method.

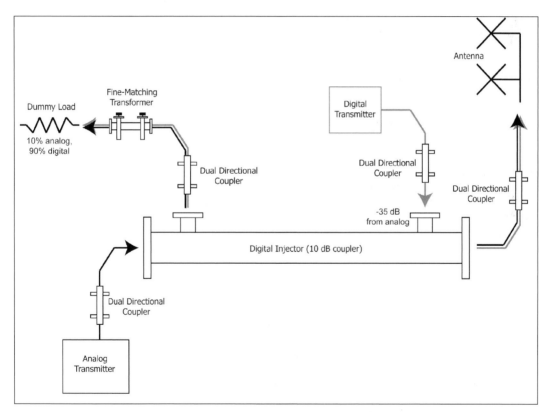

Figure 13.8 High Level Combining Diagram (Courtesy of Shively Laboratories)

The High-Level Combiner

When IBOC was in the development stage, field trials involved prototype digital transmitters that could be transported to a test station and inserted with a minimum of disruption. High-level combining provided this convenience. The most invasive part of the installation was the insertion of the high-level combiner into the path of the station's transmission line. As long a there was enough space, and a power source, the prototype and the reject load could be wheeled into place and attached to the combiner. This approach permitted the use of a digital-only prototype, avoiding the need to develop a full power hybrid prototype transmitter early on. Also, it protected the host analog signal from development glitches by isolating the old reliable analog transmitter from the digital prototype. The only thing that would have been less invasive would have been to utilize a backup antenna, if one were available, for the digital signal. This would have had the disadvantage of introducing an uncertainty into the testing—the difference in antenna placement and pattern between the digital and analog signals.

The most common way to perform high-level combining is to use a 10 dB combiner. 10% of the analog power is directed to a heat sink, while the remaining 90% goes toward the antenna. The opposite is true for the digital signal. 90% goes to the heat sink and 10% goes out toward the antenna. Table 13.1 shows the power relationships of a high-level combiner. In the example, to meet licensed ERP (effective radiated power) we need 10,000 watts analog power out of the combiner to drive the transmission line to the antenna. We are using a 10-dB combiner in the first section of the table. Digital output power is 1% of the analog. 90% of the digital power is lost in the combining process, as is 10% of the analog. The result is a reject load loss of 2011 W, which represents a combining efficiency of 83%.

The combiner is essentially a high power directional coupler. (Figure 13.8) Those familiar with the directional couplers used for sampling signals on a transmission line may see the relationship. A 50-dB coupler, for instance, sips one-tenth of a watt from a 10,000-watt signal to use as an RF sample. Only 0.001% of the passing signal is diverted to the sample port. 99.999% passes the coupler, headed for the antenna. Extending the model, assume we have two sampling ports, one for forward power and one for reverse. We can use these ports for sampling the signal or for injecting a signal. While a 50-dB coupler is useful for sampling passing signals, it is a very inefficient way to inject a second signal. To make a coupler a combiner, it makes sense to increase the coupling between the two sides of the device.

In our 10-dB combiner, the coupling is implicitly 10%. The coupler has two sides. It passes 10% of the signals on each side of the coupler to the other side. 90% of the signal stays on the same side as the source and passes to the corresponding output port. The analog source and the antenna are on one side. The digital source and the reject load, which is essentially a heat sink on the other side of the coupler. Hence, 90% of the analog power is directed toward the antenna, and 10% crosses toward the reject load. On the opposite side, 90% of the digital power is directed toward the reject load and 10% goes across the coupler toward the antenna.

The most sensible way to arrange the inputs to the 10-dB combiner is to give the high power signal (FM analog) the benefit of 90% pass-through, while the lower-power digital signal suffers a 90% loss to the reject load in order for 10% of the signal to be coupled out to the transmission line.

Why a 10-dB Combiner?

The same rationale for the 10-dB combiner would work for a 6-dB combiner. However, the trade-off is that now 25% of the analog signal is siphoned off to the reject load in order to increase the coupling of the digital signal to 25%. Figuring the total reject load power for the 6-dB combiner, over 13 kilowatts total power must be rejected. Doing the same instead for a 20-dB combiner results in a 10-kilowatt reject loss. It turns out that the selection of the 10-dB combiner was no accident. The least amount of rejected power occurs at 10.414 dB, with exactly 2000 watts rejected in our example. In addition to minimizing the size and waste heat of the reject load, minimizing the reject RF energy also reduces the transmitter-size requirements and the corresponding capital costs.

At the risk of taking the efficiency computation perhaps one step too far, consider that each digital output watt that is wasted is more costly than each analog watt wasted, because the digital power comes from a less efficient transmitter. Is minimizing the reject load power the correct objective? What happens when minimizing power consumption is the goal? Using a rough guideline of 30% overall digital-only transmitter efficiency and 60% overall analog-only efficiency, the reject load power that results in the least wasted power from the electric grid is with a 9.1 dB coupler. (No proof given here; view Table 13.1 for the results.) All told, the nominal 10-dB coupler could be a mite more efficient with power consumption if it were instead a 9.1-dB coupler, assuming the efficiency figures are correct.

Efficiency and Heat Load

The simplest assessment of heat loading at the transmitter facility is based on the total power consumption of all transmission equipment less the RF power exiting the facility on the transmission line. All power consumed, less the outgoing power of the radio signals toward the antenna, is converted to heat in the facility. Of course, transmitters are often vented outdoors, shunting much of the heat load of the power amplification process out of the equation (although the hot equipment still radiates substantial energy within the facility). The heat generated by the reject load also can be vented outside if necessary, or the load can be placed in separate location (even outdoors) to eliminate its heat contribution within the facility. The impact of any heat load can be evaluated to determine the cost/benefit of imposing a remedy.

To convert the heat generated in the reject load of the 10-dB high-level combiner from watts to BTU/hr, multiply our 2011 lost watts in this case, by the conversion factor 3.413 BTU/hr/W. Almost 6900 BTU/hr is put into the reject load. For comparison, this is about the load that a medium-size consumer window air conditioner could handle. One way to address heat loading is to install cooling and pay for the electricity to run it. (Keep in mind that this applies to the excess heat generated by all forms of combining, not just high level combining with a substantial rejected RF heat load.)

With a Seasonal Energy Efficiency Ratio (SEER) of, say, 13 (BTU/hr output per watt electricity input), it would take about 530 W of power to run 6900 BTU/hr of air conditioning. If cooling is needed at the site, add this to the electricity budget.

Meanwhile, let us consider whether it is worthwhile to fine-tune the amount of coupling from the nominal 10 dB. Compared to the 10-dB combiner, the 9.1-dB combiner (Table 13.1) would reject about 105 watts more RF energy while, ironically, saving 138 watts of power. The reduction in heat load from 138 fewer watts of power consumption is nearly offset by the additional heat load of the rejected RF. There is a slight power savings (138 W) and a slight net decrease in heating (138 – 105 = 33 W). The power savings amounts to less than 1% of the nearly 20 kilowatt total power consumption. Consequently, the energy savings of the 9.1-dB combiner compared to the 10-dB combiner are miniscule. Also, the accuracy of these calculations is limited, because air conditioners and transmitters are not necessarily operated at their nominal efficiencies or power levels. Their published energy efficiency ratios are very much like EPA mileage estimates for cars—"your mileage may be different."

In summary, for high-level combining, the nominal 10-dB combiner has nearly the ideal coupling factor to minimize electrical power consumption for RF generation and cooling. In designing an

10-dB Combiner (nearly minimized total rejected RF power)	Digital Signal		Analog Signal		Total
	Ratio	Power	Ratio	Power	Power
Electrical Power (AC)		3333 W		18519 W	21852 W
Overall Efficiency	30%		60%		
Transmitter Power (RF)		1000		11111 W	12111W
To Reject Load (RF)	90% −0.46 dB	900	10% −10 dB	1111	2011
Combiner Output (RF)	10% −10 dB	100	90% −0.46 dB	10000	10100
9.1 dB Combiner (minimized total power consumption)	Ratio	Power	Ratio	Power	Power
Electrical Power (AC)		2709 W		19005 W	21714 W
Overall Efficiency	30%		60%		
Transmitter Power (RF)		813		11479 W	12216W
To Reject Load (RF)	88% −0.6 dB	713	12% −9.1 dB	1403	2116
Combiner Output (RF)	12% −9.1 dB	100	88% −0.6 dB	10000	10100
Spreadsheet	A	B	C	D	E
1 Electrical Power		B3/A2		D3/C2	=B1 + D1
2 Overall Efficiency	30%		60%		
3 Transmitter Power		=B5/C4		=D5/C5	=B3 + D3
4 To Reject Load	=1-(10^(A5/10))	=B3*A4	=10^(A5/10)	=D3*C4	=B4 + D4
5 Combiner Output	−10 dB	=1%(D5)	=1-(10^(A5/10))	10000	=B5 + D5

The three pairs of highlighted values are the table input variables, assuming the given efficiencies. The other values are computed from these. The Combiner output value is entered in dB, representing the type of combiner (e.g., 10 dB in two cases), and in watts, representing the hypothetical desired analog power out of the combiner (e.g., 10,000 W in all three cases). The bottom half of the table includes the computations for the top cells, for entry into a spreadsheet.

Table 13.1 High-Level Combiner Power Budget

IBOC facility, apply the manufacturer-specified efficiency factors for the power levels to be used by the transmitters under consideration and run the calculations in Table 13.1. Transmitter manufacturers offer online calculators to assist with the computations. However, verify the assumptions employed in any calculation to see if they agree with the particular circumstances of a facility.

As mentioned in preceding paragraphs, the common-amplification hybrid transmitter is less efficient than the analog transmitter. Let's look at the balance of power between the hybrid transmitter and the high-level combined system. In our 10 kilowatt example, an estimated 21,042 watts of electrical power would be required for the hybrid transmitter running at 10,100 W power output. With the 10-dB combiner system, the power consumption is a little greater, estimated at 21,852 W—an 810 W increase. The extra 810 watts of high-level combining power consumption result in an approximately 2700 BTU/hr extra heat load, and about 212 W extra air conditioning power consumption. That's about 1 kW extra power consumption, or about 5% of the total power consumption. This kind of differential might be worth a few dollars a day in electrical costs, but it is not a gold mine of increased efficiency. The variables are numerous and wide-ranging in their values, which should provoke a more careful analysis of high-level combining versus other options before committing to it at a given facility. Consider the following variables:

- Efficiencies of transmitters under consideration, at the operating values required. Consider analog, hybrid, and all-digital

- Cost of new equipment, and upgrades and retrofits of existing equipment.

- Nature of and efficiency of heat elimination for each heat source: Electronic equipment, Reject load, Climate

- Cost of heat elimination for each heat source: Capital expense, Operating expense

- Required space for equipment versus available space

- System maintenance

Such computations should weigh the long-term expenses against the capital investment in the facility. The cost analysis should be weighed with other issues such as space requirements, availability of outdoor air for cooling, and system reliability and redundancy.

Mismatch and Isolation

We have painted a rosy picture of the ease with which the FM antenna system elements are put together. Nevertheless, there is still a need to attend to obtaining a proper match between sources and loads, and suitable isolation between signal paths. In the high-level combiner, the reject load may not ideally match the combiner, resulting in reflected energy. Reflected energy can find its way back *into* the output of a power amplifier. Likewise, the isolation between the forward component of the digital signal and the forward component of the analog signal must be good, to avoid the output of one transmitter from directly feeding into the other. In both cases—reflected energy and insufficient isolation—the result is the production of intermodulation products in the transmitter power amplifiers.

When the digital signal interacts with its analog host, each digital sideband's third-order inter-modulation product lands on the other digital sideband. Here's the math: If the analog signal is centered at f_c, the Primary Main digital sidebands are centered at $f_c \pm 164$ kHz. The equation for the third-order intermodulation frequencies involving the harmonic of the analog host demonstrates the self-interference problem. The solution to the equation equals the frequencies of the digital sidebands:

$$f_{IM3} = 2A - B = 2f_c - (f_c \pm 164) = f_c \pm 164$$

Eq. 13.1

In the extreme case, this intermodulation may also appear as a tilting of the OFDM sidebands on a spectrum analyzer display. This is an "amplitude tilt" of the OFDM subcarriers in which the amplitude of each subcarrier is progressively more attenuated from one end of the sideband to the other, apparently caused by the slope of the analog power spectrum as it intermodulates with the digital. In the less than extreme case, the interference may not be obvious on a spectrum analyzer, but still may be affecting the quality of the digital subcarriers.

Turn-around Loss

The amplifier interacts with the unwanted incursion of energy and sends it back out as intermodulation products. The magnitude of this phenomenon is measured by the "Turn-around Loss" or "Mixing Loss" of the transmitter. Geoff Mendenhall first studied this in relation to the use of multistation combiners (filterplexers).[4] As with other "loss" terms in RF engineering (e.g., return loss), a high turn-around loss is a good thing. To have as little unwanted energy turned around by the amplifier as possible is to have a high turn-around loss.

When the undesired signal enters the output of another power amplifier, it intermodulates with the desired signal in that power amplifier. Naturally, the higher the undesired signal level, the higher the intermodulation products. Transmitter loading and tuning also affect turnaround loss. The higher the output loading of the transmitter, the better the match to the incoming undesired signal, and the higher the resulting intermodulation products. The closer in frequency the undesired signal is to the transmitted signal, based on the "Q" of the transmitter output, the greater the intermodulation products. These characteristics jointly determine the turn-around loss. The lower the turn-around loss is, the higher are the unwanted intermodulation products.

Minimizing Unwanted Interaction

The high-level combined system is dependent on two characteristics to minimize mixing products: high turnaround loss, and high isolation. The turn-around loss, as discussed, is determined by the transmitter characteristics. The isolation, however, comes from how well the combiner handles the two signals. The digital and analog signals in the 10-dB combiner are within the same bandpass frequency. Unlike the combining of two stations on separate channels, with co-channel digital and analog signals there is no filter or transmitter selectivity to isolate the analog host amplifier from the IBOC digital amplifier, and vice versa.

---

[4] *A Study of RF Intermodulation Between Transmitters sharing Filterplexed or Co-Located Antenna Systems.*

There is little that can be done to adjust the turnaround loss of the transmitters in the combining of hybrid IBOC signals, except perhaps by optimizing the transmitter loading for maximum turnaround loss, if practicable and if necessary. Expect 10–20 dB turnaround loss in a solid state transmitter, 6–13 dB with a tube transmitter. Because the unwanted signal energy is within the passband of the transmitter (analog and digital energy is essentially on the same frequency), the effects of filters and the Q of the transmitter have little impact on the turnaround loss in an IBOC combining situation. On the other hand, the FM IBOC system designer has an opportunity to make the other component, the high-level combiner, work as well as possible. While it may appear to be another plug-and-play device, the combiner is sensitive to what is connected to it.

Previously, we discussed the coupling of the 10-dB combiner. Each input signal is split between two output ports. In theory, none of the input power is transferred to the other input port. In practice, it is. Consequently, it is important to understand *directivity* and *isolation*. (See Figure 13.9)

Directivity

Directivity is, so to speak, a front-to-back ratio of the energy on one side of the combiner. The combiner has two sides, separated in this case by a 10 dB relationship. 10% of the analog energy is coupled across to the other side. On that other side, all of the coupled analog power should go toward the forward port (the reject load). However, some of the power leaks through to the reverse port (digital in). The ratio of the coupled side's measured forward power to the crosstalk into the coupled side's reverse port is the directivity. It is a measure of the performance of one port of the coupler. The value is likely to be representative of the directivity of the other ports, assuming similar construction of the ports.

In Figure 13.9, 10% of the analog signal is coupled to the reject load port (C). Some of that coupled analog signal finds its way back toward the digital input (D). The ratio of C:D is the

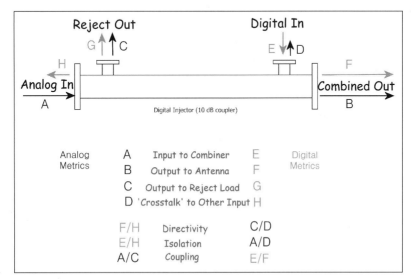

Figure 13.9 Combiner Signal Paths

directivity on that side of the combiner. Likewise, 10% of the digital input couples across to the combined output (F), and some of it leaks back toward the analog input (H). The ratio F:H is the directivity on the other side of the combiner.

Isolation

While directivity describes same-side performance, isolation measures the separation between inputs on opposite sides. Some amount of the analog input signal leaks to the digital input port (and vice versa). The level of this leakage with respect to the analog source is the isolation. As may be apparent, isolation is the product of the coupling and the directivity (the sum when using dB). For instance, in Figure 13.9, coupling (A/C) times directivity (C/D) yields isolation (A/D).

When there is an impedance mismatch between the combiner and one or more of its ports, energy traveling to the wrong ports increases, reducing the performance of the combiner. Thus, isolation is affected by the mismatch. Consequently, one cannot assume that a high-level combiner with the best factory specifications will perform to those specifications at the transmitter facility. The source impedances of the factory test sources are likely to be very well matched to the test loads. The factory tune-up of the combiner is performed under ideal conditions. At the broadcast facility, the transmitters' impedances are likely well away from the ideal, compromising how they match to the system.

When combiner mismatches cause distortion to the digital sidebands, it is likely due to unwanted energy entering the digital power amplifier the wrong way through the digital input port. The most common remedies employed are the fine matching transformer and the circulator (isolator). The circulator is placed between the digital transmitter and the combiner input port. (at point E-D in Figure 13.9) The digital signal may lose a few tenths of a dB going through to the combiner. However, the unwanted energy from the combiner, just lurking at the doorstep of the digital transmitter, is siphoned off to a separate reject load attached to the circulator. The circulator, in effect, increases the turnaround loss of the digital transmitter; or from another perspective it increases the isolation of the combiner to the digital transmitter input.

Another implementation to mitigate combiner mismatch, that may be less costly in some circumstances, is to place a fine matching transformer between the reject load and the combiner. (See the transformer depicted in Figure 13.8.) This helps improve the relative match of the reject load port with respect to the other port, thereby improving the isolation of the combiner. Tune the transformer for least distortion to the digital sidebands and to minimize their spectral regrowth products.

Directional Couplers Have the Same Issues

While the present discussion relates to the coupling, isolation and directivity of IBOC combiners, the issues apply equally to a very important diagnostic tool in the broadcast plant—the directional coupler. Directional couplers are used to obtain miniscule samples of the signals passing through transmission lines. As an indicator of power, the directional coupler's coupling factor must be accurate (and its power detector should be compatible with the type of waveform being measured). As a device that samples the forward or reverse path on the transmission line for quality assessments, the coupler's directivity must be excellent. Broadcasters are well-served by placing good-quality, calibrated directional couplers at each leg of the combining system, such as on all four ports of a high- or split-level combiner.

A general guide for transmitter isolation is to reduce undesired incoming energy to be at least 25, preferably 30 dB below the output of the transmitter to be protected. Thus on the high-level combiner, the digital transmitter puts out 1000 watts in our example, and must see fewer than 1 to 3 watts of undesired analog energy at the digital port. With an 11,111-watt analog signal on the other side of the combiner, we would require 35–40 dB combiner isolation to achieve the objective. Even well-made combiners may not be able to provide enough isolation, depending on the equipment to which they find themselves connected. To obtain good performance requires not only good combiner design and construction, but also careful attention to the performance of the combiner *in situ*.

High-level combining is advantageous when the analog transmitter power is high (about 14 kW or more), when the existing analog transmitter has 10% more power available to get through the combiner, and when the new digital transmitter, which will not be a suitable analog backup, does not force the analog backup transmitter out of the room.

Split-level Combining

Confronted with a situation where the existing analog transmitter did not have enough power to be turned up for high level combining, in 2004 Cox Radio's Director of Engineering, Steve Fluker, collaborated with George Cabrera of Harris Corporation to find another way to combine.[5] The Cox Orlando station received a class upgrade, meaning that the 5 kW tube transmitter would not have been powerful enough for the analog upgrade to 7.3 kW. It seemed unnecessary to invest in a more powerful analog transmitter plus a digital transmitter, or in a full-power analog-digital hybrid transmitter, when there was a perfectly good, but under-powered analog transmitter to begin with. Fluker pondered what would happen if the new transmitter were a lower-powered hybrid transmitter (co-generated or low-level combined) co-generation, and its output were combined with the output of the analog transmitter (see Figure 13.10).

---

[5] "Split-level Combining," Steve Fluker, Radio World, July 1, 2004..

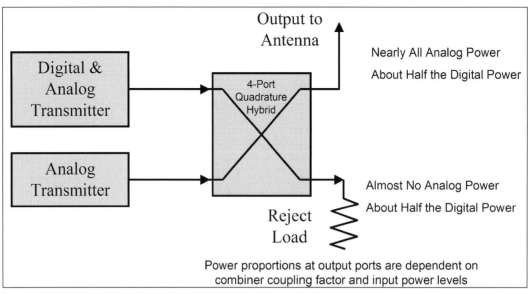

Figure 13.10 Split-level Combining Diagram

Split-level combining, also called mid-level combining, is a method by which the analog signal is split between two sources, and combined at high level, along with the digital signal. In its simplest form, the split-level combiner is a simple 3-dB hybrid. By injecting the same amount of analog energy, properly phased, into two ports, it all comes out a third port. (We'll ignore the minute power losses within the hybrid.) Ideally, the fourth port sees none of the energy. In the Cox Orlando example, the analog transmitter and the hybrid transmitter each generate 7 kW of analog signal, resulting in 14 kW out toward the antenna, and no loss to the reject load. Of course, to accomplish this, the phases of the two analog signal sources must be carefully tuned.

Meanwhile, the digital signal is generated at twice the desired 140-W power. As a single-port input, the digital signal is split to two output ports. 140 watts are sunk into the reject load and 140 watts exit the antenna port with the 14 kW analog signal. Compared to high-level combining, this split-level technique dumps far less RF energy into the reject load.

In retrospect, split-level combining is a subset or an extension of high-level combining. Both approaches take the outputs of the final power amplifiers and passively combine them before sending the signals along to the antenna. Split-level combining merely passes some analog energy through the digital transmitter (as well as the analog transmitter) to improve system efficiency.

Efficiency

The efficiencies of the split-level system are a little more complex to analyze. In the fundamental example, half the analog signal power is generated by the less efficient hybrid transmitter. Compared to an analog transmitter, substantial extra power is consumed in inefficiency in the hybrid transmitter, which offsets the couple of kilowatts saved from the reject load. It turns out there is a balance to be struck to obtain optimum efficiency, as measured by minimized electrical power consumption. Recall that in the second high-level combining example we were able to save on power consumption by balancing the system in a way that threw more power at the reject load. This was because it was more valuable to save power on generating each digital watt compared to each analog watt. In the case of the split-level combining process, the production of a digital watt still costs more than a watt from the analog transmitter. This is complicated by the fact that each analog watt from the hybrid transmitter costs more than each analog watt from the analog transmitter. Consequently, if we rearrange the balance of power between the analog transmitter and the hybrid transmitter, we can optimize system efficiency.

Combining Method	High Level	Split Level A	Split Level B	Split Level C
Coupling	10 dB	3 dB	3 dB	6 dB
	Digital Transmitter	Hybrid Transmitter		
Digital TPO	1400 W	280	280	560
FM TPO	none	5996	7000	2706
IBOC/FM dB	N/A	−13.3	−14%	−6.8
Power consumption	4878 @ 29%	12923 @ 49%	14857 @ 49%	8533 @ 38%
	Analog Transmitter			
FM TPO	15556	8082	7000	11363
Power consumption @ 60% efficiency	25926	13470	11667	18939
	System Output			
FM Power, Total	15556	14078	14000	14069
Digital Power, Total	1400	280	280	560
RF Power, Total	**16956**	**14358**	**14280**	**14629**
FM Power, Reject	1556	78	0	69
Digital Power, Reject	1260	140	140	420
Reject Power, Total	**2816**	**218**	**140**	**489**
Total Power Consumption	30804	26393	26524	27472
Combiner efficiency	83.4%	98.5%	99%	96.7%
Overall efficiency	**45.9%**	**53.6%**	**53.3%**	**51.5%**

Table 13.2 Comparison of Combining Efficiencies (Data obtained in part from Harris Coupling Coefficient Calculator, www.harris.com.)

Table 13.2 provides four examples of combining parameters. The first employs a 10-dB coupler to combine an analog signal from one transmitter and a digital signal from another. This is high-level combining. The other three examples are of split-level combining. All four columns of results are based on an ultimate output of 14 kW analog and 140 W digital power to the antenna's transmission line. The case of Split Level A obtains more analog power from the analog-only transmitter than from the hybrid transmitter. It has the best overall efficiency, based on the sum of the electric power consumption of the two transmitters. When the analog power is equally derived from each transmitter, as shown by Split Level B, the efficiency is still better than that of the high-level combiner, but not quite as good as Split Level A, which is optimized for best efficiency. Split Level A and B are based on a 3-dB coupler. Split Level C employs a 6 dB coupler. It is closer in efficiency to the other split-level examples, and better than the high-level approach.

Considering the Options

There are several dimensions in the evaluation of split-level combining efficiencies. Table 13.2 is not a universal representation of combiner performance. It is only representative of a particular arrangement of transmitter models and power levels. To design an optimal combining arrangement, consider first whether there is existing transmission equipment that might be worth incorporating in the new system; obtain its power capacity and efficiency. Then a set of calculations can be performed to obtain the key information:

- What is the best coupling factor, transmitter power, and digital-to-analog power ratio for overall efficiency?

- What are the capital cost and operating cost for various solutions involving different combinations of equipment?

However, to obtain those results, one must play with the various input dimensions, including:

- One or more analog transmitter models
  - Maximum analog transmitter power
  - Analog transmitter efficiency
- One or more hybrid transmitter models (co-generated or low-level combined)
  - Peak power capacity of transmitter (see crest factor discussion at end of chapter)
  - Maximum transmitter average power capacity at selected analog/digital power ratio
  - Hybrid transmitter efficiency-versus-analog/digital-ratio curve
- Coupling ratio
  - Vary the coupling ratio to figure where greatest efficiency lies
  - Best coupling ratio dependent on the hybrid-to-digital power ratio
- Reliability and failure modes
  - Consider reliability of the system design and what happens when a failure occurs
  - What backup schemes are acceptable?
- Heat loading
  - Consider the relative benefits in various combinations of heat loading in the facility
- Financial
  - Weigh capital and operating costs

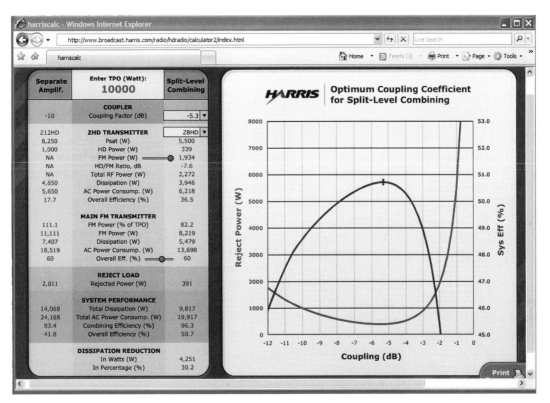

Figure 13.11 Harris Coupling Coefficient Calculator on the World Wide Web (Source: Harris.com)

In our example with a 14 kW analog transmitter power output (TPO), split-level combining could save as much as 4411 watts of wasted electricity. Some of that waste is heat produced in the transmitters and some is heat generated in the reject load. This is another dimension of the system design, "Where do you want your heat?" The design can be tinkered with to increase or decrease the amount of work the reject load is doing to absorb inefficiencies. The heat generated by the reject load can be managed differently than the heat of a transmitter. Some reject loads are installed outdoors, saving indoor heat loading as well as precious space.

Split-level combining has the potential disadvantage of forcing the analog host signal to rely on two transmitters to make licensed power. In the event of a failure of either the analog or the hybrid transmitter, the remaining transmitter is pushing out only its share of the analog power. Further, the balance in the combiner is upset by the loss of analog signal from one input port, and more analog energy is dumped into the reject load from the remaining transmitter. The reject load must be sized for the worst-case transmitter failure. These issues lead to another dimension in the analysis of a new IBOC system, "What happens when the system fails; and what is the plan for backup?" Perhaps the analog and hybrid transmitters each should be full-size so either unit can run the analog at full power, with a switch to bypass the combiner. Or perhaps a third transmitter can be standing by to replace the lost analog energy from whichever transmitter is down. The options are as many as there are creatively thinking broadcast engineers. No matter what the combining method, the implications of the IBOC system design on reliability and redundancy must be considered.

Isolation

Like its high-level cousin, split-level combining employs a passive coupler. The directivity and coupling of the coupler determine how well it isolates the outputs of the analog transmitter and the hybrid transmitter from each other. Since the design objective is to get the crosstalk components in the isolator to be low with respect to the transmitter output power, the split-level combiner has an advantage over the high-level 10-dB combiner. The high-level combiner operates with a total digital transmitter power level that is about 10% of the total analog transmitter power. This makes a 35-dB isolation impress a –25 dBc signal onto the output of the digital transmitter. (Analog TPO is ~+10 dBc with respect to the digital TPO, less 35 dB isolation yields –25 dBc analog crosstalk into the digital amplifier.) In contrast, assume the split-level combiner is running 50/50, with half the total power being contributed by each transmitter. This gives us back 10 dB of margin because the hybrid transmitter is at 0 dBc with respect to the analog. However, instead of a 10-dB coupler, we are using, say, a 3-dB coupler. We lose 7 dB of isolation due to the change in coupling. The net result is a +10 – 7 = 3 dB improvement in isolation. The split-level system can be designed to optimize the isolation by fiddling with the coupling and power ratios, based on knowledge of the coupler directivity and the transmitter's turnaround loss.

Combining with Antennas

If the ultimate goal is to radiate a clean hybrid IBOC signal with a proper ratio between analog and digital, then even if the two signals are radiated from different antennas, they are in effect combined as they propagate through free space to the receiver. Antennas may be used combine the analog and digital signals, in several ways. One form, the *dual-feed* antenna, essentially turns the antenna array into a high-level combiner. A common set of antenna bays radiates the hybrid signal. Alternatively, *separate antennas* (also called dual antennas) may be utilized to radiate the digital signal. If a licensed backup antenna (auxiliary antenna) is available on the main transmitter site, it can be put to use as the IBOC separate antenna, radiating the digital signal; or a new antenna can be installed on-site and licensed as an auxiliary antenna. Also, to conserve precious tower space, the digital antenna bays can be *interleaved* among the analog elements. The goals of antenna combining are twofold—provide the isolation required between the transmitters while generating similar antenna patterns for both the analog and digital signals.

The IBOC-to-Antenna Path

Let's identify two categories for delivering IBOC to the antenna—*common-line*, and *separate-line*. Common-line, as the name implies, carries the full hybrid signal—both the analog and digital waveforms—on one transmission line. With the separate-line category, the digital signal is segregated to a separate transmission line to the antenna. Table 13.3 shows how these two approaches compare. Figure 13.12 illustrates the differences.

Common-line transmission typically requires little or no tower work to implement. Separate-line transmission may involve tower work, if an existing backup antenna is not utilized for the digital signal. Separate-line transmission can avoid the purchase of high-level combining or common-amplification systems. Measuring separate-line hybrid signals is more challenging than common-line. Since separate-line combining occurs at the antenna, after the signals have left the transmission line, there is no place in the separate-line system to sample the combined hybrid signal to perform quality measurements. Extra care must be taken to pick up the separate-line signal over the air.

IBOC-to-Antenna Path	Common Line	Separate Line
Path of digital and analog signals to antenna(s)	IBOC and analog together on one transmission line	IBOC follows separate transmission line
Occurs in these systems	High-level combining	Dual-feed antenna
	Split-level combining	Interleaved antennas
	Low-level combining	Separate antennas
	Co-generation	
Implication	Hybrid signal is available to sample from transmission line	Hybrid signal must be intercepted over-air

Table 13.3 IBOC-to-Antenna Paths

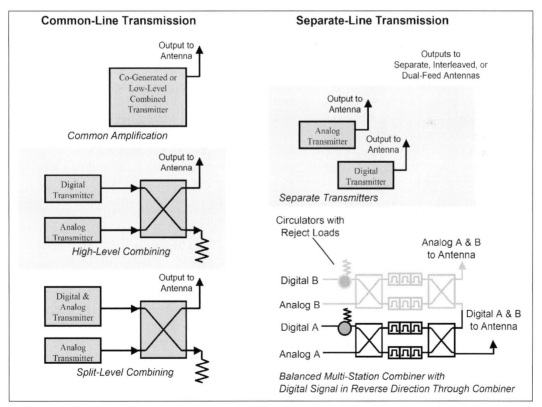

Figure 13.12 Common-Line and Separate-Line Topology

Avoiding multipath reception is the first concern in measuring a separate-line hybrid signal with an antenna. In addition, some other characteristics give common-line measurements an advantage. On common-line systems, the hybrid signal not only is combined for easy digital-to-analog ratio measurement, but also the hybrid signal is usually fairly well isolated from undesired signals at the transmitter site. This helps avoid two impacts caused by other signals at the site—high undesired signal levels can cause monitor overload, and may emit their own spurious emissions. Also, the common-line sample port on the transmission line provides a relatively high signal level, compared to the over-the-air sample for the separate-line signal. This gives the common-line sample a signal-to-noise ratio advantage over separate-line monitoring off-air.

On the separate-line system the quality of the analog and digital signals still can be independently verified with samples from their respective transmission lines. Not visible, however, is the combined signal, which would show the rest of the combining story. Only by viewing the combined signal with a test antenna, can one observe any effects on the analog and digital signals caused by their interaction in the combining process. The most important effect to observe is whether the resulting emissions show the proper power ratio between the digital signal and its analog host. This is best done at a distance from the transmitter site to avoid possible differences in antenna patterns close to the facility. In addition, assuming there is sufficient signal-to-noise ratio in the over-the-air sample, the quality of the combining can be observed by looking for spectral regrowth caused by transmitter compression and transmitter turnaround of unwanted reflected energy, as well as signal level distortions caused by bandpass filter effects.

To set up for the proper level balance between the analog and digital signals in separate-line combining methods, calculate the gains and losses of each system, and adjust the digital transmitter power accordingly. This is fundamentally the same as calculating the power budget for high-level and split-level combining, with two additional components. First is the digital transmission line. It may be smaller than the analog line, with a corresponding higher loss, or it may also be a different length than the analog. Second, with either a different antenna or a different number of antenna bays utilized for the digital signal than for the analog, the differences in gain between the two emissions must be accommodated. Before dealing with separate-antenna configurations, we'll turn next to discussing the use of a common antenna for combining digital and analog IBOC signals.

Dual-Feed Antenna

Many antenna designs incorporate 3-dB hybrids at the antenna bays. (Figure 13.13) This feature can be used to the station's advantage when implementing IBOC. The hybrid splits the analog energy to feed the antenna bay's two feed points. The two hybrid ports feed a pair of antenna elements in quadrature, which then produce a circularly polarized electromagnetic wave. For this discussion, let's say the phasing is such that the analog signal is right-hand circularly polarized. Most FM antennas consist of multiple antenna bays stacked vertically. They are separated by a calculated spacing based on the signal's wavelength. The traditional spacing is one wavelength on-center. To manage downward radiation lobes, other spacing factors are utilized as appropriate to the station's circumstances, such as 0.8-wavelength and half-wavelength spacing. Antenna spacing and number of bays determines the antenna pattern. Antenna spacing also plays a role in the interleaved antenna approach (discussed after this).

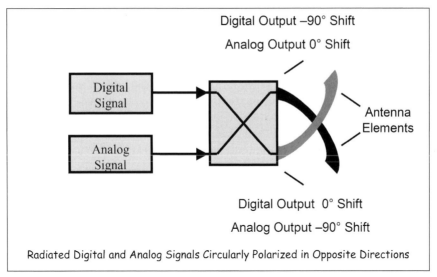

Figure 13.13 Quadrature-fed FM Antenna

With a 90-degree hybrid already present at the antenna bays, and an engineered matched load on the output ports of the hybrid (the antenna elements themselves), to use the hybrid as an analog-digital combiner is just a matter of driving the fourth port on the hybrids with the digital signal. By entering the hybrid port opposite that of the analog signal, the digital signal is forwarded to the antenna in reverse quadrature, producing, in our example, a left-polarized signal. Antennas that were previously installed with hybrids may only have three-port hybrids, with the fourth port internally terminated. This may require the replacement or modification of the hybrids. To implement a dual-feed antenna, a separate cable must be run up the tower to the antenna for the digital signal. At the same time, it is advisable to sweep and fine-tune the antenna while there is the opportunity.

There are variations to the dual-feed method. Fewer bays can be employed for the digital signal than the analog signal. This causes the digital pattern to deviate from the analog, but a pattern analysis will indicate whether the variation is significant enough to be a problem. Substantial pattern discrepancies, if any, are noted in proximity to the transmitter site due to the differences in downlobe patterns. Less antenna gain means more power is required from the digital transmitter than if all antenna bays were utilized. On the plus side, the decreased number of bays (for the digital signal, compared to the analog signal) improves isolation. With fewer bays on the digital antenna array than the analog, they are exposed to a smaller proportion of the analog emissions.

The dual-feed antenna presents other opportunities and constraints. The digital transmission line can be down-sized (compared to the analog transmission line) to save expense because of the lower digital power level, or it can be sized to act as a backup to the main analog transmission line.

The isolation between transmitters consists of several components—hybrid isolation, antenna isolation, and line loss. The antenna hybrids are measured by the same characteristics (coupling, directivity, isolation, insertion loss) that high-level combiners are. Recall that hybrids in the field may not perform as well as their factory measurements suggest, depending on how the factory does its measurements. Isolation is dependent in part on the quality of the impedances the hybrid sees on its ports. On the one hand, the antenna elements have fixed RF characteristics based on their dimensions and, by design, act as a transformer between the line and free space. On the other hand, exposed to the weather, antennas can present a varying load to their source due to deterioration and accumulation of foreign material (e.g., ice and snow). Analog energy mismatched equally to both antenna elements on a bay will find its way back out the hybrid's digital input port. It has only one way to go: in reverse toward the output of the digital transmitter. Any asymmetry in the mismatch will reflect some energy to the analog port as well.

There is also antenna isolation to consider. While the ideal antenna bay radiates all its energy and reflects none back to the input ports, the bay is still immersed in a field created by the other antenna bays. Bay spacing and bay design affect the mutual coupling between antenna bays. Some analog energy will be intercepted by each bay and sent back toward the digital port. (The same is true for digital energy reflecting back to the analog transmitter, but it is so much lower in level that problems will likely first appear in the digital transmitter.) The antenna manufacturer can provide an isolation figure based on factory tests and field experience. With the known constant load of the antenna elements, some of the uncertainty of the hybrid's behavior is eliminated. The uncertainty of the impedances at the input ports remains. The objectives for antenna isolation are the same as for high-level combining isolation—35 to 40 dB at a minimum, from transmitter to transmitter.

Separate-Antenna Operation

To make it a little easier to get IBOC on the air quickly, many stations contemplate the dual antenna approach, using their auxiliary antennas to transmit their digital signals, forgoing the expense of high-level combining. Until 2003, there had been no research into the performance of separate-antenna hybrid FM IBOC combining. The fundamental question was whether the use of a separate antenna for the digital signal could maintain the digital-to-analog power ratio required by the NRSC-5 Standard (and the FCC's rules) at the receiver. Given that the digital signal would be emitted from a place very close to the licensed analog facility, the likelihood that the digital signal would exceed protection criteria for adjacent-channel stations was negligible.

Separate-Antenna Research

The NAB convened an ad hoc committee of member station engineers and broadcast equipment specialists, which commissioned a technical study on the performance of FM IBOC using the separate antenna approach. That study, performed by the engineering consulting firm of Denny and Associates for NAB,[6] evaluated three cases of separate-antenna operation, representing a variety of separate-antenna conditions.

---

[6] *Engineering Report—Evaluation of the Use of Separate Transmitting Antennas for In-Band On-Channel Digital and Analog FM Broadcasting,* Prepared for the National Association of Broadcasters by Denny and Associates, May 28, 2003. Available at www.nrscstandards.org/drb/miscibocnonnrsc.asp.

Call Sign	WDHA-FM	WMGC-FM	KDFC-FM
City	Dover, NJ	Detroit, MI	San Francisco, CA
ERP, Class	1 kW Class A	13.5 kW, Class B	33 kW, Class B
Main – Aux = Diff Height Above Average Terrain	175 – 171 = 4 m	291 –228 = 63 m	319 – 294 = 25 m
Antenna Bays Main/Aux	1/1	2/2	4/2
Tower	Same tower	Same tower	Separate tower
Propagation	Somewhat terrain limited	Fairly open, flat terrain	Rugged terrain

Table 13.4 Three Stations Tested for Separate-antenna Performance (Source: NAB Separate-Antenna Study)

Figure 13.14 is one of the graphs from the NAB report. It contains two plots of data collected by a mobile test facility driven over a test route. First, the bold line is a plot of the station operated with hybrid on a common antenna, showing the digital-to-analog received power ratio over the test route. This provides the baseline to which the second plot is compared. The second plot shows the digital-to-analog ratio measured on the same test route with the separate antenna in operation. The comparison reveals that with the separate-antenna configuration there is a higher digital signal level close to the tower site, due to the downward radiation patterns and height differential of the two antennas. Otherwise, the plot shows good correspondence between the separate-antenna power ratios and the common-antenna power ratios. (Recall that the specified digital power level is 20 dB below analog.)

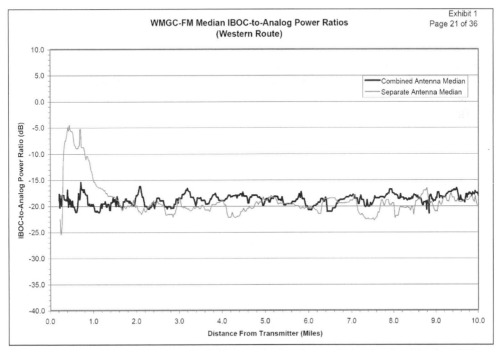

Figure 13.14 Field Test Measurements of Digital-to-Analog Power Ratios for Combined- and Separate-Antenna Operation (Source: NAB)

Some of the other plots in the report show different minor anomalies. At the sites where terrain is more of a factor, one can see brief excursions in some plots where it appears the terrain blocks either the analog or the digital signal while leaving the other less attenuated. All in all, however, the behavior of the separate antenna did not deviate very far from the naturally occurring variations in the performance of the common antenna transmission.

Mind Antenna Patterns

While the results of the NAB separate antenna study are very encouraging, the tests involved similar antennas for the digital and analog transmissions. Two tests involved main antennas paired with auxiliary antennas having the same number of bays (and bay spacing). One test involved a 4-bay main antenna and a 2-bay auxiliary antenna. The differences in the elevation patterns of these antenna pairings is negligible, so the digital-to-analog signal ratios are well maintained, even when close to the transmitter sites.

On the other hand, pairing a very high gain main antenna with a low gain aux antenna may create local reception problems. The high gain antenna emits a much lower proportion of the analog signal's power to the area surrounding the transmitter site than the low gain digital antenna. The digital-to-analog ratio can exceed the nominal 1% (–20 dB) ratio, causing interference to the reception of the host analog signal by analog receivers. Doug Vernier of V-Soft Communications[7] illustrated the problem with examples of actual IBOC implementations. One case involved a 12-bay main antenna and a 2-bay auxiliary antenna. The station received complaints from its listeners within a few miles of the transmitter site when the separate-antenna IBOC system was activated. Based on the antenna heights and vertical gain patterns, he calculated that the digital-to-analog power ratio at 11,000 feet from the transmitter site (about 2 miles) was an unacceptable 0.9:1. In other words, at that location, the digital signal was 90 times more powerful, with respect to the analog, than it should be. This is certainly capable of causing interference to analog receivers trying to acquire the host analog transmission. The station switched to a high-level combining system to eliminate the problem. Conclusion: For best performance, maintain similar antenna gains for the main and the auxiliary antennas, particularly if the transmitter is in a populated area.

---

[7] D.Vernier, IBOC Coverage and Interference, slide presented at NAB Radio Show, 2006.

Separate-Antenna Regulation

Based on the results of the NAB study, the ad hoc committee made three recommendations, which the NAB submitted to the FCC in July 2003, and reiterated in its comments to an FCC rulemaking process in January 2004. In March 2004 the FCC announced[8] that under Special Temporary Authorization (STA) it would permit separate antenna operations that meet these conditions:

1. The digital transmission must use a licensed auxiliary antenna.

2. The auxiliary antenna must be within three seconds of latitude and longitude of the main antenna; and

3. The height above average terrain of the auxiliary antennas must be between 70 and 100 percent of the height above average terrain of the main antenna.

The FCC also indicated it would consider, on a case-by-case basis, separate-antenna proposals that do not meet these criteria. The FCC further established in the Public Notice that any combining method that utilizes the same radiating elements for the digital signal and the analog, including dual-feed antennas, would not be subject to the separate-antenna filing requirements. In contrast, interleaved antennas employ separate radiating elements and are subject to the STA criteria. Since an interleaved antenna is at the same height and position as the main antenna, the only requirement for the second set of antenna elements to qualify for an STA is to be licensed as an auxiliary antenna. Once the industry and its regulators have developed a record of successful separate-antenna implementations, the FCC is likely to incorporate dual antenna operation into the IBOC rules.

MultiStation Antenna Systems

When several FM stations operate through the same antenna system, each station's IBOC combining may or may not integrate with the multistation combining. The analog signals are combined, as discussed earlier, with branch or balanced combiners. Likewise, the digital signals must be combined. Figure 13.15 shows the several ways that multistation combining and IBOC combining co-exist. In short, there is a common-line and a separate-line approach to multistation combining.

At first blush, to select an approach may appear to be simply a choice between installing an IBOC combiner for each station (common-line) or installing one multistation digital combiner for all (separate-line); however, the rubric is dependent on the hardware and facilities available at the multistation site. Consider the various configurations of the building blocks in Table 13.5.

---

[8] FCC Public Notice, MM Docket No. 99-325, USE OF SEPARATE ANTENNAS TO INITIATE DIGITAL FM TRANSMISSIONS APPROVED, DA-04-712, March 17, 2004.

	Existing antenna	Existing multi-station combiner	IBOC combining	How accomplished	Comment
1	Nonhybrid (Antenna bays with single drive points and no quadra-ture hybrid splitting the transmission feed to antenna input ports)	Branch or balanced	common-line	Each station puts a hybrid sig-nal into multistation combiner	Mind peak capacity of multistation system
2			separate- line	Separate multistation combiner for all-digital signals	Requires separate shared antenna for digital signals
3			separate- line	Reverse-feed balanced com-biner with digital signals	Requires separate shared antenna for digital signals
4			separate- line	No digital combining—each station uses its own separate antenna	e.g., when stations have individual backup antennas
5	Hybrid (Antenna bays with dual drive points fed from quadrature hybrid)	Branch	common-line	Not Applicable	
6		Branch	separate- line	Separate multistation combiner for all-digital signals	Dual-feed antenna
7		Balanced	common-line	Not Applicable	
8		Balanced	separate-line	Reverse-feed balanced com-biner with digital signals	Dual-feed antenna

Table 13.5 Multistation IBOC Combining Options

Common-Line IBOC to Multistation Combiners

One way to add digital IBOC signals to stations on a shared antenna is to use the common-line approach; the digital signal of each station is combined with its analog host, prior to multistation combining. Each station injects a complete hybrid IBOC signal into the multistation combiner. As long as the multistation combiner has the bandwidth to pass each station's full hybrid signal to the wideband side, the multistation combiner needs no modification.[9] To accomplish this, each station must install its own IBOC combining system to create a common-line IBOC signal. Each station on the multistation combiner may implement any type of common-line IBOC combining, including high-level, low-level, and co-generation. See Figure 13.15 and Table 13.5.

---

[9] Overlooked in this discussion, and in the discussion about transmitter RF peaks at the end of this chapter, is the capacity of the combiners and transmission lines. While each station on a transmission line increases its average power by 1% to add the digital signal to the analog host, the transmission line is sensitive to the peak voltages of the digital signals. This requires a 37% increase in the capacity of the transmission line over what is required for the analog signals.

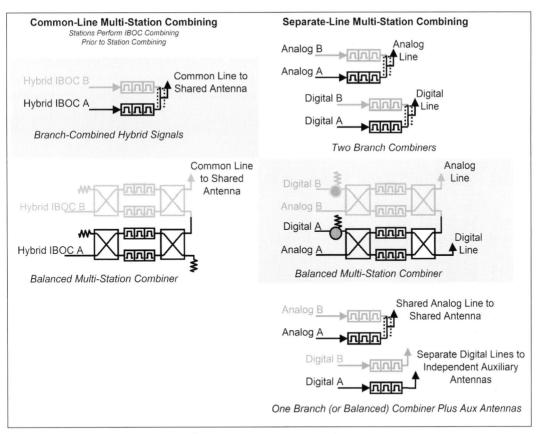

Figure 13.15 IBOC and Multistation Combiners

Separate-Line IBOC and Multistation Combining

Stations on the multistation combiner could choose to transmit their digital signals in separate-line fashion, utilizing separate, interleaved, or dual-feed antennas. The digital signals are generated independently of the analog signals, and may be combined in a separate multistation combiner just for the digital signals. This approach employs one analog multistation combiner, one digital multistation combiner, and two antenna feeds. In contrast, the common-line method employs one multistation combiner plus an IBOC combiner for each station on the system.

There is one separate-line approach that is elegantly simple. If the multistation system has both a hybrid balanced combiner and a hybrid antenna, the power of the hybrid can be used to maximum advantage. The isolation port on the narrowband side of each station's injector becomes the digital input port. This drives the digital signals in the reverse direction on the wideband side. While the analog signals propagate downstream toward the antenna in their usual way, the digital signals head upstream toward the starting point of the multistation combiner. A separate transmission line is connected to the wideband port at the very beginning of the multistation combiner to carry the multistation digital signals to the antenna. The new transmission line is connected to the fourth ports on the antenna hybrids.

Modifications to the balanced-combined/hybrid-antenna multistation system are typically limited to two major changes: adding a digital transmission line and converting the antenna hybrids to four-port models. Each station installs a low power digital transmitter at its narrowband isolation port. To absorb unwanted energy coming out the isolation ports, it may be advisable to install circulators between the narrowband isolation ports and the digital transmitters connected to them.

Crest Factor and Peak Power in Hybrid IBOC Transmission

This section contains a detailed computation of power and voltage ratios for the combined analog-digital hybrid IBOC transmitter. While it is a minor digression from the discussion of antenna topologies, those interested in the concept of the crest factor and the peak-to-average power ratio my find it illuminating. This discussion follows the accompanying table of calculations, Table 13.6. To aid the reader, each line of the table is referenced in the following narrative in this manner: [Line #].

The *crest factor* is the ratio of the peak voltage of the waveform to be amplified by the transmitter to its average (more precisely, its root-mean-square or RMS) voltage. Analog FM signals have a lower crest factor than a digital OFDM signal. Considering the crest factor, we can calculate what the demands on the transmitter ought to be. Not only do we need to know that the transmitter can deliver the average power required of it, but we also must be certain that the transmitter can handle the instantaneous voltage peaks.

Let's start with the simplest of all waveforms, the sinusoidal wave. A perfect sine wave has a peak voltage and an RMS voltage with a fixed relationship. From basic trigonometry, its RMS voltage times the square root of two is its peak voltage. The crest factor is defined as the ratio of the peak voltage to the RMS voltage [Table 13.6, Line 1]. The crest factor of a sine wave is, therefore, the square root of two (~1.41). Figure 13.16 simulates the relationship between the peaks and the RMS values of the voltages of two waveforms. By eye, the peak-to-RMS voltage ratio of the sine wave is much less than that of the complex wave. These ratios are the crest factors. The square of the crest factor is the peak-to-average power ratio (PAPR). Let's assume that the modulated FM signal, being nearly sinusoidal, has a crest factor of 1.41. [Line 2]

If we are going to sum the analog signal with the digital, we must figure out what the sums of the peak voltages of the two waveforms will be and what the sums of the average voltages will be. With a combined peak voltage and a combined average voltage, we can compute the new crest factor as the ratio of the two. In general, to find the peak voltage of two signals combined, sum the peak voltages, if their peaks are likely to occur simultaneously [Line 10]. To obtain the average (RMS) voltage, we can sum the powers[10] and take the square root, or we can perform a root mean square of the individual RMS voltages [Line 11].

---

[10] Since our objective is to work with power ratios and voltage ratios, we assume the impedance is 1.000 ohm, such that power equals voltage squared.

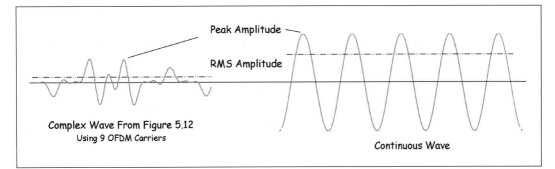

Figure 13.16 Illustration of Peak-to-RMS Relationships of Two Waveforms

	Description	Equation
1	Crest Factor	$CF = \sqrt{PAPR}$
2	Assume FM Crest Factor	$CF_{fm} = \sqrt{2} = 1.414$
3	FM Average Power	$FMP_{avg} = \left(FMV_{rms}\right)^2$
4	FM Peak Voltage	$FMV_{pk} = FMV_{rms} \times CF_{fm}$
5	OFDM Peak-to-Avg Pwr	$PAPR = 8\ dB = 6.310{:}1$
6	OFDM Crest Factor	$CF_o \sqrt{6.310} = 2.512$
7	OFDM Average Power	$OP_{avg} = -20\ dBc = 1\%\ FMP_{avg}$
8	OFDM RMS Voltage	$OV_{rms} = \sqrt{OP_{avg}} = \sqrt{1\%\ FMP_{avg}} = 10\%\ FMV_{rms}$
9	OFDM Peak Voltage	$OV_{pk} = OV_{rms} \times CF_o = 10\%\ FMV_{rms} \times 2.512 = 25.1\%\ FMV_{rms} =$ $25.1\% \left(FMV_{pk} / CF_{fm}\right) = 17.8\%\ FMV_{pk}$
10	Total Peak Voltage	$TV_{pk} = OV_{pk} + FMV_{pk} = 1.178\ FMV_{pk}$
11	Total RMS Voltage	$TV_{rms} = \sqrt{OP_{avg} + FMP_{avg}} = 1.005\ FMV_{avg}$
12	New Total Crest Factor	$CF_T = 1.178\ FMV_{pk} / \left[1.005\ FMV_{avg}\right] = CF_{fm}\ 1.178/1.005 = 1.657$
13	Resulting Total PAPR	$PAPR = 20\ \log\left(CF_T\right) = 4.387\ dB$

Table 13.6 Computation of Hybrid IBOC Peak-to-Average Power Ratio

OFDM Peak to Average

The IBOC OFDM signal in its uncompressed state has about 8 dB PAPR. Once passed through a power amplifier, the PAPR is reduced through compression[11] to about 6 dB.[12] Let's work with the 8-dB value, to preserve as much of the original waveform in our amplifier as possible. 8 dB is a 6.3:1 power ratio (PAPR) [Line 5], or a 2.5:1 voltage ratio (crest factor) [Line 6].

Relate OFDM to Analog

Next, we need to establish the relationship between the peak OFDM voltage and that of the analog host. First, tie the OFDM RMS to the analog RMS. Since the average power of the OFDM waveform is set at 1% of the analog power (–20 dBc) [Line 7], the OFDM RMS voltage is 10% (the square root of 1%) of the analog RMS voltage [Line 8]. Next, relate the OFDM peak to analog RMS. We have already determined the ratio of OFDM peak voltage to its own RMS—the crest factor of 2.5. To scale the OFDM crest factor with respect to the analog host power, we substitute 10% analog RMS voltage for OFDM RMS voltage [Line 9]. The OFDM peak voltage, then, would be 2.5 times 10% of the analog RMS voltage (25% of analog RMS). This is still the OFDM-to-OFDM crest factor, merely scaled to the analog RMS level.

OFDM Peak to Analog Peak

We need to determine the relationship between the peak voltages of the analog and digital signals, so another conversion is necessary. We must convert the OFDM-peak-voltage-to-analog-RMS ratio just calculated to a ratio between the OFDM peak and the analog peak. Divide the OFDM-peak-to-analog-RMS ratio (~25%) by the analog crest factor (1.41) to get the OFDM-peak-to-analog-peak voltage ratio 0.251/1.414 = 0.178. That is, the OFDM peak voltage is 17.8% of the analog peak voltage. Now we can add the OFDM peak voltage to the FM peak voltage to obtain the total peak voltage. The result is 117.8% of the FM peak voltage.

OFDM RMS to Analog RMS

Similarly, we can add the average power of each waveform and take the square root to obtain the RMS voltage of the combined signal—100.5% of the FM RMS voltage.

---

[11] Results may differ with waveform precorrection, also called *predstortion*, in which the complement of the amplifier compression curve is applied to the digital signal in advance of amplification.

[12] As determined by Broadcast Signal Lab measurements with Agilent power meter at various transmitter plants. Also reported by various parties in talks and the literature,

Hybrid Crest Factor

Since we are using the sum of the digital and the analog voltages in the amplifier, the new combined crest factor is a ratio that is the sum of the OFDM and FM peak voltages divided by the sum of the OFDM and FM RMS voltages. This is the same as 117.8% of the FM peak voltage divided by 100.5% of the FM RMS voltage [Line 12]. We already know the relationship between the FM peak and RMS voltages, described by the 1.41 FM crest factor. Restated, multiply the original FM crest factor by 117.8/100.5 to obtain the new combined crest factor. The crest factor of our combined signal, therefore, is 1.657, which converts to 4.387 dB.

Difference Between Hybrid and Analog Crest Factors

In comparison, recall the crest factor of the FM-only signal is 1.41; the PAPR is 2, which is 3.01 dB. Hence, changing from FM-only, with a 3.01-dB PAPR, to a combined analog-digital signal, with a 4.387 dB PAPR, requires an additional 1.39 dB headroom in the transmitter. However, the transmitter also needs to make 1% more average power to amplify the digital signal and maintain the analog power. Fortunately, that's merely a 0.04-dB increase in the average power output of the transmitter, which is barely a wiggle in the 1.39-dB increase required to cover the change in crest factor. Therefore, a combined amplifier needs about 1.3–1.4 dB more power capacity for hybrid operation than it does for analog-only.[13]

Extended Hybrid Mode

The foregoing calculation is based on hybrid FM IBOC operation with only the Primary Main OFDM subcarriers. To add all four Primary Extended partitions requires an additional 1.6 dB of digital power (Primary Main are –20 dBc; Primary Main plus Primary Extended are –18.6 dBc). This demands only 0.06 dB additional power from a combined amplifier. Adding Extended Hybrid subcarriers does not materially affect the hybrid crest factor, but it does require additional power that may be particularly important to accommodate in digital-only amplifiers.

---

[13] Dan Dickey and Alan White state it a little differently in *Development of the 816 FM-IBOC HD Transmitter*, Continental Electronics, www.contelec.com. They say, "The peak-to-average power ratio used in HD only transmitters is ~6 dB. The peak-to-average ratio used in Analog + HD transmitters is ~1.3 dB." The gist of the interpretation is the same—a combined analog-digital hybrid IBOC transmitter needs an additional 1.3 dB headroom to maintain the required power output compared to analog-only.

14 Transmission and Reception

In this chapter we diverge from the IBOC protocol stack as it is described in the NRSC-5 standard, delving into a discussion of the end points of the IBOC system: transmission system inputs at the starting end, and receivers at the destination. Chapters 3 through 11 addressed the IBOC protocol stack through the NRSC-5 standards documents themselves. Chapters 12 and 13 touched on how the IBOC waveform—the physical layer of the model—must be treated to radiate over the air properly. This chapter looks first at the IBOC broadcast facility (we'll call it Transmission), then at the IBOC receiver (Reception).

Transmission

There is only one brand of IBOC transmission system: the iBiquity HD Radio system. Numerous iBiquity-licensed manufacturers and software providers offer products that generate, process, or feed HD Radio transmissions. Transmitter manufacturers, for instance, make HD Radio products that run iBiquity firmware to process the program audio and data inputs, and generate the IBOC radio signal. Automation software companies provide interfaces to deliver program-associated data from the studio automation system to the HD Radio IBOC system. Manufacturers of studio-to-transmitter link (STL) systems configure their product lines to deliver digital information to the IBOC transmitter site. This space outside the NRSC-5 protocol stack is where manufacturers and software developers have the most opportunity to innovate. Let's have a look at the topology of the HD Radio transmission plant.

The Exciter

The etymology of the word *exciter* may have been lost to time, although the answer is probably found in early FM broadcast equipment manuals. Its context to the broadcaster has been in the generation of an FM signal at low power, apparently to *excite* the FM transmitter into oscillation. The Radio Amateur's Handbook of 1946[1] leaves this impression:

"A complete transmitter therefore may consist of an oscillator followed by one or more buffer amplifiers, frequency multipliers, or straight amplifiers, the number being determined by the output frequency and power in relation to the oscillator frequency and power. The last amplifier is called the final amplifier, and the stages up to the last comprise the exciter."

Fast-forward a couple of generations, and the term "exciter" is equated with a box that generates an analog FM radio signal at low power. It could drive a vacuum tube resonant amplifier or a broadband solid-state amplifier; or it could simply have a harmonic filter placed on its output to be a low power transmitter. Thus, the meaning of the word has evolved. Adding a new device to the category, with the second generation (GEN 2) of HD Radio transmission devices, the IBOC digital signal generator became known as an exciter. Just like an analog exciter, the GEN 2 exciter takes an audio input and puts out an IBOC digital radio signal.

The Exgine

At an FM station converting to GEN 2 HD Radio operation, the existing analog exciter was paired with a new GEN 2 HD Radio exciter, and their two independently generated signals were combined in one of the ways discussed in the previous chapter. As the products evolved, the analog exciter and digital generator could occupy the same device—the exciter would take in two audio inputs and output the hybrid signal. Then the third generation of HD Radio transmission equipment was made possible when iBiquity separated the front end from the back end of the HD Radio Exciter. On the back end, the end that generates the radio signal, transmitter manufacturers developed analog FM exciters that could accept an optional HD Radio generator board operating at the lowest layer of the IBOC protocol, designed simply to create the IBOC OFDM waveform. To provide the input to the generator, a separate unit was developed that handled the front end—processing the higher layers of the IBOC protocol, starting with the audio inputs. Considering the back-end OFDM generator be an IBOC *engine* that works inside an analog exciter, iBiquity formed a contraction of the two words, calling this IBOC building block the exciter engine, or Exgine (pronounced EX-jin). The Exgine generates the digital signal, passing on to the amplifiers in the exciter. The Exgine-equipped exciter can transmit a digital-only signal or a hybrid digital signal. (It can transmit analog-only, too, but there would be no need for the Exgine card to do that.)

Connecting the Services to the Transmitter

In this section on transmission, the focus is on the input to the Exgine and the exciter. iBiquity has a fine Application note on the subject of IBOC system input topologies, so we won't go into excruciating detail here. Look for *HD Radio Data Network Requirements*, iBiquity document number

[1] The Radio Amateur's Handbook, 1946 Edition, American Radio Relay League, p. 94, From the library of Lewis D. Collins, Sc.D.

TX_TN_2040, at www. iBiquity.com. Before reading that Application Note, the reader should be familiar with the service modes (such as MP1) and the services (such as MPS or SPS), which are threshed out in the chapters of this book.

Our focus will be on FM IBOC topology. Providing input to AM IBOC systems is a relatively uncomplicated affair compared to FM IBOC systems. AM IBOC involves transmitting only main program audio and data services (MPS and MPSD), plus the station information service (SIS). In addition to MPS, MPSD, and SIS, FM IBOC systems can transmit the optional supplemental services and advanced data services. To generate these additional services requires extra building blocks in the broadcast facility.

The simplest configuration of an IBOC input system is identical to that of an analog system. Main program audio and program-associated data are delivered to the transmitter site on the STL and are plugged into the back of the IBOC exciter. Figure 14.1 illustrates how the existing transmission infrastructure of an analog station can be utilized to transmit the host analog signal along with the IBOC MPS, MPSD, and SIS. The studio audio program is transmitted to the transmitter site in the usual way, via studio-to-transmitter link (STL). The low bit rate data for the MPSD is typically multiplexed on the STL as well, or delivered by other means. SIS data can be preprogrammed into the transmitter, requiring no STL bandwidth. Thus, with the simple addition of a slow data interface, the studio side of the system is ready for IBOC.

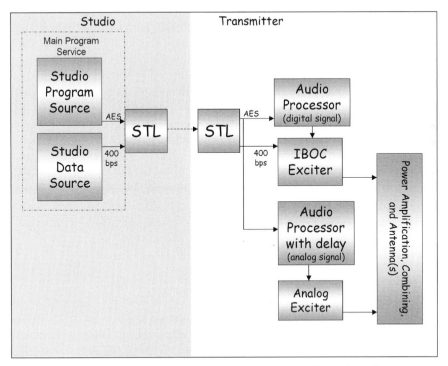

Figure 14.1 Simple IBOC Transmission Topology with All IBOC Gear at Transmitter Site

Main Program Audio

At the transmitter site, the data goes into a port in the IBOC exciter. The audio, however, is subjected to several processes before transmission. It must be split into two audio streams, one each for analog transmission and digital transmission. Of utmost importance, the analog audio must be delayed to accommodate the latency of the digital audio and to provide a diversity delay to overcome brief catastrophic reception failures. The audio clocks at studio and transmitter are best synchronized by frequency locking their clocks (often to a GPS-derived source) or processing the digital audio stream through a synchronized rate converter to avoid buffer underflows or over-flows on the air. (Audio may also be sent across an analog STL, obviating studio-transmitter clock issues by having all digitization occur at the transmitter site; this comes with the disadvantages of an analog audio plant and STL.)

Also very important, each audio stream requires an audio processor to tailor it to the transmission medium and the "sound" of the station. Processing for a digital transmission is very different than processing for an analog system. Several factors play into audio processing for analog FM audio, including the prevalence of FM noise and multipath characteristics, as well as the tension between the high frequency pre-emphasis and the 100% modulation limit. On the digital side, the codec provides a predictable and repeatable noise and distortion environment, generally unaffected by the over-the-air medium.[2] As long as the data stream is decodable, the full audio bandwidth and full signal-to-noise ratio of the audio is available to the receiver. This provides the digital audio stream with a different set of constraints on its audio processing than those that apply to the analog audio.

Analog and digital audio signals are subject to maximum levels in different ways. On the digital side, it is a numerical limit on the maximum output level of the analog-to-digital converter—the converter counts perfectly to the maximum level and can go no higher. On the analog side, audio amplifiers in the transmission chain will more gracefully overload than a digital converter does, first producing compression effects, then clipping. Also, over the air, analog transmission has a regulatory limit of 100% modulation, requiring the analog audio processor to maintain compliance by compression and/or clipping. For all these reasons, separate audio processors should be applied to the digital and the analog audio streams.

---

[2] Hybrid AM IBOC has two digital audio streams, a basic core stream and a lower reliability enhancement stream. The audio quality will change in the absence of the enhanced stream. Nevertheless, the signal-to-noise ratio of even the core audio is consistent and predictable.

Matching Audio Levels for Hybrid IBOC

Setting the Main Program Service analog and digital audio feeds on a hybrid IBOC transmission requires careful adjustment of the audio processors, the time delay of the analog audio, and the relative level setting of the digital and analog signals in the IBOC system.

Omnia Audio and iBiquity conducted a study[3] of listeners' perceptions of the relative levels of the analog and digital audio to determine what the optimum setting should be on the IBOC transmitter. They found that highly compressed analog audio, compared to more lightly compressed IBOC digital audio, was generally perceived as being about 3.5 dB louder. They recommended that the relative level settings of the IBOC transmitter boost the digital audio reference point by a total of 5 dB—the 3.5 dB perceptual difference between light and heavy processing, plus 1.5 dB for "broadcaster flexibility." This provides for a good level match in the blend to and from analog, on the average, while fostering a more open and dynamic IBOC listening experience. For an excellent discussion of the thinking on audio processing for hybrid IBOC operation, look for an article by Frank Foti of Omnia Audio, *Audio Processing and HD Radio.*[4]

Among other issues, Foti points out that the digital and analog audio processors should be of matched characteristics (such as the frequency crossover points and number of bands in multi-band processing) to avoid processor-induced phase anomalies in the transition when blending to or from analog audio. (Also see Chapter 9 for a discussion of blend issues with respect to phasing and timing.) Also, when processing audio that will be bit-rate-reduced by a codec, it is important to process the audio in a manner that is compatible with the way the codec works. This helps avoid overtaxing the codec and inducing unnecessary audio artifacts.

Finally, with respect to Supplemental Program Services, once a receiver is locked onto the digital audio stream, it can switch seamlessly from MPS to SPS and vice versa. Therefore, it is also important to assure that there is also no appreciable level disparity between each program service. The Audio Transport protocol (NRSC-5 reference document 4) provides a separate audio level offset setting for each audio program stream (MPS or any additional SPS). SPS program streams can be given their own receiver level offset values. This may come in handy when the processing and program content on an SPS is substantially different than on the MPS, enabling the perceived difference in program levels to be tweaked for best listener experience.

---

[3] Normalizing The IBOC And FM/AM-Analog Audio Signal Paths, Frank Foti, Glynn Walden, Omnia Audio October, 2002, http://www.omniaaudio.com/tech/IBOC_level.pdf.

[4] AUDIO PROCESSING and HD RADIO, Frank Foti, Omnia Audio, 2003, www.omniaaudio.com/tech/Audio_Processing&HD-Radio.htm.

Economizing for Multicasting

With the advent of multicasting, the demands placed on the STL increased substantially. If full-bandwidth audio streams were required for the supplemental audio channels, broadcasters would have to double up on their STL equipment and bandwidths. Why not take advantage of the bit-rate reduction of the HDC coder at the studio? Analog audio for the main program would still need to be delivered to the transmitter site, but with no such requirement for supplemental services, the concept made sense as a way to minimize the bandwidth required of the STL.

To support SPS channel coding at the studio, the protocols for generating an HD Radio signal would have to be divided between two locations—the studio and transmitter sites. Doing so could also benefit the broadcaster who wanted to control the main program digital and analog audio streams at the studio. By encoding the MPS audio at the studio, the station's audio processors and time alignment functions could remain at the studio. The extra bandwidth required for the MPS digital stream over the STL is about 120 kBps.

A distinction is made here between the NRSC-5 protocol stack and the HD Radio protocol stack. The NRSC-5 stack begins by receiving encoded audio from outside NRSC-5 and placing it on the audio transport, within NRSC-5. HD Radio transmission devices start by encoding the audio with the HDC coder, then passing it to the audio transport. As we talk about the input stages of the IBOC system, the HD Radio protocol stack includes audio encoding processes not included in NRSC-5.

The Exporter

To separate protocol functions between studio and transmitter, a new device has to be installed at the studio, and some of the functions normally performed at the transmitter must be stripped and moved to the studio. Clearly, the HDC coder must now be resident at the studio. It also makes sense to, at the studio, combine the program service data with the audio, making it ready for transport to the transmitter site and eventually over the air. The *HD Radio Data Network Requirements* document describes the management of data flow from studio to transmitter by logical channel (P1, P3, PIDS). Recall from Chapter 5 that these logical channels are formed by the Layer 2 multiplexing process. Therefore, it can be inferred that some or all of Layer 2 processing occurs at the studio side of this split system.

In Figure 14.2, the division of the HD Radio protocol stack between studio and transmitter sites is illustrated. A new device, the Exporter, performs the HD Radio processing tasks for the MPS, MPSD and SIS. The Exporter concept and software is an iBiquity creation that transmitter manufacturers employ in their HD Radio products. The Exporter performs several functions. It passes the incoming main program audio feed to the digital audio processor and the analog audio processor. The diversity delay is applied to analog audio. Digital outputs include the audio stream for analog transmission (not coded) and an Ethernet feed of the IBOC digital logical channels. These can be conveyed to the transmitter site by conventional private STL methods or by commercial digital telecommunications links. Alternatively the Exporter can be installed at the transmitter site as if it were part of the transmitter.

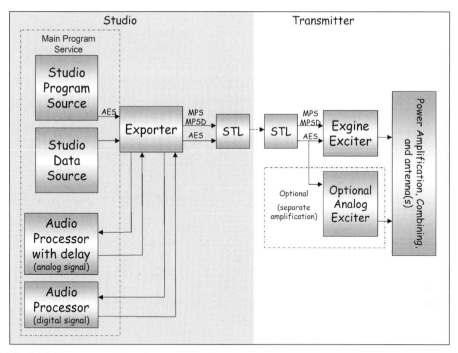

Figure 14.2 IBOC Transmission Topology with HD Radio Exporter, and Exgine Modules

Not shown is the optional use of a GPS receiver to drive the studio AES/EBU audio clock at the same rate as the transmitter's. (AES/EBU is the familiar name for a series of digital audio signaling formats jointly adopted by the Audio Engineering Society and the European Broadcasting Union.) In the functional block of the Exporter in Figure 14.3, the Exporter is depicted as a single block containing several processes. One of the processes depicted in the figure is not an original Exporter function. It is the function of the Exciter Auxiliary Service Unit (EASU), also called a *Synchronizer*. The EASU is available as a separate device, but can be integrated into one package with the Exporter. Functionally, the main program audio goes into the EASU/Synchronizer stage for clock synchronization, and goes out for audio processing. The block marked "sync" illustrates that. Then the EAS/EBU streams are processed by the Exporter functions. The EASU is GPS-synchronized to provide the both the AES/EBU digital audio stream and the Exporter a clock that matches the clock at the transmitter. The Exporter inputs labeled "From Importer" are discussed in the next section titled Importer.

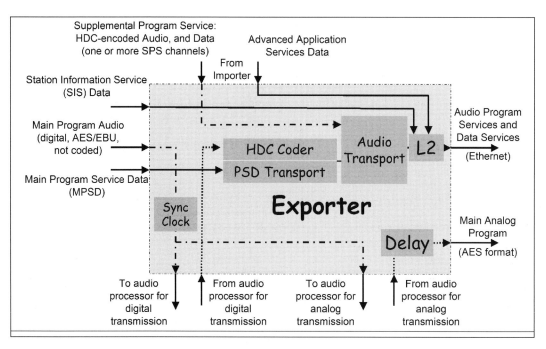

Figure 14.3 Key Functions of Exporter

Breaking into the Protocol Stack

The output of the Exporter is delivered to the Transmitter by a transfer protocol (UDP or TCP—discussed further below) over a private network isolated, as a subnetwork, from all unnecessary traffic. The *HD Radio Data Network Requirements* document assesses bandwidth requirements for various configurations of the IBOC signal. It uses the convention "E2X" to describe Exporter to Exgine data flow. For the MP1 service mode (all Primary Main OFDM subcarriers in operation with Logical Channels P1 and PIDS), iBiquity's analysis concludes 119.7 kbps is required on the average to handle the flow of logical channels P1 and PIDS (plus clock words). A required bandwidth of 176.1 kbps is required to handle bursty-ness of the traffic. (This assumes the use of the UDP transfer protocol; the numbers go up for TCP: 139.3 average, 232.0 peak.)

Where does the Exporter fit in the NRSC-5 protocol stack? This might be gleaned from the data rates required by the Exporter for the Logical Channels. For a comparison of the Exporter data rates to the IBOC protocol stack, let us consider the bandwidth required for the Logical Channels in Layer 1 and Layer 2. Looking back at Table 5.3, the output of the Layer 2 logical channels P1 and PIDS in this mode have rates of 98.4 and 0.9 kbps, respectively. The Exporter clock consumes an additional 1.024 kb per IBOC frame, or 0.7 kbps. Therefore, the net payload of a Layer 2 PDU plus the Exporter clock would run about 100.0 kbps. This is slightly less than, but in the same order of magnitude as, the required average rate for UDP transmission—119.7 kbps—supporting the inference that Layer 2 functions are incorporated in the Exporter. On the other hand, Layer 1 convolutional coding of P1 increases the bandwidth by the 2/5 coding rate, to about 246 kbps, more than the required average bandwidth would allow on the STL. We can infer that Layer 1, with its convolutional coding, is executed at the transmitter.

This splitting of IBOC protocols between two sites presents two critical challenges—timing and bit-accuracy. If the information does not make its way to the transmitter in a consistent and timely manner, the IBOC transmission will hiccup. There will be a discontinuity in the audio. If the information is inaccurate and compromised by errors along the way, packets may be rejected or possibly sent with errors, resulting in irregular performance as well.

A New Transport Where None Had Been Necessary Before

To split elements of the IBOC protocol stack (in this case, Layers 1 and 2) between two geographic locations requires yet another transport protocol. Initially, to move information in a timely manner, employing a one-way STL, the User Datagram Protocol (UDP) was chosen to transfer the information across the STL. UDP is one of the Internet protocols,[5] and might be more aptly indicated as UDP/IP, the way the more familiar TCP/IP protocol pair often is. UDP is a low-overhead protocol that simply embeds a checksum in its packets for error detection and it requires no response from the recipient. It is useful in situations where speed is valued over accuracy, on one-way links, and in a network broadcast where the overhead of responses from multiple recipients would be burdensome. Early adopters of the UDP transmission for their IBOC signals quickly learned how important it is for the STL to have as high reliability as possible.

HD Radio Data Network Requirements spells out the reliability issues. Running a 48 kbps coded audio stream via UDP, "any dropped IP packet will result in the loss of 1.5 seconds of HD Radio programming." A 0.1% packet loss would result in 873 dropouts per day. A 0.001% packet loss reduces that to 9 per day, and 0.0001% to about one per day.

On the other hand, with a bidirectional STL, and a little more bandwidth, the TCP protocol employs a feedback mechanism to retry lost or failed packets. So long as there is enough time to resend missing packets, TCP provides a much more robust link. *HD Radio Data Network Requirements* says as much as 1% packet loss can be accommodated on a TCP STL, with a 20-frame buffer and an average stream rate less than 60% of maximum. 1% loss is regarded as an "unhealthy LAN." Less than 0.1% loss is regarded as healthy. TCP is demonstrably the more reliable way to transmit IBOC frames from studio to transmitter, but it, too, has its limitations. For instance, by the time a discarded packet is retransmitted, it may be too late, wasting bandwidth on information that cannot be utilized.

---

[5] Request for Comments 768, Internet Engineering Task Force, tools.ietf.org/html/rfc768, August 1980.

Network Analysis

iBiquity commissioned a specialist in networking, MTM Technologies Inc., in 2006 to evaluate the UDP and TCP options for transporting IBOC data streams across the STL. they produced two reports, available on the iBiquity website.[6] One report, *HD Radio Networking Implementation Recommendations*, summarizes their conclusions after studying several HD Radio transmission facilities' data networks. Following are their key recommendations for the broadcast facility with some commentary on each:

- **Recommendation 1**
  Provision the WAN Link with Adequate Bandwidth

  MTM observes that the network designer should total all the anticipated traffic rates on the link and ensure that there is additional headroom in the bandwidth of the link. For UDP transmission, plan for the total traffic to consume no more than 75% of the available bandwidth of the link. This allows for the possible peakiness of the traffic when so much of the information is time-sensitive. With the greater reliability of TCP comes greater overhead; TCP links should be provisioned to consume no more than 60% of the network bandwidth. Total traffic is figured by summing the bandwidths of the various Logical Channels, plus the sync clock words, plus any other traffic planned for the link.

- **Recommendation 2**
  Make the WAN Link a Separate IP Subnet

  The second MTM report, *HD Radio Networking Best Practices*, goes into detail on the workings of hubs, switches and routers. It explains how hubs are simple repeaters—all packets coming into one port are repeated out all other ports. There is much bandwidth wasted on sending packets to ports where the information is not needed. MTM also observed a large amount of unnecessary housekeeping traffic on some stations' STL's due to their being connected to other networks at the office.

  Switches are smarter than hubs, monitoring which ports are connected to which network devices (by MAC Address). When a switch is sufficiently fast for the networks connected to it, it can maintain maximum flow on each port without sending unneeded information to any port. The switch occasionally polls all ports to verify what devices are present, and when asked to deliver a packet to a device number of which it is not aware, it polls all ports. Thus, the switch works well when it receives information intended for known clients, but if connected to a busy network, it may spin its wheels looking for clients that are not on its ports.

  The Layer 3 (L3) switch and the router are more sophisticated and require more effort to set up. The L3 switch operates on a homogenous network where all the ports employ the same interface (such as Fast Ethernet). The router is nonhomogenous and is capable of being configured to communicate with a variety of network interfaces on its ports. In both cases, the network

---

[6] Kurt VanderSluis, HD Radio Networking Implementation Recommendations, MTM Technologies and iBiquity Digital Corporation, July 27, 2006; Treiu Vu, HD Radio Networking Best Practices, MTM Technologies and iBiquity Digital Corporation, July 27, 2006.

administrator sets up each port as a *subnetwork* (subnet). Information is passed only to the subnet to which it is addressed. No bandwidth is wasted on housekeeping broadcasts not intended for a given subnet. Noting that although the subnet approach is more work to set up, MTM says, "However, the advantage of a predictable, well behaved network far exceeds the initial setup of the router/subnet." They recommend separating the office, studio, and transmission operations on separate subnets to ensure no leakage of packets that could cause congestion on mission-critical links. At the transmitter site, they suggest that the number of devices on the network, coupled with the less than 512 kbps HD Radio data traffic coming from the studio, do not preclude the use of a simple hub or switch. Keep in mind the possibility that a 1.5 Mbps AES/EBU audio stream may also be on the transmitter net, depending on how the STL is configured.

- **Recommendation 3**
  Achieve and Maintain Infrastructure Quality

  HD Radio Networking Implementation Recommendations recommends, "To successfully deliver the data stream using TCP and 20 receive buffers, the WAN link may have no more than 80 milliseconds of latency (measured on the unloaded link) and may not have more than a 1% error rate. With 3 receive buffers; the WAN link may have no more than 0.01% packet loss and no more than 50 milliseconds latency."

- **Recommendation 4**
  Use Receive Buffering When Available

  Buffering is helpful with TCP links when the recipient can request a replacement for a corrupted packet.

- **Recommendation 5**
  Use TCP When Available

  Because of its ability to request a replacement packet, TCP is substantially more robust than UDP. Timing is a critical element of the TCP configuration. If one of the last packets in a 1.49-second IBOC frame needs replacement, there is little time to request and receive a replacement before the frame must go on the air. Any additional link bandwidth allows 1.49-second frame PDU to arrive more quickly, buying more time for lost packets to be replaced.

Quality of Service

HD Radio Networking Best Practices also makes suggestions about quality of service (QoS), which is the application of rules for the delivery of data on the network. At the Exporter, each Logical Channel of the HD Radio stream is assigned a unique port number for delivery to the transmitter site. MTM recommends that the router or L3 switch be configured to give these port numbers priority over other traffic, assigning them a high priority, defined as Precedence 3. Telnet, which might be used for network administration, would be given the lesser-priority, Precedence 2, and all other traffic would have Precedence 0. Routers also manage queues. MTM recommends that HD Radio traffic be assigned Low Latency Queuing and a fixed bandwidth allocation to ensure that it moves quickly even when there is congestion. They suggest this is particularly important when the STL includes a path that is on a Wide Area Network sharing capacity with other traffic.

It is less critical when the STL is dedicated to the HD Radio traffic and on its own reserved subnet, in which case even a 10 Mbps network is "more than plentiful."

Those who have observed the output of the Exporter have noted the high burst of packets that comes once a frame period. Initially there was some concern that the STL would require enough capacity to replicate the bandwidth of the burst. However, the only reason for the burst lies in the manner in which IBOC Layer 2 works. Recall from Chapter 5 that it accumulates an entire frame of data to pass along to Layer 1 as a monolithic PDU. Once the PDU is ready, it is shoved out the door at the maximum rate the Exporter and its network interface can handle. MTM looked into this phenomenon to see how to ensure broadcast network configurations were compatible with it. They conclude that the burst bandwidth concern is unfounded. Networking devices are designed with bandwidth disparities in mind. When a faster link (the Exporter to a switch or bridge) is connected to a slower link (the STL), MTM explains that Ethernet specifications (IEEE 802.1)[7] require the slower link to be able to buffer 2 seconds of input. The burst from the Exporter is smoothed out by the buffer in the bridging device (the switch) and allowed to trickle through to the STL at its rate. Since each frame is less than 2 seconds duration, and the STL has the bandwidth to handle the required average data rate, the buffered data will make it across the STL without congestion. This conclusion presumes that all traffic on the STL has been accounted for in selecting the STL bandwidth, and that the bridging device is actually compliant with the 802.1 buffering criterion.

Network Security

MTM also discusses network security in *HD Radio Networking Best Practices*. While its study of several HD Radio facility networks was not a security audit, MTM did notice that security on the radio stations' networks was "practically nonexistent." At best stations had assigned passwords to administrative features, but they were often the same password on all parts of the network. MTM recommends among other things, diverse passwords across the network, maintaining most up-to-date patches and bug fixes for any network code in use, centralized authentication, authorization and accounting (AAA) to control and audit network activity, encryption of network management traffic, limit administrative access between subnets to only those paths that are necessary, assign read-only privileges where appropriate.

Another Approach

In a paper presented at the 2007 NAB Broadcast Engineering Conference, Philipp Schmid of Nautel Limited, revealed his analysis of the Exporter transport weaknesses.[8] Nautel developed an E2X Transport Protocol that utilizes UDP to move data and a new protocol as a transport to wrap around the UDP. It employs two UDP forward streams—one for timing and control and one for

---

[7] IEEE Standard for Information technology- Telecommunications and information exchange between systems- Local and metropolitan area networks. Part 5: Remote Media Access Control (MAC) bridging; IEEE Std. 802.1G, Institute of Electrical and Electronics Engineers, standards.ieee.org.

[8] E2X Bandwidth and Bit Error Requirements for Ethernet Synchronization; Introducing a Reliable Real-Time Point-to-Multipoint E2X Transport Protocol, *NAB Broadcast Engineering Conference Proceedings*, Philipp Schmid, 2007, National Association of Broadcasters.

the station's data content. It also adds a response path to request missing or discarded packets. It is smart enough not to retransmit packets for which it is simply too late. If there is no response (uni-directional STL or a return path failure) the protocol continues to function, only it is without the benefit of the ability to call for replacement packets. The timing transmitted from the studio to the transmitter site is less affected by delays and system jitter. Clock packets are not queued with the data packets, to ensure the timing has priority. Failed clock packets are not retransmitted, since doing so at the wrong time only adds noise to the clock signal.

Figure 14.4 shows the various "planes" of the E2X Transport protocol. In addition to the features discussed in the previous paragraph, the protocol is capable of supporting, and providing timing to multiple simultaneous transmitters from one Exporter. Requests for repeated packets are managed to avoid unnecessary multiple retransmissions of the same packet.

Nautel prepared a bit error rate graph comparing the E2X Transport operating with each of two buffer sizes, with an ordinary E2X UDP arrangement. It is shown in Figure 14.5 According to Nautel's analysis, to push the packet failure rate to a tolerable level, the reliability of the UDP STL must be extremely high—on the order of one bit error in 10^{10}. With the Nautel E2X protocol, including 16 to 20-packet buffering, one bit error per million is tolerable. Schmid indicates the TCP curve falls somewhere between the UDP and the Nautel 16-packet curve on Figure 14.5, closer to the Nautel curve. TCP, however, is not optimized for the nature of the transmission and might run into timing and congestion problems, notwithstanding the bit error rate analysis.

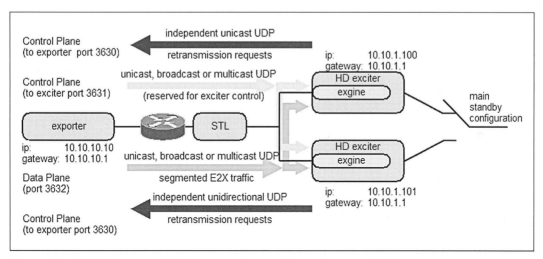

Figure 14.4 Block Diagram of E2X Transport Protocol Expanding upon UDP (Source: Nautel, The Proceedings of the 2007 NAB Broadcast Engineering Conference)

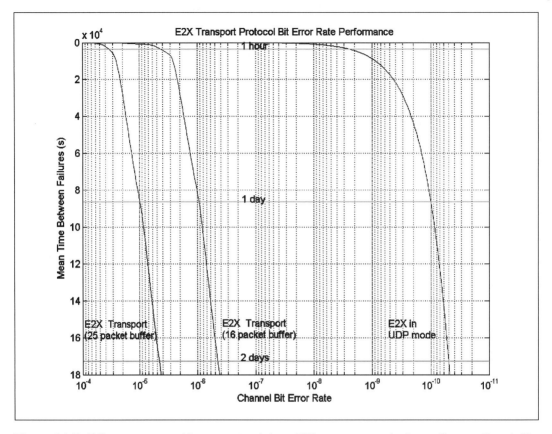

Figure 14.5 Failure rate versus bit error rate of three E2X transport mechanisms. (Source: Nautel, The Proceedings of the 2007 NAB Broadcast Engineering Conference

This effort by Nautel to improve on the technology, as well as Harris' development of split-level combining (Chapter 13), are just two examples of innovation from licensed HD Radio product manufacturers. IBOC technology as a whole benefits each time a product developer tries to "build a better mousetrap."

The Importer

To this point, the Exporter and Exgine have been exposed. An additional device is required to insert supplemental program services or additional data services. It is called the *Importer*. Like the Exporter and the Exgine, the Importer is part of the iBiquity topology for HD Radio transmission that is implemented by equipment manufacturers who are HD Radio licensees. Figure 14.6 illustrates the addition of the Importer to the HD Radio IBOC system. Figure 14.7 illustrates the key functions of the Importer.

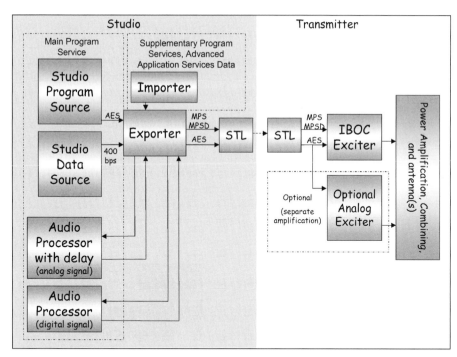

Figure 14.6 IBOC Transmission Topology with HD Radio Importer, Exporter, and Exgine Modules

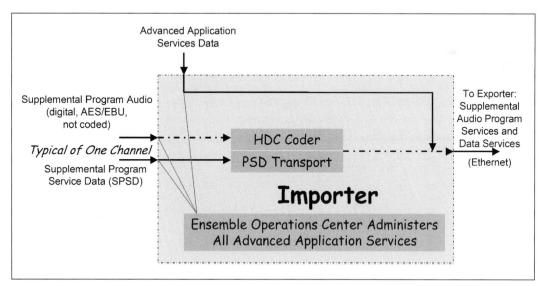

Figure 14.7 Key Functions of Importer

According to the Importer User's Guide,[9] the "Supplemental Program Service (SPS) forms an essential part of the AAS framework." The Importer is controlled by the iBiquity Advanced Application Services interface, the Ensemble Operations Center (EOC). All supplemental programs and all data services other than MPSD and SIS are controlled by the Importer. The Importer contains the HDC coder for one (or more) SPS programs, and the protocols necessary for requesting and receiving, and forwarding data for permitted data services. The EOC provides the ability to provision the HD Radio transmission for the requisite SPS bandwidth and data services bandwidth. Data service providers can be added or removed through the EOC. In addition to MPS (through the Exporter) and SPS, early services available for provisioning on the Importer included the RDS Traffic Message Channel (which is also being made available on HD Radio reception devices), a Visteon traffic application, a Reading Services for the Visually Impaired (RSVI) function, an On-Demand Interactive Audio Services (ODIA) function, and TeleAtlas gas price, point of interest, and traffic functions (TA GAS, TA POI, TA Traffic).

Secure the Critical Network

As discussed above, it takes a little more effort and better quality network components to set up an IBOC transmission network well. The Importer is a critical part of the network, passing its information on to the Exporter, where the Exporter bundles it into the packages destined for the transmitter. Recall that Logical Channel P1, for instance, can carry SPS, SPSD, MPS, MPSD and Advanced Data services. The Exporter melds its main program information with the incoming P1 information from the Importer to produce a complete Logical Channel P1. If P3 is employed for either supplemental audio or advanced data, then the Exporter will take it from the Importer and handle its delivery to the transmitter as well.

Figure 14.8 shows a recommended configuration of the studio-side networks. The mission-critical broadcast components—Importer, Exporter, and STL—are protected on their own subnetwork. The network switch is programmed to keep unnecessary traffic from where it does not belong. Note the curved arrows depicting the manner in which the switch routes the data flow. Similarly, studio operations, from which audio and data feeds might originate, can be isolated from the business office network with another subnet. Likewise, the traffic on the office network (not shown) would be switched to the studio network as necessary, avoiding being routed into the critical realm of the HD Radio data network. If necessary, the Importer can reside on the studio subnetwork, so long as a traffic analysis ensures there is enough bandwidth to handle peak traffic and keep the Importer stream flowing in a timely manner.

---

[9] Importer User's Guide, iBiquity Document No. TX-MAN-5078, Sept 2005.

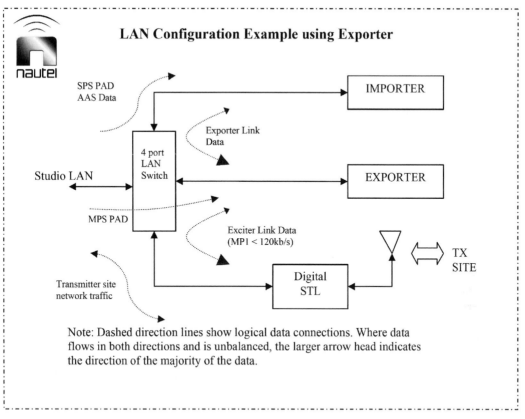

Figure 14.8 Linking Studio, Importer, Exporter and STL with Network Switch (Source: Nautel)

Reception

The NRSC-5 standard is fundamentally a *transmission standard*. There are very few criteria specified in the standard for receivers. Numerous mentions of the receiver do appear in the NRSC-5 reference documents. However, mostly they explain the purpose of features and specifications by describing how a receiver *could* take advantage of a feature. Control over receiver performance rests in iBiquity's licensing of HD Radio manufacturers. Licensed HD Radio receiver designs must pass iBiquity's certification process, ensuring that anything with the HD Radio name on it will meet a minimum standard of performance.

Core Receiver Components

iBiquity is in the business of developing software for IBOC platforms, among other things. On the receiver side, iBiquity develops code and assists with chip design for licensed receiver chipsets. Texas Instruments developed the first "digital baseband solution" for HD Radio receivers. Figure 14.9 shows a block diagram of one of their HD Radio chips, the TMA320DRI350. It illustrates how all the functions of demodulating both the analog and digital parts of the IBOC signal have been integrated into the chip. Initially, the first generation TI chip was called "bolt-on" because it contained only the digital signal receiver and was to be "bolted on" an existing analog receiver platform. The DRI350 goes to the next level, integrating all demodulating functions on the single chip, requiring only the receiver RF front end and audio back end to form a complete receiver.

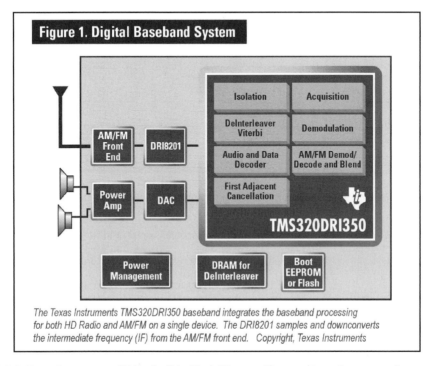

Figure 14.9 Texas Instruments HD Radio Chip Block Diagram (Source: Texas Instruments)

Other manufacturers have also developed HD Radio chipsets using iBiquity executable code or chip designs. One manufacturer, however, intends to be the first to make an IBOC receiver chip using its own power-efficient executable code and chip design. SiPort, a Silicon Valley company, develops IC designs optimized for the portable multimedia product market. Its HD Radio chip design is expected to be miserly with battery consumption, breaking the portable product barrier for HD Radio receivers.

In developing its chips, SiPort decided to start with the NRSC-5 protocol and develop its own custom IBOC reception technology. To make a small, efficient digital radio receiver chip, the designers evaluate each step of the reception process to determine which should execute as program code on the chip and which are given their own dedicated circuits. These decisions help define the power consumption and size of the chip. Then, incorporating the iBiquity HDC decoder into the IC design, a complete HD Radio receiver chip is created. Assuming they are successful, SiPort IBOC technology may become commonplace in portable multimedia devices.

In addition to the performance of the IBOC chip, receivers are dependent upon the architecture of the RF front end. Mike Bergman of Kenwood U.S.A. Corporation described[10] the design elements that receiver manufacturers consider. He makes an important observation about the economics of receiver manufacturing, "Cost drives much of the performance, in the end, since consumers are, unfortunately, more able to discern a slight difference in price than they are able to detect differences in performance." This is the crux of the tension between the broadcaster, who wants as much coverage as possible, and the receiver manufacturer who has to sell radios, at an attractive price-point, that must only perform well enough to sell.

Bergman lists a number of characteristics that are part of a matrix of performance trade-offs that manufacturers must make to sell a radio receiver. The automatic gain control (AGC) must be optimized for the type of use the receiver will see; for instance will the receiver be in motion while in use? How fast? Will it have a fixed outdoor antenna (on-vehicle), a headset cord, or a wad of wire indoors behind the cabinet? With high signal levels, will the linearity of the front end be able minimize distortion of the incoming signal? How high a noise floor can the design tolerate? To provide good digital performance, the receiver's phase noise and frequency accuracy must be well managed; how much money can go into these?

Receiver performance is part of the calculus of assessing IBOC coverage.

IBOC Coverage

In this section of the chapter, observations about AM and FM IBOC coverage are based on data from two key sources—NRSC and NPR Labs. During its evaluation of IBOC technology, the NRSC included among its review parameters the potential coverage area obtained by the IBOC digital signal. Initial studies were conducted on the iBiquity test stations equipped with prototype IBOC signal generators. Since the testing pre-dated the availability of factory-produced receivers, the mobile test platform utilized a laboratory-grade reception and measurement system. On the one hand, such systems are typically built with high-quality components from the lab bench and can be expected to perform as well as can be expected. On the other hand, a mobile laboratory platform is susceptible to noise and performance glitches that might not plague production receivers. A key component of field testing is the routine characterization and monitoring of the system performance to ensure it remains good. With careful attention to the test platforms, iBiquity measured IBOC performance in the field.

Expressing an early interest in the prospects for multicasting on the Supplemental Program Service, National Public Radio's Tomorrow Radio project followed the iBiquity field tests by two years, employing early production IBOC receivers to evaluate the FM IBOC performance in comparison to analog service.

---

[10] Mike Bergman, *A Look at Receiver Design Elements that Affect Your FM HD Coverage Areas*, Radio World, July 5, 2006.

FM Evaluation

The NRSC FM IBOC system evaluation completed in 2001 determined that the "digital service area of a radio station broadcasting FM IBOC should be an improvement with respect to existing analog service."[11] This assessment was based on the analysis conducted not only in field testing but also in the controlled environment of laboratory testing. The field testing was conducted on the eight FM stations listed in Table 14.1. They represent a variety of station power classes, geographic areas, and terrain conditions.

Station	Format	Location	Principle Test Condition(s) †	Comments
WETA 90.9	Talk and classical	Washington, D.C.	(a) low interference and low multipath	• Chan. 215B – # of radials – 8 • Host compatibility
WPOC 93.1	Country	Baltimore, MD	(c) single first adjacent interferer	• Chan. 226B – # of radials – 5 • Host, 1st-adj. compatibility (WMMR, WFLS)
WD2XAB 93.5	Test	Columbia, MD	(d) single second adjacent interferer	• Chan. 228A – limited testing • 2nd-adj. tests (WPOC is 2nd-adj. IBOC interferer)
KLLC 97.3	"Alice" (contemporary rock)	San Francisco, CA	(b) low interference, moderate/strong multipath (f) terrain obstructions	• Chan. 247B – # of test loops – 5 • EIA/NRSC test routes used (from 1996 tests) – routes are loops (not radials)
WHFS 99.1	Rock	Annapolis, MD	(e) simultaneous dual interferers, to the extent feasible	• Chan. 256B – # of radials – 1 (towards 2nd-adj's) • Two strong 2nd-adj. interferers (WMZQ, WJMO)
KWNR 95.5	Country	Las Vegas, NV	(b) low interference, moderate/strong multipath (f) terrain obstructions	• Chan. 238C – # of radials – 8 • "Specular" multipath (Las Vegas "Strip")
WNEW 102.7	Talk and Rock	New York, NY	(b) low interference, moderate/strong multipath (g) centrally located urban antenna (h) combined antenna (i) strong single 1st adjacent interferer	• Chan. 274B – # of radials – 4 (also "urban circles") • 1st-adj. compatibility (WMGK) • "Specular" multipath (downtown NYC) • Antenna located on top of Empire State Building
WWIN 95.9	Urban (pop)	Baltimore, MD	(d) single second adjacent interferer (j) low power combiner/common amp. (k) class A FM facility	• Chan. 240A – # of radials – 4 • Only station to use low power combiner (other stations all use high-power combiner)

† *letters in parentheses refer to test condition designations used in FM field test procedures.*

Table 14.1 FM IBOC Field Test Stations (Source: NRSC FM IBOC Evaluation Report, Table 4, p. 16).

[11] *Evaluation of the iBiquity Digital Corporation IBOC System: Part 1- FM IBOC*, p. 31, adopted November 2001, National Radio Systems Committee, www.nrscstandards.org.

Analog FM radio station coverage is characterized by signal strength contours in decibels with respect to one micro-volt per meter (dBμ). 70 dBμ is considered a comfortably strong signal that provides the main "city-grade" coverage. Reasonable coverage is maintained farther away from the transmitter site to the 60 dBμ contour and beyond. An FM station's coverage area is protected from overlap by strong signals on the same or certain adjacent channels. This area is bounded by the protected contour, which, depending on the power class of the FM station, is 60, 57, or 54 dBμ. These boundaries provide useful points of reference when evaluating IBOC digital coverage. Under ideal interference-free conditions, a monaural analog FM signal is considered to have coverage at signal levels as low as 34 dBμ.[12]

The FM IBOC field tests indicated that IBOC digital signals could be received at the analog host's signal level of 45 to 50 dBμ. This proved that the IBOC digital signal had the potential to cover the entire area within a station's protected contour, and more. The testing also indicated that with first-adjacent channel interference, the analog audio would deteriorate before the digital audio, effectively improving service where the analog is affected by such interference. This is no doubt due in a large part to the iBiquity first-adjacent cancellation technique employed in HD Radio reception technology. With second-adjacent interference, the IBOC reception under the controlled conditions of the testing laboratory remained excellent, even with the interferer set at the maximum level available on the test bed—42 dB stronger than the desired IBOC signal. This provided reassurance that IBOC second-adjacent interference performance would be equal to or better than the performance of analog receivers under the same conditions.

One of the techniques employed to test IBOC reception was mobile drive testing in a specially equipped van. Figure 14.10 shows one of the data plots that NRSC reviewed.[13] Numerous such plots were provided to the NRSC in the August 2001 iBiquity FM test report.[14] It shows the analog signal strength of the IBOC station as the test van drove away from the transmitter site on a route that approximated a radial with a compass bearing of 45 degrees. Below the desired signal level trace are two traces indicating the level of energy on the first-adjacent channels. Note that for most of the route, the "first-adjacent" signal levels simply mirror the desired signal level, but offset by about 13 dB. this is indicative of the selectivity of the test instrumentation—any first-adjacent signal will be masked by the crosstalk from the desired signal, until it is within about 13 dB or less of the desired signal level. This is visible to the right of the graph, when the van is a substantial distance from the desired transmitter.

---

[12] Sid Shumate, *Determining FM Coverage Area for Car Radio Reception in the Hybrid Era*, presented at the NAB Broadcast Engineering Conference, April 2006.

[13] Evaluation of the iBiquity Digital Corporation IBOC System, Part 1, FM IBOC, NRSC DAB Subcommittee Evaluation Working Group, Dr. H. Donald Messer, Chairman, November 2001, Available at www.nrscstandards.org.

[14] Report to the National Radio Systems Committee: FM IBOC DAB Laboratory and Field Testing, iBiquity Digital Corporation, August 2001, Available at www.nrscstandards.org.

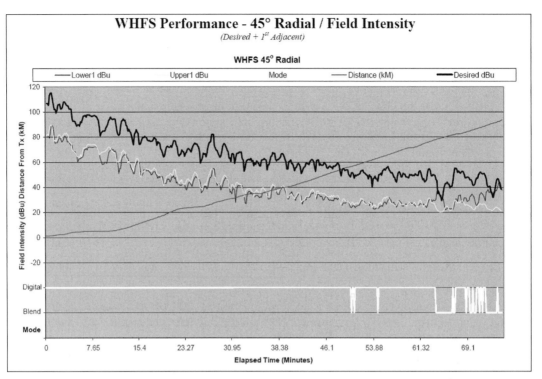

Figure 14.10 WHFS IBOC Field Test Signal Strength Graph with Audio Service Indication

The diagonal line on the graph indicates radial distance from the transmitter while the horizontal axis represents elapsed time. At the bottom of the chart is a dual-mode indicator. It is a horizontal line that indicates when the station is receiving the digital IBOC signal (the upper position of the line) or has switched to playing the analog signal (lower position of the line) when the digital signal is not performing reliably. Note how this drive test shows reliable digital service until the level drops to about 50 dBμ. Only a few dropouts occur until a first-adjacent channel signal begins to impinge on the desired signal and the desired signal level is quite low. Not all radials performed this well, depending on terrain, distance and interference conditions. However the overall sense of the data resulted in a positive evaluation by the NRSC.

Further FM Testing

With the arrival of early IBOC production receivers, NPR seized the opportunity to perform more field testing. As might be expected with relatively inexpensive (at least compared to the original prototypes), first-generation IBOC receivers, the serviceable coverage area of the digital signal was not as great as it was with the laboratory-grade field test apparatus. However, digital coverage was found to fall between the 60 and 70 dBµ contours.[15] The study observed that in optimum terrain and interference conditions IBOC digital performance was maintained at signal levels outside the 60 dBµ contour. This suggests that with continuing improvements in IBOC receiver design, for rejecting interference and equalizing signals distorted by rugged terrain paths, production receivers should be able to progress in providing digital service farther from the transmitter site.

NPR Labs continued the research into FM IBOC coverage by sharing an automated test device among numerous NPR stations. Four test rigs were shared among 26 stations, each of which mounted a rig in a vehicle, connected it to a roof-mounted antenna, and performed a drive test of the station. NPR Labs combined the data to assess digital coverage performance of FM IBOC. John Kean reported their findings[16] in 2006.

To this point, the measure of digital coverage did not particularly discriminate between Main Program Service and Supplemental Program Service reception. Since both services are conveyed on the same transport with the same codec, it is reasonable to conclude that where an SPS dropout occurs, an MPS dropout is likely as well, and vice versa. NPR Labs makes the observation, however, that with an analog backup, an assessment of the MPS digital service area is tolerant of a lower availability before considering the service to be disrupted and heavily reliant on the analog. SPS, without an analog backup service, has very abrupt interruptions when the reception fails. Therefore, it is fair to assume that a higher availability is required to define the service area of SPS.

NPR Labs employed two thresholds—90% availability and 97% availability—in its analysis of the 26 stations' coverage data. Availability is simply a geographic assessment of where digital program is or is not available. In an area identified as a 90% availability service area, an IBOC receiver can be expected to receive the digital program service at least 90% of the time. This became the NPR Labs target for evaluating MPS coverage, while 97% availability was applied to SPS assessment. Figure 14.11 is from the Kean paper. It shows, with three curves, how availability varied by signal strength for three stations; a fourth curve shows the same for the aggregate of the 26 stations. Due to propagation effects, interfering radio stations, and interfering ambient RF noise, each station had somewhat different results. The results show that there is no universal signal strength to define IBOC signal coverage.

---

[15] *National Public Radio 2003 Field Testing of Tomorrow Radio FM HD Radio Enhancement*, Hammett and Edison, Inc. available at www.nrscstandards.org.

[16] *HD Radio Coverage Measurement and Prediction*, NAB Broadcast engineering Conference Proceedings, 2006, John Kean, NPR Labs, National Public Radio.

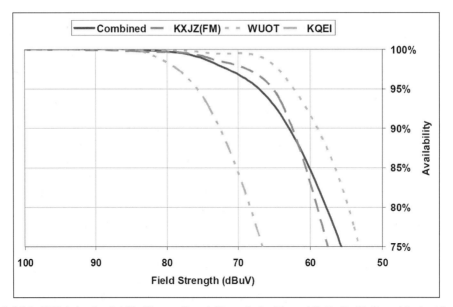

Figure 14.11 NPR Labs Availability Versus Signal Strength for Three HD Radio Stations (dashed lines) plus Combined Results for 26 Stations (solid line). (Source: NPR Labs, The Proceedings of the 2006 NAB Broadcast Engineering Conference)

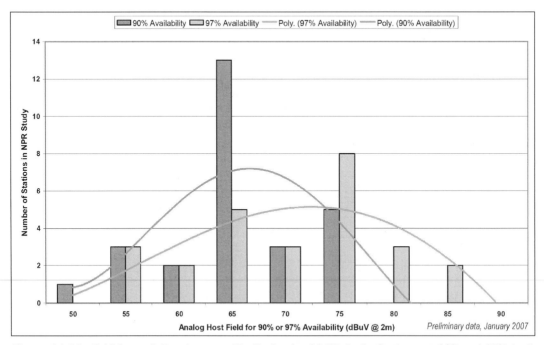

Figure 14.12 Field Strength Requirements Distribution for 26 HD Radio Stations, at 90% and 97% Availability. (Source: NPR Labs, The Proceedings of the 2006 NAB Broadcast Engineering Conference.)

Figure 14.12 shows a histogram of the 26 stations. Two sets of data are shown—90% availability and 97% availability. The horizontal axis is divided into signal level bins, each representing a 5 dB range. Each bar of the histogram represents the number of stations that have that signal strength as their 90% (or 97%) availability level. Two polynomial curves are overlaid on the histogram; each is a polynomial curve that best fits the distribution of the stations across the graph for the 90% and 97% availability values.

The NPR Labs results suggest that the 60–70 dBμ estimate of digital coverage is a reasonable estimate for MPS on many IBOC stations, at least for the receiver employed in the test. The 97% availability distribution (for SPS) sways well into the 70-dBμ or greater region. Clearly, more analysis would be necessary. How do different receiver models perform? How does receiver design affect the results, and are design improvements likely to make a difference in the consumer market? What are the controlling characteristics that affect performance—noise, interference, terrain? What about the quality of the digital signal leaving the broadcast facility?

The Corporation for Public Broadcasting issued a request for proposals[17] in 2006 to further study IBOC issues. In early 2007, NPR Labs was awarded the contract to execute the study. While the request presented a wide palette of analog and digital coverage issues to study with respect to public radio stations, it included attention to IBOC coverage impairments and improvements. The year-long study is expected to be complete in 2008.

Adjacent Channel Interference

Returning to the earlier discussion about receiver performance, Kenwood's Mike Bergman presented the chart in Figure 14.13 to illustrate the variability in receiver performance among brand and models. The bars show the desired-to-undesired signal ratio (D/U) at which each IBOC receiver blends to analog. Three receivers are depicted, with values for the upper and lower first- and second-adjacent channels. The lower the bar, the better the performance. This bench test shows that, particularly with first-adjacent interference, one model was markedly less resistant to interference than the other two. Based on the design trade-offs, the one receiver was affected by an undesired first-adjacent signal just 15 dB stronger than the desired. The good news is that even this IBOC receiver outperforms most analog radios in the same circumstance. However, the chart illustrates the variability of just three IBOC receivers under the same interference conditions.

The Kenwood chart only takes into account the receivers sitting still on a bench. Bergman observes that when one of the receivers represented in the chart was employed in the Tomorrow Radio test, it appeared to be more susceptible to the second-adjacent interference present on one of the radial routes than the chart would have suggested. Rather than surviving as much as a nominal -40 dB D/U second adjacent interferer suggested by the chart, Bergman estimates that in this case in the field, the receiver was overwhelmed at –10 dB D/U. The receiver did better on the bench than in that particular field route. This is another example of why more study is being sought on the topic. The causes of the variability of IBOC availability in the field are simply hypotheses until

---

[17] Request for Proposals for a Digital Radio Coverage and Interference Analysis Project, Corporation for Public Broadcasting, April 2006, www.cpb.org.

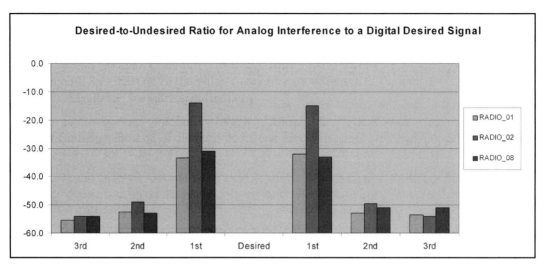

Figure 14.13 Desired-to-Undesired Ratio of Three IBOC Receivers at Point of Blend to Analog, Tested on Six Adjacencies (Source: Kenwood U.S.A. Corporation)

tested. One possible contributing cause is the hypothesis that as one travels away from the desired station, its signal level changes significantly from the front to the back of each hill, with respect to the desired station; meanwhile, the receiver is approaching the undesired station and its signal level might be doing just the opposite, being significantly stronger when the desired signal is significantly weaker. This might not show up in coverage maps but should be measurable in the field. Environmental noise and vehicular motion may also confound receiver performance, independently or in conjunction with the other signal impairments.

AM Evaluation

AM IBOC has received less attention with respect to actual coverage area with production receivers. With the bulk of NPR affiliates operating in the noncommercial FM band, plus the interest in the potential of Supplemental Program Services on FM IBOC, there has been less impetus for studies of IBOC coverage in the AM band. In Chapter 12 we discussed channelization and pattern issues with respect to the quality of the AM IBOC signal. Analysis of the potential for nighttime interference was performed by iBiquity and reviewed by NAB, resulting in the NAB recommendation to the FCC to authorize with nighttime AM IBOC operations.

The NRSC AM IBOC Evaluation Report[18] was adopted in April 2002. Table 14.2 lists the four AM stations on which the tests were conducted. With respect to AM IBOC coverage, the report concluded that during daytime IBOC operation, "The digital IBOC signals appear to provide coverage generally in areas where the analog signal strength is at useable levels. The stations may

---

[18] *Evaluation of the iBiquity Digital Corporation IBOC System: Part 2- AM IBOC*, adopted April 2002, National Radio Systems Committee, www.nrscstandards.org.

be subjected to interference from adjacent channels in some locations." Coverage data indicated that the AM IBOC test platform was capable of consistently receiving out to at least the analog AM station's 2-mV/m contour. Figure 14.14 illustrates one measurement radial during daytime operation on WTOP, Washington, D.C. The desired analog signal level is the highest, with its level indicated on the left axis. Time progresses from left to right. The right-hand vertical axis indicates the distance from transmitter, referenced to the diagonal line lower left to upper right. The signal drops out mid-test due to a tunnel. First- and second-adjacent channel signal levels are indicated on the other traces. The energy in the first-adjacent channels naturally mirrors the desired channel due to the channel overlaps. At about 65 km distance, a real first-adjacent channel signal begins to close the gap with the desired signal.

STATION	FORMAT	LOCATION	PRINCIPAL TEST CONDITION(S)†	COMMENTS
WD2XAM 1660	Test	Cincinnati, OH	(a) low interference and no grounded conductive structures (b) low interference and grounded conductive structures (f) power lines (not high-tension) overhead in urban areas	10.0 kW, 1 tower Daytime 1660 kHz 1 kW, 1 tower Nighttime 1650 kHz Experimental
WWJ 950	News/talk	Detroit, MI	(a) low interference and no grounded conductive structures (b) low interference and grounded conductive structures (f) power lines (not high-tension) overhead in urban areas	50 kW (day), 50 kW (night) DA2 5 towers
WTOP 1500	News/talk	Washington, DC	(a) low interference and no grounded conductive structures (b) low interference and grounded conductive structures (c) single first adjacent interferer (d) single second adjacent interferer (f) power lines (not high-tension) overhead in urban areas	50 kW (day/night) DA2 3 towers
KABL 960	Adult Standards	Oakland, CA	(a) low interference and no grounded conductive structures (b) low interference and grounded conductive structures (f) power lines (not high-tension) overhead in urban areas	5 kW (day/night) DA1 3 towers

†*letters in parentheses refer to test condition designations used in AM field test procedures*

Table 14.2 AM IBOC Field Test Stations (Source: NRSC AM IBOC Evaluation Report, Table 4, p. 19)

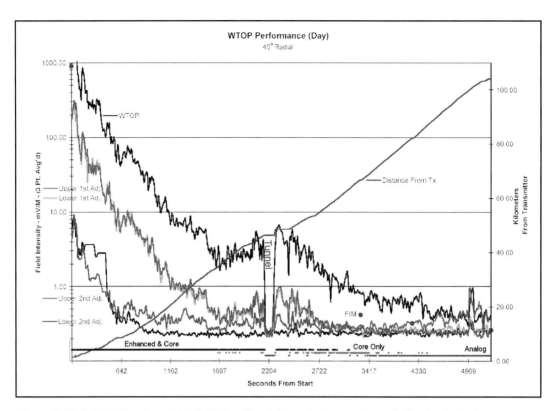

Figure 14.14 WTOP Daytime IBOC Field Test Signal Strength Graph with Audio Service Indication

Core and Enhanced

Recall that AM IBOC transmits a core and an enhanced digital audio stream. When the enhanced stream is compromised, the receiver reverts to core. Across the bottom of the chart in Figure 14.14 are three horizontal lines, each broken at various points. the top line indicates the receiver is presenting enhanced and core audio together. The second line indicates core only, and the bottom line indicates that analog audio has been switched in. Reading from left to right, the receiver is in enhanced and core mode, and begins to toggle to and from core only at about 40 km. In the tunnel, the receiver drops back to analog, but there is no tunnel radio rebroadcast evident, so the analog audio would have been nonexistent as well. Once out of the tunnel, the enhanced and core audio is restored, but more and more frequently reverts to core only. Finally, at about 65 km analog reception begins to dominate. At this point a field intensity measurement is taken with a calibrated instrument (dots marked "FIM"). The FIM suggests the signal level is actually lower than the automated measurements indicate. Thus, in this example, the AM signal level at the general area of core audio failure is approximately 0.3 to 0.8 mV/m.

Nighttime

The raised level of background noise in the AM nighttime spectrum constricts the digital coverage area. The NRSC found the digital signals consistently did not reach as far as the analog AM Nighttime Interference-Free (NIF) contour. NRSC pointed out in its evaluation that the field testing was conducted on a limited number of AM facilities, indicating that only "careful generalizations" could be made about digital coverage area, so long as the laboratory tests supported them as well.

Effect of Adjacencies on AM IBOC Coverage

The NRSC evaluation gave consideration to first- and second-adjacent channel interference to IBOC reception. The evaluation noted that the subjective listener testing of recorded analog and digital audio transmissions under first-adjacent interference conditions favored the IBOC digital signal. In other words, at a station's 0.5 mV/m contour, where ground wave allocations limit the first-adjacent interferer to 0.25 mV/m (a +6 dB D/U ratio) the digital reception was favored over the analog reception. Going further out from the 0.5 mV/m contour, the interference increases, and the digital continues to perform better than the analog. The evaluation concludes that AM IBOC coverage is "significantly more robust" to first-adjacent interference than analog reception. Even with dual first-adjacent interferers, the digital was "moderately more robust" than the analog. The same conclusions were made regarding second-adjacent channel interferers—significantly more robust than analog with a single interferer and moderately more robust with dual interferers. Based on these results, the coverage area of the AM IBOC digital signal will not generally be affected by adjacent-channel interferers any more than the analog coverage already is.

Conclusion of the IBOC Handbook

This concludes the chapters in this Handbook. During its journey through the IBOC world, the book has touched on the historical and the theoretical. This was not so much of a "how-to" book as a "how-it-works" book. I hope it has provided some useful background in the many facets of the technology. Following is an Appendix that contains a review of the building blocks of the technology from the perspective of a receiver. Reading it may be a helpful exercise to cement some of the knowledge shared in the chapters of the book. At the very least, it is a fine treatment of the receiver topology by Dave Wilson of the Consumer Electronics Association.

For all the material in this book, it is by no means everything about IBOC. Much has fallen on the cutting room floor (if I may make a cinematic metaphor for a radio book). Much continues to break anew into the marketplace, demanding vigilance from those who want to keep up with the technology. Please let me know what you think at www.ibocbook.com.

David Maxson
June 2007

A IBOC Receivers

In contemplating writing about IBOC receivers, we recalled Dave Wilson's technical paper presented at the National Association of Broadcasters 2006 Broadcast Engineering Conference and realized we could not have said it any better. This paper looks at IBOC from the receiver architecture side. The reader also may find it a useful overview of the IBOC building blocks that are covered in excruciating detail in Chapters 4 through 11. Here the building blocks are described with a focus on the receiver. We have excerpted Dave's paper with his generous permission.

IBOC Digital Radio Receiver Fundamentals

By DAVE WILSON
Consumer Electronics Association
Arlington, Virginia, USA

IBOC DIGITAL RADIO vs. HD RADIO™ Branded Products

HD Radio™ is a trademark of iBiquity Digital Corporation. In order to carry the HD Radio™ trademark a product must comply with technical specifications defined by iBiquity. There is no NRSC-sponsored certification program, or certification mark, associated with the NRSC-5 standard.

While NRSC-5 is very similar to iBiquity's HD Radio™ specification, there are important differences. One very important difference between products built to the NRSC-5 specification and products built to iBiquity's HD Radio™ specification is that NRSC-5 allows any audio codec to be used, while iBiquity's HD Radio™ specification requires the use of iBiquity's proprietary HDC Codec. Thus, transmitters and receivers designed to use other codecs (*e.g.*, Windows Media, MPEG II AAC, Lucent PAC, etc.) would be in compliance with NRSC-5. However, these products could not be called HD Radio™ products

It is also possible for receiver manufacturers to produce products that are not eligible to carry the HD Radio™ mark, but that are capable of receiving HD Radio™ transmissions. This would be the case for products that use iBiquity's HDC Codec, but that do not use the receiver integrated circuit software developed by iBiquity. Some manufacturers have expressed an interest in producing such products, indicating that they would like to develop their own software in order to optimize integrated circuit performance for specific applications (*e.g.*, portable battery powered products requiring minimal power consumption).

MAJOR COMPONENTS OF IBOC RECEIVERS

IBOC digital radio receivers differ significantly from analog receivers not only because of their ability to decode the digital IBOC signal, but also because they process the analog portion of the broadcast signal differently than most traditional analog radios. The major components of an IBOC receiver are illustrated in Figure A.1. The following paragraphs follow the incoming signal as it flows through the receiver and summarize the function of each component in the radio.

Front End

As is the case with traditional analog receivers, the first thing the incoming signal encounters when it enters the radio from the antenna is an amplifier. This amplifier boosts the level of the signal coming off of the antenna leads.

Tuning is achieved by mixing the amplified incoming signal with the output of a tunable local oscillator in the receiver. Typically, the tuned-to station is the one for which the combination of the two signals results in a 450 or 455 kHz signal (for AM) or a 10.7 MHz signal (for FM). These frequencies are referred to as the intermediate frequencies (IFs), and are specified in CEA-109-D,

Intermediate Frequencies for Entertainment Receivers.[1] CEA-109-D is a voluntary industry standard, and some receiver makers may choose to use different IF frequencies. The IF signal is then fed through a band pass filter, which attenuates most of the unwanted signals except for the one centered on the IF.

For years it has been common practice in many AM and FM receivers to address adjacent channel interference problems by narrowing the IF filter. This results in a narrowing of the bandwidth of the audio output for AM receivers, and can be accompanied by a discarding of the stereo information in FM receivers. In an IBOC digital radio receiver, however, narrowing of the IF signal cannot occur right away because, in the early stages of the signal's progression through the receiver it is not just an analog signal. It is a hybrid signal that includes the digital information, and this information is ±14.7 kHz around the center frequency (for AM) and ±198.4 kHz around the center frequency (for FM). The first IF band pass filter must be wide enough to pass both the analog and digital portions of the hybrid signal, and thus must have a bandwidth of approximately ±15 kHz (for AM) or ±275 kHz (for FM). In the FM case the filter is wider than the approximately ±200 kHz needed to pass the desired signal in order to also pass any analog first adjacent signals that might exist. Passing analog first adjacent signals like this gives the receiver an opportunity to analyze them and cancel them out.

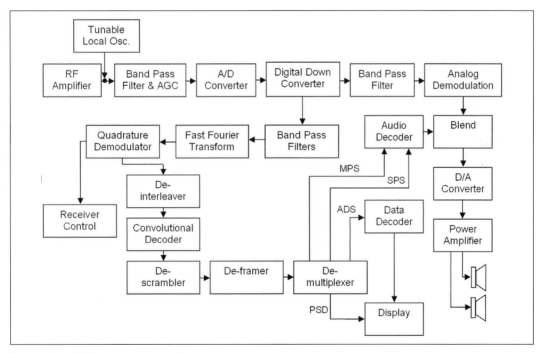

Figure A.1 IBOC Receiver Block Diagram

---

[1] CEA-109-D, *Intermediate Frequencies for Entertainment Receivers,* November, 2004.

After the IF filter it is typical to find the automatic gain control (AGC) circuit. Its two basic elements are amplification and feedback. This circuit increases or decreases the level of the signal, as needed, so that the signal level fed to the rest of the receiver is as consistent as possible. It does this by comparing the output of its amplifier with the desired signal level and feeding the result of the comparison back to the amplifier so it will know when amplification or attenuation is needed. The AGC function is even more important in an IBOC digital radio receiver because the receiver must be within its linear operating range to accurately decode the information in the IBOC sidebands. Non-linear variations of the signal levels in the IBOC sidebands will corrupt the information that they contain and result in higher error rates in the decoded signal. The AGC helps to address this problem by keeping the amplitude of the incoming signal within the linear operating range of the receiver.

Analog-to-Digital Converter

After the RF front end, the operation of an IBOC digital radio receiver begins to depart significantly from most traditional analog receivers. The filtered IF signal is fed into an analog-to-digital (A/D) converter, which converts the entire incoming signal into digital form (commonly referred to as "digitizing" or "sampling"). This may sound a little confusing because the traditional AM and FM portions of the hybrid waveforms are typically referred to as the "analog portion" of the hybrid signal, and the orthogonal frequency division multiplexed (OFDM) sidebands that carry the IBOC digital information are typically referred to as the "digital portion" of the hybrid signal. While this is all true, it is important to remember that the signal coming into the receiver from the antenna, which then passes through the amplifier and the filter, is entirely an analog signal with a single specific value associated with every instant in time. That single, specific value is the result of the combination of the AM (or FM) and OFDM signals at that specific instant in time. Converting the entire hybrid signal from analog-to-digital involves sampling the incoming signal at a frequency that is high enough to avoid aliasing. Aliasing is what happens when the periodic samples of a signal could be interpreted as samples from two very different signals, and therefore are ambiguous. This can happen if the sampling frequency used to sample a sinusoidal signal is too low. The samples could be interpreted as representing the original signal, or as representing a different signal with a much lower frequency, as illustrated in Figure A.2.

To avoid aliasing, signals must be appropriately filtered before sampling, and must be sampled at a high enough rate, which is twice the bandwidth of the signal being sampled (*e.g.*, at least 2 × 30 kHz = 60 kHz for AM, or 2 × 550 kHz = 1,100 kHz for FM), and at a resolution that results in sufficient dynamic range. Because most radios are capable of receiving both AM and FM signals, it is likely that the higher sampling rate needed for the FM band will be used for both AM and FM signals in most cases.

Of course, the IBOC digital information ultimately has to be processed digitally by the rest of the receiver. There are two reasons for sampling the analog AM/FM portion of the incoming signal and generating a digital equivalent. The first is that it creates new opportunities to use computer processing power to improve this portion of the signal, and the second is that it is necessary for implementing the blend function, which will be discussed later.

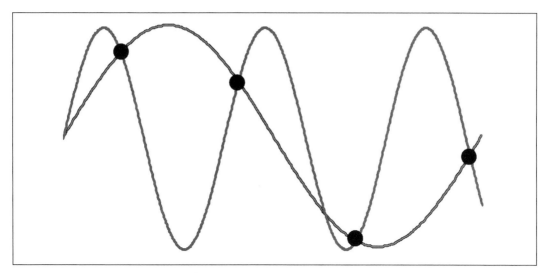

Figure A.2 Example of aliasing

Digital Down Converter

The function of the digital down converter is to eliminate the IF frequency and bring the signal down to baseband. It takes the output of the A/D converter and mixes it with an internally generated version of the IF frequency. Once this is done the signal can be split.

The AM or FM portion of the signal (as appropriate) is band pass filtered and demodulated. AM stereo signals are not compatible with IBOC digital radio because the quadrature signal that carries AM stereo information is used to carry digital information in the IBOC system, so analog AM stereo demodulation is an unlikely feature for an IBOC digital radio receiver. The ability to decode the 57 kHz RDS subcarrier in an analog FM signal is a feature in some IBOC digital radio receivers. This enables these receivers to display RDS data such as call signs, song title and artist information for analog FM signals. Once the AM or FM analog signal has been demodulated, a pulse code modulated (PCM) audio signal is fed into the blend circuit.

The other output of the digital down converter might be fed through a band pass filter to remove any extraneous energy that is not within the frequency limits of the baseband signal. The fast Fourier transform (FFT) can also do this filtering, so it is not absolutely necessary at this stage. Receiver manufacturers make the decision about where to do this filtering as part of their efforts to optimize integrated circuit designs. The next step for the signal is the FFT.

Fast Fourier Transform (FFT)

Now the signal is a digital baseband signal so the processing power needed to handle it has been reduced. However, the signal in each digital sideband is still the combined result of the combining together of all of the subcarriers within the sideband. The FFT takes the signal in each sideband and splits it up into the individual subcarriers that were combined at the transmitter. An FFT is an algorithm, essentially a computer program that takes the single combined signal in each sideband and re-expresses it in terms of the complex code bits that were imposed on the subcarriers. The output of the FFT is a group of parallel data streams, each one representing an individual subcarrier.

Subcarrier Demodulator

The data streams that come out of the FFT are fed into the subcarrier demodulator. Most of the subcarriers for both the AM and the FM IBOC system use some form of quadrature modulation. Each of these subcarriers is really the combination of two signals, the in-phase signal (commonly called the *I signal*) and the quadrature signal (commonly called the *Q signal*), which is shifted in phase from the in-phase signal by 90 degrees. The quadrature demodulator uses complex arithmetic to simultaneously decode the I and Q signals for each subcarrier.

At the transmitter, complex math is used to encode the digital ones and zeros of the IBOC data stream onto the subcarriers. All of the subcarriers carrying audio, ancillary data and station information in the FM IBOC signal use Quadrature Phase Shift Keying (QPSK) modulation for this purpose, and the reference subcarriers in the FM IBOC signal use binary phase shift keying (BPSK). In the AM IBOC signal there are three different sideband types – primary, secondary and tertiary. The subcarriers carrying audio, data and station information in the primary sidebands use 64 Quadrature Amplitude Modulation (QAM), the ones in the secondary sidebands use 16 QAM modulation, and the ones in the tertiary sidebands use QPSK modulation. The reference subcarriers in the AM IBOC signal use BPSK modulation. The combination of complex math and QAM/QPSK/BPSK modulation is an efficient way to convey data.

The location of the sidebands containing the subcarriers is illustrated in Figure A.3.

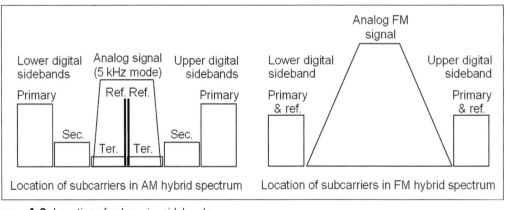

Figure A.3 Location of subcarrier sidebands

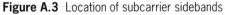

AM band subcarrier demodulation

As just described above, the primary and secondary AM IBOC sidebands use 64 QAM and 16 QAM modulation, respectively. In QAM modulation complex numbers are used to represent groups of code bits. Each OFDM subcarrier is modulated by a complex signal that consists of a real component and an imaginary component. Although the latter component is called "imaginary," it really does exist, and it is in quadrature (90 degrees out of phase) with the real component. It is called "imaginary" because complex arithmetic is used to generate the modulating signal, and complex arithmetic makes use of the imaginary number j, which represents the square root of negative one.

The two components of the modulating signal are represented by two quadrature pulse amplitude modulated (PAM) signals, one representing the value of the real portion and the other representing the value of the imaginary portion. In 16 QAM modulation there are 16 different combinations of real and imaginary values.

Figure A.4 illustrates what the different 16 QAM values mean in the secondary sideband of the AM IBOC system.

In the 16 QAM sidebands, if the receiver receives a signal on one of the subcarriers that is 1.5 units in amplitude in the direction of the real component of the complex number, and –0.5 units in amplitude in the direction of the imaginary component of the complex number, then the transmitted code bits are 1001. If, during the next symbol period, the amplitude in the direction of the real component changes to 0.5 units, and the amplitude in the direction of the imaginary component changes to 0.5 units, then the transmitted code bits are 1111. There are no phase changes in the signals representing the real and imaginary components of the complex number, only amplitude variations

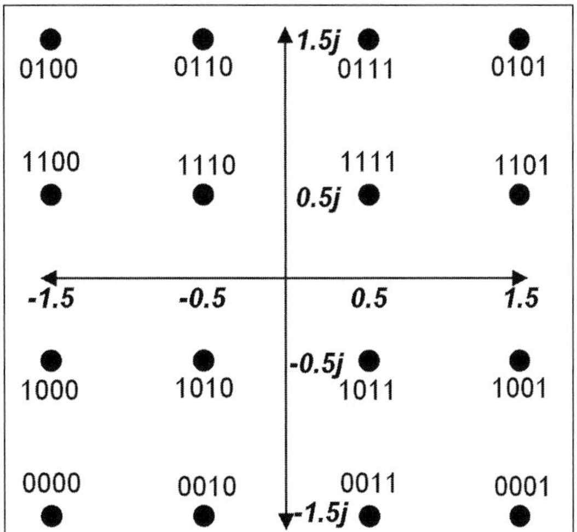

Figure A.4 AM IBOC 16 QAM constellation

The signals in the 64 QAM sidebands are similar to those in the 16 QAM sidebands, with the difference being that each PAM modulating signal has eight possible amplitude values instead of the four available in the 16 QAM sidebands. For the receiver to successfully distinguish between these eight different values the overall amplitude of the pulses in the 64 QAM sidebands is higher than the amplitude of the pulses in the 16 QAM sidebands. This is why the signal level of the primary sidebands is higher than the signal level of the secondary sidebands in the AM IBOC hybrid system. The code bits represented by the different combinations of real and imaginary carrier pulse amplitudes in the 64 QAM sidebands are described in Figure A.5.

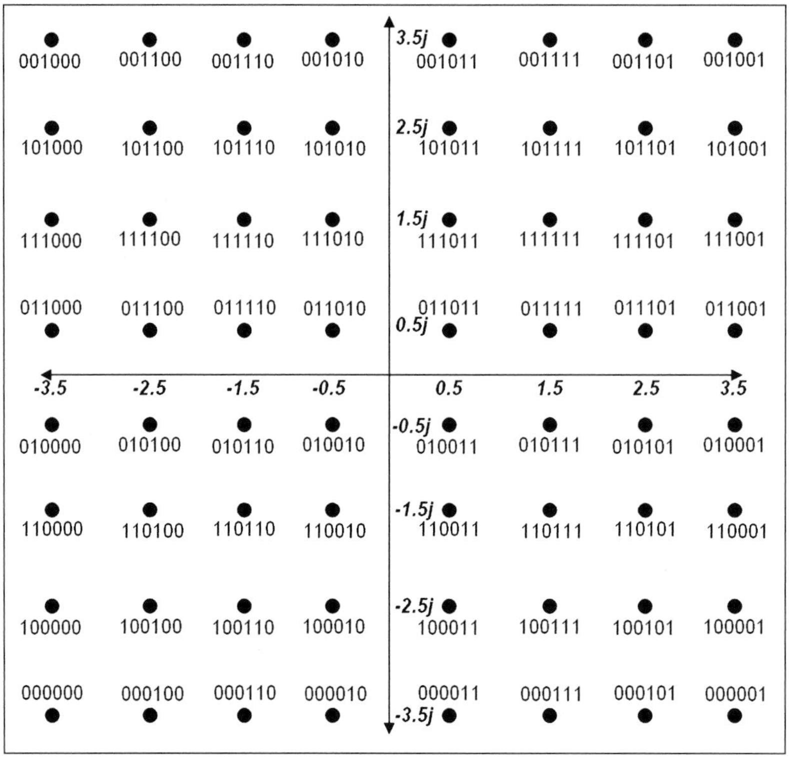

	-3.5	-2.5	-1.5	-0.5	0.5	1.5	2.5	3.5
3.5j	001000	001100	001110	001010	001011	001111	001101	001001
2.5j	101000	101100	101110	101010	101011	101111	101101	101001
1.5j	111000	111100	111110	111010	111011	111111	111101	111001
0.5j	011000	011100	011110	011010	011011	011111	011101	011001
-0.5j	010000	010100	010110	010010	010011	010111	010101	010001
-1.5j	110000	110100	110110	110010	110011	110111	110101	110001
-2.5j	100000	100100	100110	100010	100011	100111	100101	100001
-3.5j	000000	000100	000110	000010	000011	000111	000101	000001

Figure A.5 AM IBOC 64 QAM constellation

The tertiary sidebands of the AM IBOC signal contain QPSK and BPSK modulated subcarriers. The QPSK and BPSK modulation in these sidebands can also be called 4 QAM and 2 QAM, respectively. For the AM QPSK subcarriers a real value of 0.5 corresponds to a digital one, and a real value of –0.5 corresponds to a digital zero. An imaginary value of 0.5j corresponds to a digital one, and an imaginary value of –0.5j corresponds to a digital zero. In the BPSK case, for the AM IBOC signal, a real value of zero *and* an imaginary value of 0.5j correspond to a digital one, while a real value of zero *and* an imaginary value of –0.5j correspond to a digital zero.

In the AM IBOC system each QPSK, 16 QAM and 64 QAM subcarrier transmits 172.3 symbols every second. Thus, each QPSK subcarrier conveys 344.6 code bits every second, each 16 QAM subcarrier conveys 689.2 code bits every second, and each 64 QAM subcarrier conveys 1033.8 code bits every second. In the hybrid mode there are 50 tertiary (QPSK) subcarriers, 50 secondary (16 QAM) subcarriers, 50 primary (64 QAM) subcarriers, two reference (BPSK) subcarriers, and four station information (16 QAM) subcarriers. Thus, were it not for redundant symbols, the total code bit rate of the AM hybrid IBOC signal would be $(50 \times 344.6) + (50 \times 689.2) + (50 \times 1033.8) + (2 \times 172.3) + (4 \times 689.2) = 106{,}481.4$ b/s. However, the symbols transmitted over the lower secondary sideband subcarriers are redundant with the symbols transmitted over the upper secondary sideband subcarriers, and the symbols transmitted over the lower tertiary sideband subcarriers are redundant with the symbols transmitted over the upper tertiary sideband subcarriers. Also, the symbols transmitted over the upper station information subcarriers are redundant with the symbols transmitted over the lower station information subcarriers. "Redundant" in this case does not mean exactly equal, but rather perfectly correlated (barring any signal corruption in the path from transmitter to receiver). For these "redundant" sidebands and subcarriers the lower sideband data elements are the negated complex conjugates of the upper sideband elements. That is, if the upper sideband element is $a + jb$, then the corresponding lower sideband element is $-(a - jb)$, or $-a + jb$. Thus, the effective code bit rate coming out of the subcarrier demodulator is $(25 \times 344.6) + (25 \times 689.2) + (50 \times 1033.8) + (2 \times 172.3) + (2 \times 689.2) = 79{,}258$ b/s. These code bits are used for error correction coded information, which is why the actual payload data rate of the AM IBOC system in the hybrid mode is only around 36 kb/s. The error correction phase of the receiver will be discussed later.

The redundant data in the secondary and tertiary sidebands allows the receiver to compare the data from both sidebands to confirm accuracy, if desired. In the event of loss of data in one of the sidebands due to signal corruption, the receiver may use the data in the other sideband.

FM band subcarrier demodulation

In the FM IBOC system QPSK and BPSK is used to modulate the subcarriers in the digital sidebands. As with the QPSK and BPSK modulation in the AM IBOC system, complex math is used to calculate the value of the modulating signal. In the QPSK case, for the FM IBOC signal, a real value of one corresponds to a digital one, and a real value of negative one corresponds to a digital zero (see Figure A.6). An imaginary value of j corresponds to a digital one, and an imaginary value of –j corresponds to a digital zero. In the BPSK case, for the FM IBOC signal, a real value of one *and* an imaginary value of j correspond to a digital one. A real value of negative one *and* an imaginary value of –j correspond to a digital zero. Thus, in the IBOC version of BPSK two symbols are used to convey a single code bit of information

In the FM IBOC system each QPSK and BPSK subcarrier transmits 344.5 symbols every second. Thus, each QPSK subcarrier conveys 689 code bits every second and each BPSK subcarrier conveys 344.5 code bits every second. In the hybrid mode (mode MP1) there are 180 QPSK subcarriers in each sideband carrying audio, data and station information, and 11 BPSK reference subcarriers in each sideband. Thus, the total code bit rate of the FM hybrid IBOC signal is $2 \times ((180 \times 689) + (11 \times 344.5)) = 255{,}619$ b/s. These code bits are used for error correction coded information, which is why the actual payload data rate of the FM IBOC system in the hybrid mode is only around 96 kb/s. The error correction phase of the receiver will be discussed later.

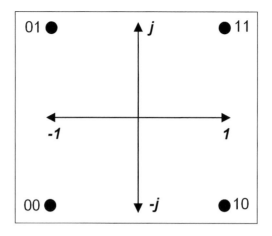

Figure A.6 FM IBOC QPSK constellation

The data comes out of the BPSK/QPSK/QAM demodulator in parallel streams, with each stream containing the symbols from one subcarrier.

The data is not yet ready for audio decoding. Most of it is still scrambled, convolutionally encoded and interleaved, all of which were done at the transmitter to help minimize the effects of channel impairments. At this point the symbols that represent the code bits being received must be complementary combined (where appropriate) and formed into soft decision values. Soft symbols are multi-leveled. That is, they have more than two possible values. For example, instead of a symbol having a value of either +1 or -1, it might have a range of values. The value of the symbol within this range indicates to the receiver how much confidence it should have in the symbol being either positive or negative. By demodulating the symbols in this manner the receiver can better understand the extent to which the symbols may have been corrupted. The use of soft decision values instead of hard decision values in the receiver improves the bit error rate performance of the system. The data must be de-interleaved, de-encoded and descrambled next. The data coming from the reference subcarriers, however, is majority decoded, error checked, and used immediately for receiver control.

Receiver Control

A few of the subcarriers in both the AM and FM system are dedicated for basic system control information. The receiver uses the information in these subcarriers (referred to earlier as the "reference" subcarriers) to determine the mode in which the station is broadcasting (hybrid, all-digital, etc.). For AM stations in hybrid mode the data from these subcarriers is also used to determine whether the analog portion of the signal is 5 kHz or 8 kHz wide. For FM stations in hybrid mode it is used to determine if the station is using the extended hybrid sidebands. These reference subcarriers convey other information about the characteristics of the digital signal as well.

The data from the reference subcarriers is used immediately by the receiver, and does not pass through the de-interleaving, decoding or descrambling processes.

De-interleaver

Interleaving is performed at the transmitter to add time and frequency diversity to mitigate the effects of signal corruption. The non-reference OFDM subcarriers are divided into frequency partitions, and de-interleaving involves taking the soft symbols from the subcarriers in each frequency partition and inserting them into rows of a two-dimensional matrix. Once the matrix is full the soft symbols are read out in a different order than they were put in. This reading out process follows a specific pattern, one that is the inverse of the pattern used at the transmitter to interleave the symbols. The interleaving pattern differs depending on the service mode of the transmitter (hybrid, extended hybrid, all-digital, etc.) The end results of the de-interleaving process are parallel one-dimensional series of soft symbols that are convolutionally encoded and scrambled. The number of series of symbols is a function of the service mode of the transmitter. In the FM band hybrid mode there are two series of symbols – one that carries the audio and/or ancillary data payload, and one that carries station information. In the AM band hybrid mode there are three series of symbols – two that carry audio and/or ancillary data payload, and one that carries station information.

Convolutional Decoder

The next step for the receiver is to undo the convolutional encoding (commonly called forward error correction) performed by the transmitter. As with interleaving, the specific method used to convolutionally encode the transmitted bit stream is dependent on the service mode of the transmitter. In all service modes, however, the coding operation is similar. A serial stream of bits is fed into the encoder and three new bit streams are created. Each is created by modulo-2 adding several incoming bits that are in close proximity to one another. In modulo-2 addition the result is a one if there are an odd number of ones among the single-digit binary numbers that are added, otherwise the result is a zero. Precisely which bits are modulo-2 added is different for each of the three output streams. A new calculation occurs after each new bit enters the encoder. Before exiting the encoder the three output streams pass through a filter that removes some of their bits (precisely which ones varies by service mode), and then through a parallel-to-serial converter. For example, for both streams (audio and/or ancillary data payload, and station information) in the FM hybrid mode one code bit is removed from every other group of three before the parallel-to-serial converter, making the ratio of outgoing code bits to incoming bits five to two.

The ultimate output of the encoder is a serial stream of data with more bits in it than the incoming stream. The bit stream coming out of the encoder does not contain the same bits as the incoming bit stream. The value of each code bit coming out of the encoder is a function of several bits that went into the encoder. Expanding the bit stream like this helps the receiver correct errors that may occur.

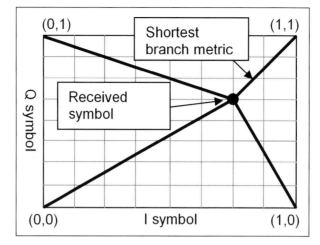

Figure A.7 The branch metric concept

To undo the convolutional encoding the receiver uses a Viterbi decoder.[2] This decoder analyzes the incoming symbols in groups called branch words, and compares them with all of the possible words that could be transmitted to determine which is the most likely match to the word that was created by the encoder at the transmitter. For example, if each branch word contained two code bits, then the incoming word would be compared with 00, 01, 10 and 11 to determine which is the closest match. Remember, the symbols coming into the decoder have been formed into multi-level soft decision values. So, what started out at the transmitter as a "1" might end up in the decoder as "0.75" after symbol corruption in the transmission path, if the soft decision values were formed by quantizing the incoming signal to the nearest $1/8^{th}$ increment between 0 and 1. The comparison between the incoming symbols and each possible word results in something called a branch metric, which is a measure of how closely the incoming symbols match the possible branch words. This is illustrated in Figure A.7.

As successive words come into the decoder they are used to feed a matrix called a trellis diagram. Once the trellis diagram has been filled a path through it that results in the fewest discrepancies becomes apparent, and leads to a received symbol value that is most likely to be correct. This is the "error corrected" value. Figure A.8 shows, conceptually, how this process works. The decoding that goes on inside an IBOC digital radio receiver is more complicated than the example shown here, but this is the general concept.

In the Figure A.8 example the path through the trellis begins at 00. When the first code bit is received it could be either a 1 or a 0, so the two possible paths from 00 are to 00 and 01. Once the first code bit is received the bits are shifted and the two code bits now being analyzed are compared against the possible values at the end of the two possible paths from 00. If the first received code bit were a 1, then the two code bits to be analyzed would be 01, and the path leading to 00 would

---

[2] Viterbi, Andrew, "Error bounds for convolutional codes and an asymptotically optimum decoding Algorithm," *IEEE Transactions on Information Theory*, Volume IT 13, April 1967, p 260.

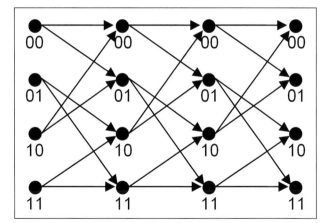

Figure A.8 Trellis diagram concept

have one discrepancy while the path leading to 01 would have no discrepancies. The values used to keep track of the discrepancies are called "path metrics." If the second code bit received were a 1 then, after shifting, the two code bits to be analyzed would be 11. This pair is compared against the pairs at the ends of the four possible paths from the two previous possible endpoints (two from 00 and two from 01). The path from 01 to 11 results in no discrepancies, so it is the most likely. The path from 01 to 10 results in one discrepancy, as does the path from 00 to 01. The path from 00 to 00 results in two discrepancies. Although in the second step the paths from 00 to 01 and 01 to 10 both result in one discrepancy, the *cumulative* discrepancies in the former path are greater because there was also a discrepancy in first step going from 00 to 00, while going from 00 to 01 in the first step resulted in no discrepancies.

This process continues until the end of the trellis is reached. At that point, the path through the trellis that results in the fewest *cumulative* discrepancies (*i.e.*, the combination of path metrics and branch metrics that results in the fewest discrepancies) identifies the bits that are most likely to represent the original bits that were fed into the encoder at the transmitter.

In short, the decoder estimates the values of the transmitted symbols based on the received symbols, and then checks this estimation several times by analyzing successive received symbols and how they relate to the ones that preceded them. Remember, when the code bits were generated by the encoder their values were dependent on several incoming bits that were in close proximity to one another. In this manner the decoder can use the values of the symbols both before and after a particular received symbol to ascertain what is most likely to be the correct value of a received symbol. When a corrupt symbol arrives at the receiver the decoder is often able to detect and fix the corruption using this method.

In the hybrid mode in the FM system the bit rate at the output of both convolutional decoders is 60 percent less than the bit rate at the input of the decoders, resulting in a total bit rate at the decoder output of $255,619 \times 0.4 = 102,247.6$ b/s. This is not the rate of the payload being sent through the system, but rather the combined bit rate of the audio, ancillary data and station information data, as well as the bits used to organize this data into frames. So, when the signal was encoded at the transmitter additional bits totaling 150 percent of the incoming bit streams were added by the convolutional encoders to guard against errors. This resulted in a total bit rate that was two and a half times that of the bit rate going into the convolutional encoders.

In the hybrid mode in the AM system the bit rate at the output of the convolutional decoder for bits coming from the secondary and tertiary sidebands is 33.3% less than the bit rate at the input of this decoder. For the decoder for the primary sideband the bit rate is 58.3% less at the output, and for the decoder for the station information subcarrier data the output bit rate is 66.7% less. This results in a total bit rate of $(25 \times 344.6 \times 0.667) + (25 \times 689.2 \times 0.667) + (50 \times 1033.8 \times 0.417) + (2 \times 689.2 \times 0.333) = 39,252.3$ b/s coming out of the decoder. This is not the rate of the payload being sent through the system, but rather the combined bit rate of the audio, ancillary data and station information data, as well as the bits used to organize this data into frames.

The convolutional encoders and decoders are the reason that the audio bit rate is so much lower than the bit rate of the raw data coming directly from the OFDM subcarriers. It is also one of the important system elements that helps to ensure error free reception in challenging mobile environments.

De-scrambler

After being de-interleaved and decoded the parallel bit streams consist of a series of transfer frames that have each been scrambled. The next step for the receiver is to descramble each transfer frame. During the scrambling process at the transmitter a scrambling sequence is imposed on each transfer frame by performing an exclusive or (XOR) operation on a bit-by-bit basis. Thus, if a bit in the transfer frame is a zero, and the corresponding bit of the scrambling sequence is a one, the result is a one. If a bit in the transfer frame is a one and the corresponding bit of the scrambling sequence is a zero, the result is a one. If the two bits are both zero, or both one, then the result is a zero. This modulo-2 method of addition evaluates each bit independently from its neighbors, so there is no carrying or borrowing. Because of this, the receiver can simply perform the same operation as the transmitter, since ((frame bit) XOR (scrambling sequence bit)) xor (scrambling sequence bit) = (frame bit). This process is illustrated in Figure A.9.

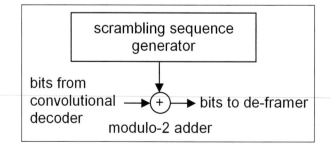

Figure A.9 Descrambling process

As noted earlier, after the de-interleaver there are multiple streams of data being processed in parallel by the receiver. In the case of the hybrid mode for the FM band system there are two streams, one that carries the audio and/or ancillary data payload, and one that carries station information. In the case of the AM band system there are three streams, two that carry the audio and/or ancillary data payload, and one that carries station information. In the receiver multiple descramblers operate in parallel to descramble each bit stream simultaneously.

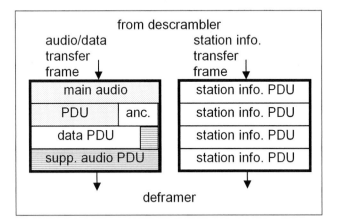

Figure A.10 PDUs in transfer frames

De-framer

After the descrambling process the receiver has multiple streams of transfer frames. These transfer frames consist of station information plus audio and/or ancillary data. The stream(s) that contain station information consist of a series of blocks of data called Station Information Service (SIS) Protocol Data Units (PDUs). Each of these PDUs is 80 bits long. SIS PDUs carry general station information, such as the three-dimensional geographic location of the transmitter, time of day, call letters, slogan, etc.

In the streams that contain audio and/or ancillary data each transfer frame includes control information that indicates whether the transfer frame contains main channel audio, supplemental audio and/or ancillary data PDUs. This control information also indicates the size of the PDUs in the stream, which is not constant. The control information is spread throughout the transfer frame in small chunks between the audio and/or ancillary data PDUs. The types of audio/data PDUs are: Main Program Service (MPS PDUs), which carry main program service audio; Supplemental Program Service (SPS PDUs), which carry supplemental program service audio; Main Program Service Data (MPSD PDUs), which carry data associated with the main program service audio, like song title and artist information; Supplemental Program Service Data (SPSD PDUs), which carry data associated with the supplemental program service audio; and Advanced Application Service (AAS PDUs).

The de-framer extracts the PDUs from the transfer frames, leaving each stream of data to consist of a series of PDUs. After removal of the transfer frame control information the bit rate is less than 39,252.3 b/s for the AM hybrid mode, and less than 102,523 b/s for the FM hybrid mode.

De-multiplexer

The streams of PDUs coming out of the de-framer pass through the de-multiplexer, which routes PDUs of similar types to the appropriate location. MPS PDUs carrying the main channel audio are routed to the main channel audio decoder. SPS PDUs are routed to the supplemental channel audio decoder (which may or may not be the same as the main channel audio decoder). MPSD and SPSD PDUs contain program associated data such as song title and artist, and these are routed to a decoder that stores them in the appropriate memory location for display on the receiver's screen. The broadcaster synchronizes transmission of PSD packets with associated audio packets to ensure that the information displayed on the receiver's screen matches the audio programming. The PSD (M or S) that is routed to the receiver display is determined by the program service the listener has selected.

AAS PDUs are routed to the appropriate place (*e.g.*, a display screen for displaying images, internal memory for storing audio, pictures or other data, etc.). To date there are no IBOC receivers on the market capable of handling AAS data, though there have been demonstrations at trade shows of receivers that use AAS data.

SIS PDUs are decoded and their information is inserted into the appropriate memory locations in the receiver (*e.g.*, the call letter and station slogan information is inserted into memory locations that are used to store information for the receiver display).

Audio Decoder

One of the controversial aspects of NRSC-5 is that it does not define an audio codec. It does not include a codec because iBiquity chose to keep its technology proprietary due to legal issues surrounding the public disclosure of its HDC codec technology. Implementers of the standard may use any codec they wish and still comply with the standard. Obviously, in order for a receiver to receive a transmitted signal both the receiver and the transmitter must be using the same codec.

Although NRSC-5 does not define an audio codec it does define how to split coded audio into two streams of differing levels of importance. These two stream types are called "core" and "enhanced." The most important encoded audio bits are included in the core stream. They can be decoded by themselves, but the result is lower quality audio than is achievable when the enhanced stream is also decoded. The enhanced stream cannot be decoded by itself. Dividing the coded audio like this provides better signal coverage and faster tuning times because the receiver can fall back to the core stream when impairments in the channel are causing too many data errors, and receivers can tune in to the core stream slightly faster upon initial acquisition of the signal.

In the receiver the output of the audio decoder is a linear PCM digital audio signal that is fed into the blend circuit.

Blend Circuit

As described earlier in the section on the digital down converter, the "analog" portion of the hybrid IBOC signal is demodulated and converted to a PCM digital audio signal before it is fed into the blend circuit. As was just discussed above the digital portion of the hybrid IBOC signal comes out of the audio decoder in PCM form. When the receiver is decoding MPS audio the two signals that are fed into the blend circuit contain the same audio. When the receiver is decoding SPS audio there is no "analog" input signal, and no blending occurs. In MPS mode the two signals are aligned in time so that the blend circuit can mix them together without the listener hearing any hiccups, clicks, pops or other artifacts. The only thing the listener should notice is an improvement in audio quality when the circuit blends from analog-to-digital.

Five of the bits in the header of each MPS PDU define the amount of gain that the receiver should apply to the incoming hybrid IBOC digital audio in order to ensure that the listener does not notice a difference in level between the analog signal and the digital signal when the receiver is blending. These bits are set by the broadcaster, and define values ranging from -8 dB to +7 dB, with the remaining bit combinations reserved for future use.

The blend circuit performs two important functions. First, it allows tuning to an MPS audio stream to be instantaneous for the listener because the "analog" signal can be sent to the speaker immediately upon tuning, and the listener can listen to that until processing and buffering of the IBOC digital portion is complete and audio is available at the output of the decoder. Second, as long as there are hybrid IBOC transmissions with low power digital signals accompanying high power analog signals the blend feature enables the receiver to gracefully fade to the analog signal at the edge of digital coverage, giving the listener an edge-of-coverage experience that is familiar.

It is because of the blend circuit in the receiver that the analog audio must be delayed at the radio station. If the analog audio were not delayed at the station the "analog" audio entering the blend circuit in the receiver would be too far ahead of its IBOC digital version coming out of the audio decoder, making blending very difficult. Conceivably the system could have been designed with no analog delay. While this would have allowed on-air talent to continue to receive real time off-air audio at the studio using traditional analog receivers, it would have required IBOC receivers to delay the analog signal in order to match it up in time with the digital version, and this would have meant that listeners with IBOC digital radios listening to IBOC digital stations would have heard a few seconds of silence after tuning to each station.

Having a time delay between the analog and digital versions of the signal provides important diversity reception advantages. Outages in the digital and analog audio are de-correlated, enabling one to "pick up the slack" when the other experiences an outage.

Most of the processing time in the receiver is fixed, and is based on the clock rates of the digital circuitry. However, the time it takes to decode the audio signal at the audio decoder is variable because the size of the encoded audio packets is not constant, as discussed in the earlier section on the de-framer. The transmitted signal includes a parameter that tells the receiver how much buffering is needed at the audio decoder to make the encode/decode process appear as a fixed delay. This does not mean that all makes and models of receiver will have synchronized audio outputs when tuned to the same station. Receivers may differ in their processing times because of different circuit designs. A specific receiver will have a constant delay for a specific station, however.

CHALLENGES FOR IBOC RECEIVERS

Tuning

Once a receiver is tuned to the main channel programming of an FM IBOC station, switching to that station's supplemental audio stream(s) can happen instantaneously. For the receiver this action simply involves deselecting the MPS PDUs from the de-multiplexer and selecting the appropriate SPS PDUs instead. Furthermore, when moving from a station's last supplemental audio feed to the main channel audio of the next station up the dial the receiver's acquisition can be instantaneous as well because it can feed the analog portion of the signal to the speakers while it works on decoding the digital signal.

When scanning down the dial, however, the receiver's acquisition of a supplemental channel cannot be instantaneous if the receiver manufacturer wants the stations found when scanning down the dial to be in reverse order from the way they are found when scanning up the dial. This is because, when scanning down the dial, the receiver has to acquire a station's RF carrier and decode the station's IBOC data stream before it can feed supplemental audio to the speakers. So, for example, if a receiver were scanning down the dial and stopped on the MPS for a station at 103.5 MHz, and the next audio stream available below it on the dial were a supplemental audio stream at 101.3 MHz, the receiver would have to leave 103.5 MHz, lock onto the 101.3 MHz carrier, decode the digital signal at 101.3 MHz to determine if it contained any supplemental audio and, once it has determined the presence of supplemental audio, decode the highest numbered supplemental stream and feed the audio to the speakers.

Making the tuning experience appear consistent for all audio streams (MPS and SPS) is a challenge for IBOC receivers, and is dependent on the implementation.

Noise

For years, to minimize interference to licensed services, the FCC has published rules limiting the emissions from non-licensed digital products that use RF energy (e.g., personal computers).[3] Generally speaking these rules have attempted to keep digital devices from interfering with licensed services as long as the digital device is more than about ten feet away from the receiver for the licensed service. With IBOC digital radio, digital circuitry must be added *inside* the receiver in close proximity to the circuitry that detects and decodes the analog signal. Thus, receiver manufacturers must pay particular attention to the possibility that the digital circuits inside the receiver may interfere with desired analog signals, and must include safeguards to keep this from happening. This is no simple challenge, particularly for analog AM reception.

IBOC digital circuits are not the only concern when it comes to noise. Any noise source that generates interference that couples into the antenna can cause reception problems. Interference

---

[3] *Code of Federal Regulations*, Title 47, Part 15, October 1, 2005.

can come from the host microprocessor, the display, switching power supplies, or digital amplifiers. All of these components can be found in non-IBOC receivers today.

A number of radio tuner cards have been produced for personal computers over the years, but they have generally included only FM tuners because of the difficulty of receiving noise-free analog AM in such close proximity to computer circuits.

Of course, the circuitry that demodulates the analog portion of the hybrid signal must now deal with the additional IBOC digital energy in the band as well. As far as the analog signal is concerned, this is noise.

THE FUTURE FOR IBOC RECEIVERS

There are many possibilities for future developments in IBOC digital radio receivers.

Portable Battery-Powered Receivers

Most likely the next big development in IBOC receivers will come after the development of new chipsets that minimize power consumption and thus make battery-powered portable receivers more practical. Several companies have expressed interest in using the NRSC-5 standard to develop their own chipsets for this purpose.

Receivers with Pictures

Beyond battery-powered portable receivers future developments may involve advanced applications that make use of the ancillary data capacity in the IBOC signal. While the ancillary data capacity in the hybrid AM IBOC signal is minimal, the potential for data transmissions in the FM band is significant.

It is well documented that the throughput of the FM band IBOC signal is sufficient to sustain two stereo audio signals of acceptable quality. Many FM stations have deployed, or are planning to deploy, so-called HD2 broadcasts. This is a very important feature, and critical for terrestrial radio broadcasters in the near term as they seek to create public excitement about IBOC digital radio. Ultimately, however, radio broadcasters may find that dedicating some of that bandwidth to pictures, both still and moving, may be more important to their future success.

Dedicating some bandwidth to pictures would not mean that supplemental audio streams like HD2 programming would have to be abandoned. The key to successful use of pictures via IBOC digital radio is caching of the pictures in the receiver, which means that the pictures would not be broadcast "live" to the "listener," but rather downloaded to the receiver and viewed by the listener, either on demand, or upon the broadcaster's command. For this type of operation the broadcaster might choose to dedicate bandwidth to HD2 broadcasts from, say, 5:00 AM to midnight, and use the period from midnight to 5:00 AM to push data out to receivers. If the broadcaster dedicated 48 kb/s to this for five hours each day, then approximately 100 MB of data could be transferred every night. [Ed. Note: Impulse Radio's early demonstrations showed that stations could provide a rich real time multimedia PAD experience with as little as 2 or 3 kbps reserved for data.]

To make this work only two things are needed. The first is a standardized codec for still pictures (*e.g.*, gif, jpeg, etc.) and the second is a standardized codec for moving pictures (*e.g.*, H.264/AVC, MPEG-4, etc.). The IBOC digital radio AAT PDUs that would carry this picture information would need to include header bits that indicate if there is a particular MPS/SPS audio stream with which they are associated, and if they should be stored in the receiver for display at a specific time, or simply stored for future on-demand recall by the consumer.

Radio on Demand

Ancillary data capacity could also be used to transmit stored audio files to the receiver, ready for recall by the consumer on demand. As with pictures, appropriate standards would have to be defined so that receivers would know what type of audio files were being transmitted, and how and when they should be available for playback. Having on-demand news, weather and traffic reports are obvious uses for such an application. Other uses might include premium advertising time where the advertiser gets to have a long-form advertisement stored on the receiver for a specific length of time.

Within the consumer electronics marketplace portable digital audio devices have been very popular in recent years, and consumers are becoming accustomed to downloading content to these devices. If the radio broadcasting industry had a standardized method to push stored content onto these portable devices it would be able to connect with the millions of consumers who are using them.

Future Receiver Developments are up to Broadcasters

According to CEA data, revenue from AM/FM receiver sales accounts for less than half of one percent of all consumer electronics industry revenue. Thus, the potential rewards for the consumer electronics industry in general are modest when it comes to introducing new terrestrial radio features. If the radio broadcast industry wants to expand its offerings to still pictures, video and/or other new services it will need to drive the development of these features itself. The addition of such features would help radio broadcasters capitalize on the growing market for portable multimedia products, a market into which cellular phone companies, satellite radio companies, and portable audio device makers have already started moving.

CONCLUSION

IBOC digital radio is an exciting technology that will transform the AM and FM radio broadcasting business. New receivers are now on the market that use this technology, and allow radio broadcasters to offer new services to their customers. The features that most people now recognize as the greatest improvements over today's analog systems are likely to be just the first of many enhancements made possible by IBOC digital radio. This technology has the ability to expand radio broadcasters' offerings beyond real-time audio information to include on-demand audio, still pictures and video. For radio broadcasters to fully realize the potential of their digital future they must take the lead in developing and promoting new features.

Glossary

Absolute Layer 1 Frame Number (ALFN) – A sequential number assigned to every Layer 1 frame. The start time of ALFN 0 was 00:00:00 Universal Coordinated Time (UTC) on January 6, 1980. Each subsequent ALFN is incremented by one from the previous ALFN. The present time can be calculated by multiplying the next frame's ALFN times the frame duration, T_f, and adding the total to the start time of ALFN 0.

All-Digital Waveform (or Signal) – The IBOC waveform intended to be broadcast without an accompanying host analog signal. In the absence of an analog signal for fast audio acquisition upon tune-in, the All-Digital signal contains a fast-acquisition digital audio stream that is reinforced when the more robust copy of the digital audio stream has time to de-interleave and blend in. This waveform is the planned successor to the hybrid waveform, although its use remains to be authorized by the FCC. (See *Hybrid waveform* and *Extended Hybrid waveform.*)

Allotment (of a Broadcast Frequency) – the creation of an availability for the placement of a certain class broadcast signal on a certain frequency in a certain area indicated (in the U.S.A.) by a city of license. (See also *assignment.*)

Amplitude Modulation (AM) – Modulation in which the amplitude of a carrier wave is varied in accordance with the amplitude of the modulating signal.

Amplitude Scale Factor – A factor by which the level of a particular OFDM subcarrier is multiplied to obtain its desired power with respect to a reference power level.

Analog Audio Bandwidth Control (AAB) – A parameter that indicates whether the 5 kHz or the 8 kHz audio bandwidth has been selected when an AM IBOC station is in hybrid mode.

Analog Signal (or Waveform) – The frequency-modulated or amplitude-modulated signal, consisting of a modulated RF carrier and accompanying sidebands, that is incumbent in the FM and AM broadcast bands and is receivable by both IBOC and non-IBOC receivers. (See *digital signal.*)

Assignment (of a Broadcast Frequency) – The licensing of a certain allotment to a specific entity (the licensee) with a specific set of parameters (power, height, location, directionality, gain, and so forth).

Audio Encoder – The process on the transmission side of the IBOC system that ingests an uncompressed digital audio stream and reduces the bit rate using a perceptual coding algorithm. It is the coder side of the two-step process called a codec. Decoding occurs at the receiver.

Audio Frame – The audio information processed as a unit by the Audio Encoder, consisting of 2048 audio samples at a sampling rate of 44.1 kHz.

Binary Phase Shift Keying (BPSK) – A form of digital phase modulation that assigns one of two discrete phases, differing by 180 degrees, to the OFDM subcarrier. Each BPSK symbol conveys one bit of information.

Bit Mapping – The assignment of certain bits of information to specific positions within a vector or matrix. At higher layers bit mapping creates a structure for conveying such information as headers, payload, data fields, error checking, and the like. At Layer 1, bit mapping assigns bits to the various OFDM subcarriers.

Block Encoding – The process of generating a forward error correction codeword for a block of data and appending it to that block. The encoded block consists of N symbols, containing K information symbols ($K < N$) and N-K redundant check symbols, such that most naturally occurring errors can be detected and/or corrected. (See *Reed-Solomon encoding.* Contrast with *convolutional encoding.*)

Channel Encoding – The process used to add redundancy to each of the logical channels to improve the reliability of the transmitted information; not related to audio encoding.

Code Rate – The ratio (m/n) of the amount of information input to a channel encoder (m) to the amount of information output by the channel encoder (n). The lower the rate, the higher the degree of information redundancy. Example: a rate 2/5 encoder conveys two bits of information with five bits of coded data. (See *convolutional code.*)

Complex Conjugate – The mathematical operation where the sign of the imaginary component of a complex number is inverted: conj(a + jb) = a – jb This operation is implicit in the generation of a radio signal with symmetrical sidebands above and below center frequency.

Configuration Administrator – The configuration administrator is an IBOC system function that configures each of the layers using SCCH information or parameters which do not change often.

Convolutional Code – A type of error-correction code in which m input bits of information are convolved through shift registers and adders to produce an n-bit output, where $n > m$. For each of the m bits, the encoder looks at k adjacent bits in the input vector and produces n/m output bits. The complexity of the convolution is determined, in part, by k, the constraint length, of the code, which indicates how many input bits are processed in each step. In contrast with *block encoding*, convolutional encoding does not append a parity codeword to the input data; rather, it transforms the input data into a larger codeword, within which the original input data may not be recognizable until decoded. See *code rate*.

Crest Factor – The ratio of the peak voltage to the RMS voltage of a signal. The crest factor of a sinusoidal waveform is 1.41 (the square root of 2).

Differential Encoding – Encoding process in which signal states are represented as changes to succeeding values rather than absolute values.

Digital Signal – With respect to IBOC, the digitally modulated OFDM waveform. In the hybrid mode, the term *digital signal* is exclusive of the host analog signal.

Diversity Delay – The fixed time delay imposed on one of two channels carrying the same information. It increases the probability of successful reception of the information in the presence of channel impairments such as fading and impulsive noise.

Emissions Mask – A specification for the maximum permissible power spectral density of radio frequency emissions, including those within the necessary bandwidth, out-of-band domain, and spurious domain.

Extended Hybrid Waveform (or Signal) – The FM IBOC waveform composed of the analog FM signal plus digitally modulated Primary Main OFDM subcarriers (subcarriers +356 to +546 and –356 to –546) and some or all Primary Extended subcarriers (subcarriers +280 to +355 and –280 to –355). (See *All-Digital waveform* and *Hybrid waveform*.)

Fading – The variation (over time) of the amplitude or relative phase (or both) of one or more frequency components of a received signal, as the result of propagation conditions and/or receiver motion.

Frequency Modulation (FM) – Modulation in which the instantaneous frequency of a continuous wave carrier is caused to depart from the channel center frequency by an amount proportional to the instantaneous amplitude of the modulating signal.

Frequency Partition – For FM IBOC, a group of 19 OFDM subcarriers containing 18 data subcarriers and one reference subcarrier.

Hermitian Symmetry – A characteristic of radio frequency sidebands in which the frequency responses of the In-phase (real) components above and below center frequency are symmetrical, while the frequency responses of the Quadrature (imaginary) components above and below center frequency would be symmetrical but for the fact that the sign of one Quadrature sideband's response is inverted with respect to the other. Mathematically, this is also called conjugate symmetry, in which the sign of the imaginary component is negated on one sideband with respect to the other: conj(a + jb) = a − jb. In terms of phase and amplitude response, the amplitude response is symmetrical while the phase rotates in opposite directions above and below center frequency. (After Charles Hermite.)

Hybrid Waveform – This waveform supports operation of both analog and digital receivers and may be used in an interim phase preceding conversion to the All-Digital waveform. (See *All-Digital waveform.*)

Host Signal – The analog signal that is part of the hybrid waveform, acting as a "host" to the digital portion of the hybrid waveform.

Hybrid Waveform – The AM and FM IBOC signals that consist of the host analog signal and an IBOC digital signal. It is considered hybrid because it mixes analog and digital transmission in the same channel. For AM IBOC, it is the transmitted waveform composed of the analog AM signal, plus digitally modulated primary, secondary, and tertiary OFDM subcarriers. For FM IBOC it is the transmitted waveform composed of the host analog FM signal, plus digitally modulated Primary Main OFDM subcarriers (subcarriers +356 to +546 and −356 to −546). Also, the FM IBOC *Extended Hybrid Waveform* may be distinguished from *Hybrid Waveform*, although for convenience the term *Hybrid Waveform* is often used in a context that includes the *Extended Hybrid Waveform* as a subset. All forms of *Hybrid Waveform* are distinguished from the *All-Digital Waveform*.

In-Band Adjacent-Channel – Technology never fully developed that employed digital transmission in the AM and FM broadcast bands in which the digital signals are asymmetrical to the analog host and consequently may not be compatible with the existing analog emissions and frequency assignments and may fail to provide a digital channel for every analog host.

In-Band On-Channel – Technology that employs digital transmission in the AM and FM broadcast bands in which the digital transmissions are symmetrical about the center frequency of the host analog signal; they maintain compatibility with reception of existing analog emissions and frequency assignments; and have an implicit one-for-one correspondence between digital signal and analog host.

Interleaving – A reordering of the message bits to distribute them in time (over different OFDM symbols) and frequency (over different OFDM subcarriers) to mitigate the effects of signal fading and interference.

L1 Block – A unit of time of duration T_b. Each FM IBOC L1 frame comprises 16 L1 blocks. Each AM IBOC L1 frame comprises 8 L1 blocks.

L1 Block Pair – Two contiguous FM IBOC L1 blocks. There is no AM IBOC counterpart. A unit of time duration T_p.

L1 Block Pair Rate – The rate, equal to the reciprocal of the Layer 1 block pair duration, at which T_p selected transfer frames are conducted through Layer 1.

L1 Block Rate – The rate, R_b, equal to the reciprocal of, T_b.

L1 Frame – A complere unit of information transmitted within a specific time slot of duration T_f identified by an ALFN. The IBOC digital signal consists of a series of L1 frames.

L1 Frame Rate – The rate, R_f, equal to the reciprocal of the L1 frame duration, T_f at which selected

L2 PDU (Protocol Data Unit) – Units of upper-layer content and protocol control information transferred from Layer 2 to Layer 1.

Latency – The inherent time delay that a logical channel imposes on a transfer frame as it traverses Layer 1, being the sum of the interleaver depth and any diversity delay applied. One of the three characterization parameters. (see *robustness* and *transfer*).

Layer 1 (L1) – The lowest protocol layer in the IBOC protocol stack (also known as the waveform/transmission layer). Primarily concerned with the preparation for and transmission of data over the communication channel. Includes framing, channel coding, interleaving, and signal generation according to the specified service mode.

Layer 2 (L2) – The protocol layer above Layer 1 at which the multiple services entering Layer 2 are multiplexed to Logical Channels for passage to Layer 1.

Logical Channel – Information conveyed from transmitter to receiver bearing common encoding, interleaving, and OFDM spectrum.

Lower Sideband (LSB) – The frequencies below the center frequency of the channel. IBOC digital waveforms are subdivided into groups, half of which occupy the Lower Sideband (see Upper Sideband)

Main Program Service (MPS) – The Main Program Service replicates the host analog audio program on the digital signal. MPS consists of Main Program Audio and Main Program Service Data.

Matrix – A two-dimensional block of data indicated by a double underscore; for example, a $\underline{u}$ or $\underline{V}$. If accompanied by a subscript, the subscript elements represent matrix row and column numbers, respectively; for example, $\underline{V}_{r,c}$

MPS PDU – The output of the Audio Transport consisting of protocol information followed by a sequence of encoded audio packets and MPSD.

Multicast – In the context of IBOC, the transmission of supplemental program audio channels in addition to the main program audio channel.

Multistream – An encoded audio stream split into two components in which one consists of a moderate fidelity *core* stream that is independently decodable and another that consists of an *enhanced* audio stream that supplements the *core*, but cannot be decoded independently. The *core* stream is more robust by being transmitted with a higher quality of service than the *enhanced*, and faster to acquire by being transmitted at the block rate rater than the frame rate. Different from *multicast*.

Necessary Bandwidth – The bandwidth sufficient to ensure transmission and reception of a signal with a specified minimum quality or performance under defined conditions.

OFDM Subcarrier – A discrete frequency-domain signal within the IBOC necessary sidebands that is phase or phase-and-amplitude modulated. The IBOC digital waveform consists of numerous subcarriers uniformly spaced at multiples of Δf. All subcarriers are modulated synchronously at the symbol rate, R_s. (See *OFDM symbol.*)

OFDM Symbol – Time domain pulse of duration T_s, containing all the active subcarriers and conveying all the data in one row from the interleaver and system control data sequence matrices. The transmitted waveform is the concatenation of successive OFDM symbols.

Orthogonal Frequency Division Multiplexing (OFDM) – A parallel multiplexing scheme that modulates a data stream onto a large number of orthogonal subcarriers that are transmitted simultaneously. (See *OFDM symbol.*)

Out-of-Band Emissions (or Domain) – Emissions on frequencies immediately outside the *necessary bandwidth* which results from the modulation process, but excluding *spurious emissions*. The out-of-band domain is the region within which such emissions occur for a given waveform.

P3 Interleaver Select (P3 IS) – In FM IBOC service modes MP2 – MP5, the P3 logical channel may utilize either a short or long interleaver depth (time span) depending on the state of P3 interleaver select. This control bit is received from L2 via the SCCH. When the state of P3 IS changes (as detected on an L I frame boundary) while transmitting in service mode MP2 – MP5, there will be a discontinuity in the transmission of the P3 logical channel.

Parity – In a binary-coded data vector, a condition maintained with a "parity bit" so that, the total number of "1s" or "0s" is always odd, or always even.

Peak-to-Average Power Ratio (PAPR) – The square of the *crest factor*, representing the ratio of the peak power to the average power of a waveform. The PAPR of a sinusoidal waveform is 2.

Power Level Control (PL) – In the AM IBOC Hybrid Waveform, the nominal level of the secondary, PIDS, and tertiary sidebands (relative to the analog carrier) as indicated by one of two settings, where PL=0 selects the low level amplitude scale factors and PL=1 selects the high level amplitude scale factors.

Primary Extended (PX) Sidebands – The portion of the FM IBOC primary sideband that additional optional frequency partitions occupy closer to center frequency from the Primary Main sidebands. PX sidebands are activated in the Extended Hybrid and All-Digital waveforms. They consists, at most, of subcarriers 280 through 355 and –280 through –355.

Primary Main (PM) Sidebands – The ten partitions in the FM IBOC primary sideband consisting of subcarriers 356 through 545 and –356 through –545, available in Hybrid, Extended Hybrid and All-Digital modes. Also, in the AM IBOC signal, subcarriers 57 through 81 and –57 through –81 in the Hybrid waveform and subcarriers 2 through 26 and –2 through –26 in the All-Digital waveform.

Protocol Control Information (PCI) – Information about the payload data, including: Stream ID, length of payload, and Cyclic Redundancy Check (CRC) for the PCI.

Protocol Data Unit (PDU) – A Protocol Data Unit (PDU) is the generic name for any assembled data element in the IBOC protocol stack that is produced by a specific layer (or process within a layer). The PDUs of a given layer may encapsulate one or more PDUs from the next higher layer of the stack and/or include content data and protocol-control information originating in the layer (or process) itself. The sequence of assembling PDUs within PDUs as they propagate down the transmission protocol stack is reversed, recovering PDUs from within PDUs as they propagate up the protocol stack at the receiver.

Protocol Stack – The organization of the various protocols for services and transports into a hierarchical structure such that the sequence of information flow is downward through the stack for transmission and upward upon reception.

Pulse-Shaping Function – A time-domain pulse superimposed on the OFDM symbol to improve its spectral characteristics.

Puncturing – The process of removing selected bits from the mother codeword to increase FEC code rate.

Quadrature Amplitude Modulation (QAM) – A form of digital phase and amplitude modulation that assigns one of m discrete phase-and-amplitude combinations to a carrier (or to an OFDM subcarrier) with each phase-and-amplitude state representing one symbol. mQAM has m possible symbols. For instance, 16 QAM has 16 possible symbols, each representing 4 bits per symbol ($2^4 = 16$).

Quadrature Phase Shift Keying (QPSK) – A form of digital phase modulation that assigns one of four discrete phases, differing by 90 degrees, to the carrier, with each phase representing a unique symbol value. Each QPSK symbol conveys two bits of information.

Reed-Solomon Encoding (RS) – A type of block encoding that encodes a block of information symbol by symbol (e.g., byte by byte). It is especially robust against burst errors because it does not matter how many bits in a given symbol are erroneous. There are k symbols encoded with n-k parity symbols, resulting in an encoder output of n symbols. The degree of redundancy of the RS encoder determines how many erroneous symbols can be fixed in a block of data: up to $(n-k)/2$ erroneous symbols can be corrected. (After Irving S. Reed and Gustave Solomon.)

Reference Subcarrier – A dedicated OFDM subcarrier that conveys L1 system control and status information contained in the system control data sequence. It also contains synchronization information from which the receiver determines the frame and block structure of the IBOC signal.

Robustness – The relative ability of a Logical Channel to withstand channel impairments such as noise, interference, and fading. FM IBOC Logical Channels are classified in one of eleven possible values. AM IBOC Logical Channels have eight possible classifications. One of the three characterization parameters. (See *latency* and *transfer*.)

Scrambling – The process of modulo 2 summing the input data bits with a pseudo-random bit stream to randomize the time domain bit stream.

Secondary Sidebands – The AM IBOC OFDM subcarrier groups consisting of subcarriers 27 through 53 and –27 through –53 in the Hybrid mode and subcarriers 27 through 52 in the All-Digital mode. The FM IBOC subcarrier groups that replace the analog signal in All-Digital mode. The FM IBOC secondary sidebands consist of FM IBOC subcarriers –279 through +279. These sidebands are divided into the Secondary Main (SM) sidebands containing ten frequency partitions, Secondary Extended (SX) sidebands containing four frequency partitions, and the Secondary Protected (SP) sidebands containing two groups of twelve protected subcarriers.

Service Mode – A specific configuration of operating parameters specifying throughput, performance level, and selected logical channels.

Signal – Detectable transmitted energy that can be used to carry information. In the radio frequency spectrum a signal has a characteristic *waveform*.

Spurious Emissions (Domain) – Emissions on frequencies which are outside the *necessary bandwidth* and the level of which may be reduced without affecting the corresponding transmission of information. Spurious emissions include harmonic emissions, parasitic emissions, intermodulation products and frequency conversion products, but exclude *out-of-band emissions*. The spurious domain is the region within which such emissions occur for a given waveform.

Supplemental Program Service (SPS) – The program service consisting or one or more Supplemental Program Audio streams paired with Supplemental Program Service Data. Unlike MPS, the SPS services do not have a corresponding host analog audio broadcast as a backup.

System Control Channel (SCCH) – A channel which transports control information from the Configuration Administrator to Layer 1 and also conveys status information from Layer 1 to Layer 2, through the system control processing.

Symbol – A modulated waveform having a duration of one symbol period, T_s that conveys one vector of binary data. For instance, a QPSK-modulated OFDM subcarrier conveys two bits per symbol, while an IBOC logical channel consisting of, say, 50 QPSK subcarriers, would convey $50 \times 2 = 100$ bits per symbol.

Transfer – A measure of the data throughput through a logical channel. One of the three characterization parameters. (See *latency* and *robustness*.)

Tertiary Sidebands – The AM IBOC OFDM subcarrier groups consisting of subcarriers 2 through 26 and –2 through –26 with the Hybrid Waveform and subcarriers –27 through –52 with the All-Digital waveform.

Training Bits – A pre-determined pattern or sequence of bits, the training pattern or training sequence, that is intermingled in the transmitted information at predetermined positions to allow the receiver to detect and correct for the effects of nonuniform channel effects over the transmission path and receiver front end.

Upper Sideband (USB) – The frequencies above the center frequency of the channel. IBOC digital waveforms are subdivided into groups, half of which occupy the Upper Sideband (See *Lower Sideband*.)

Waveform – The amplitude-versus-time representation of a *signal*. The term "waveform" is often employed in the context of a set of time and frequency characteristics that describe a specific type of signal. (See *Hybrid Waveform, Extended Hybrid Waveform, All-Digital Waveform*.)

Vector – A one-dimensional string of data (typically presented as a binary number). In the text they are represented by a letter with a single underscore: e.g., $\underline{u}$ or $\underline{V}$.

Abbreviations: Acronyms and Units

AAA	Authentication, Authorization and Accounting
AAB	Analog Audio Bandwidth
AAS	Advanced Application Services
AAT	AAS Data Transport
ADC	Analog-to-Digital Converter
AES	Audio Engineering Society
ALFN	Absolute L1 Frame Number
α	Alpha: cyclic prefix width (ratio)
AM	Amplitude Modulation
ASCII	American Standard Code for Information Interchange
ASF	Amplitude Scale Factor
ATTC	Advanced Television Technology Center
AWGN	Additive White Gaussian Noise
BBM	Block Boundary Marker

BC	Block Count
BPSK	Binary Phase Shift Keying
BTU	British Thermal Unit
CEA	Consumer Electronics Association
CCC	Configuration Control Channel
CODEC	Coder/Decoder
CPP	Comment Period (Pre-vote)
CRC	Cyclic Redundancy Check
DAB	Digital Audio Broadcasting
DAC	Digital-to-Analog Converter
DRB	Digital Radio Broadcasting
dB	Decibel
dBµ	dBµV/m, decibels with respect to one millivolt per meter
DDL	Data Delimiter
Δf	Delta-f: difference in frequency, change in frequency
DFT	Discrete Fourier Transform
DSP	Digital Signal Processor, Digital Signal Processing
DST	Daylight Saving Time
DTPF	Data Transport Packet Format
D/U	Desired-to-Undesired (ratio)
E2X	Exporter-to-Exgine
EASU	Exciter Auxiliary Service Unit
EBU	European Broadcasting Union
EOC	Ensemble Operations Center
EPG	Electronic Program Guide
ESG	Electronic Service Guide
EWG	Evaluation Working Group
f_c	Center Frequency
FCC	Federal Communications Commission (USA)
FEC	Forward Error Correction

FFT	Fast Fourier Transform
FM	Frequency Modulation
GPS	Global Positioning System
HD BML	HD Broadcast Multimedia Language (HD BML is an iBiquity Trademark)
HDC	HD Codec (HDC is an iBiquity trademark)
HDLC	High-Level Data Link Control
HTTP	Hypertext Transfer Protocol
Hz	Hertz
IAAIS	International Association of Audio Information Services
IBOC	In-Band On-Channel
IBAC	In-Band Adjacent-Channel
I2E	Importer to Exporter
IANA	Internet Assigned Numbers Authority
IAT	International Atomic Time
I	In-phase (real component)
IC	Integrated Circuit
ID3	Tag Embedded In MPEG I Layer III Files
IDFT	Inverse Discrete Fourier Transform
IEC	International Electrotechnical Commission
IETF	Internet Engineering Task Force
IP	Interleaving Process or Internet Protocol
ISO	International Organization for Standardization
ITU	International Telecommunications Union
ITU-R	ITU Radiocommunications Bureau
ITU-T	ITU Telecommunications Bureau
kbps	Kilobits per second
L1	Layer 1
L2	Layer 2
LSB	Least Significant Bit, Lower Sideband
MA1	AM Hybrid Service Mode

MA3	AM All-Digital Service Mode
MB	Megabyte: 10^6 bytes
MHz	Megahertz: 10^6 hertz
MP1-MP6	FM IBOC Primary Service Modes 1 through 6
MS1-MS4	FM IBOC Secondary Service Modes I through 4
MPA	Main Program Service Audio
MPEG	Moving Picture Experts Group
MPS	Main Program Service
MPSA	Main Program Service Audio
MPSD	Main Program Service Data
MS1-MS4	FM IBOC Secondary Service Modes 1 through 4
mV/m	Millivolts per meter
N/A	Not Applicable
NAB	National Association of Broadcasters
NIF	Nighttime Interference-Free (contour)
NOP	Number of Packets
NPR	National Public Radio
NRSC	National Radio Systems Committee
NRSC-1	NRSC Standard: AM pre-emphasis/de-emphasis and transmission bandwidth specifications
NRSC-2	NRSC Standard: AM emissions limit specifications
NRSC-3	NRSC Standard: AM receiver audio bandwidth and distortion recommendations
NRSC-4	NRSC Standard: RBDS data subcarrier standard
NRSC-5	AM and FM IBOC transmission standard (note: NRSC standards revisions have a letter appended to the standard number, e.g., NRSC-5-A)
ODA	Open Data Application
OFDM	Orthogonal Frequency Division Multiplexing
OSI	Open Systems Interconnection (model)
P1-P3	Primary Logical Channels 1 through 3

PA	Power Amplifier	
PAD	Program Associated Data	
PAPR	Peak-to-Average Power Ratio	
PCI	Protocol Control Information	
PCM	Pulse Code Modulation	
PDU	Protocol Data Unit	
PIDS	AM and FM IBOC Primary IBOC Data Service Logical Channel	
PL	Power Level	
PSD	Program Service Data	
PM	FM IBOC Primary Main Subcarrier Group	
PPP	Point-to-Point Protocol	
PSIP	Program and System Information Protocol	
PTY	Program Type	
PX	FM IBOC Primary Extended Subcarrier Group	
Q	Quadrature (imaginary component)	
QAM	Quadrature Amplitude Modulation	
QoS, QOS	Quality of Service	
QPSK	Quadrature Phase Shift Keying	
R_b	Block Rate	
R_f	Frame Rate	
R_p	Block Pair Rate	
R_a	Symbol Rate	
RBDS	Radio Broadcast Data Standard (NRSC Subcommittee, NRSC-4 Standard)	
RC	Raised Cosine	
RDS	Radio Data System	
RF	Radio Frequency	
RFC	Request For Comment	
RMS	Root-Mean-Square	
RRC	Root Raised Cosine	
RS	Reed-Solomon	

RSS	Root-Sum-Square
RT	Radiotext
S1-S5	FM IBOC Secondary Logical Channels 1 through 5
SCA	Subsidiary Communications Authorization
SCCH	System Control Channel
SEER	Seasonal Energy Efficiency Ratio
SIDS	FM IBOC Secondary IBOC Data Service Logical Channel
SIDTG	Supplemental Audio Identification Task Group
SIS	Station Information Service
SM	FM IBOC Secondary Main Subcarrier Group
SP	FM IBOC Secondary Protected Subcarrier Group
SPS	Supplemental Program Service
SPSA	Supplemental Program Service Audio
SPSD	Supplemental Program Service Data
SSATG	Surround Sound Audio Task Group
STA	Special Temporary Authorization by the FCC
STL	Studio-to-Transmitter Link
SX	Secondary Extended
T_b	Block Time (duration)
T_{dd}	Diversity Delay Time (duration)
T_f	Frame Time (duration)
T_p	Block Pair Time (duration)
T_a	Symbol Time (duration)
TCP	Transmission Control Protocol
TPO	Transmitter Power Output
TPWG	Test Procedures Working Group
UDP	User Datagram Protocol, also called Universal Datagram Protocol
URL	Uniform Resource Locator
USB	Upper Sideband
UTC	Coordinated Universal Time

UTF	Unicode Transformation Format
μV	Microvolt
W	Watt
XDS	Extensible Data Service
XML	Extensible Markup Language

Bibliography

4D, Inc. March 1, 1999. "Understanding Cyclic Redundancy Check." Tech Note, ID # 11874. Available: www.4d.com/knowledgebase.

4i2i Communications Ltd. 2004. "An Introduction to Reed-Solomon codes: Principles, Architecture and Implementation." Available: www.4i2i.com/reed_solomon_codes.htm.

Agilent Technologies. 2000. "Spectrum Analysis Amplitude and Frequency Modulation." *Application Note 150-1*. Available: cp.literature.agilent.com/litweb/pdf/5954-9130.pdf.

Ala-Fossi, M., and A. Stavitsky. 2003. "Understanding IBOC: Digital Technology for Analog Economics." *Journal of Radio Studies*, Vol. 10, No. 1, pp. 63–79.

American Standards Association. 1963. "American Standard Code for Information Interchange (ASCII)."

Astronomical Applications, US Naval Observatory. "When Does Daylight Time Begin and End?" Available: aa.usno.navy.mil/faq/docs/daylight_time.html.

Beezley, B. "HD Radio Self Noise Levels." Available: http://users.tns.net/~bb/iboc.htm.

Bouchard, G. June, 2006. "First Canadian Encounter with the New Radio Transmission Technology." In *CBC Technology Review*, CBC Radio-Canada.

Bower, A. J. April 1998. "Digital Radio—The Eureka 147 DAB System." *Electronic Engineering*, BBC Research and Development Publications.

Breebaart, J. et al. October 2005. "MPEG Spatial Audio Coding / MPEG Surround: Overview and Current Status." Paper presented at the 119th Audio Engineering Society Convention, New York, NY.

"Coded Orthogonal Frequency Division Multiplexing (COFDM)." www.digitalradiotech.co.uk/cofdm.htm.

Coding Technologies. September 8, 2006. "MPEG Surround to Bring Surround Sound to Digital Broadcasting." Press Release. Available: www.codingtechnologies.com.

Communications Research Centre Canada. 1997. "Digital Radio Broadcasting and CRC."

Computer Lab. 2002. "Mathematics, Complex Numbers and Functions, Tech Note: Complex Arithmetic, efg's." Available: www.efg2.com/Lab/Mathematics/Complex/Arithmetic.htm.

Crutchfield, S. 1996. "Signals, Systems, Control—Demonstrations: The Joy of Convolution." Johns Hopkins University. Available: http://www.jhu.edu/~signals/convolve/index.html.

Denny and Associates. 2003. "Evaluation of the Use of Separate Transmitting Antennas for In-Band On-Channel Digital and Analog FM Broadcasting." Prepared for the National Association of Broadcasters.

Dickey, D., and A. White. "Development of the 816HD FM-IBOC Transmitter." White Paper, Continental Electronics. Available: www.contelec.com/fm_white_papers.htm.

Downs, H. "IBOC Considerations for Multi-Channel Installations." Technical Paper, Dielectric Communications. Available: www.dielectric.com/broadcast/support_technical_papers.asp.

duTreil, Lundin & Rackley, and Hatfield & Dawson Joint Venture. 2005. "AM IBOC Ascertainment Project." Slides presented at the National Association of Broadcasters Broadcast Engineering Conference, Las Vegas, NV.

EarLevel Engineering. "A Gentle Introduction to the FFT." Available: www.earlevel.com/Digital%20Audio/FFT.html.

Electronic Industries Association Consumer Electronics Group, Thomas B. Keller, Chairman, Working Group B (Testing). August 11, 1995. Report on Digital Audio Radio Laboratory Tests; Transmission Quality, Failure Characterization, and Analog Compatibility.

Federal Communications Commission. Adopted November 1, 1999. In the Matter of Digital Audio Broadcasting Systems and Their Impact on the Terrestrial Radio Broadcast Service. MM Docket No. 99-325.

Federal Communications Commission. Adopted October 10, 2002. In the Matter of Digital Audio Broadcasting Systems And Their Impact on the Terrestrial Radio Broadcast Service. First Report and Order, MM Docket No. 99 325.

Federal Communications Commission. Amendment of the Rules with Regard to the Establishment and Regulation of New Digital Audio Radio Services, 5 FCC Rcd 5237 (1990).

Federal Communications Commission. November 1, 1999. Notice of Proposed Rulemaking, in the Matter of Digital Audio Broadcasting Systems and Their Impact on the Terrestrial Radio Broadcast Service. FCC 99-327.

Federal Communications Commission. November 6, 1998. Public Notice DA 98-2244.

Fisher, R., S. Perkins, A. Walker and E. Wolfart. 2003. "Convolution." Available: homepages.inf.ed.ac.uk/rbf/HIPR2/convolve.htm.

Fleming, C. 2006. "A Tutorial on Convolutional Coding with Viterbi Decoding." Spectrum Applications. Available: home.netcom.com/~chip.f/viterbi/tutorial.html.

Fluker, S. July 1, 2004. "Split-level Combining." *Radio World*, IMAS Publishing.

Foti, F. 2003. "Audio Processing & HD Radio." *Omnia Audio*. Available: www.omniaaudio.com/tech/Audio_Processing&HD-Radio.htm.

Foti, F. May, 2005. "5.1 Surround Sound Compatibility Within HD Radio and The Existing FM-Stereo Environment." *Omnia Audio*. Available: www.omniaaudio.com/tech/compatible.htm.

Foti, F. and G. Walden. October, 2002. "Normalizing The IBOC And FM/AM-Analog Audio Signal Paths." *Omnia Audio*. Available: www.omniaaudio.com/tech/IBOC_level.pdf.

Goldsmith, D., and M. Davis. May 1997. "UTF-7 A Mail-Safe Transformation Format of Unicode." Internet Engineering Task Force RFC2152.

Henry, L. October 2006. "Extra! Extra! FMeXtra!" In Radio Guide, *Media Magazines, Inc.*

Howard W. Sams & Co. 1999. Reference Data for Radio Engineers.

Hypertext Transfer Protocol, W3C. 2003. Available: www.w3.org/Protocols.

iBiquity Digital Corporation. "IBOC FM Transmission Specification, August 2001." Filed with the FCC and referenced as Appendix B in the First Report and Order, in the matter of Digital Audio Broadcasting Systems and Their Impact on the Terrestrial Radio Broadcast Service, MM Docket No. 99-325, adopted October 10, 2002.

iBiquity Digital Corporation. "IBOC AM Transmission Specification, November 2001." Filed with the FCC and referenced as Appendix C in the First Report and Order, in the matter of Digital Audio Broadcasting Systems and Their Impact on the Terrestrial Radio Broadcast Service, MM Docket No. 99-325, adopted October 10, 2002.

iBiquity Digital Corporation. May 2003. AM Nighttime Compatibility Study Report.

iBiquity Digital Corporation. October 2003. Field Report: AM IBOC Nighttime Performance. Available: www.nrscstandards.org.

iBiquity Digital Corporation. October 2003. Field Report: AM Nighttime Compatibility. Available: www.nrscstandards.org.

iBiquity Digital Corporation. September 2005. "Importer User's Guide." Document No. TX-MAN-5078.

International Organization for Standardization and International Electrotechnical Commission. ISO/IEC 7498-1; 1994. *Information Technology—Open Systems Interconnection—Basic Reference Model: The Basic Model*, 2nd Edition. November 15, 1994.

International Telecommunications Union. 1999. *Recommendation ITU-R SM.328.10 Spectra and Bandwidth of Emissions* (Question ITU-R 76/1).

Jampro RF Systems, Inc. "Bandpass Combiner Principles and Theory of Operation." Available: www.jampro.com/tech/combinertheory.pdf.

Johannesson, R., and K. S. Zigangirov. 1996. *Fundamentals of Convolutional Coding*. John Wiley and Sons.

Joyce, D. E. 1999. "Dave's Short Course on Complex Numbers, Reciprocals, Conjugates, and Division." Available: www.clarku.edu/~djoyce/complex/div.html.

Kahn v. iBiquity Digital Corp., No. 06 Civ. 1536 (NRB) (S.D.N.Y. Dec. 7, 2006).

Krieger, M. September 15, 2004. "IBOC Update: Insight on HD Radio." In *Radio Magazine*, Prism Business Media, Inc.

Lawrey, E. "OFDM Results." Available: www.skydsp.com/publications/4thyrthesis/chapter2.htm.

Lockwood, S. S. May 26, 2005. "So, What Have We Learned, or What to Do about IBOC." Slides available: www.hatdaw.com.

M/A-COM, an AMP Company. Application Note M561, "Power Dividers/Combiners." Available: www.macom.com/Application%20Notes/index.htm.

M/ACOM, an AMP Company. Application Note M568, "RF Hybrid Devices." Available: www.macom.com/Application%20Notes/index.htm.

Maxson, D. 2003. "Applying the Principles of Data Communications to the Development of an Open and Universal IBOC Data Protocol." Proceedings, National Association of Broadcasters Broadcast Engineering Conference, Las Vegas, NV.

Maxson, D. 2004. "Considering Measurement Requirements for IBOC Radio." Slides presented at the IEEE Broadcast Technology Society. Available: www.broadcastsignallab.com.

Maxson, D. 2004. "Interference Potential of Hybrid Digital Transmission: An IBOC Occupied Bandwidth Case Study." Proceedings, National Association of Broadcasters Broadcast Engineering Conference, Las Vegas, NV.

Maxson, D. 2006. "Beyond Spectral Occupancy: An Investigation of IBOC Signal Quality Metrics." Proceedings, National Association of Broadcasters Broadcast Engineering Conference, Las Vegas, NV.

Maxson, D. April 2005. "IBOC Spectrum Occupancy Measurements." Slides presented at the National Association of Broadcasters Broadcast Engineering Conference, Las Vegas, NV. Application notes by Agilent and Tektronix. Available: www.broadcastsignallab.com.

Maxson, D. April 6, 2005. "Evaluating Emissions of Your New IBOC Transmitter, Measuring Digital Signals Requires New Methods." In *Radio World*, IMAS Publishing.

Maxson, D. May 9, 2001. "The Future of Bitcasting." In *Radio World*, IMAS Publishing. Available: www.broadcastsignallab.com/white_papers/bitcasting.pdf.

Maxson, D., and P. Signorelli. 2002. "How Data Transmitted over an IBOC Station Will Be Managed: Using A Gateway To Generate Data Revenue." Proceedings, National Association of Broadcasters Broadcast Engineering Conference, Las Vegas, NV.

Mendenhall, G. "A Study of RF Intermodulation Between Transmitters sharing Filterplexed or Co-Located Antenna Systems." Technical Paper, Broadcast Electronics, Inc. Available: www.vallee.com/Tech%20paper/rfintrmd.pdf.

Merrimac Industries. "Quadrature Hybrids 90° Power Dividers/Combiners 10 kHz to 40 GHz General Information." Available: www.merrimacind.com/rfmw/05intro_quadhybrids.pdf.

NASA Lewis Research Center. 1996. "Digital Audio Radio Broadcast Systems Laboratory Testing Nearly Complete." Available: www.lerc.nasa.gov/WWW/RT1995/5000/5610h.htm.

National Association of Broadcasters. 1997. "FM Subcarrier Report/Technology Guide."

National Communications System Technology and Standards Division Secretariat: U.S. Department of Commerce, National Telecommunications and Information Administration, Institute for Telecommunication Sciences. August 7, 1996. "Federal Standard 1037C, Telecommunications: Glossary of Telecommunications Terms Published by General Services Administration Information Technology Service."

National Instruments Corporation. "Pulse-Shape Filtering in Communications Systems." Available: zone.ni.com/devzone/cda/tut/p/id/3876.

National Instruments Corporation. "Gaining Spectral Efficiency with OFDM." Available: www.zone.ni.com/devzone/cda/tut/p/id/3370.

National Instruments Corporation. "Multicarrier Modulation and OFDM." Available: www.zone.ni.com/devzone/cda/ph/p/id/150.

National Instruments Corporation. "RF and Communications Fundamentals." Available: www.zone.ni.com/devzone/cda/tut/p/id/3992.

National Instruments Corporation. "The Fundamentals of FFT-Based Signal Analysis and Measurement in LabVIEW and LabWindows/CVI." Available: www.zone.ni.com/devzone/cda/tut/p/id/4278.

National Instruments Corporation. "What is I/Q Data?" Available: www.zone.ni.com/devzone/cda/tut/p/id/4805.

National Public Radio. October 14, 2004. "Perceptual Tests of iBiquity's HD Coder at Multiple Bit Rates." Available: www.nrscstandards.org.

National Radio Systems Committee (NRSC). April, 2005. "NRSC-4-A: United States RBDS Standard. Specification of the radio broadcast data system (RBDS). Part I – Standard Document." Available: www.nrscstandards.org.

National Radio Systems Committee (NRSC). April, 2005. "NRSC-4-A: United States RBDS Standard. Specification of the radio broadcast data system (RBDS). Part II – Annexes." Available: www.nrscstandards.org.

National Radio Systems Committee (NRSC). July, 1998. "NRSC-1: NRSC AM Preemphasis/de-emphasis and Broadcast Audio Transmission Bandwidth Specifications." Available: www.nrscstandards.org.

National Radio Systems Committee (NRSC). June, 1990. "NRSC-3: Audio Bandwidth and Distortion Recommendations for AM Broadcast Receivers." Available: www.nrscstandards.org.

National Radio Systems Committee (NRSC). June, 1998. "NRSC-2: Emission Limitation for AM Broadcast Transmission." Available: www.nrscstandards.org.

National Radio Systems Committee (NRSC). September, 2005. "NRSC-5-A: In-band/on-channel Digital Radio Broadcasting Standard." Available: www.nrscstandards.org.

National Radio Systems Committee DAB Subcommittee Test Procedures Working Group. October 2000. "Proposed NRSC IBOC Test Program."

National Radio Systems Committee DAB Subcommittee. Adopted January 9, 2003. "NRSC DAB Subcommittee Goals and Objectives."

National Radio Systems Committee DAB Subcommittee. April 2002. "Evaluation of the iBiquity Digital Corporation IBOC System, Part 2, AM IBOC." Available: www.nrscstandards.org.

National Radio Systems Committee DAB Subcommittee. May 1999. "In-band/On-channel (IBOC) Digital Audio Broadcasting (DAB) System Evaluation Guidelines."

National Radio Systems Committee DAB Subcommittee. November 2001. "Evaluation of the iBiquity Digital Corporation IBOC System, Part 1, FM IBOC." Available: www.nrscstandards.org.

National Radio Systems Committee DAB Subcommittee. Adopted April 2000. "Evaluation of Lucent Digital Radio's Submission To The NRSC DAB Subcommittee of Selected Laboratory and Field Test Results for Its FM and AM Band IBOC System." Available: www.nrscstandards.org.

National Radio Systems Committee DAB Subcommittee. Adopted April 2000. "Evaluation of USA Digital Radio's Submission To The NRSC DAB Subcommittee of Selected Laboratory and Field Test Results for Its FM and AM Band IBOC System." Available: www.nrscstandards.org.

National Radio Systems Committee DAB Subcommittee. Adopted December 3, 1998. "In-band/On-channel (IBOC) Digital Audio Broadcasting (DAB) System Test Guidelines Part I – Laboratory Tests." Available: www.nscstandards.org.

National Radio Systems Committee. Adopted January 20, 2006. "National Radio Systems Committee Procedures Manual, Rev 1.2." Available: www.nrscstandards.org.

National Radio Systems Committee. Adopted September 24, 2003. "National Radio Systems Committee Procedures Manual, Section 7.2.5.1, Patent Policy." Available: www.nrscstandards.org.

National Radio Systems Committee. August 25, 2000. Standards setting process-----NRSC Standard project initiation – IBOC DAB standards development.

Network Working Group. July 1994. Request for Comments #1662, STD 51, PPP in HDLC-like Framing. IETF Secretariat, Reston, VA.

Neural Audio Press Release. August 29, 2006. "WGUC-FM Begins 5.1 Broadcasting With Neural Surround™."

Nilsson, M. "ID3v2.3.0 Informal Standard." Available: http://www.ID3.org.

NPR Labs. September 8, 2006. "Consumer Testing of AM Broadcast Transmission Bandwidth and Audio Performance Measurements of Broadcast AM receivers."

Proakis, J. G. 1995. *Digital Communications*, 3rd Edition. McGraw-Hill.

Rackley, R.D., P.E. 2004. "Evaluation And Improvement Of AM Antenna Characteristics For Optimal Digital Performance." Proceedings, National Association of Broadcasters Broadcast Engineering Conference, Las Vegas, NV.

Rhoads, Eric. August 30, 1999. "Can Radio Survive the New Millennium?" In *Radio Ink*.

Rappaport, T. 2002. *Wireless Communications Principles and Practice*, 2nd Edition. Prentice Hall.

Reed, I. S., and G. Solomon. 1960. "Polynomial codes over certain finite fields." *Journal of the Society of Industrial and Applied Mathematics* 8(10):300–304.

Reeves, A. 2006. Imperial College Lectures.

Reply Comments of the National Association of Broadcasters. August 17, 2005. In the Matter of Digital Audio Broadcasting Systems MM Docket No. 99-325 and their Impact on the Terrestrial Radio Broadcast Service.

Salek, S., and D. Mansergh. 1997. "Field Testing of Proposed Digital Audio Radio Systems, Part 1: Mobile Data Collection System." Proceedings, National Association of Broadcasters Broadcast Engineering Conference, Las Vegas, NV.

Schurgers, C., and M. B. Srivastava. "A Systematic Approach to Peak-to-Average Power Ratio in OFDM." Electrical Engineering Department, UCLA. Available: http://fleece.ucsd.edu/~curts/papers/SPIE01.pdf.

Shannon, C. 1948. *A Mathematical Theory of Communications*. University of Illinois Press.

Sklar, B. 2001. *Digital Communications: Fundamentals and Applications*, 2nd Edition. Prentice Hall PTR.

Smith, J. O. 2003. "Mathematics of the Discrete Fourier Transform (DFT) with Audio Applications." W3K Publishing. Available: ccrma.stanford.edu/~jos/mdft/.

Smith, J. O. 2003. "Mathematics of the Discrete Fourier Transform (DFT)," W3K Publishing. Available: ccrma.stanford.edu/~jos/mdft/.

Smith, S. W., Ph.D. 1997. *The Scientist and Engineer's Guide to Digital Signal Processing*.

California Technical Publishing. Available: http://www.dspguide.com.

Thakral, P. et al. "OFDM Adaptive Modulation Reduction of Peak-to-Average Power Ratio"; "Channel Estimation"; "OFDM in Frequency Selective Fading." Available: www.winlab. rutgers.edu/~spasojev/courses/projects/PAR_OFDM.ppt.

Title 47, US Code of Federal Regulations, Parts 2.1 and 73.

Tomorrow Radio. January 6, 2004. "Tomorrow Radio[SM] Field Testing in the Washington, D.C., New York City, San Francisco, and Los Angeles (Long Beach) Radio Markets." Available: www.nrscstandards.org.

University of California Observatories, Lick Observatories. "The Future of Leap Seconds." Available: www.ucolick.org.

Viterbi, A. J. April, 1967. "Error Bounds for Convolutional Codes and an Asymptotically Optimum Decoding Algorithm." *IEEE Transactions on Information Theory*, vol. IT-13, 260–269.

Williams, R.N. 1993. "A Painless Guide To CRC Error Detection Algorithms." Available: www.repairfaq.org/filipg/LINK/F_crc_v31.html.

Wire, G. August 14, 2002. "iBiquity Charts a New Course." In *Radio World*, IMAS Publishing. Available: www.rwonline.com/reference-room/guywire/gw-08-28-03.shtml.

Web Sites

- psd.publicbroadcasting.net. Public Radio International PSD Consortium.

- tycho.usno.navy.mil. US Naval Observatory.

- www.agilent.com. Agilent Technologies, Inc., Application Notes.

- www.astronautix.com/craft/hs702.htm. Hughes HS702 communications satellite.

- www.bbc.co.uk/digitalradio/. British Broadcasting Corporation.

- www.bdcast.com. Broadcast Electronics.

- www.beradio.com. Radio Magazine, Prism Business Media, Inc.

- www.Bird-Technologies.com. Bird Technologies.

- www.broadcast.harris.com. Harris Corporation.

- www.broadcastsignallab.com. Broadcast Signal Lab, LLP.

- www.cbc.radio-canada.ca. CBC Radio-Canada.

- www.cisco.com. Cisco Systems.

- www.complextoreal.com. Charan Langton. Complex Communications Technology Made Easy.

- www.dcita.gov.au/media_broadcasting/radio/digital_radio/. Australian Government, Department of Communications, Information Technology and the Arts, Digital Radio Advisory Committee.

- www.dielectric.com. Dielectric Communications.

- www.drm.org. Digital Radio Mondial.

- www.dspguru.com. Iowegian International Corporation.

- www.eriinc.com. ERI Inc.

- www.hatdaw.com. Hatfield and Dawson.

- www.hdradioalliance.com. HD Digital Radio Alliance.

- www.hdradioplaybook.com. HD Radio Playbook.

- www.h-e.com. Hammett and Edison.

- www.howstuffworks.com. How Stuff Works, Inc.

- www.iana.org. Internet Assigned Numbers Authority.

- www.id3.org. ID³.

- www.ilabamerica.com. iLAB America, Inc.

- www.itu.int. International Telecommunications Union.

- www.jampro.com. Jampro RF Systems, Inc.

- www.mathworks.com. Wolfram Research.

- www.mathworld.wolfram.com. The Mathworks, Inc.

- www.nautel.com. Nautel Corporation.

- www.nrscstandards.org. National Radio Systems Committee Standards.

- www.psd.publicbroadcasting.net. PRI PSD Consortium.

- www.radioink.com. Radio Ink.

- www.rfcafe.com/references/electrical/directional%20coupler.htm. RF Café.

- www.rwonline.com. Radio World.

- www.shively.com. Shively Laboratories.

- www.stratosinteractive.com. StratosInteractive, Inc.

- www.tek.com. Tektronix, Inc., Application Notes.

- www.uspto.gov. US Patent and Trademark Office.

- www.worlddab.org. Formerly World DAB Forum, now World DMB Forum.

- www.wrathofkahn.org. Leonard Kahn.

About the Author

As a lad in the 1960s, David Maxson was captivated by the magic of electronic media. His fascination with tape recordings, LP's, dictaphones, film, and radio and TV broadcasting led to his exposure to the world of electronics. One of the first electronic projects he succeded at building was the quintessential crystal radio set. Growing up in the Connecticut suburbs of New York City, David was exposed not only to the technology of the day, but the rich content that radiates out of a major city. With an interest in media firmly in place by the end of his high school years, David went on to Boston University's College of Communication and obtained a degree in Broadcasting and Film. He reports that when he was on an audio or video production or film shoot, his peers seemed to rely on his knack for putting things together, and fixing them when they went wrong. He learned broadcast engineering the way many of his colleagues do, through hands-on experience, reading, and relying on mentors.

With a college degree and an FCC First Class Radiotelephone license, David hit the streets looking for a first step to a career. He was snapped up by Boston's storied classical music radio broadcaster, Charles River Broadcasting Company, where he entered as assistant chief engineer of the flagship station WCRB, and quickly rose to the role of Vice President, Director of Engineering of the parent company. That first job, found through a simple classified ad in the Boston Globe, evolved into a twenty-year career with Charles River Broadcasting. In addition to his work with the radio station, David gained experience with the classical music recording and syndication arm of the company, as well as their satellite and FM subcarrier-delivered background music service and sound system company. In 1995, David collaborated with a development team at Lockheed Sanders to create a digital audio transmission system employing the FM subcarrier spectrum, presenting technical papers at broadcast conferences. This signalled the beginning of his digital broadcasting career.

Early in his time at WCRB, in 1982, David also launched his radio frequency measurement and compliance business, Broadcast Signal Lab, LLP with partner Rick Levy, providing broadcasters in the northeastern USA with precision measurements and analysis. Leaving Charles River Broadcasting in 1998, David then devoted his full attention to BSL. At that time he began to represent his company at the National Radio Systems Committee, which was just resuming tracking IBOC developments. It was David's active participation in NRSC activities over the ensuing eight years that lead him to think he "knew enough about IBOC to write a book." Meanwhile, David also consults to emerging media technology companies and in the wireless facility deployment arena.

David has remained in the Boston metropolitan area since his college days, and continues to seek ways to participate in technological innovation in media.

Index